T0178593

Principles of Distributed Database Systems

M. Tamer Özsu • Patrick Valduriez

Principles of Distributed Database Systems

Fourth Edition

 Springer

M. Tamer Özsu
Cheriton School of Computer Science
University of Waterloo
Waterloo, ON, Canada

Patrick Valduriez
Inria and LIRMM
University of Montpellier
Montpellier, France

The first two editions of this book were published by: Pearson Education, Inc.

ISBN 978-3-030-26255-6   ISBN 978-3-030-26253-2   (eBook)
https://doi.org/10.1007/978-3-030-26253-2

3rd edition: © Springer Science+Business Media, LLC 2011
© Springer Nature Switzerland AG 2020, corrected publication 2020
This work is subject to copyright. All rights are reserved by the Publisher, whether the whole or part of the material is concerned, specifically the rights of translation, reprinting, reuse of illustrations, recitation, broadcasting, reproduction on microfilms or in any other physical way, and transmission or information storage and retrieval, electronic adaptation, computer software, or by similar or dissimilar methodology now known or hereafter developed.
The use of general descriptive names, registered names, trademarks, service marks, etc. in this publication does not imply, even in the absence of a specific statement, that such names are exempt from the relevant protective laws and regulations and therefore free for general use.
The publisher, the authors, and the editors are safe to assume that the advice and information in this book are believed to be true and accurate at the date of publication. Neither the publisher nor the authors or the editors give a warranty, expressed or implied, with respect to the material contained herein or for any errors or omissions that may have been made. The publisher remains neutral with regard to jurisdictional claims in published maps and institutional affiliations.

This Springer imprint is published by the registered company Springer Nature Switzerland AG.
The registered company address is: Gewerbestrasse 11, 6330 Cham, Switzerland

*To our families
and our parents
M.T.Ö. and P.V.*

Preface

The first edition of this book appeared in 1991 when the technology was new and there were not too many products. In the Preface to the first edition, we had quoted Michael Stonebraker who claimed in 1988 that in the following 10 years, centralized DBMSs would be an "antique curiosity" and most organizations would move towards distributed DBMSs. That prediction has certainly proved to be correct, and a large proportion of the systems in use today are either distributed or parallel—commonly referred to as scale-out systems. When we were putting together the first edition, undergraduate and graduate database courses were not as prevalent as they are now; so the initial version of the book contained lengthy discussions of centralized solutions before introducing their distributed/parallel counterparts. Times have certainly changed on that front as well, and now, it is hard to find a graduate student who does not have at least some rudimentary knowledge of database technology. Therefore, a graduate-level textbook on distributed/parallel database technology needs to be positioned differently today. That was our objective in this edition while maintaining the many new topics we introduced in the third edition. The main revisions introduced in this fourth edition are the following:

1. Over the years, the motivations and the environment for this technology have somewhat shifted (Web, cloud, etc.). In light of this, the introductory chapter needed a serious refresh. We revised the introduction with the aim of a more contemporary look at the technology.
2. We have added a new chapter on big data processing to cover distributed storage systems, data stream processing, MapReduce and Spark platforms, graph analytics, and data lakes. With the proliferation of these systems, systematic treatment of these topics is essential.
3. Similarly, we addressed the growing influence of NoSQL systems by devoting a new chapter to it. This chapter covers the four types of NoSQL (key-value stores, document stores, wide column systems, and graph DBMSs), as well as NewSQL systems and polystores.
4. We have combined the database integration and multidatabase query processing chapters from the third edition into a uniform chapter on database integration.

5. We undertook a major revision of the web data management discussion that previously focused mostly on XML to refocus on RDF technology, which is more prevalent at this time. We now discuss, in this chapter, web data integration approaches, including the important issue of data quality.

6. We have revised and updated the peer-to-peer data management chapter and included a lengthy discussion of blockchain.

7. As part of our cleaning the previous chapters, we condensed the query processing and transaction management chapters by removing the fundamental centralized techniques and focused these chapters on distributed/parallel techniques. In the process, we included some topics that have since gained importance, such as dynamic query processing (eddies) and Paxos consensus algorithm and its use in commit protocols.

8. We updated the parallel DBMS chapter by clarifying the objectives, in particular, scale-up versus scale-out, and discussing parallel architectures that include UMA or NUMA. We also added a new section of parallel sorting algorithms and variants of parallel join algorithms to exploit large main memories and multicore processors that are prevalent today.

9. We updated the distribution design chapter by including a lengthy discussion of modern approaches that combine fragmentation and allocation. By rearranging material, this chapter is now central to data partitioning for both the distributed and parallel data management discussions in the remainder of the book.

10 Although object technology continues to play a role in information systems, its importance in distributed/parallel data management has declined. Therefore, we removed the chapter on object databases from this edition.

As is evident, the entire book and every chapter have seen revisions and updates for a more contemporary treatment. The material we removed in the process is not lost—they are included as online appendices and appear on the book's web page: https://cs.uwaterloo.ca/ddbs. We elected to make these available online rather than in the print version to keep the size of the book reasonable (which also keeps the price reasonable). The web site also includes presentation slides that can be used to teach from the book as well as solutions to most of the exercises (available only to instructors who have adopted the book for teaching).

As in previous editions, many colleagues helped with this edition of the book whom we would like to thank (in no specific order). Dan Olteanu provided a nice discussion of two optimizations that can significantly reduce the maintenance time of materialized views in Chap. 3. Phil Bernstein provided leads for new papers on the multiversion transaction management that resulted in updates to that discussion in Chap. 5. Khuzaima Daudjee was also helpful in providing a list of more contemporary publications on distributed transaction processing that we include in the bibliographic notes section of that chapter. Ricardo Jimenez-Peris contributed text on high-performance transaction systems that is included in the same chapter. He also contributed a section on LeanXcale in the NoSQL, NewSQL, and polystores chapter. Dennis Shasha reviewed the new blockchain section in the P2P chapter. Michael Carey read the big data, NoSQL, NewSQL and polystores, and parallel DBMS chapters and provided extremely detailed comments that improved those chapters considerably. Tamer's students Anil Pacaci, Khaled Ammar and postdoc Xiaofei Zhang provided extensive reviews of the big data chapter, and texts from their publications are included in this chapter. The NoSQL, NewSQL, and polystores chapter includes text from publications of Boyan Kolev and Patrick's student Carlyna Bondiombouy. Jim Webber reviewed the section on Neo4j in that chapter. The characterization of graph analytics systems in that chapter is partially based on Minyang Han's master's thesis where he also proposes GiraphUC approach that is discussed in that chapter. Semih Salihoglu and Lukasz Golab also reviewed and provided very helpful comments on parts of this chapter. Alon Halevy provided comments on the WebTables discussion in Chap. 12. The data quality discussion in web data integration is contributed by Ihab Ilyas and Xu Chu. Stratos Idreos was very helpful in clarifying how database cracking can be used as a partitioning approach and provided text that is included in Chap. 2. Renan Souza and Fabian Stöter reviewed the entire book.

The third edition of the book introduced a number of new topics that carried over to this edition, and a number of colleagues were very influential in writing those chapters. We would like to, once again, acknowledge their assistance since their impact is reflected in the current edition as well. Renée Miller, Erhard Rahm, and Alon Halevy were critical in putting together the discussion on database integration, which was reviewed thoroughly by Avigdor Gal. Matthias Jarke, Xiang Li, Gottfried Vossen, Erhard Rahm, and Andreas Thor contributed exercises to this chapter. Hubert Naacke contributed to the section on heterogeneous cost modeling and Fabio Porto to the section on adaptive query processing. Data replication (Chap. 6) could not have been written without the assistance of Gustavo Alonso and Bettina Kemme. Esther Pacitti also contributed to the data replication chapter, both by reviewing it and by providing background material; she also contributed to the section on replication in database clusters in the parallel DBMS chapter. Peer-to-peer data management owes a lot to the discussions with Beng Chin Ooi. The section of this chapter on query processing in P2P systems uses material from the PhD work of Reza Akbarinia and Wenceslao Palma, while the section on replication uses material from the PhD work of Vidal Martins.

We thank our editor at Springer Susan Lagerstrom-Fife for pushing this project within Springer and also pushing us to finish it in a timely manner. We missed almost all of her deadlines, but we hope the end result is satisfactory.

Finally, we would be very interested to hear your comments and suggestions regarding the material. We welcome any feedback, but we would particularly like to receive feedback on the following aspects:

1. Any errors that may have remained despite our best efforts (although we hope there are not many);

2. Any topics that should no longer be included and any topics that should be added or expanded;
3. Any exercises that you may have designed that you would like to be included in the book.

Waterloo, Canada   M. Tamer Özsu (tamer.ozsu@uwaterloo.ca)
Montpellier, France   Patrick Valduriez (patrick.valduriez@inria.fr)
June 2019

Contents

The original version of this book was revised. The correction to this book is available at https://doi.org/10.1007/978-3-030-26253-2_13

Chapter 1
Introduction

The current computing environment is largely distributed—computers are connected to Internet to form a worldwide distributed system. Organizations have
geographically distributed and interconnected data centers, each with hundreds or
thousands of computers connected with high-speed networks, forming mixture of
distributed and parallel systems (Fig. 1.1). Within this environment, the amount of
data that is captured has increased dramatically. Not all of this data is stored in
database systems (in fact a small portion is) but there is a desire to provide some
sort of data management capability on these widely distributed data. This is the
scope of distributed and parallel database systems, which have moved from a small
part of the worldwide computing environment a few decades ago to mainstream.
In this chapter, we provide an overview of this technology, before we examine the
details in subsequent chapters.

1.1 What Is a Distributed Database System?

We define a *distributed database* as *a collection of multiple, logically interrelated
databases located at the nodes of a distributed system*. A *distributed database
management system* (distributed DBMS) is then defined as *the software system that
permits the management of the distributed database and makes the distribution
transparent to the users*. Sometimes "distributed database system" (distributed
DBMS) is used to refer jointly to the distributed database and the distributed DBMS.
The two important characteristics are that data is logically interrelated and that it
resides on a distributed system.

The original version of this chapter was revised. The correction to this chapter is available at https://
doi.org/10.1007/978-3-030-26253-2_13

© Springer Nature Switzerland AG 2020   1
M. T. Özsu, P. Valduriez, *Principles of Distributed Database Systems*,
https://doi.org/10.1007/978-3-030-26253-2_1

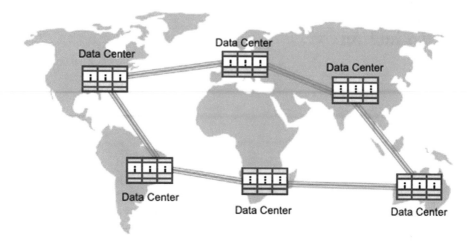

Fig. 1.1 Geographically distributed data centers

The existence of a distributed system is an important characteristic. In this context, we define a *distributed computing system* as a number of interconnected autonomous processing elements (PEs). The capabilities of these processing elements may differ, they may be heterogeneous, and the interconnections might be different, but the important aspect is that PEs do not have access to each other's state, which they can only learn by exchanging messages that incur a communication cost. Therefore, when data is distributed, its management and access in a logically integrated manner requires special care from the distributed DBMS software.

A distributed DBMS is not a "collection of files" that can be individually stored at each PE of a distributed system (usually called "site" of a distributed DBMS); data in a distributed DBMS is interrelated. We will not try to be very specific with what we mean by interrelated, because the requirements differ depending on the type of data. For example, in the case of relational data, different relations or their partitions might be stored at different sites (more on this in Chap. 2), requiring join or union operations to answer queries that are typically expressed in SQL. One can usually define a *schema* of this distributed data. At the other extreme, data in NoSQL systems (discussed further in Chap. 11) may have a much looser definition of interrelatedness; for example, it may be vertices of a graph that might be stored at different sites.

The upshot of this discussion is that a distributed DBMS is *logically integrated* but *physically distributed*. What this means is that a distributed DBMS gives the users the view of a unified database, while the underlying data is physically distributed.

As noted above, we typically consider two types of distributed DBMSs: geographically distributed (commonly referred to as *geo-distributed*) and single location (or single site) . In the former, the sites are interconnected by wide area networks that are characterized by long message latencies and higher error rates. The latter consist of systems where the PEs are located in close proximity allowing much faster exchanges leading to shorter (even negligible with new technologies) message latencies and very low error rates. Single location distributed DBMSs are typically characterized by computer clusters in one data center, and are commonly known as parallel DBMSs (and the PEs are referred to as "nodes" to distinguish from "sites"). As noted above, it is now quite common to find distributed DBMSs that have multiple single site clusters interconnected by wide area networks, leading to hybrid, multisite systems. For most of this book, we will focus on the problems of data management among the sites of a geo-distributed DBMS; we will focus on the problems of single site systems in Chaps. 8, 10, and 11 where we discuss parallel DBMSs, big data systems, and NoSQL/NewSQL systems.

1.2   History of Distributed DBMS

Before the advent of database systems in the 1960s, the prevalent mode of computation was one where each application defined and maintained its own data (Fig. 1.2). In this mode, each application defined the data that it used, its structure and access methods, and managed the file in the storage system. The end result was significant uncontrolled redundancy in the data, and high overhead for the programmers to manage this data within their applications.

Database systems allow data to be defined and administered centrally (Fig. 1.3). This new orientation results in *data independence*, whereby the application programs are immune to changes in the logical or physical organization of the data and vice versa. Consequently, programmers are freed from the task of managing and maintaining the data that they need, and the redundancy of the data can be eliminated (or reduced).

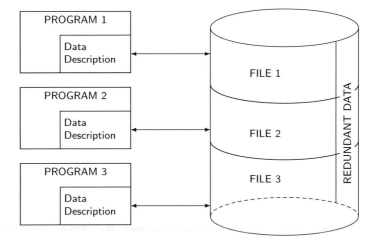

Fig. 1.2 Traditional file processing

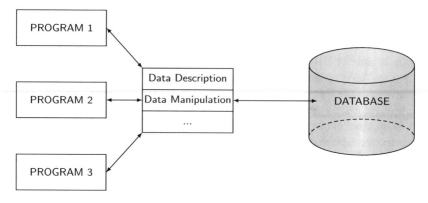

Fig. 1.3 Database processing

One of the original motivations behind the use of database systems was the desire to integrate the operational data of an enterprise and to provide integrated, thus controlled access to that data. We carefully use the term "integrated" rather than "centralized" because, as discussed earlier, the data can physically be located on different machines that might be geographically distributed. This is what the distributed database technology provides. As noted earlier, this physical distribution can be concentrated at one geographic location or it can be at multiple locations. Therefore, each of the locations in Fig. 1.5 might be a data center that is connected to other data centers over a communication network. These are the types of distributed environments that are now common and that we study in this book.

Over the years, distributed database system architectures have undergone significant changes. The original distributed database systems such as Distributed INGRES and SDD-1 were designed as geographically distributed systems with very slow network connections; consequently they tried to optimize operations to reduce network communication. They were early *peer-to-peer systems* (P2P) in the sense that each site had similar functionality with respect to data management. With the development of personal computers and workstations, the prevailing distribution model shifted to *client/server* where data operations were moved to a back-end server, while user applications ran on the front-end workstations. These systems became dominant in particular for distribution at one particular location where the network speeds would be higher, enabling frequent communication between the clients and the server(s). There was a reemergence of P2P systems in the 2000s, where there is no distinction of client machines versus servers. These modern P2P systems have important differences from the earlier systems that we discuss later in this chapter. All of these architectures can still be found today and we discuss them in subsequent chapters.

The emergence of the World Wide Web (usually called the web) as a major collaboration and sharing platform had a profound impact on distributed data management research. Significantly more data was opened up for access, but this was not the well-structured, well-defined data DBMSs typically handle; instead, it is unstructured or semistructured (i.e., it has some structure but not at the level of a database schema), with uncertain provenance (so it might be "dirty" or unreliable), and conflicting. Furthermore, a lot of the data is stored in systems that are not easily accessible (what is called the *dark web*). Consequently, distributed data management efforts focus on accessing this data in meaningful ways.

This development added particular impetus to one thread of research that existed since the beginning of distributed database efforts, namely *database integration*. Originally, these efforts focused on finding ways to access data in separate databases (thus the terms *federated database* and *multidatabase*), but with the emergence of web data, these efforts shifted to virtual integration of different data types (and the term *data integration* became more popular). The term that is in vogue right now is *data lake* which implies that all of the data is captured in a logically single store, from which relevant data is extracted for each application. We discuss the former in Chap. 7 and the latter in Chaps. 10 and 12.

A significant development in the last ten years has been the emergence of cloud computing. Cloud computing refers to a computing model where a number of service providers make available shared and geo-distributed computing resources such that users can rent some of these resources based on their needs. Clients can rent the basic computing infrastructure on which they could develop their own software, but then decide on the operating system they wish to use and create virtual machines (VMs) to create the environment in which they wish to work—the so-called *Infrastructure-as-a-Service* (IaaS) approach. A more sophisticated cloud environment involves renting, in addition to basic infrastructure, the full computing platform leading to *Platform-as-a-Service* (PaaS) on which clients can develop their own software. The most sophisticated version is where service providers make available specific software that the clients can then rent; this is called *Software-as-a-Service* (SaaS). There has been a trend in providing distributed database management services on the cloud as part of SaaS offering, and this has been one of the more recent developments.

In addition to the specific chapters where we discuss these architectures in depth, we provide an overview of all of them in Sect. 1.6.1.2.

1.3 Data Delivery Alternatives

In distributed databases, data delivery occurs between sites—either from server sites to client sites in answer to queries or between multiple servers. We characterize the data delivery alternatives along three orthogonal dimensions: *delivery modes*, *frequency*, and *communication methods*. The combinations of alternatives along each of these dimensions provide a rich design space.

The alternative delivery modes are pull-only, push-only, and hybrid. In the *pull-only* mode of data delivery, the transfer of data is initiated by a pull (i.e., request) from one site to a data provider—this may be a client requesting data from a server or a server requesting data from another server. In the following we use the terms "receiver" and "provider" to refer to the machine that received the data and the machine that sends the data, respectively. When the request is received by the provider, the data is located and transferred. The main characteristic of pull-based delivery is that receivers become aware of new data items or updates at the provider only when they explicitly poll. Also, in pull-based mode, providers must be interrupted continuously to deal with requests. Furthermore, the data that receivers can obtain from a provider is limited to when and what clients know to ask for. Conventional DBMSs offer primarily pull-based data delivery.

In the *push-only* mode of data delivery, the transfer of data from providers is initiated by a push without a specific request. The main difficulty of the push-based approach is in deciding which data would be of common interest, and when to send it to potentially interested receivers—alternatives are periodic, irregular, or conditional. Thus, the usefulness of push depends heavily upon the accuracy of a provider to predict the needs of receivers. In push-based mode, providers disseminate information to either an unbounded set of receivers (random broadcast) who can listen to a medium or selective set of receivers (multicast), who belong to some categories of recipients.

The *hybrid* mode of data delivery combines the pull and push mechanisms. The persistent query approach (see Sect. 10.3) presents one possible way of combining the pull and push modes, namely: the transfer of data from providers to receivers is first initiated by a pull (by posing the query), and the subsequent transfer of updated data is initiated by a push by the provider.

There are three typical frequency measurements that can be used to classify the regularity of data delivery. They are periodic, conditional, and ad hoc (or irregular).

In *periodic delivery*, data is sent from the providers at regular intervals. The intervals can be defined by system default or by receivers in their profiles. Both pull and push can be performed in periodic fashion. Periodic delivery is carried out on a regular and prespecified repeating schedule. A request for a company's stock price every week is an example of a periodic pull. An example of periodic push is when an application can send out stock price listing on a regular basis, say every morning. Periodic push is particularly useful for situations in which receivers might not be available at all times, or might be unable to react to what has been sent, such as in the mobile setting where clients can become disconnected.

In *conditional delivery*, data is sent by providers whenever certain conditions specified by receivers in their profiles are satisfied. Such conditions can be as simple as a given time span or as complicated as event-condition-action rules. Conditional delivery is mostly used in the hybrid or push-only delivery systems. Using conditional push, data is sent out according to a prespecified condition, rather than any particular repeating schedule. An application that sends out stock prices only when they change is an example of conditional push. An application that sends out a balance statement only when the total balance is 5% below the predefined balance threshold is an example of hybrid conditional push. Conditional push assumes that changes are critical to the receivers who are always listening and need to respond to what is being sent. Hybrid conditional push further assumes that missing some update information is not crucial to the receivers.

Ad hoc delivery is irregular and is performed mostly in a pure pull-based system. Data is pulled from providers in an ad hoc fashion in response to requests. In contrast, periodic pull arises when a requestor uses polling to obtain data from providers based on a regular period (schedule).

The third component of the design space of information delivery alternatives is the communication method. These methods determine the various ways in which providers and receivers communicate for delivering information to clients. The alternatives are unicast and one-to-many. In *unicast*, the communication from a provider to a receiver is one-to-one: the provider sends data to one receiver using a particular delivery mode with some frequency. In *one-to-many*, as the name implies, the provider sends data to a number of receivers. Note that we are not referring here to a specific protocol; one-to-many communication may use a multicast or broadcast protocol.

We should note that this characterization is subject to considerable debate. It is not clear that every point in the design space is meaningful. Furthermore, specification of alternatives such as conditional **and** periodic (which may make sense) is difficult. However, it serves as a first-order characterization of the complexity of emerging distributed data management systems. For the most part, in this book, we are concerned with pull-only, ad hoc data delivery systems, and discuss push-based and hybrid modes under streaming systems in Sect. 10.3.

1.4 Promises of Distributed DBMSs

Many advantages of distributed DBMSs can be cited; these can be distilled to four fundamentals that may also be viewed as promises of distributed DBMS technology: transparent management of distributed and replicated data, reliable access to data through distributed transactions, improved performance, and easier system expansion. In this section, we discuss these promises and, in the process, introduce many of the concepts that we will study in subsequent chapters.

1.4.1 Transparent Management of Distributed and Replicated Data

Transparency refers to separation of the higher-level semantics of a system from lower-level implementation issues. In other words, a transparent system "hides" the implementation details from users. The advantage of a fully transparent DBMS is the high level of support that it provides for the development of complex applications. Transparency in distributed DBMS can be viewed as an extension of the data independence concept in centralized DBMS (more on this below).

EMP(<u>ENO</u>, ENAME, TITLE)
PROJ(<u>PNO</u>, PNAME, BUDGET, LOC)
ASG(<u>ENO, PNO</u>, RESP, DUR)
PAY(<u>TITLE</u>, SAL)

Fig. 1.4 Example engineering database

Let us start our discussion with an example. Consider an engineering firm that has offices in Boston, Waterloo, Paris, and San Francisco. They run projects at each of these sites and would like to maintain a database of their employees, the projects, and other related data. Assuming that the database is relational, we can store this information in a number of relations (Fig. 1.4): EMP stores employee information with employee number, name, and title[1]; PROJ holds project information where LOC records where the project is located. The salary information is stored in PAY (assuming everyone with the same title gets the same salary) and the assignment of people to projects is recorded in ASG where DUR indicates the duration of the assignment and the person's responsibility on that project is maintained in RESP. If all of this data were stored in a centralized DBMS, and we wanted to find out the names and employees who worked on a project for more than 12 months, we would specify this using the following SQL query:

```
SELECT ENAME, AMT
FROM EMP NATURAL JOIN ASG, EMP NATURAL JOIN PAY
WHERE ASG.DUR > 12
```

However, given the distributed nature of this firm's business, it is preferable, under these circumstances, to localize data such that data about the employees in Waterloo office is stored in Waterloo, those in the Boston office is stored in Boston, and so forth. The same applies to the project and salary information. Thus, what we are engaged in is a process where we partition each of the relations and store each partition at a different site. This is known as *data partitioning* or *data fragmentation* and we discuss it further below and in detail in Chap. 2.

Furthermore, it may be preferable to duplicate some of this data at other sites for performance and reliability reasons. The result is a distributed database which is fragmented and replicated (Fig. 1.5). Fully transparent access means that the users can still pose the query as specified above, without paying any attention to the fragmentation, location, or replication of data, and let the system worry about resolving these issues. For a system to adequately deal with this type of query over a distributed, fragmented, and replicated database, it needs to be able to deal with a number of different types of transparencies as discussed below.

Data Independence.   This notion carries over from centralized DBMSs and refers to the immunity of user applications to changes in the definition and organization of data, and vice versa.

---

[1]Primary key attributes are underlined.

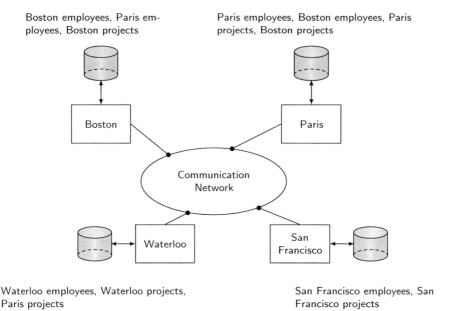

Boston employees, Paris employees, Boston projects

Paris employees, Boston employees, Paris projects, Boston projects

Waterloo employees, Waterloo projects, Paris projects

San Francisco employees, San Francisco projects

Fig. 1.5 Distributed database

Two types of data independence are usually cited: logical data independence and physical data independence. *Logical data independence* refers to the immunity of user applications to changes in the logical structure (i.e., schema) of the database. *Physical data independence*, on the other hand, deals with hiding the details of the storage structure from user applications. When a user application is written, it should not be concerned with the details of physical data organization. Therefore, the user application should not need to be modified when data organization changes occur due to performance considerations.

Network Transparency.   Preferably, users should be protected from the operational details of the communication network that connects the sites; possibly even hiding the existence of the network. Then there would be no difference between database applications that would run on a centralized database and those that would run on a distributed database. This type of transparency is referred to as *network transparency* or *distribution transparency*.

Sometimes two types of distribution transparency are identified: location transparency and naming transparency. *Location transparency* refers to the fact that the command used to perform a task is independent of both the location of the data and the system on which an operation is carried out. *Naming transparency* means that a unique name is provided for each object in the database. In the absence of naming transparency, users are required to embed the location name (or an identifier) as part of the object name.

Fragmentation Transparency.   As discussed above, it is commonly desirable to divide each database relation into smaller fragments and treat each fragment as a separate database object (i.e., another relation). This is commonly done for reasons of performance, availability, and reliability—a more in-depth discussion is in Chap. 2. It would be preferable for the users not to be aware of data fragmentation in specifying queries, and let the system deal with the problem of mapping a user query that is specified on full relations as specified in the schema to a set of queries executed on subrelations. In other words, the issue is one of finding a query processing strategy based on the fragments rather than the relations, even though the queries are specified on the latter.

Replication Transparency.   For performance, reliability, and availability reasons, it is usually desirable to be able to distribute data in a replicated fashion across the machines on a network. Assuming that data is replicated, the transparency issue is whether the users should be aware of the existence of copies or whether the system should handle the management of copies and the user should act as if there is a single copy of the data (note that we are not referring to the placement of copies, only their existence). From a user's perspective it is preferable not to be involved with handling copies and having to specify the fact that a certain action can and/or should be taken on multiple copies. The issue of replicating data within a distributed database is introduced in Chap. 2 and discussed in detail in Chap. 6.

1.4.2 Reliability Through Distributed Transactions

Distributed DBMSs are intended to improve reliability since they have replicated components and thereby eliminate single points of failure. The failure of a single site, or the failure of a communication link which makes one or more sites unreachable, is not sufficient to bring down the entire system. In the case of a distributed database, this means that some of the data may be unreachable, but with proper care, users may be permitted to access other parts of the distributed database. The "proper care" comes mainly in the form of support for distributed transactions.

A DBMS that provides full transaction support guarantees that concurrent execution of user transactions will not violate database consistency, i.e., each user thinks their query is the only one executing on the database (called *concurrency transparency*) even in the face of system failures (called *failure transparency*) as long as each transaction is correct, i.e., obeys the integrity rules specified on the database.

Providing transaction support requires the implementation of distributed concurrency control and distributed reliability protocols—in particular, two-phase commit (2PC) and distributed recovery protocols—which are significantly more complicated than their centralized counterparts. These are discussed in Chap. 5. Supporting replicas requires the implementation of replica control protocols that enforce a specified semantics of accessing them. These are discussed in Chap. 6.

1.4.3 Improved Performance

The case for the improved performance of distributed DBMSs is typically made based on two points. First, a distributed DBMS fragments the database, enabling data to be stored in close proximity to its points of use (also called *data locality*). This has two potential advantages:

1. Since each site handles only a portion of the database, contention for CPU and I/O services is not as severe as for centralized databases.
2. Locality reduces remote access delays that are usually involved in wide area networks.

This point relates to the overhead of distributed computing if the data resides at remote sites and one has to access it by remote communication. The argument is that it is better, in these circumstances, to distribute the data management functionality to where the data is located rather than moving large amounts of data. This is sometimes a topic of contention. Some argue that with the widespread use of high-speed, high-capacity networks, distributing data and data management functions no longer makes sense and that it may be much simpler to store data at a central site using a very large machine and access it over high-speed networks. This is commonly referred to as *scale-up* architecture. It is an appealing argument, but misses an important point of distributed databases. First, in most of today's applications, data is distributed; what may be open for debate is how and where we process it. Second, and more important, point is that this argument does not distinguish between bandwidth (the capacity of the computer links) and latency (how long it takes for data to be transmitted). Latency is inherent in distributed environments and there are physical limits to how fast we can send data over computer networks. Remotely accessing data may incur latencies that might not be acceptable for many applications.

The second point is that the inherent parallelism of distributed systems may be exploited for interquery and intraquery parallelism. *Interquery parallelism* enables the parallel execution of multiple queries generated by concurrent transactions, in order to increase the transactional throughput. The definition of intraquery parallelism is different in distributed versus parallel DBMSs. In the former, intraquery parallelism is achieved by breaking up a single query into a number of subqueries, each of which is executed at a different site, accessing a different part of the distributed database. In parallel DBMSs, it is achieved by *interoperator* and *intraoperator* parallelism. Interoperator parallelism is obtained by executing in parallel different operators of the query tree on different processors, while with intraoperator parallelism, the same operator is executed by many processors, each one working on a subset of the data. Note that these two forms of parallelism also exist in distributed query processing.

Intraoperator parallelism is based on the decomposition of one operator in a set of independent suboperators, called *operator instances*. This decomposition is done using partitioning of relations. Each operator instance will then process one relation partition. The operator decomposition frequently benefits from the initial partitioning of the data (e.g., the data is partitioned on the join attribute). To illustrate intraoperator parallelism, let us consider a simple select-join query. The select operator can be directly decomposed into several select operators, each on a different partition, and no redistribution is required (Fig. 1.6). Note that if the relation is partitioned on the select attribute, partitioning properties can be used to eliminate some select instances. For example, in an exact-match select, only one select instance will be executed if the relation was partitioned by hashing (or range) on the select attribute. It is more complex to decompose the join operator. In order to have independent joins, each partition of one relation R may be joined to the entire other relation S. Such a join will be very inefficient (unless S is very small) because it will imply a broadcast of S on each participating processor. A more efficient way is to use partitioning properties. For example, if R and S are partitioned by hashing on the join attribute and if the join is an equijoin, then we can partition the join into independent joins. This is the ideal case that cannot be always used, because it depends on the initial partitioning of R and S. In the other cases, one or two operands may be repartitioned. Finally, we may notice that the partitioning function (hash, range, round robin—discussed in Sect. 2.3.1) is independent of the local algorithm (e.g., nested loop, hash, sort merge) used to process the join operator (i.e., on each processor). For instance, a hash join using a hash partitioning needs two hash functions. The first one, h_1, is used to partition the two base relations on the join attribute. The second one, h_2, which can be different for each processor, is used to process the join on each processor.

Two forms of interoperator parallelism can be exploited. With *pipeline parallelism*, several operators with a producer–consumer link are executed in parallel. For instance, the two select operators in Fig. 1.7 will be executed in parallel with the join operator. The advantage of such execution is that the intermediate result does not need to be entirely materialized, thus saving memory and disk accesses. *Independent*

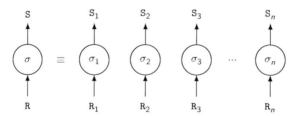

Fig. 1.6 Intraoperator parallelism. σ_i is instance i of the operator; n is the degree of parallelism

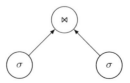

Fig. 1.7 Interoperator parallelism

parallelism is achieved when there is no dependency between the operators that are executed in parallel. For instance, the two select operators of Fig. 1.7 can be executed in parallel. This form of parallelism is very attractive because there is no interference between the processors.

1.4.4 Scalability

In a distributed environment, it is much easier to accommodate increasing database sizes and bigger workloads. System expansion can usually be handled by adding processing and storage power to the network. Obviously, it may not be possible to obtain a linear increase in "power," since this also depends on the overhead of distribution. However, significant improvements are still possible. That is why distributed DBMSs have gained much interest in *scale-out* architectures in the context of cluster and cloud computing. Scale-out (also called *horizontal scaling*) refers to adding more servers, called "scale-out servers" in a loosely coupled fashion, to scale almost infinitely. By making it easy to add new component database servers, a distributed DBMS can provide scale-out.

1.5 Design Issues

In the previous section, we discussed the promises of distributed DBMS technology, highlighting the challenges that need to be overcome in order to realize them. In this section, we build on this discussion by presenting the design issues that arise in building a distributed DBMS. These issues will occupy much of the remainder of this book.

1.5.1 Distributed Database Design

The question that is being addressed is how the data is placed across the sites. The starting point is one global database and the end result is a distribution of the data across the sites. This is referred to as *top-down design*. There are two basic alternatives to placing data: *partitioned* (or *nonreplicated*) and *replicated*. In the partitioned scheme the database is divided into a number of disjoint partitions each of which is placed at a different site. Replicated designs can be either *fully replicated* (also called *fully duplicated*) where the entire database is stored at each site, or *partially replicated* (or *partially duplicated*) where each partition of the database is stored at more than one site, but not at all the sites. The two fundamental design issues are *fragmentation*, the separation of the database into partitions called *fragments*, and *distribution*, the optimum distribution of fragments.

A related problem is the design and management of system directory. In centralized DBMSs, the *catalog* contains metainformation (i.e., description) about the data.

In a distributed system, we have a directory that contains additional information such as where data is located. Problems related to directory management are similar in nature to the database placement problem discussed in the preceding section. A directory may be global to the entire distributed DBMS or local to each site; it can be centralized at one site or distributed over several sites; there can be a single copy or multiple copies. Distributed database design and directory management are topics of Chap. 2.

1.5.2 Distributed Data Control

An important requirement of a DBMS is to maintain data consistency by controlling how data is accessed. This is called *data control* and involves view management, access control, and integrity enforcement. Distribution imposes additional challenges since data that is required to check rules is distributed to different sites requiring distributed rule checking and enforcement. The topic is covered in Chap. 3.

1.5.3 Distributed Query Processing

Query processing deals with designing algorithms that analyze queries and convert them into a series of data manipulation operations. The problem is how to decide on a strategy for executing each query over the network in the most cost-effective way, however, cost is defined. The factors to be considered are the distribution of data, communication costs, and lack of sufficient locally available information. The objective is to optimize where the inherent parallelism is used to improve the performance of executing the transaction, subject to the above-mentioned constraints. The problem is NP-hard in nature, and the approaches are usually heuristic. Distributed query processing is discussed in detail in Chap. 4.

1.5.4 Distributed Concurrency Control

Concurrency control involves the synchronization of accesses to the distributed database, such that the integrity of the database is maintained. The concurrency control problem in a distributed context is somewhat different than in a centralized framework. One not only has to worry about the integrity of a single database, but also about the consistency of multiple copies of the database. The condition that requires all the values of multiple copies of every data item to converge to the same value is called *mutual consistency*.

The two general classes of solutions are *pessimistic*, synchronizing the execution of user requests before the execution starts, and *optimistic*, executing the requests and then checking if the execution has compromised the consistency of the database. Two fundamental primitives that can be used with both approaches are *locking*, which is based on the mutual exclusion of accesses to data items, and *timestamping*, where the transaction executions are ordered based on timestamps. There are variations of these schemes as well as hybrid algorithms that attempt to combine the two basic mechanisms.

In locking-based approaches deadlocks are possible since there is mutually exclusive access to data by different transactions. The well-known alternatives of prevention, avoidance, and detection/recovery also apply to distributed DBMSs. Distributed concurrency control is covered in Chap. 5.

1.5.5   Reliability of Distributed DBMS

We mentioned earlier that one of the potential advantages of distributed systems is improved reliability and availability. This, however, is not a feature that comes automatically. It is important that mechanisms be provided to ensure the consistency of the database as well as to detect failures and recover from them. The implication for distributed DBMSs is that when a failure occurs and various sites become either inoperable or inaccessible, the databases at the operational sites remain consistent and up-to-date. Furthermore, when the computer system or network recovers from the failure, the distributed DBMSs should be able to recover and bring the databases at the failed sites up-to-date. This may be especially difficult in the case of network partitioning, where the sites are divided into two or more groups with no communication among them. Distributed reliability protocols are the topic of Chap. 5.

1.5.6   Replication

If the distributed database is (partially or fully) replicated, it is necessary to implement protocols that ensure the consistency of the replicas, i.e., copies of the same data item have the same value. These protocols can be *eager* in that they force the updates to be applied to all the replicas before the transaction completes, or they may be *lazy* so that the transaction updates one copy (called the *master*) from which updates are propagated to the others after the transaction completes. We discuss replication protocols in Chap. 6.

1.5.7   Parallel DBMSs

As earlier noted, there is a strong relationship between distributed databases and parallel databases. Although the former assumes each site to be a single logical computer, most of these installations are, in fact, parallel clusters. This is the distinction that we highlighted earlier between single site distribution as in data center clusters and geo-distribution. Parallel DBMS objectives are somewhat different from distributed DBMSs in that the main objectives are high scalability and performance. While most of the book focuses on issues that arise in managing data in geo-distributed databases, interesting data management issues exist within a single site distribution as a parallel system. We discuss these issues in Chap. 8.

1.5.8   Database Integration

One of the important developments has been the move towards "looser" federation among data sources, which may also be heterogeneous. As we discuss in the next section, this has given rise to the development of multidatabase systems (also called *federated database systems*) that require reinvestigation of some of the fundamental database techniques. The input here is a set of already distributed databases and the objective is to provide easy access by (physically or logically) integrating them. This involves *bottom-up design*. These systems constitute an important part of today's distributed environment. We discuss multidatabase systems, or as more commonly termed now *database integration*, including design issues and query processing challenges in Chap. 7.

1.5.9   Alternative Distribution Approaches

The growth of the Internet as a fundamental networking platform has raised important questions about the assumptions underlying distributed database systems. Two issues are of particular concern to us. One is the re-emergence of peer-to-peer computing, and the other is the development and growth of the World Wide Web. Both of these aim at improving data sharing, but take different approaches and pose different data management challenges. We discuss peer-to-peer data management in Chap. 9 and web data management in Chap. 12.

1.5.10   Big Data Processing and NoSQL

The last decade has seen the explosion of "big data" processing. The exact definition of big data is elusive, but they are typically accepted to have four characteristics dubbed the "four V's": data is very high *volume*, is multimodal (*variety*), usually comes at very high speed as data streams (*velocity*), and may have quality concerns due to uncertain sources and conflicts (*veracity*). There have been significant efforts to develop systems to deal with "big data," all spurred by the perceived unsuitability of relational DBMSs for a number of new applications. These efforts typically take two forms: one thread has developed general purpose computing platforms (almost always scale-out) for processing, and the other special DBMSs that do not have the full relational functionality, with more flexible data management capabilities (the so-called NoSQL systems). We discuss the big data platforms in Chap. 10 and NoSQL systems in Chap. 11.

1.6   Distributed DBMS Architectures

The architecture of a system defines its structure. This means that the components of the system are identified, the function of each component is specified, and the interrelationships and interactions among these components are defined. The specification of the architecture of a system requires identification of the various modules, with their interfaces and interrelationships, in terms of the data and control flow through the system.

In this section, we develop four "reference" architectures[2] for a distributed DBMS: client/server, peer-to-peer, multidatabase, and cloud. These are "idealized" views of a DBMS in that many of the commercially available systems may deviate from them; however, the architectures will serve as a reasonable framework within which the issues related to distributed DBMS can be discussed.

We start with a discussion of the design space to better position the architectures that will be presented.

1.6.1   Architectural Models for Distributed DBMSs

We use a classification (Fig. 1.8) that recognizes three dimensions according to which distributed DBMSs may be architected: (1) the autonomy of local systems, (2) their distribution, and (3) their heterogeneity. These dimensions are orthogonal as we discuss shortly and in each dimension we identify a number of alternatives. Consequently, there are 18 possible architectures in the design space; not all of these architectural alternatives are meaningful, and most are not relevant from the perspective of this book. The three on which we focus are identified in Fig. 1.8.

---

[2]A reference architecture is commonly created by standards developers to clearly define the interfaces that need to be standardized.

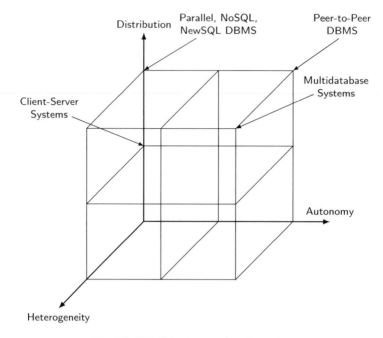

Fig. 1.8 DBMS implementation alternatives

1.6.1.1   Autonomy

Autonomy, in this context, refers to the distribution of control, not of data. It indicates the degree to which individual DBMSs can operate independently. Autonomy is a function of a number of factors such as whether the component systems (i.e., individual DBMSs) exchange information, whether they can independently execute transactions, and whether one is allowed to modify them.

We will use a classification that covers the important aspects of these features. This classification highlights three alternatives. One alternative is *tight integration*, where a single-image of the entire database is available to any user who wants to share the data that may reside in multiple databases. From the users' perspective, the data is logically integrated in one database. In these tightly integrated systems, the data managers are implemented so that one of them is in control of the processing of each user request even if that request is serviced by more than one data manager. The data managers do not typically operate as independent DBMSs even though they usually have the functionality to do so.

Next, we identify *semiautonomous* systems that consist of DBMSs that can (and usually do) operate independently, but have decided to participate in a federation to make their local data sharable. Each of these DBMSs determines what parts of their own database they will make accessible to users of other DBMSs. They are not fully autonomous systems because they need to be modified to enable them to exchange information with one another.

The last alternative that we consider is *total isolation*, where the individual systems are stand-alone DBMSs that know neither of the existence of other DBMSs nor how to communicate with them. In such systems, the processing of user transactions that access multiple databases is especially difficult since there is no global control over the execution of individual DBMSs.

1.6.1.2   Distribution

Whereas autonomy refers to the distribution (or decentralization) of control, the distribution dimension of the taxonomy deals with data. Of course, we are considering the physical distribution of data over multiple sites; as we discussed earlier, the user sees the data as one logical pool. There are a number of ways DBMSs have been distributed. We abstract these alternatives into two classes: *client/server* distribution and *peer-to-peer* distribution (or *full* distribution). Together with the nondistributed option, the taxonomy identifies three alternative architectures.

The client/server distribution concentrates data management duties at servers, while the clients focus on providing the application environment including the user interface. The communication duties are shared between the client machines and servers. Client/server DBMSs represent a practical compromise to distributing functionality. There are a variety of ways of structuring them, each providing a different level of distribution. We leave detailed discussion to Sect. 1.6.2.

In *peer-to-peer systems*, there is no distinction of client machines versus servers. Each machine has full DBMS functionality and can communicate with other machines to execute queries and transactions. Most of the very early work on distributed database systems have assumed peer-to-peer architecture. Therefore, our main focus in this book is on peer-to-peer systems (also called *fully distributed*), even though many of the techniques carry over to client/server systems as well.

1.6.1.3   Heterogeneity

Heterogeneity may occur in various forms in distributed systems, ranging from hardware heterogeneity and differences in networking protocols to variations in data managers. The important ones from the perspective of this book relate to data models, query languages, and transaction management protocols. Representing data with different modeling tools creates heterogeneity because of the inherent expressive powers and limitations of individual data models. Heterogeneity in query languages not only involves the use of completely different data access paradigms in different data models (set-at-a-time access in relational systems versus record-at-a-time access in some object-oriented systems), but also covers differences in languages even when the individual systems use the same data model. Although SQL is now the standard relational query language, there are many different implementations and every vendor's language has a slightly different flavor (sometimes even different semantics, producing different results). Furthermore, big data platforms and NoSQL systems have significantly variable access languages and mechanisms.

1.6.2   Client/Server Systems

Client/server entered the computing scene at the beginning of 1990s and has made a significant impact on the DBMS technology. The general idea is very simple and elegant: distinguish the functionality that needs to be provided on a server machine from those that need to be provided on a client. This provides a *two-level architecture* which makes it easier to manage the complexity of modern DBMSs and the complexity of distribution.

In relational client/server DBMSs, the server does most of the data management work. This means that all of query processing and optimization, transaction management, and storage management are done at the server. The client, in addition to the application and the user interface, has a *DBMS client* module that is responsible for managing the data that is cached to the client and (sometimes) managing the transaction locks that may have been cached as well. It is also possible to place consistency checking of user queries at the client side, but this is not common since it requires the replication of the system catalog at the client machines. This architecture, depicted in Fig. 1.9, is quite common in relational systems where the communication between the clients and the server(s) is at the level of SQL

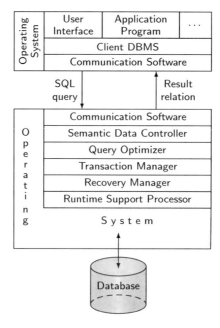

Fig. 1.9 Client/server reference architecture

statements. In other words, the client passes SQL queries to the server without trying to understand or optimize them. The server does most of the work and returns the result relation to the client.

There are a number of different realizations of the client/server architecture. The simplest is the case where there is only one server which is accessed by multiple clients. We call this *multiple client/single server*. From a data management perspective, this is not much different from centralized databases since the database is stored on only one machine (the server) that also hosts the software to manage it. However, there are important differences from centralized systems in the way transactions are executed and caches are managed—since data is cached at the client, it is necessary to deploy cache coherence protocols.

A more sophisticated client/server architecture is one where there are multiple servers in the system (the so-called *multiple client/multiple server* approach). In this case, two alternative management strategies are possible: either each client manages its own connection to the appropriate server or each client knows of only its "home server" which then communicates with other servers as required. The former approach simplifies server code, but loads the client machines with additional responsibilities. This leads to what has been called "heavy client" systems. The latter approach, on the other hand, concentrates the data management functionality at the servers. Thus, the transparency of data access is provided at the server interface, leading to "light clients."

In the multiple server systems, data is partitioned and may be replicated across the servers. This is transparent to the clients in the case of light client approach, and servers may communicate among themselves to answer a user query. This approach is implemented in parallel DBMS to improve performance through parallel processing.

Client/server can be naturally extended to provide for a more efficient function distribution on different kinds of servers: *clients* run the user interface (e.g., web servers), *application servers* run application programs, and *database servers* run database management functions. This leads to the three-tier distributed system architecture.

The application server approach (indeed, an n-tier distributed approach) can be extended by the introduction of multiple database servers and multiple application servers (Fig. 1.10), as can be done in classical client/server architectures. In this case, it is typically the case that each application server is dedicated to one or a few applications, while database servers operate in the multiple server fashion discussed above. Furthermore, the interface to the application is typically through a load balancer that routes the client requests to the appropriate servers.

The database server approach, as an extension of the classical client/server architecture, has several potential advantages. First, the single focus on data management makes possible the development of specific techniques for increasing data reliability and availability, e.g., using parallelism. Second, the overall performance of database management can be significantly enhanced by the tight integration of the database system and a dedicated database operating system. Finally, database servers can also exploit advanced hardware assists such as GPUs and FPGAs to enhance both performance and data availability.

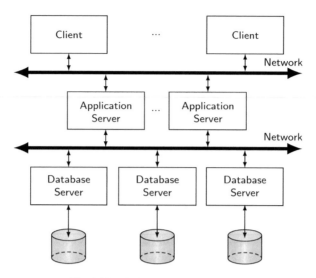

Fig. 1.10 Distributed database servers

Although these advantages are significant, there is the additional overhead introduced by another layer of communication between the application and the data servers. The communication cost can be amortized if the server interface is sufficiently high level to allow the expression of complex queries involving intensive data processing.

1.6.3 Peer-to-Peer Systems

The early works on distributed DBMSs all focused on peer-to-peer architectures where there was no differentiation between the functionality of each site in the system. Modern peer-to-peer systems have two important differences from their earlier relatives. The first is the massive distribution in more recent systems. While in the early days the focus was on a few (perhaps at most tens of) sites, current systems consider thousands of sites. The second is the inherent heterogeneity of every aspect of the sites and their autonomy. While this has always been a concern of distributed databases, as discussed earlier, coupled with massive distribution, site heterogeneity and autonomy take on an added significance, disallowing some of the approaches from consideration. In this book we initially focus on the classical meaning of peer-to-peer (the same functionality at each site), since the principles and fundamental techniques of these systems are very similar to those of client/server systems, and discuss the modern peer-to-peer database issues in a separate chapter (Chap. 9).

In these systems, the database design follows a top-down design as discussed earlier. So, the input is a (centralized) database with its own schema definition (*global conceptual schema*—GCS). This database is partitioned and allocated to sites of the distributed DBMS. Thus, at each site, there is a local database with its own schema (called the *local conceptual schema*—LCS). The user formulates queries according to the GCS, irrespective of its location. The distributed DBMS translates global queries into a group of local queries, which are executed by distributed DBMS components at different sites that communicate with one another. From a querying perspective, peer-to-peer systems and client/server DBMSs provide the same view of data. That is, they give the user the appearance of a logically single database, while at the physical level data is distributed.

The detailed components of a distributed DBMS are shown in Fig. 1.11. One component handles the interaction with users, and another deals with the storage.

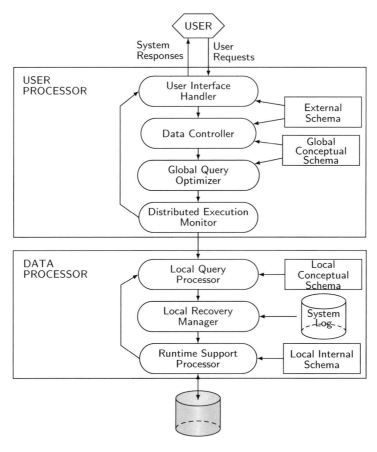

Fig. 1.11 Components of a distributed DBMS

The first major component, which we call the *user processor*, consists of four elements:

1. The *user interface handler* is responsible for interpreting user commands as they come in, and formatting the result data as it is sent to the user.
2. The *data controller* uses the integrity constraints and authorizations that are defined as part of the global conceptual schema to check if the user query can be processed. This component, which is studied in detail in Chap. 3, is also responsible for authorization and other functions.
3. The *global query optimizer and decomposer* determines an execution strategy to minimize a cost function, and translates the global queries into local ones using the global and local conceptual schemas as well as the global directory. The global query optimizer is responsible, among other things, for generating the best strategy to execute distributed join operations. These issues are discussed in Chap. 4.
4. The *distributed execution monitor* coordinates the distributed execution of the user request. The execution monitor is also called the *distributed transaction manager*. In executing queries in a distributed fashion, the execution monitors at various sites may, and usually do, communicate with one another. Distributed transaction manager functionality is covered in Chap. 5.

The second major component of a distributed DBMS is the *data processor* and consists of the following three elements. These are all issues that centralized DBMSs deal with, so we do not focus on them in this book.

1. The *local query optimizer*, which actually acts as the *access path selector*, is responsible for choosing the best access path[3] to access any data item.
2. The *local recovery manager* is responsible for making sure that the local database remains consistent even when failures occur.
3. The *runtime support processor* physically accesses the database according to the physical commands in the schedule generated by the query optimizer. The runtime support processor is the interface to the operating system and contains the *database buffer* (or *cache*) *manager*, which is responsible for maintaining the main memory buffers and managing the data accesses.

It is important to note that our use of the terms "user processor" and "data processor" does not imply a functional division similar to client/server systems. These divisions are merely organizational and there is no suggestion that they should be placed on different machines. In peer-to-peer systems, one expects to find both the user processor modules and the data processor modules on each machine. However, there can be "query-only sites" that only have the user processor.

---

[3]The term *access path* refers to the data structures and the algorithms that are used to access the data. A typical access path, for example, is an index on one or more attributes of a relation.

1.6.4 Multidatabase Systems

Multidatabase systems (MDBSs) represent the case where individual DBMSs are fully autonomous and have no concept of cooperation; they may not even "know" of each other's existence or how to talk to each other. Our focus is, naturally, on distributed MDBSs, which refers to the MDBS where participating DBMSs are located on different sites. Many of the issues that we discussed are common to both single-node and distributed MDBSs; in those cases we will simply use the term MDBS without qualifying it as single node or distributed. In most current literature, one finds the term *database integration* used instead. We discuss these systems further in Chap. 7. We note, however, that there is considerable variability in the use of the term "multidatabase" in literature. In this book, we use it consistently as defined above, which may deviate from its use in some of the existing literature.

The differences in the level of autonomy between the MDBSs and distributed DBMSs are also reflected in their architectural models. The fundamental difference relates to the definition of the global conceptual schema. In the case of logically integrated distributed DBMSs, the global conceptual schema defines the conceptual view of the *entire* database, while in the case of MDBSs, it represents only the collection of *some* of the local databases that each local DBMS wants to share. The individual DBMSs may choose to make some of their data available for access by others. Thus the definition of a *global database* is different in MDBSs than in distributed DBMSs. In the latter, the global database is equal to the union of local databases, whereas in the former it is only a (possibly proper) subset of the same union. In an MDBS, the GCS (which is also called a *mediated schema*) is defined by integrating (possibly parts of) local conceptual schemas.

The component-based architectural model of a distributed MDBS is significantly different from a distributed DBMS, because each site is a full-fledged DBMS that manages a different database. The MDBS provides a layer of software that runs on top of these individual DBMSs and provides users with the facilities of accessing various databases (Fig. 1.12). Note that in a distributed MDBS, the MDBS layer may run on multiple sites or there may be central site where those services are offered. Also note that as far as the individual DBMSs are concerned, the MDBS layer is simply another application that submits requests and receives answers.

A popular implementation architecture for MDBSs is the mediator/wrapper approach (Fig. 1.13). A *mediator* "is a software module that exploits encoded knowledge about certain sets or subsets of data to create information for a higher layer of applications" [Wiederhold 1992]. Thus, each mediator performs a particular function with clearly defined interfaces. Using this architecture to implement an MDBS, each module in the MDBS layer of Fig. 1.12 is realized as a mediator. Since mediators can be built on top of other mediators, it is possible to construct a layered implementation. The mediator level implements the GCS. It is this level that handles user queries over the GCS and performs the MDBS functionality.

The mediators typically operate using a common data model and interface language. To deal with potential heterogeneities of the source DBMSs, *wrappers*

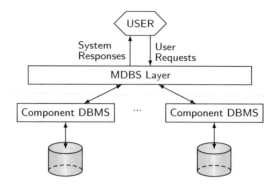

Fig. 1.12   Components of an MDBS

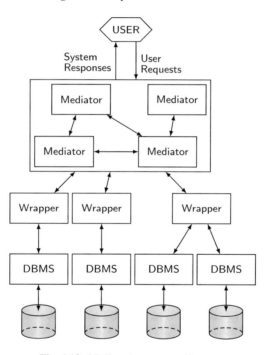

Fig. 1.13   Mediator/wrapper architecture

are implemented whose task is to provide a mapping between a source DBMSs view and the mediators' view. For example, if the source DBMS is a relational one, but the mediator implementations are object-oriented, the required mappings are established by the wrappers. The exact role and function of mediators differ from one implementation to another. In some cases, mediators do nothing more than translation; these are called "thin" mediators. In other cases, wrappers take over the execution of some of the query functionality.

One can view the collection of mediators as a middleware layer that provides services above the source systems. Middleware is a topic that has been the subject of significant study in the past decade and very sophisticated middleware systems have been developed that provide advanced services for development of distributed applications. The mediators that we discuss only represent a subset of the functionality provided by these systems.

1.6.5 Cloud Computing

Cloud computing has caused a significant shift in how users and organizations deploy scalable applications, in particular, data management applications. The vision encompasses on demand, reliable services provided over the Internet (typically represented as a cloud) with easy access to virtually infinite computing, storage, and networking resources. Through very simple web interfaces and at small incremental cost, users can outsource complex tasks, such as data storage, database management, system administration, or application deployment, to very large data centers operated by cloud providers. Thus, the complexity of managing the software/hardware infrastructure gets shifted from the users' organization to the cloud provider.

Cloud computing is a natural evolution, and combination, of different computing models proposed for supporting applications over the web: service-oriented architectures (SOA) for high-level communication of applications through web services, utility computing for packaging computing and storage resources as services, cluster and virtualization technologies to manage lots of computing and storage resources, and autonomous computing to enable self-management of complex infrastructure. The cloud provides various levels of functionality such as:

- Infrastructure-as-a-Service (IaaS): the delivery of a computing infrastructure (i.e., computing, networking, and storage resources) as a service;
- Platform-as-a-Service (PaaS): the delivery of a computing platform with development tools and APIs as a service;
- Software-as-a-Service (SaaS): the delivery of application software as a service; or
- Database-as-a-Service (DaaS): the delivery of database as a service.

What makes cloud computing unique is its ability to provide and combine all kinds of services to best fit the users' requirements. From a technical point of view, the grand challenge is to support in a cost-effective way, the very large scale of the infrastructure that has to manage lots of users and resources with high quality of service.

Agreeing on a precise definition of cloud computing is difficult as there are many different perspectives (business, market, technical, research, etc.). However, a good working definition is that a "cloud provides on demand resources and services over the Internet, usually at the scale and with the reliability of a data center" [Grossman and Gu 2009]. This definition captures well the main objective (providing on-demand resources and services over the Internet) and the main requirements for supporting them (at the scale and with the reliability of a data center). Since the resources are accessed through services, everything gets delivered as a service. Thus, as in the services industry, this enables cloud providers to propose a pay-as-you-go pricing model, whereby users only pay for the resources they consume.

The main functions provided by clouds are: security, directory management, resource management (provisioning, allocation, monitoring), and data management (storage, file management, database management, data replication). In addition, clouds provide support for pricing, accounting, and service level agreement management.

The typical advantages of cloud computing are the following:

- **Cost.** The cost for the customer can be greatly reduced since the infrastructure does not need to be owned and managed; billing is only based on resource consumption. As for the cloud provider, using a consolidated infrastructure and sharing costs for multiple customers reduces the cost of ownership and operation.
- **Ease of access and use.** The cloud hides the complexity of the IT infrastructure and makes location and distribution transparent. Thus, customers can have access to IT services anytime, and from anywhere with an Internet connection.
- **Quality of service.** The operation of the IT infrastructure by a specialized provider that has extensive experience in running very large infrastructures (including its own infrastructure) increases quality of service and operational efficiency.
- **Innovation.** Using state-of-the-art tools and applications provided by the cloud encourages modern practice, thus increasing the innovation capabilities of the customers.
- **Elasticity.** The ability to scale resources out, up and down dynamically to accommodate changing conditions is a major advantage. This is typically achieved through server virtualization, a technology that enables multiple applications to run on the same physical computer as virtual machines (VMs), i.e., as if they would run on distinct physical computers. Customers can then require computing instances as VMs and attach storage resources as needed.

However, there are also disadvantages that must be well-understood before moving to the cloud. These disadvantages are similar to when outsourcing applications and data to an external company.

- **Provider dependency.** Cloud providers tend to lock in customers, through proprietary software, proprietary format, or high outbound data transfer costs, thus making cloud service migration difficult.
- **Loss of control.** Customers may lose managerial control over critical operations such as system downtime, e.g., to perform a software upgrade.
- **Security.** Since a customer's cloud data is accessible from anywhere on the Internet, security attacks can compromise business's data. Cloud security can be improved using advanced capabilities, e.g., virtual private cloud, but may be complex to integrate with a company's security policy.

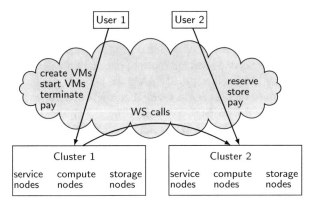

Fig. 1.14 Simplified cloud architecture

- **Hidden costs.** Customizing applications to make them cloud-ready using SaaS/-PaaS may incur significant development costs.

There is no standard cloud architecture and there will probably never be one, since different cloud providers provide different cloud services (IaaS, PaaS, SaaS, etc.) in different ways (public, private, virtual private, etc.) depending on their business models. Thus, in this section, we discuss a simplified cloud architecture with emphasis on database management.

A cloud is typically multisite (Fig. 1.14), i.e., made of several geographically distributed sites (or data centers), each with its own resources and data. Major cloud providers divide the world in several regions, each with several sites. There are three major reasons for this. First, there is low latency access in a user's region since user requests can be directed to the closest site. Second, using data replication across sites in different regions provides high availability, in particular, resistance from catastrophic (site) failures. Third, some national regulations that protect citizen's data privacy force cloud providers to locate data centers in their region (e.g., Europe). Multisite transparency is generally a default option, so the cloud appears "centralized" and the cloud provider can optimize resource allocation to users. However, some cloud providers (e.g., Amazon and Microsoft) make their sites visible to users (or application developers). This allows choosing a particular data center to install an application with its database, or to deploy a very large application across multiple sites communicating through web services (WS). For instance, in Fig. 1.14, we could imagine that Client 1 first connects to an application at Data Center 1, which would call an application at Data Center 2 using WS.

The architecture of a cloud site (data center) is typically 3-tier. The first tier consists of web clients that access cloud web servers, typically via a router or load balancer at the cloud site. The second tier consists of web/application servers that support the clients and provide business logic. The third tier consists of database servers. There can be other kinds of servers, e.g., cache servers between the application servers and database servers. Thus, the cloud architecture provides two levels of distribution: geographical distribution across sites using a WAN and within a site, distribution across the servers, typically in a computer cluster. The techniques used at the first level are those of geographically distributed DBMS, while the techniques used at the second level are those of parallel DBMS.

Cloud computing has been originally designed by web giants to run their very large scale applications on data centers with thousands of servers. Big data systems (Chap. 10) and NoSQL/NewSQL systems (Chap. 11) specifically address the requirements of such applications in the cloud, using distributed data management techniques. With the advent of SaaS and PaaS solutions, cloud providers also need to serve small applications for very high numbers of customers, called *tenants*, each with its own (small) database accessed by its users. Dedicating a server for each tenant is wasteful in terms of hardware resources. To reduce resource wasting and operation cost, cloud providers typically share resources among tenants using a "multitenancy" architecture in which a single server can accommodate multiple tenants. Different multitenant models yield different trade-offs between performance, isolation (both security and performance isolation), and design complexity. A straightforward model used in IaaS is hardware sharing, which is typically achieved through server virtualization, with a VM for each tenant database and operating system. This model provides strong security isolation. However, resource utilization is limited because of redundant DBMS instances (one per VM) that do not cooperate and perform independent resource management. In the context of SaaS, PaaS, or DaaS, we can distinguish three main multitenant database models with increasing resource sharing and performance at the expense of less isolation and increased complexity.

- **Shared DBMS server.** In this model, tenants share a server with one DBMS instance, but each tenant has a different database. Most DBMSs provide support for multiple databases in a single DBMS instance. Thus, this model can be easily supported using a DBMS. It provides strong isolation at the database level and is more efficient than shared hardware as the DBMS instance has full control over hardware resources. However, managing each of these databases separately may still lead to inefficient resource management.
- **Shared database.** In this model, tenants share a database, but each tenant has its own schema and tables. Database consolidation is typically provided by an additional abstraction layer in the DBMS. This model is implemented by some DBMS (e.g., Oracle) using a single container database hosting multiple databases. It provides good resource usage and isolation at schema level. However, with lots (thousands) of tenants per server, there is a high number of small tables, which induces much overhead.
- **Shared tables.** In this model, tenants share a database, schema, and tables. To distinguish the rows of different tenants in a table, there is usually an additional column tenant_id. Although there is better resource sharing (e.g., cache memory), there is less isolation, both in security and performance. For instance, bigger customers will have more rows in shared tables, thus hurting the performance for smaller customers.

1.7 Bibliographic Notes

There are not many books on distributed DBMSs. The two early ones by Ceri and Pelagatti [1983] and Bell and Grimson [1992] are now out of print. A more recent book by Rahimi and Haug [2010] covers some of the classical topics that are also covered in this book. In addition, almost every database book now has a chapter on distributed DBMSs.

The pioneering systems Distributed INGRES and SDD-1 are discussed in [Stonebraker and Neuhold 1977] and [Wong 1977], respectively.

Database design is discussed in an introductory manner in [Levin and Morgan 1975] and more comprehensively in [Ceri et al. 1987]. A survey of the file distribution algorithms is given in [Dowdy and Foster 1982]. Directory management has not been considered in detail in the research community, but general techniques can be found in [Chu and Nahouraii 1975] and [Chu 1976]. A survey of query processing techniques can be found in [Sacco and Yao 1982]. Concurrency control algorithms are reviewed in [Bernstein and Goodman 1981] and [Bernstein et al. 1987]. Deadlock management has also been the subject of extensive research; an introductory paper is [Isloor and Marsland 1980] and a widely quoted paper is [Obermack 1982]. For deadlock detection, good surveys are [Knapp 1987] and [Elmagarmid 1986]. Reliability is one of the issues discussed in [Gray 1979], which is one of the landmark papers in the field. Other important papers on this topic are [Verhofstadt 1978] and [Härder and Reuter 1983]. [Gray 1979] is also the first paper discussing the issues of operating system support for distributed databases; the same topic is addressed in [Stonebraker 1981]. Unfortunately, both papers emphasize centralized database systems. A very good early survey of multidatabase systems is by Sheth and Larson [1990]; Wiederhold [1992] proposes the mediator/wrapper approach to MDBSs. Cloud computing has been the topic of quite a number of recent books; perhaps [Agrawal et al. 2012] is a good starting point and [Cusumano 2010] is a good short overview. The architecture we used in Sect. 1.6.5 is from [Agrawal et al. 2012]. Different multitenant models in cloud environments are discussed in [Curino et al. 2011] and [Agrawal et al. 2012].

There have been a number of architectural framework proposals. Some of the interesting ones include Schreiber's quite detailed extension of the ANSI/SPARC framework which attempts to accommodate heterogeneity of the data models [Schreiber 1977], and the proposal by Mohan and Yeh [1978]. As expected, these date back to the early days of the introduction of distributed DBMS technology. The detailed component-wise system architecture given in Fig. 1.11 derives from [Rahimi 1987]. An alternative to the classification that we provide in Fig. 1.8 can be found in [Sheth and Larson 1990].

The book by Agrawal et al. [2012] gives a very good presentation of the challenges and concepts of data management in the cloud, including distributed transactions, big data systems, and multitenant databases.

Chapter 2
Distributed and Parallel Database Design

A typical database design is a process which starts from a set of requirements and results in the definition of a schema that defines the set of relations. The distribution design starts from this global conceptual schema (GCS) and follows two tasks: *partitioning* (*fragmentation*) and *allocation*. Some techniques combine these two tasks in one algorithm, while others implement them in two separate tasks as depicted in Fig. 2.1. The process typically makes use of some auxiliary information that is depicted in the figure although some of this information is optional (hence the dashed lines in the figure).

The main reasons and objectives for fragmentation in distributed versus parallel DBMSs are slightly different. In the case of the former, the main reason is *data locality*. To the extent possible, we would like queries to access data at a single site in order to avoid costly remote data access. A second major reason is that fragmentation enables a number of queries to execute concurrently (through *interquery parallelism*). The fragmentation of relations also results in the parallel execution of a single query by dividing it into a set of subqueries that operate on fragments, which is referred to as *intraquery parallelism*. Therefore, in distributed DBMSs, fragmentation can potentially reduce costly remote data access and increase inter and intraquery parallelism.

In parallel DBMSs, data localization is not that much of a concern since the communication cost among nodes is much less than in geo-distributed DBMSs. What is much more of a concern is load balancing as we want each node in the system to be doing more or less the same amount of work. Otherwise, there is the danger of the entire system thrashing since one or a few nodes end up doing a majority of the work, while many nodes remain idle. This also increases the latency of queries and transactions since they have to wait for these overloaded nodes to finish. Inter and intraquery parallelism are both important as we discuss in Chap. 8,

The original version of this chapter was revised. The correction to this chapter is available at https://doi.org/10.1007/978-3-030-26253-2_13

© Springer Nature Switzerland AG 2020
M. T. Özsu, P. Valduriez, *Principles of Distributed Database Systems*,
https://doi.org/10.1007/978-3-030-26253-2_2

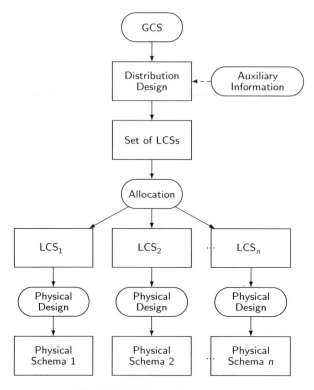

Fig. 2.1 Distribution design process

although some of the modern big data systems (Chap. 10) pay more attention to interquery parallelism.

Fragmentation is important for system performance, but it also raises difficulties in distributed DBMSs. It is not always possible to entirely localize queries and transactions to only access data at one site—these are called *distributed queries* and *distributed transactions*. Processing them incurs a performance penalty due to, for example, the need to perform distributed joins and the cost of distributed transaction commitment (see Chap. 5). One way to overcome this penalty for read-only queries is to replicate the data in multiple sites (see Chap. 6), but that further exacerbates the overhead of distributed transactions. A second problem is related to semantic data control, specifically to integrity checking. As a result of fragmentation, attributes participating in a constraint (see Chap. 3) may be decomposed into different fragments that are allocated to different sites. In this case, integrity checking itself involves distributed execution, which is costly. We consider the issue of distributed data control in the next chapter. Thus, the challenge is to partition[1] and allocate

---

[1]A minor point related to terminology is the use of terms "fragmentation" and "partitioning": in distributed DBMSs, the term fragmentation is more commonly used, while in parallel DBMSs, data partitioning is preferred. We do not prefer one over the other and will use them interchangeably in this chapter and in this book.

EMP

ENO	ENAME	TITLE
E1	J. Doe	Elect. Eng.
E2	M. Smith	Syst. Anal.
E3	A. Lee	Mech. Eng.
E4	J. Miller	Programmer
E5	B. Casey	Syst. Anal.
E6	L. Chu	Elect. Eng.
E7	R. Davis	Mech. Eng.
E8	J. Jones	Syst. Anal.

ASG

ENO	PNO	RESP	DUR
E1	P1	Manager	12
E2	P1	Analyst	24
E2	P2	Analyst	6
E3	P3	Consultant	10
E3	P4	Engineer	48
E4	P2	Programmer	18
E5	P2	Manager	24
E6	P4	Manager	48
E7	P3	Engineer	36
E8	P3	Manager	40

PROJ

PNO	PNAME	BUDGET	LOC
P1	Instrumentation	150000	Montreal
P2	Database Develop.	135000	New York
P3	CAD/CAM	250000	New York
P4	Maintenance	310000	Paris

PAY

TITLE	SAL
Elect. Eng.	40000
Syst. Anal.	34000
Mech. Eng.	27000
Programmer	24000

Fig. 2.2 Example database

the data in such a way that most user queries and transactions are local to one site, minimizing distributed queries and transactions.

Our discussion in this chapter will follow the methodology of Fig. 2.1: we will first discuss fragmentation of a global database (Sect. 2.1), and then discuss how to allocate these fragments across the sites of a distributed database (Sect. 2.2). In this methodology, the unit of distribution/allocation is a fragment. There are also approaches that combine the fragmentation and allocation steps and we discuss these in Sect. 2.3. Finally we discuss techniques that are adaptive to changes in the database and the user workload in Sect. 2.4.

In this chapter, and throughout the book, we use the engineering database introduced in the previous chapter. Figure 2.2 depicts an instance of this database.

2.1 Data Fragmentation

Relational tables can be partitioned either *horizontally* or *vertically*. The basis of horizontal fragmentation is the select operator where the selection predicates determine the fragmentation, while vertical fragmentation is performed by means of the project operator. The fragmentation may, of course, be nested. If the nestings are of different types, one gets *hybrid fragmentation*.

Example 2.1 Figure 2.3 shows the PROJ relation of Fig. 2.2 divided horizontally into two fragments: PROJ$_1$ contains information about projects whose budgets are less than $200,000, whereas PROJ$_2$ stores information about projects with larger budgets. ♦

PROJ$_1$

PNO	PNAME	BUDGET	LOC
P1	Instrumentation	150000	Montreal
P2	Database Develop.	135000	New York

PROJ$_2$

PNO	PNAME	BUDGET	LOC
P3	CAD/CAM	255000	New York
P4	Maintenance	310000	Paris

Fig. 2.3 Example of horizontal partitioning

PROJ$_1$

PNO	BUDGET
P1	150000
P2	135000
P3	250000
P4	310000

PROJ$_2$

PNO	PNAME	LOC
P1	Instrumentation	Montreal
P2	Database Develop.	New York
P3	CAD/CAM	New York
P4	Maintenance	Paris

Fig. 2.4 Example of vertical partitioning

Example 2.2 Figure 2.4 shows the PROJ relation of Fig. 2.2 partitioned vertically into two fragments: PROJ$_1$ and PROJ$_2$. PROJ$_1$ contains only the information about project budgets, whereas PROJ$_2$ contains project names and locations. It is important to notice that the primary key to the relation (PNO) is included in both fragments.   ◆

Horizontal fragmentation is more prevalent in most systems, in particular in parallel DBMSs (where the literature prefers the term *sharding*). The reason for the prevalence of horizontal fragmentation is the *intraquery parallelism*[2] that most recent big data platforms advocate. However, vertical fragmentation has been successfully used in *column-store* parallel DBMSs, such as MonetDB and Vertica, for analytical applications, which typically require fast access to a few attributes.

The systematic fragmentation techniques that we discuss in this chapter ensure that the database does not undergo semantic change during fragmentation, such as losing data as a consequence of fragmentation. Therefore, it is necessary to be able to argue about the *completeness* and *reconstructability*. In the case of horizontal fragmentation, *disjointness* of fragments may also be a desirable property (unless we explicitly wish to replicate individual tuples as we will discuss later).

1. *Completeness.* If a relation instance R is decomposed into fragments $F_R = \{R_1, R_2, \ldots, R_n\}$, each data item that is in R can also be found in one or more of R_i's. This property, which is identical to the *lossless decomposition* property of

---

[2]In this chapter, we use the terms "query" and "transaction" interchangeably as they both refer to the system workload that is one of the main inputs to distribution design. As highlighted in Chap. 1 and as will be discussed in length in Chap. 5, transactions provide additional guarantees, and therefore their overhead is higher and we will incorporate this into our discussion where needed.

normalization (Appendix A), is also important in fragmentation since it ensures that the data in a global relation is mapped into fragments without any loss. Note that in the case of horizontal fragmentation, the "item" typically refers to a tuple, while in the case of vertical fragmentation, it refers to an attribute.

2. *Reconstruction*. If a relation R is decomposed into fragments $F_R = \{R_1, R_2, \ldots, R_n\}$, it should be possible to define a relational operator $\triangledown$ such that

$$R = \triangledown R_i, \quad \forall R_i \in F_R$$

The operator $\triangledown$ will be different for different forms of fragmentation; it is important, however, that it can be identified. The reconstructability of the relation from its fragments ensures that constraints defined on the data in the form of dependencies are preserved.

3. *Disjointness*. If a relation R is horizontally decomposed into fragments $F_R = \{R_1, R_2, \ldots, R_n\}$ and data item d_i is in R_j, it is not in any other fragment R_k ($k \neq j$). This criterion ensures that the horizontal fragments are disjoint. If relation R is vertically decomposed, its primary key attributes are typically repeated in all its fragments (for reconstruction). Therefore, in case of vertical partitioning, disjointness is defined only on the nonprimary key attributes of a relation.

2.1.1 Horizontal Fragmentation

As we explained earlier, horizontal fragmentation partitions a relation along its tuples. Thus, each fragment has a subset of the tuples of the relation. There are two versions of horizontal partitioning: primary and derived. *Primary horizontal fragmentation* of a relation is performed using predicates that are defined on that relation. *Derived horizontal fragmentation*, on the other hand, is the partitioning of a relation that results from predicates being defined on another relation.

Later in this section, we consider an algorithm for performing both of these fragmentations. However, we first investigate the information needed to carry out horizontal fragmentation activity.

2.1.1.1 Auxiliary Information Requirements

The database information that is required concerns the global conceptual schema, primarily on how relations are connected to one another, especially with joins. One way of capturing this information is to explicitly model primary key–foreign key join relationships in a *join graph*. In this graph, each relation R_i is represented as a vertex and a directed edge L_k exists from R_i to R_j if there is a primary key–foreign key equijoin from R_i to R_j. Note that L_k also represents a one-to-many relationship.

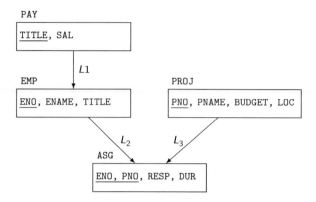

Fig. 2.5 Join graph representing relationships among relations

Example 2.3 Figure 2.5 shows the edges among the database relations given in
Fig. 2.2. Note that the direction of the edge shows a one-to-many relationship. For
example, for each title there are multiple employees with that title; thus, there is an
edge between the PAY and EMP relations. Along the same lines, the many-to-many
relationship between the EMP and PROJ relations is expressed with two edges to
the ASG relation.   ◆

The relation at the tail of an edge is called the *source* of the edge and the relation
at the head is called the *target*. Let us define two functions: *source* and *target*, both
of which provide mappings from the set of edges to the set of relations. Considering
L_1 of Fig. 2.5, $source(L_1) =$ PAY and $target(L_1) =$ EMP.

Additionally, the cardinality of each relation R denoted by $card(R)$ is useful in
horizontal fragmentation.

These approaches also make use of the workload information, i.e., the queries
that are run on the database. Of particular importance are the predicates used in
user queries. In many cases, it may not be possible to analyze the full workload,
so the designer would normally focus on the important queries. There is a well-
known "80/20" rule-of-thumb in computer science that applies in this case as well:
the most common 20% of user queries account for 80% of the total data accesses,
so focusing on that 20% is usually sufficient to get a fragmentation that improves
most distributed database accesses.

At this point, we are interested in determining *simple predicates*. Given a relation
$R(A_1, A_2, \ldots, A_n)$, where A_i is an attribute defined over domain D_i, a simple
predicate p_j defined on R has the form

$$p_j : A_i \ \theta \ Value$$

where $\theta \in \{=, <, \neq, \leq, >, \geq\}$ and *Value* is chosen from the domain of
A_i ($Value \in D_i$). We use Pr_i to denote the set of all simple predicates defined
on a relation R_i. The members of Pr_i are denoted by p_{ij}.

Example 2.4 Given the relation instance PROJ of Fig. 2.2,

$$\text{PNAME} = \text{"Maintenance" and BUDGET} \leq 200000$$

is a simple predicate. ◆

User queries often include more complicated predicates, which are Boolean combinations of simple predicates. One such combination, called a *minterm predicate*, is the conjunction of simple predicates. Since it is always possible to transform a Boolean expression into conjunctive normal form, the use of minterm predicates in the design algorithms does not cause any loss of generality.

Given a set $Pr_i = \{p_{i1}, p_{i2}, \ldots, p_{im}\}$ of simple predicates for relation R_i, the set of minterm predicates $M_i = \{m_{i1}, m_{i2}, \ldots, m_{iz}\}$ is defined as

$$M_i = \{m_{ij} = \bigwedge_{p_{ik} \in Pr_i} p_{ik}^*\}, \ 1 \leq k \leq m, \ 1 \leq j \leq z$$

where $p_{ik}^* = p_{ik}$ or $p_{ik}^* = \neg p_{ik}$. So each simple predicate can occur in a minterm predicate in either its natural form or its negated form.

Negation of a predicate is straightforward for equality predicates of the form *Attribute = Value*. For inequality predicates, the negation should be treated as the complement. For example, the negation of the simple predicate *Attribute ≤ Value* is *Attribute > Value*. There are theoretical problems of finding the complement in infinite sets, and also the practical problem that the complement may be difficult to define. For example, if two simple predicates are defined of the form *Lower_bound ≤ Attribute_*1, and *Attribute_*1 ≤ *Upper_bound*, their complements are ¬(*Lower_bound ≤ Attribute_*1) and ¬(*Attribute_*1 ≤ *Upper_bound*). However, the original two simple predicates can be written as *Lower_bound ≤ Attribute_*1 ≤ *Upper_bound* with a complement ¬(*Lower_bound ≤ Attribute_*1 ≤ *Upper_bound*) that may not be easy to define. Therefore, we limit ourselves to simple predicates.

Example 2.5 Consider relation PAY of Fig. 2.2. The following are some of the possible simple predicates that can be defined on PAY.

$$p_1 : \text{TITLE} = \text{"Elect. Eng."}$$

$$p_2 : \text{TITLE} = \text{"Syst. Anal."}$$

$$p_3 : \text{TITLE} = \text{"Mech. Eng."}$$

$$p_4 : \text{TITLE} = \text{"Programmer"}$$

$$p_5 : \text{SAL} \leq 30000$$

The following are *some* of the minterm predicates that can be defined based on these simple predicates.

$$m_1 : \text{TITLE} = \text{``Elect. Eng.''} \land \text{SAL} \le 30000$$

$$m_2 : \text{TITLE} = \text{``Elect. Eng.''} \land \text{SAL} > 30000$$

$$m_3 : \neg(\text{TITLE} = \text{``Elect. Eng.''}) \land \text{SAL} \le 30000$$

$$m_4 : \neg(\text{TITLE} = \text{``Elect. Eng.''}) \land \text{SAL} > 30000$$

$$m_5 : \text{TITLE} = \text{``Programmer''} \land \text{SAL} \le 30000$$

$$m_6 : \text{TITLE} = \text{``Programmer''} \land \text{SAL} > 30000$$

◆

These are only a representative sample, not the entire set of minterm predicates. Furthermore, some of the minterms may be meaningless given the semantics of relation PAY, in which case they are removed from the set. Finally, note that these are simplified versions of the minterms. The minterm definition requires each predicate to be in a minterm in either its natural or its negated form. Thus, m_1, for example, should be written as

$$m_1 : \text{TITLE} = \text{``Elect. Eng.''} \land \text{TITLE} \ne \text{``Syst. Anal.''} \land \text{TITLE} \ne \text{``Mech. Eng.''}$$

$$\land \text{TITLE} \ne \text{``Programmer''} \land \text{SAL} \le 30000$$

This is clearly not necessary, and we use the simplified form.

We also need quantitative information about the workload:

1. *Minterm selectivity*: number of tuples of the relation that would satisfy a given minterm predicate. For example, the selectivity of m_2 of Example 2.5 is 0.25 since one of the four tuples in PAY satisfies m_2. We denote the selectivity of a minterm m_i as $sel(m_i)$.
2. *Access frequency*: frequency with which user applications access data. If $Q = \{q_1, q_2, \ldots, q_q\}$ is a set of user queries, $acc(q_i)$ indicates the access frequency of query q_i in a given period.

Note that minterm access frequencies can be determined from the query frequencies. We refer to the access frequency of a minterm m_i as $acc(m_i)$.

2.1.1.2 Primary Horizontal Fragmentation

Primary horizontal fragmentation applies to the relations that have no incoming edges in the join graph and performed using the predicates that are defined on that relation. In our examples, relations PAY and PROJ are subject to primary horizontal fragmentation, and EMP and ASG are subject to derived horizontal fragmentation. In this section, we focus on primary horizontal fragmentation and devote the next section to derived horizontal fragmentation.

A primary horizontal fragmentation is defined by a selection operation on the source relations of a database schema. Therefore, given relation R its horizontal fragments are given by

$$R_i = \sigma_{F_i}(R), \ 1 \le i \le w$$

where F_i is the selection formula used to obtain fragment R_i (also called the *fragmentation predicate*). Note that if F_i is in conjunctive normal form, it is a minterm predicate (m_i). The algorithm requires that F_i be a minterm predicate.

Example 2.6 The decomposition of relation PROJ into horizontal fragments PROJ$_1$ and PROJ$_2$ in Example 2.1 is defined as follows[3]:

$$PROJ_1 = \sigma_{BUDGET \le 200000}(PROJ)$$

$$PROJ_2 = \sigma_{BUDGET > 200000}(PROJ)$$

◆

Example 2.6 demonstrates one of the problems of horizontal partitioning. If the domain of the attributes participating in the selection formulas is continuous and infinite, as in Example 2.6, it is quite difficult to define the set of formulas $F = \{F_1, F_2, \ldots, F_n\}$ that would fragment the relation properly. One possible solution is to define ranges as we have done in Example 2.6. However, there is always the problem of handling the two endpoints. For example, if a new tuple with a BUDGET value of, say, \$600,000 were to be inserted into PROJ, one would have to review the fragmentation to decide if the new tuple is to go into PROJ$_2$ or if the fragments need to be revised and a new fragment needs to be defined as

$$PROJ_2 = \sigma_{200000 < BUDGET \wedge BUDGET \le 400000}(PROJ)$$

$$PROJ_3 = \sigma_{BUDGET > 400000}(PROJ)$$

Example 2.7 Consider relation PROJ of Fig. 2.2. We can define the following horizontal fragments based on the project location. The resulting fragments are shown in Fig. 2.6.

$$PROJ_1 = \sigma_{LOC="Montreal"}(PROJ)$$

$$PROJ_2 = \sigma_{LOC="New York"}(PROJ)$$

$$PROJ_3 = \sigma_{LOC="Paris"}(PROJ)$$

◆

Now we can define a horizontal fragment more carefully. A horizontal fragment R_i of relation R consists of all the tuples of R that satisfy a minterm predicate m_i.

---

[3] We assume that the nonnegativity of the BUDGET values is a feature of the relation that is enforced by an integrity constraint. Otherwise, a simple predicate of the form $0 \le$ BUDGET also needs to be included in Pr. We assume this to be true in all our examples and discussions in this chapter.

PROJ$_1$

PNO	PNAME	BUDGET	LOC
P1	Instrumentation	150000	Montreal

PROJ$_2$

PNO	PNAME	BUDGET	LOC
P2	Database Develop.	135000	New York
P3	CAD/CAM	255000	New York
P4	Maintenance	310000	Paris

PROJ$_3$

PNO	PNAME	BUDGET	LOC
P4	Maintenance	310000	Paris

Fig. 2.6 Primary horizontal fragmentation of relation PROJ

Hence, given a set of minterm predicates M, there are as many horizontal fragments of relation R as there are minterm predicates. This set of horizontal fragments is also commonly referred to as the set of *minterm fragments*.

We want the set of simple predicates that form the minterm predicates to be *complete* and *minimal*. A set of simple predicates Pr is said to be *complete* if and only if there is an equal probability of access by every application to any tuple belonging to any minterm fragment that is defined according to Pr.[4]

Example 2.8 Consider the fragmentation of relation PROJ given in Example 2.7. If the only query that accesses PROJ wants to access the tuples according to the location, the set is complete since each tuple of each fragment PROJ$_i$ has the same probability of being accessed. If, however, there is a second query that accesses only those project tuples where the budget is less than or equal to $200,000, then Pr is not complete. Some of the tuples within each PROJ$_i$ have a higher probability of being accessed due to this second application. To make the set of predicates complete, we need to add (BUDGET $\leq$ 200000, BUDGET $>$ 200000) to Pr:

$$Pr = \{\text{LOC} = \text{``Montreal''}, \text{LOC} = \text{``New York''}, \text{LOC} = \text{``Paris''},$$

$$\text{BUDGET} \leq 200000, \text{BUDGET} > 200000\}$$

◆

Completeness is desirable because fragments obtained according to a complete set of predicates are logically uniform, since they all satisfy the minterm predicate. They are also statistically homogeneous in the way applications access them. These

---

[4]Clearly the definition of completeness of a set of simple predicates is different from the completeness rule of fragmentation we discussed earlier.

characteristics ensure that the resulting fragmentation results in a balanced load (with respect to the given workload) across all the fragments.

Minimality states that if a predicate influences how fragmentation is performed (i.e., causes a fragment f to be further fragmented into, say, f_i and f_j), there should be at least one application that accesses f_i and f_j differently. In other words, the simple predicate should be *relevant* in determining a fragmentation. If all the predicates of a set Pr are relevant, Pr is *minimal*.

A formal definition of relevance can be given as follows. Let m_i and m_j be two minterm predicates that are identical in their definition, except that m_i contains the simple predicate p_i in its natural form, while m_j contains $\neg p_i$. Also, let f_i and f_j be two fragments defined according to m_i and m_j, respectively. Then p_i is *relevant* if and only if

$$\frac{acc(m_i)}{card(f_i)} \neq \frac{acc(m_j)}{card(f_j)}$$

Example 2.9 The set Pr defined in Example 2.8 is complete and minimal. If, however, we were to add the predicate PNAME = "Instrumentation" to Pr, the resulting set would not be minimal since the new predicate is not relevant with respect to Pr—there is no application that would access the resulting fragments any differently. ◆

We now present an iterative algorithm that would generate a complete and minimal set of predicates Pr' given a set of simple predicates Pr. This algorithm, called COM_MIN, is given in Algorithm 2.1 where we use the following notation:

Rule 1: each fragment is accessed differently by at least one application.

f_i *of* Pr': fragment f_i defined according to a minterm predicate defined over the predicates of Pr'.

COM_MIN begins by finding a predicate that is relevant and that partitions the input relation. The **repeat-until** loop iteratively adds predicates to this set, ensuring minimality at each step. Therefore, at the end the set Pr' is both minimal and complete.

The second step in the primary horizontal design process is to derive the set of minterm predicates that can be defined on the predicates in set Pr'. These minterm predicates determine the fragments that are used as candidates in the allocation step. Determination of individual minterm predicates is trivial; the difficulty is that the set of minterm predicates may be quite large (in fact, exponential on the number of simple predicates). We look at ways of reducing the number of minterm predicates that need to be considered in fragmentation.

This reduction can be achieved by eliminating some of the minterm fragments that may be meaningless. This elimination is performed by identifying those minterms that might be contradictory to a set of implications I. For example, if $Pr' = \{p_1, p_2\}$, where

---

Algorithm 2.1: COM_MIN

Input: R: relation; Pr: set of simple predicates
Output: Pr': set of simple predicates
Declare: F: set of minterm fragments
begin
    $Pr' \leftarrow \emptyset; F \leftarrow \emptyset$ {initialize}
    find $p_i \in Pr$ such that p_i partitions R according to *Rule* 1
    $Pr' \leftarrow Pr' \cup p_i$
    $Pr \leftarrow Pr - p_i$
    $F \leftarrow F \cup f_i$ {f_i is the minterm fragment according to p_i}
    repeat
        find $p_j \in Pr$ such that p_j partitions some f_k of Pr' according to *Rule* 1
        $Pr' \leftarrow Pr' \cup p_j$
        $Pr \leftarrow Pr - p_j$
        $F \leftarrow F \cup f_j$
        if $\exists p_k \in Pr'$ *which is not relevant* **then**
            $Pr' \leftarrow Pr' - p_k$
            $F \leftarrow F - f_k$
        end if
    until Pr' *is complete*
end

$$p_1 : \quad att = value\_1$$
$$p_2 : \quad att = value\_2$$

and the domain of *att* is $\{value\_1, value\_2\}$, so I contains two implications:

$$i_1 : \quad (att = value\_1) \Rightarrow \neg(att = value\_2)$$
$$i_2 : \quad \neg(att = value_1) \Rightarrow (att = value\_2)$$

The following four minterm predicates are defined according to Pr':

$$m_1 : \quad (att = value\_1) \wedge (att = value\_2)$$
$$m_2 : \quad (att = value\_1) \wedge \neg(att = value\_2)$$
$$m_3 : \quad \neg(att = value\_1) \wedge (att = value\_2)$$
$$m_4 : \quad \neg(att = value\_1) \wedge \neg(att = value\_2)$$

In this case the minterm predicates m_1 and m_4 are contradictory to the implications I and can therefore be eliminated from M.

The algorithm for primary horizontal fragmentation, called PHORIZONTAL, is given in Algorithm 2.2. The input is a relation R that is subject to primary horizontal fragmentation, and Pr, which is the set of simple predicates that have been determined according to applications defined on relation R.

Example 2.10 We now consider relations PAY and PROJ that are subject to primary horizontal fragmentation as depicted in Fig. 2.5.

Suppose that there is only one query that accesses PAY, which checks the salary information and determines a raise accordingly. Assume that employee records are managed in two places, one handling the records of those with salaries less than or equal to $30,000, and the other handling the records of those who earn more than $30,000. Therefore, the query is issued at two sites.

The simple predicates that would be used to partition relation PAY are

$$p_1 : \text{SAL} \leq 30000$$

$$p_2 : \text{SAL} > 30000$$

thus giving the initial set of simple predicates $Pr = \{p_1, p_2\}$. Applying the COM_MIN algorithm with $i = 1$ as initial value results in $Pr' = \{p_1\}$. This is complete and minimal since p_2 would not partition f_1 (which is the minterm fragment formed with respect to p_1) according to Rule 1. We can form the following minterm predicates as members of M:

$$m_1 : \text{SAL} < 30000$$

$$m_2 : \neg(\text{SAL} \leq 30000) = \text{SAL} > 30000$$

Therefore, we define two fragments $F_{\text{PAY}} = \{\text{PAY}_1, \text{PAY}_2\}$ according to M (Fig. 2.7).

Algorithm 2.2: PHORIZONTAL

Input: R: relation; Pr: set of simple predicates
Output: F_R: set of horizontal fragments of R
begin
    $Pr' \leftarrow$ COM_MIN(R, Pr)
    determine the set M of minterm predicates
    determine the set I of implications among $p_i \in Pr'$
    foreach $m_i \in M$ **do**
        if m_i *is contradictory according to* I **then**
            $M \leftarrow M - m_i$
        end if
    end foreach
    $F_R = \{R_i | R_i = \sigma_{m_i} R\}, \forall m_i \in M$
end

PAY$_1$

TITLE	SAL
Mech. Eng.	27000
Programmer	24000

PAY$_2$

TITLE	SAL
Elect. Eng.	40000
Syst. Anal.	34000

Fig. 2.7 Horizontal fragmentation of relation PAY

Let us next consider relation PROJ. Assume that there are two queries. The first is issued at three sites and finds the names and budgets of projects given their location. In SQL notation, the query is

```
SELECT PNAME, BUDGET
FROM   PROJ
WHERE  LOC=Value
```

For this application, the simple predicates that would be used are the following:

$$p_1 : \text{LOC} = \text{``Montreal''}$$

$$p_2 : \text{LOC} = \text{``New York''}$$

$$p_3 : \text{LOC} = \text{``Paris''}$$

The second query is issued at two sites and has to do with the management of the projects. Those projects that have a budget of less than or equal to \$200,000 are managed at one site, whereas those with larger budgets are managed at a second site. Thus, the simple predicates that should be used to fragment according to the second application are

$$p_4 : \text{BUDGET} \leq 200000$$

$$p_5 : \text{BUDGET} > 200000$$

Using COM_MIN, we get the complete and minimal set $Pr' = \{p_1, p_2, p_4\}$. Actually COM_MIN would add any two of p_1, p_2, p_3 to Pr'; in this example we have selected to include p_1, p_2.

Based on Pr', the following six minterm predicates that form M can be defined:

$$m_1 : (\text{LOC} = \text{``Montreal''}) \wedge (\text{BUDGET} \leq 200000)$$

$$m_2 : (\text{LOC} = \text{``Montreal''}) \wedge (\text{BUDGET} > 200000)$$

$$m_3 : (\text{LOC} = \text{``New York''}) \wedge (\text{BUDGET} \leq 200000)$$

$$m_4 : (\text{LOC} = \text{``New York''}) \wedge (\text{BUDGET} > 200000)$$

$$m_5 : (\text{LOC} = \text{``Paris''}) \wedge (\text{BUDGET} \leq 200000)$$

$$m_6 : (\text{LOC} = \text{``Paris''}) \wedge (\text{BUDGET} > 200000)$$

As noted in Example 2.5, these are not the only minterm predicates that can be generated. It is, for example, possible to specify predicates of the form

$$p_1 \wedge p_2 \wedge p_3 \wedge p_4 \wedge p_5$$

However, the obvious implications (e.g., $p_1 \Rightarrow \neg p_2 \wedge \neg p_3$, $\neg p_5 \Rightarrow p_4$) eliminate these minterm predicates and we are left with m_1 to m_6.

Looking at the database instance in Fig. 2.2, one may be tempted to claim that the following implications hold:

$$i_8 : \text{LOC} = \text{"Montreal"} \Rightarrow \neg(\text{BUDGET} > 200000)$$

$$i_9 : \text{LOC} = \text{"Paris"} \Rightarrow \neg(\text{BUDGET} \leq 200000)$$

$$i_{10} : \neg(\text{LOC} = \text{"Montreal"}) \Rightarrow \text{BUDGET} \leq 200000$$

$$i_{11} : \neg(\text{LOC} = \text{"Paris"}) \Rightarrow \text{BUDGET} > 200000$$

However, remember that implications should be defined according to the semantics of the database, not according to the current values. There is nothing in the database semantics that suggest that the implications i_8–i_{11} hold. Some of the fragments defined according to $M = \{m_1, \dots, m_6\}$ may be empty, but they are, nevertheless, fragments.

The result of the primary horizontal fragmentation of PROJ is to form six fragments $F_{\text{PROJ}} = \{\text{PROJ}_1, \text{PROJ}_2, \text{PROJ}_3, \text{PROJ}_4, \text{PROJ}_5, \text{PROJ}_6\}$ of relation PROJ according to the minterm predicates M (Fig. 2.8). Since fragments PROJ$_2$ and PROJ$_5$ are empty, they are not depicted in Fig. 2.8. ◆

2.1.1.3 Derived Horizontal Fragmentation

A derived horizontal fragmentation applies to the target relations in the join graph and is performed based on predicates defined over the source relation of the join graph edge. In our examples, relations EMP and ASG are subject to derived horizontal fragmentation. Recall that the edge between the source and the target relations is defined as an equijoin that can be implemented by means of semijoins.

PROJ$_1$

PNO	PNAME	BUDGET	LOC
P1	Instrumentation	150000	Montreal

PROJ$_3$

PNO	PNAME	BUDGET	LOC
P2	Database Develop.	135000	New York

PROJ$_4$

PNO	PNAME	BUDGET	LOC
P3	CAD/CAM	255000	New York

PROJ$_6$

PNO	PNAME	BUDGET	LOC
P4	Maintenance	310000	Paris

Fig. 2.8 Horizontal fragmentation of relation PROJ

This second point is important, since we want to partition a target relation according to the fragmentation of its source, but we also want the resulting fragment to be defined *only* on the attributes of the target relation.

Accordingly, given an edge L where $source(L) = $ S and $target(L) = $ R, the derived horizontal fragments of R are defined as

$$R_i = R \ltimes S_i, 1 \leq i \leq w$$

where w is the maximum number of fragments that will be defined on R and $S_i = \sigma_{F_i}(S)$, where F_i is the formula according to which the primary horizontal fragment S_i is defined.

Example 2.11 Consider edge L_1 in Fig. 2.5, where $source(L_1) = $ PAY and $target(L_1) = $ EMP. Then, we can group engineers into two groups according to their salary: those making less than or equal to \$30,000, and those making more than \$30,000. The two fragments EMP$_1$ and EMP$_2$ are defined as follows:

$$EMP_1 = EMP \ltimes PAY_1$$

$$EMP_2 = EMP \ltimes PAY_2$$

where

$$PAY_1 = \sigma_{SAL \leq 30000}(PAY)$$

$$PAY_2 = \sigma_{SAL > 30000}(PAY)$$

The result of this fragmentation is depicted in Fig. 2.9.   ◆

Derived horizontal fragmentation applies to the target relations in the join graph and are performed based on predicates defined over the source relation of the join graph edge. In our examples, relations EMP and ASG are subject to derived horizontal fragmentation. To carry out a derived horizontal fragmentation, three inputs are needed: the set of partitions of the source relation (e.g., PAY$_1$ and PAY$_2$ in Example 2.11), the target relation, and the set of semijoin predicates between

EMP$_1$

ENO	ENAME	TITLE
E3	A. Lee	Mech. Eng.
E4	J. Miller	Programmer
E7	R. Davis	Mech. Eng.

EMP$_2$

ENO	ENAME	TITLE
E1	J. Doe	Elect. Eng.
E2	M. Smith	Syst. Anal.
E5	B. Casey	Syst. Anal.
E6	L. Chu	Elect. Eng.
E8	J. Jones	Syst. Anal.

Fig. 2.9 Derived horizontal fragmentation of relation EMP

the source and the target (e.g., `EMP.TITLE = PAY.TITLE` in Example 2.11). The fragmentation algorithm, then, is quite trivial, so we will not present it in any detail.

There is one potential complication that deserves some attention. In a database schema, it is common that there are multiple edges into a relation R (e.g., in Fig. 2.5, `ASG` has two incoming edges). In this case, there is more than one possible derived horizontal fragmentation of R. The choice of candidate fragmentation is based on two criteria:

1. The fragmentation with better join characteristics;
2. The fragmentation used in more queries.

Let us discuss the second criterion first. This is quite straightforward if we take into consideration the frequency that the data is accessed by the workload. If possible, one should try to facilitate the accesses of the "heavy" users so that their total impact on system performance is minimized.

Applying the first criterion, however, is not that straightforward. Consider, for example, the fragmentation we discussed in Example 2.1. The effect (and the objective) of this fragmentation is that the join of the `EMP` and `PAY` relations to answer the query is assisted (1) by performing it on smaller relations (i.e., fragments), and (2) by potentially performing joins in parallel.

The first point is obvious. The second point deals with intraquery parallelism of join queries, i.e., executing each join query in parallel, which is possible under certain circumstances. Consider, for example, the edges between the fragments (i.e., the join graph) of `EMP` and `PAY` derived in Example 2.9. We have $PAY_1 \rightarrow EMP_1$ and $PAY_2 \rightarrow EMP_2$; there is only one edge coming in or going out of a fragment, so this is a *simple* join graph. The advantage of a design where the join relationship between fragments is simple is that the target and source of an edge can be allocated to one site and the joins between different pairs of fragments can proceed independently and in parallel.

Unfortunately, obtaining simple join graphs is not always possible. In that case, the next desirable alternative is to have a design that results in a *partitioned* join graph. A partitioned graph consists of two or more subgraphs with no edges between them. Fragments so obtained may not be distributed for parallel execution as easily as those obtained via simple join graphs, but the allocation is still possible.

Example 2.12 Let us continue with the distribution design of the database we started in Example 2.10. We already decided on the fragmentation of relation `EMP` according to the fragmentation of `PAY` (Example 2.11). Let us now consider `ASG`. Assume that there are the following two queries:

1. The first query finds the names of engineers who work at certain places. It runs on all three sites and accesses the information about the engineers who work on local projects with higher probability than those of projects at other locations.
2. At each administrative site where employee records are managed, users would like to access the responsibilities on the projects that these employees work on and learn how long they will work on those projects.

The first query results in a fragmentation of ASG according to the (nonempty) fragments PROJ$_1$, PROJ$_3$, PROJ$_4$, and PROJ$_6$ of PROJ obtained in Example 2.10:

$$PROJ_1 : \sigma_{LOC=\text{“Montreal”} \wedge BUDGET \leq 200000}(PROJ)$$

$$PROJ_3 : \sigma_{LOC=\text{“New York”} \wedge BUDGET \leq 200000}(PROJ)$$

$$PROJ_4 : \sigma_{LOC=\text{“New York”} \wedge BUDGET > 200000}(PROJ)$$

$$PROJ_6 : \sigma_{LOC=\text{“Paris”} \wedge BUDGET > 200000}(PROJ)$$

Therefore, the derived fragmentation of ASG according to {PROJ$_1$, PROJ$_3$, PROJ$_4$, PROJ$_6$} is defined as follows:

$$ASG_1 = ASG \ltimes PROJ_1$$

$$ASG_2 = ASG \ltimes PROJ_3$$

$$ASG_3 = ASG \ltimes PROJ_4$$

$$ASG_4 = ASG \ltimes PROJ_6$$

These fragment instances are shown in Fig. 2.10.

The second query can be specified in SQL as

```
SELECT RESP, DUR
FROM    ASG NATURAL JOIN EMPᵢ
```

where $i = 1$ or $i = 2$, depending on the site where the query is issued. The derived fragmentation of ASG according to the fragmentation of EMP is defined below and depicted in Fig. 2.11.

$$ASG_1 = ASG \ltimes EMP_1$$

$$ASG_2 = ASG \ltimes EMP1_2$$

ASG$_1$

ENO	PNO	RESP	DUR
E1	P1	Manager	12
E2	P1	Analyst	24

ASG$_2$

ENO	PNO	RESP	DUR
E2	P2	Analyst	6
E4	P2	Programmer	18
E5	P2	Manager	24

ASG$_3$

ENO	PNO	RESP	DUR
E3	P3	Consultant	10
E7	P3	Engineer	36
E8	P3	Manager	40

ASG$_4$

ENO	PNO	RESP	DUR
E3	P4	Engineer	48
E6	P4	Manager	48

Fig. 2.10 Derived fragmentation of ASG with respect to PROJ

ASG$_1$

ENO	PNO	RESP	DUR
E3	P3	Consultant	10
E3	P4	Engineer	48
E4	P2	Programmer	18
E7	P3	Engineer	36

ASG$_2$

ENO	PNO	RESP	DUR
E1	P1	Manager	12
E2	P1	Analyst	24
E2	P2	Analyst	6
E5	P2	Manager	24
E6	P4	Manager	48
E8	P3	Manager	40

Fig. 2.11 Derived fragmentation of ASG with respect to EMP

◆

This example highlights two observations:

1. Derived fragmentation may follow a chain where one relation is fragmented as a result of another one's design and it, in turn, causes the fragmentation of another relation (e.g., the chain PAY → EMP → ASG).
2. Typically, there will be more than one candidate fragmentation for a relation (e.g., relation ASG). The final choice of the fragmentation scheme is a decision problem that may be addressed during allocation.

2.1.1.4   Checking for Correctness

We now check the fragmentation algorithms discussed so far with respect to the three correctness criteria we discussed earlier.

Completeness

The completeness of a primary horizontal fragmentation is based on the selection predicates used. As long as the selection predicates are complete, the resulting fragmentation is guaranteed to be complete as well. Since the basis of the fragmentation algorithm is a set of *complete* and *minimal* predicates (Pr'), completeness is guaranteed if Pr' is properly determined.

The completeness of a derived horizontal fragmentation is somewhat more difficult to define since the predicate determining the fragmentation involves two relations.

Let R be the target relation of an edge whose source is relation S, where R and S are fragmented as $F_R = \{R_1, R_2, \ldots, R_w\}$ and $F_S = \{S_1, S_2, \ldots, S_w\}$, respectively. Let A be the join attribute between R and S. Then for each tuple t of R_i, there should be a tuple t' of S_i such that $t[A] = t'[A]$. This is the well-known *referential integrity* rule, which ensures that the tuples of any fragment of the target relation are also in the source relation. For example, there should be no ASG tuple which has a project number that is not also contained in PROJ. Similarly, there should be no EMP tuples with TITLE values where the same TITLE value does not appear in PAY as well.

Reconstruction

Reconstruction of a global relation from its fragments is performed by the union operator in both the primary and the derived horizontal fragmentation. Thus, for a relation R with fragmentation $F_R = \{R_1, R_2, \ldots, R_w\}$, $R = \bigcup R_i$, $\forall R_i \in F_R$.

Disjointness

It is easier to establish disjointness of fragmentation for primary than for derived horizontal fragmentation. In the former case, disjointness is guaranteed as long as the minterm predicates determining the fragmentation are mutually exclusive.

In derived fragmentation, however, there is a semijoin involved that adds considerable complexity. Disjointness can be guaranteed if the join graph is simple. Otherwise, it is necessary to investigate actual tuple values. In general, we do not want a tuple of a target relation to join with two or more tuples of the source relation when these tuples are in different fragments of the source. This may not be very easy to establish, and illustrates why derived fragmentation schemes that generate a simple join graph are always desirable.

Example 2.13 In fragmenting relation PAY (Example 2.10), the minterm predicates $M = \{m_1, m_2\}$ were

$$m_1 : \text{SAL} \leq 30000$$

$$m_2 : \text{SAL} > 30000$$

Since m_1 and m_2 are mutually exclusive, the fragmentation of PAY is disjoint.
For relation EMP, however, we require that

1. Each engineer has a single title.
2. Each title has a single salary value associated with it.

Since these two rules follow from the semantics of the database, the fragmentation of EMP with respect to PAY is also disjoint.   ◆

2.1.2 Vertical Fragmentation

Recall that a vertical fragmentation of a relation R produces fragments $R_1, R_2,$ $\ldots, R_r$, each of which contains a subset of R's attributes as well as the primary key of RÄs in the case of horizontal fragmentation, the objective is to partition a relation into a set of smaller relations so that many of the user applications will run on only one fragment. Primary key is included in each fragment to enable reconstruction, as we discuss later. This is also beneficial for integrity enforcement since the primary key functionally determines all the relation attributes; having it in each fragment eliminates distributed computation to enforce primary key constraint.

Vertical partitioning is inherently more complicated than horizontal partitioning, mainly due to the total number of possible alternatives. For example, in horizontal partitioning, if the total number of simple predicates in Pr is n, there are 2^n possible minterm predicates. In addition, we know that some of these will contradict the existing implications, further reducing the candidate fragments that need to be considered. In the case of vertical partitioning, however, if a relation has m nonprimary key attributes, the number of possible fragments is equal to $B(m)$, which is the mth Bell number. For large values of m, $B(m) \approx m^m$; for example, for $m = 10$, $B(m) \approx 115,000$, for $m = 15$, $B(m) \approx 10^9$, for $m = 30$, $B(m) = 10^{23}$.

These values indicate that it is futile to attempt to obtain optimal solutions to the vertical partitioning problem; one has to resort to heuristics. Two types of heuristic approaches exist for the vertical fragmentation of global relations[5]:

1. *Grouping:* starts by assigning each attribute to one fragment, and at each step, joins some of the fragments until some criteria are satisfied.
2. *Splitting:* starts with a relation and decides on beneficial partitionings based on the access behavior of applications to the attributes.

In what follows we discuss only the splitting technique, since it fits more naturally within the design methodology we discussed earlier, since the "optimal" solution is probably closer to the full relation than to a set of fragments each of which consists of a single attribute. Furthermore, splitting generates nonoverlapping fragments, whereas grouping typically results in overlapping fragments. We prefer nonoverlapping fragments for disjointness. Of course, nonoverlapping refers only to nonprimary key attributes.

2.1.2.1 Auxiliary Information Requirements

We again require workload information. Since vertical partitioning places in one fragment those attributes usually accessed together, there is a need for some measure that would define more precisely the notion of "togetherness." This measure is the *affinity* of attributes, which indicates how closely related the attributes are. It is not realistic to expect the designer or the users to be able to easily specify these values. We present one way they can be obtained from more primitive data.

Let $Q = \{q_1, q_2, \ldots, q_q\}$ be the set of user queries that access relation $R(A_1, A_2, \ldots, A_n)$. Then, for each query q_i and each attribute A_j, we associate an *attribute usage value*, denoted as $use(q_i, A_j)$:

---

[5]There is also a third, extreme approach in column-oriented DBMS (like MonetDB and Vertica) where each column is mapped to one fragment. Since we do not cover column-oriented DBMSs in this book, we do not discuss this approach further.

$$use(q_i, A_j) = \begin{cases} 1 \text{ if attribute } A_j \text{ is referenced by query } q_i \\ 0 \text{ otherwise} \end{cases}$$

The $use(q_i, \bullet)$ vectors for each query are easy to determine.

Example 2.14 Consider relation PROJ of Fig. 2.2. Assume that the following queries are defined to run on this relation. In each case, we also give the SQL expression.

q_1: Find the budget of a project, given its identification number.

```
SELECT  BUDGET
FROM    PROJ
WHERE   PNO=Value
```

q_2: Find the names and budgets of all projects.

```
SELECT  PNAME, BUDGET
FROM    PROJ
```

q_3: Find the names of projects located at a given city.

```
SELECT  PNAME
FROM    PROJ
WHERE   LOC=Value
```

q_4: Find the total project budgets for each city.

```
SELECT  SUM(BUDGET)
FROM    PROJ
WHERE   LOC=Value
```

According to these four queries, the attribute usage values can be defined in matrix form (Fig. 2.12), where entry (i, j) denotes $use(q_i, A_j)$.   ◆

Attribute usage values are not sufficiently general to form the basis of attribute splitting and fragmentation, because they do not represent the weight of application frequencies. The frequency measure can be included in the definition of the attribute affinity measure $aff(A_i, A_j)$, which measures the bond between two attributes of a relation according to how they are accessed by queries.

	PNO	PNAME	BUDGET	LOC
q_1	0	1	1	0
q_2	1	1	1	0
q_3	1	0	0	1
q_4	0	0	1	0

Fig. 2.12 Example attribute usage matrix

The attribute affinity measure between two attributes A_i and A_j of a relation $R(A_1, A_2, \ldots, A_n)$ with respect to the set of queries $Q = \{q_1, q_2, \ldots, q_q\}$ is defined as

$$aff(A_i, A_j) = \sum_{k|use(q_k,A_i)=1 \wedge use(q_k,A_j)=1} \sum_{\forall S_l} ref_l(q_k)acc_l(q_k)$$

where $ref_l(q_k)$ is the number of accesses to attributes (A_i, A_j) for each execution of application q_k at site S_l and $acc_l(q_k)$ is the application access frequency measure previously defined and modified to include frequencies at different sites.

The result of this computation is an $n \times n$ matrix, each element of which is one of the measures defined above. This matrix is called the *attribute affinity matrix (AA)*.

Example 2.15 Let us continue with the case that we examined in Example 2.14. For simplicity, let us assume that $ref_l(q_k) = 1$ for all q_k and S_l. If the application frequencies are

$$acc_1(q_1) = 15 \qquad\qquad acc_1(q_2) = 5$$
$$acc_1(q_3) = 25 \qquad\qquad acc_1(q_4) = 3$$
$$acc_2(q_1) = 20 \qquad\qquad acc_2(q_2) = 0$$
$$acc_2(q_3) = 25 \qquad\qquad acc_3(q_4) = 0$$
$$acc_3(q_1) = 10 \qquad\qquad acc_3(q_2) = 0$$
$$acc_3(q_3) = 25 \qquad\qquad acc_2(q_4) = 0$$

then the affinity measure between attributes PNO and BUDGET can be measured as

$$aff(\text{PNO}, \text{BUDGET}) = \sum_{k=1}^{1} \sum_{l=1}^{3} acc_l(q_k) = acc_1(q_1) + acc_2(q_1) + acc_3(q_1) = 45$$

since the only application that accesses both of the attributes is q_1. The complete attribute affinity matrix is shown in Fig. 2.13. Note that the diagonal values are not computed since they are meaningless. ♦

	PNO	PNAME	BUDGET	LOC
PNO	–	0	45	0
PNAME	0	–	5	75
BUDGET	45	5	–	3
LOC	0	75	3	–

Fig. 2.13 Attribute affinity matrix

The attribute affinity matrix will be used in the rest of this chapter to guide the fragmentation effort. The process first clusters together the attributes with high affinity for each other, and then splits the relation accordingly.

2.1.2.2   Clustering Algorithm

The fundamental task in designing a vertical fragmentation algorithm is to find some means of grouping the attributes of a relation based on the attribute affinity values in AA. We will discuss the bond energy algorithm (BEA) that has been proposed for this purpose. Other clustering algorithms can also be used.

BEA takes as input the attribute affinity matrix for relation $R(A_1, \ldots, A_n)$, permutes its rows and columns, and generates a *clustered affinity matrix* (CA). The permutation is done in such a way as to *maximize* the following *global affinity measure* (AM):

$$AM = \sum_{i=1}^{n} \sum_{j=1}^{n} aff(A_i, A_j)[aff(A_i, A_{j-1}) + aff(A_i, A_{j+1})$$

$$+ aff(A_{i-1}, A_j) + aff(A_{i+1}, A_j)]$$

where

$$aff(A_0, A_j) = aff(A_i, A_0) = aff(A_{n+1}, A_j) = aff(A_i, A_{n+1}) = 0$$

The last set of conditions takes care of the cases where an attribute is being placed in CA to the left of the leftmost attribute or to the right of the rightmost attribute during column permutations, and prior to the topmost row and following the last row during row permutations. We denote with A_0 the attribute to the left of the leftmost attribute and the row prior to the topmost row, and with A_{n+1} the attribute to the right of the rightmost attribute or the row following the last row. In these cases, we set to 0 *aff* values between the attribute being considered for placement and its left or right (top or bottom) neighbors, since they do not exist in CA.

The maximization function considers the nearest neighbors only, thereby resulting in the grouping of large values with large ones, and small values with small ones. Also, the attribute affinity matrix (AA) is symmetric, which reduces the objective function to

$$AM = \sum_{i=1}^{n} \sum_{j=1}^{n} aff(A_i, A_j)[aff(A_i, A_{j-1}) + aff(A_i, A_{j+1})]$$

Algorithm 2.3: BEA

Input: AA: attribute affinity matrix
Output: CA: clustered affinity matrix
begin
    {initialize; remember that AA is an $n \times n$ matrix}
    $CA(\bullet, 1) \leftarrow AA(\bullet, 1)$
    $CA(\bullet, 2) \leftarrow AA(\bullet, 2)$
    $index \leftarrow 3$
    while $index \le n$ **do**   {choose the "best" location for attribute AA_{index}}
        for i *from 1 to index* $- 1$ *by 1* **do** calculate $cont(A_{i-1}, A_{index}, A_i)$
        calculate $cont(A_{index-1}, A_{index}, A_{index+1})$ {boundary condition}
        $loc \leftarrow$ placement given by maximum $cont$ value
        for j *from index to loc by* -1 **do**
           | $CA(\bullet, j) \leftarrow CA(\bullet, j-1)$ {shuffle the two matrices}
        end for
        $CA(\bullet, loc) \leftarrow AA(\bullet, index)$
        $index \leftarrow index + 1$
    end while
    order the rows according to the relative ordering of columns
end

The details of BEA are given in Algorithm 2.3. Generation of the clustered affinity matrix (CA) is done in three steps:

1. *Initialization.* Place and fix one of the columns of AA arbitrarily into CA. Column 1 was chosen in the algorithm.
2. *Iteration.* Pick each of the remaining $n - i$ columns (where i is the number of columns already placed in CA) and try to place them in the remaining $i + 1$ positions in the CA matrix. Choose the placement that makes the greatest contribution to the global affinity measure described above. Continue this step until no more columns remain to be placed.
3. *Row ordering.* Once the column ordering is determined, the placement of the rows should also be changed so that their relative positions match the relative positions of the columns.[6]

For the second step of the algorithm to work, we need to define what is meant by the contribution of an attribute to the affinity measure. This contribution can be derived as follows. Recall that the global affinity measure AM was previously defined as

---

[6]From now on, we may refer to elements of the AA and CA matrices as $AA(i, j)$ and $CA(i, j)$, respectively. The mapping to the affinity measures is $AA(i, j) = aff(A_i, A_j)$ and $CA(i, j) = aff$(attribute placed at column i in CA, attribute placed at column j in CA). Even though AA and CA matrices are identical except for the ordering of attributes, since the algorithm orders all the CA columns before it orders the rows, the affinity measure of CA is specified with respect to columns. Note that the endpoint condition for the calculation of the affinity measure (AM) can be specified, using this notation, as $CA(0, j) = CA(i, 0) = CA(n+1, j) = CA(i, n+1) = 0$.

$$AM = \sum_{i=1}^{n} \sum_{j=1}^{n} aff(A_i, A_j)[aff(A_i, A_{j-1}) + aff(A_i, A_{j+1})]$$

which can be rewritten as

$$AM = \sum_{i=1}^{n} \sum_{j=1}^{n} [aff(A_i, A_j)aff(A_i, A_{j-1}) + aff(A_i, A_j)aff(A_i, A_{j+1})]$$

$$= \sum_{j=1}^{n} \left[\sum_{i=1}^{n} aff(A_i, A_j)aff(A_i, A_{j-1}) + \sum_{i=1}^{n} aff(A_i, A_j)aff(A_i, A_{j+1}) \right]$$

Let us define the *bond* between two attributes A_x and A_y as

$$bond(A_x, A_y) = \sum_{z=1}^{n} aff(A_z, A_x)aff(A_z, A_y)$$

Then *AM* can be written as

$$AM = \sum_{j=1}^{n} [bond(A_j, A_{j-1}) + bond(A_j, A_{j+1})]$$

Now consider the following n attributes:

$$\underbrace{A_1 \ A_2 \ \ldots \ A_{i-1}}_{AM'} \ A_i \ A_j \ \underbrace{A_{j+1} \ \ldots \ A_n}_{AM^1}$$

The global affinity measure for these attributes can be written as

$$AM_{old} = AM' + AM^1$$
$$+ bond(A_{i-1}, A_i) + bond(A_i, A_j) + bond(A_j, A_i) + bond(A_j, A_{j+1})$$
$$= \sum_{l=1}^{i} [bond(A_l, A_{l-1}) + bond(A_l, A_{l+1})]$$
$$+ \sum_{l=i+2}^{n} [bond(A_l, A_{l-1}) + bond(A_l, A_{l+1})]$$
$$+ 2bond(A_i, A_j)$$

Now consider placing a new attribute A_k between attributes A_i and A_j in the clustered affinity matrix. The new global affinity measure can be similarly written as

$$AM_{new} = AM' + AM^1 + bond(\mathbb{A}_i, \mathbb{A}_k) + bond(\mathbb{A}_k, \mathbb{A}_i)$$
$$+ bond(\mathbb{A}_k, \mathbb{A}_j) + bond(\mathbb{A}_j, \mathbb{A}_k)$$
$$= AM' + AM^1 + 2bond(\mathbb{A}_i, \mathbb{A}_k) + 2bond(\mathbb{A}_k, \mathbb{A}_j)$$

Thus, the net *contribution* to the global affinity measure of placing attribute $\mathbb{A}_k$ between $\mathbb{A}_i$ and $\mathbb{A}_j$ is

$$cont(\mathbb{A}_i, \mathbb{A}_k, \mathbb{A}_j) = AM_{new} - AM_{old}$$
$$= 2bond(\mathbb{A}_i, \mathbb{A}_k) + 2bond(\mathbb{A}_k, \mathbb{A}_j) - 2bond(\mathbb{A}_i, \mathbb{A}_j)$$

Example 2.16 Let us consider the AA matrix given in Fig. 2.13 and study the contribution of moving attribute LOC between attributes PNO and PNAME, given by the formula

$$cont(\text{PNO}, \text{LOC}, \text{PNAME}) = 2bond(\text{PNO}, \text{LOC}) + 2bond(\text{LOC}, \text{PNAME})$$
$$- 2bond(\text{PNO}, \text{PNAME})$$

Computing each term, we get

$$bond(\text{PNO}, \text{LOC}) = 45 * 0 + 0 * 75 + 45 * 3 + 0 * 78 = 135$$
$$bond(\text{LOC}, \text{PNAME}) = 11865$$
$$bond(\text{PNO}, \text{PNAME}) = 225$$

Therefore,

$$cont(\text{PNO}, \text{LOC}, \text{PNAME}) = 2 * 135 + 2 * 11865 - 2 * 225 = 23550$$

$\blacklozenge$

The algorithm and our discussion so far have both concentrated on the columns of the attribute affinity matrix. It is possible to redesign the algorithm to operate on the rows. Since the AA matrix is symmetric, both of these approaches will generate the same result.

Note that Algorithm 2.3 places the second column next to the first one during the initialization step. This obviously works since the bond between the two, however, is independent of their positions relative to one another.

Computing *cont* at the endpoints requires care. If an attribute $\mathbb{A}_i$ is being considered for placement to the left of the leftmost attribute, one of the bond equations to be calculated is between a nonexistent left element and $\mathbb{A}_k$ [i.e., $bond(\mathbb{A}_0, \mathbb{A}_k)$]. Thus we need to refer to the conditions imposed on the definition of the global affinity measure AM, where $CA(0, k) = 0$. Similar arguments hold for the placement to the right of the rightmost attribute.

Example 2.17 We consider the clustering of the PROJ relation attributes and use the attribute affinity matrix AA of Fig. 2.13.

According to the initialization step, we copy columns 1 and 2 of the AA matrix to the CA matrix (Fig. 2.14a) and start with column 3 (i.e., attribute BUDGET). There are three alternative places where column 3 can be placed: to the left of column 1, resulting in the ordering (3-1-2), in between columns 1 and 2, giving (1-3-2), and to the right of 2, resulting in (1-2-3). Note that to compute the contribution of the last ordering we have to compute $cont$(PNAME, BUDGET, LOC) rather than $cont$(PNO, PNAME, BUDGET). However, note that attribute LOC has not yet been placed into the CA matrix (Fig. 2.14b), thus requiring special computation as outlined above. Let us calculate the contribution to the global affinity measure of each alternative.

Ordering (0-3-1):

$$cont(\text{A}_0, \text{BUDGET}, \text{PNO}) = 2bond(\text{A}_0, \text{BUDGET}) + 2bond(\text{BUDGET}, \text{PNO})$$
$$- 2bond(\text{A}_0, \text{PNO})$$

We know that

$$bond(\text{A}_0, \text{PNO}) \quad = bond(\text{A}_0, \text{BUDGET}) = 0$$
$$bond(\text{BUDGET}, \text{PNO}) = 45 * 45 + 5 * 0 + 53 * 45 + 3 * 0 = 4410$$

	PNO	PNAME
PNO	45	0
PNAME	0	80
BUDGET	45	5
LOC	0	75

(a)

	PNO	BUDGET	PNAME
PNO	45	45	0
PNAME	0	5	80
BUDGET	45	53	5
LOC	0	3	75

(b)

	PNO	BUDGET	PNAME	LOC
PNO	45	45	0	0
PNAME	0	5	80	75
BUDGET	45	53	5	3
LOC	0	3	75	78

(c)

	PNO	BUDGET	PNAME	LOC
PNO	45	45	0	0
BUDGET	45	53	5	3
PNAME	0	5	80	75
LOC	0	3	75	78

(d)

Fig. 2.14 Calculation of the clustered affinity (CA) matrix

Thus

$$cont(A_0, \text{BUDGET}, \text{PNO}) = 8820$$

Ordering (1-3-2):

$$cont(\text{PNO}, \text{BUDGET}, \text{PNAME}) = 2bond\,\text{PNO}, \text{BUDGET}) + 2bond(\text{BUDGET}, \text{PNAME})$$
$$- 2bond(\text{PNO}, \text{PNAME})$$

$bond(\text{PNO}, \text{BUDGET})$ $\quad = bond(\text{BUDGET}, \text{PNO}) = 4410$

$bond(\text{BUDGET}, \text{PNAME})$ $\quad = 890$

$bond(\text{PNO}, \text{PNAME})$ $\quad = 225$

Thus

$$cont(\text{PNO}, \text{BUDGET}, \text{PNAME}) = 10150$$

Ordering (2-3-4):

$$cont(\text{PNAME}, \text{BUDGET}, \text{LOC}) = 2bond(\text{PNAME}, \text{BUDGET}) + 2bond(\text{BUDGET}, \text{LOC})$$
$$- 2bond(\text{PNAME}, \text{LOC})$$

$bond(\text{PNAME}, \text{BUDGET})$ $\quad = 890$

$bond(\text{BUDGET}, \text{LOC})$ $\quad = 0$

$bond(\text{PNAME}, \text{LOC})$ $\quad = 0$

Thus

$$cont(\text{PNAME}, \text{BUDGET}, \text{LOC}) = 1780$$

Since the contribution of the ordering (1-3-2) is the largest, we select to place BUDGET to the right of PNO (Fig. 2.14b). Similar calculations for LOC indicate that it should be placed to the right of PNAME (Fig. 2.14c).

Finally, the rows are organized in the same order as the columns and the result is shown in Fig. 2.14d.   ♦

In Fig. 2.14d we see the creation of two clusters: one is in the upper left corner and contains the smaller affinity values and the other is in the lower right corner and contains the larger affinity values. This clustering indicates how the attributes of relation PROJ should be split. However, in general the border for this split may not be this clear-cut. When the CA matrix is big, usually more than two clusters are formed and there are more than one candidate partitionings. Thus, there is a need to approach this problem more systematically.

2.1.2.3 Splitting Algorithm

The objective of splitting is to find sets of attributes that are accessed solely, or for the most part, by distinct sets of queries. For example, if it is possible to identify two attributes A_1 and A_2 that are accessed only by query q_1, and attributes A_3 and A_4 that are accessed by, say, two queries q_2 and q_3, it would be quite straightforward to decide on the fragments. The task lies in finding an algorithmic method of identifying these groups.

Consider the clustered attribute matrix of Fig. 2.15. If a point along the diagonal is fixed, two sets of attributes are identified. One set $\{A_1, A_2, \ldots, A_i\}$ is at the upper left-hand corner (denoted TA) and the second set $\{A_{i+1}, \ldots, A_n\}$ is at the lower right corner (denoted TB) relative to this point.

We now partition the set of queries $Q = \{q_1, q_2, \ldots, q_q\}$ that access only TA, only BA, or both. These sets are defined as follows:

$$AQ(q_i) = \{A_j | use(q_i, A_j) = 1\}$$

$$TQ = \{q_i | AQ(q_i) \subseteq TA\}$$

$$BQ = \{q_i | AQ(q_i) \subseteq BA\}$$

$$OQ = Q - \{TQ \cup BQ\}$$

The first of these equations defines the set of attributes accessed by query q_i; TQ and BQ are the sets of queries that only access TA or BA, respectively, and OQ is the set of queries that access both.

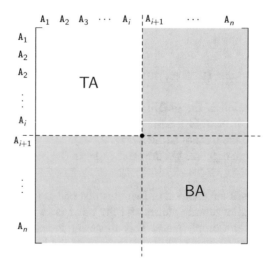

Fig. 2.15 Locating a splitting point

There is an optimization problem here. If there are n attributes of a relation, there are $n - 1$ possible positions where the dividing point can be placed along the diagonal of the clustered attribute matrix for that relation. The best position for division is one which produces the sets TQ and BQ such that the total accesses to *only one* fragment are maximized, while the total accesses to *both* fragments are minimized. We therefore define the following cost equations:

$$CQ = \sum_{q_i \in Q} \sum_{\forall S_j} ref_j(q_i) acc_j(q_i)$$

$$CTQ = \sum_{q_i \in TQ} \sum_{\forall S_j} ref_j(q_i) acc_j(q_i)$$

$$CBQ = \sum_{q_i \in BQ} \sum_{\forall S_j} ref_j(q_i) acc_j(q_i)$$

$$COQ = \sum_{q_i \in OQ} \sum_{\forall S_j} ref_j(q_i) acc_j(q_i)$$

Each of the equations above counts the total number of accesses to attributes by queries in their respective classes. Based on these measures, the optimization problem is defined as finding the point x $(1 \leq x \leq n)$ such that the expression

$$z = CTQ * CBQ - COQ^2$$

is maximized. The important feature of this expression is that it defines two fragments such that the values of CTQ and CBQ are as nearly equal as possible. This enables the balancing of processing loads when the fragments are distributed to various sites. It is clear that the partitioning algorithm has linear complexity in terms of the number of attributes of the relation, that is, $O(n)$.

This procedure splits the set of attributes two-way. For larger sets of attributes, it is quite likely that m-way partitioning may be necessary. Designing an m-way partitioning is possible but computationally expensive. Along the diagonal of the CA matrix, it is necessary to try $1, 2, \ldots, m - 1$ split points, and for each of these, it is necessary to check which point maximizes z. Thus, the complexity of such an algorithm is $O(2^m)$. Of course, the definition of z has to be modified for those cases where there are multiple split points. The alternative solution is to recursively apply the binary partitioning algorithm to each of the fragments obtained during the previous iteration. One would compute TQ, BQ, and OQ, as well as the associated access measures for each of the fragments, and partition them further.

Our discussion so far assumed that the split point is unique and single and divides the CA matrix into an upper left-hand partition and a second partition formed by the rest of the attributes. The partition, however, may also be formed in the middle of the matrix. In this case, we need to modify the algorithm slightly. The leftmost column of the CA matrix is shifted to become the rightmost column and the topmost row is

---

Algorithm 2.4: SPLIT

Input: CA: clustered affinity matrix; R: relation; ref: attribute usage matrix; acc: access
      frequency matrix
Output: F: set of fragments
begin
    | {determine the z value for the first column}
    | {the subscripts in the cost equations indicate the split point}
    | calculate CTQ_{n-1}
    | calculate CBQ_{n-1}
    | calculate COQ_{n-1}
    | $best \leftarrow CTQ_{n-1} * CBQ_{n-1} - (COQ_{n-1})^2$
    | **repeat**
    | | {determine the best partitioning}
    | | **for** i *from* $n - 2$ *to* 1 *by* -1 **do**
    | | | calculate CTQ_i
    | | | calculate CBQ_i
    | | | calculate COQ_i
    | | | $z \leftarrow CTQ * CBQ - COQ_i^2$
    | | | **if** $z > best$ **then** $best \leftarrow z$ {record the split point within shift}
    | | **end for**
    | | call SHIFT(CA)
    | **until** *no more SHIFT is possible*
    | reconstruct the matrix according to the shift position
    | $R_1 \leftarrow \Pi_{TA}(R) \cup K$ {K is the set of primary key attributes of R}
    | $R_2 \leftarrow \Pi_{BA}(R) \cup K$
    | $F \leftarrow \{R_1, R_2\}$
end

---

shifted to the bottom. The shift operation is followed by checking the $n - 1$ diagonal positions to find the maximum z. The idea behind shifting is to move the block of attributes that should form a cluster to the topmost left corner of the matrix, where it can easily be identified. With the addition of the shift operation, the complexity of the partitioning algorithm increases by a factor of n and becomes $O(n^2)$.

Assuming that a shift procedure, called SHIFT, has already been implemented, the splitting algorithm is given in Algorithm 2.4. The input of the algorithm is the clustered affinity matrix CA, the relation R to be fragmented, and the attribute usage and access frequency matrices. The output is a set of fragments $F_R = \{R_1, R_2\}$, where $R_i \subseteq \{A_1, A_2 \dots, A_n\}$ and $R_1 \cap R_2 =$ the key attributes of relation R.Note that for n-way partitioning, this routine should be either invoked iteratively or implemented as a recursive procedure.

Example 2.18 When the SPLIT algorithm is applied to the CA matrix obtained for relation PROJ (Example 2.17), the result is the definition of fragments $F_{\text{PROJ}} = \{\text{PROJ}_1, \text{PROJ}_2\}$, where

$$\text{PROJ}_1 = \{\text{PNO, BUDGET}\}$$

$$\text{PROJ}_2 = \{\text{PNO, PNAME, LOC}\}$$

Note that in this exercise we performed the fragmentation over the entire set of attributes rather than only on the nonkey ones. The reason for this is the simplicity of the example. For that reason, we included PNO, which is the key of PROJ in PROJ$_2$ as well as in PROJ$_1$.   ◆

2.1.2.4 Checking for Correctness

We follow arguments similar to those of horizontal partitioning to prove that the SPLIT algorithm yields a correct vertical fragmentation.

Completeness

Completeness is guaranteed by the SPLIT algorithm since each attribute of the global relation is assigned to one of the fragments. As long as the set of attributes A over which the relation R is defined consists of $A = \bigcup R_i$, completeness of vertical fragmentation is ensured.

Reconstruction

We have already mentioned that the reconstruction of the original global relation is made possible by the join operation. Thus, for a relation R with vertical fragmentation $F_R = \{R_1, R_2, \ldots, R_r\}$ and key attribute(s) K, $R = \bowtie_K R_i, \forall R_i \in F_R$. Therefore, as long as each R_i is complete, the join operation will properly reconstruct R. Another important point is that either each R_i should contain the key attribute(s) of R or it should contain the system assigned tuple IDs (TIDs).

Disjointness

As noted earlier, the primary key attributes are replicated in each fragment. Excluding these, the SPLIT algorithm finds mutually exclusive clusters of attributes, leading to disjoint fragments with respect to the attributes.

2.1.3 Hybrid Fragmentation

In some cases a simple horizontal or vertical fragmentation of a database schema may not be sufficient to satisfy the requirements of user applications. In this case a vertical fragmentation may be followed by a horizontal one, or vice versa, producing a tree-structured partitioning (Fig. 2.16). Since the two types of

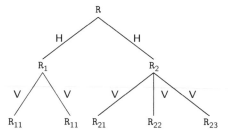

Fig. 2.16 Hybrid fragmentation

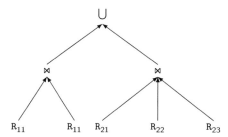

Fig. 2.17 Reconstruction of hybrid fragmentation

partitioning strategies are applied one after the other, this alternative is called *hybrid* fragmentation. It has also been named *mixed* fragmentation or *nested* fragmentation.

A good example for the necessity of hybrid fragmentation is relation PROJ. In Example 2.10 we partitioned it into six horizontal fragments based on two applications. In Example 2.18 we partitioned the same relation vertically into two. What we have, therefore, is a set of horizontal fragments, each of which is further partitioned into two vertical fragments.

The correctness rules and conditions for hybrid fragmentation follow naturally from those for vertical and horizontal fragmentations. For example, to reconstruct the original global relation in case of hybrid fragmentation, one starts at the leaves of the partitioning tree and moves upward by performing joins and unions (Fig. 2.17). The fragmentation is complete if the intermediate and leaf fragments are complete. Similarly, disjointness is guaranteed if intermediate and leaf fragments are disjoint.

2.2   Allocation

Following fragmentation, the next decision problem is to allocate fragments to the sites of the distributed DBMS. This can be done by either placing each fragment at a single site or replicating it on a number of sites. The reasons for replication are reliability and efficiency of read-only queries. If there are multiple copies of a fragment, there is a good chance that some copy of the data will be accessible somewhere even when system failures occur. Furthermore, read-only queries that access the same data items can be executed in parallel since copies exist on multiple sites. On the other hand, the execution of update queries causes trouble since the system has to ensure that all the copies of the data are updated properly. Hence the decision regarding replication is a trade-off that depends on the ratio of the read-only queries to the update queries. This decision affects almost all of the distributed DBMS algorithms and control functions.

A nonreplicated database (commonly called a *partitioned* database) contains fragments that are allocated to sites such that each fragment is placed at one site. In case of replication, either the database exists in its entirety at each site (*fully replicated* database), or fragments are distributed to the sites in such a way that copies of a fragment may reside in multiple sites (*partially replicated* database). In the latter the number of copies of a fragment may be an input to the allocation algorithm or a decision variable whose value is determined by the algorithm. Figure 2.18 compares these three replication alternatives with respect to various distributed DBMS functions. We will discuss replication at length in Chap. 6.

The file allocation problem has long been studied within the context of distributed computing systems where the unit of allocation is a file. This is commonly referred as the *file allocation problem* (FAP) and the formulations are usually quite simple, reflecting the simplicity of file APIs. Even this simple version has been shown to be NP-complete, resulting in a search for reasonable heuristics.

FAP formulations are not suitable for distributed database design, due fundamentally to the characteristics of DBMSs: fragments are not independent of each other so they cannot simply be mapped to individual files; the access to data in a database is more complex than simple access to files; and DBMSs enforce integrity and transactional properties whose costs need to be considered.

There are no general heuristic models that take as input a set of fragments and produce a near-optimal allocation subject to the types of constraints discussed here. The models developed to date make a number of simplifying assumptions and are applicable to certain specific formulations. Therefore, instead of presenting one or

	Full replication	Partial replication	Partitioning
QUERY PROCESSING	Easy	Same difficulty	
DIRECTORY MANAGEMENT	Easy or nonexistent	Same difficulty	
CONCURRENCY CONTROL	Moderate	Difficult	Easy
RELIABILITY	Very high	High	Low
REALITY	Possible application	Realistic	Possible application

Fig. 2.18 Comparison of replication alternatives

more of these allocation algorithms, we present a relatively general model and then discuss a number of possible heuristics that might be employed to solve it.

2.2.1 Auxiliary Information

We need the quantitative data about the database, the workload, the communication network, the processing capabilities, and storage limitations of each site on the network.

To perform horizontal fragmentation, we defined the selectivity of minterms. We now need to extend that definition to fragments, and define the selectivity of a fragment F_j with respect to query q_i. This is the number of tuples of F_j that need to be accessed in order to process q_i. This value will be denoted as $sel_i(F_j)$.

Another piece of necessary information on the database fragments is their size. The size of a fragment F_j is given by

$$size(F_j) = card(F_j) * length(F_j)$$

where $length(F_j)$ is the length (in bytes) of a tuple of fragment F_j.

Most of the workload-related information is already compiled during fragmentation, but a few more are required by the allocation model. The two important measures are the number of read accesses that a query q_i makes to a fragment F_j during its execution (denoted as RR_{ij}), and its counterpart for the update accesses (UR_{ij}). These may, for example, count the number of block accesses required by the query.

We also need to define two matrices UM and RM, with elements u_{ij} and r_{ij}, respectively, which are specified as follows:

$$u_{ij} = \begin{cases} 1 \text{ if query } q_i \text{ updates fragment } F_j \\ 0 \text{ otherwise} \end{cases}$$

$$r_{ij} = \begin{cases} 1 \text{ if query } q_i \text{ retrieves from fragment } F_j \\ 0 \text{ otherwise} \end{cases}$$

A vector O of values $o(i)$ is also defined, where $o(i)$ specifies the originating site of query q_i. Finally, to define the response-time constraint, the maximum allowable response time of each application should be specified.

For each computer site, we need to know its storage and processing capacity. Obviously, these values can be computed by means of elaborate functions or by simple estimates. The unit cost of storing data at site S_k will be denoted as USC_k. There is also a need to specify a cost measure LPC_k as the cost of processing one unit of work at site S_k. The work unit should be identical to that of the RR and UR measures.

In our model we assume the existence of a simple network where the cost of communication is defined in terms of one message that contains a specific amount of data. Thus g_{ij} denotes the communication cost per message between sites S_i and S_j. To enable the calculation of the number of messages, we use *msize* as the size (in bytes) of one message. There are more elaborate network models that take into consideration the channel capacities, distances between sites, protocol overhead, and so on, but this simple model is sufficient for our purposes.

2.2.2 Allocation Model

We discuss an allocation model that attempts to minimize the total cost of processing and storage while trying to meet certain response time restrictions. The model we use has the following form:

   min(Total Cost)

subject to

   response-time constraint
   storage constraint
   processing constraint

In the remainder of this section, we expand the components of this model based on the information requirements discussed in Sect. 2.2.1. The decision variable is x_{ij}, which is defined as

$$x_{ij} = \begin{cases} 1 \text{ if the fragment } F_i \text{ is stored at site } S_j \\ 0 \text{ otherwise} \end{cases}$$

2.2.2.1 Total Cost

The total cost function has two components: query processing and storage. Thus it can be expressed as

$$TOC = \sum_{\forall q_i \in Q} QPC_i + \sum_{\forall S_k \in S} \sum_{\forall F_j \in F} STC_{jk}$$

where QPC_i is the query processing cost of query q_i, and STC_{jk} is the cost of storing fragment F_j at site S_k.

Let us consider the storage cost first. It is simply given by

$$STC_{jk} = USC_k * size(F_j) * x_{jk}$$

and the two summations find the total storage costs at all the sites for all the fragments.

The query processing cost is more difficult to specify. We specify it as consisting of the processing cost (PC) and the transmission cost (TC). Thus the query processing cost (QPC) for application q_i is

$$QPC_i = PC_i + TC_i$$

The processing component, PC, consists of three cost factors, the access cost (AC), the integrity enforcement cost (IE), and the concurrency control cost (CC):

$$PC_i = AC_i + IE_i + CC_i$$

The detailed specification of each of these cost factors depends on the algorithms used to accomplish these tasks. However, to demonstrate the point, we specify AC in some detail:

$$AC_i = \sum_{\forall S_k \in S} \sum_{\forall F_j \in F} (u_{ij} * UR_{ij} + r_{ij} * RR_{ij}) * x_{jk} * LPC_k$$

The first two terms in the above formula calculate the number of accesses of user query q_i to fragment F_j. Note that $(UR_{ij} + RR_{ij})$ gives the total number of update and retrieval accesses. We assume that the local costs of processing them are identical. The summation gives the total number of accesses for all the fragments referenced by q_i. Multiplication by LPC_k gives the cost of this access at site S_k. We again use x_{jk} to select only those cost values for the sites where fragments are stored.

The access cost function assumes that processing a query involves decomposing it into a set of subqueries, each of which works on a fragment stored at the site, followed by transmitting the results back to the site where the query has originated. Reality is more complex; for example, the cost function does not take into account the cost of performing joins (if necessary), which may be executed in a number of ways (see Chap. 4).

The integrity enforcement cost factor can be specified much like the processing component, except that the unit local processing cost would likely change to reflect the true cost of integrity enforcement. Since the integrity checking and concurrency control methods are discussed later in the book, we do not study these cost components further here. The reader should refer back to this section after reading Chaps. 3 and 5 to be convinced that the cost functions can indeed be derived.

The transmission cost function can be formulated along the lines of the access cost function. However, the data transmission overhead for update and that for retrieval requests may be quite different. In update queries it is necessary to inform all the sites where replicas exist, while in retrieval queries, it is sufficient to access only one of the copies. In addition, at the end of an update request, there is no data transmission back to the originating site other than a confirmation message, whereas the retrieval-only queries may result in significant data transmission.

The update component of the transmission function is

$$TCU_i = \sum_{\forall S_k \in S} \sum_{\forall F_j \in F} u_{ij} * x_{jk} * g_{o(i),k} + \sum_{\forall S_k \in S} \sum_{\forall F_j \in F} u_{ij} * x_{jk} * g_{k,o(i)}$$

The first term is for sending the update message from the originating site $o(i)$ of q_i to all the fragment replicas that need to be updated. The second term is for the confirmation.

The retrieval cost can be specified as

$$TCR_i = \sum_{\forall F_j \in F} \min_{S_k \in S} (r_{ij} * x_{jk} * g_{o(i),k} + r_{ij} * x_{jk} * \frac{sel_i(F_j) * length(F_j)}{msize} * g_{k,o(i)})$$

The first term in TCR represents the cost of transmitting the retrieval request to those sites which have copies of fragments that need to be accessed. The second term accounts for the transmission of the results from these sites to the originating site. The equation states that among all the sites with copies of the same fragment, only the site that yields the minimum total transmission cost should be selected for the execution of the operation.

Now the transmission cost function for query q_i can be specified as

$$TC_i = TCU_i + TCR_i$$

which fully specifies the total cost function.

2.2.2.2 Constraints

The constraint functions can be specified in similar detail. However, instead of describing these functions in depth, we will simply indicate what they should look like. The response-time constraint should be specified as

execution time of $q_i \leq$ maximum response time of $q_i, \forall q_i \in Q$

Preferably, the cost measure in the objective function should be specified in terms of time, as it makes the specification of the execution time constraint relatively straightforward.

The storage constraint is

$$\sum_{\forall F_j \in F} STC_{jk} \leq \text{storage capacity at site } S_k, \forall S_k \in S$$

whereas the processing constraint is

$$\sum_{\forall q_i \in Q} \text{processing load of } q_i \text{ at site } S_k \leq \text{processing capacity of } S_k, \forall S_k \in S$$

This completes our development of the allocation model. Even though we have not developed it entirely, the precision in some of the terms indicates how one goes about formulating such a problem. In addition to this aspect, we have indicated the important issues that need to be addressed in allocation models.

2.2.3   Solution Methods

As noted earlier, simple file allocation problem is NP-complete. Since the model we developed in the previous section is more complex, it is likely to be NP-complete as well. Thus one has to look for heuristic methods that yield suboptimal solutions. The test of "goodness" in this case is, obviously, how close the results of the heuristic algorithm are to the optimal allocation.

It was observed early on that there is a correspondence between the file allocation and the facility location problems. In fact, the isomorphism of the simple file allocation problem and the single commodity warehouse location problem has been shown. Thus, heuristics developed for the latter have been used for the former. Examples are the knapsack problem solution, branch-and-bound techniques, and network flow algorithms.

There have been other attempts to reduce the complexity of the problem. One strategy has been to assume that all the candidate partitionings have been determined together with their associated costs and benefits in terms of query processing. The problem, then, is modeled as choosing the optimal partitioning and placement for each relation. Another simplification frequently employed is to ignore replication at first and find an optimal nonreplicated solution. Replication is handled at the second step by applying a greedy algorithm which starts with the nonreplicated solution as the initial feasible solution, and tries to improve upon it. For these heuristics, however, there is not enough data to determine how close the results are to the optimal.

2.3   Combined Approaches

The design process depicted in Fig. 2.1 on which we based our discussion separates the fragmentation and allocation steps. The methodology is linear where the output of fragmentation is input to allocation; we call this the *fragment-then-allocate approach*. This simplifies the formulation of the problem by reducing the decision space, but the isolation of the two steps may in fact contribute to the complexity of the allocation models. Both steps have similar inputs, differing only in that fragmentation works on global relations, whereas allocation considers fragments. They both require workload information, but ignore how each other makes use of these inputs. The end result is that the fragmentation algorithms decide how to partition a relation based partially on how queries access it, but the allocation models ignore the part that this input plays in fragmentation. Therefore, the allocation models have to include all over again detailed specification of the relationship among the fragment relations and how user applications access them. There are approaches that combine the fragmentation and allocation steps in such a way that the data partitioning algorithm also dictates allocation, or the allocation algorithm dictates how the data is partitioned; we call these the *combined approaches*. These mostly consider horizontal partitioning, since that is the common method for obtaining significant parallelism. In this section we present these approaches, classified as either workload-agnostic or workload-aware.

2.3.1   Workload-Agnostic Partitioning Techniques

This class of techniques ignores the workload that will run on the data and simply focus on the database, often not even paying attention to the schema definition. These approaches are mostly used in parallel DBMSs where data dynamism is higher than distributed DBMSs, so simpler techniques that can be quickly applied are preferred.

The simplest form of these algorithms is *round-robin partitioning* (Fig. 2.19). With n partitions, the ith tuple in insertion order is assigned to partition (i mod n). This strategy enables the sequential access to a relation to be done in parallel. However, the direct access to individual tuples, based on a predicate, requires accessing the entire relation. Thus, round-robin partitioning is appropriate for full scan queries, as in data mining.

An alternative is *hash partitioning*, which applies a hash function to some attribute that yields the partition number (Fig. 2.20). This strategy allows exact-match queries on the selection attribute to be processed by exactly one node and all

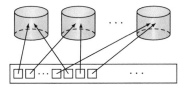

Fig. 2.19   Round-robin partitioning

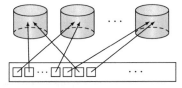

Fig. 2.20   Hash partitioning

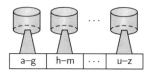

Fig. 2.21 Range partitioning

other queries to be processed by all the nodes in parallel. However, if the attribute used for partitioning has nonuniform data distribution, e.g., as with people's names, the resulting placement may be unbalanced, with some partitions much bigger than some others. This is called *data skew* and it is an important issue that can cause unbalanced load.

Finally, there is *range partitioning* (Fig. 2.21) that distributes tuples based on the value intervals (ranges) of some attribute and thus can deal with nonuniform data distributions. Unlike hashing, which relies on hash functions, ranges must be maintained in an index structure, e.g., a B-tree. In addition to supporting exact-match queries (as in hashing), it is well-suited for range queries. For instance, a query with a predicate "A between A_1 and A_2" may be processed by the only node(s) containing tuples whose A value is in range $[A_1, A_2]$.

These techniques are simple, can be computed quickly and, as we discuss in Chap. 8, nicely fit the dynamicity of data in parallel DBMSs. However, they have indirect ways of handling the semantic relationships among relations in the database. For example, consider two relations that have a foreign key–primary key join relationship such as R $\bowtie_{R.A=S.B}$ S, hash partitioning would use the same function over attribute R.A and S.B to ensure that they are located at the same node, thereby localizing the joins and parallelizing the join execution. A similar approach can be used in range partitioning, but round-robin would not take this relationship into account.

2.3.2 Workload-Aware Partitioning Techniques

This class of techniques considers the workload as input and performs partitioning to localize as much of the workload on one site as possible. As noted at the beginning of this chapter, their objective is to minimize the amount of distributed queries.

One approach that has been proposed in a system called Schism uses the database and workload information to build a graph $G = V, E$ where each vertex v in V represents a tuple in the database, and each edge $e = (v_i, v_j)$ in E represents a query that accesses both tuples v_i and v_j. Each edge is assigned a weight that is the count of the number of transactions that access both tuples.

In this model, it is also easy to take into account replicas, by representing each copy by a separate vertex. The number of replica vertices is determined by the number of transactions accessing the tuple; i.e., each transaction accesses one

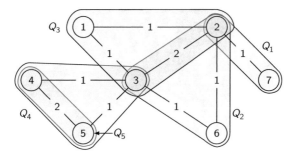

Fig. 2.22 Graph representation for partitioning in schism

copy. A replicated tuple is represented in the graph by a star-shaped configuration consisting of $n+1$ vertices where the "central" vertex represents the logical tuple and the other n vertices represent the physical copies. The weight of an edge between the physical copy vertex and the central vertex is the number of transactions that update the tuple; the weights of other edges remain as the number of queries that access the tuple. This arrangement makes sense since the objective is to localize transactions as much as possible and this technique uses replication to achieve localization.

Example 2.19 Let us consider a database with one relation consisting of seven tuples that are accessed by five transactions. In Fig. 2.22 we depict the graph that is constructed: there are seven vertices corresponding to the tuples, and the queries that access them together are shown as cliques. For example, query Q_1 accesses tuples 2 and 7, query Q_2 accesses tuples 2, 3, and 6, query Q_3 accesses tuples 1, 2, and 3, query Q_4 accesses tuples 3, 4, and 5, and query Q_5 accesses tuples 4 and 5. Edge weights capture the number of transaction accesses.

Replication can be incorporated into this graph but replicating the tuples that are accessed by multiple transactions; this is shown in Fig. 2.23. Note that tuples 1, 6, and 7 are not replicated since they are only accessed by one transaction each, tuples 4 and 5 are replicated twice, and tuples 2 and 3 are replicated three times. We represent the "replication edges" between the central vertex and each physical copy by dashed lines and omit the weights for these edges in this example. ♦

Once the database and the workload are captured by this graph representation, the next step is to perform a vertex-disjoint graph partitioning. Since we discuss these techniques in detail in Sect. 10.4.1, we do not get into the details here, but simply state that vertex-disjoint partitioning allocates each vertex of the graph to a separate partition such that partitions are mutually exclusive. These algorithms have, as their objective function, a balanced (or nearly balanced) set of partitions while minimizing the cost of edge cuts. The cost of an edge cut takes into account the weights of each edge so as to minimize the number of distributed queries.

The advantage of the Schism approach is its fine-grained allocation—it treats each tuple as an allocation unit and the partitioning "emerges" as the allocation decision is made for each tuple. Thus, the mapping of sets of tuples to queries can

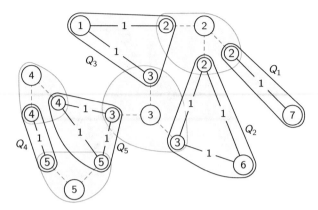

Fig. 2.23 Schism graph incorporating replication

be controlled and many of them can execute at one site. However, the downside of
the approach is that the graph becomes very large as the database size increases, in
particular when replicas are added to the graph. This makes the management of the
graph difficult and its partitioning expensive. Another issue to consider is that the
mapping tables that record where each tuple is stored (i.e., the directory) become
very large and may pose a management problem of their own.

One approach to overcome these issues has been proposed as part of the SWORD
system that employs a hypergraph model[7] where each clique in Fig. 2.22 is represented as a hyperedge. Each hyperedge represents one query and the set of vertices
spanned by the hyperedge represents the tuples accessed by it. Each hyperedge has
a weight that represents the frequency of that query in the workload. Therefore what
we have is a weighted hypergraph. This hypergraph is then partitioned using a k-way
balanced min-cut partitioning algorithm that produces k balanced partitions, each of
which is allocated to a site. This minimizes the number of distributed queries since
the algorithm is minimizing the cuts in hyperedges and each of these cuts indicates
a distributed query.

Of course, this change in the model is not sufficient to address the issues
discussed above. In order to reduce the size of the graph, and the overhead of
maintaining the associated mapping table, SWORD compresses this hypergraph as
follows. The set of vertices V in the original hypergraph G is mapped to a set of
virtual vertices V' using a hash or other function that operates on the primary keys
of the tuples. Once the set of virtual vertices are determined, the edges in the original
hypergraph are now mapped to hyperedges in the compressed graph (E') such that
if the vertices spanned by a hyperedge $e \in E$ are mapped to different virtual vertices
in the compressed graph, then there will be a hyperedge $e' \in E'$.

---

[7]A hypergraph allows each edge (called a hyperedge) to connect more than two vertices as is the
case with regular graphs. The details of the hypergraph model are beyond our scope.

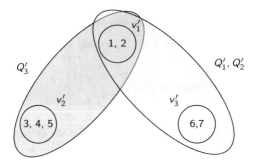

Fig. 2.24 Sword compressed hypergraph

Of course for this compression to make sense, $|V'| < |V|$, so a critical issue is
to determine how much compression is desired—too much compression will reduce
the number of virtual vertices, but will increase the number of hyperedges, and
therefore the possibility of distributed queries. The resulting compressed hypergraph
$G' = (V', E')$ is going to be smaller than the original hypergraph so easier to
manage and partition, and the mapping tables will also be smaller since they will
only consider the mapping of sets of virtual vertices.

Example 2.20 Let us revisit the case in Example 2.19 and consider that we are
compressing the hypergraph into three virtual vertices: $v'_1 = 1, 2, v'_2 = 3, 4, 5, v'_3 =$
$6, 7$. Then there would be two hyperedges: $e'_1 = (v'_1, v'_3)$ with frequency 2
(corresponding to Q_1 and Q_2 in the original hypergraph) and $e'_2 = (v'_1, v'_2)$ with
frequency 1 (corresponding to Q_3). The hyperedges representing queries Q_4 and
Q_5 would be local (i.e., not spanning virtual vertices) so no hyperedges are required
in the compressed hypergraph. This is shown in Fig. 2.24.   ◆

Performing the k-way balanced min-cut partitioning on the compressed hypergraph can be performed much faster and the resulting mapping table will be smaller
due to the reduced size of the graph.

SWORD incorporates replication in the compressed hypergraph. It first determines, for each virtual vertex, how many replicas are required. It does this by using
the tuple-level access pattern statistics for each tuple t_j in each virtual vertex v'_i,
namely its read frequency f^r_{ij} and its write frequency f^w_{ij}. Using these, it computes
the average read and write frequencies (ARF and AWF, respectively) of virtual
vertex v'_i as follows:

$$ARF(v'_i) = \frac{\sum_j f^r_{ij}}{\log S(v'_i)} \quad \text{and} \quad AWF(v'_i) = \frac{\sum_j f^w_{ij}}{\log S(v'_i)}$$

$S(v'_i)$ is the size of each virtual vertex (in terms of the number of actual vertices
mapped to it) and its log is taken to compensate for the skew in the sizes of virtual
vertices (so, these are size-compensated averages). From these, SWORD defines a

replication factor, $\mathcal{R} = \frac{AWF(v'_i)}{ARWF(v'_i)}$ and a user-specified threshold δ ($0 < \delta < 1$) is defined. The number of replicas (#_*rep*) for virtual vertex v'_i is then given as

$$\#\_rep(v'_i) = \begin{cases} 1 & \text{if } \mathcal{R} \geq \delta \\ ARF(v'_i) & \text{otherwise} \end{cases}$$

Once the number of replicas for each virtual vertex is determined, these are added to the compressed hypergraph and assigned to hyperedges in a way that minimizes the min-cut in the partitioning algorithm. We ignore the details of this assignment.

2.4 Adaptive Approaches

The work described in this chapter generally assumes a static environment where design is conducted only once and this design can persist. Reality, of course, is quite different. Both physical (e.g., network characteristics, available storage at various sites) and logical (e.g., workload) changes occur necessitating redesign of the database. In a dynamic environment, the process becomes one of design-redesign-materialization of the redesign. When things change, the simplest approach is to redo the distribution design from scratch. For large or highly dynamic systems, this is not quite realistic as the overhead of redesign is likely to be very high. A preferred approach is to perform incremental redesign, focusing only on the parts of the database that are likely to be affected by the changes. The incremental redesign can either be done every time a change is detected or periodically where changes are batched and evaluated at regular intervals.

Most of the work in this area has focused on changes in the workload (queries and transactions) over time and those are what we focus in this section. While some work in this area has focused on the fragment-then-allocate approach, most follow the combined approach. In the former case one alternative that has been proposed involves a split phase where fragments are further subdivided based on the changed application requirements until no further subdivision is profitable based on a cost function. At this point, the merging phase starts where fragments that are accessed together by a set of applications are merged into one fragment. We will focus more on the dynamic combined approaches that perform incremental redesign as the workload changes.

The objective in the adaptive approaches is the same as the workload-aware partitioning strategies discussed in Sect. 2.3.2: to minimize the number of distributed queries and ensure that the data for each query is local. Within this context, there are three interrelated issues that need to be addressed in adaptive distribution design:

1. How to detect workload changes that require changes in the distribution design?
2. How to determine which data items are going to be affected in the design?
3. How to perform the changes in an efficient manner?

In the remainder we discuss each of these issues.

2.4.1   Detecting Workload Changes

This is a difficult issue on which there is not much work. Most of the adaptive techniques that have been proposed assume that the change in the workload is detected, and simply focus on the migration problem. To be able to detect workload changes, the incoming queries need to be monitored. One way to do this is to periodically examine the system logs, but this may have high overhead, especially in highly dynamic systems. An alternative is to continuously monitor the workload within the DBMS. In the SWORD system we discussed above, the system monitors the percentage increase in the number of distributed transactions and considers that the system has changed sufficiently to require a reconfiguration if this percentage increase is above a defined threshold. As another example, the E-Store system monitors both system-level metrics and tuple-level access. It starts by collecting system-level metrics at each computing node using OS facilities. E-Store currently focuses primarily on detecting workload imbalances across the computing nodes, and therefore only collects CPU utilization data. If the CPU utilization imbalance exceeds a threshold, then it invokes more fine-grained tuple-level monitoring to detect the affected items (see next section). Although imbalance in CPU utilization may be a good indicator of possible performance problems, it is too simple to capture more significant workload changes. It is possible, of course, to do more sophisticated monitoring, e.g., one can create a profile that looks at the frequency of each query in a given time period, the percentage of queries that meet (or exceed) their agreed-upon latencies (as captured in a service level agreement, perhaps), and others. Then it can be decided whether the changes in the profile require redesign, which can be done either continuously (i.e., every time the monitor registers information) or periodically. The challenge here is to do this efficiently without intruding on the system performance. This is an open research area that has not been properly studied.

2.4.2   Detecting Affected Items

Once a change is detected in the workload the next step is to determine what data items are affected and need to be migrated to address this change. How this is done is very much dependent on the detection method. For example, if the system is monitoring the frequency of queries and detects changes, then the queries will identify the data items. It is possible to generalize from individual queries to query templates in order to capture "similar" queries that might also be affected by the changes. This is done in the Apollo system where each constant is replaced by a wildcard. For example, the query

```
SELECT PNAME FROM PROJ WHERE BUDGET>200000 AND LOC = "London"
```

would be generalized to

```
SELECT PNAME FROM PROJ WHERE BUDGET>? AND LOC = "?"
```

While this reduces the granularity of determining the exact set of data items that are affected, it may allow the detection of additional data items that might be affected by similar queries and reduce the frequency of changes that are necessary.

The E-Store system starts tuple-level monitoring once it detects a system load imbalance. For a short period, it collects access data to the tuples in each computing node (i.e., each partition) and determines the "hot" tuples, which are the top-k most frequently accessed tuples within a time period. To do this, it uses a histogram for each tuple that is initialized when the tuple-level monitoring is enabled and updated as access happens within the monitoring window. At the end of this time period, the top-k list is assembled. The monitoring software gathers these lists and generates a global top-k list of hot tuples—these are the data items that need to be migrated. A side-effect is the determination of cold tuples; of particular importance are tuples that were previously hot and have since become cold. The determination of the time window for tuple-level monitoring and the value of k are parameters set by the database administrator.

2.4.3 Incremental Reconfiguration

As noted earlier, the naive approach to perform redesign is to redo the entire data partitioning and distribution. While this may be of interest in environments where workload change occurs infrequently, in most cases, the overhead of redesign is too high to do it from scratch. The preferred approach is to apply the changes incrementally by migrating data; in other words, we only look at the changed workload and the data items that are affected, and move them around.[8] So, in this section, we focus on incremental approaches.

Following from the previous section, one obvious approach is to use an incremental graph partitioning algorithm that reacts to changes in the graph representation we discussed. This has been followed in the SWORD system discussed above and in AdaptCache, both of which represent usage as hypergraphs and perform incremental partitioning on these graphs. The incremental graph partitioning initiates data migration for reconfiguration.

The E-Store system we have been discussing takes a more sophisticated approach. Once the set of hot tuples are identified, a migration plan is prepared that identifies where the hot tuples should be moved and what reallocation of cold tuples is necessary. This can be posed as an optimization problem that creates a balanced load across the computing nodes (balance is defined as average-load-across-nodes

---

[8]The research in this area has exclusively focused on horizontal partitioning, which will be our focus here as well, meaning that our units of migration are individual tuples.

± a threshold value), but solving this optimization problem in real time for online reconfiguration is not easy, so it uses approximate placement approaches (e.g., greedy, first-fit) to generate the reconfiguration plan. Basically, it first determines the appropriate computing nodes at which each hot tuple should be located, then addresses cold tuples, if necessary due to remaining imbalance, by moving them in blocks. So, the generated reconfiguration plan addresses the migration of hot tuples individually, but the migration of cold tuples as blocks. As part of the plan a coordinating node is determined to manage the migration, and this plan is an input to the Squall reconfiguration system.

Squall performs reconfiguration and data migration in three steps. In the first step, the coordinator identified in the reconfiguration plan initializes the system for migration. This step includes the coordinating obtaining exclusive access control to all of these partitions through a transaction as we will discuss in Chap. 5. Then the coordinator asks each site to identify the tuples that will be moving out of the local partition and the tuples that will be coming in. This analysis is done on the metadata so can be done quickly after which each site notifies the coordinator and the initialization transaction terminates. In the second step, the coordinator instructs each site to do the data migration. This is critical as there are queries accessing the data as it is being moved. If a query is executing at a given computing node where the data is supposed to be according to the reconfiguration plan but the required tuples are not locally available, Squall pulls the missing tuples to process the query. This is done in addition to the normal migration of the data according to the reconfiguration plan. In other words, in order to execute the queries in a timely fashion, Squall performs on-demand movement in addition to its normal migration. Once this step is completed, each node informs the coordinator, which then starts the final termination step and informs each node that reconfiguration is completed. These three steps are necessary for Squall to be able to perform migration while executing user queries at the same time rather than stopping all query execution, performing the migration and then restarting the query execution.

Another approach is *database cracking*, which is an adaptive indexing technique that targets dynamic, hard to predict workloads and scenarios where there is little or no idle time to devote to workload analysis and index building. Database cracking works by continuously reorganizing data to match the query workload. Every query is used as an advice on how the data should be stored. Cracking does this by building and refining indices partially and incrementally as part of query processing. By reacting to every single query with lightweight actions, database cracking manages to adapt to a changing workload instantly. As more queries arrive, the indices are refined, and the performance improves, eventually reaching the optimal performance, i.e., the performance we would get from a manually tuned system.

The main idea in the original database cracking approach is that the data system reorganizes one column of the data at a time and only when touched by a query. In other words, the reorganization utilizes the fact that the data is already read and decides how to refine it in the best way. Effectively the original cracking approach overloads the select operator of a database system and uses the predicates of each query to determine how to reorganize the relevant column. The first time an attribute

A is required by a query, a copy of the base column *A* is created, called the cracker column of *A*. Each select operator on *A* triggers the physical reorganization of the cracker column based on the requested range of the query. Entries with a key that is smaller than the lower bound are moved before the lower bound, while entries with a key that is greater than the upper bound are moved after the upper bound in the respective column. The partitioning information for each cracker column is maintained in an AVL-tree, the cracker index. Future queries on column *A* search the cracker index for the partition where the requested range falls. If the requested key already exists in the index, i.e., if past queries have cracked on exactly those ranges, then the select operator can return the result immediately. Otherwise, the select operator refines on the fly the column further, i.e., only the partitions/pieces of the column where the predicates fall will be reorganized (at most two partitions at the boundaries of the range). Progressively the column gets more "ordered" with more but smaller pieces.

The primary concept in database cracking and its basic techniques can be extended to partition data in a distributed setting, i.e., to store data across a set of nodes using incoming queries as an advice. Each time a node needs a specific part of the data for a local query but the data does not exist in this node, this information can be used as a hint that the data could be moved to this node. However, contrary to the in-memory database cracking methods where the system reacts immediately to every query, in a distributed setting we need to consider that moving the data is more expensive. At the same time, for the same reason, the benefit that future queries may have is going to be more significant. In fact, the same trade-off has already been studied in variations of the original database cracking approach to optimize for disk-based data. The net effect is twofold: (1) instead of reacting with every query, we should wait for more workload evidence before we embark on expensive data reorganization actions, and (2) we should apply "heavier" reorganizations to utilize the fact that reading and writing data is more expensive out of memory. We expect future approaches to explore and develop such adaptive indexing methods to benefit from effective partitioning in scenarios where the workload is not easy to predict, and there is not enough time to fully sort/partition all data before the first query arrives.

2.5 Data Directory

The final distribution design issue we discuss is related to data directory. The distributed database schema needs to be stored and maintained by the system. This information is necessary during distributed query optimization, as we will discuss later. The schema information is stored in a *catalog/data dictionary/directory* (simply directory). A directory is a metadatabase that stores a number of information such as schema and mapping definitions, usage statistics, access control information, and the like.

   In the case of a distributed DBMS, schema definition is done at the global level
(i.e., the global conceptual schema—GCS) as well as at the local sites (i.e., local
conceptual schemas—LCSs). GCS defines the overall database while each LCS
describes data at that particular site. Consequently, there are two types of directories:
a *global directory/dictionary* (GD/D)[9] that describes the database schema as the
end users see it, and the *local directory/dictionary* (LD/D) that describes the
local mappings and describes the schema at each site. Thus, the local database
management components are integrated by means of global DBMS functions.
   As stated above, the directory is itself a database that contains *metadata* about
the actual data stored in the database. Therefore, the techniques we discussed in
this chapter, with respect to distributed database design also apply to directory
management, but in much simpler manner. Briefly, a directory may be either *global*
to the entire database or *local* to each site. In other words, there might be a single
directory containing information about all the data in the database (the GD/D), or
a number of directories, each containing the information stored at one site (the
LD/D). In the latter case, we might either build hierarchies of directories to facilitate
searches or implement a distributed search strategy that involves considerable
communication among the sites holding the directories.
   A second issue is replication. There may be a *single* copy of the directory
or *multiple* copies. Multiple copies would provide more reliability, since the
probability of reaching one copy of the directory would be higher. Furthermore,
the delays in accessing the directory would be lower, due to less contention and the
relative proximity of the directory copies. On the other hand, keeping the directory
up-to-date would be considerably more difficult, since multiple copies would need
to be updated. Therefore, the choice should depend on the environment in which
the system operates and should be made by balancing such factors as the response-
time requirements, the size of the directory, the machine capacities at the sites, the
reliability requirements, and the volatility of the directory (i.e., the amount of change
experienced by the database, which would cause a change to the directory).

2.6   Conclusion

In this chapter, we presented the techniques that can be used for distributed database
design with special emphasis on the partitioning and allocation issues. We have
discussed, in detail, the algorithms that one can use to fragment a relational schema
in various ways. These algorithms have been developed quite independently and
there is no underlying design methodology that combines the horizontal and vertical
partitioning techniques. If one starts with a global relation, there are algorithms
to decompose it horizontally as well as algorithms to decompose it vertically into
a set of fragment relations. However, there are no algorithms that fragment a

---

[9]In the remainder, we will simply refer to this as the *global directory*.

global relation into a set of fragment relations some of which are decomposed horizontally and others vertically. It is commonly pointed out that most real-life fragmentations would be mixed, i.e., would involve both horizontal and vertical partitioning of a relation, but the methodology research to accomplish this is lacking. If this design methodology is to be followed, what is needed is a distribution design methodology which encompasses the horizontal and vertical fragmentation algorithms and uses them as part of a more general strategy. Such a methodology should take a global relation together with a set of design criteria and come up with a set of fragments some of which are obtained via horizontal and others obtained via vertical fragmentation.

We also discussed techniques that do not separate fragmentation and allocation steps—the way data is partitioned dictates how it is allocated or vice versa. These techniques typically have two characteristics. The first is that they exclusively focus on horizontal partitioning. The second is that they are more fine-grained and the unit of allocation is a tuple; fragments at each site "emerge" as the union of tuples from the same relation assigned to that site.

We finally discussed adaptive techniques that take into account changes in workload. These techniques again typically involve horizontal partitioning, but monitor the workload changes (both in terms of the query set and in terms of the access patterns) and adjust the data partitioning accordingly. The naïve way achieving this is by to do new batch run of the partitioning algorithm, but this is obviously not desired. Therefore, the better algorithms in this class adjust data distribution incrementally.

2.7   Bibliographic Notes

Distributed database design has been studied systematically since the early years of the technology. An early paper that characterizes the design space is [Levin and Morgan 1975]. Davenport [1981], Ceri et al. [1983], and Ceri et al. [1987] provide nice overviews of the design methodology. Ceri and Pernici [1985] discuss a particular methodology, called DATAID-D, which is similar to what we presented in Fig. 2.1. Other attempts to develop a methodology are due to Fisher et al. [1980], Dawson [1980], Hevner and Schneider [1980], and Mohan [1979].

Most of the known results about fragmentation have been covered in this chapter. Work on fragmentation in distributed databases initially concentrated on horizontal fragmentation. The discussion on that topic is mainly based on [Ceri et al. 1982b] and [Ceri et al. 1983]. Data partitioning in parallel DBMS is treated in [DeWitt and Gray 1992]. The topic of vertical fragmentation for distribution design has been addressed in several papers (e.g., Navathe et al. [1984] and Sacca and Wiederhold [1985]). The original work on vertical fragmentation goes back to Hoffer's dissertation [Hoffer 1975, Hoffer and Severance 1975] and to Niamir [1978] and Hammer and Niamir [1979]. McCormick et al. [1972] present the bond energy algorithm that has been adopted to vertical fragmentation by Hoffer and Severance [1975] and Navathe et al. [1984].

The investigation of file allocation problem on wide area networks goes back to Chu's work [Chu 1969, 1973]. Most of the early work on this has been covered in the excellent survey by Dowdy and Foster [1982]. Some theoretical results are reported by Grapa and Belford [1977] and Kollias and Hatzopoulos [1981]. The distributed data allocation work dates back to the mid-1970s to the works of Eswaran [1974] and others. In their earlier work, Levin and Morgan [1975] concentrated on data allocation, but later they considered program and data allocation together [Morgan and Levin 1977]. The distributed data allocation problem has been studied in many specialized settings as well. Work has been done to determine the placement of computers and data in a wide area network design [Gavish and Pirkul 1986]. Channel capacities have been examined along with data placement [Mahmoud and Riordon 1976] and data allocation on supercomputer systems [Irani and Khabbaz 1982] as well as on a cluster of processors [Sacca and Wiederhold 1985]. An interesting work is the one by Apers [1981], where the relations are optimally placed on the nodes of a virtual network, and then the best matching between the virtual network nodes and the physical network is found. The isomorphism of data allocation problem to single commodity warehouse location problem is due to Ramamoorthy and Wah [1983]. For other solution approaches, the sources are as follows: knapsack problem solution [Ceri et al. 1982a], branch-and-bound techniques [Fisher and Hochbaum 1980], and network flow algorithms [Chang and Liu 1982].

The Schism approach to combined partitioning (Sect. 2.3.2) is due to Curino et al. [2010] and SWORD is due to Quamar et al. [2013]. Other works along these lines are [Zilio 1998], [Rao et al. 2002], and [Agrawal et al. 2004], which mostly focus on partitioning for parallel DBMSs.

An early adaptive technique is discussed by Wilson and Navathe [1986]. Limited redesign, in particular, the materialization issue, is studied in [Rivera-Vega et al. 1990, Varadarajan et al. 1989]. Complete redesign and materialization issues have been studied in [Karlapalem et al. 1996, Karlapalem and Navathe 1994, Kazerouni and Karlapalem 1997]. Kazerouni and Karlapalem [1997] describe the stepwise redesign methodology that we referred to in Sect. 2.4. AdaptCache is described in [Asad and Kemme 2016].

The impact of workload changes on distributed/parallel DBMSs and the desirability of localizing data for each transaction have been studied by Pavlo et al. [2012] and Lin et al. [2016]. There are a number of works that address adaptive partitioning in the face of these changes. Our discussion focused on E-Store [Taft et al. 2014] as an exemplar. E-Store implements the E-Monitor and E-Planner systems, respectively, for monitoring and detecting workload changes, and for detecting affected items to create a migration plan. For actual migration it uses an optimized version of Squall [Elmore et al. 2015]. There are other works along the same vein; for example, P-Store [Taft et al. 2018] predicts load demands (as opposed to E-Store reacting to them).

The log-inspection-based determination of workload changes is due to Levandoski et al. [2013].

One work that focuses on detecting workload shifts for autonomic computing is described in Holze and Ritter [2008]. The Apollo system, which we referred to in discussion how to detect data items that are affected, and that abstracts queries to query templates in order to do predictive computation is described in Glasbergen et al. [2018].

Database cracking as a concept has been studied in the context of main-memory column-stores [Idreos et al. 2007b, Schuhknecht et al. 2013]. The cracking algorithms have been adapted to work for many core database architecture issues such as: updates to incrementally and adaptively absorb data changes [Idreos et al. 2007a], multiattribute queries to reorganize whole relations as opposed to only columns [Idreos et al. 2009], to use also the join operator as a trigger for adaptation [Idreos 2010], concurrency control to deal with the problem that cracking effectively turns reads into writes [Graefe et al. 2014, 2012], and partition-merge-like logic to provide cracking algorithms that can balance index convergence versus initialization costs [Idreos et al. 2011]. In addition, tailored benchmarks have been developed to stress-test critical features such as how quickly an algorithm adapts [Graefe et al. 2010]. Stochastic database cracking [Halim et al. 2012] shows how to be robust on various workloads, and Graefe and Kuno [2010b] show how adaptive indexing can apply to key columns. Finally, recent work on parallel adaptive indexing studies CPU-efficient implementations and proposes cracking algorithms to utilize multicores [Pirk et al. 2014, Alvarez et al. 2014] or even idle CPU time [Petraki et al. 2015].

The database cracking concept has also been extended to broader storage layout decisions, i.e., reorganizing base data (columns/rows) according to incoming query requests [Alagiannis et al. 2014], or even about which data should be loaded [Idreos et al. 2011, Alagiannis et al. 2012]. Cracking has also been studied in the context of Hadoop [Richter et al. 2013] for local indexing in each node as well as for improving more traditional disk-based indexing which forces reading data at the granularity of pages and where writing back the reorganized data needs to be considered as a major overhead [Graefe and Kuno 2010a].

Exercises

Problem 2.1 (*) Given relation EMP as in Fig. 2.2, let p_1: TITLE < "Programmer" and p_2: TITLE > "Programmer" be two simple predicates. Assume that character strings have an order among them, based on the alphabetical order.

(a) Perform a horizontal fragmentation of relation EMP with respect to $\{p_1, p_2\}$.
(b) Explain why the resulting fragmentation (EMP$_1$, EMP$_2$) does not fulfill the correctness rules of fragmentation.
(c) Modify the predicates p_1 and p_2 so that they partition EMP obeying the correctness rules of fragmentation. To do this, modify the predicates, compose

all minterm predicates and deduce the corresponding implications, and then perform a horizontal fragmentation of EMP based on these minterm predicates. Finally, show that the result has completeness, reconstruction, and disjointness properties.

Problem 2.2 (*) Consider relation ASG in Fig. 2.2. Suppose there are two applications that access ASG. The first is issued at five sites and attempts to find the duration of assignment of employees given their numbers. Assume that managers, consultants, engineers, and programmers are located at four different sites. The second application is issued at two sites where the employees with an assignment duration of less than 20 months are managed at one site, whereas those with longer duration are managed at a second site. Derive the primary horizontal fragmentation of ASG using the foregoing information.

Problem 2.3 Consider relations EMP and PAY in Fig. 2.2. EMP and PAY are horizontally fragmented as follows:

$$EMP_1 = \sigma_{TITLE=\text{"Elect. Eng."}}(EMP)$$

$$EMP_2 = \sigma_{TITLE=\text{"Syst. Anal."}}(EMP)$$

$$EMP_3 = \sigma_{TITLE=\text{"Mech. Eng."}}(EMP)$$

$$EMP_4 = \sigma_{TITLE=\text{"Programmer"}}(EMP)$$

$$PAY_1 = \sigma_{SAL \geq 30000}(PAY)$$

$$PAY_2 = \sigma_{SAL < 30000}(PAY)$$

Draw the join graph of EMP $\bowtie_{TITLE}$ PAY. Is the graph simple or partitioned? If it is partitioned, modify the fragmentation of either EMP or PAY so that the join graph of EMP $\bowtie_{TITLE}$ PAY is simple.

Problem 2.4 Give an example of a CA matrix where the split point is not unique and the partition is in the middle of the matrix. Show the number of shift operations required to obtain a single, unique split point.

Problem 2.5 (**) Given relation PAY as in Fig. 2.2, let $p_1 : SAL < 30000$ and $p_2 : SAL \geq 30000$ be two simple predicates. Perform a horizontal fragmentation of PAY with respect to these predicates to obtain PAY_1 and PAY_2. Using the fragmentation of PAY, perform further derived horizontal fragmentation for EMP. Show completeness, reconstruction, and disjointness of the fragmentation of EMP.

Problem 2.6 (**) Let $Q = \{q_1, \ldots, q_5\}$ be a set of queries, $A = \{A_1, \ldots, A_5\}$ be a set of attributes, and $S = \{S_1, S_2, S_3\}$ be a set of sites. The matrix of Fig. 2.25a describes the attribute usage values and the matrix of Fig. 2.25b gives the application access frequencies. Assume that $ref_i(q_k) = 1$ for all q_k and S_i and that A_1 is the key attribute. Use the bond energy and vertical partitioning algorithms to obtain a vertical fragmentation of the set of attributes in A.

Problem 2.7 (**) Write an algorithm for derived horizontal fragmentation.

$$
\begin{array}{ccccc}
 & A_1 & A_2 & A_3 & A_4 & A_5 \\
q_1 & 0 & 1 & 1 & 0 & 1 \\
q_2 & 1 & 1 & 1 & 0 & 1 \\
q_3 & 1 & 0 & 0 & 1 & 1 \\
q_4 & 0 & 0 & 1 & 0 & 0 \\
q_5 & 1 & 1 & 1 & 0 & 0
\end{array}
\qquad\qquad
\begin{array}{ccc}
 & S_1 & S_2 & S_3 \\
q_1 & 10 & 20 & 0 \\
q_2 & 5 & 0 & 10 \\
q_3 & 0 & 35 & 5 \\
q_4 & 0 & 10 & 0 \\
q_5 & 0 & 15 & 0
\end{array}
$$

(a)   (b)

Fig. 2.25 Attribute usage values and application access frequencies in Exercise 3.6

Problem 2.8 (**) Assume the following view definition:

```
CREATE VIEW    EMPVIEW(ENO, ENAME, PNO, RESP)
AS       SELECT EMP.ENO, EMP.ENAME, ASG.PNO, ASG.RESP
         FROM   EMP JOIN ASG
         WHERE  DUR=24
```

is accessed by application q_1, located at sites 1 and 2, with frequencies 10 and 20, respectively. Let us further assume that there is another query q_2 defined as

```
SELECT ENO, DUR
FROM   ASG
```

which is run at sites 2 and 3 with frequencies 20 and 10, respectively. Based on the above information, construct the $use(q_i, A_j)$ matrix for the attributes of both relations EMP and ASG. Also construct the affinity matrix containing all attributes of EMP and ASG. Finally, transform the affinity matrix so that it could be used to split the relation into two vertical fragments using heuristics or BEA.

Problem 2.9 (**) Formally define the three correctness criteria for derived horizontal fragmentation.

Problem 2.10 (*) Given a relation $R(K, A, B, C)$ (where K is the key) and the following query:

```
SELECT *
FROM   R
WHERE  R.A=10 AND R.B=15
```

(a) What will be the outcome of running PHF on this query?
(b) Does the COM_MIN algorithm produce in this case a complete and minimal predicate set? Justify your answer.

Problem 2.11 (*) Show that the bond energy algorithm generates the same results using either row or column operation.

Problem 2.12 (**) Modify algorithm SPLIT to allow n-way partitioning, and compute the complexity of the resulting algorithm.

Problem 2.13 (**) Formally define the three correctness criteria for hybrid fragmentation.

Problem 2.14 Discuss how the order in which the two basic fragmentation schemas are applied in hybrid fragmentation affects the final fragmentation.

Problem 2.15 (**) Describe how the following can be properly modeled in the database allocation problem.

(a) Relationships among fragments
(b) Query processing
(c) Integrity enforcement
(d) Concurrency control mechanisms

Problem 2.16 (**) Consider the various heuristic algorithms for the database allocation problem.

(a) What are some of the reasonable criteria for comparing these heuristics? Discuss.
(b) Compare the heuristic algorithms with respect to these criteria.

Problem 2.17 (*) Pick one of the heuristic algorithms used to solve the DAP, and write a program for it.

Problem 2.18 (**) Assume the environment of Exercise 3.8. Also assume that 60% of the accesses of query q_1 are updates to PNO and RESP of view EMPVIEW and that ASG.DUR is not updated through EMPVIEW. In addition, assume that the data transfer rate between site 1 and site 2 is half of that between site 2 and site 3. Based on the above information, find a reasonable fragmentation of ASG and EMP and an optimal replication and placement for the fragments, assuming that storage costs do not matter here, but copies are kept consistent.

Hint: Consider horizontal fragmentation for ASG based on DUR = 24 predicate and the corresponding derived horizontal fragmentation for EMP. Also look at the affinity matrix obtained in Example 2.7 for EMP and ASG together, and consider whether it would make sense to perform a vertical fragmentation for ASG.

Chapter 3
Distributed Data Control

An important requirement of a DBMS is the ability to support data control, i.e., controlling how data is accessed using a high-level language. Data control typically includes view management, access control, and semantic integrity control. Informally, these functions must ensure that *authorized* users perform *correct* operations on the database, thus contributing to the maintenance of database integrity. The functions necessary for maintaining the physical integrity of the database in the presence of concurrent accesses and failures are studied separately in Chap. 5 in the context of transaction management. In relational DBMSs, data control can be achieved in a uniform fashion. Views, authorizations, and semantic integrity constraints can be defined as rules that the system automatically enforces. The violation of some rules by database operations generally implies the rejection of the effects of some operations (e.g., undoing some updates) or propagating some effects (e.g., updating related data) to preserve the database integrity.

The definition of these rules is part of the administration of the database, a function generally performed by a database administrator (DBA). This person is also in charge of applying the organizational policies. Well-known solutions for data control have been proposed for centralized DBMSs. In this chapter, we discuss how these solutions can be extended to distributed DBMSs. The cost of enforcing data control, which is high in terms of resource utilization in a centralized DBMS, can be prohibitive in a distributed environment.

Since the rules for data control must be stored, the management of a distributed directory is also relevant in this chapter. The directory of a distributed DBMS can be viewed as a distributed database. There are several ways to store data control definitions, according to the way the directory is managed. Directory information can be stored differently according to its type; in other words, some information might be fully replicated, whereas other information might be distributed. For example, information that is useful at compile time, such as access control information, could

The original version of this chapter was revised. The correction to this chapter is available at https://doi.org/10.1007/978-3-030-26253-2_13

© Springer Nature Switzerland AG 2020

M. T. Özsu, P. Valduriez, *Principles of Distributed Database Systems*,
https://doi.org/10.1007/978-3-030-26253-2_3

be replicated. In this chapter, we emphasize the impact of directory management on the performance of data control mechanisms.

This chapter is organized as follows: View management is the subject of Sect. 3.1. Access control is presented in Sect. 3.2. Finally, semantic integrity control is treated in Sect. 3.3. For each section we first outline the solution in a centralized DBMS and then give the distributed solution, which is often an extension of the centralized one, although more difficult.

3.1   View Management

One of the main advantages of the relational model is that it provides full logical data independence. As introduced in Chap. 1, external schemas enable user groups to have their particular *view* of the database. In a relational system, a view is a *virtual relation*, defined as the result of a query on *base relations* (or real relations), but not materialized like a base relation in the database. A view is a dynamic window in the sense that it reflects all updates to the database. An external schema can be defined as a set of views and/or base relations. Besides their use in external schemas, views are useful for ensuring data security in a simple way. By selecting a subset of the database, views *hide* some data. If users may only access the database through views, they cannot see or manipulate the hidden data, which is therefore secure.

In the remainder of this section we look at view management in centralized and distributed systems as well as the problems of updating views. Note that in a distributed DBMS, a view can be derived from distributed relations, and the access to a view requires the execution of the distributed query corresponding to the view definition. An important issue in a distributed DBMS is to make view materialization efficient. We will see how the concept of materialized views helps in solving this problem, among others, but requires efficient techniques for materialized view maintenance.

3.1.1   Views in Centralized DBMSs

Most relational DBMSs use a view mechanism where a view is a relation derived from base relations as the result of a relational query (this was first proposed within the INGRES and System R projects). It is defined by associating the name of the view with the retrieval query that specifies it.

Example 3.1 The view of system analysts (SYSAN) derived from relation EMP can be defined by the following SQL query:

```
CREATE VIEW SYSAN(ENO, ENAME) AS
  SELECT ENO, ENAME
  FROM   EMP
  WHERE  TITLE = "Syst. Anal."
```

The single effect of this statement is the storage of the view definition in the catalog. No other information needs to be recorded. Therefore, the result of the query defining the view (i.e., a relation having the attributes ENO and ENAME for the system analysts as shown in Fig. 3.1) is *not* produced. However, the view SYSAN can be manipulated as a base relation.

Example 3.2 The query

"Find the names of all the system analysts with their project number and responsibility(ies)"

involving the view SYSAN and relation ASG can be expressed as

```
SELECT ENAME, PNO, RESP
FROM   SYSAN NATURAL JOIN ASG
```

Mapping a query expressed on views into a query expressed on base relations can be done by *query modification*. With this technique the variables are changed to range on base relations and the query qualification is merged (ANDed) with the view qualification.

Example 3.3 The preceding query can be modified to

```
SELECT ENAME, PNO, RESP
FROM   EMP NATURAL JOIN ASG
WHERE  TITLE = "Syst. Anal."
```

The result of this query is illustrated in Fig. 3.2.   ♦

The modified query is expressed on base relations and can therefore be processed by the query processor. It is important to note that view processing can be done at

SYSAN

ENO	ENAME
E2	M. Smith
E5	B. Casey
E8	J. Jones

Fig. 3.1 Relation corresponding to the view SYSAN

ENAME	PNO	RESP
M. Smith	P1	Analyst
M. Smith	P2	Analyst
B. Casey	P3	Manager
J. Jones	P4	Manager

Fig. 3.2 Result of query involving view SYSAN

compile time. The view mechanism can also be used for refining the access controls to include subsets of objects. To specify any user from whom one wants to hide data, the keyword USER generally refers to the logged-on user identifier.

Example 3.4 The view ESAME restricts the access by any user to those employees having the same title:

```
CREATE VIEW ESAME AS
  SELECT *
  FROM    EMP E1, EMP E2
  WHERE   E1.ENO = E2.ENO
  AND     E1.ENO = USER
```

In the view definition above, * stands for "all attributes" and the two tuple variables (E1 and E2) ranging over relation EMP are required to express the join of one tuple of EMP (the one corresponding to the logged-on user) with all tuples of EMP based on the same title. For example, the following query issued by the user J. Doe

```
SELECT *
FROM    ESAME
```

returns the relation of Fig. 3.3. Note that the user J. Doe also appears in the result. If the user who creates ESAME is an electrical engineer, as in this case, the view represents the set of all electrical engineers.   ◆

Views can be defined using arbitrarily complex relational queries involving selection, projection, join, aggregate functions, and so on. All views can be interrogated as base relations, but not all views can be manipulated as such. Updates through views can be handled automatically only if they can be propagated correctly to the base relations. We can classify views as being updatable and not updatable. A view is updatable only if the updates to the view can be propagated to the base relations without ambiguity. The view SYSAN above is updatable; the insertion, for example, of a new system analyst ⟨201, Smith⟩ will be mapped into the insertion of a new employee ⟨201, Smith, Syst. Anal.⟩. If attributes other than TITLE were hidden by the view, they would be assigned *null values*.

Example 3.5 However, the following view, which uses a natural join (i.e., the equijoin of two relations on a common attribute), is not updatable:

```
CREATE VIEW EG(ENAME, RESP) AS
  SELECT DISTINCT ENAME, RESP
```

ENO	ENAME	TITLE
E1	J. Doe	Elect. Eng.
E2	L. Chu	Elect. Eng.

Fig. 3.3 Result of query on view ESAME

    FROM   EMP **NATURAL JOIN** ASG

The deletion, for example, of the tuple ⟨Smith, Analyst⟩ cannot be propagated, since it is ambiguous. Deletions of Smith in relation EMP or analyst in relation ASG are both meaningful, but the system does not know which is correct.   ◆

Current systems are very restrictive about supporting updates through views. Views can be updated only if they are derived from a single relation by selection and projection. This precludes views defined by joins, aggregates, and so on. However, it is theoretically possible to automatically support updates of a larger class of views. It is interesting to note that views derived by join are updatable if they include the keys of the base relations.

3.1.2 Views in Distributed DBMSs

The definition of a view is similar in a distributed DBMS and in centralized systems. However, a view in a distributed system may be derived from fragmented relations stored at different sites. When a view is defined, its name and its retrieval query are stored in the catalog.

Since views may be used as base relations by application programs, their definition should be stored in the directory in the same way as the base relation descriptions. Depending on the degree of site autonomy offered by the system, view definitions can be centralized at one site, partially duplicated or fully duplicated. In any case, the information associating a view name to its definition site should be duplicated. If the view definition is not present at the site where the query is issued, remote access to the view definition site is necessary.

The mapping of a query expressed on views into a query expressed on base relations (which can potentially be fragmented) can also be done through query modification in the same way as in centralized DBMSs. With this technique, the qualification defining the view is found in the distributed database catalog and then merged with the query to provide a query on base relations. Such a modified query is a *distributed query*, which can be processed by the distributed query processor (see Chap. 4). The query processor maps the distributed query into a query on physical fragments.

In Chap. 2 we presented alternative ways of fragmenting base relations. The definition of fragmentation is, in fact, very similar to the definition of particular views. Thus, it is possible to manage views and fragments using a unified mechanism. Furthermore, replicated data can be handled in the same way. The value of such a unified mechanism is to facilitate distributed database administration. The objects manipulated by the database administrator can be seen as a hierarchy where the leaves are the fragments from which relations and views can be derived. Therefore, the DBA may increase locality of reference by making views in one-to-one correspondence with fragments. For example, it is possible to implement the view SYSAN illustrated in Example 3.1 by a fragment at a given site, provided that most users accessing the view SYSAN are at the same site.

Evaluating views derived from distributed relations may be costly. In a given organization it is likely that many users access the same view which must be recomputed for each user. We saw in Sect. 3.1.1 that view derivation is done by merging the view qualification with the query qualification. An alternative solution is to avoid view derivation by maintaining actual versions of the views, called *materialized views*. A *materialized view* stores the tuples of a view in a database relation, like the other database tuples, possibly with indices. Thus, access to a materialized view is much faster than deriving the view, in particular, in a distributed DBMS where base relations can be remote. Introduced in the early 1980s, materialized views have since gained much interest in the context of data warehousing to speed up Online Analytical Processing (OLAP) applications. Materialized views in data warehouses typically involve aggregate (such as **SUM** and **COUNT**) and grouping (**GROUP BY**) operators because they provide compact database summaries. Today, all major database products support materialized views.

Example 3.6 The following view over relation PROJ(PNO,PNAME,BUDGET,LOC) gives, for each location, the number of projects and the total budget.

```
CREATE VIEW PL(LOC, NBPROJ, TBUDGET) AS
   SELECT LOC, COUNT(*),SUM(BUDGET)
   FROM   PROJ
   GROUP BY LOC
```

                                                                                                                    ◆

3.1.3   *Maintenance of Materialized Views*

A materialized view is a copy of some base data and thus must be kept consistent with that base data which may be updated. *View maintenance* is the process of updating (or refreshing) a materialized view to reflect the changes made to the base data. The issues related to view materialization are somewhat similar to those of database replication which we will address in Chap. 6. However, a major difference is that materialized view expressions, in particular, for data warehousing, are typically more complex than replica definitions and may include join, group by, and aggregate operators. Another major difference is that database replication is concerned with more general replication configurations, e.g., with multiple copies of the same base data at multiple sites.

A view maintenance policy allows a DBA to specify *when* and *how* a view should be refreshed. The first question (when to refresh) is related to consistency (between the view and the base data) and efficiency. A view can be refreshed in two modes: *immediate* or *deferred*. With the immediate mode, a view is refreshed immediately as part as the transaction that updates base data used by the view. If the view and the base data are managed by different DBMSs, possibly at different sites, this requires the use of a distributed transaction, for instance, using the two-phase commit (2PC) protocol (see Chap. 5). The main advantages of immediate refreshment are that the view is always consistent with the base data and that read-only queries can be fast. However, this is at the expense of increased transaction time to update both the base data and the views within the same transactions. Furthermore, using distributed transactions may be difficult.

In practice, the deferred mode is preferred because the view is refreshed in separate (refresh) transactions, thus without performance penalty on the transactions that update the base data. The refresh transactions can be triggered at different times: *lazily*, just before a query is evaluated on the view; *periodically*, at predefined times, e.g., every day; or *forcedly*, after a predefined number of updates to the base data. Lazy refreshment enables queries to see the latest consistent state of the base data but at the expense of increased query time to include the refreshment of the view. Periodic and forced refreshment allow queries to see views whose state is not consistent with the latest state of the base data. The views managed with these strategies are also called *snapshots*.

The second question (how to refresh a view) is an important efficiency issue. The simplest way to refresh a view is to recompute it from scratch using the base data. In some cases, this may be the most efficient strategy, e.g., if a large subset of the base data has been changed. However, there are many cases where only a small subset of view needs to be changed. In these cases, a better strategy is to compute the view *incrementally*, by computing only the changes to the view. Incremental view maintenance relies on the concept of differential relation. Let u be an update of relation R. R^+ and R^- are *differential relations* of R by u, where R^+ contains the tuples inserted by u into R, and R^- contains the tuples of R deleted by u. If u is an insertion, R^- is empty. If u is a deletion, R^+ is empty. Finally, if u is a modification, relation R can be obtained by computing $(V - V^-) \cup V^+$. Computing the changes to the view, i.e., V^+ and V^-, may require using the base relations in addition to differential relations.

Example 3.7 Consider the view EG of Example 3.5 which uses relations EMP and ASG as base data and assume its state is derived from that of Example 3.1, so that EG has 9 tuples (see Fig. 3.4). Let EMP^+ consist of one tuple ⟨E9, B. Martin, Programmer⟩ to be inserted in EMP, and ASG^+ consist of two tuples ⟨E4, P3, Programmer, 12⟩ and ⟨E9, P3, Programmer, 12⟩ to be inserted in ASG. The changes to the view EG can be computed as:

```
EG+ = (SELECT ENAME, RESP
       FROM   EMP NATURAL JOIN ASG+)
           UNION
      (SELECT ENAME, RESP
       FROM   EMP+ NATURAL JOIN ASG)
           UNION
      (SELECT ENAME, RESP
       FROM   EMP+ NATURAL JOIN ASG+)
```

which yields tuples ⟨B. Martin, Programmer⟩ and ⟨J. Miller, Programmer⟩. Note that integrity constraints would be useful here to avoid useless work (see Sect. 3.3.2). Assuming that relations EMP and ASG are related by a referential constraint that says that ENO in ASG must exist in EMP, the second **SELECT** statement is useless as it produces an empty relation.   ◆

Efficient techniques have been devised to perform incremental view maintenance using both the materialized views and the base relations. The techniques essentially differ in their views' expressiveness, their use of integrity constraints, and the way they handle insertion and deletion. They can be classified along the view expressiveness dimension as nonrecursive views, views involving outerjoins, and recursive views. For nonrecursive views, i.e., select-project-join (SPJ) views that may have duplicate elimination, union, and aggregation, an elegant solution is the *counting algorithm*. One problem stems from the fact that individual tuples in the view may be derived from several tuples in the base relations, thus making deletion in the view difficult. The basic idea of the counting algorithm is to maintain a count of the number of derivations for each tuple in the view, and to increment (resp. decrement) tuple counts based on insertions (resp. deletions); a tuple in the view of which count is zero can then be deleted.

Example 3.8 Consider the view EG in Fig. 3.4. Each tuple in EG has one derivation (i.e., a count of 1) except tuple ⟨M. Smith, Analyst⟩ which has two (i.e., a count of 2). Assume now that tuples ⟨E2, P1, Analyst, 24⟩ and ⟨E3, P3, Consultant, 10⟩ are deleted from ASG. Then only tuple ⟨A. Lee, Consultant⟩ needs to be deleted from EG.   ◆

We now present the basic counting algorithm for refreshing a view V defined over two relations R and S as a query $q(R, S)$. Assuming that each tuple in V has an associated derivation count, the algorithm has three main steps (see Algorithm 3.1). First, it applies the view differentiation technique to formulate the differential views V^+ and V^- as queries over the view, the base relations, and the differential relations. Second, it computes V^+ and V^- and their tuple counts. Third, it applies the changes V^+ and V^- in V by adding positive counts and subtracting negative counts, and deleting tuples with a count of zero.

ENAME	RESP
J. Doe	Manager
M. Smith	Analyst
A. Lee	Consultant
A. Lee	Engineer
J. Miller	Programmer
B. Casey	Manager
L. Chu	Manager
R. Davis	Engineer
J. Jones	Manager

Fig. 3.4 State of view EG

Algorithm 3.1: COUNTING

Input: V: view defined as $q(\text{R}, \text{S})$; R, S: relations; R^+, R^-: changes to R
begin

    $\text{V}^+ = q^+(\text{V}, \text{R}^+, \text{R}, \text{S})$
    $\text{V}^- = q^-(\text{V}, \text{R}^-, \text{R}, \text{S})$
    compute V^+ with positive counts for inserted tuples
    compute V^- with negative counts for deleted tuples
    compute $(\text{V} - \text{V}^-) \cup \text{V}^+$ by adding positive counts and subtracting negative counts
      deleting each tuple in V with count $= 0$;

end

The counting algorithm is optimal since it computes exactly the view tuples that are inserted or deleted. However, it requires access to the base relations. This implies that the base relations be maintained (possibly as replicas) at the sites of the materialized view. To avoid accessing the base relations so the view can be stored at a different site, the view should be maintainable using only the view and the differential relations. Such views are called *self-maintainable*.

Example 3.9 Consider the view SYSAN in Example 3.1. Let us write the view definition as SYSAN=q(EMP) meaning that the view is defined by a query q on EMP. We can compute the differential views using only the differential relations, i.e., SYSAN$^+$ = q(EMP$^+$) and SYSAN$^-$ = q(EMP$^-$). Thus, the view SYSAN is self-maintainable.   ◆

Self-maintainability depends on the views' expressiveness and can be defined with respect to the update type (insertion, deletion, or modification). Most SPJ views are not self-maintainable with respect to insertion but are often self-maintainable with respect to deletion and modification. For instance, an SPJ view is self-maintainable with respect to deletion of relation R if the key attributes of R are included in the view.

Example 3.10 Consider the view EG of Example 3.5. Let us add attribute ENO (which is key of EMP) in the view definition. This view is not self-maintainable with respect to insertion. For instance, after an insertion of an ASG tuple, we need to perform the join with EMP to get the corresponding ENAME to insert in the view. However, this view is self-maintainable with respect to deletion on EMP. For instance, if one EMP tuple is deleted, the view tuples having same ENO can be deleted.   ◆

We discuss two optimizations that can significantly reduce the maintenance time of the COUNTING algorithm. The first optimization is to materialize views representing subqueries of the input query. A view is constructed by removing a subset of relations from the query. These views are increasingly smaller and build a hierarchy. F-IVM method constructs such a hierarchy, called a view tree, with the input query at the top, the relations at the leaves, and inner views defined by project-join-aggregate queries over their children. Updates to a relation are propagated bottom-up in this view tree. The views that are on the path from the updated relation to the root are maintained using the delta processing from the COUNTING algorithm. All other views remain unchanged; if they are materialized, then they may speed up this delta processing. For a restricted class of acyclic queries, called q-hierarchical, such view trees allow for constant-time updates to any of the input relations.

The second optimization exploits the skew in the data. Values that appear very often in the database are deemed heavy, while all others are light. IVM^ϵ uses evaluation strategies that are sensitive to the heavy/light skew in the data and that use materialized views and delta computation like all aforementioned maintenance algorithms.

We exemplify these two optimizations for a query that counts the number of triangles in a graph. We would like to refresh this triangle count immediately and incrementally under one update to the data graph, which can be an edge insertion or deletion. Let us consider three copies R, S, and T of the binary edge relation of a graph with N edges. We record the multiplicities of tuples in the input relations and views, that is, the number of their derivations, in a separate column P. Assuming the schemas of the relations are (A, B, P_R), (B, C, P_S), and (C, A, P_T), the triangle count query is

```
CREATE VIEW Q(CNT) AS
  SELECT SUM(P_R * P_S * P_T) as CNT
  FROM   R NATURAL JOIN S NATURAL JOIN T
```

The insertion or deletion of an edge triggers updates to each of the three relation copies. We discuss the case of updating R; the other two cases are treated similarly. We model this update as a relation deltaR consisting of a single tuple (a, b, p), where (a, b) defines the updated edge and p is the multiplicity. Following the formalism of generalized multiset relations, we model both inserts and deletes uniformly by allowing for multiplicities to be integers, that is, negative and positive numbers. Then, for inserting or deleting the edge three times, we set the multiplicity p to $+3$ or, respectively, to -3.

The COUNTING algorithm computes on the fly a delta query deltaQ that represents the change to the query result: This query is the same as Q, where we replace R by deltaR. This delta computation takes $\mathcal{O}(N)$ time since it needs to intersect two lists of possibly $\mathcal{O}(N)$ many C-values that are paired with b in S and with a in T (that is, the multiplicity of such pairs in S and T is nonzero).

The DBToaster approach speeds up the delta computation by precomputing three auxiliary views representing the update-independent parts of the delta queries for updates to the three relations:

```
CREATE VIEW V_ST(B, A, CNT) AS
  SELECT   B, A, SUM(P_S * P_T) as CNT
  FROM     S NATURAL JOIN T
  GROUP BY B, A

CREATE VIEW V_TR(C, B, CNT) AS
```

```
SELECT    C, B, SUM(P_T * P_R) as CNT
FROM      T NATURAL JOIN R
GROUP BY C, B

CREATE VIEW V_RS(A, C, CNT) AS
  SELECT    A, C, SUM(P_R * P_S) as CNT
  FROM      R NATURAL JOIN S
  GROUP BY A, C
```

The view V_ST allows to compute the delta query deltaQ in $\mathcal{O}(1)$ time, since the join of deltaR and V_ST requires a constant-time lookup for $\langle a, b \rangle$ into V_ST. However, maintaining the views V_RS and V_TR, which are defined using R, still requires $\mathcal{O}(N)$ time.

The F-IVM method materializes only one of the three views, for instance, V_ST. In this case, the maintenance under updates to R takes $\mathcal{O}(1)$ time, but the maintenance of S and T under updates still takes $\mathcal{O}(N)$ time.

IVM$^\epsilon$ algorithm partitions the nodes in the graph depending on their degree, that is, on the number of directly connected nodes: The *heavy* nodes have degree greater than or equal to $N^{1/2}$, while the *light* nodes have degree less than $N^{1/2}$. This leads to a partition of each of the three copies R, S, and T of the edge relation into a heavy part R_h (S_h, T_h) and a light part R_l (S_l, T_l): a tuple $\langle a, b, p \rangle$ is in R_h if a is heavy and in R_l otherwise; similarly, a tuple $\langle b, c, p \rangle$ is in S_h if b is heavy and in S_l otherwise; finally, $\langle c, a, p \rangle$ is in T_h if c is heavy and in T_l otherwise. We can rewrite Q by replacing each of the three relations with the union of its two parts. The query Q is then equivalent to the union of eight skew-aware views Q_r,s,t, where $r, s, t \in \{h, l\}$:

```
CREATE VIEW   Q_r,s,t(CNT) AS
  SELECT SUM(P_R * P_S * P_T) as CNT
  FROM    R_r NATURAL JOIN S_s NATURAL JOIN T_t
```

Consider a single-tuple update deltaR_r $= \{(a, b, p)\}$ to the part R_r of relation R for $r \in \{h, l\}$. The delta computation for a view Q_r,s,t is then given by the following simpler query:

```
CREATE VIEW   deltaQ_r,s,t(CNT) AS
  SELECT SUM(P_R * P_S * P_T) as CNT
  FROM    deltaR_r NATURAL JOIN S_s NATURAL JOIN T_t
  WHERE   S_s.A = a AND T_t.B = b
```

IVM$^\epsilon$ adapts its maintenance strategy to each skew-aware view to achieve the sublinear update time. While most of these views trivially achieve the $\mathcal{O}(N^{1/2})$ upper bound, there is one exception. We next explain how to achieve this bound for maintaining each of these views.

The delta computation for the four views Q_r,l,t (for $r, t \in \{h, l\}$) is expressed as follows:

```
CREATE VIEW   deltaQ_r,l,t(CNT) AS
  SELECT SUM(P_R * P_S * P_T) as CNT
  FROM   deltaR_r NATURAL JOIN S_l NATURAL JOIN T_t
  WHERE  S_l.A = a AND T_t.B = b
```

It joins the parts S_l with T_t on C. Since the update deltaR_r sets B to b in S_l and b can only be a light value in S_l, there are at most $N^{1/2}$ C-values paired with b in S_l. The intersection of the set of C-values in S_l and T_t can then take at most $\mathcal{O}(N^{1/2})$ time.

The delta computation for the views Q_r,h,h is expressed similarly. Since all C-values in T_h are heavy, each of them has at least $N^{1/2}$ A-values. This also means there are at most $N^{1/2}$ heavy C-values. The intersection of the set of the heavy C-values in T_h with the C-values in S_h can then take at most $\mathcal{O}(N^{1/2})$ time.

However, the delta computation for the views Q_r,h,l for $r \in \{h, l\}$ needs linear time, since it requires iterating over all the C-values c paired with b in S_h and with a in T_l; the number of such C-values can be linear in the size of the database. In this case, IVM^ϵ precomputes the update-independent parts of the delta queries as auxiliary materialized views and then exploits these views to speed up the delta evaluation:

```
CREATE VIEW V_ST(B, A, CNT) AS
  SELECT B, A, SUM(P_S * P_T) as CNT
  FROM   S_h NATURAL JOIN T_l
  GROUP BY B, A
```

We materialize similar views V_RS and V_TR in case of updates to T and, respectively, S. Each of these views needs $\mathcal{O}(N^{3/2})$ space. We can now compute deltaQ_r,h,l using V_ST as

```
CREATE VIEW   deltaQ_r,h,l(CNT) AS
  SELECT SUM(P_R * CNT) as CNT
  FROM   deltaR_r NATURAL JOIN V_ST
  WHERE  V_ST.B = b AND V_ST.A = a
```

This takes $\mathcal{O}(1)$ time since we only need a lookup in V_ST to fetch the multiplicity of the edge (a, b) followed by the multiplication with p from deltaR_r.

3.2 Access Control

Access control is an important aspect of data security, the function of a database system that protects data against unauthorized access. Another important aspect is *data protection*, to prevent unauthorized users from understanding the physical content of data. This function is typically provided by file systems in the context of centralized and distributed operating systems. The main data protection approach is data encryption.

Access control must guarantee that only authorized users perform operations they are allowed to perform on the database. Many different users may have access to a large collection of data under the control of a single centralized or distributed system. The centralized or distributed DBMS must thus be able to restrict the access of a subset of the database to a subset of the users. Access control has long been provided by operating systems as services of the file system. In this context, a centralized control is offered. Indeed, the central controller creates objects, and may allow particular users to perform particular operations (read, write, execute) on these objects. Also, objects are identified by their external names.

Access control in database systems differs in several aspects from that in traditional file systems. Authorizations must be refined so that different users have different rights on the same database objects. This requirement implies the ability to specify subsets of objects more precisely than by name and to distinguish between groups of users. In addition, the decentralized control of authorizations is of particular importance in a distributed context. In relational systems, authorizations can be uniformly controlled by database administrators using high-level constructs. For example, controlled objects can be specified by predicates in the same way as is a query qualification.

There are two main approaches to database access control. The first approach is called *discretionary access control (DAC)* and has long been provided by DBMS. DAC defines access rights based on the users, the type of access (e.g., `SELECT, UPDATE`), and the objects to be accessed. The second approach, called *mandatory access control (MAC)* further increases security by restricting access to classified data to cleared users. Support of MAC by major DBMSs is more recent and stems from increased security threats coming from the Internet. Other approaches go further into adding more semantics to access control, in particular, role-based access control, which considers users with different roles, and purpose-based access control, e.g., hippocratic databases, which associates purpose information with data, i.e., the reasons for data collection and access.

From solutions to access control in centralized systems, we derive those for distributed DBMSs. However, there is the additional complexity which stems from the fact that objects and users can be distributed. In what follows we first present discretionary and mandatory access control in centralized systems and then the additional problems and their solutions in distributed systems.

3.2.1 Discretionary Access Control

Three main actors are involved in DAC: the *subject* (e.g., users, groups of users) who trigger the execution of application programs; the *operations*, which are embedded in application programs; and the *database objects*, on which the operations are performed. Authorization control consists of checking whether a given triple (subject, operation, object) can be allowed to proceed (i.e., the user can execute the operation on the object). An authorization can be viewed as a triple (subject, operation type, object definition) which specifies that the subjects have the right to perform an operation of operation type on an object. To control authorizations properly, the DBMS requires the definition of subjects, objects, and access rights.

The introduction of a subject in the system is typically done by a pair (user name, password). The user name uniquely *identifies* the users of that name in the system, while the password, known only to the users of that name, *authenticates* the users. Both user name and password must be supplied in order to log in the system. This prevents people who do not know the password from entering the system with only the user name.

The objects to protect are subsets of the database. Relational systems provide finer and more general protection granularity than do earlier systems. In a file system, the protection granule is the file. In a relational system, objects can be defined by their type (view, relation, tuple, attribute) as well as by their content using selection predicates. Furthermore, the view mechanism as introduced in Sect. 3.1 permits the protection of objects simply by hiding subsets of relations (attributes or tuples) from unauthorized users.

A right expresses a relationship between a subject and an object for a particular set of operations. In an SQL-based relational DBMS, an operation is a high-level statement such as **SELECT, INSERT, UPDATE,** or **DELETE,** and rights are defined (granted or revoked) using the following statements:

> **GRANT** ⟨operation type(s)⟩ **ON** ⟨object⟩ TO ⟨subject(s)⟩
> **REVOKE** ⟨operation type(s)⟩ **FROM** ⟨object⟩ TO ⟨subject(s)⟩

The keyword *public* can be used to mean all users. Authorization control can be characterized based on who (the grantors) can grant the rights. To ease database administration, it is convenient to define user groups, as in operating systems, for the purpose of authorization. Once defined, a user group can be used as subject in **GRANT** and **REVOKE** statements.

In its simplest form, the control is centralized: a single user or user class, the database administrators, has all privileges on the database objects and is the only one allowed to use the **GRANT** and **REVOKE** statements. A more flexible form of control is decentralized: the creator of an object becomes its owner and is granted all privileges on it. In particular, there is the additional operation type **GRANT,** which transfers all the rights of the grantor performing the statement to the specified subjects. Therefore, the person receiving the right (the grantee) may subsequently grant privileges on that object. Thus, access control is discretionary in the sense that users with grant privilege can make access policy decisions. The revoking process is complex as it must be recursive. For example, if A, who granted B who granted C the **GRANT** privilege on object O, wants to revoke all the privileges of B on O, all the privileges of C on O must also be revoked. To perform revocation, the system must maintain a hierarchy of grants per object where the creator of the object is the root.

The privileges of the subjects over objects are recorded in the catalog (directory) as authorization rules. There are several ways to store the authorizations. The most convenient approach is to consider all the privileges as an *authorization matrix*, in which a row defines a subject, a column an object, and a matrix entry (for a pair ⟨subject, object⟩), the authorized operations. The authorized operations are specified by their operation type (e.g., **SELECT, UPDATE**). It is also customary to associate with the operation type a predicate that further restricts the access to the object. The latter option is provided when the objects must be base relations and cannot be views. For example, one authorized operation for the pair ⟨Jones, relation EMP⟩ could be

SELECT WHERE TITLE = "Syst.Anal."

which authorizes Jones to access only the employee tuples for system analysts. Figure 3.5 gives an example of an authorization matrix where objects are either relations (EMP and ASG) or attributes (ENAME).

The authorization matrix can be stored in three ways: by row, by column, or by element. When the matrix is stored by *row*, each subject is associated with the list of objects that may be accessed together with the related access rights. This approach makes the enforcement of authorizations efficient, since all the rights of the logged-on user are together (in the user profile). However, the manipulation of access rights per object (e.g., making an object public) is not efficient since all subject profiles must be accessed. When the matrix is stored by *column*, each object is associated with the list of subjects who may access it with the corresponding access rights. The advantages and disadvantages of this approach are the reverse of the previous approach.

The respective advantages of the two approaches can be combined in the third approach, in which the matrix is stored by *element*, that is, by relation (subject, object, right). This relation can have indices on both subject and object, thereby providing fast-access right manipulation per subject and per object.

Directly managing relationships between many subjects and many objects gets complicated for database administrators. *Role-based access control* (RBAC) addresses this problem by adding roles, as a level of independence between subjects and objects. Roles correspond to various job functions (e.g., clerk, analyst, manager, etc.), users are assigned particular roles, and authorizations on objects are assigned to specific roles. Thus, users no longer acquire authorizations directly, but only

	EMP	ENAME	ASG
Casey	UPDATE	UPDATE	UPDATE
Jones	SELECT	SELECT	SELECT WHERE RESP $\neq$ "Manager"
Casey	NONE	SELECT	NONE

Fig. 3.5 Example of authorization matrix

through their roles. Since there are not that many roles, RBAC simplifies much access control, in particular when adding or modifying user accounts.

3.2.2   Mandatory Access Control

DAC has some limitations. One problem is that a malicious user can access unauthorized data through an authorized user. For instance, consider user A who has authorized access to relations R and S and user B who has authorized access to relation S only. If B somehow manages to modify an application program used by A so it writes R data into S, then B can read unauthorized data without violating authorization rules.

MAC answers this problem and further improves security by defining different security levels for both subjects and data objects. Furthermore, unlike DAC, the access policy decisions are under the control of a single administrator, i.e., users cannot define their own policies and grant access to objects. MAC in databases is based on the well-known Bell-LaPadula model designed for operating system security. In this model, subjects are processes acting on a user's behalf; a process has a security level also called *clearance* derived from that of the user. In its simplest form, the security levels are Top Secret (TS), Secret (S), Confidential (C), and Unclassified (U), and ordered as $TS > S > C > U$, where ">" means "more secure." Access in read and write modes by subjects is restricted by two simple rules:

1. A subject T is allowed to read an object of security level l only if $level(T) \geq l$.
2. A subject T is allowed to write an object of security level l only if $class(T) \leq l$.

Rule 1 (called "no read up") protects data from unauthorized disclosure, i.e., a subject at a given security level can only read objects at the same or lower security levels. For instance, a subject with secret clearance cannot read top-secret data. Rule 2 (called "no write down") protects data from unauthorized change, i.e., a subject at a given security level can only write objects at the same or higher security levels. For instance, a subject with top-secret clearance can only write top-secret data but cannot write secret data (which could then contain top-secret data).

In the relational model, data objects can be relations, tuples, or attributes. Thus, a relation can be classified at different levels: relation (i.e., all tuples in the relation have the same security level), tuple (i.e., every tuple has a security level), or attribute (i.e., every distinct attribute value has a security level). A classified relation is thus called *multilevel relation* to reflect that it will appear differently (with different data) to subjects with different clearances. For instance, a multilevel relation classified at the tuple level can be represented by adding a security level attribute to each tuple. Similarly, a multilevel relation classified at attribute level can be represented by adding a corresponding security level to each attribute. Figure 3.6 illustrates a multilevel relation PROJ* based on relation PROJ which is classified at the attribute

PROJ*

PNO	SL1	PNAME	SL2	BUDGET	SL3	LOC	SL4
P1	C	Instrumentation	C	150000	C	Montreal	C
P2	C	Database Develop.	C	135000	S	New York	S
P3	S	CAD/CAM	S	250000	S	New York	S

Fig. 3.6 Multilevel relation PROJ* classified at the attribute level

PROJ*C

PNO	SL1	PNAME	SL2	BUDGET	SL3	LOC	SL4
P1	C	Instrumentation	C	150000	C	Montreal	C
P2	C	Database Develop.	C	Null	S	Null	S

Fig. 3.7 Confidential relation PROJ*C

PROJ**

PNO	SL1	PNAME	SL2	BUDGET	SL3	LOC	SL4
P1	C	Instrumentation	C	150000	C	Montreal	C
P2	C	Database Develop.	C	135000	S	New York	S
P3	S	CAD/CAM	S	250000	S	New York	S
P3	C	Web Develop.	C	200000	C	Paris	C

Fig. 3.8 Multilevel relation with polyinstantiation

level. Note that the additional security level attributes may increase significantly the size of the relation.

The entire relation also has a security level which is the lowest security level of any data it contains. For instance, relation PROJ* has security level *C*. A relation can then be accessed by any subject having a security level which is the same or higher. However, a subject can only access data for which it has clearance. Thus, attributes for which a subject has no clearance will appear to the subject as null values with an associated security level which is the same as the subject. Figure 3.7 shows an instance of relation PROJ* as accessed by a subject at a confidential security level.

MAC has strong impact on the data model because users do not see the same data and have to deal with unexpected side-effects. One major side-effect is called *polyinstantiation*, which allows the same object to have different attribute values depending on the users' security level. Figure 3.8 illustrates a multirelation with polyinstantiated tuples. Tuple of primary key P3 has two instantiations, each one with a different security level. This may result from a subject *T* with security level *C* inserting a tuple with key="P3" in relation PROJ* in Fig. 3.6. Because *T* (with confidential clearance level) should ignore the existence of tuple with key="P3" (classified as secret), the only practical solution is to add a second tuple with same key and different classification. However, a user with secret clearance would see both tuples with key="E3" and should interpret this unexpected effect.

3.2.3   Distributed Access Control

The additional problems of access control in a distributed environment stem from the fact that objects and subjects are distributed and that messages with sensitive data can be read by unauthorized users. These problems are: remote user authentication, management of discretionary access rules, handling of views and of user groups, and enforcing MAC.

Remote user authentication is necessary since any site of a distributed DBMS may accept programs initiated, and authorized, at remote sites. To prevent remote access by unauthorized users or applications (e.g., from a site that is not part of the distributed DBMS), users must also be identified and authenticated at the accessed site. Furthermore, instead of using passwords that could be obtained from sniffing messages, encrypted certificates could be used.

Three solutions are possible for managing authentication:

1. Authentication information is maintained at a central site for *global users* which can then be authenticated only once and then accessed from multiple sites.
2. The information for authenticating users (user name and password) is replicated at all sites in the catalog. Local programs, initiated at a remote site, must also indicate the user name and password.
3. All sites of the distributed DBMS identify and authenticate themselves similar to the way users do. Intersite communication is thus protected by the use of the site password. Once the initiating site has been authenticated, there is no need for authenticating their remote users.

The first solution simplifies password administration significantly and enables single authentication (also called single sign on). However, the central authentication site can be a single point of failure and a bottleneck. The second solution is more costly in terms of directory management given that the introduction of a new user is a distributed operation. However, users can access the distributed database from any site. The third solution is necessary if user information is not replicated. Nevertheless, it can also be used if there is replication of the user information. In this case it makes remote authentication more efficient. If user names and passwords are not replicated, they should be stored at the sites where the users access the system (i.e., the home site). The latter solution is based on the realistic assumption that users are more static, or at least they always access the distributed database from the same site.

Distributed authorization rules are expressed in the same way as centralized ones. Like view definitions, they must be stored in the catalog. They can be either fully replicated at each site or stored at the sites of the referenced objects. In the latter case the rules are duplicated only at the sites where the referenced objects are distributed. The main advantage of the fully replicated approach is that authorization can be processed by query modification at compile time. However, directory management is more costly because of data duplication. The second solution is better if locality of reference is very high. However, distributed authorization cannot be controlled at compile time.

Views may be considered to be objects by the authorization mechanism. Views are composite objects, that is, composed of other underlying objects. Therefore, granting access to a view translates into granting access to underlying objects. If view definition and authorization rules for all objects are fully replicated (as in many systems), this translation is rather simple and can be done locally. The translation is harder when the view definition and its underlying objects are all stored separately, as is the case with site autonomy assumption. In this situation, the translation is a totally distributed operation. The authorizations granted on views depend on the access rights of the view creator on the underlying objects. A solution is to record the association information at the site of each underlying object.

Handling user groups for the purpose of authorization simplifies distributed database administration. In a centralized DBMS, "all users" can be referred to as *public*. In a distributed DBMS, the same notion is useful, the public denoting all the users of the system. However an intermediate level is often introduced to specify the public at a particular site, e.g., denoted by public@site_s. More precise groups can be defined by the command

DEFINE GROUP ⟨group_id⟩ **AS** ⟨list of subject_ids⟩

The management of groups in a distributed environment poses some problems since the subjects of a group can be located at various sites and access to an object may be granted to several groups, which are themselves distributed. If group information and access rules are fully replicated at all sites, the enforcement of access rights is similar to that of a centralized system. However, maintaining this replication may be expensive. The problem is more difficult if site autonomy (with decentralized control) must be maintained. One solution enforces access rights by performing a remote query to the nodes holding the group definition. Another solution replicates a group definition at each node containing an object that may be accessed by subjects of that group. These solutions tend to decrease the degree of site autonomy.

Enforcing MAC in a distributed environment is made difficult by the possibility of indirect means, called *covert channels*, to access unauthorized data. For instance, consider a simple distributed DBMS architecture with two sites, each managing its database at a single security level, e.g., one site is confidential, while the other is secret. According to the "no write down" rule, an update operation from a subject with secret clearance could only be sent to the secret site. However, according to the "no read up" rule, a read query from the same secret subject could be sent to both the secret and the confidential sites. Since the query sent to the confidential site may contain secret information (e.g., in a select predicate), it is potentially a covert channel. To avoid such covert channels, a solution is to replicate part of the database so that a site at security level *l* contains all data that a subject at level *l* can access. For instance, the secret site would replicate confidential data so that it can entirely process secret queries. One problem with this architecture is the overhead of maintaining the consistency of replicas (see Chap. 6 on replication). Furthermore, although there are no covert channels for queries, there may still be covert channels for update operations because the delays involved in synchronizing transactions may be exploited. The complete support for MAC in distributed database systems, therefore, requires significant extensions to transaction management techniques and to distributed query processing techniques.

3.3 Semantic Integrity Control

Another important and difficult problem for a database system is how to guarantee *database consistency*. A database state is said to be consistent if the database satisfies a set of constraints, called *semantic integrity constraints*. Maintaining a consistent database requires various mechanisms such as concurrency control, reliability, protection, and semantic integrity control, which are provided as part of transaction management. Semantic integrity control ensures database consistency by rejecting update transactions that lead to inconsistent database states, or by activating specific actions on the database state, which compensate for the effects of the update transactions. Note that the updated database must satisfy the set of integrity constraints.

In general, semantic integrity constraints are rules that represent the *knowledge* about the properties of an application. They define static or dynamic application properties that cannot be directly captured by the object and operation concepts of a data model. Thus the concept of an integrity rule is strongly connected with that of a data model in the sense that more semantic information about the application can be captured by means of these rules.

Two main types of integrity constraints can be distinguished: structural constraints and behavioral constraints. *Structural constraints* express basic semantic properties inherent to a model. Examples of such constraints are unique key constraints in the relational model, or one-to-many associations between objects in the object-oriented model. *Behavioral constraints*, on the other hand, regulate the application behavior. Thus they are essential in the database design process. They can express associations between objects, such as inclusion dependency in the relational model, or describe object properties and structures. The increasing variety of database applications and the development of database design aid tools call for powerful integrity constraints that can enrich the data model.

Integrity control appeared with data processing and evolved from procedural methods (in which the controls were embedded in application programs) to declarative methods. Declarative methods have emerged with the relational model to alleviate the problems of program/data dependency, code redundancy, and poor performance of the procedural methods. The idea is to express integrity constraints using assertions of predicate calculus. Thus a set of semantic integrity assertions defines database consistency. This approach allows one to easily declare and modify complex integrity constraints.

The main problem in supporting automatic semantic integrity control is that the cost of checking for constraint violation can be prohibitive. Enforcing integrity constraints is costly because it generally requires access to a large amount of data that are not directly involved in the database updates. The problem is more difficult when constraints are defined over a distributed database.

Various solutions have been investigated to design an integrity manager by combining optimization strategies. Their purpose is to (1) limit the number of constraints that need to be enforced, (2) decrease the number of data accesses to enforce a given constraint in the presence of an update transaction, (3) define a preventive strategy that detects inconsistencies in a way that avoids undoing updates, (4) perform as much integrity control as possible at compile time. A few of these solutions have been implemented, but they suffer from a lack of generality. Either they are restricted to a small set of assertions (more general constraints would have a prohibitive checking cost) or they only support restricted programs (e.g., single-tuple updates).

In this section, we present the solutions for semantic integrity control first in centralized systems and then in distributed systems. Since our context is the relational model, we consider only declarative methods.

3.3.1   Centralized Semantic Integrity Control

A semantic integrity manager has two main components: a language for expressing and manipulating integrity constraints, and an enforcement mechanism that performs specific actions to enforce database integrity upon update transactions.

3.3.1.1   Specification of Integrity Constraints

Integrity constraints are manipulated by the database administrator using a high-level language. In this section, we illustrate a declarative language for specifying integrity constraints. This language is much in the spirit of the standard SQL language, but with more generality. It allows one to specify, read, or drop integrity constraints. These constraints can be defined either at relation creation time or at any time, even if the relation already contains tuples. In both cases, however, the syntax is almost the same. For simplicity and without lack of generality, we assume that the effect of integrity constraint violation is to abort the violating transactions. However, the SQL standard provides means to express the propagation of update actions to correct inconsistencies, with the CASCADING clause within the constraint declaration. More generally, *triggers* (event-condition-action rules) can be used to automatically propagate updates, and thus to maintain semantic integrity. However, triggers are quite powerful and thus more difficult to support efficiently than specific integrity constraints.

In relational database systems, integrity constraints are defined as assertions. An assertion is a particular expression of tuple relational calculus, in which each variable is either universally ($\forall$) or existentially ($\exists$) quantified. Thus an assertion can be seen as a query qualification that is either true or false for each tuple in the Cartesian product of the relations determined by the tuple variables. We can distinguish between three types of integrity constraints: predefined, precondition, or general constraints.

Predefined constraints are based on simple keywords. Through them, it is possible to express concisely the more common constraints of the relational model, such as nonnull attribute, unique key, foreign key, or functional dependency. Examples 3.11–3.14 demonstrate predefined constraints.

Example 3.11 Employee number in relation EMP cannot be null.

```
ENO NOT NULL IN EMP
```

◆

Example 3.12 The pair (ENO, PNO) is the unique key in relation ASG.

```
(ENO, PNO) UNIQUE IN ASG
```

◆

Example 3.13 The project number PNO in relation ASG is a foreign key matching the primary key PNO of relation PROJ. In other words, a project referred to in relation ASG must exist in relation PROJ.

```
PNO IN ASG REFERENCES PNO IN PROJ
```

◆

Example 3.14 The employee number functionally determines the employee name.

```
ENO IN EMP DETERMINES ENAME
```

◆

Precondition constraints express conditions that must be satisfied by all tuples in a relation for a given update type. The update type, which might be **INSERT, DELETE**, or **MODIFY**, permits restricting the integrity control. To identify in the constraint definition the tuples that are subject to update, two variables, NEW and OLD, are implicitly defined. They range over new tuples (to be inserted) and old tuples (to be deleted), respectively. Precondition constraints can be expressed with the SQL **CHECK** statement enriched with the ability to specify the update type. The syntax of the **CHECK** statement is

```
CHECK ON ⟨relation name⟩ WHEN ⟨change type⟩
    (⟨qualification over relation name⟩)
```

Examples of precondition constraints are the following:

Example 3.15 The budget of a project is between 500K and 1000K.

```
CHECK ON PROJ (BUDGET+ >= 500000 AND  BUDGET <= 1000000)
```

◆

Example 3.16 Only the tuples whose budget is 0 may be deleted.

```
CHECK ON PROJ WHEN DELETE (BUDGET = 0)
```

◆

Example 3.17 The budget of a project can only increase.

```
CHECK ON PROJ (NEW.BUDGET > OLD.BUDGET AND
  NEW.PNO = OLD.PNO)
```

◆

General constraints are formulas of tuple relational calculus where all variables are quantified. The database system must ensure that those formulas are always true. General constraints are more concise than precompiled constraints since the former may involve more than one relation. For instance, at least three precompiled constraints are necessary to express a general constraint on three relations. A general constraint may be expressed with the following syntax:

```
CHECK ON list of ⟨variable name⟩:⟨relation name⟩,
  (⟨qualification⟩)
```

Examples of general constraints are given below.

Example 3.18 The constraint of Example 3.8 may also be expressed as

```
CHECK ON e1:EMP, e2:EMP
  (e1.ENAME = e2.ENAME IF e1.ENO = e2.ENO)
```

◆

Example 3.19 The total duration for all employees in the CAD project is less than 100.

```
CHECK ON g:ASG, j:PROJ (SUM(g.DUR WHERE
  g.PNO=j.PNO)<100 IF j.PNAME="CAD/CAM")
```

◆

3.3.1.2 Integrity Enforcement

We now focus on enforcing semantic integrity that consists of rejecting update transactions that violate some integrity constraints. A constraint is violated when it becomes false in the new database state produced by the update transaction. A major difficulty in designing an integrity manager is finding efficient enforcement algorithms. Two basic methods permit the rejection of inconsistent update transactions. The first one is based on the *detection* of inconsistencies. The update transaction u is executed, causing a change of the database state D to D_u. The enforcement algorithm verifies, by applying tests derived from these constraints, that all relevant constraints hold in state D_u. If state D_u is inconsistent, the DBMS can try either to reach another consistent state, D'_u, by modifying D_u with compensation actions or to restore state D by undoing u. Since these tests are applied *after* having changed the database state, they are generally called *posttests*. This approach may be inefficient if a large amount of work (the update of D) must be undone in the case of an integrity failure.

The second method is based on the *prevention* of inconsistencies. An update is executed only if it changes the database state to a consistent state. The tuples subject to the update transaction are either directly available (in the case of insert) or must be retrieved from the database (in the case of deletion or modification). The enforcement algorithm verifies that all relevant constraints will hold after updating those tuples. This is generally done by applying to those tuples tests that are derived from the integrity constraints. Given that these tests are applied *before* the database state is changed, they are generally called *pretests*. The preventive approach is more efficient than the detection approach since updates never need to be undone because of integrity violation.

The query modification algorithm is an example of a preventive method that is particularly efficient at enforcing domain constraints. It adds the assertion qualification to the query qualification by an AND operator so that the modified query can enforce integrity.

Example 3.20 The query for increasing the budget of the CAD/CAM project by 10%, which would be specified as

```
UPDATE  PROJ
SET     BUDGET = BUDGET*1.1
WHERE   PNAME= "CAD/CAM"
```

will be transformed into the following query in order to enforce the domain constraint discussed in Example 3.9.

```
UPDATE  PROJ
SET     BUDGET = BUDGET * 1.1
WHERE   PNAME= "CAD/CAM"
AND     NEW.BUDGET ≥ 500000
AND     NEW.BUDGET ≤ 1000000
```

◆

The query modification algorithm, which is well-known for its elegance, produces pretests at runtime by ANDing the assertion predicates with the update predicates of each instruction of the transaction. However, the algorithm only applies to tuple calculus formulas and can be specified as follows. Consider the assertion $(\forall x \in R)F(x)$, where F is a tuple calculus expression in which x is the only free variable. An update of R can be written as $(\forall x \in R)(Q(x) \Rightarrow update(x))$, where Q is a tuple calculus expression whose only free variable is x. Roughly speaking, the query modification consists in generating the update $(\forall x \in R)((Q(x)$ and $F(x)) \Rightarrow update(x))$. Thus x needs to be universally quantified.

Example 3.21 The foreign key constraint of Example 3.13 that can be rewritten as

$$\forall g \in \text{ASG}, \exists j \in \text{PROJ} : g.\text{PNO} = j.\text{PNO}$$

could not be processed by query modification because the variable j is not universally quantified.   ◆

To handle more general constraints, pretests can be generated at constraint definition time, and enforced at runtime when updates occur. In the rest of this section, we present a general method. This method is based on the production, at constraint definition time, of pretests that are used subsequently to prevent the introduction of inconsistencies in the database. This is a general preventive method that handles the entire set of constraints introduced in the preceding section. It significantly reduces the proportion of the database that must be checked when enforcing assertions in the presence of updates. This is a major advantage when applied to a distributed environment.

The definition of pretest uses differential relations, as defined in Sect. 3.1.3. A *pretest* is a triple (R, U, C) in which R is a relation, U is an update type, and C is an assertion ranging over the differential relation(s) involved in an update of type U. When an integrity constraint I is defined, a set of pretests may be produced for the relations used by I. Whenever a relation involved in I is updated by a transaction u, the pretests that must be checked to enforce I are only those defined on I for the update type of u. The performance advantages of this approach are twofold. First, the number of assertions to enforce is minimized since only the pretests of type u need be checked. Second, the cost of enforcing a pretest is less than that of enforcing I since differential relations are, in general, much smaller than the base relations.

Pretests may be obtained by applying transformation rules to the original assertion. These rules are based on a syntactic analysis of the assertion and quantifier permutations. They permit the substitution of differential relations for base relations. Since the pretests are simpler than the original ones, the process that generates them is called *simplification*.

Example 3.22 Consider the modified expression of the foreign key constraint in Example 3.15. The pretests associated with this constraint are

(ASG, **INSERT**, C_1), (PROJ, **DELETE**, C_2), and (PROJ, **MODIFY**, C_3),

where C_1 is

$$\forall \, \text{NEW} \in \text{ASG}^+, \exists j \in \text{PROJ}: \text{NEW.PNO} = j.\text{PNO}$$

C_2 is

$$\forall g \in \text{ASG}, \forall \, \text{OLD} \in \text{PROJ}^- : g.\text{PNO} \neq \text{OLD.PNO}$$

and C_3 is

$$\forall g \in \text{ASG}, \forall \, \text{OLD} \in \text{PROJ}^- \, \exists \, \text{NEW} \in \text{PROJ}^+ : g.\text{PNO} \neq \text{OLD.PNO OR}$$
$$\text{OLD.PNO} = \text{NEW.PNO} \qquad\qquad\qquad\qquad\qquad\qquad\qquad\qquad\quad \blacklozenge$$

The advantage provided by such pretests is obvious. For instance, a deletion on relation ASG does not incur any assertion checking.

The enforcement algorithm makes use of pretests and is specialized according to the class of the assertions. Three classes of constraints are distinguished: single-relation constraints, multirelation constraints, and constraints involving aggregate functions.

Let us now summarize the enforcement algorithm. Recall that an update transaction updates all tuples of relation R that satisfy some qualification. The algorithm acts in two steps. The first step generates the differential relations R^+ and R^- from R. The second step simply consists of retrieving the tuples of R^+ and R^-, which do not satisfy the pretests. If no tuples are retrieved, the constraint is valid. Otherwise, it is violated.

Example 3.23 Suppose there is a deletion on PROJ. Enforcing (PROJ, **DELETE**, C_2) consists in generating the following statement:

result $\leftarrow$ retrieve all tuples of PROJ$^-$ where $\neg(C_2)$

Then, if the result is empty, the assertion is verified by the update and consistency is preserved. $\qquad\qquad\qquad\qquad\qquad\qquad\qquad\qquad\qquad\qquad\qquad\qquad\quad \blacklozenge$

3.3.2   *Distributed Semantic Integrity Control*

In this section, we present algorithms for ensuring the semantic integrity of distributed databases. They are extensions of the simplification method discussed previously. In what follows, we assume global transaction management capabilities, as provided for homogeneous systems or multidatabase systems. Thus, the two main problems of designing an integrity manager for such a distributed DBMS are the definition and storage of constraints, and their enforcement. We will also discuss the issues involved in integrity constraint checking when there is no global transaction support.

3.3.2.1 Definition of Distributed Integrity Constraints

An integrity constraint is supposed to be expressed in predicate calculus. Each assertion is seen as a query qualification that is either true or false for each tuple in the Cartesian product of the relations determined by the tuple variables. Since assertions can involve data stored at different sites, the storage of the constraints must be decided so as to minimize the cost of integrity checking. There is a strategy based on a taxonomy of integrity constraints that distinguishes three classes:

1. *Individual constraints*: single-relation single-variable constraints. They refer only to tuples to be updated independently of the rest of the database. For instance, the domain constraint of Example 3.15 is an individual assertion.
2. *Set-oriented constraints*: include single-relation multivariable constraints such as functional dependency (Example 3.14) and multirelation multivariable constraints such as foreign key constraints (Example 3.13).
3. *Constraints involving aggregates*: require special processing because of the cost of evaluating the aggregates. The assertion in Example 3.19 is representative of a constraint of this class.

The definition of a new integrity constraint can be started at one of the sites that store the relations involved in the assertion. Remember that the relations can be fragmented. A fragmentation predicate is a particular case of assertion of class 1. Different fragments of the same relation can be located at different sites. Thus, defining an integrity assertion becomes a distributed operation, which is done in two steps. The first step is to transform the high-level assertions into pretests, using the techniques discussed in the preceding section. The next step is to store pretests according to the class of constraints. Constraints of class 3 are treated like those of class 1 or 2, depending on whether they are individual or set-oriented.

Individual Constraints

The constraint definition is sent to all other sites that contain fragments of the relation involved in the constraint. The constraint must be compatible with the relation data at each site. Compatibility can be checked at two levels: predicate and data. First, predicate compatibility is verified by comparing the constraint predicate with the fragment predicate. A constraint C is not compatible with a fragment predicate p if "C is true" implies that "p is false," and is compatible with p otherwise. If noncompatibility is found at one of the sites, the constraint definition is globally rejected because tuples of that fragment do not satisfy the integrity constraints. Second, if predicate compatibility has been found, the constraint is tested against the instance of the fragment. If it is not satisfied by that instance, the constraint is also globally rejected. If compatibility is found, the constraint is stored at each site. Note that the compatibility checks are performed only for pretests whose update type is "insert" (the tuples in the fragments are considered "inserted").

Example 3.24 Consider relation EMP, horizontally fragmented across three sites using the predicates

$$p_1: \quad 0 \leq \text{ENO} < \text{``E3''}$$
$$p_2: \quad \text{``E3''} \leq \text{ENO} \leq \text{``E6''}$$
$$p_3: \quad \text{ENO} > \text{``E6''}$$

and the domain constraint C: ENO < "E4." Constraint C is compatible with p_1 (if C is true, p_1 is true) and p_2 (if C is true, p_2 is not necessarily false), but not with p_3 (if C is true, then p_3 is false). Therefore, constraint C should be globally rejected because the tuples at site 3 cannot satisfy C, and thus relation EMP does not satisfy C.   ♦

Set-Oriented Constraints

Set-oriented constraints are multivariable; that is, they involve join predicates. Although the assertion predicate may be multirelation, a pretest is associated with a single relation. Therefore, the constraint definition can be sent to all the sites that store a fragment referenced by these variables. Compatibility checking also involves fragments of the relation used in the join predicate. Predicate compatibility is useless here, because it is impossible to infer that a fragment predicate p is false if the constraint C (based on a join predicate) is true. Therefore C must be checked for compatibility against the data. This compatibility check basically requires joining each fragment of the relation, say R, with all fragments of the other relation, say S, involved in the constraint predicate. This operation may be expensive and, as any join, should be optimized by the distributed query processor. Three cases, given in increasing cost of checking, can occur:

1. The fragmentation of R is derived (see Chap. 2) from that of S based on a semijoin on the attribute used in the assertion join predicate.
2. S is fragmented on join attribute.
3. S is not fragmented on join attribute.

In the first case, compatibility checking is cheap since the tuple of S matching a tuple of R is at the same site. In the second case, each tuple of R must be compared with at most one fragment of S, because the join attribute value of the tuple of R can be used to find the site of the corresponding fragment of S. In the third case, each tuple of R must be compared with all fragments of S. If compatibility is found for all tuples of R, the constraint can be stored at each site.

Example 3.25 Consider the set-oriented pretest (ASG, **INSERT**, C_1) defined in Example 3.16, where C_1 is

$$\forall \text{ NEW} \in \text{ASG}^+, \exists j \in \text{PROJ}: \text{NEW.PNO} = j.\text{PNO}$$

Let us consider the following three cases:

1. ASG is fragmented using the predicate

$$\text{ASG} \ltimes_{\text{PNO}} \text{PROJ}_i$$

where PROJ$_I$ is a fragment of relation PROJ. In this case each tuple NEW of ASG has been placed at the same site as tuple j such that NEW.PNO = j.PNO. Since the fragmentation predicate is identical to that of C_1, compatibility checking does not incur communication.

2. PROJ is horizontally fragmented based on the two predicates

$$p_1: \quad \text{PNO} < \text{"P3"}$$
$$p_2: \quad \text{PNO} \geq \text{"P3"}$$

In this case each tuple NEW of ASG is compared with either fragment PROJ$_1$, if NEW.PNO < "P3," or fragment PROJ$_2$, if NEW.PNO $\geq$ "P3."

3. PROJ is horizontally fragmented based on the two predicates

$$p_1: \quad \text{PNAME} = \text{"CAD/CAM"}$$
$$p_2: \quad \text{PNAME} \neq \text{"CAD/CAM"}$$

In this case each tuple of ASG must be compared with both fragments PROJ$_1$ and PROJ$_2$.

$\blacklozenge$

3.3.2.2   Enforcement of Distributed Integrity Constraints

Enforcing distributed integrity constraints is more complex than in centralized DBMSs, even with global transaction management support. The main problem is to decide where (at which site) to enforce the integrity constraints. The choice depends on the class of the constraint, the type of update, and the nature of the site where the update is issued (called the *query master site*). This site may, or may not, store the updated relation or some of the relations involved in the integrity constraints. The critical parameter we consider is the cost of transferring data, including messages, from one site to another. We now discuss the different types of strategies according to these criteria.

Individual Constraints

Two cases are considered. If the update transaction is an insert statement, all the tuples to be inserted are explicitly provided by the user. In this case, all individual constraints can be enforced at the site where the update is submitted. If the update is a qualified update (delete or modify statements), it is sent to the sites storing the relation that will be updated. The query processor executes the update qualification for each fragment. The resulting tuples at each site are combined into one temporary relation in the case of a delete statement, or two, in the case of a modify statement (i.e., R^+ and R^-). Each site involved in the distributed update enforces the assertions relevant at that site (e.g., domain constraints when it is a delete).

Set-Oriented Constraints

We first study single-relation constraints by means of an example. Consider the functional dependency of Example 3.14. The pretest associated with update type **INSERT** is

(EMP, **INSERT**, C)

where C is

$$(\forall e \in \text{EMP})(\forall \text{NEW}1 \in \text{EMP})(\forall \text{NEW}2 \in \text{EMP}) \tag{1}$$

$$(\text{NEW}1.\text{ENO} = e.\text{ENO} \Rightarrow \text{NEW}1.\text{ENAME} = e.\text{ENAME}) \wedge \tag{2}$$

$$(\text{NEW}1.\text{ENO} = \text{NEW}2.\text{ENO} \Rightarrow \text{NEW}1.\text{ENAME} = \text{NEW}2.\text{ENAME} \tag{3}$$

The second line in the definition of C checks the constraint between the inserted tuples (NEW1) and the existing ones (e), while the third checks it between the inserted tuples themselves. That is why two variables (NEW1 and NEW2) are declared in the first line.

Consider now an update of EMP. First, the update qualification is executed by the query processor and returns one or two temporary relations, as in the case of individual constraints. These temporary relations are then sent to all sites storing EMP. Assume that the update is an **INSERT** statement. Then each site storing a fragment of EMP will enforce constraint C described above. Because e in C is universally quantified, C must be satisfied by the local data at each site. This is due to the fact that $\forall x \in \{a_1, \ldots, a_n\} f(x)$ is equivalent to $[f(a_1) \wedge f(a_2) \wedge \cdots \wedge f(a_n)]$. Thus the site where the update is submitted must receive for each site a message indicating that this constraint is satisfied and that it is a condition for all sites. If the constraint is not true for one site, this site sends an error message indicating that the constraint has been violated. The update is then invalid, and it is the responsibility of the integrity manager to decide if the entire transaction must be rejected using the global transaction manager.

Let us now consider multirelation constraints. For the sake of clarity, we assume that the integrity constraints do not have more than one tuple variable ranging over the same relation. Note that this is likely to be the most frequent case. As with single-relation constraints, the update is computed at the site where it was submitted. The enforcement is done at the query master site, using the ENFORCE algorithm given in Algorithm 3.2.

Algorithm 3.2: ENFORCE

Input: U: update type; R: relation
begin
    retrieve all compiled assertions (R, U, C_i)
    inconsistent ← **false**
    for *each compiled assertion* **do**
       | *result* ← all new (respectively, old), tuples of R where $\neg(C_i)$
    end for
    if *card(result)* $\neq$ 0 **then**
       | *inconsistent* ← **true**
    end if
    if $\neg inconsistent$ **then**
       | send the tuples to update to all the sites storing fragments of R
    else
       | reject the update
    end if
end

Example 3.26 We illustrate this algorithm through an example based on the foreign key constraint of Example 3.13. Let u be an insertion of a new tuple into ASG. The previous algorithm uses the pretest (ASG, **INSERT**, C), where C is

$$\forall \text{NEW} \in \text{ASG}^+, \exists j \in \text{PROJ}: \text{NEW.PNO} = j.\text{PNO}$$

For this constraint, the retrieval statement is to retrieve all new tuples in ASG^+, where C is not true. This statement can be expressed in SQL as

```
SELECT NEW.*
FROM    ASG+ NEW, PROJ
WHERE   COUNT(PROJ.PNO WHERE NEW.PNO = PROJ.PNO)=0
```

Note that NEW.* denotes all the attributes of ASG^+.   ◆

Thus the strategy is to send new tuples to sites storing relation PROJ in order to perform the joins, and then to centralize all results at the query master site. For each site storing a fragment of PROJ, the site joins the fragment with ASG^+ and sends the result to the query master site, which performs the union of all results. If the union is empty, the database is consistent. Otherwise, the update leads to an inconsistent state and should be rejected, using the global transaction manager. More sophisticated strategies that notify or compensate inconsistencies can also be devised.

Constraints Involving Aggregates

These constraints are among the most costly to test because they require the calculation of the aggregate functions. The aggregate functions generally manipulated are **MIN, MAX, SUM**, and **COUNT**. Each aggregate function contains a projection part and a selection part. To enforce these constraints efficiently, it is possible to produce pretests that isolate redundant data which can be stored at each site storing the associated relation. This data is what we called *materialized views* in Sect. 3.1.2.

3.3.2.3 Summary of Distributed Integrity Control

The main problem of distributed integrity control is that the communication and processing costs of enforcing distributed constraints can be prohibitive. The two main issues in designing a distributed integrity manager are the definition of the distributed assertions and of the enforcement algorithms that minimize the cost of distributed integrity checking. We have shown in this chapter that distributed integrity control can be completely achieved, by extending a preventive method based on the compilation of semantic integrity constraints into pretests. The method is general since all types of constraints expressed in first-order predicate logic can be handled. It is compatible with fragment definition and minimizes intersite communication. A better performance of distributed integrity enforcement can be obtained if fragments are defined carefully. Therefore, the specification of distributed integrity constraints is an important aspect of the distributed database design process.

The method described above assumes global transaction support. Without global transaction support as in some loosely coupled multidatabase systems, the problem is more difficult. First, the interface between the constraint manager and the component DBMS is different since constraint checking can no longer be part of the global transaction validation. Instead, the component DBMSs should notify the integrity manager to perform constraint checking after some events, e.g., as a result of local transactions' commitments. This can be done using triggers whose events are updates to relations involved in global constraints. Second, if a global constraint violation is detected, since there is no way to specify global aborts, specific correcting transactions should be provided to produce global database states that are consistent. The solution is to have a family of protocols for global integrity checking. The root of the family is a simple strategy, based on the computation of differential relations (as in the previous method), which is shown to be safe (correctly identifies constraint violations) but inaccurate (may raise an error event though there is no constraint violation). Inaccuracy is due to the fact that producing differential relations at different times at different sites may yield *phantom* states for the global database, i.e., states that never existed. Extensions of the basic protocol with either timestamping or using local transaction commands are proposed to solve that problem.

3.4 Conclusion

Data control includes view management, access control, and semantic integrity control. In relational DBMSs, these functions can be uniformly achieved by enforcing rules that specify data manipulation control. Solutions initially designed for handling these functions in centralized systems have been significantly extended and enriched for distributed systems, in particular, support for materialized views and group-based discretionary access control. Semantic integrity control has received less attention and is generally not well supported by distributed DBMS products.

Full data control is more complex and costly in terms of performance in distributed systems. The two main issues for efficiently performing data control are the definition and storage of the rules (site selection) and the design of enforcement algorithms which minimize communication costs. The problem is difficult since increased functionality (and generality) tends to increase site communication. The problem is simplified if control rules are fully replicated at all sites and harder if site autonomy is to be preserved. In addition, specific optimizations can be done to minimize the cost of data control but with extra overhead such as managing materialized views or redundant data. Thus the specification of distributed data control must be included in the distributed database design so that the cost of control for update programs is also considered.

3.5 Bibliographic Notes

Data control is well-understood in centralized systems and all major DBMSs provide extensive support for it. Research on data control in distributed systems started in the mid-1980s with the R* project at IBM Research and has increased much since then to address new important applications such as data warehousing or data integration.

Most of the work on view management has concerned updates through views and support for materialized views. The two basic papers on centralized view management are [Chamberlin et al. 1975] and [Stonebraker 1975]. The first reference presents an integrated solution for view and authorization management in the System R project at IBM Research. The second reference describes the query modification technique proposed in the INGRES project at UC Berkeley for uniformly handling views, authorizations, and semantic integrity control. This method was presented in Sect. 3.1.

Theoretical solutions to the problem of view updates are given in [Bancilhon and Spyratos 1981, Dayal and Bernstein 1978, Keller 1982]. In the seminal paper on view update semantics [Bancilhon and Spyratos 1981], the authors formalize the view invariance property after updating, and show how a large class of views including joins can be updated. Semantic information about the base relations is particularly useful for finding unique propagation of updates. However, the current commercial systems are very restrictive in supporting updates through views.

Materialized views have received much attention in the context of data warehousing. The notion of snapshot for optimizing view derivation in distributed database systems is due to [Adiba and Lindsay 1980], and generalized in Adiba [1981] as a unified mechanism for managing views and snapshots, as well as fragmented and replicated data. Self-maintainability of materialized views with respect to the kind of updates (insertion, deletion, or modification) is addressed in [Gupta et al. 1996]. A thorough paper on materialized view management can be found in Gupta and Mumick [1999], with the main techniques to perform incremental maintenance of materialized views. The counting algorithm which we presented in Sect. 3.1.3 was proposed in [Gupta et al. 1993]. We introduced two recent important optimizations that have been proposed to significantly reduce the maintenance time of the counting algorithm, following the formalism of generalized multiset relations [Koch 2010]. The first optimization is to materialize views representing subqueries of the input query [Koch et al. 2014, Berkholz et al. 2017, Nikolic and Olteanu 2018]. The second optimization exploits the skew in the data [Kara et al. 2019].

Security in computer systems in general is presented in [Hoffman 1977]. Security in centralized database systems is presented in [Lunt and Fernández 1990, Castano et al. 1995]. Discretionary access control (DAC) in distributed systems has first received much attention in the context of the R* project. The access control mechanism of System R [Griffiths and Wade 1976] is extended in [Wilms and Lindsay 1981] to handle groups of users and to run in a distributed environment. Mandatory access control (MAC) for distributed DBMS has recently gained much interest. The seminal paper on MAC is the Bell and LaPadula model originally designed for operating system security [Bell and Lapuda 1976]. MAC for databases is described in [Lunt and Fernández 1990, Jajodia and Sandhu 1991]. A good introduction to multilevel security in relational DBMS can be found in [Rjaibi 2004]. Transaction management in multilevel secure DBMS is addressed in [Ray et al. 2000, Jajodia et al. 2001]. Extensions of MAC for distributed DBMS are proposed in [Thuraisingham 2001]. Role-based access control (RBAC) [Ferraiolo and Kuhn 1992] extends DAC and MAC by adding roles, as a level of independence between subjects and objects. Hippocratic databases [Sandhu et al. 1996] associate purpose information with data, i.e., the reasons for data collection and access.

The content of Sect. 3.3 comes largely from the work on semantic integrity control described in [Simon and Valduriez 1984, 1986, 1987]. In particular, [Simon and Valduriez 1986] extend a preventive strategy for centralized integrity control based on pretests to run in a distributed environment, assuming global transaction support. The initial idea of declarative methods, that is, to use assertions of predicate logic to specify integrity constraints, is due to [Florentin 1974]. The most important declarative methods are in [Bernstein et al. 1980a, Blaustein 1981, Nicolas 1982, Simon and Valduriez 1984, Stonebraker 1975]. The notion of concrete views for storing redundant data is described in [Bernstein and Blaustein 1982]. Note that concrete views are useful in optimizing the enforcement of constraints involving aggregates. Civelek et al. [1988], Sheth et al. [1988b], and Sheth et al.

[1988a] describe systems and tools for data control, particularly view management. Semantic integrity checking in loosely coupled multidatabase systems without global transaction support is addressed in [Grefen and Widom 1997].

Exercises

Problem 3.1 Define in SQL-like syntax a view of the engineering database V(ENO, ENAME, PNO, RESP), where the duration is 24. Is view V updatable? Assume that relations EMP and ASG are horizontally fragmented based on access frequencies as follows:

$$\underline{\text{Site 1}}\ \underline{\text{Site 2}}\ \underline{\text{Site 3}}$$
$$\text{EMP}_1\ \ \text{EMP}_2$$
$$\text{ASG}_1\ \ \text{ASG}_2$$

where

$$\text{EMP}_1 = \sigma_{\text{TITLE} \neq \text{"Engineer"}}(\text{EMP})$$
$$\text{EMP}_2 = \sigma_{\text{TITLE} = \text{"Engineer"}}(\text{EMP})$$
$$\text{ASG}_1 = \sigma_{0 < \text{DUR} < 36}(\text{ASG})$$
$$\text{ASG}_2 = \sigma_{\text{DUR} \geq 36}(\text{ASG})$$

At which site(s) should the definition of V be stored without being fully replicated, to increase locality of reference?

Problem 3.2 Express the following query: names of employees in view V who work on the CAD/CAM project.

Problem 3.3 (*) Assume that relation PROJ is horizontally fragmented as

$$\text{PROJ}_1\ \ =\ \ \sigma_{\text{PNAME} = \text{"CAD/CAM"}}(\text{PROJ})$$
$$\text{PROJ}_2\ \ =\ \ \sigma_{\text{PNAME} \neq \text{"CAD/CAM"}}(\text{PROJ})$$

Modify the query obtained in Problem 3.2 to a query expressed on the fragments.

Problem 3.4 (**) Propose a distributed algorithm to efficiently refresh a snapshot at one site derived by projection from a relation horizontally fragmented at two other sites. Give an example query on the view and base relations which produces an inconsistent result.

Problem 3.5 (*) Consider the view EG of Example 3.5 which uses relations EMP and ASG as base data and assume its state is derived from that of Example 3.1, so that EG has 9 tuples (see Fig. 3.4). Assume that tuple ⟨E3, P3, Consultant, 10⟩ from ASG is updated to ⟨E3, P3, Engineer, 10⟩. Apply the basic counting algorithm for refreshing the view EG. What projected attributes should be added to view EG to make it self-maintainable?

Problem 3.6 Propose a relation schema for storing the access rights associated with user groups in a distributed database catalog, and give a fragmentation scheme for that relation, assuming that all members of a group are at the same site.

Problem 3.7 (**) Give an algorithm for executing the **REVOKE** statement in a distributed DBMS, assuming that the **GRANT** privilege can be granted only to a group of users where all its members are at the same site.

Problem 3.8 (**) Consider the multilevel relation PROJ** in Fig. 3.8. Assuming that there are only two classification levels for attributes (S and C), propose an allocation of PROJ** on two sites using fragmentation and replication that avoids covert channels on read queries. Discuss the constraints on updates for this allocation to work.

Problem 3.9 Using the integrity constraint specification language of this chapter, express an integrity constraint which states that the duration spent in a project cannot exceed 48 months.

Problem 3.10 (*) Define the pretests associated with integrity constraints covered in Examples 3.11–3.14.

Problem 3.11 Assume the following vertical fragmentation of relations EMP, ASG, and PROJ:

Site 1   Site 2   Site 3   Site 4

EMP$_1$ EMP$_2$

PROJ$_1$ PROJ$_2$

ASG$_1$ ASG$_2$

where

$$EMP_1 = \Pi_{ENO, ENAME}(EMP)$$
$$EMP_2 = \Pi_{ENO, TITLE}(EMP)$$
$$PROJ_1 = \Pi_{PNO, PNAME}(PROJ)$$
$$PROJ_2 = \Pi_{PNO, BUDGET}(PROJ)$$
$$ASG_1 = \Pi_{ENO, PNO, RESP}(ASG)$$
$$ASG_2 = \Pi_{ENO, PNO, DUR}(ASG)$$

Where should the pretests obtained in Problem 3.9 be stored?

Problem 3.12 (**) Consider the following set-oriented constraint:

```
CHECK ON e:EMP, a:ASG
  (e.ENO = a.ENO AND (e.TITLE = "Programmer")
  IF a.RESP = "Programmer")
```

What does it mean? Assuming that EMP and ASG are allocated as in the previous exercise, define the corresponding pretests and their storage. Apply algorithm ENFORCE for an update of type **INSERT** in ASG.

Problem 3.13 (**) Assume a distributed multidatabase system with no global transaction support. Assume also that there are two sites, each with a (different) EMP relation and an integrity manager that communicates with the component DBMS. Suppose that we want to have a global unique key constraint on EMP. Propose a simple strategy using differential relations to check this constraint. Discuss the possible actions when a constraint is violated.

Chapter 4
Distributed Query Processing

By hiding the low-level details about the physical organization of the data, relational database languages allow the expression of complex queries in a concise and simple manner. In particular, to construct the answer to the query, the user does not precisely specify the procedure to follow; this procedure is actually devised by a module, called a *query processor*. This relieves the user from query optimization, a time-consuming task that is best handled by the query processor, since it can exploit a large amount of useful information about the data.

Because it is a critical performance issue, query processing has received (and continues to receive) considerable attention in the context of both centralized and distributed DBMSs. However, the query processing problem is much more difficult in distributed environments, because a larger number of parameters affect the performance of distributed queries. In particular, the relations involved in a distributed query may be fragmented and/or replicated, thereby inducing communication costs. Furthermore, with many sites to access, query response time may become very high.

In this chapter, we give a detailed presentation of query processing in distributed DBMSs. The context chosen is that of relational calculus and relational algebra, because of their generality and wide use in distributed DBMSs. As we saw in Chap. 2, distributed relations are implemented by fragments, with the objective of increasing reference locality, and sometimes parallel execution for the most important queries. The role of a distributed query processor is to map a high-level query (assumed to be expressed in relational calculus) on a distributed database (i.e., a set of global relations) into a sequence of database operators (of relational algebra) on relation fragments. Several important functions characterize this mapping. First, the *calculus query* must be *decomposed* into a sequence of relational operators called an *algebraic query*. Second, the data accessed by the query must be *localized* so that the operators on relations are translated to bear on local data (fragments). Finally, the algebraic query on fragments must be extended with communication

---

The original version of this chapter was revised. The correction to this chapter is available at https://doi.org/10.1007/978-3-030-26253-2_13

© Springer Nature Switzerland AG 2020   129
M. T. Özsu, P. Valduriez, *Principles of Distributed Database Systems*,
https://doi.org/10.1007/978-3-030-26253-2_4

operators and *optimized* with respect to a cost function to be minimized. This cost function typically refers to computing resources such as disk I/Os, CPUs, and communication networks.

This chapter is organized as follows: Section 4.1 gives an overview of distributed query processing. In Sect. 4.2, we describe data localization, with emphasis on reduction and simplification techniques for the four following types of fragmentation: horizontal, vertical, derived, and hybrid. In Sect. 4.3, we discuss the major optimization issue, which deals with the join ordering in distributed queries. We also examine alternative join strategies based on semijoin. In Sect. 4.4, we discuss the distributed cost model. In Sect. 4.5, we illustrate the use of the techniques in three basic distributed query optimization approaches: dynamic, static, and hybrid. In Sect. 4.5, we discuss adaptive query processing.

We assume that the reader is familiar with basic query processing notions in centralized DBMSs as covered in most undergraduate database courses and textbooks.

4.1   Overview

This section introduces distributed query processing. First, in Sect. 4.1.1, we discuss the query processing problem. Then, in Sect. 4.1.2, we introduce query optimization. Finally, in Sect. 4.1.3, we introduce the different layers of query processing starting from a distributed query down to the execution of operators on local sites.

4.1.1   Query Processing Problem

The main function of a query processor is to transform a high-level query (typically, in relational calculus) into an equivalent lower-level query (typically, in some variation of relational algebra). The low-level query actually implements the execution strategy for the query. The transformation must achieve both correctness and efficiency. It is correct if the low-level query has the same semantics as the original query, that is, if both queries produce the same result. The well-defined mapping from relational calculus to relational algebra makes the correctness issue easy. But producing an efficient execution strategy is more difficult. A relational calculus query may have many equivalent and correct transformations into relational algebra. Since each equivalent execution strategy can lead to very different consumptions of computer resources, the main difficulty is to select the execution strategy that minimizes resource consumption.

Example 4.1 We consider the following subset of the engineering database schema:

```
EMP(ENO, ENAME, TITLE)
ASG(ENO, PNO, RESP, DUR)
```

and the following simple user query:

"Find the names of employees who are managing a project"

The expression of the query in relational calculus using the SQL syntax (with natural join) is

```
SELECT ENAME
FROM    EMP NATURAL JOIN ASG
WHERE   RESP = "Manager"
```

Two equivalent relational algebra queries that are correct transformations of the query above are

$$\Pi_{\text{ENAME}}(\sigma_{\text{RESP="Manager"} \wedge \text{EMP.ENO=ASG.ENO}}(\text{EMP} \times \text{ASG}))$$

and

$$\Pi_{\text{ENAME}}(\bowtie_{\text{ENO}} (\sigma_{\text{RESP="Manager"}}(\text{ASG})))$$

It is intuitively obvious that the second query which avoids the Cartesian product of EMP and ASG consumes much less computing resources than the first, and thus should be retained.   ◆

In a distributed system, relational algebra is not enough to express execution strategies. It must be supplemented with operators for exchanging data between sites. Besides the choice of ordering relational algebra operators, the distributed query processor must also select the best sites to process data, and possibly the way data should be transformed. This increases the solution space from which to choose the distributed execution strategy, making distributed query processing significantly more difficult than centralized query processing.

Example 4.2 This example illustrates the importance of site selection and communication for a chosen relational algebra query against a fragmented database. We consider the following query of Example 4.1:

$$\Pi_{\text{ENAME}}(\text{EMP} \bowtie_{\text{ENO}} (\sigma_{\text{RESP="Manager"}}(\text{ASG})))$$

We assume that relations EMP and ASG are horizontally fragmented as follows:

$$\text{EMP}_1 = \sigma_{\text{ENO}\leq\text{"E3"}}(\text{EMP})$$

$$\text{EMP}_2 = \sigma_{\text{ENO}>\text{"E3"}}(\text{EMP})$$

$$\text{ASG}_1 = \sigma_{\text{ENO}\leq\text{"E3"}}(\text{ASG})$$

$$\text{ASG}_2 = \sigma_{\text{ENO}>\text{"E3"}}(\text{ASG})$$

Fragments ASG_1, ASG_2, EMP_1, and EMP_2 are stored at sites 1, 2, 3, and 4, respectively, and the result is expected at site 5.

For the sake of simplicity, we ignore the project operator in the following. Two equivalent distributed execution strategies for the above query are shown in Fig. 4.1. An arrow from site i to site j labeled with R indicates that relation R is transferred from site i to site j. Strategy A exploits the fact that relations EMP and ASG are fragmented the same way in order to perform the select and join operator in parallel. Strategy B is a default strategy (always works) that simply centralizes all the operand data at the result site before processing the query.

To evaluate the resource consumption of these two strategies, we use a very simple cost model. We assume that a tuple access, denoted by *tupacc*, is 1 unit (which we leave unspecified) and a tuple transfer, denoted *tuptrans*, is 10 units. We assume that relations EMP and ASG have 400 and 1000 tuples, respectively, and that there are 20 managers in relation ASG. We also assume that data is uniformly distributed among sites. Finally, we assume that relations ASG and EMP are locally clustered on attributes RESP and ENO, respectively. Therefore, there is direct access to tuples of ASG (respectively, EMP) based on the value of attribute RESP (respectively, ENO).

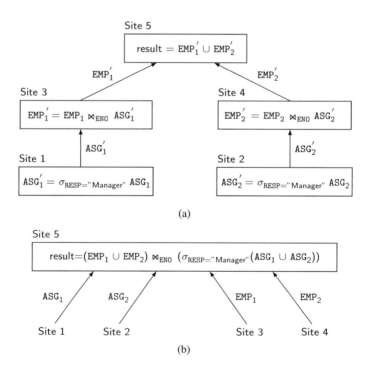

Fig. 4.1 Equivalent distributed execution strategies. (**a**) Strategy A. (**b**) Strategy B

The total cost of strategy A can be derived as follows:

1. Produce ASG′ by selecting ASG requires $(10 + 10)*$
    $tupacc$ =   20

2. Transfer ASG′ to the sites of EMP requires $(10 + 10)*$
    $tuptrans$ =   200

3. Produce EMP′ by joining ASG′ and EMP requires
    $(10 + 10) * tupacc * 2$ =   40

4. Transfer EMP′ to result site requires $(10 + 10)*$
    $tuptrans$ =   200

    The total cost is $\overline{460}$

The cost of strategy B can be derived as follows:

1. Transfer EMP to site 5 requires $400 * tuptrans$ =   4, 000
2. Transfer ASG to site 5 requires $1000 * tuptrans$ =   10, 000
3. Produce ASG′ by selecting ASG requires $1000*tupacc$ =   1, 000
4. Join EMP and ASG′ requires $400 * 20 * tupacc$ =   8, 000

    The total cost is $\overline{23, 000}$

In strategy A, the join of ASG′ and EMP (step 3) can exploit the clustered index on ENO of EMP. Thus, EMP is accessed only once for each tuple of ASG′. In strategy B, we assume that the access methods to relations EMP and ASG based on attributes RESP and ENO are lost because of data transfer. This is a reasonable assumption in practice. We assume that the join of EMP and ASG′ in step 4 is done by the default nested loop algorithm (that simply performs the Cartesian product of the two input relations). Strategy A is better by a factor of 50, which is quite significant. Furthermore, it provides better distribution of work among sites. The difference would be even higher if we assumed slower communication and/or higher degree of fragmentation.   ♦

4.1.2   Query Optimization

Query optimization refers to the process of producing a query execution plan (QEP), which represents an execution strategy for the query. This QEP minimizes an objective cost function. A query optimizer, the software module that performs query optimization, is usually seen as consisting of three components: a search space, a cost model, and a search strategy.

4.1.2.1   Search Space

The *search space* is the set of alternative execution plans that represent the input query. These plans are equivalent, in the sense that they yield the same result, but they differ in the execution order of operators and the way these operators are implemented, and therefore in their performance. The search space is obtained by applying transformation rules, such as those for relational algebra.

4.1.2.2   Cost Model

The *cost model* is used to predict the cost of any given execution plan, and to compare equivalent plans so as to choose the best one. To be accurate, the cost model must have good knowledge about the distributed execution environment, using statistics on the data and cost functions.

In a distributed database, statistics typically bear on fragments, and include fragment cardinality and size as well as the size and number of distinct values of each attribute. To minimize the probability of error, more detailed statistics such as histograms of attribute values are sometimes used at the expense of higher management cost. The accuracy of statistics is achieved by periodic updating.

A good measure of cost is the *total cost* that will be incurred in processing the query. Total cost is the sum of all times incurred in processing the operators of the query at various sites and in intersite communication. Another good measure is the *response time* of the query, which is the time elapsed for executing the query. Since operators can be executed in parallel at different sites, the response time of a query may be significantly less than its total cost.

In a distributed database system, the total cost to be minimized includes CPU, I/O, and communication costs. The CPU cost is incurred when performing operators on data in main memory. The I/O cost is the time necessary for disk accesses. This cost can be minimized by reducing the number of disk accesses through fast access methods to the data and efficient use of main memory (buffer management). The communication cost is the time needed for exchanging data between sites participating in the execution of the query. This cost is incurred in processing the messages (formatting/deformatting), and in transmitting the data over the communication network.

The communication cost component is probably the most important factor considered in distributed databases. Most of the early proposals for distributed query optimization assumed that the communication cost largely dominates local processing cost (I/O and CPU cost), and thus ignored the latter. However, modern distributed processing environments have much faster communication networks, whose bandwidth is comparable to that of disks. Therefore, the solution is to have a weighted combination of these three cost components since they all contribute significantly to the total cost of evaluating a query.

In this chapter, we consider relational algebra as a basis to express the output of query processing. Therefore, the complexity of relational algebra operators, which directly affects their execution time, dictates some principles useful to a query processor. These principles can help in choosing the final execution strategy.

The simplest way of defining complexity is in terms of relation cardinalities independent of physical implementation details such as fragmentation and storage structures. Complexity is $\mathcal{O}(n)$ for unary operators, where n denotes the relation cardinality, if the resulting tuples may be obtained independently of each other. Complexity is $\mathcal{O}(n \log n)$ for binary operators if each tuple of one relation must be compared with each tuple of the other on the basis of the equality of selected attributes. This complexity assumes that tuples of each relation must be sorted on the comparison attributes. However, using hashing and enough memory to hold one hashed relation can reduce the complexity of binary operators to $\mathcal{O}(n)$. Project with duplicate elimination and grouping operators require that each tuple of the relation be compared with each other tuple, and thus also have $\mathcal{O}(n \log n)$ complexity. Finally, complexity is $\mathcal{O}(n^2)$ for the Cartesian product of two relations because each tuple of one relation must be combined with each tuple of the other.

4.1.2.3   Search Strategy

The *search strategy* explores the search space and selects the best plan, using the cost model. It defines which plans are examined and in which order. The details of the distributed environment are captured by the search space and the cost model.

An immediate method for query optimization is to search the solution space, exhaustively predict the cost of each strategy, and select the strategy with minimum cost. Although this method is effective in selecting the best strategy, it may incur a significant processing cost for the optimization itself. The problem is that the solution space can be large; that is, there may be many equivalent strategies, even when the query involves a small number of relations. The problem becomes worse as the number of relations or fragments increases (e.g., becomes greater than 10). Having high optimization cost is not necessarily bad, particularly if query optimization is done once for many subsequent executions of the query.

The most popular search strategy used by query optimizers is *dynamic programming*, which was first proposed in the System R project at IBM Research. It proceeds by *building* plans, starting from base relations, joining one more relation at each step until complete plans are obtained. Dynamic programming builds all possible plans, breadth-first, before it chooses the "best" plan. To reduce the optimization cost, partial plans that are not likely to lead to the optimal plan are *pruned* (i.e., discarded) as soon as possible.

For very complex queries, making the search space large, *randomized* strategies such as Iterative Improvement and Simulated Annealing can be used. They try to find a very good solution, not necessarily the best one, but with a good trade-off between optimization time and execution time.

Another, complementary solution is to restrict the solution space so that only a few strategies are considered. In both centralized and distributed systems, a common heuristic is to minimize the size of intermediate relations. This can be done by performing unary operators first, and ordering the binary operators by the increasing sizes of their intermediate relations.

A query may be optimized at different times relative to the actual time of query execution. Optimization can be done *statically* before executing the query or *dynamically* as the query is executed. Static query optimization is done at query compilation time. Thus the cost of optimization may be amortized over multiple query executions. Therefore, this timing is appropriate for use with the exhaustive search method. Since the sizes of the intermediate relations of a strategy are not known until runtime, they must be estimated using database statistics. Errors in these estimates can lead to the choice of suboptimal strategies.

Dynamic query optimization proceeds at query execution time. At any point of execution, the choice of the best next operator can be based on accurate knowledge of the results of the operators executed previously. Therefore, database statistics are not needed to estimate the size of intermediate results. However, they may still be useful in choosing the first operators. The main advantage over static query optimization is that the actual sizes of intermediate relations are available to the query processor, thereby minimizing the probability of a bad choice. The main shortcoming is that query optimization, an expensive task, must be repeated for each execution of the query. Therefore, this approach is best for ad hoc queries.

Hybrid query optimization attempts to provide the advantages of static query optimization while avoiding the issues generated by inaccurate estimates. The approach is basically static, but dynamic query optimization may take place at runtime when a high difference between predicted sizes and actual size of intermediate relations is detected.

4.1.3   Layers Of Query Processing

The problem of query processing can itself be decomposed into several subproblems, corresponding to various layers. In Fig. 4.2, a generic layering scheme for query processing is shown where each layer solves a well-defined subproblem. To simplify the discussion, let us assume a static query processor that does not exploit replicated fragments. The input is a query on global data expressed in relational calculus. This query is posed on global (distributed) relations, meaning that data distribution is hidden. Four main layers are involved in distributed query processing. The first three layers map the input query into a distributed query execution plan (distributed QEP) . They perform the functions of *query decomposition*, *data localization*, and *global query optimization*. Query decomposition and data localization correspond to query rewriting. The first three layers are performed by a central control site and use schema information stored in the global directory. The fourth layer performs *distributed query execution* by executing the plan and returns the answer to the query. It is done by the local sites and the control site. In the remainder of this section, we introduce these four layers.

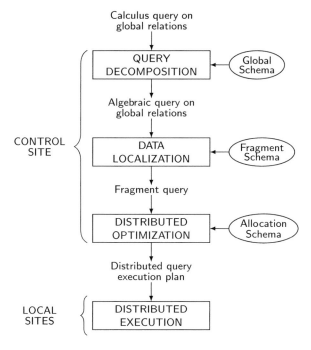

Fig. 4.2 Generic layering scheme for distributed query processing

4.1.3.1 Query Decomposition

The first layer decomposes the calculus query into an algebraic query on global relations. The information needed for this transformation is found in the global conceptual schema describing the global relations. However, the information about data distribution is not used here but in the next layer. The techniques used by this layer are those of a centralized DBMS, so we only briefly remind them in this chapter.

Query decomposition can be viewed as four successive steps. First, the calculus query is rewritten in a *normalized* form that is suitable for subsequent manipulation. Normalization of a query generally involves the manipulation of the query quantifiers and of the query qualification by applying logical operator priority.

Second, the normalized query is *analyzed* semantically so that incorrect queries are detected and rejected as early as possible. A query is semantically incorrect if components of it do not contribute in any way to the generation of the result. In the context of relational calculus, it is not possible to determine the semantic correctness of general queries. However, it is possible to do so for a large class of relational queries, i.e., those which do not contain disjunction and negation. This is based on the representation of the query as a graph, called a *query graph* or *connection graph*. We define this graph for the most useful kinds of queries involving selection, projection, and join operators. In a query graph, one node indicates the result relation, and any other node indicates an operand relation. An edge between two nodes that are not results represents a join, whereas an edge whose destination node is the result represents a project. Furthermore, a nonresult node may be labeled by a selection or a self-join (join of the relation with itself) predicate. An important subgraph of the query graph is the *join graph*, in which only the joins are considered.

Third, the correct query (still expressed in relational calculus) is *simplified*. One way to simplify a query is to eliminate redundant predicates. Note that redundant queries are likely to arise when a query is the result of system transformations applied to the user query. As seen in Chap. 3, such transformations are used for performing distributed data control (views, protection, and semantic integrity control).

Fourth, the calculus query is *restructured* as an algebraic query. Recall from Sect. 4.1.1 that several algebraic queries can be derived from the same calculus query, and that some algebraic queries are "better" than others. The quality of an algebraic query is defined in terms of expected performance. The traditional way to do this transformation towards a "better" algebraic specification is to start with an initial algebraic query and transform it in order to find a "good" one. The initial algebraic query is derived immediately from the calculus query by translating the predicates and the target statement into relational operators as they appear in the query. This directly translated algebra query is then restructured through transformation rules. The algebraic query generated by this layer is good in the sense that the worse executions are typically avoided. For instance, a relation will be accessed only once, even if there are several select predicates. However, this query is generally far from providing an optimal execution, since information about data distribution and fragment allocation is not used at this layer.

4.1.3.2 Data Localization

The input to the second layer is an algebraic query on global relations. The main role of the second layer is to localize the query's data using data distribution information in the fragment schema. In Chap. 2 we saw that relations are fragmented and stored in disjoint subsets, called fragments, each being stored at a different site. This layer determines which fragments are involved in the query and transforms the distributed query into a query on fragments. Fragmentation is defined through fragmentation rules that can be expressed as relational operators. A global relation can be reconstructed by applying the fragmentation rules, and then deriving a program, called a *materialization program*, of relational algebra operators which then acts on fragments. Localization involves two steps. First, the query is mapped into a fragment query by substituting each relation by its materialization program. Second, the fragment query is simplified and restructured to produce another "good" query. Simplification and restructuring may be done according to the same rules used in the decomposition layer. As in the decomposition layer, the final fragment query is generally far from optimal because information regarding fragments is not utilized.

4.1.3.3 Distributed Optimization

The input to the third layer is an algebraic query on fragments, i.e., a fragment query. The goal of query optimization is to find an execution strategy for the query which is close to optimal. An execution strategy for a distributed query can be described with relational algebra operators and *communication primitives* (send/receive operators) for transferring data between sites. The previous layers have already optimized the query, for example, by eliminating redundant expressions. However, this optimization is independent of fragment characteristics such as fragment allocation and cardinalities. In addition, communication operators are not yet specified. By permuting the ordering of operators within one query on fragments, many equivalent queries may be found.

Query optimization consists of finding the "best" ordering of operators in the query, including communication operators, that minimizes a cost function. The cost function, often defined in terms of time units, refers to the use of computing resources such as disk, CPU cost, and network. Generally, it is a weighted combination of I/O, CPU, and communication costs. To select the ordering of operators it is necessary to predict execution costs of alternative candidate orderings. Determining execution costs before query execution (i.e., static optimization) is based on fragment statistics and the formulas for estimating the cardinalities of results of relational operators. Thus the optimization decisions depend on the allocation of fragments and available statistics on fragments which are recorder in the allocation schema.

An important aspect of query optimization is *join ordering*, since permutations of the joins within the query may lead to improvements of orders of magnitude. The output of the query optimization layer is an optimized algebraic query with communication operators included on fragments. It is typically represented and saved (for future executions) as a distributed QEP.

4.1.3.4 Distributed Execution

The last layer is performed by all the sites that have fragments involved in the query. Each subquery executing at one site, called a *local query*, is optimized using the local schema of the site and executed. At this time, the algorithms to perform the relational operators may be chosen. Local optimization uses the algorithms of centralized systems.

The classical implementation of relational operators in database systems is based on the iterator model, which provides pipelined parallelism within operator trees. It is a simple pull model that executes operators starting from the root operator node (that produces the result) to the leaf nodes (that access the base relations). Thus, the intermediate results of operators do not need to be materialized as tuples are produced on demand and can be consumed by subsequent operators. However, it requires operators to be implemented in pipeline mode, using an open-next-close interface. Each operator must be implemented as an iterator with three functions:

1. Open(): initializes the operator's internal state, e.g., allocate a hash table;
2. Next(): produces and returns the next result tuple or null;
3. Close(): cleans up all allocated resources, after all tuples have been processed.

Thus, an iterator provides the iteration component of a while loop, i.e., initialization, increment, loop termination condition, and final cleaning. Executing a QEP proceeds as follows. First, execution is initialized by calling Open() on the root operator of the operator tree, which then forwards the Open() call through the entire plan using the operators themselves. Then the root operator iteratively produces its next result record by forwarding the Next() call through the operator tree as needed. Execution terminates when the last Open() call returns "end" to the root operator.

To illustrate the implementation of a relational operator using the open-next-close interface, let us consider the nested loop join operator that performs R ⋈ S on attribute A. The Open() and Next() functions are as follows:

```
Function Open()
     R.Open() ;
     S.Open() ;
     r := R.Next() ;

Function Next()
     while (r ≠ null) do
         (while (s:=S.Next()) ≠ null) do
             if r.A=s.A then return(r,s);
         S.close() ;
         S.open() ;
         r:=R.next() ; )
     return null;
```

It is not always possible to implement an operator in pipelined mode. Such operators are *blocking*, i.e., need to materialize their input data in memory or disk before they can produce any output. Examples of blocking operators are sorting and hash join. If the data is already sorted, then merge-join, grouping, and duplicate elimination can be implemented in pipelined mode.

4.2 Data Localization

Data localization translates an algebraic query on global relations into a fragment query using information stored in the fragment schema. A naive way to do this is to generate a query where each global relation is substituted by its materialization program. This can be viewed as replacing the leaves of the operator tree of the distributed query with subtrees corresponding to the materialized programs. In general, this approach is inefficient because important restructurings and simplifications of the fragment query can still be made. In the remainder of this section, for each type of fragmentation we present *reduction techniques* that generate simpler and optimized queries. We use the transformation rules and the heuristics, such as pushing unary operators down the tree.

4.2.1 Reduction for Primary Horizontal Fragmentation

The horizontal fragmentation function distributes a relation based on selection predicates. The following example is used in the subsequent discussions.

Example 4.3 Relation EMP(ENO, ENAME, TITLE) can be split into three horizontal fragments EMP$_1$, EMP$_2$, and EMP$_3$, defined as follows:

$$EMP_1 = \sigma_{ENO \leq "E3"}(EMP)$$

$$EMP_2 = \sigma_{"E3" < ENO \leq "E6"}(EMP)$$

$$EMP_3 = \sigma_{ENO > "E6"}(EMP)$$

The materialization program for a horizontally fragmented relation is the union of the fragments. In our example, we have

$$EMP = EMP_1 \cup EMP_2 \cup EMP_3$$

Thus the materialized form of any query specified on EMP is obtained by replacing it by (EMP$_1$ ∪ EMP$_2$ ∪ EMP$_3$).   ◆

The reduction of queries on horizontally fragmented relations consists primarily of determining, after restructuring the subtrees, those that will produce empty relations, and removing them. Horizontal fragmentation can be exploited to simplify both selection and join operators.

4.2.1.1   Reduction with Selection

Selections on fragments that have a qualification contradicting the qualification of the fragmentation rule generate empty relations. Given a relation R that has been horizontally fragmented as R$_1$, R$_2$, ..., R$_w$, where R$_j$ = σ_{p_j}(R), the rule can be stated formally as follows:

Rule 1 $\sigma_{p_i}(R_j) = \phi$ if $\forall x$ in R : $\neg(p_i(x) \wedge p_j(x))$

where p_i and p_j are selection predicates, x denotes a tuple, and $p(x)$ denotes "predicate p holds for x."

For example, the selection predicate ENO="E1" conflicts with the predicates of fragments EMP$_2$ and EMP$_3$ of Example 4.3 (i.e., no tuple in EMP$_2$ and EMP$_3$ can satisfy this predicate). Determining the contradicting predicates requires theorem-

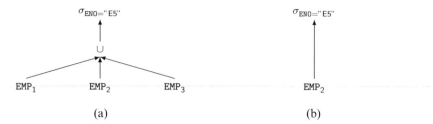

Fig. 4.3 Reduction for horizontal fragmentation (with selection). (**a**) Fragment query. (**b**) Reduced query

proving techniques if the predicates are quite general. However, DBMSs generally simplify predicate comparison by supporting only simple predicates for defining fragmentation rules (by the database administrator).

Example 4.4 We now illustrate reduction by horizontal fragmentation using the following example query:

```
SELECT *
FROM    EMP
WHERE   ENO  =  "E5"
```

Applying the naive approach to localize EMP using EMP_1, EMP_2, and EMP_3 gives the fragment query of Fig. 4.3a. By commuting the selection with the union operator, it is easy to detect that the selection predicate contradicts the predicates of EMP_1 and EMP_3, thereby producing empty relations. The reduced query is simply applied to EMP_2 as shown in Fig. 4.3b.   ◆

4.2.2 Reduction with Join

Joins on horizontally fragmented relations can be simplified when the joined relations are fragmented according to the join attribute. The simplification consists of distributing joins over unions and eliminating useless joins. The distribution of join over union can be stated as:

$$(R_1 \cup R_2) \bowtie S = (R_1 \bowtie S) \cup (R_2 \bowtie S)$$

where R_i are fragments of R and S is a relation.

With this transformation, unions can be moved up in the operator tree so that all possible joins of fragments are exhibited. Useless joins of fragments can be determined when the qualifications of the joined fragments are contradicting, thus yielding an empty result. Assuming that fragments R_i and R_j are defined, respectively, according to predicates p_i and p_j on the same attribute, the simplification rule can be stated as follows:

Rule 2 $R_i \bowtie R_j = \phi$ if $\forall x$ in $R_i, \forall y$ in $R_j : \neg(p_i(x) \wedge p_j(y))$

The determination of useless joins and their elimination using rule 2 can thus be performed by looking only at the fragment predicates. The application of this rule allows the join of two relations to be implemented as parallel partial joins of fragments. It is not always the case that the reduced query is better (i.e., simpler) than the fragment query. The fragment query is better when there are a large number of partial joins in the reduced query. This case arises when there are few contradicting fragmentation predicates. The worst case occurs when each fragment of one relation must be joined with each fragment of the other relation. This is tantamount to the Cartesian product of the two sets of fragments, with each set corresponding to one relation. The reduced query is better when the number of partial joins is small. For example, if both relations are fragmented using the same predicates, the number of partial joins is equal to the number of fragments of each relation. One advantage of the reduced query is that the partial joins can be done in parallel, and thus increase response time.

Example 4.5 Assume that relation EMP is fragmented as EMP_1, EMP_2, EMP_3, as above, and that relation ASG is fragmented as

$$ASG_1 = \sigma_{ENO \leq "E3"}(ASG)$$

$$ASG_2 = \sigma_{ENO > "E3"}(ASG)$$

EMP_1 and ASG_1 are defined by the same predicate. Furthermore, the predicate defining ASG_2 is the union of the predicates defining EMP_2 and EMP_3. Now consider the join query

```
SELECT *
FROM    EMP NATURAL JOIN ASG
```

The equivalent fragment query is given in Fig. 4.4a. The query reduced by distributing joins over unions and applying rule 2 can be implemented as a union of three partial joins that can be done in parallel (Fig. 4.4b).   ◆

4.2.3   Reduction for Vertical Fragmentation

The vertical fragmentation function distributes a relation based on projection attributes. Since the reconstruction operator for vertical fragmentation is the join, the materialization program for a vertically fragmented relation consists of the join of the fragments on the common attribute. For vertical fragmentation, we use the following example.

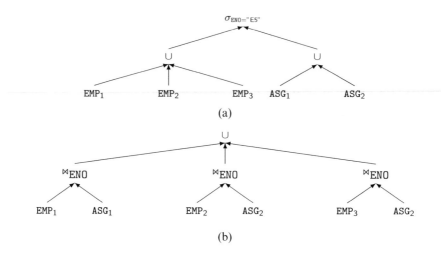

Fig. 4.4 Reduction by horizontal fragmentation (with join). (**a**) Fragment query. (**b**) Reduced query

Example 4.6 Relation EMP can be divided into two vertical fragments where the key attribute ENO is duplicated:

$$EMP_1 = \Pi_{ENO,ENAME}(EMP)$$

$$EMP_2 = \Pi_{ENO,TITLE}(EMP)$$

The materialization program is

$$EMP = EMP_1 \bowtie_{ENO} EMP_2 \qquad\blacklozenge$$

Similar to horizontal fragmentation, queries on vertical fragments can be reduced by determining the useless intermediate relations and removing the subtrees that produce them. Projections on a vertical fragment that has no attributes in common with the projection attributes (except the key of the relation) produce useless, though not empty relations. Given a relation R, defined over attributes $A = \{A_1, \ldots, A_n\}$, which is vertically fragmented as $R_i = \Pi_{A'}(R)$, where $A' \subseteq A$, the rule can be formally stated as follows:

Rule 3 $\Pi_{D,K}(R_i)$ is useless if the set of projection attributes D is not in A'.

Example 4.7 Let us illustrate the application of this rule using the following example query in SQL:

```
SELECT ENAME
FROM    EMP
```

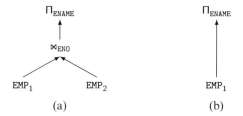

Fig. 4.5 Reduction for vertical fragmentation. (**a**) Fragment query. (**b**) Reduced query

The equivalent fragment query on EMP_1 and EMP_2 (as obtained in Example 4.4) is given in Fig. 4.5a. By commuting the projection with the join (i.e., projecting on ENO, ENAME), we can see that the projection on EMP_2 is useless because ENAME is not in EMP_2. Therefore, the projection needs to apply only to EMP_1, as shown in Fig. 4.5b. ◆

4.2.4 Reduction for Derived Fragmentation

As we saw in previous sections, the join operator, which is probably the most important operator because it is both frequent and expensive, can be optimized by using primary horizontal fragmentation when the joined relations are fragmented according to the join attributes. In this case the join of two relations is implemented as a union of partial joins. However, this method precludes one of the relations from being fragmented on a different attribute used for selection. Derived horizontal fragmentation is another way of distributing two relations so that the joint processing of selection and join is improved. Typically, if relation R is subject to derived horizontal fragmentation due to relation S, the fragments of R and S that have the same join attribute values are located at the same site. In addition, S can be fragmented according to a selection predicate.

Since tuples of R are placed according to the tuples of S, derived fragmentation should be used only for one-to-many (hierarchical) relationships of the form S → R, where a tuple of S can match with n tuples of R, but a tuple of R matches with exactly one tuple of S. Note that derived fragmentation could be used for many-to-many relationships provided that tuples of S (that match with n tuples of R) are replicated. For simplicity, we assume and advise that derived fragmentation be used only for hierarchical relationships.

Example 4.8 Given a one-to-many relationship from EMP to ASG, relation ASG(ENO, PNO, RESP, DUR) can be indirectly fragmented according to the following rules:

$$ASG_1 = ASG \ltimes_{ENO} EMP_1$$

$$ASG_2 = ASG \ltimes_{ENO} EMP_2$$

Recall from Chap. 2 that EMP_1 and EMP_2 are fragmented as follows:

$$EMP_1 = \sigma_{TITLE=\text{"Programmer"}}(EMP)$$

$$EMP_2 = \sigma_{TITLE\neq\text{"Programmer"}}(EMP)$$

The materialization program for a horizontally fragmented relation is the union of the fragments. In our example, we have

$$ASG = ASG_1 \cup ASG_2$$

◆

Queries on derived fragments can also be reduced. Since this type of fragmentation is useful for optimizing join queries, a useful transformation is to distribute joins over unions (used in the materialization programs) and to apply rule 2 introduced earlier. Because the fragmentation rules indicate what the matching tuples are, certain joins will produce empty relations if the fragmentation predicates conflict. For example, the predicates of ASG_1 and EMP_2 conflict; thus, we have

$$ASG_1 \bowtie EMP_2 = \phi$$

Contrary to the reduction with join discussed previously, the reduced query is always preferable to the fragment query because the number of partial joins usually equals the number of fragments of R.

Example 4.9 The reduction by derived fragmentation is illustrated by applying it to the following SQL query, which retrieves all attributes of tuples from EMP and ASG that have the same value of ENO and the title "Mech. Eng.":

```
SELECT *
FROM    EMP NATURAL JOIN ASG
WHERE   TITLE = "Mech. Eng."
```

The fragment query on fragments EMP_1, EMP_2, ASG_1, and ASG_2 defined previously is given in Fig. 4.6a. By pushing selection down to fragments EMP_1 and EMP_2, the query reduces to that of Fig. 4.6b. This is because the selection predicate conflicts with that of EMP_1, and thus EMP_1 can be removed. In order to discover conflicting join predicates, we distribute joins over unions. This produces the tree of Fig. 4.6c. The left subtree joins two fragments, ASG_1 and EMP_2, whose qualifications conflict because of predicates TITLE = "Programmer" in ASG_1, and TITLE $\neq$ "Programmer" in EMP_2. Therefore the left subtree which produces an empty relation can be removed, and the reduced query of Fig. 4.6d is obtained. The resulting query is made simpler, illustrating the value of fragmentation in improving the performance of distributed queries.   ◆

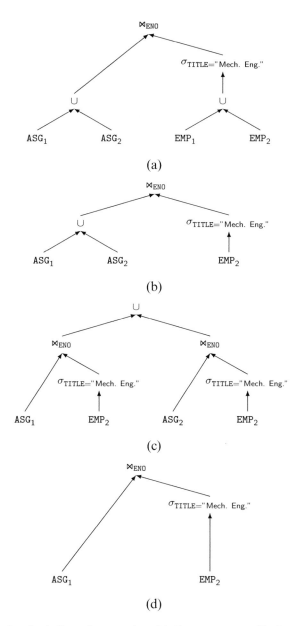

Fig. 4.6 Reduction for indirect fragmentation. (**a**) Fragment query. (**b**) Query after pushing selection down. (**c**) Query after moving unions up. (**d**) Reduced query after eliminating the left subtree

4.2.5 Reduction for Hybrid Fragmentation

Hybrid fragmentation is obtained by combining the fragmentation functions discussed above. The goal of hybrid fragmentation is to support, efficiently, queries involving projection, selection, and join. Note that the optimization of an operator or of a combination of operators is always done at the expense of other operators. For example, hybrid fragmentation based on selection–projection will make selection only, or projection only, less efficient than with horizontal fragmentation (or vertical fragmentation). The materialization program for a hybrid fragmented relation uses unions and joins of fragments.

Example 4.10 Here is an example of hybrid fragmentation of relation EMP:

$$EMP_1 = \sigma_{ENO \leq "E4"}(\Pi_{ENO,ENAME}(EMP))$$

$$EMP_2 = \sigma_{ENO > "E4"}(\Pi_{ENO,ENAME}(EMP))$$

$$EMP_3 = \Pi_{ENO,TITLE}(EMP)$$

In our example, the materialization program is

$$EMP = (EMP_1 \cup EMP_2) \bowtie_{ENO} EMP_3$$

◆

Queries on hybrid fragments can be reduced by combining the rules used, respectively, in primary horizontal, vertical, and derived horizontal fragmentation. These rules can be summarized as follows:

1. Remove empty relations generated by contradicting selections on horizontal fragments.
2. Remove useless relations generated by projections on vertical fragments.
3. Distribute joins over unions in order to isolate and remove useless joins.

Example 4.11 The following example query in SQL illustrates the application of rules (1) and (2) to the horizontal–vertical fragmentation of relation EMP into EMP_1, EMP_2, and EMP_3 given above:

```
SELECT  ENAME
FROM    EMP
WHERE   ENO="E5"
```

The fragment query of Fig. 4.7a can be reduced by first pushing selection down, eliminating fragment EMP_1, and then pushing projection down, eliminating fragment EMP_3. The reduced query is given in Fig. 4.7b.   ◆

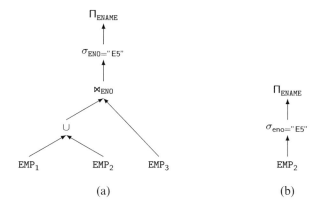

Fig. 4.7 Reduction for hybrid fragmentation. (**a**) Fragment query. (**b**) Reduced query

4.3   Join Ordering in Distributed Queries

Ordering joins is an important aspect of centralized query optimization. Join ordering in a distributed context is even more important since joins between fragments may increase the communication time. Therefore, the search space investigated by a distributed query optimizer concentrates on join trees (see next section). Two basic approaches exist to order joins in distributed queries. One tries to optimize the ordering of joins directly, whereas the other replaces joins by combinations of semijoins in order to minimize communication costs.

4.3.1   Join Trees

QEPs are typically abstracted by means of operator trees, which define the order in which the operators are executed. They are enriched with additional information, such as the best algorithm chosen for each operator. For a given query, the search space can thus be defined as the set of equivalent operator trees that can be produced using transformation rules. To characterize query optimizers, it is useful to concentrate on *join trees*, which are operator trees whose operators are join or Cartesian product. This is because permutations of the join order have the most important effect on performance of relational queries.

Example 4.12 Consider the following query:

```
SELECT ENAME, RESP
FROM   EMP NATURAL JOIN ASG NATURAL JOIN PROJ
```

Figure 4.8 illustrates three equivalent join trees for that query, which are obtained by exploiting the associativity of binary operators. Each of these join trees can be

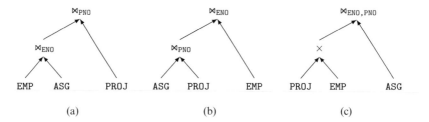

Fig. 4.8 Equivalent join trees

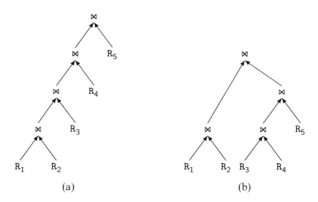

Fig. 4.9 The two major shapes of join trees. (a) Linear join tree. (b) Bushy join tree

assigned a cost based on the estimated cost of each operator. Join tree (c) which starts with a Cartesian product may have a much higher cost than the other join trees.   ♦

For a complex query (involving many relations and many operators), the number of equivalent operator trees can be very high. For instance, the number of alternative join trees that can be produced by applying the commutativity and associativity rules is $\mathcal{O}(N!)$ for N relations. Investigating a large search space may make optimization time prohibitive, sometimes much more expensive than the actual execution time. Therefore, query optimizers typically restrict the size of the search space they consider. The first restriction is to use heuristics. The most common heuristic is to perform selection and projection when accessing base relations. Another common heuristic is to avoid Cartesian products that are not required by the query. For instance, in Fig. 4.8, operator tree (c) would not be part of the search space considered by the optimizer.

Another important restriction is with respect to the shape of the join tree. Two kinds of join trees are usually distinguished: linear versus bushy trees (see Fig. 4.9). A *linear tree* is a tree such that at least one operand of each operator node is a base relation. A *left linear tree* is a linear tree where the right subtree of a join node is always a leaf node corresponding to a base relation. A *bushy tree* is more general and may have operators with no base relations as operands (i.e., both operands are intermediate relations). By considering only linear trees, the size of the search space is reduced to $\mathcal{O}(2^N)$. However, in a distributed environment, bushy trees are useful in exhibiting parallelism. For example, in join tree (b) of Fig. 4.9, operators $R_1 \bowtie R_2$ and $R_3 \bowtie R_4$ can be done in parallel.

4.3.2   Join Ordering

Some algorithms optimize the ordering of joins directly without using semijoins. The purpose of this section is to stress the difficulty that join ordering presents and to motivate the subsequent section, which deals with the use of semijoins to optimize join queries.

A number of assumptions are necessary to concentrate on the main issues. Since the query is expressed on fragments, we do not need to distinguish between fragments of the same relation and fragments of different relations. To simplify notation, we use the term *relation* to designate a fragment stored at a particular site. Also, to concentrate on join ordering, we ignore local processing time, assuming that reducers (selection, projection) are executed locally either before or during the join (remember that doing selection first is not always efficient). Therefore, we consider only join queries whose operand relations are stored at different sites. We assume that relation transfers are done in a set-at-a-time mode rather than in a tuple-at-a-time mode. Finally, we ignore the transfer time for producing the data at a result site.

Let us first concentrate on the simpler problem of operand transfer in a single join. The query is R ⋈ S, where R and S are relations stored at different sites. The obvious choice of the relation to transfer is to send the smaller relation to the site of the larger one, which gives rise to two possibilities, as shown in Fig. 4.10. To make this choice we need to evaluate the sizes of R and S (we assume there is a function $size()$). We now consider the case where there are more than two relations to join. As in the case of a single join, the objective of the join-ordering algorithm is to transmit smaller operands. The difficulty stems from the fact that the join operators may reduce or increase the size of the intermediate results. Thus, estimating the size of join results is mandatory, but also difficult. A solution is to estimate the communication costs of all alternative strategies and to choose the best one. However, as discussed earlier, the number of strategies grows rapidly with the number of relations. This approach makes optimization costly, although this overhead is amortized rapidly if the query is executed frequently.

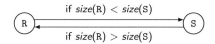

Fig. 4.10   Transfer of operands in binary operator

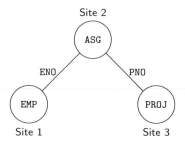

Fig. 4.11 Join graph of distributed query

Example 4.13 Consider the following query expressed in relational algebra:

$$\text{PROJ} \bowtie_{\text{PNO}} \text{ASG} \bowtie_{\text{ENO}} \text{EMP}$$

This query can be represented by its join graph in Fig. 4.11. Note that we have made certain assumptions about the locations of the three relations. This query can be executed in at least five different ways. We describe these strategies by the following programs, where (R → site *j*) stands for "relation R is transferred to site *j*."

1. EMP → site 2;
   Site 2 computes EMP′ = EMP ⋈ ASG;
   EMP′ → site 3;
   Site 3 computes EMP′ ⋈ PROJ.
2. ASG → site 1;
   Site 1 computes EMP′ = EMP ⋈ ASG;
   EMP′ → site 3;
   Site 3 computes EMP′ ⋈ PROJ.
3. ASG → site 3;
   Site 3 computes ASG′ = ASG ⋈ PROJ;
   ASG′ → site 1;
   Site 1 computes ASG′ ⋈ EMP.
4. PROJ → site 2;
   Site 2 computes PROJ′ = PROJ ⋈ ASG;
   PROJ′ → site 1;
   Site 1 computes PROJ′ ⋈ EMP.
5. EMP → site 2;
   PROJ → site 2;
   Site 2 computes EMP ⋈ PROJ ⋈ ASG

To select one of these programs, the following sizes must be known or predicted: $size(\text{EMP})$, $size(\text{ASG})$, $size(\text{PROJ})$, $size(\text{EMP} \bowtie \text{ASG})$, and $size(\text{ASG} \bowtie \text{PROJ})$. Furthermore, if it is the response time that is being considered, the optimization must take into account the fact that transfers can be done in parallel with strategy 5. An alternative to enumerating all the solutions is to use heuristics that consider only the sizes of the operand relations by assuming, for example, that the cardinality of the resulting join is the product of operand cardinalities. In this case, relations are ordered by increasing sizes and the order of execution is given by this ordering and the join graph. For instance, the order (EMP, ASG, PROJ) could use strategy 1, while the order (PROJ, ASG, EMP) could use strategy 4.   ◆

4.3.3 Semijoin-Based Algorithms

The semijoin operator has the important property of reducing the size of the operand relation. When the main cost component considered by the query processor is communication, a semijoin is particularly useful for improving the processing of distributed join operators as it reduces the size of data exchanged between sites. However, using semijoins may result in an increase in the number of messages and in the local processing time. The early distributed DBMSs, such as SDD-1, which were designed for slow wide area networks, make extensive use of semijoins. Nevertheless, semijoins are still beneficial in the context of fast networks when they induce a strong reduction of the join operand. Therefore, some algorithms aim at selecting an optimal combination of joins and semijoins.

In this section, we show how the semijoin operator can be used to decrease the total time of join queries. We are making the same assumptions as in Sect. 4.3.2. The main shortcoming of the join approach described in the preceding section is that entire operand relations must be transferred between sites. The semijoin acts as a size reducer for a relation much as a selection does.

The join of two relations R and S over attribute A, stored at sites 1 and 2, respectively, can be computed by replacing one or both operand relations by a semijoin with the other relation, using the following rules:

$$R \bowtie_A S \Leftrightarrow (R \ltimes_A S) \bowtie_A S$$

$$\Leftrightarrow R \bowtie_A (S \ltimes_A R)$$

$$\Leftrightarrow (R \ltimes_A S) \bowtie_A (S \ltimes_A R)$$

The choice between one of the three semijoin strategies requires estimating their respective costs.

The use of the semijoin is beneficial if the cost to produce and send it to the other site is less than the cost of sending the whole operand relation and of doing the actual join. To illustrate the potential benefit of the semijoin, let us compare the costs of the two alternatives: $R \bowtie_A S$ versus $(R \ltimes_A S) \bowtie_A S$, assuming that $size(R) < size(S)$.

The following program, using the notation of Sect. 4.3.2, uses the semijoin operator:

1. $\Pi_A(S) \rightarrow$ site 1
2. Site 1 computes $R' = R \ltimes_A S$

3. R′ → site 2
4. Site 2 computes R′ ⋉$_A$ S

For simplicity, let us ignore the constant T_{MSG} in the communication time assuming that the term $T_{TR} * size(R)$ is much larger. We can then compare the two alternatives in terms of the transmitted data size. The cost of the join-based algorithm is that of transferring relation R to site 2. The cost of the semijoin-based algorithm is the cost of steps 1 and 3 above. Therefore, the semijoin approach is better if

$$size(\Pi_A(S)) + size(R \ltimes_A S) < size(R)$$

The semijoin approach is better if the semijoin acts as a sufficient reducer, that is, if a few tuples of R participate in the join. The join approach is better if almost all tuples of R participate in the join, because the semijoin approach requires an additional transfer of a projection on the join attribute. The cost of the projection step can be minimized by encoding the result of the projection in bit arrays, thereby reducing the cost of transferring the joined attribute values. It is important to note that neither approach is systematically the best; they should be considered as complementary.

More generally, the semijoin can be useful in reducing the size of the operand relations involved in multiple join queries. However, query optimization becomes more complex in these cases. Consider again the join graph of relations EMP,ASG, and PROJ given in Fig. 4.11. We can apply the previous join algorithm using semijoins to each individual join. Thus an example of a program to compute EMP ⋈ ASG ⋈ PROJ is EMP′ ⋈ ASG′ ⋈ PROJ, where EMP′ = EMP ⋉ ASG and ASG′ = ASG ⋉ PROJ.

However, we may further reduce the size of an operand relation by using more than one semijoin. For example, EMP′ can be replaced in the preceding program by EMP″ derived as

$$EMP'' = EMP \ltimes (ASG \ltimes PROJ)$$

since if $size(ASG \ltimes PROJ) \leq size(ASG)$, we have $size(EMP'') \leq size(EMP')$. In this way, EMP can be reduced by the sequence of semijoins: EMP ⋉ (ASG ⋉ PROJ). Such a sequence of semijoins is called a *semijoin program* for EMP. Similarly, semijoin programs can be found for any relation in a query. For example, PROJ could be reduced by the semijoin program PROJ ⋉ (ASG ⋉ EMP). However, not all of the relations involved in a query need to be reduced; in particular, we can ignore those relations that are not involved in the final joins.

For a given relation, there exist several potential semijoin programs. The number of possibilities is in fact exponential in the number of relations. But there is one optimal semijoin program, called the *full reducer*, which reduces each relation R more than the others. The problem is to find the full reducer. A simple method is to evaluate the size reduction of all possible semijoin programs and to select the best one. The problems with the enumerative method are twofold:

1. There is a class of queries, called *cyclic queries*, that have cycles in their join graph and for which full reducers cannot be found.
2. For other queries, called *tree queries*, full reducers exist, but the number of candidate semijoin programs is exponential in the number of relations, which makes the enumerative approach NP-hard.

In what follows, we discuss solutions to these problems.

Example 4.14 Consider the following relations, where attribute CITY has been added to relations EMP (renamed ET), PROJ (renamed PT), and ASG (renamed AT) of the engineering database. Attribute CITY of AT corresponds to the city where the employee is identified by ENO lives.

```
ET(ENO, ENAME, TITLE, CITY)
AT(ENO, PNO, RESP, DUR, CITY)
PT(PNO, PNAME, BUDGET, CITY)
```

The following SQL query retrieves the names of all employees living in the city in which their project is located together with the project name.

```
SELECT ENAME, PNAME
FROM   ET NATURAL JOIN AT NATURAL JOIN PT
       NATURAL JOIN ET
```

As illustrated in Fig. 4.12a, this query is cyclic. ◆

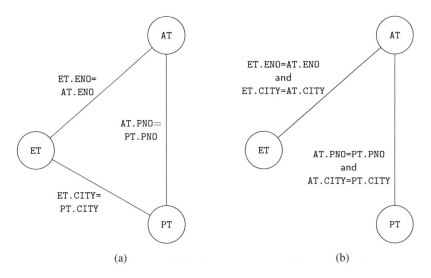

Fig. 4.12 Transformation of cyclic query. (**a**) Cyclic query. (**b**) Equivalent acyclic query

No full reducer exists for the query in Example 4.14. In fact, it is possible to derive semijoin programs for reducing it, but the number of operators is multiplied by the number of tuples in each relation, making the approach inefficient. One solution consists of transforming the cyclic graph into a tree by removing one arc of the graph and by adding appropriate predicates to the other arcs such that the removed predicate is preserved by transitivity. In the example of Fig. 4.12b, where the arc (ET, PT) is removed, the additional predicate ET.CITY = AT.CITY and AT.CITY = PT.CITY imply ET.CITY = PT.CITY by transitivity. Thus the acyclic query is equivalent to the cyclic query.

Although full reducers for tree queries exist, the problem of finding them is NP-hard. However, there is an important class of queries, called *chained queries*, for which a polynomial algorithm exists. A chained query has a join graph where relations can be ordered, and each relation joins only with the next relation in the order. Furthermore, the result of the query is at the end of the chain. For instance, the query in Fig. 4.11 is a chain query. Because of the difficulty of implementing an algorithm with full reducers, most systems use single semijoins to reduce the relation size.

4.3.4 Join Versus Semijoin

Compared with the join, the semijoin induces more operators but possibly on smaller operands. Figure 4.13 illustrates these differences with an equivalent pair of join and semijoin strategies for the query whose join graph is given in Fig. 4.11. The join EMP ⋈ ASG is done by sending one relation, e.g., ASG, to the site of the other one, e.g., EMP, to complete the join locally. When a semijoin is used, however, the

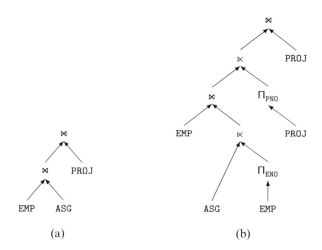

Fig. 4.13 Join versus semijoin approaches. (**a**) Join approach. (**b**) Semijoin approach

transfer of relation ASG is avoided. Instead, it is replaced by the transfer of the join attribute values of relation EMP to the site of relation ASG, followed by the transfer of the matching tuples of relation ASG to the site of relation EMP, where the join is completed. If the semijoin has good selectivity, then the semijoin approach can result in significant savings in communication time. The semijoin approach may also decrease the local processing time, by exploiting indices on the join attribute. Let us consider again the join EMP ⋈ ASG, assuming that there is a selection on ASG and an index on the join attribute of ASG. Without semijoin, we would perform the selection of ASG first, and then send the result relation to the site of EMP to complete the join. Thus, the index on the join attribute of ASG cannot be used (because the join takes place at the site of EMP). Using the semijoin approach, both the selection and the semijoin ASG ⋉ EMP would take place at the site of ASG, and can be performed efficiently using indices.

Semijoins can still be beneficial with fast networks if they have very good selectivity and are implemented with bit arrays. A bit array $BA[1 : n]$ is useful in encoding the join attribute values present in one relation. Let us consider the semijoin R ⋉ S. Then $BA[i]$ is set to 1 if there exists a join attribute value A = val in relation S such that $h(val) = i$, where h is a hash function. Otherwise, $BA[i]$ is set to 0. Such a bit array is much smaller than a list of join attribute values. Therefore, transferring the bit array instead of the join attribute values to the site of relation R saves communication time. The semijoin can be completed as follows. Each tuple of relation R, whose join attribute value is val, belongs to the semijoin if $BA[h(val)] = 1$.

4.4 Distributed Cost Model

An optimizer's cost model includes cost functions to predict the cost of operators, statistics and base data, and formulas to evaluate the sizes of intermediate results. The cost is in terms of execution time, so a cost function represents the execution time of a query.

4.4.1 Cost Functions

The cost of a distributed execution strategy can be expressed with respect to either the total time or the response time. The total time is the sum of all time (also referred to as cost) components, while the response time is the elapsed time from the initiation to the completion of the query. A general formula for determining the total time can be specified as follows:

$$Total\_time = T_{CPU} * \#insts + T_{I/O} * \#I/Os + T_{MSG} * \#msgs + T_{TR} * \#bytes$$

The first two components measure the local processing time, where T_{CPU} is the time of a CPU instruction and $T_{I/O}$ is the time of a disk I/O. The communication time is depicted by the two last components. T_{MSG} is the fixed time of initiating and receiving a message, while T_{TR} is the time it takes to transmit a data unit from one site to another. The data unit is given here in terms of bytes (*#bytes* is the sum of the sizes of all messages), but could be in different units (e.g., packets). A typical assumption is that T_{TR} is constant. This might not be true for wide area networks, where some sites are farther away than others. However, this assumption greatly simplifies query optimization. Thus the communication time of transferring *#bytes* of data from one site to another is assumed to be a linear function of *#bytes*:

$$CT(\#bytes) = T_{MSG} + T_{TR} * \#bytes$$

Costs are generally expressed in terms of time units, which in turn can be translated into other units (e.g., dollars).

The relative values of the cost coefficients characterize the distributed database environment. The topology of the network greatly influences the ratio between these components. In a wide area network such as the Internet, the communication time is generally the dominant factor. In local area networks, however, there is more of a balance among the components. Thus, most early distributed DBMSs designed for wide area networks have ignored the local processing cost and concentrated on minimizing the communication cost. Distributed DBMSs designed for local area networks, on the other hand, consider all three cost components. The new faster networks (both wide area and local area) have improved the above ratios in favor of communication cost when all things are equal. However, communication is still the dominant time factor in wide area networks such as the Internet because of the longer distances that data is retrieved from (or shipped to).

When the response time of the query is the objective function of the optimizer, parallel local processing and parallel communications must also be considered. A general formula for response time is

$$Response\_time = T_{CPU} * seq\_\#insts + T_{I/O} * seq\_\#I/Os$$
$$+ T_{MSG} * seq\_\#msgs + T_{TR} * seq\_\#bytes$$

where *seq_#x*, in which *x* can be instructions (*insts*), I/O, messages (*msgs*), or *bytes*, is the maximum number of *x* which must be done sequentially for the execution of the query. Thus any processing and communication done in parallel is ignored.

Example 4.15 Let us illustrate the difference between total cost and response time using the example of Fig. 4.14, which computes the answer to a query at site 3 with data from sites 1 and 2. For simplicity, we assume that only communication cost is considered.

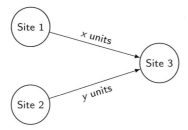

Fig. 4.14 Example of data transfers for a query

Assume that T_{MSG} and T_{TR} are expressed in time units. The total time of transferring x data units from site 1 to site 3 and y data units from site 2 to site 3 is

$$Total\_time = 2\,T_{MSG} + T_{TR} * (x + y)$$

The response time of the same query can be approximated as

$$Response\_time = max\{T_{MSG} + T_{TR} * x, T_{MSG} + T_{TR} * y\}$$

since the transfers can be done in parallel.   ◆

Minimizing response time is achieved by increasing the degree of parallel execution. This does not, however, imply that the total time is also minimized. On the contrary, it can increase the total time, for example, by having more parallel local processing and transmissions. Minimizing the total time implies that the utilization of the resources improves, thus increasing the system throughput. In practice, a compromise between the two is desired. In Sect. 4.5 we present algorithms that can optimize a combination of total time and response time, with more weight on one of them.

4.4.2   Database Statistics

The main factor affecting the performance of an execution strategy is the size of the intermediate relations that are produced during the execution. When a subsequent operator is located at a different site, the intermediate relation must be transmitted over the network. Therefore, it is of prime interest to estimate the size of the intermediate results of relational algebra operators in order to minimize the size of data transfers. This estimation is based on statistical information about the base relations and formulas to predict the cardinalities of the results of the relational operators. There is a direct trade-off between the precision of the statistics and the cost of managing them, the more precise statistics being the more costly. For a relation R fragmented as R_1, R_2, $\ldots$, R_r, the statistical data typically are the following:

1. For each attribute A of relation R its length (in number of bytes), denoted by $length(A)$, the cardinality of its domain, denoted by $card(dom[A])$, which gives the number of unique values in $dom[A]$, and in the case the domain is defined on a set of values that can be ordered (e.g., integers or reals), the minimum and maximum possible values, denoted by $min(A)$ and $max(A)$

2. For each attribute A of each fragment R_i, the number of distinct values of A, with the cardinality of the projection of fragment R_i on A, denoted by $card(\Pi_A(R_i))$.

3. The number of tuples in each fragment R_i, denoted by $card(R_i)$.

In addition, for each attribute A, there may be a histogram that approximates the frequency distribution of the attribute within a number of buckets, each corresponding to a range of values.

These statistics are useful to predict the size of intermediate relations. Remember that in Chap. 2 we defined the size of an intermediate relation R as follows:

$$size(R) = card(R) * length(R)$$

where $length(R)$ is the length (in bytes) of a tuple of R, and $card(R)$ is the number of tuples in R.

The estimation of $card(R)$ requires the use of formulas. Two simplifying assumptions are commonly made about the database. The distribution of attribute values in a relation is supposed to be uniform, and all attributes are independent, meaning that the value of an attribute does not affect the value of any other attribute. These two assumptions are often wrong in practice, but they make the problem tractable. Based on these assumptions, we can use simple formulas for estimating the cardinalities of the results of the basic relational algebra operators, based on their selectivity. The *selectivity factor* of an operator, that is, the proportion of tuples of an operand relation that participate in the result of that operation, is denoted by $SF(op)$, where op is the operation. It is a real value between 0 and 1. A low value (e.g., 0.001) corresponds to a good (or high) selectivity, while a high value (e.g., 0.5) to a bad (or low) selectivity.

Let us illustrate with the two major operators, i.e., selection and join. The cardinality of selection is

$$card(\sigma_F(R)) = SF(\sigma_F(R)) * card(R)$$

where $SF(\sigma_F(R))$ can be computed as follows for the basic predicates:

$$SF(\sigma_{A=value}(R)) = \frac{1}{card(\Pi_A(R))}$$

$$SF(\sigma_{A>value}(R)) = \frac{max(A) - value}{max(A) - min(A)}$$

$$SF(\sigma_{A<value}(R)) = \frac{value - min(A)}{max(A) - min(A)}$$

The cardinality of join is

$$card(\text{R} \bowtie \text{S}) = SF(\text{R} \bowtie_A \text{S}) * card(\text{R}) * card(\text{S})$$

There is no general way to estimate $SF(\text{R} \bowtie_A \text{S})$ without additional information. Thus, a simple approximation is to use a constant, e.g., 0.01, which reflects the known join selectivity. However, there is a case, which occurs frequently, where the estimation is accurate. If relation R is equijoined with relation S over attribute A where A is a key of R and a foreign key of S, the join selectivity factor can be approximated as

$$SF(\text{R} \bowtie_A \text{S}) = \frac{1}{card(\text{R})}$$

because each tuple of S matches with at most one tuple of R.

4.5   Distributed Query Optimization

In this section, we illustrate the use of the techniques presented in earlier sections within the context of three basic query optimization algorithms. First, we present the dynamic and static approaches. Then, we present a hybrid approach.

4.5.1   Dynamic Approach

We illustrate the dynamic approach with the algorithm of Distributed INGRES. The objective function of the algorithm is to minimize a combination of both the communication time and the response time. However, these two objectives may be conflicting. For instance, increasing communication time (by means of parallelism) may well decrease response time. Thus, the function can give a greater weight to one or the other. Note that this query optimization algorithm ignores the cost of transmitting the data to the result site. The algorithm also takes advantage of fragmentation, but only horizontal fragmentation is handled for simplicity.

Since both general and broadcast networks are considered, the optimizer takes into account the network topology. In broadcast networks, the same data unit can be transmitted from one site to all the other sites in a single transfer, and the algorithm explicitly takes advantage of this capability. For example, broadcasting is used to replicate fragments and then to maximize the degree of parallelism.

The input to the algorithm is a query expressed in tuple relational calculus (in conjunctive normal form) and schema information (the network type, as well as the location and size of each fragment). This algorithm is executed by the site, called the *master site*, where the query is initiated. The algorithm, which we call Dynamic-QOA, is given in Algorithm 4.1.

Algorithm 4.1: Dynamic-QOA

Input: MRQ: multirelation query
Output: result of the last multirelation query
begin

    for *each detachable* ORQ_i *in MRQ* **do** $\{ORQ$ is monorelation query$\}$
    | run(ORQ_i)   (1)
    end for
    $\{$MRQ replaced by n irreducible queries$\}$
    $MRQ'\_list \leftarrow$ REDUCE(MRQ)   (2)
    while $n \neq 0$ **do** $\{n$ is the number of irreducible queries$\}$ (3)
        $\{$choose next irreducible query involving the smallest fragments$\}$
        $MRQ' \leftarrow$ SELECT_QUERY(MRQ'_list)   (3.1)
        $\{$determine fragments to transfer and processing site for $MRQ'\}$
        Fragment-site-list $\leftarrow$ SELECT_STRATEGY(MRQ')   (3.2)
        $\{$move the selected fragments to the selected sites$\}$
        for *each pair* (F, S) *in Fragment-site-list* **do**
        | move fragment F to site S   (3.3)
        end for
        execute MRQ' (3.4)
        $n \leftarrow n - 1$
    end while
    $\{$output is the result of the last $MRQ'\}$
end

All monorelation queries (e.g., selection and projection) that can be detached are first processed locally (step 1). Then the reduction algorithm is applied to the original query (step 2). Reduction is a technique that isolates all irreducible subqueries and monorelation subqueries by detachment. Monorelation subqueries are ignored because they have already been processed in step 1. Thus the REDUCE procedure produces a sequence of irreducible subqueries $q_1 \rightarrow q_2 \rightarrow \cdots \rightarrow q_n$, with at most one relation in common between two consecutive subqueries.

Based on the list of irreducible queries isolated in step 2 and the size of each fragment, the next subquery, MRQ', which has at least two variables, is chosen at step 3.1 and steps 3.2–3.4 are applied to it. Steps 3.1 and 3.2 are discussed below. Step 3.2 selects the best strategy to process the query MRQ'. This strategy is described by a list of pairs (F, S), in which F is a fragment to transfer to the processing site S. Step 3.3 transfers all the fragments to their processing sites. Finally, step 3.4 executes the query MRQ'. If there are remaining subqueries, the algorithm goes back to step 3 and performs the next iteration. Otherwise, it terminates.

Optimization occurs in steps 3.1 and 3.2. The algorithm has produced subqueries with several components and their dependency order (similar to the one given by a relational algebra tree). At step 3.1, a simple choice for the next subquery is to take the next one having no predecessor and involving the smaller fragments. This minimizes the size of the intermediate results. For example, if a query q has the subqueries q_1, q_2, and q_3, with dependencies $q_1 \rightarrow q_3, q_2 \rightarrow q_3$, and if the fragments referred to by q_1 are smaller than those referred to by q_2, then q_1 is selected. Depending on the network, this choice can also be affected by the number of sites having relevant fragments.

The subquery selected must then be executed. Since the relation involved in a subquery may be stored at different sites and even fragmented, the subquery may nevertheless be further subdivided.

Example 4.16   Let us consider the following query:

"Names of employees working on the CAD/CAM project"

This query can be expressed in SQL by the following query q_1 on the engineering database:

q_1 :   **SELECT** EMP.ENAME
      FROM   EMP **NATURAL JOIN** ASG **NATURAL JOIN** PROJ
      WHERE PNAME="CAD/CAM"

Assume that relations EMP, ASG, and PROJ are stored as follows, where relation EMP is fragmented.

Site 1	Site 2
EMP_1	EMP_2
ASG	PROJ

There are several possible strategies, including the following:

1. Execute the entire query (EMP ⋈ ASG ⋈ PROJ) by moving EMP_1 and ASG to site 2.
2. Execute (EMP ⋈ ASG) ⋈ PROJ by moving (EMP_1 ⋈ ASG) and ASG to site 2, and so on.

The choice between the possible strategies requires an estimate of the size of the intermediate results. For example, if $size(\text{EMP} \bowtie \text{ASG}) > size(\text{EMP}_1)$, strategy 1 is preferred to strategy 2. Therefore, an estimate of the size of joins is required.   ♦

At step 3.2, the next optimization problem is to determine how to execute the subquery by selecting the fragments that will be moved and the sites where the processing will take place. For an n-relation subquery, fragments from $n-1$ relations must be moved to the site(s) of fragments of the remaining relation, say R_p, and then replicated there. Also, the remaining relation may be further partitioned into k "equalized" fragments in order to increase parallelism. This method is called *fragment-and-replicate* and performs a substitution of fragments rather than of tuples. The selection of the remaining relation and of the number of processing sites k on which it should be partitioned is based on the objective function and the topology of the network. Remember that replication is cheaper in broadcast networks than in point-to-point networks. Furthermore, the choice of the number of processing sites involves a trade-off between response time and total time. A larger number of sites decreases response time (by parallel processing) but increases total time, in particular increasing communication costs.

Formulas to minimize either communication time or processing time use as input the location of fragments, their size, and the network type. They can minimize both costs but with a priority to one. To illustrate these formulas, we give the rules for minimizing communication time. The rule for minimizing response time is even more complex. We use the following assumptions. There are n relations $R_1, R_2, \ldots, R_n$ involved in the query. R_i^j denotes the fragment of R_i stored at site j. There are m sites in the network. Finally, $CT_k(\#bytes)$ denotes the communication time of transferring $\#bytes$ to k sites, with $1 \leq k \leq m$. The rule for minimizing communication time considers the types of networks separately. Let us first concentrate on a broadcast network. In this case we have

$$CT_k(\#bytes) = CT_1(\#bytes)$$

The rule can be stated as

```
if   max_{j=1,m}(∑_{i=1}^{n} size(R_i^j)) > max_{i=1,n}(size(R_i))
then
     the processing site is the j with the
         largest amount of data
else
     R_p is the largest relation and
     site of R_p is the processing site
```

If the inequality predicate is satisfied, one site contains an amount of data useful to the query larger than the size of the largest relation. Therefore, this site should be the processing site. If the predicate is not satisfied, one relation is larger than the maximum useful amount of data at one site. Therefore, this relation should be the R_p, and the processing sites are those which have its fragments.

Let us now consider the case of the point-to-point networks. In this case we have

$$CT_k(\#bytes) = k * CT_1(\#bytes)$$

The choice of R_p that minimizes communication is obviously the largest relation. Assuming that the sites are arranged by decreasing order of amounts of useful data for the query, that is,

$$\sum_{i=1}^{n} size(R_i^j) > \sum_{i=1}^{n} size(R_i^{j+1})$$

the choice of k, the number of sites at which processing needs to be done, is given as

```
if ∑_{i≠p}(size(R_i) − size(R_i^1)) > size(R_p^1)
then
    k = 1
else
    k is the largest j such that ∑_{i≠p}(size(R_i) − size(R_i^j)) ≤ size(R_p^j)
```

This rule chooses a site as the processing site only if the amount of data it must receive is smaller than the additional amount of data it would have to send if it were not a processing site. Obviously, the then-part of the rule assumes that site 1 stores a fragment of R_p.

Example 4.17 Let us consider the query PROJ ⋈ ASG, where PROJ and ASG are fragmented. Assume that the allocation of fragments and their sizes are as follows (in kilobytes):

	Site 1	Site 2	Site 3	Site 4
PROJ	1000	1000	1000	1000
ASG			2000	

With a point-to-point network, the best strategy is to send each PROJ$_i$ to site 3, which requires a transfer of 3000 kbytes, versus 6000 kbytes if ASG is sent to sites 1, 2, and 4. However, with a broadcast network, the best strategy is to send ASG (in a single transfer) to sites 1, 2, and 4, which incurs a transfer of 2000 kbytes. The latter strategy is faster and maximizes response time because the joins can be done in parallel.   ◆

This dynamic query optimization algorithm is characterized by a limited search of the solution space, where an optimization decision is taken for each step without concerning itself with the consequences of that decision on global optimization. However, the algorithm is able to correct a local decision that proves to be incorrect.

4.5.2 Static Approach

We illustrate the static approach with the algorithm of R*, which has been the basis for many distributed query optimizers. This algorithm performs an exhaustive search of all alternative strategies in order to choose the one with the least cost. Although predicting and enumerating these strategies may be costly, the overhead of exhaustive search is rapidly amortized if the query is executed frequently. Query compilation is a distributed task, coordinated by a *master site*, where the query is initiated. The optimizer of the master site makes all intersite decisions, such as the selection of the execution sites and the fragments as well as the method for transferring data. The *apprentice sites*, which are the other sites that have relations involved in the query, make the remaining local decisions (such as the ordering of

---

Algorithm 4.2: Static*-QOA

Input: QT: query tree
Output: $strat$: minimum cost strategy
begin
    for *each relation* $R_i \in QT$ **do**
        for *each access path* AP_{ij} *to* R_i **do**
            compute $cost(AP_{ij})$
        end for
        $best\_AP_i \leftarrow AP_{ij}$ with minimum cost
    end for
    for *each order* $(R_{i1}, R_{i2}, \cdots, R_{in})$ *with* $i = 1, \cdots, n!$ **do**
        build strategy $(\ldots((best\, AP_{i1} \bowtie R_{i2}) \bowtie R_{i3}) \bowtie \ldots \bowtie R_{in})$
        compute the cost of strategy
    end for
    $strat \leftarrow$ strategy with minimum cost
    for *each site k storing a relation involved in* QT **do**
        $LS_k \leftarrow$ local strategy (strategy, k)
        send $(LS_k,$ site $k)$ {each local strategy is optimized at site k}
    end for
end

---

joins at a site) and generate local access plans for the query. The objective function of the optimizer is the general total time function, including local processing and communications costs.

We now summarize this query optimization algorithm. The input to the algorithm is a fragment query expressed as a relational algebra tree (the query tree), the location of relations, and their statistics. The algorithm is described by the procedure Static-QOA in Algorithm 4.2.

The optimizer must select the join ordering, the join algorithm (nested-loop or merge-join), and the access path for each fragment (e.g., clustered index, sequential scan, etc.). These decisions are based on statistics and formulas used to estimate the size of intermediate results and access path information. In addition, the optimizer must select the sites of join results and the method of transferring data between sites. To join two relations, there are three candidate sites: the site of the first relation, the site of the second relation, or a third site (e.g., the site of a third relation to be joined with). Two methods are supported for intersite data transfers.

1. *Ship-whole*. The entire relation is shipped to the join site and stored in a temporary relation before being joined. If the join algorithm is merge-join, the relation does not need to be stored, and the join site can process incoming tuples in a pipeline mode, as they arrive.
2. *Fetch-as-needed*. The external relation is sequentially scanned, and for each tuple the join value is sent to the site of the internal relation, which selects the internal tuples matching the value and sends the selected tuples to the site of the external relation. This method, also called *bindjoin*, is equivalent to the semijoin of the internal relation with each external tuple.

The trade-off between these two methods is obvious. Ship-whole generates a larger data transfer but fewer messages than fetch-as-needed. It is intuitively better to ship-whole relations when they are small. On the contrary, if the relation is large and the join has good selectivity (only a few matching tuples), the relevant tuples should be fetched as needed. The optimizer does not consider all possible combinations of join methods with transfer methods since some of them are not worthwhile. For example, it would be useless to transfer the external relation using fetch-as-needed in the nested loop join algorithm, because all the outer tuples must be processed anyway and therefore should be transferred as a whole.

Given the join of an external relation R with an internal relation S on attribute A, there are four join strategies. In what follows we describe each strategy in detail and provide a simplified cost formula for each, where LT denotes local processing time (I/O + CPU time) and CT denotes communication time. For simplicity, we ignore the cost of producing the result. For convenience, we denote by s the average number of tuples of S that match one tuple of R:

$$s = \frac{card(S \bowtie_A R)}{card(R)}$$

Strategy 1. Ship the entire external relation to the site of the internal relation. In this case the external tuples can be joined with S as they arrive. Thus we have

$$Total\_time = LT(\text{retrieve } card(R) \text{ tuples from R})$$
$$+ CT(size(R))$$
$$+ LT(\text{retrieve } s \text{ tuples from S}) * card(R)$$

Strategy 2. Ship the entire internal relation to the site of the external relation. In this case, the internal tuples cannot be joined as they arrive, and they need to be stored in a temporary relation T. Thus we have

$$Total\_time = LT(\text{retrieve } card(S) \text{ tuples from S})$$
$$+ CT(size(S))$$
$$+ LT(\text{store } card(S) \text{ tuples in T})$$
$$+ LT(\text{retrieve } card(R) \text{ tuples from R})$$
$$+ LT(\text{retrieve } s \text{ tuples from T}) * card(R)$$

Strategy 3. Fetch tuples of the internal relation as needed for each tuple of the external relation. In this case, for each tuple in R, the join attribute (A) value is sent to the site of S. Then the *s* tuples of S which match that value are retrieved and sent to the site of R to be joined as they arrive. Thus we have

$$Total\_time = LT(\text{retrieve } card(\text{R}) \text{ tuples from R})$$
$$+ CT(length(\text{A})) * card(\text{R})$$
$$+ LT(\text{retrieve } s \text{ tuples from S}) * card(\text{R})$$
$$+ CT(s * length(\text{S})) * card(\text{R})$$

Strategy 4. Move both relations to a third site and compute the join there. In this case the internal relation is first moved to a third site and stored in a temporary relation T. Then the external relation is moved to the third site and its tuples are joined with T as they arrive. Thus we have

$$Total\_time = LT(\text{retrieve } card(\text{S}) \text{ tuples from S})$$
$$+ CT(size(\text{S}))$$
$$+ LT(\text{store } card(\text{S}) \text{ tuples in T})$$
$$+ LT(\text{retrieve } card(\text{R}) \text{ tuples from R})$$
$$+ CT(size(\text{R}))$$
$$+ LT(\text{retrieve } s \text{ tuples from T}) * card(\text{R})$$

Example 4.18 Let us consider a query that consists of the join of relations PROJ, the external relation, and ASG, the internal relation, on attribute PNO. We assume that PROJ and ASG are stored at two different sites and that there is an index on attribute PNO for relation ASG. The possible execution strategies for the query are as follows:

1. Ship-whole PROJ to site of ASG.
2. Ship-whole ASG to site of PROJ.
3. Fetch ASG tuples as needed for each tuple of PROJ.
4. Move ASG and PROJ to a third site.

The optimization algorithm predicts the total time of each strategy and selects the cheapest. Given that there is no operator following the join PROJ ⋈ ASG, strategy 4 obviously incurs the highest cost since both relations must be transferred. If $size(\text{PROJ})$ is much larger than $size(\text{ASG})$, strategy 2 minimizes the communication time and is likely to be the best if local processing time is not too high compared to strategies 1 and 3. Note that the local processing time of strategies 1 and 3 is probably much better than that of strategy 2 since they exploit the index on the join attribute.

If strategy 2 is not the best, the choice is between strategies 1 and 3. Local processing costs in both of these alternatives are identical. If PROJ is large and only a few tuples of ASG match, strategy 3 probably incurs the least communication time and is the best. Otherwise, that is, if PROJ is small or many tuples of ASG match, strategy 1 should be the best.   ♦

Conceptually, the algorithm can be viewed as an exhaustive search among all alternatives that are defined by the permutation of the relation join order, join methods (including the selection of the join algorithm), result site, access path to the internal relation, and intersite transfer mode. Such an algorithm has a combinatorial complexity in the number of relations involved. Actually, the algorithm significantly reduces the number of alternatives by using dynamic programming and the heuristics. With dynamic programming, the tree of alternatives is dynamically constructed and pruned by eliminating the inefficient choices.

Performance evaluation of the algorithm in the context of both high-speed networks (similar to local networks) and medium-speed wide area networks confirms the significant contribution of local processing costs, even for wide area networks. It is shown in particular that for the distributed join, transferring the entire internal relation outperforms the fetch-as-needed method.

4.5.3   Hybrid Approach

Dynamic and static query optimization both have advantages and drawbacks. Dynamic query optimization mixes optimization and execution and thus can make accurate optimization choices at runtime. However, query optimization is repeated for each execution of the query. Therefore, this approach is best for ad hoc queries. Static query optimization, done at compilation time, amortizes the cost of optimization over multiple query executions. The accuracy of the cost model is thus critical to predict the costs of candidate QEPs. This approach is best for queries embedded in stored procedures, and has been adopted by all commercial DBMSs.

However, even with a sophisticated cost model, there is an important problem that prevents accurate cost estimation and comparison of QEPs at compile time. The problem is that the actual bindings of parameter values in embedded queries are not known until runtime. Consider, for instance, the selection predicate WHERE R.A=$a, where $a is a parameter value. To estimate the cardinality of this selection, the optimizer must rely on the assumption of uniform distribution of A values in R and cannot make use of histograms. Since there is a runtime binding of the parameter a, the accurate selectivity of $\sigma_{A=\$a}(R)$ cannot be estimated until runtime. Thus, it can make major estimation errors that can lead to the choice of suboptimal QEPs. In addition to unknown bindings of parameter values in embedded queries, sites may become unavailable or overloaded at runtime. Furthermore, relations (or relation fragments) may be replicated at several sites. Thus, site and copy selection should be done at runtime to increase availability and load balancing of the system.

Hybrid query optimization attempts to provide the advantages of static query optimization while avoiding the issues generated by inaccurate estimates. The approach is basically static, but further optimization decisions may take place at runtime. A general solution is to produce *dynamic QEPs* which include carefully selected optimization decisions to be made at runtime using "choose-plan" operators. The choose-plan operator links two or more equivalent subplans of a QEP that are incomparable at compile time because important runtime information (e.g., parameter bindings) is missing to estimate costs. The execution of a choose-plan operator yields the comparison of the subplans based on actual costs and the selection of the best one. Choose-plan nodes can be inserted anywhere in a QEP. This approach is general enough to incorporate site and copy selection decisions. However, the search space of alternative subplans linked by choose-plan operators becomes much larger and may result in heavy static plans and much higher startup time. Therefore, several hybrid techniques have been proposed to optimize queries in distributed systems. They essentially rely on the following two-step approach:

1. At compile time, generate a static plan that specifies the ordering of operators and the access methods, without considering where relations are stored.
2. At startup time, generate an execution plan by carrying out site and copy selection and allocating the operators to the sites.

Example 4.19 Consider the following query expressed in relational algebra:

$$\sigma(R_1) \bowtie R_2 \bowtie R_3$$

Figure 4.15 shows a two-step plan for this query. The static plan shows the relational operator ordering as produced by a centralized query optimizer. The runtime plan extends the static plan with site and copy selection and communication between sites. For instance, the first selection is allocated at site S_1 on copy R_{11} of relation R_1 and sends its result to site S_3 to be joined with R_{23} and so on.   ◆

The first step can be done by a centralized query optimizer. It may also include choose-plan operators so that runtime bindings can be used at startup time to make accurate cost estimations. The second step carries out site and copy selection, possibly in addition to choose-plan operator execution. Furthermore, it can optimize the load balancing of the system. In the rest of this section, we illustrate this second step.

We consider a distributed database system with a set of sites $S = \{S_1, .., S_n\}$. A query Q is represented as an ordered sequence of subqueries $Q = \{q_1, .., q_m\}$. Each subquery q_i is the maximum processing unit that accesses a single base relation and communicates with its neighboring subqueries. For instance, in Fig. 4.15, there are three subqueries, one for R_1, one for R_2, and one for R_3. Each site S_i has a load, denoted by $load(S_i)$, which reflects the number of queries currently submitted. The load can be expressed in different ways, e.g., as the number of I/O bound and CPU bound queries at the site. The average load of the system is defined as:

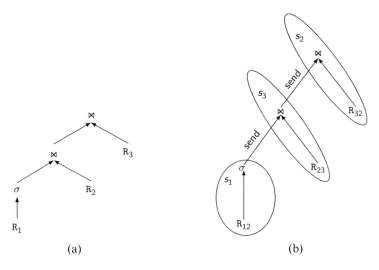

Fig. 4.15 A two-step plan. (**a**) Static plan. (**b**) Runtime plan

$$Avg\_load(S) = \frac{\sum_{i=1}^{n} load(S_i)}{n}$$

The balance of the system for a given allocation of subqueries to sites can be measured as the variance of the site loads using the following *unbalance factor*:

$$UF(S) = \frac{1}{n} \sum_{i=1}^{n} (load(S_i) - Avg\_load(S))^2$$

As the system gets balanced, its unbalance factor approaches 0 (perfect balance). For example, with $load(S_1) = 10$ and $load(S_1) = 30$, the unbalance factor of S_1, S_2 is 100 while with $load(S_1) = 20$ and $load(S_2) = 20$, it is 0.

The problem addressed by the second step of two-step query optimization can be formalized as the following subquery allocation problem. Given

1. a set of sites $S = \{S_1, .., S_n\}$ with the load of each site;
2. a query $Q = \{q_1, .., q_m\}$; and
3. for each subquery q_i in Q, a feasible allocation set of sites $S_q = \{S_1, \ldots, S_k\}$ where each site stores a copy of the relation involved in q_i;

the objective is to find an optimal allocation on Q to S such that

1. $UF(S)$ is minimized, and
2. the total communication cost is minimized.

There is an algorithm that finds near-optimal solutions in a reasonable amount
of time. The algorithm, which we describe in Algorithm 4.3 for linear join trees,
uses several heuristics. The first heuristic (step 1) is to start by allocating subqueries
with least allocation flexibility, i.e., with the smaller feasible allocation sets of sites.
Thus, subqueries with a few candidate sites are allocated earlier. Another heuristic
(step 2) is to consider the sites with least load and best benefit. The benefit of a site
is defined as the number of subqueries already allocated to the site and measures
the communication cost savings from allocating the subquery to the site. Finally, in
step 3 of the algorithm, the load information of any unallocated subquery that has a
selected site in its feasible allocation set is recomputed.

Example 4.20 Consider the following query Q expressed in relational algebra:

$$\sigma(R_1) \bowtie R_2 \bowtie R_3 \bowtie R_4$$

Figure 4.16 shows the placement of the copies of the 4 relations at the 4 sites,
and the site loads. We assume that Q is decomposed as $Q = \{q_1, q_2, q_3, q_4\}$, where
q_1 is associated with R_1, q_2 with R_2 joined with the result of q_1, q_3 with R_3 joined
with the result of q_2, and q_4 with R_4 joined with the result of q_3. The SQAllocation

---

Algorithm 4.3: SQAllocation

Input: Q: $q_1, \ldots, q_m$
    Feasible allocation sets: $F_{q_1}, \ldots, F_{q_m}$
    Loads: $load(F_1), \ldots, load(F_m)$
Output: an allocation of Q to S
begin
    for *each q in Q* **do**
    | compute($load(F_q)$)
    end for
    while *Q not empty* **do**
        {select subquery a for allocation}
        $a \leftarrow q \in Q$ with least allocation flexibility   (1)
        {select best site b for a}
        $b \leftarrow f \in F_a$ with least load and best benefit   (2)
        $Q \leftarrow Q - a$
        {recompute loads of remaining feasible allocation sets if necessary}   (3)
        for *each $q \in Q$ where $b \in F_q$* **do**
        | compute($load(F_q)$)
        end for
    end while
end

Sites	Load	R_1	R_2	R_3	R_4
s_1	1	R_{11}		R_{31}	R_{41}
s_2	2		R_{22}		
s_3	2	R_{13}		R_{33}	
s_4	2	R_{14}	R_{24}		

Fig. 4.16 Example data placement and load

algorithm performs 4 iterations. In the first one, it selects q_4 which has the least allocation flexibility, allocates it to S_1, and updates the load of S_1 to 2. In the second iteration, the next subqueries to be selected are either q_2 or q_3 since they have the same allocation flexibility. Let us choose q_2 and assume it gets allocated to S_2 (it could be allocated to S_4 which has the same load as S_2). The load of S_2 is increased to 3. In the third iteration, the next subquery selected is q_3 and it is allocated to S_1 which has the same load as S_3 but a benefit of 1 (versus 0 for S_3) as a result of the allocation of q_4. The load of S_1 is increased to 3. Finally, in the last iteration, q_1 gets allocated to either S_3 or S_4 which have the least loads. If in the second iteration q_2 was allocated to S_4 instead of to S_2, then the fourth iteration would have allocated q_1 to S_4 because of a benefit of 1. This would have produced a better execution plan with less communication. This illustrates that two-step optimization can still miss optimal plans.   ♦

This algorithm has reasonable complexity. It considers each subquery in turn, considering each potential site, selects a current one for allocation, and sorts the list of remaining subqueries. Thus, its complexity can be expressed as $\mathcal{O}(max(m * n, m^2 * log_2 m))$.

Finally, the algorithm includes a refining phase to further optimize join processing and decide whether or not to use semijoins. Although it minimizes communication given a static plan, two-step query optimization may generate runtime plans that have higher communication cost than the optimal plan. This is because the first step is carried out ignoring data location and its impact on communication cost. For instance, consider the runtime plan in Fig. 4.15 and assume that the third subquery on R_3 is allocated to site S_1 (instead of site S_2). In this case, the plan that does the join (or Cartesian product) of the result of the selection of R_1 with R_3 first at site S_1 may be better since it minimizes communication. A solution to this problem is to perform plan reorganization using operator tree transformations at startup time.

4.6 Adaptive Query Processing

The underlying assumption so far is that the distributed query processor has sufficient knowledge about query runtime conditions in order to produce an efficient QEP and the runtime conditions remain stable during execution. This is a fair assumption for queries with few database relations running in a controlled environment. However, this assumption is inappropriate for changing environments with large numbers of relations and unpredictable runtime conditions.

Example 4.21 Consider the QEP in Fig. 4.17 with relations EMP, ASG, PROJ, and PAY at sites S_1, S_2, S_3, S_4, respectively. The crossed arrow indicates that, for some reason (e.g., failure), site S_2 (where ASG is stored) is not available at the beginning of execution. Let us assume, for simplicity, that the query is to be executed according to the iterator execution model, such that tuples flow from the left most relation.

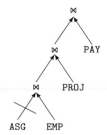

Fig. 4.17 Query execution plan with a blocked relation

Because of the unavailability of S_2, the entire pipeline is blocked, waiting for
ASG tuples to be produced. However, with some reorganization of the plan, some
other operators could be evaluated while waiting for S_2, for instance, to evaluate the
join of EMP and PAY.   ♦

This simple example illustrates that a typical static plan cannot cope with
unpredictable data source unavailability. More complex examples involve continuous queries, expensive predicates, and data skew. The main solution is to have
some adaptive behavior during query processing, i.e., *adaptive query processing*.
Adaptive query processing is a form of dynamic query processing, with a feedback
loop between the execution environment and the query optimizer in order to react to
unforeseen variations of runtime conditions. A query processing system is defined as
adaptive if it receives information from the execution environment and determines
its behavior according to that information in an iterative manner.

In this section, we first provide a general presentation of the adaptive query
processing process. Then, we present the eddy approach that provides a powerful
framework for adaptive query processing.

4.6.1   Adaptive Query Processing Process

Adaptive query processing adds to the traditional query processing process the following activities: monitoring, assessing, and reacting. These activities are logically
implemented in the query processing system by sensors, assessment components,
and reaction components, respectively. Monitoring involves measuring some environment parameters within a time window, and reporting them to the assessment
component. The latter analyzes the reports and considers thresholds to arrive at an
adaptive reaction plan. Finally, the reaction plan is communicated to the reaction
component that applies the reactions to query execution.

Typically, an adaptive process specifies the frequency with which each component will be executed. There is a trade-off between reactiveness, in which
higher values lead to eager reactions, and the overhead caused by the adaptive
process. A generic representation of the adaptive process is given by the function

$f_{adapt}(E, T) \rightarrow Ad$, where E is a set of monitored environment parameters, T is a set of threshold values, and Ad is a possibly empty set of adaptive reactions. The elements of E, T, and Ad, called adaptive elements, obviously may vary in a number of ways depending on the application. The most important elements are the monitoring parameters and the adaptive reactions. We now describe them.

4.6.1.1 Monitoring Parameters

Monitoring query runtime parameters involves placing sensors at key places of the QEP and defining observation windows, during which sensors collect information. It also requires the specification of a communication mechanism to pass collected information to the assessment component. Examples of candidates for monitoring are:

- Memory size. Monitoring available memory size allows, for instance, operators to react to memory shortage or memory increase.
- Data arrival rates. Monitoring the variation on data arrival rates may enable the query processor to do useful work while waiting for a blocked data source.
- Actual statistics. Database statistics in a distributed environment tend to be inaccurate, if at all available. Monitoring the actual size of relations and intermediate results may lead to important modifications in the QEP. Furthermore, the usual data assumptions, in which the selectivity of predicates over attributes in a relation is mutually independent, can be abandoned and real selectivity values can be computed.
- Operator execution cost. Monitoring the actual cost of operator execution, including production rates, is useful for better operator scheduling. Furthermore, monitoring the size of the queues placed before operators may avoid overloading.
- Network throughput. Monitoring network throughput may be helpful to define the block size to retrieve data. In a lower throughput network, the system may react with larger block sizes to reduce network penalty.

4.6.1.2 Adaptive Reactions

Adaptive reactions modify query execution behavior according to the decisions taken by the assessment component. Important adaptive reactions are:

- Change schedule: modifies the order in which operators in the QEP get scheduled. *Query scrambling* reacts by a *change schedule* of the plan to avoid stalling on a blocked data source during query evaluation. Eddy adopts finer reaction where operator scheduling can be decided on a tuple basis.
- Operator replacement: replaces a physical operator by an equivalent one. For example, depending on the available memory, the system may choose between a nested loop join or a hash join. Operator replacement may also change the plan by introducing a new operator to join the intermediate results produced by

a previous adaptive reaction. Query scrambling, for instance, may introduce new operators to evaluate joins between the results of *change schedule* reactions.

- Data refragmentation: considers the dynamic fragmentation of a relation. Static partitioning of a relation tends to produce load imbalance between sites. For example, information partitioned according to their associated geographical region may exhibit different access rates during the day because of the time differences in users' locations.
- Plan reformulation: computes a new QEP to replace an inefficient one. The optimizer considers actual statistics and state information, collected on the fly, to produce a new plan.

4.6.2   Eddy Approach

Eddy is a general framework for adaptive query processing over distributed relations. For simplicity, we only consider select-project-join (SPJ) queries. Select operators can include expensive predicates. The process of generating a QEP from an input SPJ query begins by producing an operator tree of the join graph G of the input query. The choice among join algorithms and relation access methods favors adaptiveness. A QEP can be modeled as a tuple $Q = \langle D, P, C \rangle$, where D is a set of database relations, P is a set of query predicates with associated algorithms, and C is a set of ordering constraints that must be followed during execution. Observe that multiple valid operator trees can be derived from G that obey the constraints in C, by exploring the search space with different predicate orders. There is no need to find an optimal QEP during query compilation. Instead, operator ordering is done on the fly on a tuple-per-tuple basis (i.e., tuple routing). The process of QEP compilation is completed by adding the *eddy operator* which is an n-ary operator placed between the relations in D and query predicates in P.

Example 4.22 Consider a three-relation query $Q = (\sigma_p(\text{R}) \bowtie \text{S} \bowtie \text{T})$, where joins are equijoins. Assume that the only access method to relation T is through an index on join attribute T.A, i.e., the second join can only be an index join over T.A. Assume also that σ_p is an expensive predicate (e.g., a predicate over the results of running a program over values of T.B). Under these assumptions, the QEP is defined as $D = \{\text{R}, \text{S}, \text{T}\}$, $P = \{\sigma_p(\text{R}), \text{R} \bowtie \text{S}, \text{S} \bowtie \text{T}\}$, and $C = \{\text{S} \prec \text{T}\}$. The constraint $\prec$ imposes S tuples to probe T tuples, based on the index on T.A.

Figure 4.18 shows a QEP produced by the compilation of query Q with eddy. An ellipse corresponds to a physical operator (i.e., either eddy operator or an algorithm implementing a predicate $p \in P$). As usual, the bottom of the plan presents the source relations. In the absence of a scan access method, the access to relation T is wrapped by the join S $\bowtie$ T, thus does not appear as a source relation. The arrows specify pipeline dataflow following a producer–consumer relationship. Finally, an arrow departing from the eddy models the production of output tuples.   ◆

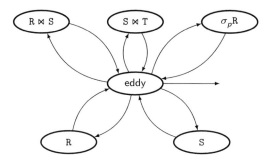

Fig. 4.18 A query execution plan with eddy

Eddy provides fine-grained adaptiveness by deciding on the fly how to route tuples through predicates according to a scheduling policy. During query execution, tuples in source relations are retrieved and staged into an input buffer managed by the eddy operator. Eddy responds to relation unavailability by simply reading from another relation and staging tuples in the buffer pool.

The flexibility of choosing the currently available source relation is obtained by relaxing the fixed order of predicates in a QEP. In eddy, there is no fixed QEP and each tuple follows its own path through predicates according to the constraints in the plan and its own history of predicate evaluation.

The tuple-based routing strategy produces a new QEP topology. The eddy operator together with its managed predicates forms a circular dataflow in which tuples leave the eddy operator to be evaluated by the predicates, which in turn bounce back output tuples to the eddy operator. A tuple leaves the circular dataflow either when it is eliminated by a predicate evaluation or the eddy operator realizes that the tuple has passed through all the predicates in its list. The lack of a fixed QEP requires each tuple to register the set of predicates it is eligible for. For example, in Fig. 4.18, S tuples are eligible for the two join predicates but are not eligible for predicate $\sigma_p(\text{R})$.

4.7 Conclusion

In this chapter, we provided a detailed presentation of query processing in distributed DBMSs. We first introduced the problem of distributed query processing. The main assumption is that the input query is expressed in relational calculus since that is the case with most current distributed DBMS. The complexity of the problem is proportional to the expressive power and the abstraction capability of the query language.

The query processing problem is very difficult to understand in distributed environments because many elements are involved. However, the problem may be divided into several subproblems which are easier to solve individually. Therefore, we have proposed a generic layering scheme for describing distributed query processing. Four main functions have been isolated: query decomposition, data localization, distributed optimization, and distributed execution. These functions successively refine the query by adding more details about the processing environment.

Then, we described data localization, with emphasis on reduction and simplification techniques for the four following types of fragmentation: horizontal, vertical, derived, and hybrid. The query produced by the data localization layer is good in the sense that the worse executions are avoided. However, the subsequent layers usually perform important optimizations, as they add to the query increasing detail about the processing environment.

Next, we discussed the major optimization issue, which deals with the join ordering in distributed queries, including alternative join strategies based on semijoin, and the definition of a distributed cost model.

We illustrated the use of the join and semijoin techniques in three basic distributed query optimization algorithms: dynamic, static, and hybrid. The static and dynamic distributed optimization approaches have the same advantages and disadvantages as in centralized systems. The hybrid approach is best in today's dynamic environments as it delays important decisions such as copy selection and allocation of subqueries to sites at query startup time. Thus, it can better increase availability and load balancing of the system. We illustrated the hybrid approach with two-step query optimization which first generates a static plan that specifies the operators ordering as in a centralized system and then generates an execution plan at startup time, by carrying out site and copy selection and allocating the operators to the sites.

Finally, we discussed adaptive query processing, to deal with the dynamic behavior of the local DBMSs. Adaptive query processing addresses this problem with a dynamic approach whereby the query optimizer communicates at runtime with the execution environment in order to react to unforeseen variations of runtime conditions.

4.8   Bibliographic Notes

There are several survey papers on query processing and query optimization in the context of the relational model. Graefe [1993] provides a detailed survey.

The iterator execution model which has been the basis for many query processor implementation was proposed in the context of the Volcano extensible query evaluation system [Graefe 1994]. The seminal paper on cost-based query optimization [Selinger et al. 1979] was the first to propose a cost model with database statistics (see Sect. 4.4.2) and the use of a dynamic programming search strategy (see Sect. 4.1.1). Randomized strategies, such as Iterative Improvement [Swami 1989] and Simulated Annealing [Ioannidis and Wong 1987] have been proposed to achieve a good trade-off between optimization time and execution time.

The most complete survey on distributed query processing is by Kossmann [2000] and deals with both distributed DBMSs and multidatabase systems. The paper presents the traditional phases of query processing in centralized and distributed systems, and describes the various techniques for distributed query processing. Distributed cost models are discussed in several papers such as [Lohman et al., Khoshafian and Valduriez 1987].

Data localization is treated in detail by Ceri and Pelagatti [1983] for horizontally partitioned relations which are referred to as multirelations. The formal properties of horizontal and vertical fragmentation are used by Ceri et al. [1986] to characterize distributed joins over fragmented relations.

The theory of semijoins and their value for distributed query processing has been covered in [Bernstein and Chiu 1981], [Chiu and Ho 1980], and [Kambayashi et al. 1982]. The semijoin-based approach to distributed query optimization was proposed by Bernstein et al. [1981] for SDD-1 system [Wong 1977]. Full reducer semijoin programs are investigated by Chiu and Ho [1980], Kambayashi et al. [1982]. The problem of finding full reducers is NP-hard. However, for chained queries, a polynomial algorithm exists [Chiu and Ho 1980, Ullman 1982]. The cost of semijoins can be minimized by using bit arrays [Valduriez 1982]. Some other query processing algorithms aim at selecting an optimal combination of joins and semijoins [Özsoyoglu and Zhou 1987, Wah and Lien 1985].

The dynamic approach to distributed query optimization was first proposed for Distributed INGRES [Epstein et al. 1978]. The algorithm takes advantage of the network topology (general or broadcast networks) and uses the reduction algorithm [Wong and Youssefi 1976] that isolates all irreducible subqueries and monorelation subqueries by detachment.

The static approach to distributed query optimization was first proposed for R* [Selinger and Adiba 1980]. It is one of the first papers to recognize the significance of local processing on the performance of distributed queries. Experimental validation by Lohman et al. and Mackert and Lohman [1986a,b] have confirmed this important statement. The method fetch-as-needed of R* is called bindjoin in [Haas et al. 1997a].

A general hybrid approach to query optimization is to use choose-plan operators [Cole and Graefe 1994]. Several hybrid approaches based on two-step query optimization have been proposed for distributed systems [Carey and Lu 1986, Du et al. 1995, Evrendilek et al. 1997]. The content of Sect. 4.5.3 is based on the seminal paper on two-step query optimization by Carey and Lu [1986]. Du et al. [1995] propose efficient operators to transform linear join trees (produced by the first step) into bushy trees which exhibit more parallelism. Evrendilek et al. [1997] propose a solution to maximize intersite join parallelism in the second step.

Adaptive query processing is surveyed in [Hellerstein et al. 2000, Gounaris et al. 2002]. The seminal paper on the eddy approach which we used to illustrate adaptive query processing in Sect. 4.6 is [Avnur and Hellerstein 2000]. Other important techniques for adaptive query processing are query scrambling [Amsaleg et al. 1996, Urhan et al. 1998], ripple joins [Haas and Hellerstein 1999b], adaptive partitioning [Shah et al. 2003], and cherry picking [Porto et al. 2003]. Major extensions to eddy are state modules [Raman et al. 2003] and distributed eddies [Tian and DeWitt 2003].

Exercises

Problem 4.1 Assume that relation PROJ of the sample database is horizontally fragmented as follows:

$$PROJ_1 = \sigma_{PNO \leq "P2"}(PROJ)$$

$$PROJ_2 = \sigma_{PNO > "P2"}(PROJ)$$

Transform the following query into a reduced query on fragments:

```
SELECT ENO, PNAME
FROM    PROJ NATURAL JOIN ASG
WHERE   PNO = "P4"
```

Problem 4.2 (*) Assume that relation PROJ is horizontally fragmented as in Problem 4.1, and that relation ASG is horizontally fragmented as

$$ASG_1 = \sigma_{PNO \leq "P2"}(ASG)$$

$$ASG_2 = \sigma_{"P2" < PNO \leq "P3"}(ASG)$$

$$ASG_3 = \sigma_{PNO > "P3"}(ASG)$$

Transform the following query into a reduced query on fragments, and determine whether it is better than the fragment query:

```
SELECT RESP, BUDGET
FROM    ASG NATURAL JOIN PROJ
WHERE   PNAME = "CAD/CAM"
```

Problem 4.3 (**) Assume that relation PROJ is fragmented as in Problem 4.1. Furthermore, relation ASG is indirectly fragmented as

$$ASG_1 = ASG \ltimes_{PNO} PROJ_1$$

$$ASG_2 = ASG \ltimes_{PNO} PROJ_2$$

and relation EMP is vertically fragmented as

$$EMP_1 = \Pi_{ENO, ENAME}(EMP)$$

$$EMP_2 = \Pi_{ENO, TITLE}(EMP)$$

vnine
Transform the following query into a reduced query on fragments:

```
SELECT ENAME
FROM    EMP NATURAL JOIN ASG NATURAL JOIN PROJ
WHERE   PNAME = "Instrumentation"
```

Problem 4.4 Consider the join graph of Fig. 4.11 and the following information: $size(\text{EMP}) = 100$, $size(\text{ASG}) = 200$, $size(\text{PROJ}) = 300$, $size(\text{EMP} \bowtie \text{ASG}) = 300$, and $size(\text{ASG} \bowtie \text{PROJ}) = 200$. Describe an optimal join program based on the objective function of total transmission time.

Problem 4.5 Consider the join graph of Fig. 4.11 and make the same assumptions as in Problem 4.4. Describe an optimal join program that minimizes response time (consider only communication).

Problem 4.6 Consider the join graph of Fig. 4.11, and give a program (possibly not optimal) that reduces each relation fully by semijoins.

Problem 4.7 (*) Consider the join graph of Fig. 4.11 and the fragmentation depicted in Fig. 4.19. Also assume that $size(\text{EMP} \bowtie \text{ASG}) = 2000$ and $size(\text{ASG} \bowtie \text{PROJ}) = 1000$. Apply the dynamic distributed query optimization algorithm in Sect. 4.5.1 in two cases, general network and broadcast network, so that communication time is minimized.

Problem 4.8 (**) Consider the following query on our engineering database:

```
SELECT  ENAME,SAL
FROM    PAY NATURAL JOIN EMP NATURAL JOIN ASG
        NATURAL JOIN PROJ
WHERE   (BUDGET>200000 OR DUR>24)
AND     (DUR>24 OR PNAME = "CAD/CAM")
```

Assume that relations EMP, ASG, PROJ, and PAY have been stored at sites 1, 2, and 3 according to the table in Fig. 4.20. Assume also that the transfer rate between any two sites is equal and that data transfer is 100 times slower than data processing performed by any site. Finally, assume that $size(\text{R} \bowtie \text{S}) = max(size(\text{R}), size(\text{S}))$ for any two relations R and ₮ and the selectivity factor of the disjunctive selection of the query is 0.5. Compose a distributed program that computes the answer to the query and minimizes total time.

Relation	Site 1	Site 2	Site 3
EMP	1000	1000	1000
ASG		2000	
PROJ	1000		

Fig. 4.19 Fragmentation

Relation	Site 1	Site 2	Site 3
EMP	2000		
ASG		3000	
PROJ			1000
PAY			500

Fig. 4.20 Fragmentation statistics

Problem 4.9 (**) In Sect. 4.5.3, we described Algorithm 4.3 for linear join trees. Extend this algorithm to support bushy join trees. Apply it to the bushy join tree in Fig. 4.9 using the data placement and site loads shown in Fig. 4.16.

Problem 4.10 (**) Consider three relations $R(A,B)$, $S(B,D)$ and $T(D,E)$, and query $Q(\sigma_p^1(R) \bowtie_1 S \bowtie_2 T)$, where $\bowtie_1$ and $\bowtie_2$ are natural joins. Assume that S has an index on attribute B and T has an index on attribute D. Furthermore, σ_p^1 is an expensive predicate (i.e., a predicate over the results of running a program over values of $R.A$). Using the eddy approach for adaptive query processing, answer the following questions:

(a) Propose the set C of constraints on Q to produce an eddy-based QEP.
(b) Give a join graph G for Q.
(c) Using C and G, propose an eddy-based QEP.
(d) Propose a second QEP that uses State Modules. Discuss the advantages obtained by using state modules in this QEP.

Problem 4.11 (**) Propose a data structure to store tuples in the eddy buffer pool to help choosing quickly the next tuple to be evaluated according to user-specified preference, for instance, produce first results earlier.

Chapter 5
Distributed Transaction Processing

The concept of a *transaction* is used in database systems as a basic unit of consistent and reliable computing. Thus, queries are executed as transactions once their execution strategies are determined and they are translated into primitive database operations. Transactions ensure that database consistency and durability are maintained when concurrent access occurs to the same data item (with at least one of these being an update) and when failures occur.

The terms *consistent* and *reliable* in transaction definition need to be defined more precisely. We differentiate between *database consistency* and *transaction consistency*.

A database is in a *consistent state* if it obeys all of the consistency (integrity) constraints defined over it (see Chap. 3). State changes occur due to modifications, insertions, and deletions (together called *updates*). Of course, we want to ensure that the database never enters an inconsistent state. Note that the database can be (and usually is) temporarily inconsistent during the execution of a transaction. The important point is that the database should be consistent when the transaction terminates (Fig. 5.1).

Transaction consistency, on the other hand, refers to the operations of concurrent transactions. We would like the database to remain in a consistent state even if there are a number of user requests that are concurrently accessing (reading or updating) the database.

Reliability refers to both the *resiliency* of a system to various types of failures and its capability to *recover* from them. A resilient system is tolerant of system failures and can continue to provide services even when failures occur. A recoverable DBMS is one that can get to a consistent state (by moving back to a previous consistent state or forward to a new consistent state) following various types of failures.

Transaction management deals with the problems of always keeping the database in a consistent state even when concurrent accesses and failures occur. The issues in

---

The original version of this chapter was revised. The correction to this chapter is available at https://doi.org/10.1007/978-3-030-26253-2_13

© Springer Nature Switzerland AG 2020
M. T. Özsu, P. Valduriez, *Principles of Distributed Database Systems*,
https://doi.org/10.1007/978-3-030-26253-2_5

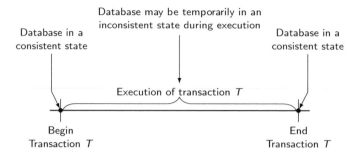

Fig. 5.1 A transaction model

managing concurrent transactions are well-known in centralized DBMSs and can be found in many textbooks. In this chapter, we investigate these issues within the context of distributed DBMSs focusing on distributed concurrency control and distributed reliability and recovery. We expect that the reader has familiarity with the basic transaction management concepts and techniques as commonly covered in undergraduate database courses and books. We provide a brief refresher in Sect. 5.1. More detailed discussion of the fundamental transaction processing concepts is in Appendix C. For now, we ignore data replication issues; the following chapter is devoted to that topic. DBMSs are typically classified as On-Line Transaction Processing (OLTP) or On-Line Analytical Processing (OLAP). *On-Line Transaction Processing* applications, such as airline reservation or banking systems, are high-throughput transaction-oriented. They need extensive data control and availability, high multiuser throughput and predictable, fast response times. In contrast, *On-line Analytical Processing* applications, such as trend analysis or forecasting, need to analyze historical, summarized data coming from a number of operational databases. They use complex queries over potentially very large tables. Most OLAP applications do not need the most current versions of the data, and thus do not need direct access to most up-to-date operational data. In this chapter, we focus on OLTP systems and consider OLAP systems in Chap. 7.

The organization of this chapter is as follows. In Sect. 5.1 we provide a quick introduction to the basic terminology that is used in this chapter, and revisit the architectural model defined in Chap. 1 to highlight the modifications that are necessary to support transaction management. Section 5.2 provides an in-depth treatment of serializability-based distributed concurrency control techniques, while Sect. 5.3 considers concurrency control under snapshot isolation. Section 5.4 discusses distributed reliability techniques focusing on distributed commit, termination, and recovery protocols.

5.1 Background and Terminology

Our objective in this section is to provide a very brief introduction to the concepts and terminology that we use in the rest of the chapter. As mentioned previously, our objective is not to provide a deep overview of the fundamental concepts—those can be found in Appendix C—but to introduce the basic terminology that will be helpful in the rest of the chapter. We also discuss how the system architecture needs to be revised to accommodate transactions.

As indicated before, a transaction is a unit of consistent and reliable computation. Each transaction begins with a Begin_transaction command, includes a series of Read and Write operations, and ends with either a Commit or an Abort. Commit, when processed, ensures that the updates that the transaction has made to the database are permanent from that point on, while Abort undoes the transaction's actions so, as far as the database is concerned, it is as if the transaction has never been executed. Each transaction is characterized by its *read set* (*RS*) that includes the data items that it reads, and its *write set* (*WS*) of the data items that it writes. The read set and write set of a transaction need not be mutually exclusive. The union of the read set and write set of a transaction constitutes its *base set* ($BS = RS \cup WS$).

Typical DBMS transaction services provide ACID properties:

1. *Atomicity* ensures that transaction executions are atomic, i.e., either all of the actions of a transaction are reflected in the database or none of it are.
2. *Consistency* refers to a transaction being a correct execution (i.e., the transaction code is correct and when it executes on a database that is consistent, it will leave it in a consistent state).
3. *Isolation* indicates that the effects of concurrent transactions are shielded from each other until they commit—this is how the correctness of concurrently executing transactions are ensured (i.e., executing transactions concurrently does not break database consistency).
4. *Durability* refers to that property of transactions that ensures that the effects of committed transactions on the database are permanent and will survive system crashes.

Concurrency control algorithms that we discuss in Sect. 5.2 enforce the isolation property so that concurrent transactions see a consistent database state and leave the database in a consistent state, while reliability measures we discuss in Sect. 5.4 enforce atomicity and durability. Consistency in terms of ensuring that a given transaction does not do anything incorrect to the database is typically handled by integrity enforcement as discussed in Chap. 3.

Concurrency control algorithms implement a notion of "correct concurrent execution." The most common correctness notion is *serializability* that requires that the history generated by the concurrent execution of transactions is equivalent to some serial history (i.e., a sequential execution of these transactions). Given that a transaction maps one consistent database state to another consistent database state, any serial execution order is, by definition, correct; if the concurrent execution history is equivalent to one of these orders, it must also be correct. In Sect. 5.3, we introduce a more relaxed correctness notion called *snapshot isolation* (SI). Concurrency control algorithms are basically concerned with enforcing different levels of isolation among concurrent transactions very efficiently.

When a transaction commits, its actions need to be made permanent. This requires management of *transaction logs* where each action of a transaction is recorded. The commit protocols ensure that database updates as well as logs are saved into persistent storage so that they are made permanent. Abort protocols, on the other hand, use the logs to erase all actions of the aborted transaction from the database. When recovery from system crashes is needed, the logs are consulted to bring the database to a consistent state.

The introduction of transactions to the DBMS workload along with read-only queries requires revisiting the architectural model introduced in Chap. 1. The revision is an expansion of the role of the distributed execution monitor.

The distributed execution monitor consists of two modules: a *transaction manager* (TM) and a *scheduler* (SC). The transaction manager is responsible for coordinating the execution of the database operations on behalf of an application. The scheduler, on the other hand, is responsible for the implementation of a specific concurrency control algorithm for synchronizing access to the database.

A third component that participates in the management of distributed transactions is the local recovery managers (LRM) that exist at each site. Their function is to implement the local procedures by which the local database can be recovered to a consistent state following a failure.

Each transaction originates at one site, which we will call its *originating site*. The execution of the database operations of a transaction is coordinated by the TM at that transaction's originating site. We refer to the TM at the originating site as the *coordinator* or the *coordinating TM*.

A transaction manager implements an interface for the application programs to the transaction commands identified earlier: Begin_transaction, Read, Write, Commit, and Abort. The processing of each of these commands in a nonreplicated distributed DBMS is discussed below at an abstract level. For simplicity, we concentrate on the interface to the TM; the details are presented in the following sections.

1. Begin_transaction. This is an indicator to the coordinating TM that a new trans-action is starting. The TM does some bookkeeping by recording the transaction's name, the originating application, and so on, in a main memory log (called the *volatile log*).
2. Read. If the data item is stored locally, its value is read and returned to the transaction. Otherwise, the coordinating TM finds where the data item is stored and requests its value to be returned (after appropriate concurrency control measures are taken). The site where the data item is read inserts a log record in the volatile log.
3. Write. If the data item is stored locally, its value is updated (in coordination with the data processor). Otherwise, the coordinating TM finds where the data item is located and requests the update to be carried out at that site (after appropriate concurrency control measures are taken). Again, the site that executes the write inserts a log record in the volatile log.

4. Commit. The TM coordinates the sites involved in updating data items on behalf of this transaction so that the updates are made durable at every site. WAL protocol is executed to move volatile log records to a log on disk (called the *stable log*).

5. Abort. The TM makes sure that no effects of the transaction are reflected in any of the databases at the sites where it updated data items. The log is used to execute the undo (rollback) protocol.

In providing these services, a TM can communicate with SCs and data processors at the same or at different sites. This arrangement is depicted in Fig. 5.2.

As we indicated in Chap. 1, the architectural model that we have described is only an abstraction that serves a pedagogical purpose. It enables the separation of many of the transaction management issues and their independent and isolated discussion. In Sect. 5.2, as we discuss the scheduling algorithm, we focus on the interface between a TM and an SC and between an SC and a data processor. In Sect. 5.4 we consider the execution strategies for the commit and abort commands in a distributed environment, in addition to the recovery algorithms that need to be implemented for the recovery manager. In Chap. 6, we extend this discussion to the case of replicated databases. We should point out that the computational model that we described here is not unique. Other models have been proposed such as, for example, using a private workspace for each transaction.

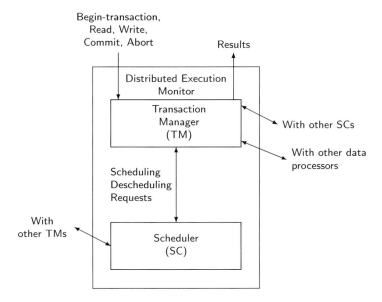

Fig. 5.2 Detailed model of the distributed execution monitor

5.2   Distributed Concurrency Control

As noted above, a concurrency control algorithm enforces a particular isolation level. In this chapter, we mainly focus on serializability among concurrent trans-actions. Serializability theory extends in a straightforward manner to the distributed databases. The history of transaction execution at each site is called a *local history*. If the database is not replicated and each local history is serializable, their union (called the *global history*) is also serializable as long as local serialization orders are identical.

Example 5.1 We give a very simple example to demonstrate the point. Consider two bank accounts, x (stored at Site 1) and y (stored at Site 2), and the following two transactions where T_1 transfers \$100 from x to y, while T_2 simply reads the balance of x and y:

T_1:   Read(x) T_2:   Read(x)
        $x \leftarrow x - 100$ Read(y)
        Write(x)   Commit
        Read(y)
        $y \leftarrow y + 100$
        Write(y)
        Commit

Obviously, both of these transactions need to run at both sites. Consider the following two histories that may be generated locally at the two sites (H_i is the history at Site i and R_j and W_j are Read and Write operations, respectively, in transaction T_j):

$$H_1 = \{R_1(x), W_1(x), R_2(x)\}$$
$$H_2 = \{R_1(y), W_1(y), R_2(y)\}$$

Both of these histories are serializable; indeed, they are serial. Therefore, each represents a correct execution order. Furthermore, the serialization order for both are the same $T_1 \rightarrow T_2$. Therefore global history that is obtained is also serializable with the serialization order $T_1 \rightarrow T_2$.

However, if the histories generated at the two sites are as follows, there is a problem:

$$H_1' = \{R_1(x), W_1(x), R_2(x)\}$$
$$H_2' = \{R_2(y), R_1(y), W_1(y)\}$$

Although each local history is still serializable, the serialization orders are different: H_1' serializes T_1 before T_2 ($T_1 \rightarrow T_2$) while H_2' serializes T_2 before T_1 ($T_2 \rightarrow T_1$). Therefore, there can be no serializable global history. ◆

Concurrency control protocols are in charge of isolation. A protocol aims at guaranteeing a particular isolation level such as serializability, snapshot isolation, or read committed. There are different aspects or dimensions of concurrency control. The first one is obviously the isolation level(s) aimed by the algorithm. The second aspect is whether a protocol prevents the isolation to be broken (pessimistic) or whether it allows it to be broken and then aborts one of the conflicting transactions to preserve the isolation level (optimistic).

The third dimension is how transactions get serialized. They can be serialized depending on the order of conflicting accesses or a predefined order, called *timestamp order*. The first case corresponds to locking algorithms where transactions get serialized based on the order they try to acquire conflicting locks. The second case corresponds to algorithms that order transactions according to a timestamp. The timestamp can either be assigned at the start of the transaction (start timestamp) when they are pessimistic or just before committing the transaction (commit timestamp) if they are optimistic. The fourth dimension that we consider is how updates are maintained. One possibility is to keep a single version of the data (that it is possible in pessimistic algorithms). Another possibility is to keep multiple versions of the data. The latter is needed for optimistic algorithms, but some pessimistic algorithms rely on it as well for recovery purposes (basically, they keep two versions: the latest committed one and the current uncommitted one). We discuss replication in the next chapter.

Most combinations of these multiple dimensions have been explored. In the remainder of this section, we focus on the seminal techniques for pessimistic algorithms, locking (Sect. 5.2.1) and timestamp ordering (Sect. 5.2.2), and the optimistic ones (Sect. 5.2.4). Understanding these techniques will also help the reader to move on to more involved algorithms of this kind.

5.2.1 Locking-Based Algorithms

Locking-based concurrency control algorithms prevent isolation violation by maintaining a "lock" for each lock unit and requiring each operation to obtain a lock on the data item before it is accessed—either in read (shared) mode or in write (exclusive) mode. The operation's access request is decided based on the compatibility of lock modes—read lock is compatible with another read lock, a write lock is not compatible with either a read or a write lock. The system manages the locks using the two-phase locking algorithm. The fundamental decision in distributed locking-based concurrency control algorithms is where and how the locks are maintained (usually called a *lock table*). The following sections provide algorithms that make different decisions in this regard.

5.2.1.1 Centralized 2PL

The 2PL algorithm can easily be extended to the distributed DBMS environment by delegating lock management responsibility to a single site. This means that only one of the sites has a lock manager; the transaction managers at the other sites communicate with it to obtain locks. This approach is also known as the *primary site* 2PL algorithm.

The communication between the cooperating sites in executing a transaction according to a centralized 2PL (C2PL) algorithm is depicted in Fig. 5.3 where the order of messages is indicated. This communication is between the *coordinating* TM, the lock manager at the central site, and the data processors (DP) at the other participating sites. The participating sites are those that store the data items on which the operation is to be carried out.

The centralized 2PL transaction management algorithm (C2PL-TM) that incorporates these changes is given at a very high level in Algorithm 5.1, while the centralized 2PL lock management algorithm (C2PL-LM) is shown in Algorithm 5.2. A highly simplified data processor algorithm (DP) is given in Algorithm 5.3, which will see major changes when we discuss reliability issues in Sect. 5.4.

These algorithms use a 5-tuple for the operation they perform: $Op : \langle Type = \{BT, R, W, A, C\}, arg :$ Data item, $val :$ Value, $tid :$ Transaction identifier, $res :$ Result$\rangle$. For an operation $o : Op, o.Type \in \{BT, R, W, A, C\}$ specifies its type where $BT = $ Begin_transaction, $R = $ Read, $W = $ Write, $A = $ Abort, and $C = $ Commit, arg is the data item that the operation accesses (reads or writes; for other operations this field is null), val is the value that has been read or to be written for data item arg

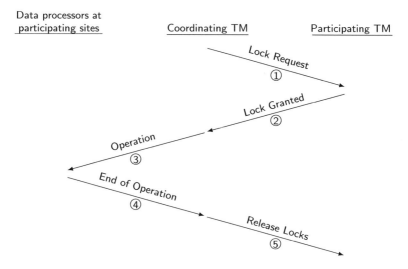

Fig. 5.3 Communication structure of centralized 2PL

Algorithm 5.1: Centralized 2PL Transaction Manager (C2PL-TM)

Input: msg : a message
begin
  repeat
    wait for a msg
    switch msg **do**
      case *transaction operation* **do**
        let op be the operation
        if $op.Type = BT$ **then** DP(op)   {call DP with operation}
        else C2PL-LM(op)   {call LM with operation}
      end case
      case *Lock Manager response* **do**   {lock request granted or locks released}
        if *lock request granted* **then**
          find site that stores the requested data item (say H_i)
          $DP_{Si}(op)$ {call DP at site S_i with operation}
        else   {must be lock release message}
          inform user about the termination of transaction
        end if
      end case
      case *Data Processor response* **do**   {operation completed message}
        switch *transaction operation* **do**
          let op be the operation
          case R **do**
            return $op.val$ (data item value) to the application
          end case
          case W **do**
            inform application of completion of the write
          end case
          case C **do**
            if *commit msg has been received from all participants* **then**
              inform application of successful completion of transaction
              C2PL-LM(op)   {need to release locks}
            else   {wait until commit messages come from all}
              record the arrival of the commit message
            end if
          end case
          case A **do**
            inform application of completion of the abort
            C2PL-LM(op)   {need to release locks}
          end case
        end switch
      end case
    end switch
  until *forever*
end

Algorithm 5.2: Centralized 2PL Lock Manager (C2PL-LM)

Input: $op : Op$
begin
 switch *op.Type* **do**
  case *R or W* **do**   {lock request; see if it can be granted}
   find the lock unit *lu* such that $op.arg \subseteq lu$
   if *lu is unlocked or lock mode of lu is compatible with op.Type* **then**
    set lock on *lu* in appropriate mode on behalf of transaction *op.tid*
    send "Lock granted" to coordinating TM of transaction
   else
    put *op* on a queue for *lu*
   end if
  end case
  case *C or A* **do**   {locks need to be released}
   foreach *lock unit lu held by transaction* **do**
    release lock on *lu* held by transaction
    if *there are operations waiting in queue for lu* **then**
     find the first operation *O* on queue
     set a lock on *lu* on behalf of *O*
     send "Lock granted" to coordinating TM of transaction *O.tid*
    end if
   end foreach
   send "Locks released" to coordinating TM of transaction
  end case
 end switch
end

(for other operations it is null), tid is the transaction that this operation belongs to (strictly speaking, this is the transaction identifier), and res indicates the completion code of operations requested of DP, which is important for reliability algorithms.

The transaction manager (C2PL-TM) algorithm is written as a process that runs forever and waits until a message arrives from either an application (with a transaction operation) or from a lock manager, or from a data processor. The lock manager (C2PL-LM) and data processor (DP) algorithms are written as procedures that are called when needed. Since the algorithms are given at a high level of abstraction, this is not a major concern, but actual implementations may, naturally, be quite different.

One common criticism of C2PL algorithms is that a bottleneck may quickly form around the central site. The communication between the cooperating sites in executing a transaction according to a centralized 2PL (C2PL) algorithm is depicted in Fig. 5.3 where the order of messages is indicated. This communication is between the *coordinating* TM, the lock manager at the central site, and the data processors (DP) at the other participating sites. The participating sites are those that store the data items on which the operation is to be carried out. Furthermore, the system may be less reliable since the failure or inaccessibility of the central site would cause major system failures.

Algorithm 5.3: Data Processor (DP)

Input: *op* : *Op*
begin
    switch *op.Type* **do**   {check the type of operation}
        case *BT* **do**   {details to be discussed in Sect. 5.4}
          | do some bookkeeping
        end case
        case *R* **do**
          | *op.res* ← READ(*op.arg*) ;   {database READ operation}
          | *op.res* ← "Read done"
        end case
        case *W* **do**   {database WRITE of *val* into data item *arg*}
          | WRITE(*op.arg*, *op.val*)
          | *op.res* ← "Write done"
        end case
        case *C* **do**
          | COMMIT ;   {execute COMMIT }
          | *op.res* ← "Commit done"
        end case
        case *A* **do**
          | ABORT ;   {execute ABORT }
          | *op.res* ← "Abort done"
         end case
    end switch
    return *op*
end

5.2.1.2   Distributed 2PL

Distributed 2PL (D2PL) requires the availability of lock managers at each site. The communication between cooperating sites that execute a transaction according to the distributed 2PL protocol is depicted in Fig. 5.4.

The distributed 2PL transaction management algorithm is similar to the C2PL-TM, with two major modifications. The messages that are sent to the central site lock manager in C2PL-TM are sent to the lock managers at all participating sites in D2PL-TM. The second difference is that the operations are not passed to the data processors by the coordinating transaction manager, but by the participating lock managers. This means that the coordinating transaction manager does not wait for a "lock request granted" message. Another point about Fig. 5.4 is the following. The participating data processors send the "end of operation" messages to the coordinating TM. The alternative is for each DP to send it to its own lock manager who can then release the locks and inform the coordinating TM. We have chosen to describe the former since it uses an LM algorithm identical to the strict 2PL lock manager that we have already discussed and it makes the discussion of the commit protocols simpler (see Sect. 5.4). Owing to these similarities, we do not give the

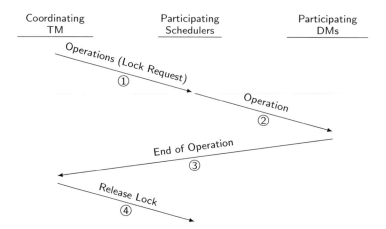

Fig. 5.4 Communication structure of distributed 2PL

distributed TM and LM algorithms here. Distributed 2PL algorithms have been used in R*and in NonStop SQL.

5.2.1.3 Distributed Deadlock Management

Locking-based concurrency control algorithms may cause deadlocks; in the case of distributed DBMSs, these could be *distributed* (or *global*) *deadlocks* due to transactions executing at different sites waiting for each other. Deadlock detection and resolution is the most popular approach to managing deadlocks in the distributed setting. The wait-for graph (WFG) can be useful for detecting deadlocks; this is a directed graph whose vertices are active transactions with an edge from T_i to T_j if an operation in T_i is waiting to access a data item that is currently locked in an incompatible mode by an operation in T_j. However, the formation of the WFG is more complicated in a distributed setting due to the distributed execution of transactions. Therefore, it is not sufficient for each site to form a *local wait-for graph* (LWFG) and check it; it is also necessary to form a *global wait-for graph* (GWFG), which is the union of all the LWFGs, and check it for cycles.

Example 5.2 Consider four transactions T_1, T_2, T_3, and T_4 with the following wait-for relationship among them: $T_1 \rightarrow T_2 \rightarrow T_3 \rightarrow T_4 \rightarrow T_1$. If T_1 and T_2 run at site 1 while T_3 and T_4 run at site 2, the LWFGs for the two sites are shown in Fig. 5.5a. Notice that it is not possible to detect a deadlock simply by examining the two LWFGs independently, because the deadlock is global. The deadlock can easily be detected, however, by examining the GWFG where intersite waiting is shown by dashed lines (Fig. 5.5b).   ◆

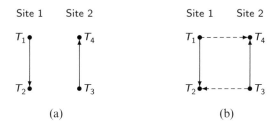

Fig. 5.5 Difference between LWFG and GWFG

The various algorithms differ in how they manage the GWFG. There are three fundamental methods of detecting distributed deadlocks, referred as *centralized, distributed*, and *hierarchical deadlock detection*. We discuss them below.

Centralized Deadlock Detection

In the centralized deadlock detection approach, one site is designated as the deadlock detector for the entire system. Periodically, each lock manager transmits its LWFG to the deadlock detector, which then forms the GWFG and looks for cycles in it. The lock managers need only send changes in their graphs (i.e., the newly created or deleted edges) to the deadlock detector. The length of intervals for transmitting this information is a system design decision: the smaller the interval, the smaller the delays due to undetected deadlocks, but the higher the deadlock detection and communication overhead.

Centralized deadlock detection is simple and would be a very natural choice if the concurrency control algorithm were centralized 2PL. However, the issues of vulnerability to failure, and high communication overhead, must also be considered.

Hierarchical Deadlock Detection

An alternative to centralized deadlock detection is the building of a hierarchy of deadlock detectors (see Fig. 5.6). Deadlocks that are local to a single site would be detected at that site using the LWFG. Each site also sends its LWFG to the deadlock detector at the next level. Thus, distributed deadlocks involving two or more sites would be detected by a deadlock detector in the next lowest level that has control over these sites. For example, a deadlock at site 1 would be detected by the local deadlock detector (DD) at site 1 (denoted DD_{21}, 2 for level 2, 1 for site 1). If, however, the deadlock involves sites 1 and 2, then DD_{11} detects it. Finally, if the deadlock involves sites 1 and 4, DD_{0x} detects it, where x is one of 1, 2, 3, or 4.

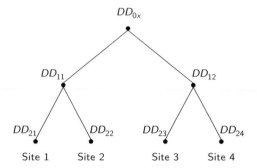

Fig. 5.6 Hierarchical deadlock detection

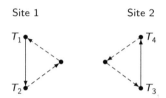

Fig. 5.7 Modified LWFGs

The hierarchical deadlock detection method reduces the dependence on the central site, thus reducing the communication cost. It is, however, considerably more complicated to implement and would involve nontrivial modifications to the lock and transaction manager algorithms.

Distributed Deadlock Detection

Distributed deadlock detection algorithms delegate the responsibility of detecting deadlocks to individual sites. Thus, as in the hierarchical deadlock detection, there are local deadlock detectors at each site that communicate their LWFGs with one another (in fact, only the potential deadlock cycles are transmitted). Among the various distributed deadlock detection algorithms, the one implemented in System R* is the more widely known and referenced, and we describe it below.

The LWFG at each site is formed and is modified as follows:

1. Since each site receives the potential deadlock cycles from other sites, these edges are added to the LWFGs.
2. The edges in the LWFG that show that local transactions are waiting for transactions at other sites are joined with edges in the LWFGs depicting that remote transactions are waiting for local ones.

Example 5.3 Consider the example in Fig. 5.5. The local WFG for the two sites are modified as shown in Fig. 5.7.   ◆

Local deadlock detectors look for two things. If there is a cycle that does not include the external edges, there is a local deadlock that can be handled locally. If, on the other hand, there is a cycle involving these external edges, there is a potential distributed deadlock and this cycle information has to be communicated to other deadlock detectors. In the case of Example 5.3, the possibility of such a distributed deadlock is detected by both sites.

A question that needs to be answered at this point is to whom to transmit the information. Obviously, it can be transmitted to all deadlock detectors in the system. In the absence of any more information, this is the only alternative, but it incurs a high overhead. If, however, one knows whether the transaction is ahead or behind in the deadlock cycle, the information can be transmitted forward or backward along the sites in this cycle. The receiving site then modifies its LWFG as discussed above, and checks for deadlocks. Obviously, there is no need to transmit along the deadlock cycle in both the forward and backward directions. In the case of Example 5.3, site 1 would send it to site 2 in both forward and backward transmission along the deadlock cycle.

The distributed deadlock detection algorithms require uniform modification to the lock managers at each site. This uniformity makes them easier to implement. However, there is the potential for excessive message transmission. This happens, for example, in the case of Example 5.3: site 1 sends its potential deadlock information to site 2, and site 2 sends its information to site 1. In this case the deadlock detectors at both sites will detect the deadlock. Besides causing unnecessary message transmission, there is the additional problem that each site may choose a different victim to abort. Obermarck's algorithm solves the problem by using transaction timestamps (monotonically increasing counter—see more details in the next section) as well as the following rule. Let the path that has the potential of causing a distributed deadlock in the local WFG of a site be $T_i \rightarrow \cdots \rightarrow T_j$. A local deadlock detector forwards the cycle information only if timestamp of T_i is smaller than the timestamp of T_j. This reduces the average number of message transmissions by one-half. In the case of Example 5.3, site 1 has a path $T_1 \rightarrow T_2 \rightarrow T_3$, whereas site 2 has a path $T_3 \rightarrow T_4 \rightarrow T_1$. Therefore, assuming that the subscripts of each transaction denote their timestamp, only site 1 will send information to site 2.

5.2.2 Timestamp-Based Algorithms

Timestamp-based concurrency control algorithms select, a priori, a serialization order and execute transactions accordingly. To establish this ordering, the transaction manager assigns each transaction T_i a unique *timestamp*, $ts(T_i)$, at its initiation.

Assignment of timestamps in a distributed DBMS requires some attention since multiple sites will be assigning timestamps, and maintaining uniqueness and monotonicity across the system is not easy. One method is to use a global (system-wide) monotonically increasing counter. However, the maintenance of global counters is a problem in distributed systems. Therefore, it is preferable that each site autonomously assigns timestamps based on its local counter. To maintain uniqueness, each site appends its own identifier to the counter value. Thus the timestamp is a two-tuple of the form ⟨local counter value, site identifier⟩. Note that the site identifier is appended in the least significant position. Hence it serves only to order the timestamps of two transactions that might have been assigned the same local counter value. If each system can access its own system clock, it is possible to use system clock values instead of counter values.

Architecturally (see Fig. 5.2), the transaction manager is responsible for assigning a timestamp to each new transaction and attaching this timestamp to each database operation that it passes on to the scheduler. The latter component is responsible for keeping track of read and write timestamps as well as performing the serializability check.

5.2.2.1 Basic TO Algorithm

In the basic TO algorithm the coordinating TM assigns the timestamp to each transaction T_i $[ts(T_i)]$, determines the sites where each data item is stored, and sends the relevant operations to these sites. It is a straightforward implementation of the TO rule.

TO Rule Given two conflicting operations O_{ij} and O_{kl} belonging, respectively, to transactions T_i and T_k, O_{ij} is executed before O_{kl} if and only if $ts(T_i) < ts(T_k)$. In this case T_i is said to be the *older* transaction and T_k is said to be the *younger* one.

A scheduler that enforces the TO rule checks each new operation against conflicting operations that have already been scheduled. If the new operation belongs to a transaction that is younger than all the conflicting ones that have already been scheduled, the operation is accepted; otherwise, it is rejected, causing the entire transaction to restart with a *new* timestamp.

To facilitate checking of the TO Rule, each data item x is assigned two timestamps: a *read timestamp* $[rts(x)]$, which is the largest of the timestamps of the transactions that have read x, and a *write timestamp* $[wts(x)]$, which is the largest of the timestamps of the transactions that have written (updated) x. It is now sufficient to compare the timestamp of an operation with the read and write timestamps of the data item that it wants to access to determine if any transaction with a larger timestamp has already accessed the same data item.

The basic TO transaction manager algorithm (BTO-TM) is depicted in Algorithm 5.4. The histories at each site simply enforce the TO rule. The scheduler

---

Algorithm 5.4: Basic Timestamp Ordering (BTO-TM)

Input: msg : a message
begin
  repeat
    wait for a msg
    switch msg *type* **do**
      case *transaction operation* **do**   {operation from application program }
        let op be the operation
        switch $op.Type$ **do**
          case BT **do**
            $S \leftarrow \emptyset$;   {S: set of sites where transaction executes }
            assign a timestamp to transaction—call it $ts(T)$
            DP(op)   {call DP with operation}
          end case
          case R, W **do**
            find site that stores the requested data item (say S_i)
            BTO-SC$_{S_i}(op, ts(T))$;   {send op and ts to SC at S_i}
            $S \leftarrow S \cup S_i$ {build list of sites where transaction runs}
          end case
          case A, C **do**   {send op to DPs that execute transaction }
            DP$_S(op)$
          end case
        end switch
      end case
      case *SC response* **do**   {operation must have been rejected by a SC}
        $op.Type \leftarrow A$;   {prepare an abort message}
        BTO-SC$_S(op, -)$;   {ask other participating SCs}
        restart transaction with a new timestamp
      end case
      case *DP response* **do**   {operation completed message}
        switch *transaction operation type* **do**
          let op be the operation
          case R **do** return $op.val$ to the application
          case W **do** inform application of completion of the write
          case C **do**
            if *commit msg has been received from all participants* **then**
             inform application of successful completion of transaction
            else   {wait until commit messages come from all}
             record the arrival of the commit message
            end if
          end case
          case A **do**
            inform application of completion of the abort
            BTO-SC(op)   {need to reset read and write ts}
          end case
        end switch
      end case
    end switch
  until *forever*
end

---

algorithm is given in Algorithm 5.5. The data manager is still the one given in
Algorithm 5.3. The same data structures and assumptions we used for centralized
2PL algorithms apply to these algorithms as well.

When an operation is rejected by a scheduler, the corresponding transaction is
restarted by the transaction manager with a new timestamp. This ensures that the
transaction has a chance to execute in its next try. Since the transactions never
wait while they hold access rights to data items, the basic TO algorithm never
causes deadlocks. However, the penalty of deadlock freedom is potential restart of
a transaction numerous times. There is an alternative to the basic TO algorithm that
reduces the number of restarts, which we discuss in the next section.

Another detail that needs to be considered relates to the communication between
the scheduler and the data processor. When an accepted operation is passed on to
the data processor, the scheduler needs to refrain from sending another conflicting,
but acceptable operation to the data processor until the first is processed and
acknowledged. This is a requirement to ensure that the data processor executes the
operations in the order in which the scheduler passes them on. Otherwise, the read
and write timestamp values for the accessed data item would not be accurate.

Algorithm 5.5: Basic Timestamp Ordering Scheduler (BTO-SC)

Input: $op : Op; ts(T) : Timestamp$
begin
    retrieve $rts(op.arg)$ and $wts(arg)$
    save $rts(op.arg)$ and $wts(arg)$;   {might be needed if aborted }
    switch *op.arg* **do**
        case *R* **do**
            if $ts(T) > wts(op.arg)$ **then**
                DP(op) ;   {operation can be executed; send it to DP}
                $rts(op.arg) \leftarrow ts(T)$
            else
                send "Reject transaction" message to coordinating TM
            end if
        end case
        case *W* **do**
            if $ts(T) > rts(op.arg)$ and $ts(T) > wts(op.arg)$ **then**
                DP(op) ;   {operation can be executed; send it to DP}
                $rts(op.arg) \leftarrow ts(T)$
                $wts(op.arg) \leftarrow ts(T)$
            else
                send"Reject transaction" message to coordinating TM
            end if
        end case
        case *A* **do**
            forall *op.arg that has been accessed by transaction* **do**
                reset $rts(op.arg)$ and $wts(op.arg)$ to their initial values
            end forall
        end case
    end switch
end

Example 5.4 Assume that the TO scheduler first receives $W_i(x)$ and then receives $W_j(x)$, where $ts(T_i) < ts(T_j)$. The scheduler would accept both operations and pass them on to the data processor. The result of these two operations is that $wts(x) = ts(T_j)$, and we then expect the effect of $W_j(x)$ to be represented in the database. However, if the data processor does not execute them in that order, the effects on the database will be wrong. ◆

The scheduler can enforce the ordering by maintaining a queue for each data item that is used to delay the transfer of the accepted operation until an acknowledgment is received from the data processor regarding the previous operation on the same data item. This detail is not shown in Algorithm 5.5.

Such a complication does not arise in 2PL-based algorithms because the lock manager effectively orders the operations by releasing the locks only after the operation is executed. In one sense the queue that the TO scheduler maintains may be thought of as a lock. However, this does not imply that the history generated by a TO scheduler and a 2PL scheduler would always be equivalent. There are some histories that a TO scheduler would generate that would not be admissible by a 2PL history.

Remember that in the case of strict 2PL algorithms, the releasing of locks is delayed further, until the commit or abort of a transaction. It is possible to develop a strict TO algorithm by using a similar scheme. For example, if $W_i(x)$ is accepted and released to the data processor, the scheduler delays all $R_j(x)$ and $W_j(x)$ operations (for all T_j) until T_i terminates (commits or aborts).

5.2.2.2 Conservative TO Algorithm

We indicated in the preceding section that the basic TO algorithm never causes operations to wait, but instead, restarts them. We also pointed out that even though this is an advantage due to deadlock freedom, it is also a disadvantage, because numerous restarts would have adverse performance implications. The conservative TO algorithms attempt to lower this system overhead by reducing the number of transaction restarts.

Let us first present a technique that is commonly used to reduce the probability of restarts. Remember that a TO scheduler restarts a transaction if a younger conflicting transaction is already scheduled or has been executed. Note that such occurrences increase significantly if, for example, one site is comparatively inactive relative to the others and does not issue transactions for an extended period. In this case its timestamp counter indicates a value that is considerably smaller than the counters of other sites. If the TM at this site then receives a transaction, the operations that are sent to the histories at the other sites will almost certainly be rejected, causing the transaction to restart. Furthermore, the same transaction will restart repeatedly until the timestamp counter value at its originating site reaches a level of parity with the counters of other sites.

The foregoing scenario indicates that it is useful to keep the counters at each site synchronized. However, total synchronization is not only costly—since it requires exchange of messages every time a counter changes—but also unnecessary. Instead, each transaction manager can send its remote operations, rather than histories, to the transaction managers at the other sites. The receiving transaction managers can then compare their own counter values with that of the incoming operation. Any manager whose counter value is smaller than the incoming one adjusts its own counter to one more than the incoming one. This ensures that none of the counters in the system run away or lag behind significantly. Of course, if system clocks are used instead of counters, this approximate synchronization may be achieved automatically as long as the clocks are synchronized with a protocol like Network Time Protocol (NTP).

Conservative TO algorithms execute each operation differently than basic TO. The basic TO algorithm tries to execute an operation as soon as it is accepted; it is therefore "aggressive" or "progressive." Conservative algorithms, on the other hand, delay each operation until there is an assurance that no operation with a smaller timestamp can arrive at that scheduler. If this condition can be guaranteed, the scheduler will never reject an operation. However, this delay introduces the possibility of deadlocks.

The basic technique that is used in conservative TO is based on the following idea: the operations of each transaction are buffered until an ordering can be established so that rejections are not possible, and they are executed in that order. We will consider one possible implementation of the conservative TO algorithm.

Assume that each scheduler maintains one queue for each transaction manager in the system. The scheduler at site s stores all the operations that it receives from the transaction manager at site t in queue Q_s^t. Scheduler at site s has one such queue for each site t. When an operation is received from a transaction manager, it is placed in its appropriate queue in increasing timestamp order. The histories at each site execute the operations from these queues in increasing timestamp order.

This scheme will reduce the number of restarts, but it will not guarantee that they will be eliminated completely. Consider the case where at site s the queue for site t (Q_s^t) is empty. The scheduler at site s will choose an operation [say, $R(x)$] with the smallest timestamp and pass it on to the data processor. However, site t may have sent to s an operation [say, $W(x)$] with a smaller timestamp which may still be in transit in the network. When this operation reaches site s, it will be rejected since it violates the TO rule: it wants to access a data item that is currently being accessed (in an incompatible mode) by another operation with a higher timestamp.

It is possible to design an extremely conservative TO algorithm by insisting that the scheduler choose an operation to be sent to the data processor only if there is at least one operation in each queue. This guarantees that every operation that the scheduler receives in the future will have timestamps greater than or equal to those currently in the queues. Of course, if a transaction manager does not have a transaction to process, it needs to send dummy messages periodically to every scheduler in the system, informing them that the operations that it will send in the future will have timestamps greater than that of the dummy message.

The careful reader will realize that the extremely conservative timestamp ordering scheduler actually executes transactions serially at each site. This is very restrictive. One method that has been employed to overcome this restriction is to group transactions into classes. Transaction classes are defined with respect to their read sets and write sets. It is therefore sufficient to determine the class that a transaction belongs to by comparing the transaction's read set and write set, respectively, with the read set and write set of each class. Thus, the conservative TO algorithm can be modified so that instead of requiring the existence, at each site, of one queue for each transaction manager, it is only necessary to have one queue for each transaction class. Alternatively, one might mark each queue with the class to which it belongs. With either of these modifications, the conditions for sending an operation to the data processor are changed. It is no longer necessary to wait until there is at least one operation in each queue; it is sufficient to wait until there is at least one operation in each class to which the transaction belongs. This and other weaker conditions that reduce the waiting delay can be defined and are sufficient. A variant of this method is used in the SDD-1 prototype system.

5.2.3   Multiversion Concurrency Control

The approaches we discussed above fundamentally address in-place updates: when a data item's value is updated, its old value is replaced with the new one in the database. An alternative is to maintain the versions of data items as they get updated. Algorithms in this class are called *multiversion concurrency control* (MVCC). Then each transaction "sees" the value of a data item based on its isolation level. Multiversion TO is another attempt at eliminating the restart overhead of transactions by maintaining multiple versions of data items and scheduling operations on the appropriate version of the data item. The availability of multiple versions of the database also allows *time travel queries* that track the change of data item values over time. A concern in MVCC is the proliferation of multiple versions of updated data items. To save space, the versions of the database may be purged from time to time. This should be done when the distributed DBMS is certain that it will no longer receive a transaction that needs to access the purged versions.

Although the original proposal dates back to 1978, it has gained popularity in recent years and is now implemented in a number of DBMSs such as IBM DB2, Oracle, SQL Server, SAP HANA, BerkeleyDB, PostgreSQL as well as systems such as Spanner. These systems enforce *snapshot isolation* that we discuss in Sect. 5.3.

MVCC techniques typically use timestamps to maintain transaction isolation although proposals exist that build multiversioning on top of a locking-based concurrency control layer. Here, we will focus on timestamp-based implementation that enforces serializability. In this implementation, each version of a data item that is created is labeled with the timestamp of the transaction that creates it. The idea is that each read operation accesses the version of the data item that is appropriate for its timestamp, thus reducing transaction aborts and restarts. This ensures that

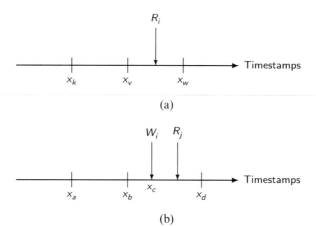

Fig. 5.8 Multiversion TO cases

each transaction operates on a state of the database that it would have seen if the transaction were executed serially in timestamp order.

The existence of versions is transparent to users who issue transactions simply by referring to data items, not to any specific version. The transaction manager assigns a timestamp to each transaction, which is also used to keep track of the timestamps of each version. The operations are processed by the histories as follows guaranteeing a serializable history:

1. A $R_i(x)$ is translated into a read on one version of x. This is done by finding a version of x (say, x_v) such that $ts(x_v)$ is the largest timestamp less than $ts(T_i)$. $R_i(x_v)$ is then sent to the data processor to read x_v. This case is depicted in Fig. 5.8a, which shows that R_i can read the version (x_v) that it would have read had it arrived in timestamp order.

2. A $W_i(x)$ is translated into $W_i(x_w)$ so that $ts(x_w) = ts(T_i)$ and sent to the data processor if and only if no other transaction with a timestamp greater than $ts(T_i)$ has read the value of a version of x (say, x_r) such that $ts(x_r) > ts(x_w)$. In other words, if the scheduler has already processed a $R_j(x_r)$ such that

$$ts(T_i) < ts(x_r) < ts(T_j)$$

then $W_i(x)$ is rejected. This case is depicted in Fig. 5.8b, which shows that if W_i is accepted, it would create a version (x_c) that R_j should have read, but did not since the version was not available when R_j was executed—it, instead, read version x_b, which results in the wrong history.

5.2.4   Optimistic Algorithms

Optimistic algorithms assume that transaction conflicts and contention for data will not be predominant, and therefore allow transactions to execute without synchronization until the very end when they are validated for correctness. Optimistic concurrency control algorithms can be based on locking or timestamping, which was the original proposal. In this section, we describe a timestamp-based distributed optimistic algorithm.

Each transaction follows five phases: read (R), execute (E), write (W), validate (V), and commit (C)—of course commit phase becomes abort if the transaction is not validated. This algorithm assigns timestamps to transactions at the beginning of their validation step rather than at the beginning of transactions as is done with (pessimistic) TO algorithms. Furthermore, it does not associate read and write timestamps with data items—it only works with transaction timestamps during the validation phase.

Each transaction T_i is subdivided (by the transaction manager at the originating site) into a number of subtransactions, each of which can execute at many sites. Notationally, let us denote by T_i^s a subtransaction of T_i that executes at site s. At the beginning of the validation phase a timestamp is assigned to the transaction, which is also the timestamp of its subtransactions. The local validation of T_i^s is performed according to the following rules, which are mutually exclusive.

Rule 1   At each site s, if all transactions T_k^s where $ts(T_k^s) < ts(T_i^s)$ have completed their write phase before T_i^s has started its read phase (Fig. 5.9a), validation succeeds, because transaction executions are in serial order.

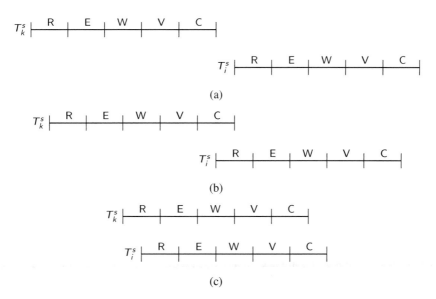

Fig. 5.9 Possible execution scenarios

Rule 2 At each site s, if there is any transaction T_k^s such that $ts(T_k^s) < ts(T_i^s)$, and which completes its write phase while T_i^s is in its read phase (Fig. 5.9b), the validation succeeds if $WS(T_k) \cap RS(T_i^s) = \emptyset$.

Rule 3 At each site s, if there is any transaction T_k^s such that $ts(T_k^s) < ts(T_i^s)$, and which completes its read phase before T_i^s completes its read phase (Fig. 5.9c), the validation succeeds if $WS(T_k^s) \cap RS(T_i^s) = \emptyset$, and $WS(T_k^s) \cap WS(T_i^s) = \emptyset$.

Rule 1 is obvious; it indicates that the transactions are actually executed serially in their timestamp order. Rule 2 ensures that none of the data items updated by T_k^s are read by T_i^s and that T_k^s finishes writing its updates into the database (i.e., commits) before T_i^s starts writing. Thus the updates of T_i^s will not be overwritten by the updates of T_k^s. Rule 3 is similar to Rule 2, but does not require that T_k^s finish writing before T_i^s starts writing. It simply requires that the updates of T_k^s not affect the read phase or the write phase of T_i^s.

Once a transaction is locally validated to ensure that the local database consistency is maintained, it also needs to be globally validated to ensure that the mutual consistency rule is obeyed. This is done by ensuring that the above rules hold at every participating site.

An advantage of optimistic concurrency control algorithms is the potential to allow a higher level of concurrency. It has been shown that when transaction conflicts are very rare, the optimistic mechanism performs better than locking. A difficulty with optimistic approaches is the maintenance of the information necessary for validation. To validate a subtransaction T_i^s the read and write sets of terminated transactions that were in progress when T_i^s arrived at site s need to be maintained.

Another problem is starvation. Consider a situation in which the validation phase of a long transaction fails. In subsequent trials it is still possible that the validation will fail repeatedly. Of course, it is possible to solve this problem by permitting the transaction exclusive access to the database after a specified number of trials. However, this reduces the level of concurrency to a single transaction. The exact mix of transactions that would cause an intolerable level of restarts is an issue that remains to be studied.

5.3   Distributed Concurrency Control Using Snapshot Isolation

Up to this point, we have discussed algorithms that enforce serializability. Although serializability is the most studied and discussed correctness criterion for concurrent transaction execution, for some applications it may be considered too strict in the sense that it disallows certain histories that might be acceptable. In particular, serializability creates a bottleneck that prevents distributed databases from scaling to large levels. The main reason is that it constrains transaction concurrency very heavily, since large read queries conflict with updates. This has led to the definition of *snapshot isolation* (SI) as an alternative. SI has been widely adopted in commercial systems, and a number of modern systems, such as Google Spanner and LeanXcale, that have managed to scale to very large levels rely on it; we discuss these approaches in Sect. 5.5. Snapshot isolation provides repeatable reads, but not serializable isolation. Each transaction "sees" a consistent snapshot of the database when it starts, and its reads and writes are performed on this snapshot—thus its writes are not visible to other transactions and it does not see the writes of other transactions once it starts executing.

Snapshot isolation is a multiversioning approach, allowing transactions to read the appropriate snapshot (i.e., version). An important advantage of SI-based concurrency control is that read-only transactions can proceed without significant synchronization overhead. For update transactions, the concurrency control algorithm (in centralized systems) is as follows:

S1. When a transaction T_i starts, it obtains a *begin timestamp* $ts_b(T_i)$.

S2. When T_i is ready to commit, it obtains a *commit timestamp* $ts_c(T_i)$ that is greater than any of the existing ts_b or ts_c.

S3. T_i commits its updates if there is no other T_j such that $ts_c(T_j) \in [ts_b(T_i), ts_c(T_i)]$ (i.e., no other transaction has committed since T_i started); otherwise T_i is aborted. This is known as the *first committer wins* rule, and it prevents lost updates.

S4. When T_i is committed, its changes become available to all transactions T_k where $ts_b(T_k) > ts_c(T_i)$.

When SI is used as the correctness criterion in distributed concurrency control, a problem that needs to be addressed is how to compute the consistent snapshot (version) on which transaction T_i operates. If the read and write sets of the transaction are known up-front, it may be possible to centrally compute the snapshot (at the coordinating TM) by collecting information from the participating sites. This, of course, is not realistic. What is needed is a global guarantee similar to the global serializability guarantee we discussed earlier. In other words,

1. Each local history is SI, and
2. The global history is SI, i.e., the commitment orders of transactions at each site are the same.

We now identify the conditions that need to be satisfied for the above guarantee to be realized. We start with defining the *dependence relationship* between two transactions, which is important in this context since the snapshot that a transaction T_i reads should include only the updates of transactions on which it depends. A transaction T_i at site s (T_i^s) is dependent on T_j^s, denoted as *dependent*(T_i^s, T_j^s), if and only if $(RS(T_i^s) \cap WS(T_j^s) \neq \emptyset) \vee (WS(T_i^s) \cap RS(T_j^s) \neq \emptyset) \vee (WS(T_i^s) \cap WS(T_j^s) \neq \emptyset)$. If there is any participating site where this dependence holds, then *dependent*(T_i, T_j) holds.

Now we are ready to more precisely specify the conditions that need to hold to ensure global SI as defined above. The conditions below are given for pairwise transactions, but they transitively hold for a set of transactions. For a transaction T_i to see a globally consistent snapshot, the following conditions have to hold for each pair of transactions:

C1.   If $dependent(T_i, T_j) \land tsb(T_i^s) < ts_c(T_j^s)$, then $tsb(T_i^t) < ts_c(T_j^t)$ at every site t where T_i and T_j execute together.

C2.   If $dependent(T_i, T_j) \land ts_c(T_i^s) < tsb(T_j^s)$, then $ts_c(T_i^t) < tsb(T_j^t)$ at every site t where T_i and T_j execute together.

C3.   If $ts_c(T_i^s) < ts_c(T_j^s)$, then $ts_c(T_i^t) < tsb(T_j^t)$ at every site t where T_i and T_j execute together.

The first two of these conditions ensure that $dependent(T_i, T_j)$ is true at all the sites, i.e., T_i always correctly sees this relationship across sites. The third condition ensures commit order among transactions is the same at all participating sites, and prevents two snapshots from including partial commits that are incompatible with each other.

Before discussing the distributed SI concurrency control algorithm, let us identify the information that each site s maintains:

- For any active transaction T_i, the set of *active* and *committed* transactions at s are categorized into two groups: those that are concurrent with T_i (i.e., any T_j where $tsb(T_i^s) < ts_c(T_j^s)$), and those that are serial (i.e., any T_j where $ts_c(T_j^s) < tsb(T_i^s)$)—note that serial is not the same as dependent; local history indicates ordering in the local history at s without any statement on dependence.
- A monotonically increasing event clock.

The basic distributed SI algorithm basically implements step S3 of the centralized algorithm presented earlier (although different implementations exist), i.e., it certifies whether transaction T_i can be committed or needs to be aborted. The algorithm proceeds as follows:

D1.   The coordinating TM of T_i asks each participating site s to send its set of transactions concurrent with T_i. It piggybacks to this message its own event clock.

D2.   Each site s responds to the coordinating TM with its local set of transactions concurrent with T_i.

D3.   The coordinating TM merges all of the local concurrent transaction sets into one global concurrent transaction set for T_i.

D4.   The coordinating TM sends this global list of concurrent transactions to all of the participating sites.

D5.   Each site s checks whether the conditions C1 and C2 hold. It does this by checking whether there is a transaction T_j in the global concurrent transaction list that is in local history serial list (i.e., in the local history of s, T_j has executed before T_i), and on which T_i is dependent (i.e., $dependent(T_i^s, T_j^s)$ holds). If that is the case, T_i does not see a consistent snapshot at site s, so it should be aborted. Otherwise T_i is validated at site s.

D6.   Each site s sends its positive or negative validation to the coordinating TM. If a positive validation message is sent, then site s updates its own event clock to the maximum of its own event clock and the event clock of the coordinating TM that it received, and it piggybacks its new clock value to the response message.

D7.   If the coordinating TM receives one negative validation message, then T_i is aborted, since there is at least one site where it does not see a consistent snapshot. Otherwise, the coordinating TM globally certifies T_i and allows it to commit its updates. If the decision is to globally validate, the coordinating TM updates its own event clock to the maximum of the event clocks it receives from the participating sites and its own clock.

D8.   The coordinating TM informs all of the participating sites that T_i is validated and can be committed. It also piggybacks its new event clock value, which becomes $ts_c(T_i)$.

D9.   Upon receipt of this message, each participant site s makes T_i's updates persistent, and also updates its own event clock as before.

In this algorithm, the certification of conditions C1 and C2 is done in step D5; the other steps serve to collect the necessary information and coordinate the certification check. The event clock synchronization among the sites serves to enforce condition C3 by ensuring that the commit orders of dependent transactions are consistent across sites so that the global snapshot will be consistent.

The algorithm we discussed is one possible approach to implementing SI in a distributed DBMS. It guarantees global SI, but requires that the global snapshot is computed upfront, thus introducing a number of scalability bottlenecks. For instance, sending all concurrent transactions in step D2 obviously does not scale since a system executing millions of concurrent transactions would have to send millions of transactions on each check that would severely limit scalability. Furthermore, it requires all transactions to follow the same certification process. This can be optimized by separating single-site transactions that only access data at one site, and, therefore, do not require the generation of a global snapshot from global transactions that execute across a number of sites. One way to accomplish this is to incrementally build the snapshot that a transaction T_i reads as the data are accessed across different sites.

5.4   Distributed DBMS Reliability

In centralized DBMSs, three types of errors can occur: transaction failures (e.g., transaction aborts), site failures (that cause the loss of data in memory, but not in persistent storage), and media failures (that may cause partial or total loss of data in persistent storage). In the distributed setting, the system needs to cope with a fourth failure type: *communication failures*. There are a number of types of communication failures; the most common ones are the errors in the messages, improperly ordered messages, lost (or undeliverable) messages, and communication line failures. The first two errors are the responsibility of the computer network, and we will not consider them further. Therefore, in our discussions of distributed DBMS reliability, we expect the underlying computer network to ensure that two messages sent from a process at some originating site to another process at some destination site are delivered without error and in the order in which they were sent; i.e., we consider each communication link to be a reliable FIFO channel.

Lost or undeliverable messages are typically the consequence of communication line failures or (destination) site failures. If a communication line fails, in addition to losing the message(s) in transit, it may also divide the network into two or more disjoint groups. This is called *network partitioning*. If the network is partitioned, the sites in each partition may continue to operate. In this case, executing transactions that access data stored in multiple partitions becomes a major issue. In a distributed system, it is generally not possible to differentiate failures of destination site versus communication lines. In both cases, a source site sends a message but does not get a response within an expected time; this is called a *timeout*. At that point, reliability algorithms need to take action.

Communication failures point to a unique aspect of failures in distributed systems. In centralized systems the system state can be characterized as all-or-nothing: either the system is operational or it is not. Thus the failures are complete: when one occurs, the entire system becomes nonoperational. Obviously, this is not true in distributed systems. As we indicated a number of times before, this is their potential strength. However, it also makes the transaction management algorithms more difficult to design, since, if a message is undelivered, it is hard to know whether the recipient site has failed or a network failure occurred that prevented the message from being delivered.

If messages cannot be delivered, we assume that the network does nothing about it. It will not buffer it for delivery to the destination when the service is reestablished and will not inform the sender process that the message cannot be delivered. In short, the message will simply be lost. We make this assumption because it represents the least expectation from the network and places the responsibility of dealing with these failures to the distributed DBMS. As a consequence, the distributed DBMS is responsible for detecting that a message is undeliverable. The detection mechanism is typically dependent on the characteristics of the communication system on which the distributed DBMS is implemented. The details are beyond our scope; in this discussion we will assume, as noted above, that the sender of a message will set a timer and wait until the end of a timeout period when it will decide that the message has not been delivered.

Distributed reliability protocols aim to maintain the atomicity and durability of distributed transactions that execute over a number of databases. The protocols address the distributed execution of the Begin_transaction, Read, Write, Abort, Commit, and recover commands. The Begin_transaction, Read, and Write commands are executed by Local Recovery Managers (LRMs) in the same way as they are in centralized DBMSs. The ones that require special care in distributed DBMSs are the Commit, Abort, and Read commands. The fundamental difficulty is to ensure that all of the sites that participate in the execution of a transaction reach the same decision (abort or commit) regarding the fate of the transaction.

The implementation of distributed reliability protocols within the architectural model we have adopted in this book raises a number of interesting and difficult issues. We discuss these in Sect. 5.4.6 after we introduce the protocols. For the time being, we adopt a common abstraction: we assume that at the originating site of a transaction there is a *coordinator* process and at each site where the transaction executes there are *participant* processes. Thus, the distributed reliability protocols are implemented between the coordinator and the participants.

The reliability techniques in distributed database systems consist of commit, termination, and recovery protocols—the commit and recovery protocols specify how the Commit and the recover commands are executed, while the termination protocols specify how the sites that are alive can terminate a transaction when they detect that a site has failed. Termination and recovery protocols are two opposite faces of the recovery problem: given a site failure, termination protocols address how the operational sites deal with the failure, whereas recovery protocols deal with the procedure that the process (coordinator or participant) at a failed site has to go through to recover its state once the site is restarted. In the case of network partitioning, the termination protocols take the necessary measures to terminate the active transactions that execute at different partitions, while the recovery protocols address how the global database consistency is reestablished following reconnection of the partitions of the network.

The primary requirement of commit protocols is that they maintain the atomicity of distributed transactions. This means that even though the execution of the distributed transaction involves multiple sites, some of which might fail while executing, the effects of the transaction on the distributed database is all-or-nothing. This is called *atomic commitment*. We would prefer the termination protocols to be *nonblocking*. A protocol is nonblocking if it permits a transaction to terminate at the operational sites without waiting for recovery of the failed site. This would significantly improve the response-time performance of transactions. We would also like the distributed recovery protocols to be *independent*. Independent recovery protocols determine how to terminate a transaction that was executing at the time of a failure without having to consult any other site. Existence of such protocols would reduce the number of messages that need to be exchanged during recovery. Note that the existence of independent recovery protocols would imply the existence of nonblocking termination protocols, but the reverse is not true.

5.4.1   Two-Phase Commit Protocol

Two-phase commit (2PC) is a very simple and elegant protocol that ensures the atomic commitment of distributed transactions. It extends the effects of local atomic commit actions to distributed transactions by insisting that all sites involved in the execution of a distributed transaction agree to commit the transaction before its

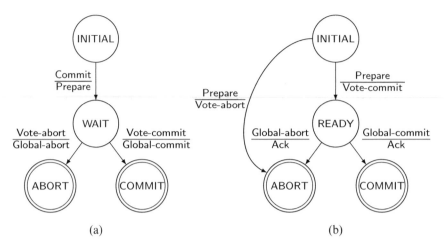

Fig. 5.10 State transitions in 2PC protocol. (**a**) Coordinator states. (**b**) Participant states

effects are made permanent. There are a number of reasons why such synchronization among sites is necessary. First, depending on the type of concurrency control
algorithm that is used, some schedulers may not be ready to terminate a transaction.
For example, if a transaction has read a value of a data item that is updated by
another transaction that has not yet committed, the associated scheduler may not
want to commit the former. Of course, strict concurrency control algorithms that
avoid cascading aborts would not permit the updated value of a data item to be read
by any other transaction until the updating transaction terminates. This is sometimes
called the *recoverability condition*.

Another possible reason why a participant may not agree to commit is due to
deadlocks that require a participant to abort the transaction. Note that, in this case,
the participant should be permitted to abort the transaction without being told to do
so. This capability is quite important and is called *unilateral abort*. Another reason
for unilateral abort may be timeouts as discussed earlier.

A brief description of the 2PC protocol that does not consider failures is given
below. This discussion is facilitated by means of the state transition diagram of the
2PC protocol (Fig. 5.10). The states are denoted by circles and the edges represent
the state transitions. The terminal states are depicted by concentric circles. The
interpretation of the labels on the edges is as follows: the reason for the state
transition, which is a received message, is given at the top, and the message that
is sent as a result of state transition is given at the bottom.

1. Initially, the coordinator writes a begin_commit record in its log, sends a
   "prepare" message to all participant sites, and enters the WAIT state.
2. When a participant receives a "prepare" message, it checks if it could commit
   the transaction. If so, the participant writes a ready record in the log, sends a
   "vote-commit" message to the coordinator, and enters READY state; otherwise,

the participant writes an abort record and sends a "vote-abort" message to the coordinator.

3. If the decision of the site is to abort, it can forget about that transaction, since an abort decision serves as a veto (i.e., unilateral abort).
4. After the coordinator has received a reply from every participant, it decides whether to commit or to abort the transaction. If even one participant has registered a negative vote, the coordinator has to abort the transaction globally. So it writes an abort record, sends a "global-abort" message to all participant sites, and enters the ABORT state; otherwise, it writes a commit record, sends a "global-commit" message to all participants, and enters the COMMIT state.
5. The participants either commit or abort the transaction according to the coordinator's instructions and send back an acknowledgment, at which point the coordinator terminates the transaction by writing an end_of_transaction record in the log.

Note the manner in which the coordinator reaches a global termination decision regarding a transaction. Two rules govern this decision, which, together, are called the *global-commit rule*:

1. If even one participant votes to abort the transaction, the coordinator has to reach a global-abort decision.
2. If all the participants vote to commit the transaction, the coordinator has to reach a global-commit decision.

The operation of the 2PC protocol between a coordinator and one participant in the absence of failures is depicted in Fig. 5.11, where the circles indicate the states and the dashed lines indicate messages between the coordinator and the participants. The labels on the dashed lines specify the nature of the message.

A few important points about the 2PC protocol that can be observed from Fig. 5.11 are as follows. First, 2PC permits a participant to unilaterally abort a transaction until it has logged an affirmative vote. Second, once a participant votes to commit or abort a transaction, it cannot change its vote. Third, while a participant is in the READY state, it can move either to abort the transaction or to commit it, depending on the nature of the message from the coordinator. Fourth, the global termination decision is taken by the coordinator according to the global-commit rule. Finally, note that the coordinator and participant processes enter certain states where they have to wait for messages from one another. To guarantee that they can exit from these states and terminate, timers are used. Each process sets its timer when it enters a state, and if the expected message is not received before the timer runs out, the process times out and invokes its timeout protocol (which will be discussed later).

There are a number of different ways to implement a 2PC protocol. The one discussed above and depicted in Fig. 5.11 is called a *centralized 2PC* since the communication is only between the coordinator and the participants; the participants do not communicate among themselves. This communication structure, which is the basis of our subsequent discussions, is depicted more clearly in Fig. 5.12.

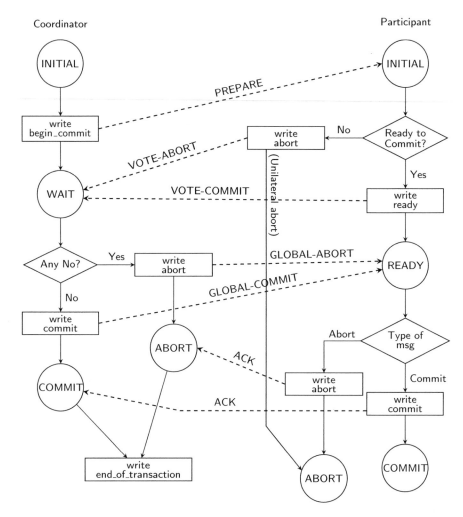

Fig. 5.11 2PC protocol actions

Another alternative is *linear 2PC* (also called *nested 2PC*) where participants can communicate with one another. There is a possibly logical ordering between the sites in the system for the purposes of communication. Let us assume that the ordering among the sites that participate in the execution of a transaction are $1, \ldots, N$, where the coordinator is the first one in the order. The 2PC protocol is implemented by a forward communication from the coordinator (number 1) to N, during which the first phase is completed, and by a backward communication from N to the coordinator, during which the second phase is completed. Thus, linear 2PC operates in the following manner.

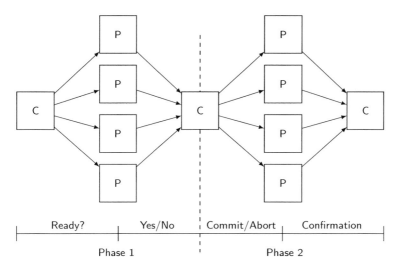

Fig. 5.12 Centralized 2PC communication structure. C: Coordinator, P: Participant

The coordinator sends the "prepare" message to participant 2. If participant 2 is not ready to commit the transaction, it sends a "vote-abort" message (VA) to participant 3 and the transaction is aborted at this point (unilateral abort by 2). If, on the other hand, participant 2 agrees to commit the transaction, it sends a "vote-commit" message (VC) to participant 3 and enters the READY state. As in the centralized 2PC implementation, each site logs its decision before sending the message to the next site. This process continues until a "vote-commit" vote reaches participant N. This is the end of the first phase. If site N decides to commit, it sends back to site $(N-1)$ "global-commit" (GC); otherwise, it sends a "global-abort" message (GA). Accordingly, the participants enter the appropriate state (COMMIT or ABORT) and propagate the message back to the coordinator.

Linear 2PC, whose communication structure is depicted in Fig. 5.13, incurs fewer messages but does not provide any parallelism. Therefore, it suffers from low response-time performance.

Another popular communication structure for implementation of the 2PC protocol involves communication among all the participants during the first phase of the protocol so that they all independently reach their termination decisions with respect to the specific transaction. This version, called *distributed 2PC*, eliminates the need for the second phase of the protocol since the participants can reach a decision on their own. It operates as follows. The coordinator sends the prepare message to all participants. Each participant then sends its decision to all the other participants (and to the coordinator) by means of either a "vote-commit" or a "vote-abort" message. Each participant waits for messages from all the other participants and makes its termination decision according to the global-commit rule. Obviously, there is no need for the second phase of the protocol (someone sending the global-abort or global-commit decision to the others), since each participant has independently

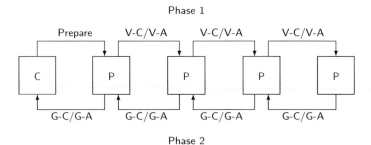

Fig. 5.13 Linear 2PC communication structure. V-C: vote.commit; V-A: vote.abort; G-C: global.commit; G-A: global.abort

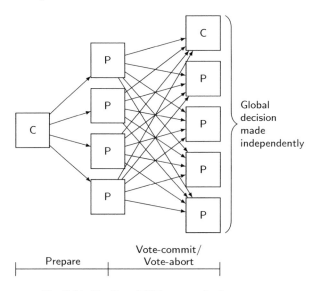

Fig. 5.14 Distributed 2PC communication structure

reached that decision at the end of the first phase. The communication structure of distributed commit is depicted in Fig. 5.14.

In linear and distributed 2PC implementation, a participant has to know the identity of either the next participant in the linear ordering (in case of linear 2PC) or of all the participants (in case of distributed 2PC). This problem can be solved by attaching the list of participants to the prepare message that is sent by the coordinator. Such an issue does not arise in the case of centralized 2PC since the coordinator clearly knows who the participants are.

The algorithm for the centralized execution of the 2PC protocol by the coordinator and by the participants are given in Algorithms 5.6 and 5.7, respectively.

Algorithm 5.6: 2PC Coordinator (2PC-C)

---

begin
  repeat
    wait for an *event*
    switch *event* **do**
      case *Msg Arrival* **do**
        Let the arrived message be *msg*
        switch *msg* **do**
          case *Commit* **do**   {commit command from scheduler}
            write begin_commit record in the log
            send "Prepared" message to all the involved participants
            set timer
          end case
          case *Vote-abort* **do** {one participant has voted to abort; unilateral abort}
            write abort record in the log
            send "Global-abort" message to the other involved participants
            set timer
          end case
          case *Vote-commit* **do**
            update the list of participants who have answered
            if *all the participants have answered* **then** {all must have voted to commit}
              write commit record in the log
              send "Global-commit" to all the involved participants
              set timer
            end if
          end case
          case *Ack* **do**
            update the list of participants who have acknowledged
            if *all the participants have acknowledged* **then**
             write end_of_transaction record in the log
            else
             send global decision to the unanswering participants
            end if
          end case
        end switch
      end case
      case *Timeout* **do**
        execute the termination protocol
      end case
    end switch
  until *forever*
end

5.4.2   Variations of 2PC

Two variations of 2PC have been proposed to improve its performance. This is accomplished by reducing (1) the number of messages that are transmitted between the coordinator and the participants, and (2) the number of times logs are written.

Algorithm 5.7: 2PC Participant (2PC-P)

---

begin
  repeat
    wait for an *event*
    switch *ev* **do**
      case *Msg Arrival* **do**
        Let the arrived message be *msg*
        switch *msg* **do**
          case *Prepare* **do**   {Prepare command from the coordinator}
            if *ready to commit* **then**
              write ready record in the log
              send "Vote-commit" message to the coordinator
              set timer
            end if
            else   {unilateral abort}
              write abort record in the log
              send "Vote-abort" message to the coordinator
              abort the transaction
            end if
          end case
          case *Global-abort* **do**
            write abort record in the log
            abort the transaction
          end case
          case *Global-commit* **do**
            write commit record in the log
            commit the transaction
          end case
        end switch
      end case
      case *Timeout* **do**
        execute the termination protocol
      end case
    end switch
  until *forever*
end

These protocols are called *presumed abort* and *presumed commit*. Presumed abort is a protocol that is optimized to handle read-only transactions as well as those update transactions, some of whose processes do not perform any updates to the database (called partially read-only). The presumed commit protocol is optimized to handle the general update transactions. We will discuss briefly both of these variations.

5.4.2.1 Presumed Abort 2PC Protocol

In the presumed abort 2PC protocol, whenever a prepared participant polls the coordinator about a transaction's outcome and there is no information about it, the response to the inquiry is to abort the transaction. This works since, in the case of a commit, the coordinator does not forget about a transaction until all participants acknowledge, guaranteeing that they will no longer inquire about this transaction.

When this convention is used, it can be seen that the coordinator can forget about a transaction immediately after it decides to abort it. It can write an abort record and not expect the participants to acknowledge the abort command. The coordinator does not need to write an end_of_transaction record after an abort record.

The abort record does not need to be forced, because if a site fails before receiving the decision and then recovers, the recovery routine will check the log to determine the fate of the transaction. Since the abort record is not forced, the recovery routine may not find any information about the transaction, in which case it will ask the coordinator and will be told to abort it. For the same reason, the abort records do not need to be forced by the participants either.

Since it saves some message transmission between the coordinator and the participants in case of aborted transactions, presumed abort 2PC is expected to be more efficient.

5.4.2.2   Presumed Commit 2PC Protocol

Presumed commit 2PC is based on the premise that if no information about the transaction exists, it should be considered committed. However, it is not an exact dual of presumed abort 2PC, since an exact dual would require that the coordinator forget about a transaction immediately after it decides to commit it, that commit records (also the ready records of the participants) not be forced, and that commit commands need not be acknowledged. Consider, however, the following scenario. The coordinator sends prepared messages and starts collecting information, but fails before being able to collect all of them and reach a decision. In this case, the participants will wait until they timeout, and then turn the transaction over to their recovery routines. Since there is no information about the transaction, the recovery routines of each participant will commit the transaction. The coordinator, on the other hand, will abort the transaction when it recovers, thus causing inconsistency.

Presumed commit 2PC solves the problem as follows. The coordinator, prior to sending the prepare message, force-writes a collecting record, which contains the names of all the participants involved in executing that transaction. The participant then enters the COLLECTING state, following which it sends the "prepare" message and enters the WAIT state. The participants, when they receive the "prepare" message, decide what they want to do with the transaction, write an abort/ready record accordingly, and respond with either a "vote-abort" or a "vote-commit" message. When the coordinator receives decisions from all the participants, it decides to abort or commit the transaction. If the decision is to abort, the coordinator writes an abort record, enters the ABORT state, and sends a "global-abort" message. If it decides to commit the transaction, it writes a commit record, sends a "global-commit" command, and forgets the transaction. When the participants receive a "global-commit" message, they write a commit record and update the database. If they receive a "global-abort" message, they write an abort record and acknowledge. The participant, upon receiving the abort acknowledgment, writes an end_of_transaction record and forgets about the transaction.

5.4.3   Dealing with Site Failures

In this section, we consider the failure of sites in the network. Our aim is to develop nonblocking termination and independent recovery protocols. As we indicated before, the existence of independent recovery protocols would imply the existence of nonblocking recovery protocols. However, our discussion addresses both aspects separately. Also note that in the following discussion we consider only the standard 2PC protocol, not its two variants presented above.

   Let us first set the boundaries for the existence of nonblocking termination and independent recovery protocols in the presence of site failures. It has been proven that such protocols exist when a single site fails. In the case of multiple site failures, however, the prospects are not as promising. A negative result indicates that it is not possible to design independent recovery protocols (and, therefore, nonblocking termination protocols) when multiple sites fail. We first develop termination and recovery protocols for the 2PC algorithm and show that 2PC is inherently blocking. We then proceed to the development of atomic commit protocols which are nonblocking in the case of single site failures.

5.4.3.1   Termination and Recovery Protocols for 2PC

Termination Protocols

The termination protocols serve the timeouts for both the coordinator and the participant processes. A timeout occurs at a destination site when it cannot get an expected message from a source site within the expected time period. In this section, we consider that this is due to the failure of the source site.

   The method for handling timeouts depends on the timing of failures as well as on the types of failures. We therefore need to consider failures at various points of 2PC execution. In the following, we again refer to the 2PC state transition diagram (Fig. 5.10).

Coordinator Timeouts

There are three states in which the coordinator can timeout: WAIT, COMMIT, and ABORT. Timeouts during the last two are handled in the same manner. So we need to consider only two cases:

1. *Timeout in the WAIT state.* In the WAIT state, the coordinator is waiting for the local decisions of the participants. The coordinator cannot unilaterally commit the transaction since the global-commit rule has not been satisfied. However, it can decide to globally abort the transaction, in which case it writes an abort record in the log and sends a "global-abort" message to all the participants.
2. *Timeout in the COMMIT or ABORT states.* In this case the coordinator is not certain that the commit or abort procedures have been completed by the local recovery managers at all of the participant sites. Thus the coordinator repeatedly sends the "global-commit" or "global-abort" commands to the sites that have not yet responded, and waits for their acknowledgement.

Participant Timeouts

A participant can time out[1] in two states: INITIAL and READY. Let us examine both of these cases.

1. *Timeout in the INITIAL state.* In this state the participant is waiting for a "prepare" message. The coordinator must have failed in the INITIAL state. The participant can unilaterally abort the transaction following a timeout. If the "prepare" message arrives at this participant at a later time, this can be handled in one of two possible ways. Either the participant would check its log, find the abort record, and respond with a "vote-abort," or it can simply ignore the "prepare" message. In the latter case the coordinator would time out in the WAIT state and follow the course we have discussed above.
2. *Timeout in the READY state.* In this state the participant has voted to commit the transaction but does not know the global decision of the coordinator. The participant cannot unilaterally reach a decision. Since it is in the READY state, it must have voted to commit the transaction. Therefore, it cannot now change its vote and unilaterally abort it. On the other hand, it cannot unilaterally decide to commit it, since it is possible that another participant may have voted to abort it. In this case, the participant will remain blocked until it can learn from someone (either the coordinator or some other participant) the ultimate fate of the transaction.

Let us consider a centralized communication structure where the participants cannot communicate with one another. In this case, the participant that is trying to terminate a transaction has to ask the coordinator for its decision and wait until it receives a response. If the coordinator has failed, the participant will remain blocked. This is undesirable.

---

[1] In some discussions of the 2PC protocol, it is assumed that the participants do not use timers and do not time out. However, implementing timeout protocols for the participants solves some nasty problems and may speed up the commit process. Therefore, we consider this more general case.

If the participants can communicate with each other, a more distributed termination protocol may be developed. The participant that times out can simply ask all the other participants to help it make a decision. Assuming that participant P_i is the one that times out, each of the other participants (P_j) responds in the following manner:

1. P_j is in the INITIAL state. This means that P_j has not yet voted and may not even have received the "prepare" message. It can therefore unilaterally abort the transaction and reply to P_i with a "vote-abort" message.
2. P_j is in the READY state. In this state P_j has voted to commit the transaction but has not received any word about the global decision. Therefore, it cannot help P_i to terminate the transaction.
3. P_j is in the ABORT or COMMIT states. In these states, either P_j has unilaterally decided to abort the transaction, or it has received the coordinator's decision regarding global termination. It can, therefore, send P_i either a "vote-commit" or a "vote-abort" message.

Consider how the participant that times out (P_i) can interpret these responses. The following cases are possible:

1. P_i receives "vote-abort" messages from all P_j. This means that none of the other participants had yet voted, but they have chosen to abort the transaction unilaterally. Under these conditions, P_i can proceed to abort the transaction.
2. P_i receives "vote-abort" messages from some P_j, but some other participants indicate that they are in the READY state. In this case P_i can still go ahead and abort the transaction, since according to the global-commit rule, the transaction cannot be committed and will eventually be aborted.
3. P_i receives notification from all P_j that they are in the READY state. In this case none of the participants knows enough about the fate of the transaction to terminate it properly.
4. P_i receives "global-abort" or "global-commit" messages from all P_j. In this case all the other participants have received the coordinator's decision. Therefore, P_i can go ahead and terminate the transaction according to the messages it receives from the other participants. Incidentally, note that it is not possible for some of the P_j to respond with a "global-abort" while others respond with "global-commit" since this cannot be the result of a legitimate execution of the 2PC protocol.
5. P_i receives "global-abort" or "global-commit" from some P_j, whereas others indicate that they are in the READY state. This indicates that some sites have received the coordinator's decision while others are still waiting for it. In this case P_i can proceed as in case 4 above .4.

These five cases cover all the alternatives that a termination protocol needs to handle. It is not necessary to consider cases where, for example, one participant sends a "vote-abort" message while another one sends "global-commit." This cannot happen in 2PC. During the execution of the 2PC protocol, no process (participant or coordinator) is more than one state transition apart from any other process. For example, if a participant is in the INITIAL state, all other participants are in either the INITIAL or the READY state. Similarly, the coordinator is either in the INITIAL or the WAIT state. Thus, all the processes in a 2PC protocol are said to be *synchronous within one state transition.*

Note that in case 3, the participant processes stay blocked, as they cannot terminate a transaction. Under certain circumstances there may be a way to overcome this blocking. If during termination all the participants realize that only the coordinator site has failed, they can elect a new coordinator, which can restart the commit process. There are different ways of electing the coordinator. It is possible either to define a total ordering among all sites and elect the next one in order, or to establish a voting procedure among the participants . This will not work, however, if both a participant site and the coordinator site fail. In this case it is possible for the participant at the failed site to have received the coordinator's decision and have terminated the transaction accordingly. This decision is unknown to the other participants; thus if they elect a new coordinator and proceed, there is the danger that they may decide to terminate the transaction differently from the participant at the failed site. It is clear that it is not possible to design termination protocols for 2PC that can guarantee nonblocking termination. The 2PC protocol is, therefore, a blocking protocol. Formally, the protocol is blocking because there is a state in Fig. 5.10 that is adjacent to both the commit and abort state, and when there is a coordinator failure participants are in the ready state. Therefore, it is impossible to determine whether the coordinator went to the abort or commit state until it recovers. The 3PC (three-phase commit) protocol solves this blocking situation by adding a new state, PRECOMMIT, between the wait and commit states to avoid the situation and preventing the blocking situation in the advent of a coordinator failure.

Since we had assumed a centralized communication structure in developing the 2PC algorithms in Algorithms 5.6 and 5.7, we will continue with the same assumption in developing the termination protocols. The portion of code that should be included in the timeout section of the coordinator and the participant 2PC algorithms is given in Algorithms 5.8 and 5.9, respectively.

Algorithm 5.8: 2PC Coordinator Terminate

```
begin
    if in WAIT state then                          {coordinator is in ABORT state}
        write abort record in the log
        send "Global-abort" message to all the participants
    else                                           {coordinator is in COMMIT state}
        check for the last log record
        if last log record = abort then
            | send "Global-abort" to all participants that have not responded
        else
            | send "Global-commit" to all the participants that have not responded
        end if
    end if
    set timer
end
```

Algorithm 5.9: 2PC-Participant Terminate

---

begin
    if *in INITIAL state* **then**
        | write abort record in the log
    else
        | send "Vote-commit" message to the coordinator
        | reset timer
    end if
end

Recovery Protocols

In the preceding section, we discussed how the 2PC protocol deals with failures from the perspective of the operational sites. In this section, we take the opposite viewpoint: we are interested in investigating protocols that a coordinator or participant can use to recover their states when their sites fail and then restart. Remember that we would like these protocols to be independent. However, in general, it is not possible to design protocols that can guarantee independent recovery while maintaining the atomicity of distributed transactions. This is not surprising given the fact that the termination protocols for 2PC are inherently blocking.

In the following discussion, we again use the state transition diagram of Fig. 5.10. Additionally, we make two interpretive assumptions: (1) the combined action of writing a record in the log and sending a message is assumed to be atomic, and (2) the state transition occurs after the transmission of the response message. For example, if the coordinator is in the WAIT state, this means that it has successfully written the begin_commit record in its log and has successfully transmitted the "prepare" command. This does not say anything, however, about successful completion of the message transmission. Therefore, the "prepare" message may never get to the participants, due to communication failures, which we discuss separately. The first assumption related to atomicity is, of course, unrealistic. However, it simplifies our discussion of fundamental failure cases. At the end of this section we show that the other cases that arise from the relaxation of this assumption can be handled by a combination of the fundamental failure cases.

Coordinator Site Failures

The following cases are possible:

1. *The coordinator fails while in the INITIAL state*. This is before the coordinator has initiated the commit procedure. Therefore, it will start the commit process upon recovery.
2. *The coordinator fails while in the WAIT state*. In this case, the coordinator has sent the "prepare" command. Upon recovery, the coordinator will restart the

commit process for this transaction from the beginning by sending the "prepare" message one more time.

3. *The coordinator fails while in the COMMIT or ABORT states.* In this case, the coordinator will have informed the participants of its decision and terminated the transaction. Thus, upon recovery, it does not need to do anything if all the acknowledgments have been received. Otherwise, the termination protocol is involved.

Participant Site Failures

There are three alternatives to consider:

1. *A participant fails in the INITIAL state.* Upon recovery, the participant should abort the transaction unilaterally. Let us see why this is acceptable. Note that the coordinator will be in the INITIAL or WAIT state with respect to this transaction. If it is in the INITIAL state, it will send a "prepare" message and then move to the WAIT state. Because of the participant site's failure, it will not receive the participant's decision and will time out in that state. We have already discussed how the coordinator would handle timeouts in the WAIT state by globally aborting the transaction.

2. *A participant fails while in the READY state.* In this case the coordinator has been informed of the failed site's affirmative decision about the transaction before the failure. Upon recovery, the participant at the failed site can treat this as a timeout in the READY state and hand the incomplete transaction over to its termination protocol.

3. *A participant fails while in the ABORT or COMMIT state.* These states represent the termination conditions, so, upon recovery, the participant does not need to take any special action.

Additional Cases

Let us now consider the cases that may arise when we relax the assumption related to the atomicity of the logging and message sending actions. In particular, we assume that a site failure may occur after the coordinator or a participant has written a log record but before it can send a message. For this discussion, the reader may wish to refer to Fig. 5.11.

1. *The coordinator fails after the* begin_commit *record is written in the log but before the "prepare" command is sent.* The coordinator would react to this as a failure in the WAIT state (case 2 of the coordinator failures discussed above) and send the "prepare" command upon recovery.

2. *A participant site fails after writing the* ready *record in the log but before sending the "vote-commit" message.* The failed participant sees this as case 2 of the participant failures discussed before.

3. *A participant site fails after writing the* Abort *record in the log but before sending the "vote-abort" message.* This is the only situation that is not covered by the fundamental cases discussed before. However, the participant does not need to do anything upon recovery in this case. The coordinator is in the WAIT state and will time out. The coordinator termination protocol for this state globally aborts the transaction.

4. *The coordinator fails after logging its final decision record* (Abort *or* Commit)*, but before sending its "global-abort" or "global-commit" message to the participants.* The coordinator treats this as its case 3, while the participants treat it as a timeout in the READY state.

5. *A participant fails after it logs an* Abort *or a* Commit *record but before it sends the acknowledgment message to the coordinator.* The participant can treat this as its case 3. The coordinator will handle this by timeout in the COMMIT or ABORT state.

5.4.3.2   Three-Phase Commit Protocol

As noted earlier, blocking commit protocols are undesirable. The three-phase commit protocol (3PC) is designed as a nonblocking protocol when failures are restricted to site failures. When network failures occur, things are complicated.

3PC is interesting from an algorithmic viewpoint, but it incurs high communication overhead in terms of latency, since it involves three rounds of messages with forced writes to the stable log. Therefore, it has not been adopted in real systems—even 2PC is criticized for its high latency due to the sequential phases with forced writes to the log. Therefore, we summarize the approach without going into detailed analysis.

Let us first consider the necessary and sufficient conditions for designing nonblocking atomic commitment protocols. A commit protocol that is synchronous within one state transition is nonblocking if and only if its state transition diagram contains neither of the following:

1. No state that is "adjacent" to both a commit and an abort state.
2. No noncommittable state that is "adjacent" to a commit state.

The term *adjacent* here means that it is possible to go from one state to the other with a single state transition.

Consider the COMMIT state in the 2PC protocol (see Fig. 5.10). If any process is in this state, we know that all the sites have voted to commit the transaction. Such states are called *committable*. There are other states in the 2PC protocol that are *noncommittable*. The one we are interested in is the READY state, which is noncommittable since the existence of a process in this state does not imply that all the processes have voted to commit the transaction.

It is obvious that the WAIT state in the coordinator and the READY state in the participant 2PC protocol violate the nonblocking conditions we have stated above.

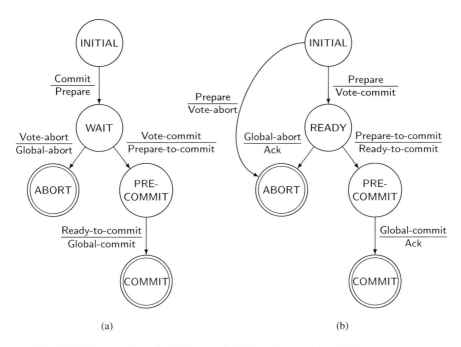

Fig. 5.15 State transitions in 3PC protocol. (**a**) Coordinator states. (**b**) Participant states

Therefore, one might be able to make the following modification to the 2PC protocol to satisfy the conditions and turn it into a nonblocking protocol.

We can add another state between the WAIT (and READY) and COMMIT states which serves as a buffer state where the process is ready to commit (if that is the final decision) but has not yet committed. The state transition diagrams for the coordinator and the participant in this protocol are depicted in Fig. 5.15. This is called the three-phase commit protocol (3PC) because there are three state transitions from the INITIAL state to a COMMIT state. The execution of the protocol between the coordinator and one participant is depicted in Fig. 5.16. Note that this is identical to Fig. 5.11 except for the addition of the PRECOMMIT state. Observe that 3PC is also a protocol where all the states are synchronous within one state transition. Therefore, the foregoing conditions for nonblocking 2PC apply to 3PC.

5.4.4   Network Partitioning

In this section, we consider how the network partitions can be handled by the atomic commit protocols that we discussed in the preceding section. Network partitions are due to communication line failures and may cause the loss of messages, depending

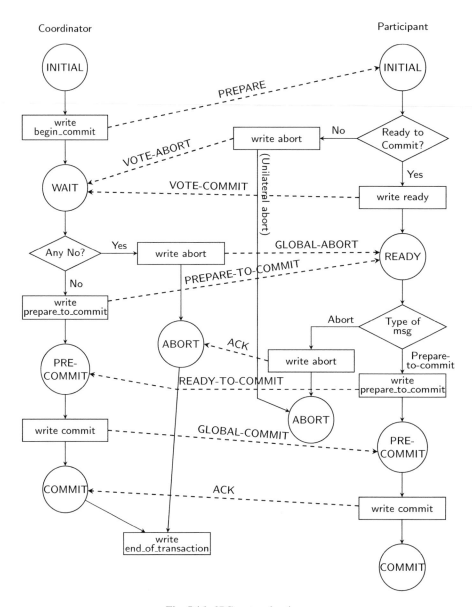

Fig. 5.16 3PC protocol actions

on the implementation of the communication network. A partitioning is called a *simple partitioning* if the network is divided into only two components; otherwise, it is called *multiple partitioning*.

The termination protocols for network partitioning address the termination of the transactions that were active in each partition at the time of partitioning. If one can develop nonblocking protocols to terminate these transactions, it is possible for the sites in each partition to reach a termination decision (for a given transaction) which is consistent with the sites in the other partitions. This would imply that the sites in each partition can continue executing transactions despite the partitioning.

Unfortunately, generally it is not possible to find nonblocking termination protocols in the presence of network partitioning. Remember that our expectations regarding the reliability of the communication network are minimal. If a message cannot be delivered, it is simply lost. In this case it can be proven that no non-blocking atomic commitment protocol exists that is resilient to network partitioning. This is quite a negative result since it also means that if network partitioning occurs, we cannot continue normal operations in all partitions, which limits the availability of the entire distributed database system. A positive counter result, however, indicates that it is possible to design nonblocking atomic commit protocols that are resilient to simple partitions. Unfortunately, if multiple partitions occur, it is again not possible to design such protocols.

In the remainder of this section we discuss a number of protocols that address network partitioning in nonreplicated databases. The problem is quite different in the case of replicated databases, which we discuss in the next chapter.

In the presence of network partitioning of nonreplicated databases, the major concern is with the termination of transactions that were active at the time of partitioning. Any new transaction that accesses a data item that is stored in another partition is simply blocked and has to await the repair of the network. Concurrent accesses to the data items within one partition can be handled by the concurrency control algorithm. The significant problem, therefore, is to ensure that the transaction terminates properly. In short, the network partitioning problem is handled by the commit protocol, and more specifically, by the termination and recovery protocols.

The absence of nonblocking protocols that would guarantee atomic commitment of distributed transactions points to an important design decision. We can either permit all the partitions to continue their normal operations and accept the fact that database consistency may be compromised, or we guarantee the consistency of the database by employing strategies that would permit operation in one of the partitions while the sites in the others remain blocked. This decision problem is the premise of a classification of partition handling strategies. The strategies can be classified as *pessimistic* or *optimistic*. Pessimistic strategies emphasize the consistency of the database, and would therefore not permit transactions to execute in a partition if there is no guarantee that the consistency of the database can be maintained. Optimistic approaches, on the other hand, emphasize the availability of the database even if this would cause inconsistencies.

The second dimension is related to the correctness criterion. If serializability is used as the fundamental correctness criterion, such strategies are called *syntactic* since the serializability theory uses only syntactic information. However, if we use a more abstract correctness criterion that is dependent on the semantics of the transactions or the database, the strategies are said to be *semantic*.

Consistent with the correctness criterion that we have adopted in this book (serializability), we consider only syntactic approaches in this section. The following two sections outline various syntactic strategies for nonreplicated databases.

All the known termination protocols that deal with network partitioning in the case of nonreplicated databases are pessimistic. Since the pessimistic approaches emphasize the maintenance of database consistency, the fundamental issue that we need to address is which of the partitions can continue normal operations. We consider two approaches.

5.4.4.1   Centralized Protocols

Centralized termination protocols are based on the centralized concurrency control algorithms discussed in Sect. 5.2. In this case, it makes sense to permit the operation of the partition that contains the central site, since it manages the lock tables.

Primary site techniques are centralized with respect to each data item. In this case, more than one partition may be operational for different queries. For any given query, only the partition that contains the primary site of the data items that are in the write set of that transaction can execute that transaction.

Both of these are simple approaches that would work well, but they are dependent on a specific concurrency control mechanism. Furthermore, they expect each site to be able to differentiate network partitioning from site failures properly. This is necessary since the participants in the execution of the commit protocol react differently to the different types of failures. Unfortunately, in general this is not possible.

5.4.4.2   Voting-Based Protocols

Voting can also be used for managing concurrent data accesses. A straightforward voting with majority has been proposed as a concurrency control method for fully replicated databases. The fundamental idea is that a transaction is executed if a majority of the sites vote to execute it.

The idea of majority voting has been generalized to voting with *quorums*. Quorum-based voting can be used as a replica control method (as we discuss in the next chapter), as well as a commit method to ensure transaction atomicity in the presence of network partitioning. In the case of nonreplicated databases, this involves the integration of the voting principle with commit protocols. We present a specific proposal along this line.

Every site in the system is assigned a vote V_i. Let us assume that the total number of votes in the system is V, and the abort and commit quorums are V_a and V_c, respectively. Then the following rules must be obeyed in the implementation of the commit protocol:

1. $V_a + V_c > V$, where $0 \leq V_a, V_c \leq V$.

2. Before a transaction commits, it must obtain a commit quorum V_c.

3. Before a transaction aborts, it must obtain an abort quorum V_a.

The first rule ensures that a transaction cannot be committed and aborted at the same time. The next two rules indicate the votes that a transaction has to obtain before it can terminate one way or the other. The integration of quorum techniques into commit protocols is left as an exercise.

5.4.5 Paxos Consensus Protocol

Up to this point, we have studied 2PC protocols for reaching agreement among transaction managers as to the resolution of a distributed transaction and discovered that it has the undesirable property of blocking when the coordinator is down as well as one other participant. We discussed how to overcome this by using 3PC protocol, which is expensive and is not resilient to network partitioning. Our treatment of network partitioning considered voting to determine the partition where a "majority" of transaction managers reside and terminate the transaction in that partition. These may seem like piece-meal solutions to the fundamental problem of finding fault-tolerant mechanisms for reaching an agreement (consensus) among transaction managers about the fate of the transaction under consideration. As it turns out, reaching a consensus among sites is a general problem in distributed computing known as *distributed consensus*. A number of algorithms have been proposed for addressing this problem; in this section, we discuss the Paxos family of algorithms and point to others in Bibliographic Notes.

We will first discuss Paxos in the general setting in which it was originally defined and then consider how it can be used in commit protocols. In the general context, the algorithm achieves a consensus among sites about the value of a variable (or decision). The important consideration is that a consensus is reached if a majority of the sites agree on the value, not all of them. So, certain number of sites may fail, but as long as a majority exists, consensus can be reached. It identifies three roles: *proposer* who recommends a value for the variable, *acceptor* who decides whether or not to accept he recommended value, and *learner* who discovers the agreed-upon value by asking one of the learners (or the value is pushed to it by an acceptor). Note that these are roles all of which can be colocated in one site, but each site can have only one instance of each. The learners are not very important so we do not consider them in any detail in our exposition.

Paxos protocol is simple if there is only one proposer, and it operates like the 2PC protocol: in the first round, the proposer suggests a value for the variable and acceptors send their responses (accept/not accept). If the proposer gets accepts from a majority of the acceptors, then it determines that particular value to be the value of the variable and notifies the acceptors who now record that value the final one. A learner can, at any point, ask an acceptor what the value of the variable is and learn the latest value.

Of course, reality is not this simple and the Paxos protocol needs to be able to deal with the following complications:

1. Since this is, by definition, a distributed consensus protocol, multiple proposers can put forward a value for the same variable. Therefore, an acceptor needs to pick one of the proposed values.
2. Given multiple proposals, it is possible to get split votes on multiple proposals with no proposed value receiving a majority.
3. It is possible that some of the acceptors fail after they accept a value. If the remaining acceptors who accepted that value do not constitute a majority, this causes a problem.

Paxos deals with the first problem by using a ballot number so that acceptors can differentiate different proposals as we discuss below. The second problem can be addressed by running multiple consensus rounds—if no proposal achieves a majority, then another round is run and this is repeated until one value achieves majority. In some cases, this can go on for a number of iterations and this can degrade its performance. Paxos deals with the problem by having a designated *leader* to which every proposer sends its value proposal. The leader then picks one value for each variable and seeks to obtain the majority. This reduces the distributed nature of the consensus protocol. In different rounds of the protocol execution, the leader could be different. The third problem is more serious. Again, this could be treated as the second issue and a new round can be started. However, the complication is that some learners may have learned the accepted value from acceptors in the previous round, and if a different value is chosen in the new round we have inconsistency. Paxos deals with this again by using ballot numbers.

We present below the steps of "basic Paxos" that focuses on determining the value of a single variable (hence the omission of the variable name in the following). Basic Paxos also simplifies the determination of ballot numbers: the ballot number in this case only needs to be unique and monotonic for each proposer; there is no attempt to make them globally unique since a consensus is reached when a majority of the acceptors settle on *some* value for the variable regardless of who proposed it. Below is the basic Paxos operation in the absence of failures:

S1. The proposer who wishes to start a consensus sends to all the acceptors a "prepare" message with its ballot number [prepare(bal)].

S2. Each acceptor that receives the prepare message performs the following:
if it had not received any proposals before
  it records prepare(bal) in its log and responds with ack(bal)
  else if bal > any ballot number that it had received from any proposer before
    then it records prepare(bal) in its log and responds with the ballot number (bal') and value (val') of the highest proposal number it had accepted prior to this: ack(bal, bal', val');
    else it ignores the prepare message.

S3. When the proposer receives an ack message from an acceptor, it logs the message.

S4. When the proposer has received acks from a majority of acceptors (i.e., it has a quorum to establish a consensus) it sends an accept($nbal$, val) message to acceptors where $nbal$ is the ballot number to accept and val is the value to accept where $nbal$ and val are determined as follows:

if all of the ack messages it received indicate that no acceptors have previously accepted a value

then the proposed value val is set to what the proposer wanted to suggest in the first place and $nbal \leftarrow bal$;

else val is set to the val' in the return ack messages with the largest bal' and $nbal \leftarrow bal$ (so everyone converges to the value with the largest ballot number);

the proposer now sends accept(bal, val) to all the acceptors (val is the proposed value).

S5. Each acceptor performs the following upon receipt of the accept($nbal$, val) message:

if $nbal$ = ack.bal (i.e., the ballot number of the accept message is the one it had promised earlier)

then it records accepted($nbal$, val)

else it ignores the message.

A number of points about the above protocol. First note that in step S2, an acceptor ignores the prepare message if it has already received a prepare message higher than the one it just received. Although the protocol works correctly in this case, the proposer may continue to communicate with this acceptor later on (e.g., in step S5) and this can be avoided if it were to send back a negative acknowledgement so that the proposer can take it off of future consideration. The second point is that when an acceptor acknowledges a prepare message, it is also acknowledging that the proposer is the Paxos leader for this round. So, in a sense, leader selection is done as part of the protocol. However, to deal with the second problem discussed earlier, it is possible to have a designated leader, which then initiates the rounds. If this is the chosen implementation, then the elected leader can choose which proposal it will put forward if it receives multiple proposals. Finally, since the protocol advances if a majority of participants (sites) are available, for a system with N sites, it can tolerate $\frac{N}{2} - 1$ simultaneous site failures.

Let us briefly analyze how Paxos deals with failures. The simplest case is when some acceptors fail but there is still the quorum for reaching a decision. In this case, the protocol proceeds as usual. If sufficient acceptors fail to eliminate the possibility of a quorum, then this is handled naturally in the protocol by running a new ballot (or multiple ballots) when a quorum can be achieved. The case that is always challenging for consensus algorithms is the failure of the proposer (which is also the leader); in this case Paxos chooses a new leader by some mechanism (there are a number of proposals in literature for this) and the new leader initiates a new round with a new ballot number.

Paxos has the multiround decision making characteristic of 2PC and 3PC and the majority voting method of quorum algorithms; it generalizes these into one coherent protocol to reach consensus in the presence of a set of distributed processes. It has been pointed out that 2PC and 3PC (and other commit protocols) are special cases of Paxos. In the following, we describe one proposal for running 2PC with Paxos in order to achieve a nonblocking 2PC protocol, called Paxos 2PC.

In Paxos 2PC, the transaction managers act as leaders—this is basically noting that what we called coordinator before is now called a leader. A main feature of the protocol is for the leader to use a Paxos protocol to reach consensus and record its decision in a replicated log. The first feature is important since the protocol does not need to have all of the participants active and participating in the decision—a majority will do and others can converge on the decided value when they recover. The second is important because leader (coordinator) failures are no longer blocking—if a leader fails, a new leader can get elected and the state of the transaction decision is available in the replicated log at other sites.

5.4.6   Architectural Considerations

In the previous sections, we have discussed the atomic commit protocols at an abstract level. Let us now look at how these protocols can be implemented within the framework of our architectural model. This discussion involves specification of the interface between the concurrency control algorithms and the reliability protocols. In that sense, the discussions of this chapter relate to the execution of Commit, Abort, and recover commands.

It is not straightforward to specify precisely the execution of these commands for two reasons. First, a significantly more detailed model of the architecture than the one we have presented needs to be considered for correct implementation of these commands. Second, the overall scheme of implementation is quite dependent on the recovery procedures that the local recovery manager implements. For example, implementation of the 2PC protocol on top of a LRM that employs a no-fix/no-flush recovery scheme is quite different from its implementation on top of a LRM that employs a fix/flush recovery scheme. The alternatives are simply too numerous. We therefore confine our architectural discussion to three areas: implementation of the coordinator and participant concepts for the commit and replica control protocols within the framework of the transaction manager-scheduler-local recovery manager architecture, the coordinator's access to the database log, and the changes that need to be made in the local recovery manager operations.

One possible implementation of the commit protocols within our architectural model is to perform both the coordinator and participant algorithms within the transaction managers at each site. This provides some uniformity in executing the distributed commit operations. However, it entails unnecessary communication between the participant transaction manager and its scheduler; this is because the scheduler has to decide whether a transaction can be committed or aborted. Therefore, it may be preferable to implement the coordinator as part of the transaction manager and the participant as part of the scheduler. If the scheduler implements a strict concurrency control algorithm (i.e., does not allow cascading aborts), it will be ready automatically to commit the transaction when the prepare message arrives. Proof of this claim is left as an exercise. However, even this alternative of implementing the coordinator and the participant outside the data processor has problems. The first issue is database log management. Recall that the database log is maintained by the LRM and the buffer manager. However, implementation of the commit protocol as described here requires the transaction manager and the scheduler to access the log as well. One possible solution to this problem is to maintain a commit log (which could be called the *distributed transaction log*) that is accessed by the transaction manager and is separate from the database log that the LRM and buffer manager maintain. The other alternative is to write the commit protocol records into the same database log. This second alternative has a number of advantages. First, only one log is maintained; this simplifies the algorithms that have to be implemented in order to save log records on stable storage. More important, the recovery from failures in a distributed database requires the cooperation of the local recovery manager and the scheduler (i.e., the participant). A single database log can serve as a central repository of recovery information for both components.

A second problem associated with implementing the coordinator within the transaction manager and the participant as part of the scheduler is integration with the concurrency control protocols. This implementation is based on the schedulers determining whether a transaction can be committed. This is fine for distributed concurrency control algorithms where each site is equipped with a scheduler. However, in centralized protocols such as the centralized 2PL, there is only one scheduler in the system. In this case, the participants may be implemented as part of the data processors (more precisely, as part of local recovery managers), requiring modification to both the algorithms implemented by the LRM and, possibly, to the execution of the 2PC protocol. We leave the details to exercises.

Storing the commit protocol records in the database log maintained by the LRM and the buffer manager requires some changes to the LRM algorithms. This is the third architectural issue we address. These changes are dependent on the type of algorithm that the LRM uses. In general, the LRM algorithms have to be modified to handle separately the prepare command and global-commit (or global-abort) decisions. Furthermore, upon recovery, the LRM should be modified to read the database log and to inform the scheduler as to the state of each transaction, in order that the recovery procedures discussed before can be followed. Let us take a more detailed look at this function of the LRM.

The LRM first has to determine whether the failed site is the host of the coordinator or of a participant. This information can be stored together with the Begin_transaction record. The LRM then has to search for the last record written in the log record during execution of the commit protocol. If it cannot even find a begin_commit record (at the coordinator site) or an abort or commit record (at the participant sites), the transaction has not started to commit. In this case, the LRM can continue with its recovery procedure. However, if the commit process has started, the recovery has to be handed over to the coordinator. Therefore, the LRM sends the last log record to the scheduler.

5.5   Modern Approaches to Scaling Out Transaction Management

All algorithms presented above introduce bottlenecks at different points in the transactional processing. Those implementing serializability severely limit the potential concurrency due to conflicts between large queries that read many data items and update transactions. For instance, an analytical query that makes a full table scan with a predicate that is not based on the primary key causes a conflict with any update on the table. All algorithms need a centralized processing step in order to commit transactions one by one.

This creates a bottleneck since they cannot process transactions at a rate higher than a single node is able to. Locking algorithms require deadlock management and many use deadlock detection, which is difficult in a distributed setting as we discussed earlier. The algorithm which we presented in the last section on snapshot isolation performs centralized certification, which again introduces a bottleneck.

Scaling transaction execution to achieve high transaction throughput in a distributed or parallel system has been a topic of interest for a long time. In recent years solutions have started to emerge; we discuss two approaches in this section: Google Spanner and LeanXcale. Both of these implement each of the ACID properties in a scalable and composable manner. In both approaches, a new technique is proposed to serialize transactions that can support very high throughput rates (millions or even billion transactions per second). Both approaches have a way to timestamp the commit of transactions and use this commit timestamp to serialize transactions. Spanner uses real time to timestamp transactions, while LeanXcale uses logical time. Real time has the advantage that it does not require any communication, but requires high accuracy and a highly reliable real-time infrastructure. The idea is to use real time as timestamp and wait for the accuracy to elapse to make the result visible to transactions.

LeanXcale adopts an approach in which transactions are timestamped with a logical time and committed transactions are made visible progressively as gaps in the serialization order are filled by newly committed transactions. Logical time avoids having to rely on creating a real-time infrastructure.

5.5.1 *Spanner*

Spanner uses traditional locking and 2PC and provides serializability as isolation level. Since locking results in high contention between large queries and update transactions, Spanner also implements multiversioning. In order to avoid the bottleneck of centralized certification, updated data items are assigned timestamps (using real time) upon commit. For this purpose, Spanner implements an internal service called TrueTime that provides the current time and its current accuracy. In order to make the TrueTime service reliable and accurate, it uses both atomic clocks and GPS since they have different failures modes that can compensate each other. For instance, atomic clocks they have a continuous drift, while GPS loses accuracy in some meteorological conditions, when the antenna gets broken, etc. The current time obtained through TrueTime is used to timestamp transactions that are going to be committed. The reported accurate is used to compensate during timestamp assignment: after obtaining the local time, there is a wait time for the length of the inaccuracy, typically around 10 milliseconds. To deal with deadlocks, Spanner adopts deadlock avoidance using a wound-and-wait approach (see Appendix C) thereby eliminating the bottleneck that deadlock detection.

Storage management in Spanner is made scalable by leveraging Google Bigtable, a key-value data store (see Chap. 11).

Multiversioning is implemented as follows. Private versions of the data items are kept at each site until commitment. Upon commit, the 2PC protocol is started during which buffered writes are propagated to each participant. Each participant sets locks on the updated data items. Once all locks have been acquired, it assigns a commit timestamp larger than any previously assigned timestamp. The coordinator also acquires the write locks. Upon acquiring all write locks and receiving the prepared message from all participants, the coordinator chooses a timestamp larger than the current time plus the inaccuracy, and bigger than any other timestamps assigned locally. The coordinator waits for the assigned timestamp to pass (recall waiting due to inaccuracy) and then communicates the commit decision to the client.

Using multiversioning, Spanner also implements read-only transactions that read over the snapshot at the current time.

5.5.2 *LeanXcale*

LeanXcale uses a totally different approach to scalable transactional management. First, it uses logical time to timestamp transactions and to set visibility over committed data. Second, it provides snapshot isolation. Third, all the functions that are intensive in resource usage such as concurrency control, logging, storage and query processing, are fully distributed and parallel, without any coordination.

For logical time, LeanXcale uses two services: the commit sequencer and the snapshot server. The commit sequencer distributes commit timestamps and the snapshot server regulates the visibility of committed data by advancing the snapshot visible to transactions.

Since LeanXcale provides snapshot isolation, it only needs to detect write-write conflicts. It implements a (possibly distributed) Conflict Manager. Each Conflict Manager takes care of checking conflicts for a subset of the data items. Basically, a Conflict Manager gets requests from LTMs to check whether a data item that is going to be updated conflicts with any concurrent updates. If there is a conflict, then the LTM will abort the transaction, otherwise it will be able to progress without aborting.

The storage functionality is provided by a relational key-value data store called KiVi. Tables are horizontally partitioned into units called *regions*. Each region is stored at one KiVi server.

When a commit is started, it is managed by an LTM that starts the commit processing as follows. First, the LTM takes a commit timestamp from the local range and uses it to timestamp the writeset of the transaction that is then logged. Logging is scaled by using multiple loggers. Each logger serves a subset of LTMs. A logger replies to the LTM when the writeset is durable. LeanXcale implements multiversioning at the storage layer. As in Spanner, private copies exist at each site. When the writeset is durable, the updates are propagated to the corresponding KiVi servers, timestamped with the commit timestamp. Once all updates have been propagated, the transaction is readable if the right start timestamp is used (equal or higher than the commit timestamp). However, it is still invisible. Then, the LTM informs to the snapshot server that the transaction is durable and readable. The snapshot server keeps track of the current snapshot, that is, the start timestamp that will be used by new transactions. It also keeps track of transactions that are durable and readable with a commit timestamp higher than the current snapshot. Whenever there are no gaps between the current snapshot and a timestamp, the snapshot server advances the snapshot to that timestamp. At that point, the committed data with a commit timestamp lower than the current snapshot becomes visible to new transactions since they will get a start timestamp at the current snapshot. Let us see how it works with an example.

Example 5.5 Consider 5 transactions committing in parallel with commit times-tamps 11 to 15. Let the current snapshot at the snapshot server be 10. The order in which the LTMs report to the snapshot server that the transactions are durable and readable is 11, 15, 14, 12, and 13. When the snapshot server is notified about transaction with commit timestamp 11, it advances the snapshot from 10 to 11 since there are no gaps. With transaction with commit timestamp 15, it cannot advance the snapshot since otherwise new transactions could observe an inconsistent state that misses updates from transactions with commit timestamps 12 to 14. Now transaction with timestamp 14 reports that its updates are durable and readable. Again, the snapshot cannot progress. But now transaction with commit timestamp 13 becomes durable and readable and now the snapshot advances till 15 since there are no gaps in the serialization order.   ◆

Note that although the algorithm so far provides snapshot isolation, it does not provide session consistency, which is a desirable feature for transactions within the same session to be able to read the writes of previously committed transactions. To provide session consistency, a new mechanism is added. Basically, when a session commits a transaction that made updates, it will wait till the snapshot progresses beyond the commit timestamp of the update transaction to start and then it will start with a snapshot that guarantees that it observes its own writes.

5.6 Conclusion

In this chapter, we discussed issues around distributed transaction processing. A transaction is an atomic unit of execution that transforms one consistent database to another consistent database. The ACID properties of transactions also indicate what the requirements for managing them are. Consistency requires a definition of integrity enforcement (which we did in Chap. 3), as well as concurrency control algorithms. Concurrency control also deals with the issue of isolation. The distributed concurrency control mechanism of a distributed DBMS ensures that the consistency of the distributed database is maintained and is therefore one of the fundamental components of a distributed DBMS. We introduced distributed concurrency control algorithms of three types: locking-based, timestamp ordering-based, and optimistic. We noted that locking-based algorithms can lead to distributed (or global) deadlocks and introduced approach for detecting and resolving these deadlocks.

Durability and atomicity properties of transactions require a discussion of distributed DBMS reliability. Specifically, durability is supported by various commit protocols and commit management, whereas atomicity requires the development of appropriate recovery protocols. We introduced two commit protocols, 2PC and 3PC, which guarantee the atomicity and durability of distributed transactions even when failures occur. One of these algorithms (3PC) can be made nonblocking, which would permit each site to continue its operation without waiting for recovery of the failed site. The performance of the distributed commit protocols with respect to the overhead they add to the concurrency control algorithms is an interesting issue.

Achieving very high transaction throughput in distributed and parallel DBMSs has been a long-standing topic of interest with some positive developments in recent years. We discussed two approaches to achieving this objective as part of Spanner and LeanXcale systems.

There are a few issues that we have omitted from this chapter:

1. *Advanced transaction models*. The transaction model that we used In this chapter, is commonly referred to as the *flat transaction* model that have a single start point (Begin_transaction) and a single termination point (End_transaction). Most of the transaction management work in databases has concentrated on flat transactions. However, there are more advanced transaction models. One of these is called the

nested transaction model where a transaction includes other transactions with their own begin and end points. The transactions that are embedded in another one are usually called *subtransactions*. The structure of a nested transaction is a tree where the outermost transaction is the root with sub transactions represented as the other nodes. These differ in their termination characteristics. One category, called *closed nested transactions* commit in a bottom-up fashion through the root. Thus, a nested subtransaction begins *after* its parent and finishes *before* it, and the commitment of the subtransactions is conditional upon the commitment of the parent. The semantics of these transactions enforce atomicity at the topmost level. The alternative is open nesting, which relaxes the top-level atomicity restriction of closed nested transactions. Therefore, an open nested transaction allows its partial results to be observed outside the transaction. Sagas and split transactions are examples of open nesting.

Even more advanced transactions are *workflows*. The term "workflow," unfortunately, does not have a clear and uniformly accepted meaning. A working definition is a set of tasks with a partial order among them that collectively perform some complicated process.

Although the management of these advanced transaction models is important, they are outside our scope, so we have not considered them in this chapter.

2. *Assumptions about transactions.* In our discussions, we did not make any distinction between read-only transactions and update transactions. It is possible to improve significantly the performance of transactions that only read data items, or of systems with a high ratio of read-only transactions to update transactions. These issues are beyond the scope of this book.

We have also treated read and write locks in an identical fashion. It is possible to differentiate between them and develop concurrency control algorithms that permit "lock conversion," whereby transactions can obtain locks in one mode and then modify their lock modes as they change their requirements. Typically, the conversion is from read locks to write locks.

3. *Transaction execution models.* The algorithms that we have described all assume a computational model where the transaction manager at the originating site of a transaction coordinates the execution of each database operation of that transaction. This is called *centralized execution*. It is also possible to consider a *distributed execution* model where a transaction is decomposed into a set of subtransactions each of which is allocated to one site where the transaction manager coordinates its execution. This is intuitively more attractive because it may permit load balancing across the multiple sites of a distributed database. However, the performance studies indicate that distributed computation performs better only under light load.

4. *Error types.* We have considered only failures that are attributable to errors. In other words, we assumed that every effort was made to design and implement the systems (hardware and software), but that because of various faults in the components, the design, or the operating environment, they failed to perform properly. Such failures are called *failures of omission*. There is another class of failures, called *failures of commission*, where the systems may not have been

designed and implemented so that they would work properly. The difference is that in the execution of the 2PC protocol, for example, if a participant receives a message from the coordinator, it treats this message as correct: the coordinator is operational and is sending the participant a correct message to go ahead and process. The only failure that the participant has to worry about is if the coordinator fails or if its messages get lost. These are failures of omission. If, on the other hand, the messages that a participant receives cannot be trusted, the participant also has to deal with failures of commission. For example, a participant site may pretend to be the coordinator and may send a malicious message. We have not discussed reliability measures that are necessary to cope with these types of failures. The techniques that address failures of commission are typically called *byzantine agreement*.

In addition to these issues there is quite a volume of recent work on transaction management in various environments (e.g., multicore, main-memory systems). We do not discuss those in this chapter, that is focused on the fundamentals, but we provide some pointers in the Bibliographic Notes.

5.7 Bibliographic Notes

Transaction management has been the topic of considerable study since DBMSs have become a significant research area. There are two excellent books on the subject: [Gray and Reuter 1993] and [Weikum and Vossen 2001]. Classical texts that focus on these topics are [Hadzilacos 1988] and [Bernstein et al. 1987]. An excellent companion to these is [Bernstein and Newcomer 1997] which provides an in-depth discussion of transaction processing principles. It also gives a view of transaction processing and transaction monitors which is more general than the database-centric view that we provide in this book. A very important work is a set of notes on database operating systems by Gray [1979]. These notes contain valuable information on transaction management, among other things.

Distributed concurrency control is extensively covered in [Bernstein and Goodman 1981], which is now out of print, but can be accessed online. The issues that are addressed In this chapter, are discussed in much more detail in [Cellary et al. 1988, Bernstein et al. 1987, Papadimitriou 1986] and [Gray and Reuter 1993].

For the fundamental techniques we have discussed in the paper, centralized 2PL was first proposed by Alsberg and Day [1976], hierarchical deadlock detection was discussed by Menasce and Muntz [1979] while distributed deadlock detection is due to Obermack [1982]. Our discussion of conservative TO algorithm is due to Herman and Verjus [1979]. The original multiversion TO algorithm was proposed by Reed [1978] with further formalization by Bernstein and Goodman [1983]. Lomet et al. [2012] discuss how to implement multiversioning on top of a concurrency layer that implements 2PL while Faleiro and Abadi [2015] do the same on top of one that implements TO. There are also approaches that implement versioning as a generic

242   5   Distributed Transaction Processing

framework on top of any concurrency control technique [Agrawal and Sengupta 1993]. Bernstein et al. [1987] discuss how to implement locking-based optimistic concurrency control algorithms while Thomas [1979] and Kung and Robinson [1981] discuss timestamp-based implementations. Our discussion in Sect. 5.2.4 is due to Ceri and Owicki [1982]. The original snapshot isolation proposal is by Berenson et al. [1995]. Our discussion of the snapshot isolation algorithm is due to Chairunnanda et al. [2014]. Binnig et al. [2014] discuss the optimization that we highlighted at the end of that section. The presumed abort and presumed commit protocols were proposed by Mohan and Lindsay [1983] and Mohan et al. [1986]. Site failures and recoverability from them is the topic of [Skeen and Stonebraker 1983] and [Skeen 1981], the latter also proposes the 3PC algorithm along with its analysis. Coordinator selection protocols that we discuss are due to Hammer and Shipman [1980] and Garcia-Molina [1982]. An early survey of consistency in the presence of network partitioning is by Davidson et al. [1985]. Thomas [1979] proposed the original majority voting technique, and the nonreplicated version of the protocol we discuss is due to Skeen [1982a]. Distributed transaction log idea in Sect. 5.4.6 is due to Bernstein et al. [1987] and Lampson and Sturgis [1976].

The transaction management in System R* discussion is due to Mohan et al. [1986]; NonStop SQL is presented in [Tandem 1987, 1988, Borr 1988]. Bernstein et al. [1980b] discusses SDD-1 in detail. The more modern systems Spanner and LeanXcale discussed in Sect. 5.5 are described in [Corbett et al. 2013] and [Jimenez-Peris and Patiño Martinez 2011], respectively.

Advanced transaction models are discussed and various examples are given in [Elmagarmid 1992]. Nested transactions are also covered in [Lynch et al. 1993]. Closed nested transactions are due to Moss [1985] while open nested transaction model sagas are proposed by Garcia-Molina and Salem [1987], Garcia-Molina et al. [1990] and split transactions by Pu [1988]. Nested transaction models and their specific concurrency control algorithms have been the subjects of some study. Specific results can be found in [Moss 1985, Lynch 1983b, Lynch and Merritt 1986, Fekete et al. 1987a,b, Goldman 1987, Beeri et al. 1989, Fekete et al. 1989] and in [Lynch et al. 1993]. A good introduction to workflow systems is given by Georgakopoulos et al. [1995] and the topic is covered in [Dogac et al. 1998] and [van Hee 2002].

The work on transaction management with semantic knowledge is presented in [Lynch 1983a, Garcia-Molina 1983], and [Farrag and Özsu 1989]. The processing of read-only transactions is discussed in [Garcia-Molina and Wiederhold 1982]. Transaction groups [Skarra et al. 1986, Skarra 1989] also exploit a correctness criterion called *semantic patterns* that is more relaxed than serializability. Furthermore, work on the ARIES system [Haderle et al. 1992] is also within this class of algorithms. In particular, [Rothermel and Mohan 1989] discusses ARIES within the context of nested transactions. Epsilon serializability [Ramamritham and Pu 1995, Wu et al. 1997] and NT/PV model [Kshemkalyani and Singhal 1994] are other "relaxed" correctness criteria. An algorithm based on ordering transactions using *serialization numbers* is discussed in [Halici and Dogac 1989].

Two books focus on the performance of concurrency control mechanisms with a focus on centralized systems [Kumar 1996, Thomasian 1996]. Kumar [1996] focuses on the performance of centralized DBMSs; the performance of distributed concurrency control methods are discussed in [Thomasian 1996] and [Cellary et al. 1988]. An early but comprehensive review of deadlock management is [Isloor and Marsland 1980]. Most of the work on distributed deadlock management has been on detection and resolution (see, e.g., [Obermack 1982, Elmagarmid et al. 1988]). Surveys of the important algorithms are included in [Elmagarmid 1986], [Knapp 1987], and [Singhal 1989].

Snapshot isolation has received significant attention in recent years. Although Oracle had implemented SI since its early versions, the concept was formally defined in [Berenson et al. 1995]. One line of work that we did not cover In this chapter, is to how to get serializable execution even when SI is used as the correctness criterion. This line of work modifies the concurrency control algorithm by detecting the anomalies that are caused by SI that lead to data inconsistency, and preventing them [Cahill et al. 2009, Alomari et al. 2009, Revilak et al. 2011, Alomari et al. 2008] and these techniques have started to be incorporated into systems, e.g., PostgreSQL [Ports and Grittner 2012]. The first SI concurrency control algorithm is due to Schenkel et al. [2000], focusing on concurrency control on data integration systems using SI. We based our discussion In this chapter, on the ConfluxDB system [Chairunnanda et al. 2014]; other work in this direction is by Binnig et al. [2014], where more refined techniques are developed.

Kohler [1981] presents a general discussion of the reliability issues in distributed database systems. Hadzilacos [1988] gives a formalization of the reliability concept. The reliability aspects of System R* are given in [Traiger et al. 1982], whereas Hammer and Shipman [1980] describe the same for the SDD-1 system.

More detailed material on the functions of the local recovery manager can be found in [Verhofstadt 1978, Härder and Reuter 1983]. Implementation of the local recovery functions in System R is described in [Gray et al. 1981].

The two-phase commit protocol is first described in [Gray 1979]. Modifications to it are presented in [Mohan and Lindsay 1983]. The definition of three-phase commit is due to Skeen [1981, 1982b]. Formal results on the existence of nonblocking termination protocols are due to Skeen and Stonebraker [1983].

Paxos was originally proposed by Lamport [1998]. This paper is considered hard to read, which has resulted in a number of different papers describing the protocol. Lamport [2001] gives a significantly simplified description, while Van Renesse and Altinbuken [2015] provide a description that is perhaps between these two points and is a good paper to study. The Paxos 2PC we briefly highlighted is proposed by Gray and Lamport [2006]. For a discussion of how to engineer a Paxos-based system, [Chandra et al. 2007] and [Kirsch and Amir 2008] are recommended. There are many different versions of Paxos—too many to list here—that has resulted in Paxos to be referred to it as a "family of protocols". We do not provide references to each of these. We also note that Paxos is not the only consensus algorithm; a number of alternatives have been proposed particularly as blockchains have become popular (see our discussion of blockchain in Chap. 9). This list is growing fast, which is why we do not give references. One algorithm, Raft, has been proposed in response to complexity and perceived difficulty in understanding Paxos. The original proposal is by Ongaro and Ousterhout [2014] and it is described nicely in Chapter 23 of [Silberschatz et al. 2019].

As noted earlier, we do not address Byzantine failures in this chapter. The Paxos protocol also does not address these failures. A good description of how to deal with these types of failures is discussed by Castro and Liskov [1999].

Regarding more recent relevant work, Tu et al. [2013] discuss scale-up transaction processing on a single multicore machine. Kemper and Neumann [2011] discuss transaction management issues in a hybrid OLAP/OLTP environment within the context of the HyPer main-memory system. Similarly, Larson et al. [2011] discuss the same issue within the context of the Hekaton system. The E-store system that we discussed in Chap. 2 as part of adaptive data partitioning also addresses transaction management in partitioned distributed DBMSs. As noted there, E-store uses Squall [Elmore et al. 2015] that considers transactions in deciding data movement. Thomson and Abadi [2010] propose Calvin that combine a deadlock avoidance technique with concurrency control algorithms to obtain histories that are guaranteed to be equivalent to a predetermined serial ordering in replicated, distributed DBMSs.

Exercises

Problem 5.1 Which of the following histories are conflict equivalent?

$$H_1 = \{W_2(x), W_1(x), R_3(x), R_1(x), W_2(y), R_3(y), R_3(z), R_2(x)\}$$
$$H_2 = \{R_3(z), R_3(y), W_2(y), R_2(z), W_1(x), R_3(x), W_2(x), R_1(x)\}$$
$$H_3 = \{R_3(z), W_2(x), W_2(y), R_1(x), R_3(x), R_2(z), R_3(y), W_1(x)\}$$
$$H_4 = \{R_2(z), W_2(x), W_2(y), W_1(x), R_1(x), R_3(x), R_3(z), R_3(y)\}$$

Problem 5.2 Which of the above histories $H_1 - H_4$ are serializable?

Problem 5.3 Give a history of two complete transactions which is not allowed by a strict 2PL scheduler but is accepted by the basic 2PL scheduler.

Problem 5.4 (*) One says that history H is *recoverable* if, whenever transaction T_i reads (some item x) from transaction T_j $(i \neq j)$ in H and C_i occurs in H, then $C_j \prec_S C_i$. T_i "reads x from" T_j in H if

1. $W_j(x) \prec_H R_i(x)$, and
2. A_j not $\prec_H R_i(x)$, and
3. if there is some $W_k(x)$ such that $W_j(x) \prec_H W_k(x) \prec_H R_i(x)$, then $A_k \prec_H R_i(x)$.

Which of the following histories are recoverable?

$$H_1 = \{W_2(x), W_1(x), R_3(x), R_1(x), C_1, W_2(y), R_3(y), R_3(z), C_3, R_2(x), C_2\}$$

$$H_2 = \{R_3(z), R_3(y), W_2(y), R_2(z), W_1(x), R_3(x), W_2(x), R_1(x), C_1, C_2, C_3\}$$

$$H_3 = \{R_3(z), W_2(x), W_2(y), R_1(x), R_3(x), R_2(z), R_3(y), C_3, W_1(x), C_2, C_1\}$$

$$H_4 = \{R_2(z), W_2(x), W_2(y), C_2, W_1(x), R_1(x), A_1, R_3(x), R_3(z), R_3(y), C_3\}$$

Problem 5.5 (*) Give the algorithms for the transaction managers and the lock managers for the distributed two-phase locking approach.

Problem 5.6 (**) Modify the centralized 2PL algorithm to handle phantom read. Phantom read occurs when two reads are executed within a transaction and the result returned by the second read contains tuples that do not exist in the first one. Consider the following example based on the airline reservation database discussed early in this chapter: Transaction T_1, during its execution, searches the FC table for the names of customers who have ordered a special meal. It gets a set of CNAME for customers who satisfy the search criteria. While T_1 is executing, transaction T_2 inserts new tuples into FC with the special meal request, and commits. If T_1 were to re-issue the same search query later in its execution, it will get back a set of CNAME that is different than the original set it had retrieved. Thus, "phantom" tuples have appeared in the database.

Problem 5.7 Timestamp ordering-based concurrency control algorithms depend on either an accurate clock at each site or a global clock that all sites can access (the clock can be a counter). Assume that each site has its own clock which "ticks" every 0.1 second. If all local clocks are resynchronized every 24 hours, what is the maximum drift in seconds per 24 hours permissible at any local site to ensure that a timestamp-based mechanism will successfully synchronize transactions?

Problem 5.8 (**) Incorporate the distributed deadlock strategy described In this chapter, into the distributed 2PL algorithms that you designed in Problem 5.5.

Problem 5.9 Explain the relationship between transaction manager storage requirement and transaction size (number of operations per transaction) for a transaction manager using an optimistic timestamp ordering for concurrency control.

Problem 5.10 (*) Give the scheduler and transaction manager algorithms for the distributed optimistic concurrency controller described in this chapter.

Problem 5.11 Recall from the discussion in Sect. 5.6 that the computational model that is used in our descriptions in this chapter is a centralized one. How would the distributed 2PL transaction manager and lock manager algorithms change if a distributed execution model were to be used?

Problem 5.12 It is sometimes claimed that serializability is quite a restrictive correctness criterion. Can you give examples of distributed histories that are correct (i.e., maintain the consistency of the local databases as well as their mutual consistency) but are not serializable?

Problem 5.13 (*) Discuss the site failure termination protocol for 2PC using a distributed communication topology.

Problem 5.14 (*)
Design a 3PC protocol using the linear communication topology.

Problem 5.15 (*) In our presentation of the centralized 3PC termination protocol, the first step involves sending the coordinator's state to all participants. The participants move to new states according to the coordinator's state. It is possible to design the termination protocol such that the coordinator, instead of sending its own state information to the participants, asks the participants to send their state information to the coordinator. Modify the termination protocol to function in this manner.

Problem 5.16 (**) In Sect. 5.4.6 we claimed that a scheduler which implements a strict concurrency control algorithm will always be ready to commit a transaction when it receives the coordinator's "prepare" message. Prove this claim.

Problem 5.17 (**) Assuming that the coordinator is implemented as part of the transaction manager and the participant as part of the scheduler, give the transaction manager, scheduler, and the local recovery manager algorithms for a nonreplicated distributed DBMS under the following assumptions.

(a) The scheduler implements a distributed (strict) two-phase locking concurrency control algorithm.
(b) The commit protocol log records are written to a central database log by the LRM when it is called by the scheduler.
(c) The LRM may implement any of the protocols that have been discussed (e.g., fix/no-flush or others). However, it is modified to support the distributed recovery procedures as we discussed in Sect. 5.4.6.

Problem 5.18 (*) Write the detailed algorithms for the no-fix/no-flush local recovery manager.

Problem 5.19 (**) Assume that

(a) The scheduler implements a centralized two-phase locking concurrency control,
(b) The LRM implements no-fix/no-flush protocol.

Give detailed algorithms for the transaction manager, scheduler, and local recovery managers.

Chapter 6
Data Replication

As we discussed in previous chapters, distributed databases are typically replicated. The purposes of replication are multiple:

1. **System availability.** As discussed in Chap. 1, distributed DBMSs may remove single points of failure by replicating data, so that data items are accessible from multiple sites. Consequently, even when some sites are down, data may be accessible from other sites.
2. **Performance.** As we have seen previously, one of the major contributors to response time is the communication overhead. Replication enables us to locate the data closer to their access points, thereby localizing most of the access that contributes to a reduction in response time.
3. **Scalability.** As systems grow geographically and in terms of the number of sites (consequently, in terms of the number of access requests), replication allows for a way to support this growth with acceptable response times.
4. **Application requirements.** Finally, replication may be dictated by the applications, which may wish to maintain multiple data copies as part of their operational specifications.

Although data replication has clear benefits, it poses the considerable challenge of keeping different copies synchronized. We will discuss this shortly, but let us first consider the execution model in replicated databases. Each replicated data item x has a number of copies $x_1, x_2, \ldots, x_n$. We will refer to x as the *logical data item* and to its copies (or *replicas*)[1] as *physical data items*. If replication transparency is to be provided, user transactions will issue read and write operations on the logical data item x. The replica control protocol is responsible for mapping these operations to reads and writes on the physical data items $x_1, \ldots, x_n$. Thus, the system behaves as if there is a single copy of each data item—referred to as *single system image* or *one-copy equivalence*. The specific implementation of the Read and Write interfaces

---

[1] In this chapter, we use the terms "replica," "copy," and "physical data item" interchangeably.

© Springer Nature Switzerland AG 2020

M. T. Özsu, P. Valduriez, *Principles of Distributed Database Systems*,

https://doi.org/10.1007/978-3-030-26253-2_6

of the transaction monitor differs according to the specific replication protocol, and we will discuss these differences in the appropriate sections.

There are a number of decisions and factors that impact the design of replication protocols. Some of these were discussed in previous chapters, while others will be discussed here.

- **Database design.** As discussed in Chap. 2, a distributed database may be fully or partially replicated. In the case of a partially replicated database, the number of physical data items for each logical data item may vary, and some data items may even be nonreplicated. In this case, transactions that access only nonreplicated data items are *local transactions* (since they can be executed locally at one site) and their execution typically does not concern us here. Transactions that access replicated data items have to be executed at multiple sites and they are *global transactions*.
- **Database consistency.** When global transactions update copies of a data item at different sites, the values of these copies may be different at a given point in time. A replicated database is said to be *mutually consistent* if all the replicas of each of its data items have identical values. What differentiates different mutual consistency criteria is how tightly synchronized replicas have to be. Some ensure that replicas are mutually consistent when an update transaction commits; thus, they are usually called *strong consistency* criteria. Others take a more relaxed approach, and are referred to as *weak consistency* criteria.
- **Where updates are performed.** A fundamental design decision in designing a replication protocol is where the database updates are first performed. The techniques can be characterized as *centralized* if they perform updates first on a *master* copy, versus *distributed* if they allow updates over any replica. Centralized techniques can be further identified as *single master* when there is only one master database copy in the system, or *primary copy* where the master copy of each data item may be different.[2]
- **Update propagation.** Once updates are performed on a replica (master or otherwise), the next decision is how updates are propagated to the others. The alternatives are identified as *eager* versus *lazy*. Eager techniques perform all of the updates within the context of the global transaction that has initiated the write operations. Thus, when the transaction commits, its updates will have been applied to all of the copies. Lazy techniques, on the other hand, propagate the updates sometime after the initiating transaction has committed. Eager techniques are further identified according to when they push each write to the other replicas—some push each write operation individually, others batch the writes and propagate them at the commit point.

---

[2]Centralized techniques are referred to, in the literature, as *single master*, while distributed ones are referred to as *multimaster* or *update anywhere*. These terms, in particular "single master," are confusing, since they refer to alternative architectures for implementing centralized protocols (more on this in Sect. 6.2.3). Thus, we prefer the more descriptive terms "centralized" and "distributed."

- **Degree of replication transparency.** Certain replication protocols require each user application to know the master site where the transaction operations are to be submitted. These protocols provide only *limited replication transparency* to user applications. Other protocols provide *full replication transparency* by involving the TM at each site. In this case, user applications submit transactions to their local TMs rather than the master site.

We discuss consistency issues in replicated databases in Sect. 6.1, and analyze centralized versus distributed update application as well as update propagation alternatives in Sect. 6.2. This will lead us to a discussion of the specific protocols in Sect. 6.3. In Sect. 6.4, we discuss the use of group communication primitives in reducing the messaging overhead of replication protocols. In these sections, we will assume that no failures occur so that we can focus on the replication protocols. We will then introduce failures and investigate how protocols are revised to handle failures in Sect. 6.5.

6.1   Consistency of Replicated Databases

There are two issues related to consistency of a replicated database. One is mutual consistency, as discussed above, that deals with the convergence of the values of physical data items corresponding to one logical data item. The second is transaction consistency as we discussed in Chap. 5. Serializability, which we introduced as the transaction consistency criterion needs to be recast in the case of replicated databases. In addition, there are relationships between mutual consistency and transaction consistency. In this section, we first discuss mutual consistency approaches and then focus on the redefinition of transaction consistency and its relationship to mutual consistency.

6.1.1   Mutual Consistency

As indicated earlier, mutual consistency criteria for replicated databases can be either strong or weak. Each is suitable for different classes of applications with different consistency requirements.

Strong mutual consistency criteria require that all copies of a data item have the same value at the end of the execution of an update transaction. This is achieved by a variety of means, but the execution of 2PC at the commit point of an update transaction is a common way to achieve strong mutual consistency.

Weak mutual consistency criteria do not require the values of replicas of a data item to be identical when an update transaction terminates. What is required is that, if the update activity ceases for some time, the values *eventually* become identical. This is commonly referred to as *eventual consistency*, which refers to the fact that replica values may diverge over time, but will eventually converge. It is hard to define this concept formally or precisely, although the following definition by Saito and Shapiro is probably as precise as one can hope to get:

> A replicated [data item] is *eventually consistent* when it meets the following conditions, assuming that all replicas start from the same initial state.
>
> - At any moment, for each replica, there is a prefix of the [history] that is equivalent to a prefix of the [history] of every other replica. We call this a *committed prefix* for the replica.
> - The committed prefix of each replica grows monotonically over time.
> - All nonaborted operations in the committed prefix satisfy their preconditions.
> - For every submitted operation α, either α or [its abort] will eventually be included in the committed prefix.

It should be noted that this definition of eventual consistency is rather strong—in particular the requirements that history prefixes are the same at any given moment and that the committed prefix grows monotonically. Many systems that claim to provide eventual consistency would violate these requirements.

Epsilon serializability (ESR) allows a query to see inconsistent data while replicas are being updated, but requires that the replicas converge to a one-copy equivalent state once the updates are propagated to all of the copies. It bounds the error on the read values by an epsilon (ϵ) value, which is defined in terms of the number of updates (write operations) that a query "misses." Given a read-only transaction (query) T_Q, let T_U be the set of all the update transactions that are executing concurrently with T_Q. If $RS(T_Q) \cap WS(T_U) \neq \emptyset$ (T_Q is reading some copy of some data items while a transaction in T_U is updating (possibly a different) copy of those data items), then there is a read–write conflict and T_Q may be reading inconsistent data. The inconsistency is bounded by the changes performed by T_U. Clearly, ESR does not sacrifice database consistency, but only allows read-only transactions (queries) to read inconsistent data. For this reason, it has been claimed that ESR does not weaken database consistency, but "stretches" it.

Other looser bounds have also been discussed. It has even been suggested that users should be allowed to specify *freshness constraints* that are suitable for particular applications and the replication protocols should enforce these. The types of freshness constraints that can be specified are the following:

- **Time-bound constraints.** Users may accept divergence of physical copy values up to a certain time interval: x_i may reflect the value of an update at time t, while x_j may reflect the value at $t - \Delta$ and this may be acceptable.
- **Value-bound constraints.** It may be acceptable to have values of all physical data items within a certain range of each other. The user may consider the database to be mutually consistent if the values do not diverge more than a certain amount (or percentage).
- **Drift constraints on multiple data items.** For transactions that read multiple data items, users may be satisfied if the time drift between the update timestamps of two data items is less than a threshold (i.e., they were updated within that threshold) or, in the case of aggregate computation, if the aggregate computed

over a data item is within a certain range of the most recent value (i.e., even if the individual physical copy values may be more out of sync than this range, as long as a particular aggregate computation is within range, it may be acceptable).

An important criterion in analyzing protocols that employ criteria that allow replicas to diverge is *degree of freshness*. The degree of freshness of a given replica x_i at time t is defined as the proportion of updates that have been applied at x_i at time t to the total number of updates.

6.1.2   *Mutual Consistency Versus Transaction Consistency*

Mutual consistency, as we have defined it here, and transactional consistency as we discussed in Chap. 5 are related, but different. Mutual consistency refers to the replicas converging to the same value, while transaction consistency requires that the global execution history be serializable. It is possible for a replicated DBMS to ensure that data items are mutually consistent when a transaction commits, but the execution history may not be globally serializable. This is demonstrated in the following example.

Example 6.1 Consider three sites (A, B, and C) and three data items (x, y, z) that are distributed as follows: site A hosts x, site B hosts x, y, site C hosts x, y, z. We will use site identifiers as subscripts on the data items to refer to a particular replica.
   Now consider the following three transactions:

T_1:	$x \leftarrow 20$	T_2:	Read(x)	T_3:	Read(x)
	Write(x)		$y \leftarrow x + y$		Read(y)
	Commit		Write(y)		$z \leftarrow (x * y)/100$
			Commit		Write(z)
					Commit

Note that T_1's Write has to be executed at all three sites (since x is replicated at all three sites), T_2's Write has to be executed at B and C, and T_3's Write has to be executed only at C. We are assuming a transaction execution model where transactions can read their local replicas, but have to update all of the replicas.
   Assume that the following three local histories are generated at the sites:

$$H_A = \{W_1(x_A), C_1\}$$

$$H_B = \{W_1(x_B), C_1, R_2(x_B), W_2(y_B), C_2\}$$

$$H_C = \{W_2(y_C), C_2, R_3(x_C), R_3(y_C), W_3(z_C), C_3, W_1(x_C), C_1\}$$

The serialization order in H_B is $T_1 \rightarrow T_2$, while in H_C it is $T_2 \rightarrow T_3 \rightarrow T_1$. Therefore, the global history is not serializable. However, the database is mutually consistent. Assume, for example, that initially $x_A = x_B = x_C = 10$, $y_B = y_C =$

15, and $z_C = 7$. With the above histories, the final values will be $x_A = x_B = x_C = 20$, $y_B = y_C = 35$, $z_C = 3.5$. All the physical copies (replicas) have indeed converged to the same value.   ◆

Of course, it is possible for the database to be mutually inconsistent and the execution history to be globally nonserializable, as demonstrated in the following example.

Example 6.2   Consider two sites (A and B), and one data item (x) that is replicated at both sites (x_A and x_B). Further consider the following two transactions:

T_1:   Read(x) T_2:   Read(x)

         $x \leftarrow x + 5$ $x \leftarrow x * 10$

         Write(x)   Write(x)

         Commit   Commit

Assume that the following two local histories are generated at the two sites (again using the execution model of the previous example):

$$H_A = \{R_1(x_A), W_1(x_A), C_1, R_2(x_A), W_2(x_A), C_2\}$$

$$H_B = \{R_2(x_B), W_2(x_B), C_2, R_1(x_B), W_1(x_B), C_1\}$$

Although both of these histories are serial, they serialize T_1 and T_2 in reverse order; thus, the global history is not serializable. Furthermore, the mutual consistency is violated as well. Assume that the value of x prior to the execution of these transactions was 1. At the end of the execution of these schedules, the value of x is 60 at site A, while it is 15 at site B. Thus, in this example, the global history is nonserializable, **and** the databases are mutually inconsistent.   ◆

Given the above observation, the transaction consistency criterion given in Chap. 5 is extended in replicated databases to define *one-copy serializability*.One-copy serializability (1SR) states that the effects of transactions on replicated data items should be the same as if they had been performed one-at-a-time on a single set of data items. In other words, the histories are equivalent to some serial execution over nonreplicated data items.

Snapshot isolation that we introduced in Chap. 5 has also been extended for replicated databases and used as an alternative transactional consistency criterion within the context of replicated databases. Similarly, a weaker form of serializability, called *relaxed concurrency (RC-)serializability* has been defined that corresponds to read-committed isolation level.

6.2   Update Management Strategies

As discussed earlier, the replication protocols can be classified according to when the updates are propagated to copies (eager versus lazy) and where updates are allowed to occur (centralized versus distributed). These two decisions are generally referred to as *update management* strategies. In this section, we discuss these alternatives before we present protocols in the next section.

6.2.1   Eager Update Propagation

The eager update propagation approaches apply the changes to all the replicas within the context of the update transaction. Consequently, when the update transaction commits, all the copies have the same value. Typically, eager propagation techniques use 2PC at commit point, but, as we will see later, alternatives are possible to achieve agreement. Furthermore, eager propagation may use *synchronous* propagation of each update by applying it on all the replicas at the same time (when the Write is issued), or *deferred* propagation whereby the updates are applied to one replica when they are issued, but their application on the other replicas is batched and deferred to the end of the transaction. Deferred propagation can be implemented by including the updates in the "Prepare-to-Commit" message at the start of 2PC execution.

Eager techniques typically enforce strong mutual consistency criteria. Since all the replicas are mutually consistent at the end of an update transaction, a subsequent read can read from any copy (i.e., one can map a $R(x)$ to $R(x_i)$ for any x_i). However, a $W(x)$ has to be applied to all replicas (i.e., $W(x_i), \forall x_i$). Thus, protocols that follow eager update propagation are known as *read-one/write-all* (ROWA) protocols.

The advantages of eager update propagation are threefold. First, they typically ensure that mutual consistency is enforced using 1SR; therefore, there are no transactional inconsistencies. Second, a transaction can read a local copy of the data item (if a local copy is available) and be certain that an up-to-date value is read. Thus, there is no need to do a remote read. Finally, the changes to replicas are done atomically; thus, recovery from failures can be governed by the protocols we have already studied in the previous chapter.

The main disadvantage of eager update propagation is that a transaction has to update all the copies before it can terminate. This has two consequences. First, the response time performance of the update transaction suffers, since it typically has to participate in a 2PC execution, and because the update speed is restricted by the slowest machine. Second, if one of the copies is unavailable, then the transaction cannot terminate since all the copies need to be updated. As discussed in Chap. 5, if it is possible to differentiate between site failures and network failures, then one can terminate the transaction as long as only one replica is unavailable (recall that more than one site unavailability causes 2PC to be blocking), but it is generally not possible to differentiate between these two types of failures.

6.2.2   Lazy Update Propagation

In lazy update propagation the replica updates are not all performed within the context of the update transaction. In other words, the transaction does not wait until its updates are applied to all the copies before it commits—it commits as soon as one replica is updated. The propagation to other copies is done *asynchronously* from the original transaction, by means of *refresh transactions* that are sent to the replica sites some time after the update transaction commits. A refresh transaction carries the sequence of updates of the corresponding update transaction.

Lazy propagation is used in those applications for which strong mutual consistency may be unnecessary and too restrictive. These applications may be able to tolerate some inconsistency among the replicas in return for better performance. Examples of such applications are Domain Name Service (DNS), databases over geographically widely distributed sites, mobile databases, and personal digital assistant databases. In these cases, usually weak mutual consistency is enforced.

The primary advantage of lazy update propagation techniques is that they generally have lower response times for update transactions, since an update transaction can commit as soon as it has updated one copy. The disadvantages are that the replicas are not mutually consistent and some replicas may be out-of-date, and consequently, a local read may read stale data and does not guarantee to return the up-to-date value. Furthermore, under some scenarios that we will discuss later, transactions may not see their own writes, i.e., $R_i(x)$ of an update transaction T_i may not see the effects of $W_i(x)$ that was executed previously. This has been referred to as *transaction inversion*. Strong one-copy serializability (strong 1SR) and strong snapshot isolation (strong SI) prevent all transaction inversions at 1SR and SI isolation levels, respectively, but are expensive to provide. The weaker guarantees of 1SR and global SI, while being much less expensive to provide than their stronger counterparts, do not prevent transaction inversions. Session-level transactional guarantees at the 1SR and SI isolation levels have been proposed that address these shortcomings by preventing transaction inversions within a client session but not necessarily across sessions. These session-level guarantees are less costly to provide than their strong counterparts while preserving many of the desirable properties of the strong counterparts.

6.2.3   Centralized Techniques

Centralized update propagation techniques require that updates are first applied at a master copy and then propagated to other copies (which are called *slaves*). The site that hosts the master copy is similarly called the *master site*, while the sites that host the slave copies for that data item are called *slave sites*.

In some techniques, there is a single master for all replicated data. We refer to these as *single master* centralized techniques. In other protocols, the master copy for each data item may be different (i.e., for data item x, the master copy may be x_i stored at site S_i, while for data item y, it may be y_j stored at site S_j). These are typically known as *primary copy* centralized techniques.

The advantages of centralized techniques are twofold. First, application of the updates is easy since they happen at only the master site, and they do not require synchronization among multiple replica sites. Second, there is the assurance that at least one site—the site that holds the master copy—has up-to-date values for a data item. These protocols are generally suitable in data warehouses and other applications where data processing is centralized at one or a few master sites.

The primary disadvantage is that, as in any centralized algorithm, if there is one central site that hosts all of the masters, this site can be overloaded and can become a bottleneck. Distributing the master site responsibility for each data item as in primary copy techniques is one way of reducing this overhead, but it raises consistency issues, in particular with respect to maintaining global serializability in lazy replication techniques, since the refresh transactions have to be executed at the replicas in the same serialization order. We discuss these further in relevant sections.

6.2.4 Distributed Techniques

Distributed techniques apply the update on the local copy at the site where the update transaction originates, and then the updates are propagated to the other replica sites. These are called distributed techniques since different transactions can update different copies of the same data item located at different sites. They are appropriate for collaborative applications with distributive decision/operation centers. They can more evenly distribute the load, and may provide the highest system availability if coupled with lazy propagation techniques.

A serious complication that arises in these systems is that different replicas of a data item may be updated at different sites (masters) concurrently. If distributed techniques are coupled by eager propagation methods, then the distributed concurrency control methods can adequately address the concurrent updates problem. However, if lazy propagation methods are used, then transactions may be executed in different orders at different sites causing non-1SR global history. Furthermore, various replicas will get out of sync. To manage these problems, a reconciliation method is applied involving undoing and redoing transactions in such a way that transaction execution is the same at each site. This is not an easy issue since reconciliation is generally application dependent.

6.3 Replication Protocols

In the previous section, we discussed two dimensions along which update management techniques can be classified. These dimensions are orthogonal; therefore, four combinations are possible: eager centralized, eager distributed, lazy centralized, and lazy distributed. We discuss each of these alternatives in this section. For simplicity of exposition, we assume a fully replicated database, which means that all update transactions are global. We further assume that each site implements a 2PL-based concurrency control technique.

6.3.1   Eager Centralized Protocols

In eager centralized replica control, a master site controls the operations on a data item. These protocols are coupled with strong consistency techniques, so that updates to a logical data item are applied to all of its replicas within the context of the update transaction, which is committed using the 2PC protocol (although non-2PC alternatives exist as we discuss shortly). Consequently, once the update transaction completes, all replicas have the same values for the updated data items (i.e., mutually consistent), and the resulting global history is 1SR.

The two design parameters that we discussed earlier determine the specific implementation of eager centralized replica protocols: where updates are performed, and degree of replication transparency. The first parameter, which was discussed in Sect. 6.2.3, refers to whether there is a single master site for all data items (single master), or different master sites for each, or, more likely, for a group of data items (primary copy). The second parameter indicates whether each application knows the location of the master copy (limited application transparency) or whether it can rely on its local TM for determining the location of the master copy (full replication transparency).

6.3.1.1   Single Master with Limited Replication Transparency

The simplest case is to have a single master for the entire database (i.e., for all data items) with limited replication transparency so that user applications know the master site. In this case, global update transactions (i.e., those that contain at least one $W(x)$ operation, where x is a replicated data item) are submitted directly to the master site—more specifically, to the TM at the master site. At the master, each $R(x)$ operation is performed on the master copy (i.e., $R(x)$ is converted to $R(x_M)$, where M signifies master copy) and executed as follows: a read lock is obtained on x_M, the read is performed, and the result is returned to the user. Similarly, each $W(x)$ causes an update of the master copy [i.e., executed as $W(x_M)$] by first obtaining a write lock and then performing the write operation. The master TM then forwards the Write to the slave sites either synchronously or in a deferred fashion (Fig. 6.1). In either case, it is important to propagate updates such that conflicting updates are executed at the slaves in the same order they are executed at the master. This can be achieved by timestamping or by some other ordering scheme.

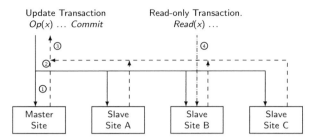

Fig. 6.1 Eager single master replication protocol actions. (1) A Write is applied on the master copy; (2) Write is then propagated to the other replicas; (3) Updates become permanent at commit time; (4) Read-only transaction's Read goes to any slave copy

The user application may submit a read-only transaction (i.e., all operations are Read) to any slave site. The execution of read-only transactions at the slaves can follow the process of centralized concurrency control algorithms, such as C2PL (Algorithms 5.1–5.3), where the centralized lock manager resides at the master replica site. Implementations within C2PL require minimal changes to the TM at the nonmaster sites, primarily to deal with the Write operations as described above, and its consequences (e.g., in the processing of Commit command). Thus, when a slave site receives a Read operation (from a read-only transaction), it forwards it to the master site to obtain a read lock. The Read can then be executed at the master and the result returned to the application, or the master can simply send a "lock granted" message to the originating site, which can then execute the Read on the local copy.

It is possible to reduce the load on the master by performing the Read on the local copy without obtaining a read lock from the master site. Whether synchronous or deferred propagation is used, the local concurrency control algorithm ensures that the local read–write conflicts are properly serialized, and since the Write operations can only be coming from the master as part of update propagation, local write–write conflicts will not occur as the propagation transactions are executed in each slave in the order dictated by the master. However, a Read may read data item values at a slave either before an update is installed or after. The fact that a Read from one transaction at one slave site may read the value of one replica before an update, while another Read from another transaction reads another replica at another slave after the same update is inconsequential from the perspective of ensuring global 1SR histories. This is demonstrated by the following example.

Example 6.3 Consider a data item x whose master site is at site A with slaves at sites B and C. Consider the following three transactions:

T_1: Write(x) T_2: Read(x) T_3: Read(x)
    Commit   Commit   Commit

Assume that T_2 is sent to slave at site B and T_3 to slave at site C. Assume that T_2 reads x at B [$R_2(x_B)$] before T_1's update is applied at B, while T_3 reads x at C

$[R_3(x_C)]$ after T_1's update at C. Then the histories generated at the two slaves will be as follows:

$$H_B = \{R_2(x), C_2, W_1(x), C_1\}$$
$$H_C = \{W_1(x), C_1, R_3(x), C_3\}$$

The serialization order at site B is $T_2 \rightarrow T_1$, while at site C it is $T_1 \rightarrow T_3$. The global serialization order, therefore, is $T_2 \rightarrow T_1 \rightarrow T_3$, which is fine. Therefore the history is 1SR.   ◆

Consequently, if this approach is followed, read transactions may read data that are concurrently updated at the master, but the global history will still be 1SR.

In this alternative protocol, when a slave site S_i receives a $R(x)$, it obtains a local read lock, reads from its local copy [i.e., $R(x_i)$], and returns the result to the user application; this can only come from a read-only transaction. When it receives a $W(x)$, if this is coming from the master site, then it performs it on the local copy [i.e., $W_i(x_i)$]. If it is from a user application, then it rejects $W(x)$, since this is obviously an error given that update transactions have to be submitted to the master site.

These alternatives of a single master eager centralized protocol are simple to implement. One important issue to address is how one recognizes a transaction as "update" or "read-only"—it may be possible to do this by explicit declaration within the Begin_transaction command.

6.3.1.2   Single Master with Full Replication Transparency

Single master eager centralized protocols require each user application to know the master site, and they put significant load on the master that has to deal with (at least) the Read operations within update transactions as well as acting as the coordinator for these transactions during 2PC execution. These issues can be addressed, to some extent, by involving, in the execution of the update transactions, the TM at the site where the application runs. Thus, the update transactions are not submitted to the master, but to the TM at the site where the application runs (since they do not need to know the master). This TM can act as the coordinating TM for both update and read-only transactions. Applications can simply submit their transactions to their local TM, providing full transparency.

There are alternatives to implementing full transparency—the coordinating TM may only act as a "router," forwarding each operation directly to the master site. The master site can then execute the operations locally (as described above) and return the results to the application. Although this alternative implementation provides full transparency and has the advantage of being simple to implement, it does not address the overloading problem at the master. An alternative implementation may be as follows:

1. The coordinating TM sends each operation, as it gets it, to the central (master) site. This requires no change to the C2PL-TM algorithm (Algorithm 5.1).
2. If the operation is a $R(x)$, then the centralized lock manager (C2PL-LM in Algorithm 5.2) can proceed by setting a read lock on its copy of x (call it x_M) on behalf of this transaction and informs the coordinating TM that the read lock is granted. The coordinating TM can then forward the $R(x)$ to any slave site that holds a replica of x [i.e., converts it to a $R(x_i)$]. The read can then be carried out by the data processor (DP) at that slave.
3. If the operation is a $W(x)$, then the centralized lock manager (master) proceeds as follows:

   (a) It first sets a write lock on its copy of x_M.
   (b) It then calls its local DP to perform $W(x_M)$ on its own copy.
   (c) Finally, it informs the coordinating TM that the write lock is granted.

   The coordinating TM, in this case, sends the $W(x)$ to all the slaves where a copy of x exists; the DPs at these slaves apply the Write to their local copies.

The fundamental difference in this case is that the master site does not deal with Read or with the coordination of the updates across replicas. These are left to the TM at the site where the user application runs.

It is straightforward to see that this algorithm guarantees that the histories are 1SR since the serialization orders are determined at a single master (similar to centralized concurrency control algorithms). It is also clear that the algorithm follows the ROWA protocol, as discussed above—since all the copies are ensured to be up-to-date when an update transaction completes, a Read can be performed on any copy.

To demonstrate how eager algorithms combine replica control and concurrency control, we show the Transaction Management algorithm for the coordinating TM (Algorithm 6.1) and the Lock Management algorithm for the master site (Algorithm 6.2). We show only the revisions to the centralized 2PL algorithms (Algorithms 5.1 and 5.2 in Chap. 5).

Note that in the algorithm fragments that we have given, the LM simply sends back a "Lock granted" message and not the result of the update operation. Consequently, when the update is forwarded to the slaves by the coordinating TM, they need to execute the update operation themselves. This is sometimes referred to as *operation transfer*. The alternative is for the "Lock granted" message to include the result of the update computation, which is then forwarded to the slaves who simply need to apply the result and update their logs. This is referred to as *state transfer*. The distinction may seem trivial if the operations are simply in the form $W(x)$, but recall that this Write operation is an abstraction; each update operation may require the execution of an SQL expression, in which case the distinction is quite important.

The above implementation of the protocol relieves some of the load on the master site and alleviates the need for user applications to know the master. However, its implementation is more complicated than the first alternative we discussed. In

---

Algorithm 6.1: Eager Single Master Modifications to C2PL-TM

begin

    ⋮

    if *lock request granted* **then**

        if *op.Type* = W **then**

            | *S* ← set of **all** sites that are slaves for the data item

        else

            | *S* ← **any** one site which has a copy of data item

        end if

        $\mathrm{DP}_S(op)$ {send operation to all sites in set *S*}

    else

      | inform user about the termination of transaction

    end if

    ⋮

end

Algorithm 6.2: Eager Single Master Modifications to C2PL-LM

begin

    ⋮

    switch *op.Type* **do**

        case *R or W* **do**   {lock request; see if it can be granted}

            find the lock unit *lu* such that *op.arg* ⊆ *lu* ;

            if *lu is unlocked or lock mode of lu is compatible with op.Type* **then**

                set lock on *lu* in appropriate mode on behalf of transaction *op.tid* ;

                if *op.Type* = W **then**

                  | $\mathrm{DP}_M(op)$ {call local DP (M for "master") with operation}

                send "Lock granted" to coordinating TM of transaction

            else

                | put *op* on a queue for *lu*

            end if

        end case

        ⋮

    end switch

end

---

particular, now the TM at the site where transactions are submitted has to act as the 2PC coordinator and the master site becomes a participant. This requires some care in revising the algorithms at these sites.

6.3.1.3   Primary Copy with Full Replication Transparency

Let us now relax the requirement that there is one master for all data items; each data item can have a different master. In this case, for each replicated data item, one of the replicas is designated as the *primary copy*. Consequently, there is no single master to determine the global serialization order, so more care is required. In the case of fully replicated databases, any replica can be primary copy for a data item; however, for partially replicated databases, limited replication transparency option only makes sense if an update transaction accesses only data items whose primary sites are at the same site. Otherwise, the application program cannot forward the update transactions to one master; it will have to do it operation-by-operation, and, furthermore, it is not clear which primary copy master would serve as the coordinator for 2PC execution. Therefore, the reasonable alternative is the full transparency support, where the TM at the application site acts as the coordinating TM and forwards each operation to the primary site of the data item that it acts on. Figure 6.2 depicts the sequence of operations in this case where we relax our previous assumption of fully replication. Site A is the master for data item x and sites B and C hold replicas (i.e., they are slaves); similarly data item y's master is site C with slave sites B and D.

Recall that this version still applies the updates to all the replicas within transactional boundaries, requiring integration with concurrency control techniques. A very early proposal is the *primary copy two-phase locking* (PC2PL) algorithm proposed for the prototype distributed version of INGRES. PC2PL is a straightforward extension of the single master protocol discussed above in an attempt to counter the latter's potential performance problems. Basically, it implements lock managers at a number of sites and makes each lock manager responsible for managing the locks for a given set of lock units for which it is the master site. The transaction managers then send their lock and unlock requests to the lock managers that are responsible for that specific lock unit. Thus the algorithm treats one copy of each data item as its primary copy.

As a combined replica control/concurrency control technique, primary copy approach demands a more sophisticated directory at each site, but it also improves the previously discussed approaches by reducing the load of the master site without causing a large amount of communication among the transaction managers and lock managers.

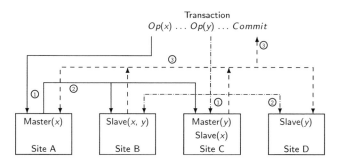

Fig. 6.2 Eager primary copy replication protocol actions. (1) Operations (Read or Write) for each data item are routed to that data item's master and a Write is first applied at the master; (2) Write is then propagated to the other replicas; (3) Updates become permanent at commit time

6.3.2   Eager Distributed Protocols

In eager distributed replica control, the updates can originate anywhere, and they are
first applied on the local replica, then the updates are propagated to other replicas.
If the update originates at a site where a replica of the data item does not exist, it is
forwarded to one of the replica sites, which coordinates its execution. Again, all of
these are done within the context of the update transaction, and when the transaction
commits, the user is notified and the updates are made permanent. Figure 6.3 depicts
the sequence of operations for one logical data item x with copies at sites A, B, C,
and D, and where two transactions update two different copies (at sites A and D).

As can be clearly seen, the critical issue is to ensure that concurrent conflicting
Write operations initiated at different sites are executed in the same order at every
site where they execute together (of course, the local executions at each site also
have to be serializable). This is achieved by means of the concurrency control
techniques that are employed at each site. Consequently, read operations can be
performed on any copy, but writes are performed on all copies within transactional
boundaries (e.g., ROWA) using a concurrency control protocol.

6.3.3   Lazy Centralized Protocols

Lazy centralized replication algorithms are similar to eager centralized replication
ones in that the updates are first applied to a master replica and then propagated
to the slaves. The important difference is that the propagation does not take place
within the update transaction, but after the transaction commits as a separate refresh
transaction. Consequently, if a slave site performs a $R(x)$ operation on its local copy,
it may read stale (nonfresh) data, since x may have been updated at the master, but
the update may not have yet been propagated to the slaves.

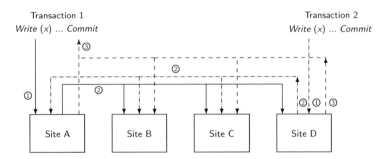

Fig. 6.3 Eager distributed replication protocol actions. (1) Two Write operations are applied on
two local replicas of the same data item; (2) The Write operations are independently propagated to
the other replicas; (3) Updates become permanent at commit time (shown only for Transaction 1)

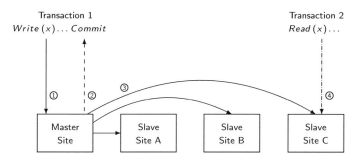

Fig. 6.4 Lazy single master replication protocol actions. (1) Update is applied on the local replica; (2) Transaction commit makes the updates permanent at the master; (3) Update is propagated to the other replicas in refresh transactions; (4) Transaction 2 reads from local copy

6.3.3.1   Single Master with Limited Transparency

In this case, the update transactions are submitted and executed directly at the master site (as in the eager single master); once the update transaction commits, the refresh transaction is sent to the slaves. The sequence of execution steps is as follows: (1) an update transaction is first applied to the master replica, (2) the transaction is committed at the master, and then (3) the refresh transaction is sent to the slaves (Fig. 6.4).

When a slave site receives a $R(x)$, it reads from its local copy and returns the result to the user. Notice that, as indicated above, its own copy may not be up-to-date if the master is being updated and the slave has not yet received and executed the corresponding refresh transaction. A $W(x)$ received by a slave is rejected (and the transaction aborted), as this should have been submitted directly to the master site. When a slave receives a refresh transaction from the master, it applies the updates to its local copy. When it receives a Commit or Abort (Abort can happen for only locally submitted read-only transactions), it locally performs these actions.

The case of primary copy with limited transparency is similar, so we do not discuss it in detail. Instead of going to a single master site, $W(x)$ is submitted to the primary copy of x; the rest is straightforward.

How can it be ensured that the refresh transactions can be applied at all of the slaves in the same order? In this architecture, since there is a single master copy for all data items, the ordering can be established by simply using timestamps. The master site would attach a timestamp to each refresh transaction according to the commit order of the actual update transaction, and the slaves would apply the refresh transactions in timestamp order.

A similar approach may be followed in the primary copy, limited transparency case. In this case, a site contains slave copies of a number of data items, causing it to get refresh transactions from multiple masters. The execution of these refresh transactions need to be ordered the same way at all of the involved slaves to ensure that the database states eventually converge. There are a number of alternatives that can be followed.

One alternative is to assign timestamps such that refresh transactions issued from different masters have different timestamps (by appending the site identifier to a monotonic counter at each site). Then the refresh transactions at each site can be executed in their timestamp order. However, those that come out of order cause difficulty. In traditional timestamp-based techniques discussed in Chap. 5, these transactions would be aborted; however, in lazy replication, this is not possible since the transaction has already been committed at the primary copy site. The only possibility is to run a compensating transaction (which, effectively, aborts the transaction by rolling back its effects) or to perform update reconciliation that will be discussed shortly. The issue can be addressed by a more careful study of the resulting histories. An approach is to use a serialization graph approach that builds a *replication graph* whose nodes consist of transactions (T) and sites (S) and an edge $\langle T_i, S_j \rangle$ exists in the graph if and only if T_i performs a Write on a (replicated) physical copy that is stored at S_j. When an operation (op_k) is submitted, the appropriate nodes (T_k) and edges are inserted into the replication graph, which is checked for cycles. If there is no cycle, then the execution can proceed. If a cycle is detected and it involves a transaction that has committed at the master, but whose refresh transactions have not yet committed at all of the involved slaves, then the current transaction (T_k) is aborted (to be restarted later) since its execution would cause the history to be non-1SR. Otherwise, T_k can wait until the other transactions in the cycle are completed (i.e., they are committed at their masters and their refresh transactions are committed at all of the slaves). When a transaction is completed in this manner, the corresponding node and all of its incident edges are removed from the replication graph. This protocol is proven to produce 1SR histories. An important issue is the maintenance of the replication graph. If it is maintained by a single site, then this becomes a centralized algorithm. We leave the distributed construction and maintenance of the replication graph as an exercise.

Another alternative is to rely on the group communication mechanism provided by the underlying communication infrastructure (if it can provide it). We discuss this alternative in Sect. 6.4.

Recall from Sect. 6.3.1 that, in the case of partially replicated databases, eager primary copy with limited replication transparency approach makes sense if the update transactions access only data items whose master sites are the same, since the update transactions are run completely at a master. The same problem exists in the case of lazy primary copy, limited replication approach. The issue that arises in both cases is how to design the distributed database so that meaningful transactions can be executed. This problem has been studied within the context of lazy protocols and a primary site selection algorithm was proposed that, given a set of transactions, a set of sites, and a set of data items, finds a primary site assignment to these data items (if one exists) such that the set of transactions can be executed to produce a 1SR global history.

6.3.3.2   Single Master or Primary Copy with Full Replication Transparency

We now turn to alternatives that provide full transparency by allowing (both read and update) transactions to be submitted at any site and forwarding their operations to either the single master or to the appropriate primary master site. This is tricky and involves two problems: the first is that, unless one is careful, 1SR global history may not be guaranteed; the second problem is that a transaction may not see its own updates. The following two examples demonstrate these problems.

Example 6.4 Consider the single master scenario and two sites M and B, where M holds the master copies of x and y and B holds their slave copies. Now consider the following two transactions: T_1 submitted at site B, while transaction T_2 submitted at site M:

$$T_1: \quad \text{Read}(x) \quad T_2: \quad \text{Write}(x)$$
$$\text{Write}(y) \qquad\qquad \text{Write}(y)$$
$$\text{Commit} \qquad\qquad \text{Commit}$$

One way these would be executed under full transparency is as follows. T_2 would be executed at site M since it contains the master copies of both x and y. Sometime after it commits, refresh transactions for its Write operations are sent to site B to update the slave copies. On the other hand, T_1 would read the local copy of x at site B $[R_1(x_B)]$, but its $W_1(x)$ would be forwarded to x's master copy, which is at site M. Some time after $W_1(x)$ is executed at the master site and commits there, a refresh transaction would be sent back to site B to update the slave copy. The following is a possible sequence of steps of execution (Fig. 6.5):

1. $R_1(x)$ is submitted at site B, where it is performed $[R_1(x_B)]$;
2. $W_2(x)$ is submitted at site M, and it is executed $[W_2(x_M)]$;
3. $W_2(y)$ is submitted at site M, and it is executed $[W_2(y_B)]$;
4. T_2 submits its Commit at site M and commits there;
5. $W_1(x)$ is submitted at site B; since the master copy of x is at site M, the Write is forwarded to M;
6. $W_1(x)$ is executed at site M $[W_1(x_M)]$; and the confirmation is sent back to site B;
7. T_1 submits Commit at site B, which forwards it to site M; it is executed there and B is informed of the commit where T_1 also commits;
8. Site M now sends refresh transaction for T_2 to site B where it is executed and commits;
9. Site M finally sends refresh transaction for T_1 to site B (this is for T_1's Write that was executed at the master), it is executed at B and commits.

The following two histories are now generated at the two sites where the superscript r on operations indicates that they are part of a refresh transaction:

$$H_B = \{W_2(x_M), W_2(y_M), C_2, W_1(y_M), C_1\}$$
$$H_B = \{R_1(x_B), C_1, W_2^r(x_B), W_2^r(y_B), C_2^r, W_1^r(x_B), C_1^r\}$$

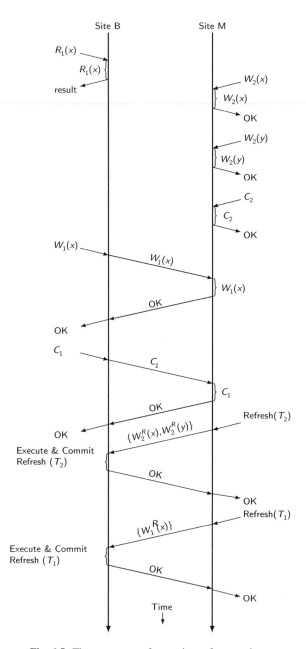

Fig. 6.5 Time sequence of executions of transactions

The resulting global history over the *logical* data items x and y is non-1SR. ◆

Example 6.5 Again consider a single master scenario, where site M holds the master copy of x and site D holds its slave. Consider the following simple transaction:

T_3: Write(x)
        Read(x)
        Commit

Following the same execution model as in Example 6.4, the sequence of steps would be as follows:

1. $W_3(x)$ is submitted at site D, which forwards it to site M for execution;
2. The Write is executed at M $[W_3(x_M)]$ and the confirmation is sent back to site D;
3. $R_3(x)$ is submitted at site D and is executed on the local copy $[R_3(x_D)]$;
4. T_3 submits commit at D, which is forwarded to M, executed there and a notification is sent back to site D, which also commits the transaction;
5. Site M sends a refresh transaction to site D for the $W_3(x)$ operation;
6. Site D executes the refresh transaction and commits it.

Note that, since the refresh transaction is sent to site D sometime after T_3 commits at site M, at step 3 when it reads the value of x at site D, it reads the old value and does not see the value of its own Write that just precedes Read. ◆

Because of these problems, there are not too many proposals for full transparency in lazy replication algorithms. A notable exception is an algorithm that considers the single master case and provides a method for validity testing by the master site, at commit point, similar to optimistic concurrency control. The fundamental idea is the following. Consider a transaction T that writes a data item x. At commit time of transaction T, the master generates a timestamp for it and uses this timestamp to set a timestamp for the master copy (x_M) that records the timestamp of the last transaction that updated it $(last\_modified(x_M))$. This is appended to refresh transactions as well. When refresh transactions are received at slaves they also set their copies to this same value, i.e., $last\_modified(x_i) \leftarrow last\_modified(x_M)$. The timestamp generation for T at the master follows the following rule:

> The timestamp for transaction T should be greater than all previously issued timestamps and should be less than the $last\_modified$ timestamps of the data items it has accessed. If such a timestamp cannot be generated, then T is aborted.[3]

This test ensures that read operations read correct values. For example, in Example 6.4, master site M would not be able to assign an appropriate timestamp

---

[3]The original proposal handles a wide range of freshness constraints, as we discussed earlier; therefore, the rule is specified more generically. However, since our discussion primarily focuses on 1SR behavior, this (more strict) recasting of the rule is appropriate.

to transaction T_1 when it commits, since the $last\_modified(x_M)$ would reflect the update performed by T_2. Therefore, T_1 would be aborted.

Although this algorithm handles the first problem we discussed above, it does not automatically handle the problem of a transaction not seeing its own writes (what we referred to as transaction inversion earlier). To address this issue, it has been suggested that a list be maintained of all the updates that a transaction performs and this list is consulted when a Read is executed. However, since only the master knows the updates, the list has to be maintained at the master and all the Read and Write operations have to be executed at the master.

6.3.4   Lazy Distributed Protocols

Lazy distributed replication protocols are the most complex ones owing to the fact that updates can occur on any replica and they are propagated to the other replicas lazily (Fig. 6.6).

The operation of the protocol at the site where the transaction is submitted is straightforward: both Read and Write operations are executed on the local copy, and the transaction commits locally. Sometime after the commit, the updates are propagated to the other sites by means of refresh transactions.

The complications arise in processing these updates at the other sites. When the refresh transactions arrive at a site, they need to be locally scheduled, which is done by the local concurrency control mechanism. The proper serialization of these refresh transactions can be achieved using the techniques discussed in previous sections. However, multiple transactions can update different copies of the same data item concurrently at different sites, and these updates may conflict with each other. These changes need to be reconciled, and this complicates the ordering of refresh

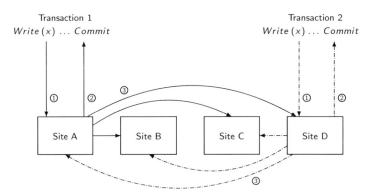

Fig. 6.6 Lazy distributed replication protocol actions. (1) Two updates are applied on two local replicas; (2) Transaction commit makes the updates permanent; (3) The updates are independently propagated to the other replicas

transactions. Based on the results of reconciliation, the order of execution of the refresh transactions is determined and updates are applied at each site.

The critical issue here is reconciliation. One can design a general purpose reconciliation algorithm based on heuristics. For example, updates can be applied in timestamp order (i.e., those with later timestamps will always win) or one can give preference to updates that originate at certain sites (perhaps there are more important sites). However, these are ad hoc methods and reconciliation is really dependent upon application semantics. Furthermore, whatever reconciliation technique is used, some of the updates are lost. Note that timestamp-based ordering will only work if timestamps are based on local clocks that are synchronized. As we discussed earlier, this is hard to achieve in large-scale distributed systems. Simple timestamp-based approach, which concatenates a site number and local clock, gives arbitrary preference between transactions that may have no real basis in application logic. The reason timestamps work well in concurrency control and not in this case is because in concurrency control we are only interested in determining *some* order; here we are interested in determining a *particular* order that is consistent with application semantics.

6.4 Group Communication

As discussed in the previous section, the overhead of replication protocols can be high—particularly in terms of message overhead. A very simple cost model for the replication algorithms is as follows. If there are n replicas and each transaction consists of m update operations, then each transaction issues $n * m$ messages (if multicast communication is possible, m messages would be sufficient). If the system wishes to maintain a throughput of k transactions-per-second, this results in $k * n * m$ messages per second (or $k * m$ in the case of multicasting). One can add sophistication to this cost function by considering the execution time of each operation (perhaps based on system load) to get a cost function in terms of time. The problem with many of the replication protocols discussed above (in particular the distributed ones) is that their message overhead is high.

A critical issue in efficient implementation of these protocols is to reduce the message overhead. Solutions have been proposed that use group communication protocols together with nontraditional techniques for processing local transactions. These solutions introduce two modifications: they do not employ 2PC at commit time, but rely on the underlying group communication protocols to ensure agreement, and they use deferred update propagation rather than synchronous.

Let us first review the group communication idea. A group communication system enables a node to multicast a message to all nodes of a group with a delivery guarantee, i.e., the message is eventually delivered to all nodes. Furthermore, it can provide multicast primitives with different delivery orders only one of which is important for our discussion: total order. In total ordered multicast, all messages sent by different nodes are delivered in the same total order at all nodes. This is important in understanding the following discussion.

We will demonstrate the use of group communication by considering two protocols. The first one is an alternative eager distributed protocol, while the second one is a lazy centralized protocol.

The group communication-based eager distributed protocol uses a local processing strategy where Write operations are carried out on local shadow copies where the transaction is submitted and utilizes total ordered group communication to multicast the set of write operations of the transaction to all the other replica sites. Total ordered communication guarantees that all sites receive the write operations in exactly the same order, thereby ensuring identical serialization order at every site. For simplicity of exposition, in the following discussion, we assume that the database is fully replicated and that each site implements a 2PL concurrency control algorithm.

The protocol executes a transaction T_i in four steps (local concurrency control actions are not indicated):

I. **Local processing phase.** A $R_i(x)$ operation is performed at the site where it is submitted (this is the master site for this transaction). A $W_i(x)$ operation is also performed at the master site, but on a shadow copy (see the previous chapter for a discussion of shadow paging).

II. **Communication phase.** If T_i consists only of Read operations, then it can be committed at the master site. If it involves Write operations (i.e., if it is an update transaction), then the TM at T_i's master site (i.e., the site where T_i is submitted) assembles the writes into one *write message* WM_i[4] and multicasts it to all the replica sites (including itself) using total ordered group communication.

III. **Lock phase.** When WM_i is delivered at a site S_j, it requests all locks in WM_i in an atomic step. This can be done by acquiring a latch (lighter form of a lock) on the lock table that is kept until all the locks are granted or requests are enqueued. The following actions are performed:

   1. For each $W(x)$ in WM_i (let x_j refer to the copy of x that exists at site S_j), the following are performed:

   (a) If there are no other transactions that have locked x_j, then the write lock on x_j is granted.

   (b) Otherwise a conflict test is performed:

   - If there is a local transaction T_k that has already locked x_j, but is in its local read or communication phases, then T_k is aborted. Furthermore, if T_k is in its communication phase, a final decision message "abort" is multicast to all the sites. At this stage, read/write conflicts are detected and local read transactions are simply aborted. Note that only local read operations obtain locks during the local

---

[4]What is being sent are the updated data items (i.e., state transfer).

execution phase, since local writes are only executed on shadow copies. Therefore, there is no need to check for write/write conflicts at this stage.

- Otherwise, $W_i(x_j)$ lock request is put on queue for x_j.

2. If T_i is a local transaction (recall that the message is also sent to the site where T_i originates, in which case $j = i$), then the site can commit the transaction, so it multicasts a "commit" message. Note that the commit message is sent as soon as the locks are requested and not after writes; thus, this is not a 2PC execution.

IV. **Write phase.** When a site is able to obtain the write lock, it applies the corresponding update (for the master site, this means that the shadow copy is made the valid version). The site where T_i is submitted can commit and release all the locks. Other sites have to wait for the decision message and terminate accordingly.

Note that in this protocol, the important thing is to ensure that the lock phases of the concurrent transactions are executed in the same order at each site; that is what total ordered multicasting achieves. Also note that there is no ordering requirement on the decision messages (step III.2) and these may be delivered in any order, even before the delivery of the corresponding WM. If this happens, then the sites that receive the decision message before WM simply register the decision, but do not take any action. When WM message arrives, they can execute the lock and write phases and terminate the transaction according to the previously delivered decision message.

This protocol is significantly better, in terms of performance, than the naive one discussed in Sect. 6.3.2. For each transaction, the master site sends two messages: one when it sends the WM and the second one when it communicates the decision. Thus, if we wish to maintain a system throughput of k transactions-per-second, the total number of messages is $2k$ rather than $k*m$, as is the case with the naive protocol (assuming multicast in both cases). Furthermore, system performance is improved by the use of deferred eager propagation since synchronization among replica sites for all Write operations is done once at the end rather than throughout the transaction execution.

The second example of the use of group communication that we will discuss is in the context of lazy centralized algorithms. Recall that an important issue in this case is to ensure that the refresh transactions are ordered the same way at all the involved slaves so that the database states converge. If totally ordered multicasting is available, the refresh transactions sent by different master sites would be delivered in the same order at all the slaves. However, total order multicast has high messaging overhead which may limit its scalability. It is possible to relax the ordering requirement of the communication system and let the replication protocol take responsibility for ordering the execution of refresh transactions. We will demonstrate this alternative by means of a protocol that assumes FIFO ordered multicast communication with a bounded delay for communication (call it *Max*), and assumes that the clocks are loosely synchronized so that they may only be out of sync by up to ϵ. It further assumes that there is an appropriate transaction management functionality at each site. The result of the replication protocol at each slave is to maintain a "running queue" that holds an ordered list of refresh transactions, which is the input to the transaction manager for local execution. Thus, the protocol ensures that the orders in the running queues at each slave site where a set of refresh transactions run are the same.

At each slave site, a "pending queue" is maintained for each master site of this slave (i.e., if the slave site has replicas of x and y whose master sites are S_1 and S_2, respectively, then there are two pending queues, q_1 and q_2, corresponding to master sites S_1 and S_2, respectively). When a refresh transaction RT_i^k is created at a master site $site_k$, it is assigned a timestamp $ts(RT_i)$ that corresponds to the real time value at the commit time of the corresponding update transaction T_i. When RT_i arrives at a slave, it is put on queue q_k. At each message arrival the top elements of all pending queues are scanned and the one with the lowest timestamp is chosen as the new RT (new_RT) to be handled. If the new_RT has changed since the last cycle (i.e., a new RT arrived with a lower timestamp than what was chosen in the previous cycle), then the one with the lower timestamp becomes the new_RT and is considered for scheduling.

When a refresh transaction is chosen as the new_RT, it is not immediately put on the "running queue" for the transaction manager; the scheduling of a refresh transaction takes into account the maximum delay and the possible drift in local clocks. This is done to ensure that any refresh transaction that may be delayed has a chance of reaching the slave. The time when an RT_i is put into the "running queue" at a slave site is $delivery\_time = ts(new\_RT) + Max + \epsilon$. Since the communication system guarantees an upper bound of Max for message delivery and since the maximum drift in local clocks (that determine timestamps) is ϵ, a refresh transaction cannot be delayed by more than the $delivery\_time$ before reaching all of the intended slaves. Thus, the protocol guarantees that a refresh transaction is scheduled for execution at a slave when the following holds: (1) all the write operations of the corresponding update transaction are performed at the master, (2) according to the order determined by the timestamp of the refresh transaction (which reflects the commit order of the update transaction), and (3) at the earliest at real time equivalent to its $delivery\_time$. This ensures that the updates on secondary copies at the slave sites follow the same chronological order in which their primary copies were updated and this order will be the same at all of the involved slaves, assuming that the underlying communication infrastructure can guarantee Max and ϵ. This is an example of a lazy algorithm that ensures 1SR global history, but weak mutual consistency, allowing the replica values to diverge by up to a predetermined time period.

6.5   Replication and Failures

Up to this point, we have focused on replication protocols in the absence of any failures. What happens to mutual consistency concerns if there are system failures?

The handling of failures differs between eager replication and lazy replication approaches.

6.5.1   Failures and Lazy Replication

Let us first consider how lazy replication techniques deal with failures. This case is relatively easy since these protocols allow divergence between the master copies and the replicas. Consequently, when communication failures make one or more sites unreachable (the latter due to network partitioning), the sites that are available can simply continue processing. Even in the case of network partitioning, one can allow operations to proceed in multiple partitions independently and then worry about the convergence of the database states upon repair using the conflict resolution techniques discussed in Sect. 6.3.4. Before the merge, databases at multiple partitions diverge, but they are reconciled at merge time.

6.5.2   Failures and Eager Replication

Let us now focus on eager replication, which is considerably more involved. As we noted earlier, all eager techniques implement some sort of ROWA protocol, ensuring that, when the update transaction commits, all of the replicas have the same value. ROWA family of protocols is attractive and elegant. However, as we saw during the discussion of commit protocols, it has one significant drawback. Even if one of the replicas is unavailable, the update transaction cannot be terminated. So, ROWA fails in meeting one of the fundamental goals of replication, namely providing higher availability.

An alternative to ROWA, which attempts to address the low availability problem, is the Read-One/Write-All Available (ROWA-A) protocol. The general idea is that the write commands are executed on all the available copies and the transaction terminates. The copies that were unavailable at the time will have to "catch up" when they become available.

There have been various versions of this protocol, two of which we will discuss. The first one is known as the *available copies protocol*. The coordinator of an update transaction T_i (i.e., the master where the transaction is executing) sends each $W_i(x)$ to all the slave sites where replicas of x reside, and waits for confirmation of execution (or rejection). If it times out before it gets acknowledgement from all the sites, it considers those that have not replied as unavailable and continues with the update on the available sites. The unavailable slave sites update their databases to the latest state when they recover. Note, however, that these sites may not even be aware of the existence of T_i and the update to x that T_i has made if they had become unavailable before T_i started.

There are two complications that need to be addressed. The first one is the possibility that the sites that the coordinator thought were unavailable were in fact up and running and may have already updated x but their acknowledgement may not have reached the coordinator before its timer ran out. Second, some of these sites may have been unavailable when T_i started and may have recovered since then and have started executing transactions. Therefore, the coordinator undertakes a validation procedure before committing T_i:

1. The coordinator checks to see if all the sites it thought were unavailable are still unavailable. It does this by sending an inquiry message to every one of these sites. Those that are available reply. If the coordinator gets a reply from one of these sites, it aborts T_i since it does not know the state that the previously unavailable site is in: it could have been that the site was available all along and had performed the original $W_i(x)$ but its acknowledgement was delayed (in which case everything is fine), or it could be that it was indeed unavailable when T_i started but became available later on and perhaps even executed $W_j(x)$ on behalf of another transaction T_j. In the latter case, continuing with T_i would make the execution schedule nonserializable.
2. If the coordinator of T does not get any response from any of the sites that it thought were unavailable, then it checks to make sure that all the sites that were available when $W_i(x)$ executed are still available. If they are, then T can proceed to commit. Naturally, this second step can be integrated into a commit protocol.

The second ROWA-A variant that we will discuss is the distributed ROWA-A protocol. In this case, each site S maintains a set, V_S, of sites that it believes to be available; this is the "view" that S has of the system configuration. In particular, when a transaction T_i is submitted, its coordinator's view reflects all the sites that the coordinator knows to be available (let us denote this as $V_C(T_i)$ for simplicity). A $R_i(x)$ is performed on any replica in $V_C(T_i)$ and a $W_i(x)$ updates all copies in $V_C(T_i)$. The coordinator checks its view at the end of T_i, and if the view has changed since T_i's start, then T_i is aborted. To modify V, a special atomic transaction is run at all sites, ensuring that no concurrent views are generated. This can be achieved by assigning timestamps to each V when it is generated and ensuring that a site only accepts a new view if its version number is greater than the version number of that site's current view.

The ROWA-A class of protocols are more resilient to failures, including network partitioning, than the simple ROWA protocol.

Another class of eager replication protocols are those based on voting. The fundamental characteristics of voting were presented in the previous chapter when we discussed network partitioning in nonreplicated databases. The general ideas hold in the replicated case. Fundamentally, each read and write operation has to obtain a sufficient number of votes to be able to commit. These protocols can be pessimistic or optimistic. In what follows we discuss only pessimistic protocols. An optimistic version compensates transactions to recover if the commit decision cannot be confirmed at completion. This version is suitable wherever compensating transactions are acceptable (see Chap. 5).

The earliest voting algorithm (known as Thomas's algorithm) works on fully replicated databases and assigns an equal vote to each site. For any operation of a transaction to execute, it must collect affirmative votes from a majority of the sites. This was revisited in Gifford's algorithm, which also works with partially replicated databases and assigns a vote to each copy of a replicated data item. Each operation then has to obtain a *read quorum* (V_r) or a *write quorum* (V_w) to read or write a data item, respectively. If a given data item has a total of V votes, the quorums have to obey the following rules:

1. $V_r + V_w > V$
2. $V_w > V/2$

As the reader may recall from the preceding chapter, the first rule ensures that a data item is not read and written by two transactions concurrently (avoiding the read–write conflict). The second rule, on the other hand, ensures that two write operations from two transactions cannot occur concurrently on the same data item (avoiding write–write conflict). Thus the two rules ensure that serializability and one-copy equivalence are maintained.

In the case of network partitioning, the quorum-based protocols work well since they basically determine which transactions are going to terminate based on the votes that they can obtain. The vote allocation and threshold rules given above ensure that two transactions that are initiated in two different partitions and access the same data cannot terminate at the same time.

The difficulty with this version of the protocol is that transactions are required to obtain a quorum even to read data. This significantly and unnecessarily slows down read access to the database. We describe below another quorum-based voting protocol that overcomes this serious performance drawback.

The protocol makes certain assumptions about the underlying communication layer and the occurrence of failures. The assumption about failures is that they are "clean." This means two things:

1. Failures that change the network's topology are detected by all sites instantaneously.
2. Each site has a view of the network consisting of all the sites with which it can communicate.

Based on the presence of a communication network that can ensure these two conditions, the replica control protocol is a simple implementation of the ROWA-A principle. When the replica control protocol attempts to read or write a data item, it first checks if a majority of the sites are in the same partition as the site at which the protocol is running. If so, it implements the ROWA rule within that partition: it reads any copy of the data item and writes all copies that are in that partition.

Notice that the read or the write operation will execute in only one partition. Therefore, this is a pessimistic protocol that guarantees one-copy serializability, *but only within that partition*. When the partitioning is repaired, the database is recovered by propagating the results of the update to the other partitions.

A fundamental question with respect to implementation of this protocol is whether or not the failure assumptions are realistic. Unfortunately, they may not be, since most network failures are not "clean." There is a time delay between the occurrence of a failure and its detection by a site. Because of this delay, it is possible for one site to think that it is in one partition when in fact subsequent failures have placed it in another partition. Furthermore, this delay may be different for various sites. Thus two sites that were in the same partition but are now in different partitions may proceed for a while under the assumption that they are still in the same partition. The violations of these two failure assumptions have significant negative consequences on the replica control protocol and its ability to maintain one-copy serializability.

The suggested solution is to build on top of the physical communication layer another layer of abstraction which hides the "unclean" failure characteristics of the physical communication layer and presents to the replica control protocol a communication service that has "clean" failure properties. This new layer of abstraction provides *virtual partitions* within which the replica control protocol operates. A virtual partition is a group of sites that have agreed on a common view of who is in that partition. Sites join and depart from virtual partitions under the control of this new communication layer, which ensures that the clean failure assumptions hold.

The advantage of this protocol is its simplicity. It does not incur any overhead to maintain a quorum for read accesses. Thus the reads can proceed as fast as they would in a nonpartitioned network. Furthermore, it is general enough so that the replica control protocol does not need to differentiate between site failures and network partitions.

Given alternative methods for achieving fault-tolerance in the case of replicated databases, a natural question is what the relative advantages of these methods are. There have been a number of studies that analyze these techniques, each with varying assumptions. A comprehensive study suggests that ROWA-A implementations achieve better scalability and availability than quorum techniques.

6.6   Conclusion

In this chapter, we discussed different approaches to data replication and presented protocols that are appropriate under different circumstances. Each of the alternative protocols we have discussed has their advantages and disadvantages. Eager centralized protocols are simple to implement, they do not require update coordination across sites, and they are guaranteed to lead to one-copy serializable histories. However, they put a significant load on the master sites, potentially causing them to become bottlenecks. Consequently, they are harder to scale, in particular in the single master site architecture—primary copy versions have better scalability properties since the master responsibilities are somewhat distributed. These protocols result in long response times (the longest among the four alternatives), since the access to any data has to wait until the commit of any transaction that is currently updating it (using 2PC, which is expensive). Furthermore, the local copies are used sparingly, only for read operations. Thus, if the workload is update-intensive, eager centralized protocols are likely to suffer from bad performance.

Eager distributed protocols also guarantee one-copy serializability and provide an elegant symmetric solution where each site performs the same function. However, unless there is communication system support for efficient multicasting, they result in very high number of messages that increase network load and result in high transaction response times. This also constrains their scalability. Furthermore, naive implementations of these protocols will cause significant number of deadlocks since update operations are executed at multiple sites concurrently.

Lazy centralized protocols have very short response times since transactions execute and commit at the master, and do not need to wait for completion at the slave sites. There is also no need to coordinate across sites during the execution of an update transaction, thus reducing the number of messages. On the other hand, mutual consistency (i.e., freshness of data at all copies) is not guaranteed as local copies can be out of date. This means that it is not possible to do a local read and be assured that the most up-to-date copy is read.

Finally, lazy multimaster protocols have the shortest response times and the highest availability. This is because each transaction is executed locally, with no distributed coordination. Only after they commit are the other replicas updated through refresh transactions. However, this is also the shortcoming of these protocols—different replicas can be updated by different transactions, requiring elaborate reconciliation protocols and resulting in lost updates.

Replication has been studied extensively within the distributed computing community as well as the database community. Although there are considerable similarities in the problem definition in the two environments, there are also important differences. Perhaps the two more important differences are the following. Data replication focuses on data, while replication of computation is equally important in distributed computing. In particular, concerns about data replication in mobile environments that involve disconnected operation have received considerable attention. Secondly, database and transaction consistency is of paramount importance in data replication; in distributed computing, consistency concerns are not as high on the list of priorities. Consequently, considerably weaker consistency criteria have been defined.

Replication has been studied within the context of parallel database systems, in particular within parallel database clusters. We discuss these separately in Chap. 8. We also defer to Chap. 7 replication issues that arise in multidatabase systems.

6.7 Bibliographic Notes

Replication and replica control protocols have been the subject of significant investigation since early days of distributed database research. This work is summarized well in [Helal et al. 1997]. Replica control protocols that deal with network partitioning are surveyed in [Davidson et al. 1985].

A landmark paper that defined a framework for various replication algorithms and argued that eager replication is problematic (thus opening up a torrent of activity on lazy techniques) is [Gray et al. 1996]. The characterization that we use in this chapter is based on this framework. A more detailed characterization is given in [Wiesmann et al. 2000].

Eventual consistency definition is from [Saito and Shapiro 2005], epsilon serializability is due to Pu and Leff [1991] and also discussed by Ramamritham and Pu [1995] and Wu et al. [1997]. A recent survey on optimistic (or lazy) replication techniques is [Saito and Shapiro 2005]. The entire topic is discussed at length in [Kemme et al. 2010].

Freshness, in particular for lazy techniques, has been a topic of some study. Alternative techniques to ensure "better" freshness are discussed in [Pacitti et al. 1998, 1999, Pacitti and Simon 2000, Röhm et al. 2002, Pape et al. 2004, Akal et al. 2005, Bernstein et al. 2006].

Extension of snapshot isolation to replicated databases is due to Lin et al. [2005] and its use in replicated databases is discussed in [Plattner and Alonso 2004, Daudjee and Salem 2006]. RC-serializability as another weaker form of serializability is introduced by Bernstein et al. [2006]. Strong one-copy serializability is discussed in [Daudjee and Salem 2004] and strong snapshot isolation in [Daudjee and Salem 2006]—these prevent transaction inversion.

An early eager primary copy replication protocol has been implemented in distributed INGRES and described in [Stonebraker and Neuhold 1977].

In single master lazy replication approach, using a replication graph to dealing with ordering of refresh transactions is due to Breitbart and Korth [1997]. Dealing with deferred updates by finding appropriate primary site assignment for data items is due to Chundi et al. [1996].

Bernstein et al. [2006] propose a lazy replication algorithm with full transparency.

The use of group communication has been discussed in [Chockler et al. 2001, Stanoi et al. 1998, Kemme and Alonso 2000a,b, Patiño-Martínez et al. 2000, Jiménez-Peris et al. 2002]. The eager distributed protocol we discuss in Sect. 6.4 is due to Kemme and Alonso [2000b] and the lazy centralized one is due to Pacitti et al. [1999].

The available copies protocol in Sect. 6.5.2 is due to Bernstein and Goodman [1984] and Bernstein et al. [1987].

There are many different versions of quorum-based protocols. Some of these are discussed in [Triantafillou and Taylor 1995, Paris 1986, Tanenbaum and van Renesse 1988]. The initial voting algorithm was proposed by Thomas [1979] and an early suggestion to use quorum-based voting for replica control is due to Gifford [1979]. The algorithm we present in Sect. 6.5.2 that overcomes the performance problems of Gifford's algorithm is by El Abbadi et al. [1985]. The comprehensive study we report in the same section that indicates the benefits of ROWA-A is [Jiménez-Peris et al. 2003]. Besides the algorithms we have described here, some notable others are given in [Davidson 1984, Eager and Sevcik 1983, Herlihy 1987, Minoura and Wiederhold 1982, Skeen and Wright 1984, Wright 1983]. These algorithms are generally called *static* since the vote assignments and read/write quorums are fixed a priori. An analysis of one such protocol (such analyses are rare) is given in [Kumar and Segev 1993]. Examples of *dynamic replication protocols* are in [Jajodia and Mutchler 1987, Barbara et al. 1986, 1989] among others. It is also possible to change the way data is replicated. Such protocols are called *adaptive* and one example is described in [Wolfson 1987].

An interesting replication algorithm based on economic models is described in [Sidell et al. 1996].

Exercises

Problem 6.1 For each of the four replication protocols (eager centralized, eager distributed, lazy centralized, lazy distributed), give a scenario/application where the approach is more suitable than the other approaches. Explain why.

Problem 6.2 A company has several geographically distributed warehouses storing and selling products. Consider the following partial database schema:

```
ITEM(ID, ItemName, Price, ...)
STOCK(ID, Warehouse, Quantity, ...)
CUSTOMER(ID, CustName, Address, CreditAmt, ...)
CLIENT-ORDER(ID, Warehouse, Balance, ...)
ORDER(ID, Warehouse, CustID, Date)
ORDER-LINE(ID, ItemID, Amount, ...)
```

The database contains relations with product information (ITEM contains the general product information, STOCK contains, for each product and for each warehouse, the number of pieces currently on stock). Furthermore, the database stores information about the clients/customers, e.g., general information about the clients is stored in the CUSTOMER table. The main activities regarding the clients are the ordering of products, the payment of bills, and general information requests. There exist several tables to register the orders of a customer. Each order is registered in the ORDER and ORDER-LINE tables. For each order/purchase, one entry exists in the order table, having an ID, indicating the customer-id, the warehouse at which the order was submitted, the date of the order, etc. A client can have several orders pending at a warehouse. Within each order, several products can be ordered. ORDER-LINE contains an entry for each product of the order, which may include one or more products. CLIENT-ORDER is a summary table that lists, for each client and for each warehouse, the sum of all existing orders.

(a) The company has a customer service group consisting of several employees
that receive customers' orders and payments, query the data of local customers
to write bills or register paychecks, etc. Furthermore, they answer any type
of requests which the customers might have. For instance, ordering products
changes (update/insert) the CLIENT-ORDER, ORDER, ORDER-LINE, and
STOCK tables. To be flexible, each employee must be able to work with any
of the clients. The workload is estimated to be 80% queries and 20% updates.
Since the workload is query oriented, the management has decided to build a
cluster of PCs each equipped with its own database to accelerate queries through
fast local access. How would you replicate the data for this purpose? Which
replica control protocol(s) would you use to keep the data consistent?

(b) The company's management has to decide each fiscal quarter on their product
offerings and sales strategies. For this purpose, they must continually observe
and analyze the sales of the different products at the different warehouses as
well as observe consumer behavior. How would you replicate the data for this
purpose? Which replica control protocol(s) would you use to keep the data
consistent?

Problem 6.3 (*) An alternative to ensuring that the refresh transactions can be
applied at all of the slaves in the same order in lazy single master protocols with
limited transparency is the use of a replication graph as discussed in Sect. 6.3.3.
Develop a method for distributed management of the replication graph.

Problem 6.4 Consider data items x and y replicated across the sites as follows:

Site 1	Site 2	Site 3	Site 4
x	x		x
	y	y	y

(a) Assign votes to each site and give the read and write quorum.
(b) Determine the possible ways that the network can partition and for each specify
in which group of sites a transaction that updates (reads and writes) x can be
terminated and what the termination condition would be.
(c) Repeat **(b)** for y.

Chapter 7
Database Integration—Multidatabase Systems

Up to this point, we considered distributed DBMSs that are designed in a top-down fashion. In particular, Chap. 2 focuses on techniques for partitioning and allocating a database, while Chap. 4 focuses on distributed query processing over such a database. These techniques and approaches are suitable for tightly integrated, homogeneous distributed DBMSs. In this chapter, we focus on distributed databases that are designed in a bottom-up fashion—we referred to these as multidatabase systems in Chap. 1. In this case, a number of databases already exist, and the design task involves integrating them into one database. The starting point of bottom-up design is the set of individual local conceptual schemas (LCSs). The process consists of integrating local databases with their (local) schemas into a global database and generating a global conceptual schema (GCS) (also called the *mediated schema*). Querying over a multidatabase system is more complicated in that applications and users can either query using the GCS (or views defined on it) or through the LCSs since each existing local database may already have applications running on it. Therefore, the techniques required for query processing require adjustments to the approach we discussed in Chap. 4 although many of those techniques carry over.

Database integration, and the related problem of querying multidatabases, is only one part of the more general *interoperability* problem, which includes nondatabase data sources and interoperability at the application level in addition to the database level. We separate this discussion into three pieces: in this chapter, we focus on the database integration and querying issues, we discuss the concerns related to web data integration and access in Chap. 12, and we discuss the more general issue of integrating data from arbitrary data sources in Chap. 10 under the title *data lakes*.

This chapter consists of two main sections. In Sect. 7.1, we discuss database integration—the bottom-up design process. In Sect. 7.2 we discuss approaches to querying these systems.

The original version of this chapter was revised. The correction to this chapter is available at https://doi.org/10.1007/978-3-030-26253-2_13

© Springer Nature Switzerland AG 2020
M. T. Özsu, P. Valduriez, *Principles of Distributed Database Systems*,
https://doi.org/10.1007/978-3-030-26253-2_7

7.1 Database Integration

Database integration can be either physical or logical. In the former, the source databases are integrated and the integrated database is *materialized*. These are known as *data warehouses*. The integration is aided by *extract–transform–load* (ETL) tools that enable extraction of data from sources, its transformation to match the GCS, and its loading (i.e., materialization). This process is depicted in Fig. 7.1. In logical integration, the global conceptual (or mediated) schema is entirely *virtual* and not materialized.

These two approaches are complementary and address differing needs. Data warehousing supports decision-support applications, which are commonly termed *Online Analytical Processing* (OLAP). Recall from Chap. 5 that OLAP applications analyze historical, summarized data coming from a number of operational databases through complex queries over potentially very large tables. Consequently, data warehouses gather data from a number of operational databases and materialize it. As updates happen on the operational databases, they are propagated to the data warehouse, which is known as *materialized view maintenance*.

By contrast, in logical data integration, the integration is only virtual and there is no materialized global database (see Fig. 1.13). The data resides in the operational databases and the GCS provides a virtual integration for querying over the multiple databases. In these systems, GCS may either be defined up-front and local databases (i.e., LCSs) mapped to it, or it may be defined bottom-up, by integrating parts of the LCSs of the local databases. Consequently, it is possible for the GCS not to capture

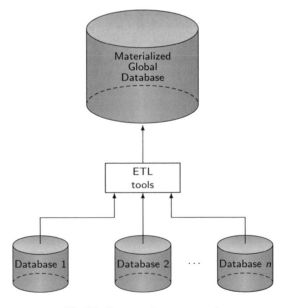

Fig. 7.1 Data warehouse approach

all of the information in each of the LCSs. User queries are posed over this global
schema, which are then decomposed and shipped to the local operational databases
for processing as is done in tightly integrated systems, with the main difference
being the autonomy and potential heterogeneity of the local systems. These have
important effects on query processing that we discuss in Sect. 7.2. Although there
is ample work on transaction management in these systems, supporting global
updates is quite difficult given the autonomy of the underlying operational DBMSs.
Therefore, they are primarily read-only.

Logical data integration and the resulting systems are known by a variety of
names; *data integration* and *information integration* are perhaps the most common
terms used in literature although these generally refer to more than database
integration and incorporate data from a variety of sources. In this chapter, we focus
on the integration of autonomous and (possibly) heterogeneous databases; thus, we
will use the term *database integration* or *multidatabase systems* (MDBSs).

7.1.1   Bottom-Up Design Methodology

Bottom-up design involves the process by which data from participating databases
can be (physically or logically) integrated to form a single cohesive global database.
As noted above, in some cases, the global conceptual (or mediated) schema is
defined first, in which case the bottom-up design involves mapping LCSs to this
schema. In other cases, the GCS is defined as an integration of parts of LCSs. In
this case, the bottom-up design involves both the generation of the GCS and the
mapping of individual LCSs to this GCS.

If the GCS is defined upfront, the relationship between the GCS and the LCSs
can be of two fundamental types: local-as-view and global-as-view. In local-as-
view (LAV) systems, the GCS definition exists, and each LCS is treated as a view
definition over it. In global-as-view systems (GAV), on the other hand, the GCS is
defined as a set of views over the LCSs. These views indicate how the elements
of the GCS can be derived, when needed, from the elements of LCSs. One way to
think of the difference between the two is in terms of the results that can be obtained
from each system . In GAV, the query results are constrained to the set of objects
that are defined in the GCS, although the local DBMSs may be considerably richer
(Fig. 7.2a). In LAV, on the other hand, the results are constrained by the objects
in the local DBMSs, while the GCS definition may be richer (Fig. 7.2b). Thus, in
LAV systems, it may be necessary to deal with incomplete answers. A combination
of these two approaches has also been proposed as global-local-as-view (GLAV)
where the relationship between GCS and LCSs is specified using both LAV and
GAV.

Bottom-up design occurs in two general steps (Fig. 7.3): *schema translation*
(or simply *translation*) and *schema generation*. In the first step, the component
database schemas are translated to a common intermediate canonical representation
(InS_1, InS_2,..., InS_n). The use of a canonical representation facilitates the trans-

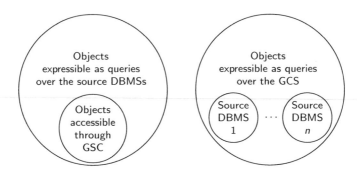

Fig. 7.2 GAV and LAV mappings (based on [Koch 2001])

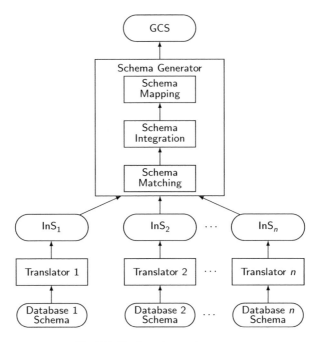

Fig. 7.3 Database integration process

lation process by reducing the number of translators that need to be written. The choice of the canonical model is important. As a principle, it should be one that is sufficiently expressive to incorporate the concepts available in all the databases that will later be integrated. Alternatives that have been used include the entity-relationship model, object-oriented model, or a graph that may be simplified to a tree or XML. In this chapter, we will simply use the relational model as our canonical data model despite its known deficiencies in representing rich semantic concepts. This choice does not affect in any fundamental way the discussion of the major issues of data integration. In any case, we will not discuss the specifics of translating various data models to relational; this can be found in many database textbooks.

Clearly, the translation step is necessary only if the component databases are heterogeneous and local schemas are defined using different data models. There has been some work on the development of system federation, in which systems with similar data models are integrated together (e.g., relational systems are integrated into one conceptual schema and, perhaps, object databases are integrated to another schema) and these integrated schemas are "combined" at a later stage (e.g., AURORA project). In this case, the translation step is delayed, providing increased flexibility for applications to access underlying data sources in a manner that is suitable for their needs.

In the second step of bottom-up design, the intermediate schemas are used to generate a GCS. The schema generation process consists of the following steps:

1. Schema matching to determine the syntactic and semantic correspondences among the translated LCS elements or between individual LCS elements and the predefined GCS elements (Sect. 7.1.2).
2. Integration of the common schema elements into a global conceptual (mediated) schema if one has not yet been defined (Sect. 7.1.3).
3. Schema mapping that determines how to map the elements of each LCS to the other elements of the GCS (Sect. 7.1.4).

It is also possible that the schema mapping step be divided into two phases: mapping constraint generation and transformation generation. In the first phase, given correspondences between two schemas, a transformation function such as a query or view definition over the source schema is generated that would "populate" the target schema. In the second phase, an executable code is generated corresponding to this transformation function that would actually generate a target database consistent with these constraints. In some cases, the constraints are implicitly included in the correspondences, eliminating the need for the first phase.

Example 7.1   To facilitate our discussion of global schema design in multidatabase systems, we will use an example that is an extension of the engineering database we have been using throughout the book. To demonstrate both phases of the database integration process, we introduce some data model heterogeneity into our example.

Consider two organizations, each with their own database definitions. One is the (relational) database example that we introduced in Chap. 2. We repeat that definition in Fig. 7.4 for completeness. The second database also defines similar data, but is specified according to the entity-relationship (E-R) data model as depicted in Fig. 7.5.[1]

We assume that the reader is familiar with the entity-relationship data model. Therefore, we will not describe the formalism, except to make the following points regarding the semantics of Fig. 7.5. This database is similar to the relational

---

[1] In this chapter, we continue our notation of typesetting relation names in `typewriter` font, but we will use normal font for E-R model components to be able to easily differentiate them.

```
EMP(ENO, ENAME, TITLE)
PROJ(PNO, PNAME, BUDGET, LOC)
ASG(ENO, PNO, RESP, DUR)
PAY(TITLE, SAL)
```

Fig. 7.4 Relational engineering database representation

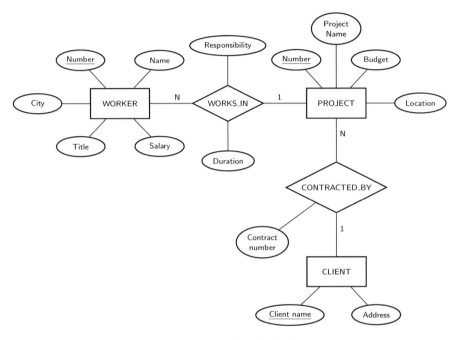

Fig. 7.5 Entity-relationship database

engineering database definition of Fig. 7.4, with one significant difference: it also maintains data about the clients for whom the projects are conducted. The rectangular boxes in Fig. 7.5 represent the entities modeled in the database, and the diamonds indicate a relationship between the entities to which they are connected. The relationship type is indicated around the diamonds. For example, the CONTRACTED-BY relation is a many-to-one from the PROJECT entity to the CLIENT entity (e.g., each project has a single client, but each client can have many projects). Similarly, the WORKS-IN relationship indicates a many-to-many relationship between the two connected relations. The attributes of entities and the relationships are shown as ellipses.   ◆

Example 7.2 The mapping of the E-R model to the relational model is given in Fig. 7.6. Note that we have renamed some of the attributes in order to ensure name uniqueness.   ◆

```
WORKER(WNUMBER, NAME, TITLE, SALARY,CITY)
PROJECT(PNUMBER, PNAME, BUDGET)
CLIENT(CNAME, ADDRESS)
WORKS_IN(WNUMBER, PNUMBER, RESPONSIBILITY, DURATION)
CONTRACTED_BY(PNUMBER, CNAME, CONTRACTNO)
```

Fig. 7.6 Relational mapping of E-R schema

7.1.2 Schema Matching

Given two schemas, schema matching determines for each concept in one schema what concept in the other matches it. As discussed earlier, if the GCS has already been defined, then one of these schemas is typically the GCS, and the task is to match each LCS to the GCS. Otherwise, matching is done over two LCSs. The matches that are determined in this phase are then used in schema mapping to produce a set of directed mappings, which, when applied to the source schema, would map its concepts to the target schema.

The matches that are defined or discovered during schema matching are specified as a set of rules where each rule (r) identifies a *correspondence* (c) between two elements, a *predicate* (p) that indicates when the correspondence may hold, and a *similarity value* (s) between the two elements identified in the correspondence. A correspondence may simply identify that two concepts are similar (which we will denote by $\approx$) or it may be a function that specifies that one concept may be derived by a computation over the other one (for example, if the budget value of one project is specified in US dollars, while the other one is specified in Euros, the correspondence may specify that one is obtained by multiplying the other one with the appropriate exchange rate). The predicate is a condition that qualifies the correspondence by specifying when it might hold. For example, in the budget example specified above, p may specify that the rule holds only if the location of one project is in US, while the other one is in the Euro zone. The similarity value for each rule can be specified or calculated. Similarity values are real values in the range [0,1]. Thus, a set of matches can be defined as $M = \{r\}$, where $r = \langle c, p, s \rangle$.

As indicated above, correspondences may either be discovered or specified. As much as it is desirable to automate this process, there are many complicating factors. The most important is schema heterogeneity, which refers to the differences in the way real-world phenomena are captured in different schemas. This is a critically important issue, and we devote a separate section to it (Sect. 7.1.2.1). Aside from schema heterogeneity, other issues that complicate the matching process are the following:

- *Insufficient schema and instance information:* Matching algorithms depend on the information that can be extracted from the schema and the existing data instances. In some cases there may be ambiguity due to the insufficient information provided about these items. For example, using short names or ambiguous abbreviations for concepts, as we have done in our examples, can lead to incorrect matching.

- *Unavailability of schema documentation:* In most cases, the database schemas are not well documented or not documented at all. Quite often, the schema designer is no longer available to guide the process. The lack of these vital information sources adds to the difficulty of matching.
- *Subjectivity of matching:* Finally, it is important to recognize that matching schema elements can be highly subjective; two designers may not agree on a single "correct" mapping. This makes the evaluation of a given algorithm's accuracy significantly difficult.

Nevertheless, algorithmic approaches have been developed to the matching problem, which we discuss in this section. A number of issues affect the particular matching algorithm. The more important ones are the following:

- *Schema versus instance matching.* So far in this chapter, we have been focusing on schema integration; thus, our attention has naturally been on matching concepts of one schema to those of another. A large number of algorithms have been developed that work on schema elements. There are others, however, that have focused instead on the data instances or a combination of schema information and data instances. The argument is that considering data instances can help alleviate some of the semantic issues discussed above. For example, if an attribute name is ambiguous, as in "contact-info," then fetching its data may help identify its meaning; if its data instances have the phone number format, then obviously it is the phone number of the contact agent, while long strings may indicate that it is the contact agent name. Furthermore, there are a large number of attributes, such as postal codes, country names, email addresses, that can be defined easily through their data instances.

  Matching that relies solely on schema information may be more efficient, because it does not require a search over data instances to match the attributes. Furthermore, this approach is the only feasible one when few data instances are available in the matched databases, in which case learning may not be reliable. However, in some cases, e.g., peer-to-peer systems (see Chap. 9), there may not be a schema, in which case instance-based matching is the only appropriate approach.
- *Element-level vs. structure-level.* Some matching algorithms operate on individual schema elements, while others also consider the structural relationships between these elements. The basic concept of the element-level approach is that most of the schema semantics are captured by the elements' names. However, this may fail to find complex mappings that span multiple attributes. Match algorithms that also consider structure are based on the belief that, normally, the structures of matchable schemas tend to be similar.
- *Matching cardinality.* Matching algorithms exhibit various capabilities in terms of cardinality of mappings. The simplest approaches use 1:1 mapping, which means that each element in one schema is matched with exactly one element in

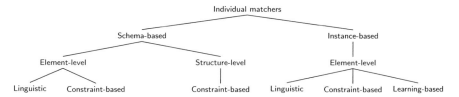

Fig. 7.7 Taxonomy of schema matching techniques

the other schema. The majority of proposed algorithms belong to this category, because problems are greatly simplified in this case. Of course there are many cases where this assumption is not valid. For example, an attribute named "Total price" could be mapped to the sum of two attributes in another schema named "Subtotal" and "Taxes." Such mappings require more complex matching algorithms that consider 1:M and N:M mappings.

These criteria, and others, can be used to come up with a taxonomy of matching approaches. According to this taxonomy (which we will follow in this chapter with some modifications), the first level of separation is between schema-based matchers versus instance-based matchers (Fig. 7.7). Schema-based matchers can be further classified as element-level and structure-level, while for instance-based approaches, only element-level techniques are meaningful. At the lowest level, the techniques are characterized as either linguistic or constraint-based. It is at this level that fundamental differences between matching algorithms are exhibited and we focus on these algorithms in the remainder, discussing linguistic approaches in Sect. 7.1.2.2, constraint-based approaches in Sect. 7.1.2.3, and learning-based techniques in Sect. 7.1.2.4. These are referred as *individual matcher* approaches, and their combinations are possible by developing either *hybrid matchers* or *composite matchers* (Sect. 7.1.2.5).

7.1.2.1 Schema Heterogeneity

Schema matching algorithms deal with both structural heterogeneity and semantic heterogeneity among the matched schemas. We discuss these in this section before presenting the different match algorithms.

Structural conflicts occur in four possible ways: as *type conflicts*, *dependency conflicts*, *key conflicts*, or *behavioral conflicts*. Type conflicts occur when the same object is represented by an attribute in one schema and an entity (relation) in another. Dependency conflicts occur when different relationship modes (e.g., one-to-one versus many-to-many) are used to represent the same thing in different schemas. Key conflicts occur when different candidate keys are available and different primary keys are selected in different schemas. Behavioral conflicts are implied by the modeling mechanism. For example, deleting the last item from one database may cause the deletion of the containing entity (i.e., deletion of the last employee causes the dissolution of the department).

Example 7.3 We have two structural conflicts in the running example of this chapter. The first is a type conflict involving clients of projects. In the schema of Fig. 7.5, the client of a project is modeled as an entity. In the schema of Fig. 7.4, however, the client is included as an attribute of the PROJ entity.

The second structural conflict is a dependency conflict involving the WORKS_IN relationship in Fig. 7.5 and the ASG relation in Fig. 7.4. In the former, the relationship is many-to-one from the WORKER to the PROJECT, whereas in the latter, the relationship is many-to-many.   ◆

Structural differences among schemas are important, but their identification and resolution is not sufficient. Schema matching has to take into account the (possibly different) semantics of the schema concepts. This is referred to as *semantic hetero-geneity*, which is a fairly loaded term without a clear definition. It basically refers to the differences among the databases that relate to the meaning, interpretation, and intended use of data. There are attempts to formalize semantic heterogeneity and to establish its link to structural heterogeneity; we will take a more informal approach and discuss some of the semantic heterogeneity issues intuitively. The following are some of these problems that the match algorithms need to deal with.

- *Synonyms, homonyms, hypernyms.* Synonyms are multiple terms that all refer to the same concept. In our database example, PROJ relation and PROJECT entity refer to the same concept. Homonyms, on the other hand, occur when the same term is used to mean different things in different contexts. Again, in our example, BUDGET may refer to the gross budget in one database and it may refer to the net budget (after some overhead deduction) in another, making their simple comparison difficult. Hypernym is a term that is more generic than a similar word. Although there is no direct example of it in the databases we are considering, the concept of a Vehicle in one database is a hypernym for the concept of a Car in another (incidentally, in this case, Car is a *hyponym* of Vehicle). These problems can be addressed by the use of *domain ontologies* that define the organization of concepts and terms in a particular domain.
- *Different ontology:* Even if domain ontologies are used to deal with issues in one domain, it is quite often the case that schemas from different domains may need to be matched. In this case, one has to be careful of the meaning of terms across ontologies, as they can be highly domain dependent. For example, an attribute called LOAD may imply a measure of resistance in an electrical ontology, but in a mechanical ontology, it may represent a measure of weight.
- *Imprecise wording:* Schemas may contain ambiguous names. For example, the LOCATION (from E-R) and LOC (from relational) attributes in our example database may refer to the full address or just part of it. Similarly, an attribute named "contact-info" may imply that the attribute contains the name of the contact agent or his/her telephone number. These types of ambiguities are common.

7.1.2.2 Linguistic Matching Approaches

Linguistic matching approaches, as the name implies, use element names and other textual information (such as textual descriptions/annotations in schema definitions) to perform matches among elements. In many cases, they may use external sources, such as thesauri, to assist in the process.

Linguistic techniques can be applied in both schema-based approaches and instance-based ones. In the former case, similarities are established among schema elements, whereas in the latter, they are specified among elements of individual data instances. To focus our discussion, we will mostly consider schema-based linguistic matching approaches, briefly mentioning instance-based techniques. Consequently, we will use the notation $\langle$SC1.element-1 $\approx$ SC2.element-2, $p, s\rangle$ to represent that element-1 in schema SC1 corresponds to element-2 in schema SC2 if predicate p holds, with a similarity value of s. Matchers use these rules and similarity values to determine the similarity value of schema elements.

Linguistic matchers that operate at the schema element-level typically deal with the names of the schema elements and handle cases such as synonyms, homonyms, and hypernyms. In some cases, the schema definitions can have annotations (natural language comments) that may be exploited by the linguistic matchers. In the case of instance-based approaches, linguistic matchers focus on information retrieval techniques such as word frequencies, key terms, etc. In these cases, the matchers "deduce" similarities based on these information retrieval measures.

Schema linguistic matchers use a set of linguistic (also called terminological) rules that can be handcrafted or may be "discovered" using auxiliary data sources such as thesauri, e.g., WordNet. In the case of handcrafted rules, the designer needs to specify the predicate p and the similarity value s as well. For discovered rules, these may either be specified by an expert following the discovery, or they may be computed using one of the techniques we will discuss shortly.

The handcrafted linguistic rules may deal with issues such as capitalization, abbreviations, and concept relationships. In some systems, the handcrafted rules are specified for each schema individually (*intraschema rules*) by the designer, and *interschema rules* are then "discovered" by the matching algorithm. However, in most cases, the rule base contains both intra and interschema rules.

Example 7.4 In the relational database of Example 7.2, the set of rules may have been defined (quite intuitively) as follows where RelDB refers to the relational schema and ERDB refers to the translated E-R schema:

$\langle$uppercase names $\approx$ lower case names, $true$, 1.0$\rangle$
$\langle$uppercase names $\approx$ capitalized names, $true$, 1.0$\rangle$
$\langle$capitalized names $\approx$ lower case names, $true$, 1.0$\rangle$
$\langle$RelDB.ASG $\approx$ ERDB.WORKS_IN, $true$, 0.8$\rangle$

...

The first three rules are generic ones specifying how to deal with capitalizations, while the fourth one specifies a similarity between the ASG of RelDB and the WORKS_IN of ERDB. Since these correspondences always hold, $p = true$.   ♦

As indicated above, there are ways of determining the element name similarities automatically. For example, COMA uses the following techniques to determine similarity of two element names:

- The *affixes* which are the common prefixes and suffixes between the two element name strings are determined.
- The *n-grams* of the two element name strings are compared. An *n*-gram is a substring of length *n* and the similarity is higher if the two strings have more *n*-grams in common.
- The *edit distance* between two element name strings is computed. The edit distance (also called the Levenshtein metric) determines the number of character modifications (additions, deletions, insertions) that one has to perform on one string to convert it to the second string.
- The *soundex code* of the element names is computed. This gives the phonetic similarity between names based on their soundex codes. Soundex code of English words is obtained by hashing the word to a letter and three numbers. This hash value (roughly) corresponds to how the word would sound. The important aspect of this code in our context is that two words that sound similar will have close soundex codes.

Example 7.5 Consider matching the RESP and the RESPONSIBILITY attributes in the two example schemas we are considering. The rules defined in Example 7.4 take care of the capitalization differences, so we are left with matching RESP with RESPONSIBILITY. Let us consider how the similarity between the two strings can be computed using the edit distance and the *n*-gram approaches.

The number of editing changes that one needs to do to convert one of these strings to the other is 10 (either we add the characters "O," "N," "S," "I," "B," "I," "L," "I," "T," "Y," to string "RESP" or delete the same characters from string "RESPONSIBILITY"). Thus the ratio of the required changes is 10/14, which defines the edit distance between these two strings; $1 - (10/14) = 4/14 = 0.29$ is then their similarity.

For *n*-gram computation, we need to first fix the value of *n*. For this example, let $n = 3$, so we are looking for 3-grams. The 3-grams of string "RESP" are "RES" and "ESP." Similarly, there are twelve 3-grams of "RESPONSIBILITY": "RES," "ESP," "SPO," "PON," "ONS," "NSI," "SIB," "IBI," "BIP," "ILI," "LIT," and "ITY." There are two matching 3-grams out of twelve, giving a 3-gram similarity of $2/12 = 0.17$.   ♦

The examples we have covered in this section all fall into the category of 1:1 matches—we matched one element of a particular schema to an element of another schema. As discussed earlier, it is possible to have 1:N (e.g., Street address, City, and Country element values in one database can be extracted from a single Address element in another), N:1 (e.g., Total_price can be calculated from Subtotal and Taxes elements), or N:M (e.g., Book_title, Rating information can be extracted via a join of two tables one of which holds book information and the other maintains reader reviews and ratings). 1:1, 1:N, and N:1 matchers are typically used in element-level matching, while schema-level matching can also use N:M matching, since, in the latter case the necessary schema information is available.

7.1.2.3   Constraint-Based Matching Approaches

Schema definitions almost always contain semantic information that constrain the values in the database. These are typically data type information, allowable ranges for data values, key constraints, etc. In the case of instance-based techniques, the existing ranges of the values can be extracted as well as some patterns that exist in the instance data. These can be used by matchers.

Consider data types that capture a large amount of semantic information. This information can be used to disambiguate concepts and also focus the match. For example, RESP and RESPONSIBILITY have relatively low similarity values according to calculations in Example 7.5. However, if they have the same data type definition, this may be used to increase their similarity value. Similarly, the data type comparison may differentiate between elements that have high lexical similarity. For example, ENO in Fig. 7.4 has the same edit distance and n-gram similarity values to the two NUMBER attributes in Fig. 7.5 (of course, we are referring to the *names* of these attributes). In this case, the data types may be of assistance—if the data type of both ENO and worker number (WORKER.NUMBER) is integer, while the data type of project number (PROJECT.NUMBER) is a string, the likelihood of ENO matching WORKER.NUMBER is significantly higher.

In structure-based approaches, the structural similarities in the two schemas can be exploited to determine the similarity of the schema elements. If two schema elements are structurally similar, this enhances our confidence that they indeed represent the same concept. For example, if two elements have very different names and we have not been able to establish their similarity through element matchers, but they have the same properties (e.g., same attributes) that have the same data types, then we can be more confident that these two elements may be representing the same concept.

The determination of structural similarity involves checking the similarity of the "neighborhoods" of the two concepts under consideration. Definition of the neighborhood is typically done using a graph representation of the schemas where each concept (relation, entity, attribute) is a vertex and there is a directed edge between two vertices if and only if the two concepts are related (e.g., there is an edge from a relation vertex to each of its attributes, or there is an edge from a foreign key attribute vertex to the primary key attribute vertex it is referencing). In this case, the neighborhood can be defined in terms of the vertices that can be reached within a certain path length of each concept, and the problem reduces to checking the similarity of the subgraphs in this neighborhood. Many of these algorithms consider the tree rooted at the concept that is being examined and compute the similarity of the concepts represented by the root vertices in the two trees. The fundamental idea is that if the subgraphs (subtrees) are similar, this increases the similarity of the concepts represented by the "root" vertex in the two graphs. The similarity of the subgraphs is typically determined in a bottom-up process, starting at the leaves whose similarity is determined using element matching (e.g., name similarity to the level of synonyms or data type compatibility). The similarity of the two subtrees is recursively determined based on the similarity of the vertices in the subtree. The similarity of two subgraphs (subtrees) is then defined as the fraction of leaves in the two subtrees that are strongly linked. This is based on the assumption that leaf vertices carry more information and that the structural similarity of two nonleaf schema elements is determined by the similarity of the leaf vertices in their respective subtrees, even if their immediate children are not similar. These are heuristic rules and it is possible to define others.

Another interesting approach to considering neighborhood in directed graphs while computing similarity of vertices is *similarity flooding*. It starts from an initial graph where the vertex similarities are already determined by means of an element matcher, and propagates, iteratively, to determine the similarity of each vertex to its neighbors. Hence, whenever any two elements in two schemas are found to be similar, the similarity of their adjacent vertices increases. The iterative process stops when the vertex similarities stabilize. At each iteration, to reduce the amount of work, a subset of the vertices are selected as the "most plausible" matches, which are then considered in the subsequent iteration.

Both of these approaches are agnostic to the edge semantics. In some graph representations, there is additional semantics attached to these edges. For example, *containment edges* from a relation or entity vertex to its attributes may be distinguished from *referential edges* from a foreign key attribute vertex to the corresponding primary key attribute vertex. Some systems (e.g., DIKE) exploit these edge semantics.

7.1.2.4 Learning-Based Matching

A third alternative approach that has been proposed is to use machine learning techniques to determine schema matches. Learning-based approaches formulate the problem as one of classification where concepts from various schemas are classified into classes according to their similarity. The similarity is determined by checking the features of the data instances of the databases that correspond to these schemas. How to classify concepts according to their features is learned by studying the data instances in a training dataset.

The process is as follows (Fig. 7.8). A training set (τ) is prepared that consists of instances of example correspondences between the concepts of two databases D_i and D_j. This training set can be generated after manual identification of the schema correspondences between two databases followed by extraction of example training data instances or by the specification of a query expression that converts data from one database to another. The learner uses this training data to acquire probabilistic

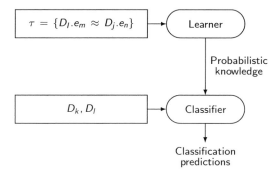

Fig. 7.8 Learning-based matching approach

information about the features of the datasets. The classifier, when given two other database instances (D_k and D_l), then uses this knowledge to go through the data instances in D_k and D_l and make predictions about classifying the elements of D_k and D_l.

This general approach applies to all of the proposed learning-based schema matching approaches. Where they differ is the type of learner that they use and how they adjust this learner's behavior for schema matching. Some have used neural networks (e.g., SEMINT), others have used Naïve Bayesian learner/classifier (Autoplex , LSD) and decision trees. We do not discuss the details of these learning techniques.

7.1.2.5   Combined Matching Approaches

The individual matching techniques that we have considered so far have their strong points and their weaknesses. Each may be more suitable for matching certain cases. Therefore, a "complete" matching algorithm or methodology usually needs to make use of more than one individual matcher.

There are two possible ways in which matchers can be combined: hybrid and composite. *Hybrid* algorithms combine multiple matchers within one algorithm. In other words, elements from two schemas can be compared using a number of element matchers (e.g., string matching as well as data type matching) and/or structural matchers within one algorithm to determine their overall similarity. Careful readers will have noted that in discussing the constraint-based matching algorithms that focused on structural matching, we followed a hybrid approach since they were based on an initial similarity determination of, for example, the leaf nodes using an element matcher, and these similarity values were then used in structural matching. *Composite* algorithms, on the other hand, apply each matcher to the elements of the two schemas (or two instances) individually, obtaining individual similarity scores, and then they apply a method for combining these similarity scores. More precisely, if $s_i(C_j^k, C_l^m)$ is the similarity score using matcher

i ($i = 1, \ldots, q$) over two concepts C_j from schema k and C_l from schema m, then the composite similarity of the two concepts is given by $s(C_j^k, C_l^m) = f(s_1, \ldots, s_q)$, where f is the function that is used to combine the similarity scores. This function can be as simple as average, max, or min, or it can be an adaptation of more complicated ranking aggregation functions that we will discuss further in Sect. 7.2. Composite approach has been proposed in the LSD and iMAP systems for handling 1:1 and N:M matches, respectively.

7.1.3 Schema Integration

Once schema matching is done, the correspondences between the various LCSs have been identified. The next step is to create the GCS, and this is referred to as *schema integration*. As indicated earlier, this step is only necessary if a GCS has not already been defined and matching was performed on individual LCSs. If the GCS was defined upfront, then the matching step would determine correspondences between it and each of the LCSs and there would be no need for the integration step. If the GCS is created as a result of the integration of LCSs based on correspondences identified during schema matching, then, as part of integration, it is important to identify the correspondences between the GCS and the LCSs. Although tools have been developed to aid in the integration process, human involvement is clearly essential.

Example 7.6 There are a number of possible integrations of the two example LCSs we have been discussing. Figure 7.9 shows one possible GCS that can be generated as a result of schema integration. We use this in the remainder of this chapter.   ◆

Integration methodologies can be classified as binary or n-ary mechanisms based on the manner in which the local schemas are handled in the first phase (Fig. 7.10). Binary integration methodologies involve the manipulation of two schemas at a time. These can occur in a stepwise (ladder) fashion (Fig. 7.11a) where intermediate schemas are created for integration with subsequent schemas, or in a purely binary fashion (Fig. 7.11b), where each schema is integrated with one other, creating an intermediate schema for integration with other intermediate schemas.

EMP(<u>E#</u>, ENAME, TITLE, CITY)

PAY(<u>TITLE</u>, SAL)

PR(<u>P#</u>, PNAME, BUDGET, LOC)

CL(<u>CNAME</u>, ADDR, CT#, P#)

WORKS(<u>E#</u>, <u>P#</u>, RESP, DUR)

Fig. 7.9 Example integrated GCS (EMP is employee, PR is project, CL is client)

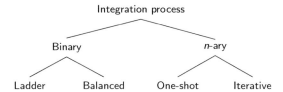

Fig. 7.10 Taxonomy of integration methodologies

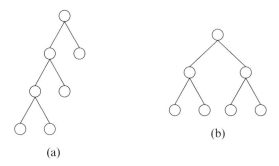

Fig. 7.11 Binary integration methods. (**a**) Stepwise. (**b**) Pure binary

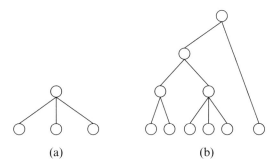

Fig. 7.12 *N*-ary integration methods. (**a**) One-pass. (**b**) Iterative

N-ary integration mechanisms integrate more than two schemas at each iteration. One-pass integration (Fig. 7.12a) occurs when all schemas are integrated at once, producing the global conceptual schema after one iteration. Benefits of this approach include the availability of complete information about all databases at integration time. There is no implied priority for the integration order of schemas, and the trade-offs, such as the best representation for data items or the most understandable structure, can be made between all schemas rather than between a few. Difficulties with this approach include increased complexity and difficulty of automation.

Iterative n-ary integration (Fig. 7.12b) offers more flexibility (typically, more information is available) and is more general (the number of schemas can be varied depending on the integrator's preferences). Binary approaches are a special case of iterative n-ary. They decrease the potential integration complexity and lead towards automation techniques, since the number of schemas to be considered at each step is more manageable. Integration by an n-ary process enables the integrator to perform the operations on more than two schemas. For practical reasons, the majority of systems utilize binary methodology, but a number of researchers prefer the n-ary approach because complete information is available.

7.1.4 Schema Mapping

Once a GCS (or mediated schema) is defined, it is necessary to identify how the data from each of the local databases (source) can be mapped to GCS (target) while preserving semantic consistency (as defined by both the source and the target). Although schema matching has identified the correspondences between the LCSs and the GCS, it may not have identified explicitly how to obtain the global database from the local ones. This is what schema mapping is about.

In the case of data warehouses, schema mappings are used to explicitly extract data from the sources, and translate them to the data warehouse schema for populating it. In the case of data integration systems, these mappings are used in query processing phase by both the query processor and the wrappers (see Sect. 7.2).

There are two issues related to schema mapping that we will study: *mapping creation* and *mapping maintenance*. Mapping creation is the process of creating explicit queries that map data from a local database to the global one. Mapping maintenance is the detection and correction of mapping inconsistencies resulting from schema evolution. Source schemas may undergo structural or semantic changes that invalidate mappings. Mapping maintenance is concerned with the detection of broken mappings and the (automatic) rewriting of mappings such that semantic consistency with the new schema and semantic equivalence with the current mapping are achieved.

7.1.4.1 Mapping Creation

Mapping creation starts with a source LCS, the target GCS, and a set of schema matches M and produces a set of queries that, when executed, will create GCS data instances from the source data. In data warehouses, these queries are actually executed to create the data warehouse (global database), while in data integration systems, they are used in the reverse direction during query processing (Sect. 7.2).

Let us make this more concrete by referring to the canonical relational representation that we have adopted. The source LCS under consideration consists of a set of relations $Source = \{O_1, \ldots, O_m\}$, the GCS consists of a set of global (or target) relations $Target = \{T_1, \ldots, T_n\}$, and M consists of a set of schema match rules as defined in Sect. 7.1.2. We are looking for a way to generate, for each T_k, a query

Q_k that is defined on a (possibly proper) subset of the relations in *Source* such that, when executed, it will generate data for T_k from the source relations.

This can be accomplished iteratively by considering each T_k in turn. It starts with $M_k \subseteq M$ (M_k is the set of rules that only apply to the attributes of T_k) and divides it into subsets $\{M_k^1, \ldots, M_k^s\}$ such that each M_k^j specifies one possible way that values of T_k can be computed. Each M_k^j can be mapped to a query q_k^j that, when executed, would generate *some* of T_k's data. The union of all of these queries gives $Q_k (= \cup_j q_k^j)$ that we are looking for.

The algorithm proceeds in four steps that we discuss below. It does not consider the similarity values in the rules. It can be argued that the similarity values would be used in the final stages of the matching process to finalize correspondences, so that their use during mapping is unnecessary. Furthermore, by the time this phase of the integration process is reached, the concern is how to map source relation (LCS) data to target relation (GCS) data. Consequently, correspondences are not symmetric equivalences ($\approx$), but mappings ($\mapsto$): attribute(s) from (possibly multiple) source relations are mapped to an attribute of a target relation (i.e., $(O_i.attribute_k, O_j.attribute_l) \mapsto T_w.attribute_z)$).

Example 7.7 To demonstrate the algorithm, we will use a different example database than what we have been working with, because it does not incorporate all the complexities that we wish to demonstrate. Instead, we will use the following abstract example.

Source relations (LCS):

$O_1(A_1, A_2)$
$O_2(B_1, B_2, B_3)$
$O_3(C_1, C_2, C_3)$
$O_4(D_1, D_2)$

Target relation (GCS):

$T(W_1, W_2, W_3, W_4)$

We consider only one relation in GCS since the algorithm iterates over target relations one-at-a-time; this is sufficient to demonstrate the operation of the algorithm.

The foreign key relationships between the attributes are as follows:

Foreign key	Refers to
A_1	B_1
A_2	B_1
C_1	B_1

Assume that the following matches have been discovered for attributes of relation T (these make up M_T). In the subsequent examples, we will not be concerned with the predicates, so they are not explicitly specified.

$$r_1 = \langle A_1 \mapsto W_1, p \rangle$$
$$r_2 = \langle A_2 \mapsto W_2, p \rangle$$
$$r_3 = \langle B_2 \mapsto W_4, p \rangle$$
$$r_4 = \langle B_3 \mapsto W_3, p \rangle$$
$$r_5 = \langle C_1 \mapsto W_1, p \rangle$$
$$r_6 = \langle C_2 \mapsto W_2, p \rangle$$
$$r_7 = \langle D_1 \mapsto W_4, p \rangle$$

◆

In the first step, M_k (corresponding to T_k) is partitioned into its subsets $\{M_k^1, \ldots, M_k^n\}$ such that each M_k^j contains at most one match for each attribute of T_k. These are called *potential candidate sets*, some of which may be *complete* in that they include a match for every attribute of T_k, but others may not be. The reasons for considering incomplete sets are twofold. First, it may be the case that no match is found for one or more attributes of the target relation (i.e., none of the match sets is complete). Second, for large and complex database schemas, it may make sense to build the mapping iteratively so that the designer specifies the mappings incrementally.

Example 7.8 M_T is partitioned into fifty-three subsets (i.e., potential candidate sets). The first eight of these are complete, while the rest are not. We show some of these below. To make it easier to read, the complete rules are listed in the order of the target attributes to which they map (e.g., the third rule in M_T^1 is r_4, because this rule maps to attribute W_3):

$$M_T^1 = \{r_1, r_2, r_4, r_3\} \quad M_T^2 = \{r_1, r_2, r_4, r_7\}$$

$$M_T^3 = \{r_1, r_6, r_4, r_3\} \quad M_T^4 = \{r_1, r_6, r_4, r_7\}$$

$$M_T^5 = \{r_5, r_2, r_4, r_3\} \quad M_T^6 = \{r_5, r_2, r_4, r_7\}$$

$$M_T^7 = \{r_5, r_6, r_4, r_3\} \quad M_T^8 = \{r_5, r_6, r_4, r_7\}$$

$$M_T^9 = \{r_1, r_2, r_3\} \quad M_T^{10} = \{r_1, r_2, r_4\}$$

$$M_T^{11} = \{r_1, r_3, r_4\} \quad M_T^{12} = \{r_2, r_3, r_4\}$$

$$M_T^{13} = \{r_1, r_3, r_6\} \quad M_T^{14} = \{r_3, r_4, r_6\}$$

$$\cdots \qquad\qquad \cdots$$

$$M_T^{47} = \{r_1\} \qquad M_T^{48} = \{r_2\}$$

$$M_T^{49} = \{r_3\} \qquad M_T^{50} = \{r_4\}$$

$$M_T^{51} = \{r_5\} \qquad M_T^{52} = \{r_6\}$$

$$M_T^{53} = \{r_7\}$$

◆

In the second step, the algorithm analyzes each potential candidate set M_k^j to see if a "good" query can be produced for it. If all the matches in M_k^j map values from a single source relation to T_k, then it is easy to generate a query corresponding to M_k^j. Of particular concern are matches that require access to multiple source relations. In this case the algorithm checks to see if there is a referential connection between these relations through foreign keys (i.e., whether there is a join path through the source relations). If there is not, then the potential candidate set is eliminated from further consideration. In case there are multiple join paths through foreign key relationships, the algorithm looks for those paths that will produce the most number of tuples (i.e., the estimated difference in size of the outer and inner joins is the smallest). If there are multiple such paths, then the database designer needs to be involved in selecting one (tools such as Clio, OntoBuilder, and others facilitate this process and provide mechanisms for designers to view and specify correspondences). The result of this step is a set $\overline{M_k} \subseteq M_k$ of *candidate sets*.

Example 7.9 In this example, there is no M_k^j where the values of all of T's attributes are mapped from a single source relation. Among those that involve multiple source relations, rules that involve O_1, O_2, and O_3 can be mapped to "good" queries since there are foreign key relationships between them. However, the rules that involve O_4 (i.e., those that include rule r_7) cannot be mapped to a "good" query since there is no join path from O_4 to the other relations (i.e., any query would involve a cross product, which is expensive). Thus, these rules are eliminated from the potential candidate set. Considering only the complete sets, M_k^2, M_k^4, M_k^6, and M_k^8 are pruned from the set. In the end, the candidate set ($\overline{M_k}$) contains thirty-five rules (the readers are encouraged to verify this to better understand the algorithm).   ◆

In the third step, the algorithm looks for a cover of the candidate sets $\overline{M_k}$. The cover $C_k \subseteq \overline{M_k}$ is a set of candidate sets such that each match in $\overline{M_k}$ appears in C_k at least once. The point of determining a cover is that it accounts for all of the matches and is, therefore, sufficient to generate the target relation T_k. If there are multiple covers (a match can participate in multiple covers), then they are ranked in increasing number of the candidate sets in the cover. The fewer the number of candidate sets in the cover, the fewer are the number of queries that will be generated in the next step; this improves the efficiency of the mappings that are generated. If there are multiple covers with the same ranking, then they are further ranked in decreasing order of the total number of unique target attributes that are used in the candidate sets constituting the cover. The point of this ranking is that covers with higher number of attributes generate fewer null values in the result. At this stage, the designer may need to be consulted to choose from among the ranked covers.

Example 7.10 First note that we have six rules that define matches in $\overline{M_k}$ that we need to consider, since M_k^j that include rule r_7 have been eliminated. There are a large number of possible covers; let us start with those that involve M_k^1 to demonstrate the algorithm:

$$C_{\mathrm{T}}^1 = \{\underbrace{\{r_1, r_2, r_4, r_3\}}_{M_{\mathrm{T}}^1}, \underbrace{\{r_1, r_6, r_4, r_3\}}_{M_{\mathrm{T}}^3}, \underbrace{\{r_2\}}_{M_{\mathrm{T}}^{48}}\}$$

$$C_{\mathrm{T}}^2 = \{\underbrace{\{r_1, r_2, r_4, r_3\}}_{M_{\mathrm{T}}^1}, \underbrace{\{r_5, r_2, r_4, r_3\}}_{M_{\mathrm{T}}^5}, \underbrace{\{r_6\}}_{M_{\mathrm{T}}^{50}}\}$$

$$C_{\mathrm{T}}^3 = \{\underbrace{\{r_1, r_2, r_4, r_3\}}_{M_{\mathrm{T}}^1}, \underbrace{\{r_5, r_6, r_4, r_3\}}_{M_{\mathrm{T}}^7}\}$$

$$C_{\mathrm{T}}^4 = \{\underbrace{\{r_1, r_2, r_4, r_3\}}_{M_{\mathrm{T}}^1}, \underbrace{\{r_5, r_6, r_4\}}_{M_{\mathrm{T}}^{12}}\}$$

$$C_{\mathrm{T}}^5 = \{\underbrace{\{r_1, r_2, r_4, r_3\}}_{M_{\mathrm{T}}^1}, \underbrace{\{r_5, r_6, r_3\}}_{M_{\mathrm{T}}^{19}}\}$$

$$C_{\mathrm{T}}^6 = \{\underbrace{\{r_1, r_2, r_4, r_3\}}_{M_{\mathrm{T}}^1}, \underbrace{\{r_5, r_6\}}_{M_{\mathrm{T}}^{32}}\}$$

At this point we observe that the covers consist of either two or three candidate sets. Since the algorithm prefers those with fewer candidate sets, we only need to focus on those involving two sets. Furthermore, among these covers, we note that the number of target attributes in the candidate sets differ. Since the algorithm prefers covers with the largest number of target attributes in each candidate set, C_{T}^3 is the preferred cover.

Note that due to the two heuristics employed by the algorithm, the only covers we need to consider are those that involve M_{T}^1, M_{T}^3, M_{T}^5, and M_{T}^7. Similar covers can be defined involving M_{T}^3, M_{T}^5, and M_{T}^7; we leave that as an exercise. In the remainder, we will assume that the designer has chosen to use C_{T}^3 as the preferred cover.   ◆

The final step of the algorithm builds a query q_k^j for each of the candidate sets in the cover selected in the previous step. The union of all of these queries (UNION ALL) results in the final mapping for relation T_k in the GCS.

Query q_k^j is built as follows:

- **SELECT** clause includes all correspondences (c) in each of the rules (r_k^i) in M_k^j.
- **FROM** clause includes all source relations mentioned in r_k^i and in the join paths determined in Step 2 of the algorithm.
- **WHERE** clause includes conjunct of all predicates (p) in r_k^i and all join predicates determined in Step 2 of the algorithm.
- If r_k^i contains an aggregate function either in c or in p
  - **GROUP BY** is used over attributes (or functions on attributes) in the **SELECT** clause that are not within the aggregate;

- If aggregate is in the correspondence c, it is added to **SELECT**, else (i.e., aggregate is in the predicate p) a **HAVING** clause is created with the aggregate.

Example 7.11 Since in Example 7.10 we have decided to use cover C_T^3 for the final mapping, we need to generate two queries: q_T^1 and q_T^7 corresponding to M_T^1 and M_T^7, respectively. For ease of presentation, we list the rules here again:

$$r_1 = \langle A_1 \mapsto W_1, p \rangle$$
$$r_2 = \langle A_2 \mapsto W_2, p \rangle$$
$$r_3 = \langle B_2 \mapsto W_4, p \rangle$$
$$r_4 = \langle B_3 \mapsto W_3, p \rangle$$
$$r_5 = \langle C_1 \mapsto W_1, p \rangle$$
$$r_6 = \langle C_2 \mapsto W_2, p \rangle$$

The two queries are as follows:

q_k^1 : **SELECT** A_1, A_2, B_2, B_3
     FROM O_1, O_2
     WHERE p_1 **AND** $O_1.A_2 = O_2.B_1$

q_k^7 : **SELECT** B_2, B_3, C_1, C_2
     FROM O_2, O_3
     WHERE p_3 **AND** p_4 **AND** p_5 **AND** p_6
     AND $O_3.c_1 = O_2.B_1$

Thus, the final query Q_k for target relation T becomes q_k^1 **UNION ALL** q_k^7. ◆

The output of this algorithm after it is iteratively applied to each target relation T_k is a set of queries $Q = \{Q_k\}$ that, when executed, produce data for the GCS relations. Thus, the algorithm produces GAV mappings between relational schemas—recall that GAV defines a GCS as a view over the LCSs and that is exactly what the set of mapping queries do. The algorithm takes into account the semantics of the source schema since it considers foreign key relationships in determining which queries to generate. However, it does not consider the semantics of the target, so that the tuples that are generated by the execution of the mapping queries are not guaranteed to satisfy target semantics. This is not a major issue in the case when the GCS is integrated from the LCSs; however, if the GCS is defined independent of the LCSs, then this is problematic.

It is possible to extend the algorithm to deal with target semantics as well as source semantics. This requires that interschema tuple-generating dependencies be considered. In other words, it is necessary to produce GLAV mappings. A GLAV mapping, by definition, is not simply a query over the source relations; it is a relationship between a query over the source (i.e., LCS) relations and a query over the target (i.e., GCS) relations. Let us be more precise. Consider a schema match v that specifies a correspondence between attribute A of a source LCS relation R and attribute B of a target GCS relation T (in the notation we used in this section we have $v = \langle R.A \approx T.B, p, s \rangle$). Then the source query specifies how to retrieve R.A and the target query specifies how to obtain T.B. The GLAV mapping, then, is a relationship between these two queries.

This can be accomplished by starting with a source schema, a target schema, and M, and "discovering" mappings that satisfy both the source and the target schema semantics. This algorithm is also more powerful than the one we discussed in this section in that it can handle nested structures that are common in XML, object databases, and nested relational systems.

The first step in discovering all of the mappings based on schema match correspondences is *semantic translation*, which seeks to interpret schema matches in M in a way that is consistent with the semantics of both the source and target schemas as captured by the schema structure and the referential (foreign key) constraints. The result is a set of *logical mappings* each of which captures the design choices (semantics) made in both source and target schemas. Each logical mapping corresponds to one target schema relation. The second step is *data translation* that implements each logical mapping as a rule that can be translated into a query that would create an instance of the target element when executed.

Semantic translation takes as inputs the source *Source* and target schemas *Target*, and M and performs the following two steps:

- It examines intraschema semantics within the *Source* and *Target* separately and produces for each a set of *logical relations* that are semantically consistent.
- It then interprets interschema correspondences M in the context of logical relations generated in Step 1 and produces a set of queries into Q that are semantically consistent with *Target*.

7.1.4.2 Mapping Maintenance

In dynamic environments where schemas evolve over time, schema mappings can be made invalid as the result of structural or constraint changes of the schemas. Thus, the detection of invalid/inconsistent schema mappings and the adaptation of such schema mappings to new schema structures/constraints are important.

In general, automatic detection of invalid/inconsistent schema mappings is desirable as the complexity of the schemas and the number of schema mappings used in database applications increase. Likewise, (semi-)automatic adaptation of mappings to schema changes is also a goal. It should be noted that automatic adaptation of schema mappings is not the same as automatic schema matching. Schema adaptation aims to resolve semantic correspondences using known changes in intraschema semantics, semantics in existing mappings, and detected semantic inconsistencies (resulting from schema changes). Schema matching must take a much more "from scratch" approach at generating schema mappings and does not have the ability (or luxury) of incorporating such contextual knowledge.

Detecting Invalid Mappings

In general, detection of invalid mappings resulting from schema change can either happen proactively or reactively. In proactive detection environments, schema mappings are tested for inconsistencies as soon as schema changes are made by a user. The assumption (or requirement) is that the mapping maintenance system is completely aware of any and all schema changes, as soon as they are made. The ToMAS system, for example, expects users to make schema changes through its own schema editors, making the system immediately aware of any schema changes. Once schema changes have been detected, invalid mappings can be detected by doing a semantic translation of the existing mappings using the logical relations of the updated schema.

In reactive detection environments, the mapping maintenance system is unaware of when and what schema changes are made. To detect invalid schema mappings in this setting, mappings are tested at regular intervals by performing queries against the data sources and translating the resulting data using the existing mappings. Invalid mappings are then determined based on the results of these mapping tests.

An alternative method that has been proposed is to use machine learning techniques to detect invalid mappings (as in the Maveric system). What has been proposed is to build an ensemble of trained *sensors* (similar to multiple learners in schema matching) to detect invalid mappings. Examples of such sensors include value sensors for monitoring distribution characteristics of target instance values, trend sensors for monitoring the average rate of data modification, and layout and constraint sensors that monitor translated data against expected target schema syntax and semantics. A weighted combination of the findings of the individual sensors is then calculated where the weights are also learned. If the combined result indicates changes and follow-up tests suggest that this may indeed be the case, an alert is generated.

Adapting Invalid Mappings

Once invalid schema mappings are detected, they must be adapted to schema changes and made valid once again. Various high-level mapping adaptation approaches have been proposed. These can be broadly described as *fixed rule approaches* that define a remapping rule for every type of expected schema change, *map bridging approaches* that compare original schema S and the updated schema S', and generate new mapping from S to S' in addition to existing mappings, and *semantic rewriting approaches*, which exploit semantic information encoded in existing mappings, schemas, and semantic changes made to schemas to propose map rewritings that produce semantically consistent target data. In most cases, multiple such rewritings are possible, requiring a ranking of the candidates for presentation to users who make the final decision (based on scenario- or business-level semantics not encoded in schemas or mappings).

Arguably, a complete remapping of schemas (i.e., from scratch, using schema matching techniques) is another alternative to mapping adaption. However, in most cases, map rewriting is cheaper than map regeneration as rewriting can exploit knowledge encoded in existing mappings to avoid computation of mappings that would be rejected by the user anyway (and to avoid redundant mappings).

7.1.5 Data Cleaning

Errors in source databases can always occur, requiring cleaning in order to correctly answer user queries. Data cleaning is a problem that arises in both data warehouses and data integration systems, but in different contexts. In data warehouses where data is actually extracted from local operational databases and materialized as a global database, cleaning is performed as the global database is created. In the case of data integration systems, data cleaning is a process that needs to be performed during query processing when data is returned from the source databases.

The errors that are subject to data cleaning can generally be broken down into either schema-level or instance-level concerns. Schema-level problems can arise in each individual LCS due to violations of explicit and implicit constraints. For example, values of attributes may be outside the range of their domains (e.g., 14th month or negative salary value), attribute values may violate implicit dependencies (e.g., the age attribute value may not correspond to the value that is computed as the difference between the current date and the birth date), uniqueness of attribute values may not hold, and referential integrity constraints may be violated. Furthermore, in the environment that we are considering in this chapter, the schema-level heterogeneities (both structural and semantic) among the LCSs that we discussed earlier can all be considered problems that need to be resolved. At the schema level, it is clear that the problems need to be identified at the schema match stage and fixed during schema integration.

Instance level errors are those that exist at the data level. For example, the values of some attributes may be missing although they were required, there could be misspellings and word transpositions (e.g., "M.D. Mary Smith" versus "Mary Smith, M.D.") or differences in abbreviations (e.g., "J. Doe" in one source database, while "J.N. Doe" in another), embedded values (e.g., an aggregate address attribute that includes street name, value, province name, and postal code), values that were erroneously placed in other fields, duplicate values, and contradicting values (the salary value appearing as one value in one database and another value in another database). For instance-level cleaning, the issue is clearly one of generating the mappings such that the data is cleaned through the execution of the mapping functions (queries).

The popular approach to data cleaning has been to define a number of operators that operate either on schemas or on individual data. The operators can be composed into a data cleaning plan. Example schema operators add or drop columns from table, restructure a table by combining columns or splitting a column into two, or define more complicated schema transformation through a generic "map" operator that takes a single relation and produces one or more relations. Example data level operators include those that apply a function to every value of one attribute, merging values of two attributes into the value of a single attribute and its converse split operator, a matching operator that computes an approximate join between tuples of two relations, clustering operator that groups tuples of a relation into clusters, and a tuple merge operator that partitions the tuples of a relation into groups and collapses the tuples in each group into a single tuple through some aggregation over them, as well as basic operators to find duplicates and eliminate them. Many of the data level operators compare individual tuples of two relations (from the same or different schemas) and decide whether or not they represent the same fact. This is similar to what is done in schema matching, except that it is done at the individual data level and what is considered are not individual attribute values, but entire tuples. However, the same techniques we studied under schema matching (e.g., use of edit distance or soundex value) can be used in this context. There have been proposals for special techniques for handling this efficiently within the context of data cleaning such as fuzzy matching that computes a similarity function to determine whether the two tuples are identical or reasonably similar.

Given the large amount of data that needs to be handled, data level cleaning is expensive and efficiency is a significant issue. The physical implementation of each of the operators we discussed above is a considerable concern. Although cleaning can be done off-line as a batch process in the case of data warehouses, for data integration systems, cleaning may need to be done online as data is retrieved from the sources. The performance of data cleaning is, of course, more critical in the latter case.

7.2   Multidatabase Query Processing

We now turn our attention to querying and accessing an integrated database obtained through the techniques discussed in the previous section—this is known as the multidatabase querying problem. As previously noted, many of the distributed query processing and optimization techniques that we discussed in Chap. 4 carry over to multidatabase systems, but there are important differences. Recall from that chapter that we characterized distributed query processing in four steps: query decomposition, data localization, global optimization, and local optimization. The nature of multidatabase systems requires slightly different steps and different techniques. The component DBMSs may be autonomous and have different database languages and query processing capabilities. Thus, an MDBS layer (see Fig. 1.12) is necessary to communicate with component DBMSs in an effective way, and this requires

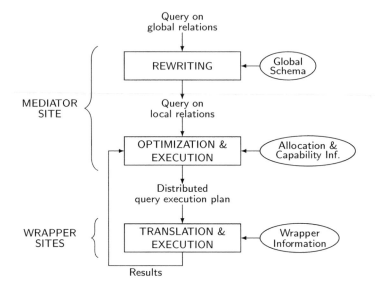

Fig. 7.13 Generic layering scheme for multidatabase query processing

additional query processing steps (Fig. 7.13). Furthermore, there may be many component DBMSs, each of which may exhibit different behavior, thereby posing new requirements for more adaptive query processing techniques.

7.2.1 Issues in Multidatabase Query Processing

Query processing in a multidatabase system is more complex than in a distributed DBMS for the following reasons:

1. The computing capabilities of the component DBMSs may be different, which prevents uniform treatment of queries across multiple DBMSs. For example, some DBMSs may be able to support complex SQL queries with join and aggregation, while some others cannot. Thus the multidatabase query processor should consider the various DBMS capabilities. The capabilities of each component is recorded in the directory along with data allocation information.
2. Similarly, the cost of processing queries may be different on different DBMSs, and the local optimization capability of each DBMS may be quite different. This increases the complexity of the cost functions that need to be evaluated.
3. The data models and languages of the component DBMSs may be quite different, for instance, relational, object-oriented, semi-structured, etc. This creates difficulties in translating multidatabase queries to component DBMS and in integrating heterogeneous results.

4. Since a multidatabase system enables access to very different DBMSs that may
have different performance and behavior, distributed query processing techniques
need to adapt to these variations.

The autonomy of the component DBMSs poses problems. DBMS autonomy can
be defined along three main dimensions: communication, design, and execution.
Communication autonomy means that a component DBMS communicates with
others at its own discretion, and, in particular, it may terminate its services at
any time. This requires query processing techniques that are tolerant to system
unavailability. The question is how the system answers queries when a component
system is either unavailable from the beginning or shuts down in the middle of
query execution. Design autonomy may restrict the availability and accuracy of cost
information that is needed for query optimization. The difficulty of determining
local cost functions is an important issue. The execution autonomy of multidatabase
systems makes it difficult to apply some of the query optimization strategies
we discussed in previous chapters. For example, semijoin-based optimization of
distributed joins may be difficult if the source and target relations reside in different
component DBMSs, since, in this case, the semijoin execution of a join translates
into three queries: one to retrieve the join attribute values of the target relation and
to ship it to the source relation's DBMS, the second to perform the join at the source
relation, and the third to perform the join at the target relation's DBMS. The problem
arises because communication with component DBMSs occurs at a high level of the
DBMS API.

In addition to these difficulties, the architecture of a distributed multidatabase
system poses certain challenges. The architecture depicted in Fig. 1.12 points to
an additional complexity. In distributed DBMSs, query processors have to deal
only with data distribution across multiple sites. In a distributed multidatabase
environment, on the other hand, data is distributed not only across sites but also
across multiple databases, each managed by an autonomous DBMS. Thus, while
there are two parties that cooperate in the processing of queries in a distributed
DBMS (the control site and local sites), the number of parties increases to three
in the case of a distributed MDBS: the MDBS layer at the control site (i.e., the
mediator) receives the global query, the MDBS layers at the sites (i.e., the wrappers)
participate in processing the query, and the component DBMSs ultimately optimize
and execute the query.

7.2.2 *Multidatabase Query Processing Architecture*

Most of the work on multidatabase query processing has been done in the context
of the mediator/wrapper architecture (see Fig. 1.13). In this architecture, each
component database has an associated wrapper that exports information about the
source schema, data, and query processing capabilities. A mediator centralizes the
information provided by the wrappers in a unified view of all available data (stored

in a global data dictionary) and performs query processing using the wrappers to access the component DBMSs. The data model used by the mediator can be relational, object-oriented, or even semi-structured. In this chapter, for consistency with the previous chapters on distributed query processing, we continue to use the relational model, which is quite sufficient to explain the multidatabase query processing techniques.

The mediator/wrapper architecture has several advantages. First, the specialized components of the architecture allow the various concerns of different kinds of users to be handled separately. Second, mediators typically specialize in a related set of component databases with "similar" data, and thus export schemas and semantics related to a particular domain. The specialization of the components leads to a flexible and extensible distributed system. In particular, it allows seamless integration of different data stored in very different components, ranging from full-fledged relational DBMSs to simple files.

Assuming the mediator/wrapper architecture, we can now discuss the various layers involved in query processing in distributed multidatabase systems as shown in Fig. 7.13. As before, we assume the input is a query on global relations expressed in relational calculus. This query is posed on global (distributed) relations, meaning that data distribution and heterogeneity are hidden. Three main layers are involved in multidatabase query processing. This layering is similar to that of query processing in homogeneous distributed DBMSs (see Fig. 4.2). However, since there is no fragmentation, there is no need for the data localization layer.

The first two layers map the input query into an optimized distributed query execution plan (QEP). They perform the functions of query rewriting, query optimization, and some query execution. The first two layers are performed by the mediator and use metainformation stored in the global directory (global schema, allocation, and capability information). Query rewriting transforms the input query into a query on local relations, using the global schema. Recall that there are two main approaches for database integration: global-as-view (GAV) and local-as-view (LAV). Thus, the global schema provides the view definitions (i.e., mappings between the global relations and the local relations stored in the component databases) and the query is rewritten using the views.

Rewriting can be done at the relational calculus or algebra levels. In this chapter, we will use a generalized form of relational calculus called Datalog that is well-suited for such rewriting. Thus, there is an additional step of calculus to algebra translation that is similar to the decomposition step in homogeneous distributed DBMSs.

The second layer performs query optimization and (some) execution by considering the allocation of the local relations and the different query processing capabilities of the component DBMSs exported by the wrappers. The allocation and capability information used by this layer may also contain heterogeneous cost information. The distributed QEP produced by this layer groups within subqueries the operations that can be performed by the component DBMSs and wrappers. Similar to distributed DBMSs, query optimization can be static or dynamic. However, the lack of homogeneity in multidatabase systems (e.g., some component

DBMSs may have unexpectedly long delays in answering) makes dynamic query optimization more critical. In the case of dynamic optimization, there may be subsequent calls to this layer after execution by the subsequent layer as illustrated by the arrow showing results coming from the translation and execution layer. Finally, this layer integrates the results coming from the different wrappers to provide a unified answer to the user's query. This requires the capability of executing some operations on data coming from the wrappers. Since the wrappers may provide very limited execution capabilities, e.g., in the case of very simple component DBMSs, the mediator must provide the full execution capabilities to support the mediator interface.

The third layer performs *query translation and execution* using the wrappers. Then it returns the results to the mediator that can perform result integration from different wrappers and subsequent execution. Each wrapper maintains a *wrapper schema* that includes the local export schema and mapping information to facilitate the translation of the input subquery (a subset of the QEP) expressed in a common language into the language of the component DBMS. After the subquery is translated, it is executed by the component DBMS and the local result is translated back to the common format.

The wrapper information describes how mappings from/to participating local schemas and global schema can be performed. It enables conversions between components of the database in different ways. For example, if the global schema represents temperatures in Fahrenheit degrees, but a participating database uses Celsius degrees, the wrapper information must contain a conversion formula to provide the proper presentation to the global user and the local databases. If the conversion is across types and simple formulas cannot perform the translation, complete mapping tables could be used in the wrapper information stored in the directory.

7.2.3 Query Rewriting Using Views

Query rewriting reformulates the input query expressed on global relations into a query on local relations. It uses the global schema, which describes in terms of views the correspondences between the global relations and the local relations. Thus, the query must be rewritten using views. The techniques for query rewriting differ in major ways depending on the database integration approach that is used, i.e., GAV or LAV. In particular, the techniques for LAV (and its extension GLAV) are much more involved. Most of the work on query rewriting using views has been done using Datalog, which is a logic-based database language. Datalog is more concise than relational calculus and thus more convenient for describing complex query rewriting algorithms. In this section, we first introduce Datalog terminology. Then, we describe the main techniques and algorithms for query rewriting in the GAV and LAV approaches.

7.2.3.1 Datalog Terminology

Datalog can be viewed as an in-line version of domain relational calculus. Let us first define *conjunctive queries*, i.e., select-project-join queries, which are the basis for more complex queries. A conjunctive query in Datalog is expressed as a rule of the form:

$$Q(t) : -\mathrm{R}_1(t_1), \ldots, \mathrm{R}_n(t_n)$$

The atom $Q(t)$ is the *head* of the query and denotes the result relation. The atoms $\mathrm{R}_1(t_1), \ldots, \mathrm{R}_n(t_n)$ are the *subgoals* in the body of the query and denote database relations. Q and $\mathrm{R}_1, \ldots, \mathrm{R}_n$ are predicate names and correspond to relation names. $t, t_1, \ldots, t_n$ refer to the relation tuples and contain variables or constants. The variables are similar to domain variables in domain relational calculus. Thus, the use of the same variable name in multiple predicates expresses equijoin predicates. Constants correspond to equality predicates. More complex comparison predicates (e.g., using comparators such as $\neq$, $\leq$, and $<$) must be expressed as other subgoals. We consider queries that are *safe*, i.e., those where each variable in the head also appears in the body. Disjunctive queries can also be expressed in Datalog using unions, by having several conjunctive queries with the same head predicate.

Example 7.12 Let us consider GCS relations EMP and WORKS defined in Fig. 7.9. Consider the following SQL query:

```
SELECT E#, TITLE, P#
FROM    EMP NATURAL JOIN WORKS
WHERE   TITLE = "Programmer" OR DUR = 24
```

The corresponding query in Datalog can be expressed as:

$$Q(\text{E\#}, \text{TITLE}, \text{P\#}) : -\text{EMP}(\text{E\#}, \text{ENAME}, \text{``Programmer''}, \text{CITY}),$$
$$\text{WORKS}(\text{E\#}, \text{P\#}, \text{RESP}, \text{DUR})$$
$$Q(\text{E\#}, \text{TITLE}, \text{P\#}) : -\text{EMP}(\text{E\#}, \text{ENAME}, \text{TITLE}, \text{CITY}),$$
$$\text{WORKS}(\text{E\#}, \text{P\#}, \text{RESP}, 24)$$

◆

7.2.3.2 Rewriting in GAV

In the GAV approach, the global schema is expressed in terms of the data sources and each global relation is defined as a view over the local relations. This is similar to the global schema definition in tightly integrated distributed DBMS. In particular, the local relations (i.e., relations in a component DBMS) can correspond to fragments. However, since the local databases preexist and are autonomous, it may happen that tuples in a global relation do not exist in local relations or that a tuple in a global relation appears in different local relations. Thus, the properties of completeness and disjointness of fragmentation cannot be guaranteed. The lack of completeness may yield incomplete answers to queries. The lack of disjointness may yield duplicate results that may still be useful information and may not need to be eliminated. Similar to queries, view definitions can use Datalog notation.

Example 7.13 Let us consider the global relations EMP and WORKS in Fig. 7.9, with a slight modification: the default responsibility of an employee in a project corresponds to its title, so that attribute TITLE is present in relation WORKS but absent in relation EMP. Let us consider the local relations EMP1 and EMP2 each with attributes E#, ENAME, TITLE, and CITY, and local relation WORKS1 with attributes E#, P#, and DUR. The global relations EMP and WORKS can be simply defined with the following Datalog rules:

$$\text{EMP(E\#, ENAME, CITY)} : -\text{EMP1(E\#, ENAME, TITLE, CITY)} \qquad (d_1)$$

$$\text{EMP(E\#, ENAME, CITY)} : -\text{EMP2(E\#, ENAME, TITLE, CITY)} \qquad (d_2)$$

$$\text{WORKS(E\#, P\#, TITLE, DUR)} : -\text{EMP1(E\#, ENAME, TITLE, CITY),}$$

$$\text{WORKS1(E\#, P\#, DUR)} \qquad (d_3)$$

$$\text{WORKS(E\#, P\#, TITLE, DUR)} : -\text{EMP2(E\#, ENAME, TITLE, CITY)),}$$

$$\text{WORKS1(E\#, P\#, DUR)} \qquad (d_4)$$

$\blacklozenge$

Rewriting a query expressed on the global schema into an equivalent query on the local relations is relatively simple and similar to data localization in tightly integrated distributed DBMS (see Sect. 4.2). The rewriting technique using views is called *unfolding*, and it replaces each global relation invoked in the query with its corresponding view. This is done by applying the view definition rules to the query and producing a union of conjunctive queries, one for each rule application. Since a global relation may be defined by several rules (see Example 7.13), unfolding can generate redundant queries that need to be eliminated.

Example 7.14 Let us consider the global schema in Example 7.13 and the following query q that asks for assignment information about the employees living in Paris:

$$Q(e, p) : -\text{EMP}(e, \text{ENAME, "Paris"}), \text{WORKS}(e, p, \text{TITLE, DUR}).$$

Unfolding q produces q' as follows:

$Q'(e, p) : -\text{EMP1}(e, \text{ENAME}, \text{TITLE}, \text{"Paris"}), \text{WORKS1}(e, p, \text{DUR}).$ (q_1)

$Q'(e, p) : -\text{EMP2}(e, \text{ENAME}, \text{TITLE}, \text{"Paris"}), \text{WORKS1}(e, p, \text{DUR}).$ (q_2)

Q' is the union of two conjunctive queries labeled as q_1 and q_2. q_1 is obtained by applying GAV rule d_3 or both rules d_1 and d_3. In the latter case, the query obtained is redundant with respect to that obtained with d_3 only. Similarly, q_2 is obtained by applying rule d_4 or both rules d_2 and d_4.   ◆

Although the basic technique is simple, rewriting in GAV becomes difficult when local databases have limited access patterns. This is the case for databases accessed over the web where relations can be only accessed using certain binding patterns for their attributes. In this case, simply substituting the global relations with their views is not sufficient, and query rewriting requires the use of recursive Datalog queries.

7.2.3.3 Rewriting in LAV

In the LAV approach, the global schema is expressed independent of the local databases and each local relation is defined as a view over the global relations. This enables considerable flexibility for defining local relations.

Example 7.15 To facilitate comparison with GAV, we develop an example that is symmetric to Example 7.13 with EMP and WORKS defined in that example as global relations as. In the LAV approach, the local relations EMP1, EMP2, and WORKS1 can be defined with the following Datalog rules:

$\text{EMP1}(\text{E\#}, \text{ENAME}, \text{TITLE}, \text{CITY}) : -\text{EMP}(\text{E\#}, \text{ENAME}, \text{CITY}),$

                           $\text{WORKS}(\text{E\#}, \text{P\#}, \text{TITLE}, \text{DUR})$ (d_5)

$\text{EMP2}(\text{E\#}, \text{ENAME}, \text{TITLE}, \text{CITY}) : -\text{EMP}(\text{E\#}, \text{ENAME}, \text{CITY}),$

                           $\text{WORKS}(\text{E\#}, \text{P\#}, \text{TITLE}, \text{DUR})$ (d_6)

$\text{WORKS1}(\text{E\#}, \text{P\#}, \text{DUR}) : -\text{WORKS}(\text{E\#}, \text{P\#}, \text{TITLE}, \text{DUR})$ (d_7)

    ◆

Rewriting a query expressed on the global schema into an equivalent query on the views describing the local relations is difficult for three reasons. First, unlike in the GAV approach, there is no direct correspondence between the terms used in the global schema, (e.g., EMP, ENAME) and those used in the views (e.g., EMP1, EMP2, ENAME). Finding the correspondences requires comparison with each view. Second, there may be many more views than global relations, thus making view comparison time consuming. Third, view definitions may contain complex predicates to reflect the specific contents of the local relations, e.g., view EMP3 containing only programmers. Thus, it is not always possible to find an equivalent rewriting of the query. In this case, the best that can be done is to find a *maximally contained* query, i.e., a query that produces the maximum subset of the answer. For instance, EMP3 could only return a subset of all employees, those who are programmers.

Rewriting queries using views has received much attention because of its relevance to both logical and physical data integration problems. In the context of physical integration (i.e., data warehousing), using materialized views may be much more efficient than accessing base relations. However, the problem of finding a rewriting using views is NP-complete in the number of views and the number of subgoals in the query. Thus, algorithms for rewriting a query using views essentially try to reduce the numbers of rewritings that need to be considered. Three main algorithms have been proposed for this purpose: the bucket algorithm, the inverse rule algorithm, and the MinCon algorithm. The bucket algorithm and the inverse rule algorithm have similar limitations that are addressed by the MinCon algorithm.

The bucket algorithm considers each predicate of the query independently to select only the views that are relevant to that predicate. Given a query Q, the algorithm proceeds in two steps. In the first step, it builds a bucket b for each subgoal q of Q that is not a comparison predicate and inserts in b the heads of the views that are relevant to answer q. To determine whether a view V should be in b, there must be a mapping that unifies q with one subgoal v in V.

For instance, consider query Q in Example 7.14 and the views in Example 7.15. The following mapping unifies the subgoal EMP(e, ENAME, "Paris") of Q with the subgoal EMP(E#, ENAME, CITY) in view EMP1:

$$e \rightarrow E\#, \text{"Paris"} \rightarrow CITY$$

In the second step, for each view V of the Cartesian product of the nonempty buckets (i.e., some subset of the buckets), the algorithm produces a conjunctive query and checks whether it is contained in Q. If it is, the conjunctive query is kept as it represents one way to answer part of Q from V. Thus, the rewritten query is a union of conjunctive queries.

Example 7.16 Let us consider query Q in Example 7.14 and the views in Example 7.15. In the first step, the bucket algorithm creates two buckets, one for each subgoal of Q. Let us denote by b_1 the bucket for the subgoal EMP(e, ENAME, "Paris") and by b_2 the bucket for the subgoal WORKS(e, p, TITLE, DUR). Since the algorithm inserts only the view heads in a bucket, there may be variables in a view head that are not in the unifying mapping. Such variables are simply primed. We obtain the following buckets:

$$b_1 = \{\text{EMP1}(E\#, ENAME, TITLE', CITY),$$
$$\text{EMP2}(E\#, ENAME, TITLE', CITY)\}$$
$$b_2 = \{\text{WORKS1}(E\#, P\#, DUR')\}$$

In the second step, the algorithm combines the elements from the buckets, which produces a union of two conjunctive queries:

$$Q'(e, p) : -\texttt{EMP1}(e, \texttt{ENAME}, \texttt{TITLE}, \text{``Paris''}), \texttt{WORKS1}(e, p, \texttt{DUR}) \qquad (q_1)$$

$$Q'(e, p) : -\texttt{EMP2}(e, \texttt{ENAME}, \texttt{TITLE}, \text{``Paris''}), \texttt{WORKS1}(e, p, \texttt{DUR}) \qquad (q_2)$$

◆

The main advantage of the bucket algorithm is that, by considering the predicates in the query, it can significantly reduce the number of rewritings that need to be considered. However, considering the predicates in the query in isolation may yield the addition of a view in a bucket that is irrelevant when considering the join with other views. Furthermore, the second step of the algorithm may still generate a large number of rewritings as a result of the Cartesian product of the buckets.

Example 7.17 Let us consider query Q in Example 7.14 and the views in Example 7.15 with the addition of the following view that gives the projects for which there are employees who live in Paris.

$$\texttt{PROJ1(P\#)} : -\texttt{EMP1}(\texttt{E\#}, \texttt{ENAME}, \text{``Paris''}),$$

$$\texttt{WORKS}(\texttt{E\#}, \texttt{P\#}, \texttt{TITLE}, \texttt{DUR}) \qquad (d_8)$$

Now, the following mapping unifies the subgoal $\texttt{WORKS}(e, p, \texttt{TITLE}, \texttt{DUR})$ of Q with the subgoal $\texttt{WORKS}(\texttt{E\#}, \texttt{P\#}, \texttt{TITLE}, \texttt{DUR})$ in view $\texttt{PROJ1}$:

$$p \rightarrow \texttt{PNAME}$$

Thus, in the first step of the bucket algorithm, $\texttt{PROJ1}$ is added to bucket b_2. However, $\texttt{PROJ1}$ cannot be useful in a rewriting of Q since the variable $\texttt{ENAME}$ is not in the head of $\texttt{PROJ1}$ and thus makes it impossible to join $\texttt{PROJ1}$ on the variable e of Q. This can be discovered only in the second step when building the conjunctive queries. ◆

The MinCon algorithm addresses the limitations of the bucket algorithm (and the inverse rule algorithm) by considering the query globally and considering how each predicate in the query interacts with the views. It proceeds in two steps like the bucket algorithm. The first step starts by selecting the views that contain subgoals corresponding to subgoals of query Q. However, upon finding a mapping that unifies a subgoal q of Q with a subgoal v in view V, it considers the join predicates in Q and finds the minimum set of additional subgoals of Q that must be mapped to subgoals in V. This set of subgoals of Q is captured by a *MinCon description* (MCD) associated with V. The second step of the algorithm produces a rewritten query by combining the different MCDs. In this second step, unlike in the bucket algorithm, it is not necessary to check that the proposed rewritings are contained in the query

because the way the MCDs are created guarantees that the resulting rewritings will
be contained in the original query.

Applied to Example 7.17, the algorithm would create 3 MCDs: two for the views
EMP1 and EMP2 containing the subgoal EMP of Q and one for ASG1 containing the
subgoal ASG. However, the algorithm cannot create an MCD for PROJ1 because
it cannot apply the join predicate in Q. Thus, the algorithm would produce the
rewritten query Q' of Example 7.16. Compared with the bucket algorithm, the
second step of the MinCon algorithm is much more efficient since it performs fewer
combinations of MCDs than buckets.

7.2.4   Query Optimization and Execution

The three main problems of query optimization in multidatabase systems are
heterogeneous cost modeling, heterogeneous query optimization (to deal with
different capabilities of component DBMSs), and adaptive query processing (to deal
with strong variations in the environment—failures, unpredictable delays, etc.). In
this section, we describe the techniques for the first two problems. In Sect. 4.6, we
presented the techniques for adaptive query processing. These techniques can be
used in multidatabase systems as well, provided that the wrappers are able to collect
information regarding execution within the component DBMSs.

7.2.4.1   Heterogeneous Cost Modeling

Global cost function definition, and the associated problem of obtaining cost-related
information from component DBMSs, is perhaps the most-studied of the three
problems. A number of possible solutions have emerged, which we discuss below.

The first thing to note is that we are primarily interested in determining the cost
of the lower levels of a query execution tree that correspond to the parts of the query
executed at component DBMSs. If we assume that all local processing is "pushed
down" in the tree, then we can modify the query plan such that the leaves of the tree
correspond to subqueries that will be executed at individual component DBMSs. In
this case, we are talking about the determination of the costs of these subqueries that
are input to the first level (from the bottom) operators. Cost for higher levels of the
query execution tree may be calculated recursively, based on the leaf node costs.

Three alternative approaches exist for determining the cost of executing queries
at component DBMSs:

1. **Black-Box Approach.** This approach treats each component DBMS as a black
   box, running some test queries on it, and from these determines the necessary
   cost information.

2. **Customized Approach.** This approach uses previous knowledge about the component DBMSs, as well as their external characteristics, to subjectively determine the cost information.

3. **Dynamic Approach.** This approach monitors the runtime behavior of component DBMSs, and dynamically collects the cost information.

We discuss each approach, focusing on the proposals that have attracted the most attention.

Black-Box Approach

In the black-box approach, the cost functions are expressed logically (e.g., aggregate CPU and I/O costs, selectivity factors), rather than on the basis of physical characteristics (e.g., relation cardinalities, number of pages, number of distinct values for each column). Thus, the cost functions for component DBMSs are expressed as

$$Cost = initialization\ cost + cost\ to\ find\ qualifying\ tuples$$
$$+ \ cost\ to\ process\ selected\ tuples$$

The individual terms of this formula will differ for different operators. However, these differences are not difficult to specify a priori. The fundamental difficulty is the determination of the term coefficients in these formulas, which change with different component DBMSs. One way to deal with this is to construct a synthetic database (called a *calibrating database*), run queries against it in isolation, and measure the elapsed time to deduce the coefficients.

A problem with this approach is that the results obtained by using a synthetic database may not apply well to real DBMSs. An alternative is based on running probing queries on component DBMSs to determine cost information. Probing queries can, in fact, be used to gather a number of cost information factors. For example, probing queries can be issued to retrieve data from component DBMSs to construct and update the multidatabase catalog. Statistical probing queries can be issued that, for example, count the number of tuples of a relation. Finally, performance measuring probing queries can be issued to measure the elapsed time for determining cost function coefficients.

A special case of probing queries is sample queries. In this case, queries are classified according to a number of criteria, and sample queries from each class are issued and measured to derive component cost information. Query classification can be performed according to query characteristics (e.g., unary operation queries, two-way join queries), characteristics of the operand relations (e.g., cardinality, number of attributes, information on indexed attributes), and characteristics of the underlying component DBMSs (e.g., the access methods that are supported and the policies for choosing access methods).

Classification rules are defined to identify queries that execute similarly, and thus could share the same cost formula. For example, one may consider that two queries that have similar algebraic expressions (i.e., the same algebraic tree shape), but different operand relations, attributes, or constants, are executed the same way if their attributes have the same physical properties. Another example is to assume that join order of a query has no effect on execution since the underlying query optimizer applies reordering techniques to choose an efficient join ordering. Thus, two queries that join the same set of relations belong to the same class, whatever ordering is expressed by the user. Classification rules are combined to define query classes. The classification is performed either top-down by dividing a class into more specific ones or bottom-up by merging two classes into a larger one. In practice, an efficient classification is obtained by mixing both approaches. The global cost function consists of three components: initialization cost, cost of retrieving a tuple, and cost of processing a tuple. The difference is in the way the parameters of this function are determined. Instead of using a calibrating database, sample queries are executed and costs are measured. The global cost equation is treated as a regression equation, and the regression coefficients are calculated using the measured costs of sample queries. The regression coefficients are the cost function parameters. Eventually, the cost model quality is controlled through statistical tests (e.g., F-test): if the tests fail, the query classification is refined until quality is sufficient.

The above approaches require a preliminary step to instantiate the cost model (either by calibration or sampling). This may not be always appropriate, because it would slow down the system each time a new DBMS component is added. One way to address this problem is to progressively learn the cost model from queries. The assumption is that the mediator invokes the underlying component DBMSs by a function call. The cost of a call is composed of three values: the response time to access the first tuple, the whole result response time, and the result cardinality. This allows the query optimizer to minimize either the time to receive the first tuple or the time to process the whole query, depending on end-user requirements. Initially the query processor does not know any statistics about component DBMSs. Then it monitors ongoing queries: it collects processing time of every call and stores it for future estimation. To manage the large amount of collected statistics, the cost manager summarizes them, either without loss of precision or with less precision at the benefit of lower space use and faster cost estimation. Summarization consists of aggregating statistics: the average response time is computed for all the calls that match the same pattern, i.e., those with identical function name and zero or more identical argument values. The cost estimator module is implemented in a declarative language. This allows adding new cost formulas describing the behavior of a particular component DBMS. However, the burden of extending the mediator cost model remains with the mediator developer.

The major drawback of the black-box approach is that the cost model, although adjusted by calibration, is common for all component DBMSs and may not capture their individual specifics. Thus it might fail to estimate accurately the cost of a query executed at a component DBMS that exposes unforeseen behavior.

Customized Approach

The basis of this approach is that the query processors of the component DBMSs are too different to be represented by a unique cost model as used in the black-box approach. It also assumes that the ability to accurately estimate the cost of local subqueries will improve global query optimization. The approach provides a framework to integrate the component DBMSs' cost model into the mediator query optimizer. The solution is to extend the wrapper interface such that the mediator gets some specific cost information from each wrapper. The wrapper developer is free to provide a cost model, partially or entirely. Then, the challenge is to integrate this (potentially partial) cost description into the mediator query optimizer. There are two main solutions.

A first solution is to provide the logic within the wrapper to compute three cost estimates: the time to initiate the query process and receive the first result item (called *reset_cost*), the time to get the next item (called *advance_cost*), and the result cardinality. Thus, the total query cost is

$$Total\_access\_cost = reset\_cost + (cardinality - 1) * advance\_cost$$

This solution can be extended to estimate the cost of database procedure calls. In that case, the wrapper provides a cost formula that is a linear equation depending on the procedure parameters. This solution has been successfully implemented to model a wide range of heterogeneous components DBMSs, ranging from a relational DBMS to an image server. It shows that a little effort is sufficient to implement a rather simple cost model and this significantly improves distributed query processing over heterogeneous sources.

A second solution is to use a hierarchical generic cost model. As shown in Fig. 7.14, each node represents a cost rule that associates a query pattern with a cost function for various cost parameters.

The node hierarchy is divided into five levels depending on the genericity of the cost rules (in Fig. 7.14, the increasing width of the boxes shows the increased focus of the rules). At the top level, cost rules apply by default to any DBMS. At the underlying levels, the cost rules are increasingly focused on: specific DBMS, relation, predicate, or query. At the time of wrapper registration, the mediator receives wrapper metadata including cost information, and completes its built-in cost model by adding new nodes at the appropriate level of the hierarchy. This framework is sufficiently general to capture and integrate both general cost knowledge declared as rules given by wrapper developers and specific information derived from recorded past queries that were previously executed. Thus, through an inheritance hierarchy, the mediator cost-based optimizer can support a wide variety of data sources. The mediator benefits from specialized cost information about each component DBMS, to accurately estimate the cost of queries and choose a more efficient QEP.

Example 7.18 Consider the GCS relations EMP and WORKS (Fig. 7.9). EMP is stored at component DBMS db_1 and contains 1,000 tuples. ASG is stored at component DBMS db_2 and contains 10,000 tuples. We assume uniform distribution

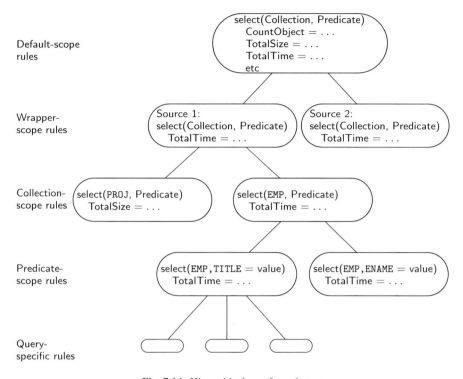

Default-scope
rules

Wrapper-
scope rules

Collection-
scope rules

Predicate-
scope rules

Query-
specific rules

Fig. 7.14 Hierarchical cost formula tree

of attribute values. Half of the WORKS tuples have a duration greater than 6. We detail below some parts of the mediator generic cost model where R and S are two relations, A is the join attribute and we use superscripts to indicate the access method:

$$cost(R) = |R|$$

$$cost(\sigma_{predicate}(R)) = cost(R) \text{ (access to R by sequential scan—by default)}$$

$$cost(R \bowtie_A^{ind} S) = cost(R) + |R| * cost(\sigma_{A=v}(S)) \text{ (using an index based } (ind)$$
join with the index on S.A)

$$cost(R \bowtie_A^{nl} S) = cost(R) + |R| * cost(S) \text{ (using a nested-loop } (nl) \text{ join)}$$

Consider the following global query Q:

```
SELECT *
FROM    EMP NATURAL JOIN WORKS
WHERE   WORKS.DUR>6
```

The cost-based query optimizer generates the following plans to process Q:

$$P_1 = \sigma_{\text{DUR}>6}(\text{EMP} \bowtie_{\text{E\#}}^{ind} \text{WORKS})$$

$$P_2 = \text{EMP} \bowtie_{\text{E\#}}^{nl} \sigma_{\text{DUR}>6}(\text{WORKS})$$

$$P_3 = \sigma_{\text{DUR}>6}(\text{WORKS}) \bowtie_{\text{E\#}}^{ind} \text{EMP}$$

$$P_4 = \sigma_{\text{DUR}>6}(\text{WORKS}) \bowtie_{\text{E\#}}^{nl} \text{EMP}$$

Based on the generic cost model, we compute their cost as:

$$cost(P_1) = cost(\sigma_{\text{DUR}>6}(\text{EMP} \bowtie_{\text{E\#}}^{ind} \text{WORKS})$$

$$= cost(\text{EMP} \bowtie_{\text{E\#}}^{ind} \text{WORKS})$$

$$= cost(\text{EMP}) + |\text{EMP}| * cost(\sigma_{\text{E\#}=v}(\text{WORKS}))$$

$$= |\text{EMP}| + |\text{EMP}| * |\text{WORKS}| = 10,001,000$$

$$cost(P_2) = cost(\text{EMP}) + |\text{EMP}| * cost(\sigma_{\text{DUR}>6}(\text{WORKS}))$$

$$= cost(\text{EMP}) + |\text{EMP}| * cost(\text{WORKS})$$

$$= |\text{EMP}| + |\text{EMP}| * |\text{WORKS}| = 10,001,000$$

$$cost(P_3) = cost(P_4) = |\text{WORKS}| + \frac{|\text{WORKS}|}{2} * |\text{EMP}|$$

$$= 5,010,000$$

Thus, the optimizer discards plans P_1 and P_2 to keep either P_3 or P_4 for processing Q. Let us assume now that the mediator imports specific cost information about component DBMSs. db_1 exports the cost of accessing EMP tuples as:

$$cost(\sigma_{\text{A}=v}(\text{R})) = |\sigma_{\text{A}=v}(\text{R})|$$

db_2 exports the specific cost of selecting WORKS tuples that have a given E\# as:

$$cost(\sigma_{\text{E\#}=v}(\text{WORKS})) = |\sigma_{\text{E\#}=v}(\text{WORKS})|$$

The mediator integrates these cost functions in its hierarchical cost model, and can now estimate more accurately the cost of the QEPs:

$$cost(P_1) = |\text{EMP}| + |\text{EMP}| * |\sigma_{\text{E\#}=v}(\text{WORKS})|$$

$$= 1,000 + 1,000 * 10$$

$$= 11,000$$

$$cost(P_2) = |\text{EMP}| + |\text{EMP}| * |\sigma_{\text{DUR}>6}(\text{WORKS})|$$

$$= |\text{EMP}| + |\text{EMP}| * \frac{|\text{ASG}|}{2}$$

$$= 5,001,000$$

$$cost(P_3) = |\text{WORKS}| + \frac{|\text{WORKS}|}{2} * |\sigma_{\text{E\#}=v}(\text{EMP})|$$

$$= 10,000 + 5,000 * 1$$

$$= 15,000$$

$$cost(P_4) = |\text{WORKS}| + \frac{|\text{WORKS}|}{2} * |\text{EMP}|$$

$$= 10,000 + 5,000 * 1,000$$

$$= 5,010,000$$

The best QEP is now P_1 which was previously discarded because of lack of cost information about component DBMSs. In many situations P_1 is actually the best alternative to process Q_1. ♦

The two solutions just presented are well-suited to the mediator/wrapper architecture and offer a good trade-off between the overhead of providing specific cost information for diverse component DBMSs and the benefit of faster heterogeneous query processing.

Dynamic Approach

The above approaches assume that the execution environment is stable over time. However, in most cases, the execution environment factors are frequently changing. Three classes of environmental factors can be identified based on their dynamicity. The first class for frequently changing factors (every second to every minute) includes CPU load, I/O throughput, and available memory. The second class for slowly changing factors (every hour to every day) includes DBMS configuration parameters, physical data organization on disks, and database schema. The third class for almost stable factors (every month to every year) includes DBMS type, database location, and CPU speed. We focus on solutions that deal with the first two classes.

One way to deal with dynamic environments where network contention, data storage, or available memory changes over time is to extend the sampling method and consider user queries as new samples. Query response time is measured to adjust the cost model parameters at runtime for subsequent queries. This avoids the overhead of processing sample queries periodically, but still requires heavy computation to solve the cost model equations and does not guarantee that cost model precision improves over time. A better solution, called qualitative, defines the system contention level as the combined effect of frequently changing factors on query cost. The system contention level is divided into several discrete categories: high, medium, low, or no system contention. This allows for defining a multicategory cost model that provides accurate cost estimates, while dynamic factors are varying. The cost model is initially calibrated using probing queries. The current system contention level is computed over time, based on the most significant system parameters. This approach assumes that query executions are short, so the environment factors remain rather constant during query execution. However, this solution does not apply to long running queries, since the environment factors may change rapidly during query execution.

To manage the case where the environment factor variation is predictable (e.g., the daily DBMS load variation is the same every day), the query cost is computed for successive date ranges. Then, the total cost is the sum of the costs for each range. Furthermore, it may be possible to learn the pattern of the available network bandwidth between the MDBS query processor and the component DBMS. This allows adjusting the query cost depending on the actual date.

7.2.4.2 Heterogeneous Query Optimization

In addition to heterogeneous cost modeling, multidatabase query optimization must deal with the issue of the heterogeneous computing capabilities of component DBMSs. For instance, one component DBMS may support only simple select operations, while another may support complex queries involving join and aggregate. Thus, depending on how the wrappers export such capabilities, query processing at the mediator level can be more or less complex. There are two main approaches to deal with this issue depending on the kind of interface between mediator and wrapper: query-based and operator-based.

1. **Query-based.** In this approach, the wrappers support the same query capability, e.g., a subset of SQL, which is translated to the capability of the component DBMS. This approach typically relies on a standard DBMS interface such as Open Database Connectivity (ODBC) and its extensions for the wrappers or SQL Management of External Data (SQL/MED). Thus, since the component DBMSs appear homogeneous to the mediator, query processing techniques designed for homogeneous distributed DBMS can be reused. However, if the component DBMSs have limited capabilities, the additional capabilities must be implemented in the wrappers, e.g., join queries may need to be handled at the wrapper, if the component DBMS does not support join.

2. **Operator-based.** In this approach, the wrappers export the capabilities of the component DBMSs through compositions of relational operators. Thus, there is

more flexibility in defining the level of functionality between the mediator and the wrapper. In particular, the different capabilities of the component DBMSs can be made available to the mediator. This makes wrapper construction easier at the expense of more complex query processing in the mediator. In particular, any functionality that may not be supported by component DBMSs (e.g., join) will need to be implemented at the mediator.

In the rest of this section, we present, in more detail, the approaches to query optimization in these systems.

Query-Based Approach

Since the component DBMSs appear homogeneous to the mediator, one approach is to use a distributed cost-based query optimization algorithm (see Chap. 4) with a heterogeneous cost model (see Sect. 7.2.4.1). However, extensions are needed to convert the distributed execution plan into subqueries to be executed by the component DBMSs and into subqueries to be executed by the mediator. The hybrid two-step optimization technique is useful in this case (see Sect. 4.5.3): in the first step, a static plan is produced by a centralized cost-based query optimizer; in the second step, at startup time, an execution plan is produced by carrying out site selection and allocating the subqueries to the sites. However, centralized optimizers restrict their search space by eliminating bushy join trees from consideration. Almost all the systems use left linear join orders. Consideration of only left linear join trees gives good results in centralized DBMSs for two reasons: it reduces the need to estimate statistics for at least one operand, and indexes can still be exploited for one of the operands. However, in multidatabase systems, these types of join execution plans are not necessarily the preferred ones as they do not allow any parallelism in join execution. As we discussed in earlier chapters, this is also a problem in homogeneous distributed DBMSs, but the issue is more serious in the case of multidatabase systems, because we wish to push as much processing as possible to the component DBMSs.

A way to resolve this problem is to somehow generate bushy join trees and consider them at the expense of left linear ones. One way to achieve this is to apply a cost-based query optimizer to first generate a left linear join tree, and then convert it to a bushy tree. In this case, the left linear join execution plan can be optimal with respect to total time, and the transformation improves the query response time without severely impacting the total time. A hybrid algorithm that concurrently performs a bottom-up and top-down sweep of the left linear join execution tree, transforming it, step-by-step, to a bushy one is possible. The algorithm maintains two pointers, called *upper anchor nodes* (UAN) on the tree. At the beginning, one of these, called the bottom UAN (UAN_B), is set to the grandparent of the leftmost root node (join with R_3 in Fig. 4.9), while the second one, called the top UAN (UAN_T), is set to the root (join with R_5). For each UAN the algorithm selects a *lower anchor node* (LAN). This is the node closest to the UAN and whose right child subtree's response time is within a designer-specified range, relative to that of the UAN's right child subtree. Intuitively, the LAN is chosen such that its right child subtree's response time is **close** to the corresponding UAN's right child subtree's response time. As we will see shortly, this helps in keeping the transformed bushy tree balanced, which reduces the response time.

At each step, the algorithm picks one of the UAN/LAN pairs (strictly speaking, it picks the UAN and selects the appropriate LAN, as discussed above), and performs the following translation for the segment between that LAN and UAN pair:

1. The left child of UAN becomes the new UAN of the transformed segment.
2. The LAN remains unchanged, but its right child vertex is replaced with a new join node of two subtrees, which were the right child subtrees of the input UAN and LAN.

The UAN mode that will be considered in that particular iteration is chosen according to the following heuristic: choose UAN_B if the response time of its left child subtree is smaller than that of UAN_T's subtree; otherwise, choose UAN_T. If the response times are the same, choose the one with the more unbalanced child subtree.

At the end of each transformation step, the UAN_B and UAN_T are adjusted. The algorithm terminates when $UAN_B = UAN_T$, since this indicates that no further transformations are possible. The resulting join execution tree will be almost balanced, producing an execution plan whose response time is reduced due to parallel execution of the joins.

The algorithm described above starts with a left linear join execution tree that is generated by a centralized DBMS optimizer. These optimizers are able to generate very good plans, but the initial linear execution plan may not fully account for the peculiarities of the distributed multidatabase characteristics, such as data replication. A special global query optimization algorithm can take these into consideration. One proposed algorithm starts from an initial plan and checks for different parenthesizations of this linear join execution order to produce a parenthesized order that is optimal with respect to response time. The result is an (almost) balanced join execution tree. This approach is likely to produce better quality plans at the expense of longer optimization time.

Operator-Based Approach

Expressing the capabilities of the component DBMSs through relational operators allows tight integration of query processing between the mediator and the wrappers. In particular, the mediator/wrapper communication can be in terms of subplans. We illustrate the operator-based approach via the planning functions proposed in the Garlic project. In this approach, the capabilities of the component DBMSs are expressed by the wrappers as planning functions that can be directly called by a centralized query optimizer. It extends a rule-based optimizer with operators to create temporary relations and retrieve locally stored data. It also creates the

PushDown operator that pushes a portion of the work to the component DBMSs where it will be executed. The execution plans are represented, as usual, as operator trees, but the operator nodes are annotated with additional information that specifies the source(s) of the operand(s), whether the results are materialized, and so on. The Garlic operator trees are then translated into operators that can be directly executed by the execution engine.

Planning functions are considered by the optimizer as enumeration rules. They are called by the optimizer to construct subplans using two main functions: accessPlan to access a relation, and joinPlan to join two relations using the access plans. These functions precisely reflect the capabilities of the component DBMSs with a common formalism.

Example 7.19 We consider three component databases, each at a different site. Component database db_1 stores relation EMP(ENO, ENAME, CITY) and component database db_2 stores relation WORKS(ENO, PNAME, DUR). Component database db_3 stores only employee information with a single relation of schema EMPASG(ENAME, CITY, PNAME, DUR), whose primary key is (ENAME, PNAME). Component databases db_1 and db_2 have the same wrapper w_1, whereas db_3 has a different wrapper w_2.

Wrapper w_1 provides two planning functions typical of a relational DBMS. The accessPlan rule

> accessPlan(R: relation, A: attribute list, P: select predicate) =
> scan(R, A, P, db(R))

produces a scan operator that accesses tuples of R from its component database db(R) (here we can have db(R) $= db_1$ or db(R) $= db_2$), applies select predicate P, and projects on the attribute list A. The joinPlan rule

> joinPlan(R$_1$, R$_2$: relations, A: attribute list, P: join predicate) =
> join(R$_1$, R$_2$, A, P)
> condition: db(R$_1$) $\neq db$(R$_2$)

produces a join operator that accesses tuples of relations R$_1$ and R$_2$ and applies join predicate P and projects on attribute list A. The condition expresses that R$_1$ and R$_2$ are stored in different component databases (i.e., db_1 and db_2). Thus, the join operator is implemented by the wrapper.

Wrapper w_2 also provides two planning functions. The accessPlan rule

> accessPlan(R: relation, A: attribute list, P: select predicate) =
> fetch(CITY="c")
> condition: (CITY="c") $\subseteq P$

produces a fetch operator that directly accesses (entire) employee tuples in component database db_3 whose CITY value is "c." The accessPlan rule

> accessPlan(R: relation, A: attribute list, P: select predicate) =
> scan(R, A, P)

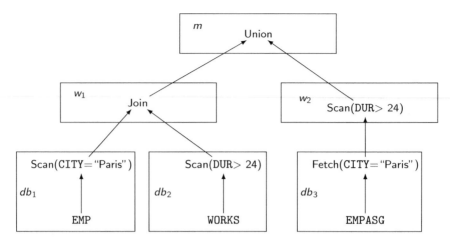

Fig. 7.15 Heterogeneous query execution plan

produces a scan operator that accesses tuples of relation R in the wrapper and applies select predicate P and attribute project list A. Thus, the scan operator is implemented by the wrapper, not the component DBMS.

Consider the following SQL query submitted to mediator m:

```
SELECT ENAME, PNAME, DUR
FROM    EMPASG
WHERE   CITY = "Paris" AND DUR > 24
```

Assuming the GAV approach, the global view EMPASG(ENAME, CITY, PNAME, DUR) can be defined as follows (for simplicity, we prefix each relation by its component database name):

$$\text{EMPASG} = (db_1.\text{EMP} \bowtie db_2.\text{WORKS}) \cup db_3.\text{EMPASG}$$

After query rewriting in GAV and query optimization, the operator-based approach could produce the QEP shown in Fig. 7.15. This plan shows that the operators that are not supported by the component DBMS are to be implemented by the wrappers or the mediator.   ◆

Using planning functions for heterogeneous query optimization has several advantages in MDBSs. First, planning functions provide a flexible way to express precisely the capabilities of component data sources. In particular, they can be used to model nonrelational data sources such as web sites. Second, since these rules are declarative, so they make wrapper development easier. The only important development for wrappers is the implementation of specific operators, e.g., the scan operator of db_3 in Example 7.19. Finally, this approach can be easily incorporated in an existing, centralized query optimizer.

The operator-based approach has also been successfully used in DIMDBS, an MDBS designed to access multiple databases over the web. DISCO uses the

GAV approach and supports an object data model to represent both mediator and component database schemas and data types. This allows easy introduction of new component databases, easily handling potential type mismatches. The component DBMS capabilities are defined as a subset of an algebraic machine (with the usual operators such as scan, join, and union) that can be partially or entirely supported by the wrappers or the mediator. This gives much flexibility for the wrapper implementors in deciding where to support component DBMS capabilities (in the wrapper or in the mediator). Furthermore, compositions of operators, including specific datasets, can be specified to reflect component DBMS limitations. However, query processing is more complicated because of the use of an algebraic machine and compositions of operators. After query rewriting on the component schemas, there are three main steps:

1. **Search space generation.** The query is decomposed into a number of QEPs, which constitutes the search space for query optimization. The search space is generated using a traditional search strategy such as dynamic programming.
2. **QEP decomposition.** Each QEP is decomposed into a forest of *n wrapper QEPs* and a *composition QEP*. Each wrapper QEP is the largest part of the initial QEP that can be entirely executed by the wrapper. Operators that cannot be performed by a wrapper are moved up to the composition QEP. The composition QEP combines the results of the wrapper QEPs in the final answer, typically through unions and joins of the intermediate results produced by the wrappers.
3. **Cost evaluation.** The cost of each QEP is evaluated using a hierarchical cost model discussed in Sect. 7.2.4.1.

7.2.5 Query Translation and Execution

Query translation and execution is performed by the wrappers using the component DBMSs. A wrapper encapsulates the details of one or more component databases, each supported by the same DBMS (or file system). It also exports to the mediator the component DBMS capabilities and cost functions in a common interface. One of the major practical uses of wrappers has been to allow an SQL-based DBMS to access non-SQL databases.

The main function of a wrapper is conversion between the common interface and the DBMS-dependent interface. Figure 7.16 shows these different levels of interfaces between the mediator, the wrapper, and the component DBMSs. Note that, depending on the level of autonomy of the component DBMSs, these three components can be located differently. For instance, in the case of strong autonomy, the wrapper should be at the mediator site, possibly on the same server. Thus, communication between a wrapper and its component DBMS incurs network cost. However, in the case of a cooperative component database (e.g., within the same organization), the wrapper could be installed at the component DBMS site, much

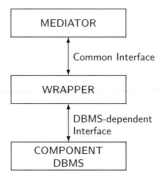

Fig. 7.16 Wrapper interfaces

like an ODBC driver. Thus, communication between the wrapper and the component DBMS is much more efficient.

The information necessary to perform conversion is stored in the wrapper schema that includes the local schema exported to the mediator in the common interface (e.g., relational) and the schema mappings to transform data between the local schema and the component database schema and vice versa. We discussed schema mappings in Sect. 7.1.4. Two kinds of conversion are needed. First, the wrapper must translate the input QEP generated by the mediator and expressed in a common interface into calls to the component DBMS using its DBMS-dependent interface. These calls yield query execution by the component DBMS that return results expressed in the DBMS-dependent interface. Second, the wrapper must translate the results to the common interface format so that they can be returned to the mediator for integration. In addition, the wrapper can execute operations that are not supported by the component DBMS (e.g., the scan operation by wrapper w_2 in Fig. 7.15).

As discussed in Sect. 7.2.4.2, the common interface to the wrappers can be query-based or operator-based. The problem of translation is similar in both approaches. To illustrate query translation in the following example, we use the query-based approach with the SQL/MED standard that allows a relational DBMS to access external data represented as foreign relations in the wrapper's local schema. This example illustrates how a very simple data source can be wrapped to be accessed through SQL.

Example 7.20 We consider relation EMP(ENO, ENAME, CITY) stored in a very simple component database, in server *Component DB*, built with Unix text files. Each EMP tuple can then be stored as a line in a file, e.g., with the attributes separated by ":". In SQL/MED, the definition of the local schema for this relation together with the mapping to a Unix file can be declared as a foreign relation with the following statement:

```
CREATE  FOREIGN TABLE EMP
        ENO INTEGER,
        ENAME VARCHAR(30),
```

```
               CITY VARCHAR(20)
     SERVER    ComponentDB
     OPTIONS   (Filename '/usr/EngDB/emp.txt',
               Delimiter ':')
```

Then, the mediator can send SQL statements to the wrapper that supports access to this relation. For instance, the query

```
     SELECT  ENAME
     FROM    EMP
```

can be translated by the wrapper using the following Unix shell command to extract the relevant attribute:

```
    cut -d: -f2 /usr/EngDB/emp
```

Additional processing, e.g., for type conversion, can then be done using programming code.   ♦

Wrappers are mostly used for read-only queries, which makes query translation and wrapper construction relatively easy. Wrapper construction typically relies on tools with reusable components to generate most of the wrapper code. Furthermore, DBMS vendors provide wrappers for transparently accessing their DBMS using standard interfaces. However, wrapper construction is much more difficult if updates to component databases are to be supported through wrappers (as opposed to directly updating the component databases through their DBMS). A major problem is due to the heterogeneity of integrity constraints between the common interface and the DBMS-dependent interface. As discussed in Chap. 3, integrity constraints are used to reject updates that violate database consistency. In modern DBMSs, integrity constraints are explicit and specified as rules that are part of the database schema. However, in older DBMSs or simpler data sources (e.g., files), integrity constraints are implicit and implemented by specific code in the applications. For instance, in Example 7.20, there could be applications with some embedded code that rejects insertions of new lines with an existing ENO in the EMP text file. This code corresponds to a unique key constraint on ENO in relation EMP but is not readily available to the wrapper. Thus, the main problem of updating through a wrapper is guaranteeing component database consistency by rejecting all updates that violate integrity constraints, whether they are explicit or implicit. A software engineering solution to this problem uses a tool with reverse engineering techniques to identify within application code the implicit integrity constraints that are then translated into validation code in the wrappers.

Another major problem is wrapper maintenance. Query translation relies heavily on the mappings between the component database schema and the local schema. If the component database schema is changed to reflect the evolution of the component database, then the mappings can become invalid. For instance, in Example 7.20, the administrator may switch the order of the fields in the EMP file. Using invalid mappings may prevent the wrapper from producing correct results. Since the component databases are autonomous, detecting and correcting invalid mappings is important. The techniques to do so are those for mapping maintenance that we discussed in this chapter.

7.3 Conclusion

In this chapter, we discussed the bottom-up database design process, which we called database integration and how to execute queries over databases constructed in this manner. Database integration is the process of creating a GCS (or a mediated schema) and determining how each LCS maps to it. A fundamental separation is between data warehouses where the GCS is instantiated and materialized, and data integration systems where the GCS is merely a virtual view.

Although the topic of database integration has been studied extensively for a long time, almost all of the work has been fragmented. Individual projects focus either on schema matching, or data cleaning, or schema mapping. What is needed is an end-to-end methodology for database integration that is semiautomatic with sufficient hooks for expert involvement. One approach to such a methodology is the work of Bernstein and Melnik [2007], which provides the beginnings of a comprehensive "end-to-end" methodology.

A related concept that has received considerable discussion in literature is *data exchange*, which is defined as "the problem of taking data structured under a source schema and creating an instance of a target schema that reflects the source data as accurately as possible" [Fagin et al. 2005]. This is very similar to the physical integration (i.e., materialized) data integration, such as data warehouses, that we discussed in this chapter. A difference between data warehouses and the materialization approaches as addressed in data exchange environments is that data warehouse data typically belongs to one organization and can be structured according to a well-defined schema, while in data exchange environments data may come from different sources and contain heterogeneity.

Our focus in this chapter has been on integrating *databases*. Increasingly, however, the data that are used in distributed applications involve those that are not in a database. An interesting new topic of discussion among researchers is the integration of *structured* data that is stored in databases and *unstructured* data that is maintained in other systems (web servers, multimedia systems, digital libraries, etc.). We discuss these in Chap. 12 where we focus on the integration of data from different web repositories and introduce the recent concept of *data lakes*.

Another issue that we ignored in this chapter is data integration when a GCS does not exist or cannot be specified. The issue arises particularly in the peer-to-peer systems where the scale and the variety of data sources make it quite difficult (if not impossible) to design a GCS. We will discuss data integration in peer-to-peer systems in Chap. 9.

The second part of this chapter focused on query processing in multidatabase systems, which is significantly more complex than in tightly integrated and homogeneous distributed DBMSs. In addition to being distributed, component databases may be autonomous, have different database languages and query processing capabilities, and exhibit varying behavior. In particular, component databases may range from full-fledged SQL databases to very simple data sources (e.g., text files).

In this chapter, we addressed these issues by extending and modifying the distributed query processing architecture presented in Chap. 4. Assuming the popular mediator/wrapper architecture, we isolated the three main layers by which a query is successively rewritten (to bear on local relations) and optimized by the mediator, and then translated and executed by the wrappers and component DBMSs. We also discussed how to support OLAP queries in a multidatabase, an important requirement of decision-support applications. This requires an additional layer of translation from OLAP multidimensional queries to relational queries. This layered architecture for multidatabase query processing is general enough to capture very different variations. This has been useful to describe various query processing techniques, typically designed with different objectives and assumptions.

The main techniques for multidatabase query processing are query rewriting using multidatabase views, multidatabase query optimization and execution, and query translation and execution. The techniques for query rewriting using multidatabase views differ in major ways depending on whether the GAV or LAV integration approach is used. Query rewriting in GAV is similar to data localization in homogeneous distributed database systems. But the techniques for LAV (and its extension GLAV) are much more involved and it is often not possible to find an equivalent rewriting for a query, in which case a query that produces a maximum subset of the answer is necessary. The techniques for multidatabase query optimization include cost modeling and query optimization for component databases with different computing capabilities. These techniques extend traditional distributed query processing by focusing on heterogeneity. Besides heterogeneity, an important problem is to deal with the dynamic behavior of the component DBMSs. Adaptive query processing addresses this problem with a dynamic approach whereby the query optimizer communicates at runtime with the execution environment in order to react to unforeseen variations of runtime conditions. Finally, we discussed the techniques for translating queries for execution by the components DBMSs and for generating and managing wrappers.

The data model used by the mediator can be relational, object-oriented, or others. In this chapter, for simplicity, we assumed a mediator with a relational model that is sufficient to explain the multidatabase query processing techniques. However, when dealing with data sources on the Web, a richer mediator model such as object-oriented or semistructured (e.g., XML- or RDF-based) may be preferred. This requires significant extensions to query processing techniques.

7.4 Bibliographic Notes

A large volume of literature exists on the topic of this chapter. The work goes back to early 1980s and which is nicely surveyed by Batini et al. [1986]. Subsequent work is nicely covered by Elmagarmid et al. [1999] and Sheth and Larson [1990]. Another more recent good review of the field is by Jhingran et al. [2002].

The book by Doan et al. [2012] provides the broadest coverage of the subject. There are a number of overview papers on the topic. Bernstein and Melnik [2007] provide a very nice discussion of the integration methodology. It goes further by comparing the model management work with some of the data integration research. Halevy et al. [2006] review the data integration work in the 1990s, focusing on the Information Manifold system [Levy et al. 1996a], that uses a LAV approach. The paper provides a large bibliography and discusses the research areas that have been opened in the intervening years. Haas [2007] takes a comprehensive approach to the entire integration process and divides it into four phases: understanding that involves discovering relevant information (keys, constraints, data types, etc.), analyzing it to assess quality, and to determine statistical properties; standardization whereby the best way to represent the integrated information is determined; specification that involves the configuration of the integration process; and execution, which is the actual integration. The specification phase includes the techniques defined in this paper.

The LAV and GAV approaches are introduced and discussed by Lenzerini [2002], Koch [2001], and Calì and Calvanese [2002]. The GLAV approach is discussed in [Friedman et al. 1999] and [Halevy 2001]. A large number of systems have been developed that have tested the LAV versus GAV approaches. Many of these focus on querying over integrated systems. Examples of LAV approaches are described in the papers [Duschka and Genesereth 1997, Levy et al. 1996b, Manolescu et al. 2001], while examples of GAV are presented in papers [Adali et al. 1996a, Garcia-Molina et al. 1997, Haas et al. 1997b].

Topics of structural and semantic heterogeneity have occupied researchers for quite some time. While the literature on this topic is quite extensive, some of the interesting publications that discuss structural heterogeneity are [Dayal and Hwang 1984, Kim and Seo 1991, Breitbart et al. 1986, Krishnamurthy et al. 1991, Batini et al. 1986] (Batini et al. [1986] also discuss the structural conflicts introduced in this chapter) and those that focus on semantic heterogeneity are [Sheth and Kashyap 1992, Hull 1997, Ouksel and Sheth 1999, Kashyap and Sheth 1996, Bright et al. 1994, Ceri and Widom 1993, Vermeer 1997]. We should note that this list is seriously incomplete.

Various proposals for the canonical model for the GCS exist. The ones we discussed in this chapter and their sources are the ER model [Palopoli et al. 1998, Palopoli 2003, He and Ling 2006], object-oriented model [Castano and Antonellis 1999, Bergamaschi 2001], graph model (which is also used for determining structural similarity) [Palopoli et al. 1999, Milo and Zohar 1998, Melnik et al. 2002,

Do and Rahm 2002, Madhavan et al. 2001], tree model [Madhavan et al. 2001], and XML [Yang et al. 2003].

Doan and Halevy [2005] provide a very good overview of the various schema matching techniques, proposing a different, and simpler, classification of the techniques as rule-based, learning-based, and combined. More works in schema matching are surveyed by Rahm and Bernstein [2001], which gives a very nice comparison of various proposals. The interschema rules we discussed in this chapter are due to Palopoli et al. [1999]. The classical source for the ranking aggregation functions used in matching is [Fagin 2002].

A number of systems have been developed demonstrating the feasibility of various schema matching approaches. Among rule-based techniques, one can cite DIKE [Palopoli et al. 1998, Palopoli 2003, Palopoli et al. 2003], DIPE, which is an earlier version of this system [Palopoli et al. 1999], TranSCM [Milo and Zohar 1998], ARTEMIS [Bergamaschi 2001], similarity flooding [Melnik et al. 2002], CUPID [Madhavan et al. 2001], and COMA [Do and Rahm 2002]. For learning-based matching, Autoplex [Berlin and Motro 2001] implements a naïve Bayesian classifier, which is also the approach proposed by Doan et al. [2001, 2003a] and Naumann et al. [2002]. In the same class, decision trees are discussed in [Embley et al. 2001, 2002], and iMAP in [Dhamankar et al. 2004].

Roth and Schwartz [1997], Tomasic et al. [1997], and Thiran et al. [2006] focus on various aspects of wrapper technology. A software engineering solution to the problem of wrapper creation and maintenance, considering integrity control, is proposed in [Thiran et al. 2006].

Some sources for binary integration are [Batini et al. 1986, Pu 1988, Batini and Lenzirini 1984, Dayal and Hwang 1984, Melnik et al. 2002], while n-ary mechanisms are discussed in [Elmasri et al. 1987, Yao et al. 1982, He et al. 2004]. For some database integration tools the readers can consult [Sheth et al. 1988a], [Miller et al. 2001] that discuss Clio, and [Roitman and Gal 2006] that describes OntoBuilder.

Mapping creation algorithm in Sect. 7.1.4.1 is due to Miller et al. [2000], Yan et al. [2001], and [Popa et al. 2002]. Mapping maintenance is discussed by Velegrakis et al. [2004].

Data cleaning has gained significant interest in recent years as the integration efforts opened up to data sources more widely. The literature is rich on this topic and is well discussed in the book by Ilyas and Chu [2019]. In this context, the distinction between schema-level and instance-level cleaning is due to Rahm and Do [2000]. The data cleaning operators we discussed are column splitting [Raman and Hellerstein 2001], map operator [Galhardas et al. 2001], and fuzzy match [Chaudhuri et al. 2003].

Work on multidatabase query processing started in the early 1980s with the first multidatabase systems (e.g., [Brill et al. 1984, Dayal and Hwang 1984] and [Landers and Rosenberg 1982]). The objective then was to access different databases within an organization. In the 1990s, the increasing use of the Web for accessing all kinds of data sources triggered renewed interest and much more work in multidatabase query processing, following the popular mediator/wrapper architecture [Wiederhold

1992]. A brief overview of multidatabase query optimization issues can be found in [Meng et al. 1993]. Good discussions of multidatabase query processing can be found in [Lu et al. 1992, 1993], in Chapter 4 of [Yu and Meng 1998] and in [Kossmann 2000].

Query rewriting using views is discussed in [Levy et al. 1995] and surveyed in [Halevy 2001]. In [Levy et al. 1995], the general problem of finding a rewriting using views is shown to be NP-complete in the number of views and the number of subgoals in the query. The unfolding technique for rewriting a query expressed in Datalog in GAV was proposed in [Ullman 1997]. The main techniques for query rewriting using views in LAV are the bucket algorithm [Levy et al. 1996b], the inverse rule algorithm [Duschka and Genesereth 1997], and the MinCon algorithm [Pottinger and Levy 2000].

The three main approaches for heterogeneous cost modeling are discussed in [Zhu and Larson 1998]. The black-box approach is used in [Du et al. 1992, Zhu and Larson 1994]; the techniques in this group are probing queries: [Zhu and Larson 1996a], sample queries (which are a special case of probing) [Zhu and Larson 1998], and learning the cost over time as queries are posed and answered [Adali et al. 1996b]. The customized approach is developed in [Zhu and Larson 1996b, Roth et al. 1999, Naacke et al. 1999]; in particular cost computation can be done within the wrapper (as in Garlic) [Roth et al. 1999] or a hierarchical cost model can be developed (as in Disco) [Naacke et al. 1999]. The dynamic approach is used in [Zhu et al. 2000], [Zhu et al. 2003], and [Rahal et al. 2004] and also discussed by Lu et al. [1992]. Zhu [1995] discusses a dynamic approaching sampling and Zhu et al. [2000] present a qualitative approach.

The algorithm we described to illustrate the query-based approach to heterogeneous query optimization (Sect. 7.2.4.2) has been proposed in [Du et al. 1995] and also discussed in [Evrendilek et al. 1997]. To illustrate the operator-based approach, we described the popular solution with planning functions proposed in the Garlic project [Haas et al. 1997a]. The operator-based approach has been also used in DISCO, a multidatabase system to access component databases over the web [Tomasic et al. 1996, 1998].

The case for adaptive query processing is made by a number of researchers in a number of environments. Amsaleg et al. [1996] show why static plans cannot cope with unpredictability of data sources; the problem exists in continuous queries [Madden et al. 2002b], expensive predicates [Porto et al. 2003], and data skew [Shah et al. 2003]. The adaptive approach is surveyed in [Hellerstein et al. 2000, Gounaris et al. 2002]. The best-known dynamic approach is eddy (see Chap. 4), which is discussed in [Avnur and Hellerstein 2000]. Other important techniques for adaptive query processing are query scrambling [Amsaleg et al. 1996, Urhan et al. 1998], Ripple joins [Haas and Hellerstein 1999b], adaptive partitioning [Shah et al. 2003], and Cherry picking [Porto et al. 2003]. Major extensions to eddy are state modules [Raman et al. 2003] and distributed Eddies [Tian and DeWitt 2003].

In this chapter, we focused on the integration of structured data captured in databases. The more general problem of integrating both structured and unstructured data is discussed by Halevy et al. [2003] and Somani et al. [2002]. A different generality direction is investigated by Bernstein and Melnik [2007], who propose a model management engine that "supports operations to match schemas, compose mappings, diff schemas, merge schemas, translate schemas into different data models, and generate data transformations from mappings."

In addition to the systems we noted above, in this chapter we referred to a number of other systems. These and their main sources are the following: SEMINT [Li and Clifton 2000, Li et al. 2000], ToMAS [Velegrakis et al. 2004], Maveric [McCann et al. 2005], and Aurora [Yan 1997, Yan et al. 1997].

Exercises

Problem 7.1 Distributed database systems and distributed multidatabase systems represent two different approaches to systems design. Find three real-life applications for which each of these approaches would be more appropriate. Discuss the features of these applications that make them more favorable for one approach or the other.

Problem 7.2 Some architectural models favor the definition of a global conceptual schema, whereas others do not. What do you think? Justify your selection with detailed technical arguments.

Problem 7.3 (*) Give an algorithm to convert a relational schema to an entity-relationship one.

Problem 7.4 (**) Consider the two databases given in Figs. 7.17 and 7.18 and described below. Design a global conceptual schema as a union of the two databases by first translating them into the E-R model.

Figure 7.17 describes a relational race database used by organizers of road races and Fig. 7.18 describes an entity-relationship database used by a shoe manufacturer. The semantics of each of these database schemas is discussed below. Figure 7.17 describes a relational road race database with the following semantics:

DIRECTOR is a relation that defines race directors who organize races; we assume that each race director has a unique name (to be used as the key), a phone number, and an address.

```
DIRECTOR(NAME, PHONE_NO, ADDRESS)
LICENSES(LIC_NO, CITY, DATE, ISSUES, COST, DEPT, CONTACT)
RACER(NAME, ADDRESS, MEM_NUM)
SPONSOR(SP_NAME, CONTACT)
RACE(R_NO, LIC_NO, DIR, MAL_WIN, FRM_WIN, SP_NAME)
```

Fig. 7.17 Road race database

LICENSES   is required because all races require a governmental license, which is issued by a CONTACT in a department who is the ISSUER, possibly contained within another government department DEPT; each license has a unique LIC_NO (the key), which is issued for use in a specific CITY on a specific DATE with a certain COST.

RACER   is a relation that describes people who participate in a race. Each person is identified by NAME, which is not sufficient to identify them uniquely, so a compound key formed with the ADDRESS is required. Finally, each racer may have a MEM_NUM to identify him or her as a member of the racing fraternity, but not all competitors have membership numbers.

SPONSOR   indicates which sponsor is funding a given race. Typically, one sponsor funds a number of races through a specific person (CONTACT), and a number of races may have different sponsors.

RACE   uniquely identifies a single race which has a license number (LIC_NO) and race number (R_NO) (to be used as a key, since a race may be planned without acquiring a license yet); each race has a winner in the male and female groups (MAL_WIN and FEM_WIN) and a race director (DIR).

Figure 7.18 illustrates an entity-relationship schema used by the sponsor's database system with the following semantics:

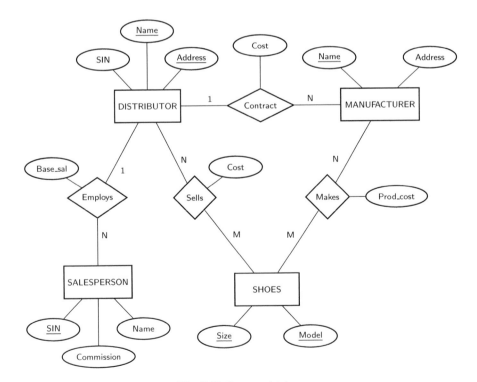

Fig. 7.18 Sponsor database

SHOES   are produced by sponsors of a certain MODEL and SIZE, which forms the key to the entity.

MANUFACTURER   is identified uniquely by NAME and resides at a certain ADDRESS.

DISTRIBUTOR   is a person that has a NAME and ADDRESS (which are necessary to form the key) and a SIN number for tax purposes.

SALESPERSON   is a person (entity) who has a NAME, earns a COMMISSION, and is uniquely identified by his or her SIN number (the key).

Makes   is a relationship that has a certain fixed production cost (PROD_COST). It indicates that a number of different shoes are made by a manufacturer, and that different manufacturers produce the same shoe.

Sells   is a relationship that indicates the wholesale COST to a distributor of shoes. It indicates that each distributor sells more than one type of shoe, and that each type of shoe is sold by more than one distributor.

Contract   is a relationship whereby a distributor purchases, for a COST, exclusive rights to represent a manufacturer. Note that this does not preclude the distributor from selling different manufacturers' shoes.

Employs   indicates that each distributor hires a number of salespeople to sell the shoes; each earns a BASE_SALARY.

Problem 7.5 (*)   Consider three sources:

- Database 1 has one relation `Area(Id, Field)` providing areas of specialization of employees; the Id field identifies an employee.
- Database 2 has two relations, `Teach(Professor, Course)` and `In(Course, Field)`; `Teach` indicates the courses that each professor teaches and `In` specifies possible fields that a course can belong to.
- Database 3 has two relations, `Grant(Researcher, GrantNo)` for grants given to researchers, and `For(GrantNo, Field)` indicating which fields the grants are for.

The objective is to build a GCS with two relations: `Works(Id, Project)` stating that an employee works for a particular project, and `Area(Project, Field)` associating projects with one or more fields.

(a) Provide a LAV mapping between Database 1 and the GCS.
(b) Provide a GLAV mapping between the GCS and the local schemas.
(c) Suppose one extra relation, `Funds(GrantNo, Project)`, is added to Database 3. Provide a GAV mapping in this case.

Problem 7.6   Consider a GCS with the following relation: `Person(Name, Age, Gender)`. This relation is defined as a view over three LCSs as follows:

```
CREATE VIEW Person AS
SELECT Name, Age, "male" AS Gender
FROM   SoccerPlayer
UNION
SELECT Name, NULL AS Age, Gender
```

```
FROM    Actor
UNION
SELECT Name, Age, Gender
FROM    Politician
WHERE   Age > 30
```

For each of the following queries, discuss which of the three local schemas (SoccerPlayer, Actor, and Politician) contributes to the global query result.

(a) **SELECT** Name **FROM** Person
(b) **SELECT** Name **FROM** Person **WHERE** Gender = "female"
(c) **SELECT** Name **FROM** Person **WHERE** Age > 25
(d) **SELECT** Name **FROM** Person **WHERE** Age < 25
(e) **SELECT** Name **FROM** Person **WHERE** Gender = "male"
    AND Age = 40

Problem 7.7 A GCS with the relation Country(Name, Continent, Population, HasCoast) describes countries of the world. The attribute HasCoast indicates if the country has direct access to the sea. Three LCSs are connected to the global schema using the LAV approach as follows:

```
CREATE VIEW EuropeanCountry AS
SELECT Name, Continent, Population, HasCoast
FROM    Country
WHERE   Continent = "Europe"

CREATE VIEW BigCountry AS
SELECT Name, Continent, Population, HasCoast
FROM    Country
WHERE   Population >= 30000000

CREATE VIEW MidsizeOceanCountry AS
SELECT Name, Continent, Population, HasCoast
FROM    Country
WHERE   HasCoast = true AND Population > 10000000
```

(a) For each of the following queries, discuss the results with respect to their completeness, i.e., verify if the (combination of the) local sources cover all relevant results.

  1. **SELECT** Name **FROM** Country
  2. **SELECT** Name **FROM** Country **WHERE** Population > 40
  3. **SELECT** Name **FROM** Country **WHERE** Population > 20

(b) For each of the following queries, discuss which of the three LCSs are necessary for the global query result.

  1. **SELECT** Name **FROM** Country

2. **SELECT** Name **FROM** Country **WHERE** Population > 30
   AND Continent = "Europe"
3. **SELECT** Name **FROM** Country **WHERE** Population < 30
4. **SELECT** Name **FROM** Country **WHERE** Population > 30
   AND HasCoast = **true**

Problem 7.8 Consider the following two relations PRODUCT and ARTICLE that are specified in a simplified SQL notation. The perfect schema matching correspondences are denoted by arrows.

PRODUCT		ARTICLE
Id: int PRIMARY KEY	$\longrightarrow$	Key: varchar(255) PRIMARY KEY
Name: varchar(255)	$\longrightarrow$	Title: varchar(255)
DeliveryPrice: float	$\longrightarrow$	Price: real
Description: varchar(8000)	$\longrightarrow$	Information: varchar(5000)

(a) For each of the five correspondences, indicate which of the following match approaches will probably identify the correspondence:

1. Syntactic comparison of element names, e.g., using edit distance string similarity
2. Comparison of element names using a synonym lookup table
3. Comparison of data types
4. Analysis of instance data values

(b) Is it possible for the listed matching approaches to determine false correspondences for these match tasks? If so, give an example.

Problem 7.9 Consider two relations S(a, b, c) and T(d, e, f). A match approach determines the following similarities between the elements of S and T:

	T.d	T.e	T.f
S.a	0.8	0.3	0.1
S.b	0.5	0.2	0.9
S.c	0.4	0.7	0.8

Based on the given matcher's result, derive an overall schema match result with the following characteristics:

• Each element participates in exactly one correspondence.
• There is no correspondence where both elements match an element of the opposite schema with a higher similarity than its corresponding counterpart.

Problem 7.10 (*) Figure 7.19 illustrates the schema of three different data sources:

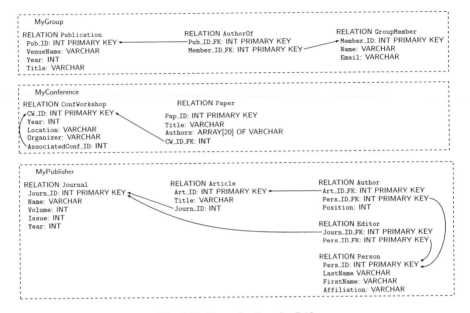

Fig. 7.19 Figure for Exercise 7.10

- MyGroup contains publications authored by members of a working group;
- MyConference contains publications of a conference series and associated workshops;
- MyPublisher contains articles that are published in journals.

The arrows show the foreign key-to-primary key relationships; note that we do not follow the proper SQL syntax of specifying foreign key relationships to save space—we resort to arrows.

The sources are defined as follows:

MyGroup

- `Publication`

    - `Pub_ID`: unique publication ID
    - `VenueName`: name of the journal, conference, or workshop
    - `VenueType`: "journal," "conference," or "workshop"
    - `Year`: year of publication
    - `Title`: publication's title

- `AuthorOf`

    - many-to-many relationship representing "group member is author of publication"

- `GroupMember`

    - `Member_ID`: unique member ID

- Name: name of the group member
- Email: email address of the group member

MyConference

- ConfWorkshop

  - CW_ID: unique ID for the conference/workshop
  - Name: name of the conference or workshop
  - Year: year when the event takes place
  - Location: event's location
  - Organizer: name of the organizing person
  - AssociatedConf_ID_FK: value is NULL if it is a conference, ID of the associated conference if the event is a workshop (this is assuming that workshops are organized in conjunction with a conference)

- Paper

  - Pap_ID: unique paper ID
  - Title: paper's title
  - Author: array of author names
  - CW_ID_FK: conference/workshop where the paper is published

MyPublisher

- Journal

  - Journ_ID: unique journal ID
  - Name: journal's name
  - Year: year when the event takes place
  - Volume: journal volume
  - Issue: journal issue

- Article

  - Art_ID: unique article ID
  - Title: title of the article
  - Journ_ID_FK: journal where the article is published

- Person

  - Pers_ID: unique person ID
  - LastName: last name of the person
  - FirstName: first name of the person
  - Affiliation: person's affiliation (e.g., the name of a university)

- Author

  - represents the many-to-many relationship for "person is author of article"
  - Position: author's position in the author list (e.g., first author has Position 1)

- Editor

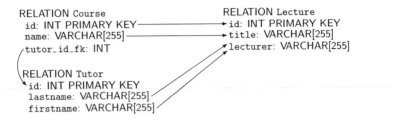

Fig. 7.20 Figure for Exercise 7.11

- represents the many-to-many relationship for "person is editor of journal issue"

(a) Identify all schema matching correspondences between the schema elements of the sources. Use the names and data types of the schema elements as well as the given description.

(b) Classify your correspondences along the following dimensions:

    1. Type of schema elements (e.g., attribute–attribute or attribute–relation)
    2. Cardinality (e.g., 1:1 or 1:N)

(c) Give a consolidated global schema that covers all information of the source schemas.

Problem 7.11 (*) Figure 7.20 illustrates (using a simplified SQL syntax) two sources $Source_1$ and $Source_2$. $Source_1$ has two relations, Course and Tutor, and $Source_2$ has only one relation, Lecture. The solid arrows denote schema matching correspondences. The dashed arrow represents a foreign key relationship between the two relations in $Source_1$.

The following are four schema mappings (represented as SQL queries) to transform $Source_1$'s data into $Source_2$.

```
1. SELECT  C.id, C.name as Title, CONCAT(T.lastname,
          T.firstname) AS Lecturer
   FROM    Course AS C
   JOIN    Tutor AS T ON (C.tutor_id_fk = T.id)
2. SELECT  C.id, C.name AS Title, NULL AS Lecturer
   FROM    Course AS C
   UNION
   SELECT  T.id AS ID, NULL AS Title, T,
          lastname AS Lecturer
   FROM    Course AS C
   FULL OUTER JOIN Tutor AS T ON(C.tutor_id_fk=T.id)
3. SELECT  C.id, C.name as Title, CONCAT(T.lastname,
          T.firstname) AS Lecturer
   FROM    Course AS C
   FULL OUTER JOIN Tutor AS T ON(C.tutor_id_fk=T.id)
```

Discuss each of these schema mappings with respect to the following questions:

(a) Is the mapping meaningful?
(b) Is the mapping complete (i.e., are all data instances of O_1 transformed)?
(c) Does the mapping potentially violate key constraints?

Problem 7.12 (*) Consider three data sources:

- Database 1 has one relation AREA(ID, FIELD) providing areas of specialization of employees where ID identifies an employee.
- Database 2 has two relations: TEACH(PROFESSOR, COURSE) and IN(COURSE, FIELD) specifying possible fields a course can belong to.
- Database 3 has two relations: GRANT(RESEARCHER, GRANT#) for grants given to researchers, and FOR(GRANT#, FIELD) indicating the fields that the grants are in.

Design a global schema with two relations: WORKS(ID, PROJECT) that records which projects employees work in, and AREA(PROJECT, FIELD) that associates projects with one or more fields for the following cases:

(a) There should be a LAV mapping between Database 1 and the global schema.
(b) There should be a GLAV mapping between the global schema and the local schemas.
(c) There should be a GAV mapping when one extra relation FUNDS(GRANT#, PROJECT) is added to Database 3.

Problem 7.13 (**) Logic (first-order logic, to be precise) has been suggested as a uniform formalism for schema translation and integration. Discuss how logic can be useful for this purpose.

Problem 7.14 (**) Can any type of global optimization be performed on global queries in a multidatabase system? Discuss and formally specify the conditions under which such optimization would be possible.

Problem 7.15 (**) Consider the global relations EMP(ENAME, TITLE, CITY) and ASG(ENAME, PNAME, CITY, DUR). CITY in ASG is the location of the project of name PNAME (i.e., PNAME functionally determines CITY). Consider the local relations EMP1(ENAME,TITLE, CITY), EMP2(ENAME, TITLE, CITY), PROJ1(PNAME, CITY), PROJ2(PNAME, CITY), and ASG1(ENAME, PNAME, DUR). Consider query Q which selects the names of the employees assigned to a project in Rio de Janeiro for more than 6 months and the duration of their assignment.

(a) Assuming the GAV approach, perform query rewriting.
(b) Assuming the LAV approach, perform query rewriting using the bucket algorithm.
(c) Same as (b) using the MinCon algorithm.

Problem 7.16 (*) Consider relations EMP and ASG of Example 7.18. We denote by $|R|$ the number of pages to store R on disk. Consider the following statistics about the data:

$$|EMP| = 100$$
$$|ASG| = 2\,000$$
$$selectivity(ASG.DUR > 36) = 1\%$$

The mediator generic cost model is

$cost(\sigma_{A=v}(R)) = |R|$
$cost(\sigma(X)) = cost(X)$, where X contains at least one operator.
$cost(R \bowtie_A^{ind} S) = cost(R) + |R| * cost(\sigma_{A=v}(S))$ using an indexed join algorithm.
$cost(R \bowtie_A^{nl} S) = cost(R) + |R| * cost(S)$ using a nested loop join algorithm.

Consider the MDBS input query Q:

```
SELECT *
FROM    EMP NATURAL JOIN ASG
WHERE   ASG.DUR>36
```

Consider four plans to process Q:

$$P_1 = \quad EMP \bowtie_{ENO}^{ind} \sigma_{DUR>36}(ASG)$$
$$P_2 = \quad EMP \bowtie_{ENO}^{nl} \sigma_{DUR>36}(ASG)$$
$$P_3 = \quad \sigma_{DUR>36}(ASG) \bowtie_{ENO}^{ind} EMP$$
$$P_4 = \quad \sigma_{DUR>36}(ASG) \bowtie_{ENO}^{nl} EMP$$

(a) What is the cost of plans P_1 to P_4?
(b) Which plan has the minimal cost?

Problem 7.17 (*) Consider relations EMP and ASG of the previous exercise. Suppose now that the mediator cost model is completed with the following cost information issued from the component DBMSs.
 The cost of accessing EMP tuples at db_1 is

$$cost(\sigma_{A=v}(R)) = |\sigma_{A=v}(R)|$$

The specific cost of selecting ASG tuples that have a given ENO at db_2 is

$$cost(\sigma_{ENO=v}(ASG)) = |\sigma_{ENO=v}(ASG)|$$

(a) What is the cost of plans P_1 to P_4?
(b) Which plan has the minimal cost?

Problem 7.18 (**) What are the respective advantages and limitations of the query-based and operator-based approaches to heterogeneous query optimization from the points of view of query expressiveness, query performance, development cost of wrappers, system (mediator and wrappers) maintenance, and evolution?

Problem 7.19 (**) Consider Example 7.19 by adding, at a new site, component database db_4 which stores relations EMP(ENO, ENAME, CITY) and ASG(ENO, PNAME, DUR). db_4 exports through its wrapper w_3 join and scan capabilities. Let us assume that there can be employees in db_1 with corresponding assignments in db_4 and employees in db_4 with corresponding assignments in db_2.

(a) Define the planning functions of wrapper w_3.
(b) Give the new definition of global view EMPASG(ENAME, CITY, PNAME, DUR).
(c) Give a QEP for the same query as in Example 7.19.

Chapter 8
Parallel Database Systems

Many data-intensive applications require support for very large databases (e.g., hundreds of terabytes or exabytes). Supporting very large databases efficiently for either OLTP or OLAP can be addressed by combining parallel computing and distributed database management.

A parallel computer, or multiprocessor, is a form of distributed system made of a number of nodes (processors, memories, and disks) connected by a very fast network within one or more cabinets in the same room. There are two kinds of multiprocessors depending on how these nodes are coupled: tightly coupled and loosely coupled. Tightly coupled multiprocessors contain multiple processors that are connected at the bus level with a shared-memory. Mainframe computers, supercomputers, and the modern multicore processors all use tight-coupling to boost performance. Loosely coupled multiprocessors, now referred to as computer clusters, or clusters for short, are based on multiple commodity computers interconnected via a high-speed network. The main idea is to build a powerful computer out of many small nodes, each with a very good cost/performance ratio, at a much lower cost than equivalent mainframe or supercomputers. In its cheapest form, the interconnect can be a local network. However, there are now fast standard interconnects for clusters (e.g., Infiniband and Myrinet) that provide high bandwidth (e.g., 100 Gigabits/sec) with low latency for message traffic.

As already discussed in previous chapters, data distribution can be exploited to increase performance (through parallelism) and availability (through replication). This principle can be used to implement *parallel database systems*, i.e., database systems on parallel computers. Parallel database systems can exploit the parallelism in data management in order to deliver high-performance and high-availability database servers. Thus, they can support very large databases with very high loads.

Most of the research on parallel database systems has been done in the context of the relational model because it provides a good basis for parallel data processing. In

---

The original version of this chapter was revised. The correction to this chapter is available at https://doi.org/10.1007/978-3-030-26253-2_13

© Springer Nature Switzerland AG 2020
M. T. Özsu, P. Valduriez, *Principles of Distributed Database Systems*,
https://doi.org/10.1007/978-3-030-26253-2_8

this chapter, we present the parallel database system approach as a solution to high-performance and high-availability data management. We discuss the advantages and disadvantages of the various parallel system architectures and we present the generic implementation techniques.

Implementation of parallel database systems naturally relies on distributed database techniques. However, the critical issues are data placement, parallel query processing, and load balancing because the number of nodes may be much higher than the number of sites in a distributed DBMS. Furthermore, a parallel computer typically provides reliable, fast communication that can be exploited to efficiently implement distributed transaction management and replication. Therefore, although the basic principles are the same as in distributed DBMS, the techniques for parallel database systems are fairly different.

This chapter is organized as follows: In Sect. 8.1, we clarify the objectives of parallel database systems. In Sect. 8.2, we discuss architectures, in particular, shared-memory, shared-disk, and shared-nothing. Then, we present the techniques for data placement in Sect. 8.3, query processing in Sect. 8.4, load balancing in Sect. 8.5, and fault-tolerance in Sect. 8.6. In Sect. 8.7, we present the use of parallel data management techniques in database clusters, an important type of parallel database system.

8.1 Objectives

Parallel processing exploits multiprocessor computers to run application programs by using several processors cooperatively, in order to improve performance. Its prominent use has long been in scientific computing to improve the response time of numerical applications. The developments in both general-purpose parallel computers using standard microprocessors and parallel programming techniques have enabled parallel processing to break into the data processing field.

Parallel database systems combine database management and parallel processing to increase performance and availability. Note that performance was also the objective of *database machines* in the 1980s. The problem faced by conventional database management has long been known as "I/O bottleneck," induced by high disk access time with respect to main memory access time (typically hundreds of thousands times faster). Initially, database machine designers tackled this problem through special-purpose hardware, e.g., by introducing data filtering devices within the disk heads. However, this approach failed because of poor cost/performance compared to the software solution, which can easily benefit from hardware progress in silicon technology. The idea of pushing database functions closer to disk has received renewed interest with the introduction of general-purpose microprocessors in disk controllers, thus leading to intelligent disks. For instance, basic functions that require costly sequential scan, e.g., select operations on tables with fuzzy predicates, can be more efficiently performed at the disk level since they avoid overloading the DBMS memory with irrelevant disk blocks. However, exploiting intelligent disks requires adapting the DBMS, in particular, the query processor to decide whether to use the disk functions. Since there is no standard intelligent disk technology, adapting to different intelligent disk technologies hurts DBMS portability.

An important result, however, is in the general solution to the I/O bottleneck. We can summarize this solution as *increasing the I/O bandwidth through parallelism*. For instance, if we store a database of size D on a single disk with throughput T, the system throughput is bounded by T. On the contrary, if we partition the database across n disks, each with capacity D/n and throughput T' (hopefully equivalent to T), we get an ideal throughput of $n * T'$ that can be better consumed by multiple processors (ideally n). Note that the main memory database system solution, which tries to maintain the database in main memory, is complementary rather than alternative. In particular, the "memory access bottleneck" in main memory systems can also be tackled using parallelism in a similar way. Therefore, parallel database system designers have strived to develop software-oriented solutions in order to exploit parallel computers.

A parallel database system can be loosely defined as a DBMS implemented on a parallel computer. This definition includes many alternatives ranging from the straightforward porting of an existing DBMS, which may require only rewriting the operating system interface routines, to a sophisticated combination of parallel processing and database system functions into a new hardware/software architecture. As always, we have the traditional trade-off between portability (to several platforms) and efficiency. The sophisticated approach is better able to fully exploit the opportunities offered by a multiprocessor at the expense of portability. Interestingly, this gives different advantages to computer manufacturers and software vendors. It is therefore important to characterize the main points in the space of alternative parallel system architectures. In order to do so, we will make precise the parallel database system solution and the necessary functions. This will be useful in comparing the parallel database system architectures.

The objectives of parallel database systems are similar to those of distributed DBMSs (performance, availability, extensibility), but have somewhat different focus due to the tighter coupling of computing/storage nodes. We highlight these below.

1. **High performance.** This can be obtained through several complementary solutions: parallel data management, query optimization, and load balancing. Parallelism can be used to increase throughput and decrease transaction response times. However, decreasing the response time of a complex query through large-scale parallelism may well increase its total time (by additional communication) and hurt throughput as a side-effect. Therefore, it is crucial to optimize and parallelize queries in order to minimize the overhead of parallelism, e.g., by constraining the degree of parallelism for the query. *Load balancing* is the ability of the system to divide a given workload equally among all processors. Depending on the parallel system architecture, it can be achieved statically by appropriate physical database design or dynamically at runtime.

2. **High availability.** Because a parallel database system consists of many redundant components, it can well increase data availability and fault-tolerance. In a highly parallel system with many nodes, the probability of a node failure at

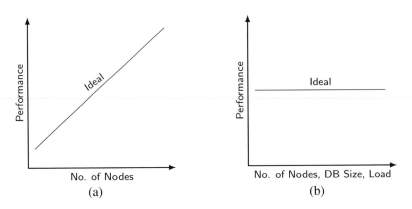

Fig. 8.1 Extensibility metrics. (**a**) Linear speed-up. (**b**) Linear scale-up

any time can be relatively high. Replicating data at several nodes is useful to support *failover*, a fault-tolerance technique that enables automatic redirection of transactions from a failed node to another node that stores a copy of the data. This provides uninterrupted service to users.

3. **Extensibility.** In a parallel system, accommodating increasing database sizes or increasing performance demands (e.g., throughput) should be easier. Extensibility is the ability to expand the system smoothly by adding processing and storage power to the system. Ideally, the parallel database system should demonstrate two extensibility advantages: *linear speed-up* and *linear scale-up* (see Fig. 8.1). Linear speed-up refers to a linear increase in performance for a constant database size and load while the number of nodes (i.e., processing and storage power) is increased linearly. Linear scale-up refers to a sustained performance for a linear increase in both database size, load and number of nodes. Furthermore, extending the system should require minimal reorganization of the existing database.

The increasing use of clusters in large-scale applications, e.g., web data management, has led to the use of the term *scale-out* versus *scale-up*. Figure 8.2 shows a cluster with 4 servers, each with a number of processing nodes ("Ps"). In this context, scale-up (also called vertical scaling) refers to adding more nodes to a server and thus gets limited by the maximum size of the server. Scale-out (also called horizontal scaling) refers to adding more servers, called "scale-out servers" in a loosely coupled fashion, to scale almost infinitely.

8.2 Parallel Architectures

A parallel database system represents a compromise in design choices in order to provide the aforementioned advantages with a good cost/performance. One guiding design decision is the way the main hardware elements, i.e., processors,

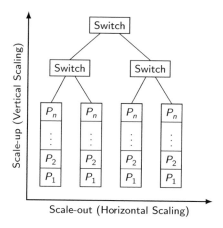

Fig. 8.2 Scale-up versus scale-out

main memory, and disks, are connected through some interconnection network. In this section, we present the architectural aspects of parallel database systems. In particular, we present and compare the three basic parallel architectures: *shared-memory*, *shared-disk*, and *shared-nothing*. Shared-memory is used in tightly coupled multiprocessors, while shared-nothing and shared-disk are used in clusters. When describing these architectures, we focus on the four main hardware elements: interconnect, processors (P), main memory modules (M), and disks. For simplicity, we ignore other elements such as processor cache, processor cores, and I/O bus.

8.2.1 General Architecture

Assuming a client/server architecture, the functions supported by a parallel database system can be divided into three subsystems much like in a typical DBMS. The differences, though, have to do with implementation of these functions, which must now deal with parallelism, data partitioning and replication, and distributed transactions. Depending on the architecture, a processor node can support all (or a subset) of these subsystems. Figure 8.3 shows the architecture using these subsystems, which is based on the architecture of Fig. 1.11 with the addition of a client manager.

1. **Client manager.** It provides support for client interactions with the parallel database system. In particular, it manages the connections and disconnections between the client processes, which run on different servers, e.g., application servers, and the query processors. Therefore, it initiates client queries (which may be transactions) at some query processors, which then become responsible for interacting directly with the clients and perform query processing and transaction management. The client manager also performs load balancing, using

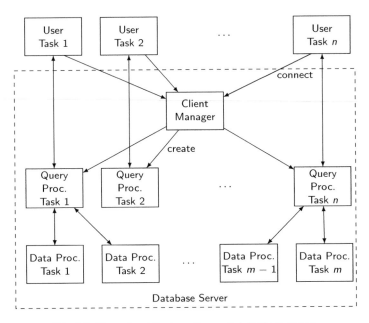

Fig. 8.3 General architecture of a parallel database system

a catalog that maintains information on processor nodes' load and precompiled queries (including data location). This allows triggering precompiled query executions at query processors that are located close to the data that is accessed. The client manager is a lightweight process, and thus not a bottleneck. However, for fault-tolerance, it can be replicated at several nodes.

2. **Query processor.** It receives and manages client queries, such as compile query, execute query, and start transaction. It uses the database directory that holds all metainformation about data, queries, and transactions. The directory itself should be managed as a database, which can be replicated at all query processor nodes. Depending on the request, it activates the various compilation phases, including semantic data control and query optimization and parallelization, triggers and monitors query execution using the data processors, and returns the results as well as error codes to the client. It may also trigger transaction validation at the data processors.

3. **Data processor.** It manages the database's data and system data (system log, etc.) and provides all the low-level functions needed to execute queries in parallel, i.e., database operator execution, parallel transaction support, cache management, etc.

8.2.2 Shared-Memory

In the shared-memory approach, any processor has access to any memory module or disk unit through an interconnect. All the processors are under the control of a single operating system.

One major advantage is simplicity of the programming model based on shared virtual memory. Since metainformation (directory) and control information (e.g., lock tables) can be shared by all processors, writing database software is not very different than for single processor computers. In particular, interquery parallelism comes for free. Intraquery parallelism requires some parallelization but remains rather simple. Load balancing is also easy since it can be achieved at runtime using the shared-memory by allocating each new task to the least busy processor.

Depending on whether physical memory is shared, two approaches are possible: Uniform Memory Access (UMA) and Non-Uniform Memory Access (NUMA), which we present below.

8.2.2.1 Uniform Memory Access (UMA)

With UMA, the physical memory is shared by all processors, so access to memory is in constant time (see Fig. 8.4). Thus, it has also been called *symmetric multiprocessor (SMP)*. Common network topologies to interconnect processors include bus, crossbar, and mesh.

The first SMPs appeared in the 1960s for mainframe computers and had a few processors. In the 1980s, there were larger SMP machines with tens of processors. However, they suffered from high cost and limited scalability. High cost was incurred by the interconnect that requires fairly complex hardware because of the need to link each processor to each memory module or disk. With faster and faster processors (even with larger caches), conflicting accesses to the shared-memory

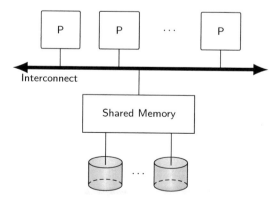

Fig. 8.4 Shared-memory

increase rapidly and degrade performance. Therefore, scalability has been limited to less than ten processors. Finally, since the memory space is shared by all processors, a memory fault may affect most processors, thereby hurting data availability.

Multicore processors are also based on SMP, with multiple processing cores and shared-memory on a single chip. Compared to the previous multichip SMP designs, they improve the performance of cache operations, require much less printed circuit board space, and consume less energy. Therefore, the current trend in multicore processor development is towards an ever increasing number of cores, as processors with hundreds of cores become feasible.

Examples of SMP parallel database systems include XPRS, DBS3, and Volcano.

8.2.2.2 Non-Uniform Memory Access (NUMA)

The objective of NUMA is to provide a shared-memory programming model and all its benefits, in a scalable architecture with distributed memory. Each processor has its own local memory module, which it can access efficiently. The term NUMA reflects the fact that accesses to the (virtually) shared-memory have a different cost depending on whether the physical memory is local or remote to the processor.

The oldest class of NUMA systems is Cache Coherent NUMA (CC-NUMA) multiprocessors (see Fig. 8.5). Since different processors can access the same data in a conflicting update mode, global cache consistency protocols are needed. In order to make remote memory access efficient, one solution is to have cache consistency done in hardware through a special consistent cache interconnect. Because shared-memory and cache consistency are supported by hardware, remote memory access is very efficient, only several times (typically up to 3 times) the cost of local access.

A more recent approach to NUMA is to exploit the Remote Direct Memory Access (RDMA) capability that is now provided by low latency cluster interconnects such as Infiniband and Myrinet. RDMA is implemented in the network card hardware and provides zero-copy networking, which allows a cluster node to directly access the memory of another node without any copying between operating system buffers. This yields typical remote memory access at latencies of the order of 10 times a local memory access. However, there is still room for improvement.

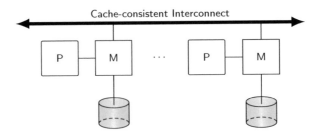

Fig. 8.5 Cache coherent non-uniform memory architecture (CC-NUMA)

For instance, the tighter integration of remote memory control into the node's local coherence hierarchy yields remote access at latencies that are within 4 times a local access. Thus, RDMA can be exploited to improve the performance of parallel database operations. However, it requires new algorithms that are NUMA aware in order to deal with the remote memory access bottleneck. The basic approach is to maximize local memory access by careful scheduling of DBMS tasks close to the data and to interleave computation and network communication.

Modern multiprocessors use a hierarchical architecture that mixes NUMA and UMA, i.e., a NUMA multiprocessor where each processor is a multicore processor. In turn, each NUMA multiprocessor can be used as a node in a cluster.

8.2.3 Shared-Disk

In a shared-disk cluster (see Fig. 8.6), any processor has access to any disk unit through the interconnect but exclusive (nonshared) access to its main memory. Each processor–memory node, which can be a shared-memory node is under the control of its own copy of the operating system. Then, each processor can access database pages on the shared-disk and cache them into its own memory. Since different processors can access the same page in conflicting update modes, global cache consistency is needed. This is typically achieved using a distributed lock manager that can be implemented using the techniques described in Chap. 5. The first parallel DBMS that used shared-disk is Oracle with an efficient implementation of a distributed lock manager for cache consistency. It has evolved to the Oracle Exadata database machine. Other major DBMS vendors such as IBM, Microsoft, and Sybase also provide shared-disk implementations, typically for OLTP workloads.

Shared-disk requires disks to be globally accessible by the cluster nodes. There are two main technologies to share disks in a cluster: network-attached storage (NAS) and storage-area network (SAN). A NAS is a dedicated device to shared-disks over a network (usually TCP/IP) using a distributed file system protocol such as Network File System (NFS). NAS is well-suited for low throughput applications such as data backup and archiving from PC's hard disks. However, it is relatively slow and not appropriate for database management as it quickly

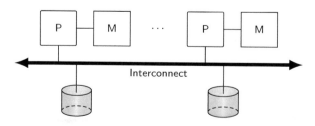

Fig. 8.6 Shared-disk architecture

becomes a bottleneck with many nodes. A storage-area network (SAN) provides similar functionality but with a lower level interface. For efficiency, it uses a block-based protocol, thus making it easier to manage cache consistency (at the block level). As a result, SAN provides high data throughput and can scale up to large numbers of nodes.

Shared-disk has three main advantages: simple and cheap administration, high availability, and good load balance. Database administrators do not need to deal with complex data partitioning, and the failure of a node only affects its cached data while the data on disk is still available to the other nodes. Furthermore, load balancing is easy as any request can be processed by any processor–memory node. The main disadvantages are cost (because of SAN) and limited scalability, which is caused by the potential bottleneck and overhead of cache coherence protocols for very large databases. A solution is to rely on data partitioning as in shared-nothing, at the expense of more complex administration.

8.2.4   Shared-Nothing

In a shared-nothing cluster (see Fig. 8.7), each processor has exclusive access to its main memory and disk, using Directly Attached Storage (DAS).

Each processor–memory–disk node is under the control of its own copy of the operating system. Shared-nothing clusters are widely used in practice, typically using NUMA nodes, because they can provide the best cost/performance ratio and scale up to very large configurations (thousands of nodes).

Each node can be viewed as a local site (with its own database and software) in a distributed DBMS. Therefore, most solutions designed for those systems such as database fragmentation, distributed transaction management, and distributed query processing may be reused. Using a fast interconnect, it is possible to accommodate large numbers of nodes. As opposed to SMP, this architecture is often called Massively Parallel Processor (MPP).

By favoring the smooth incremental growth of the system by the addition of new nodes, shared-nothing provides extensibility and scalability. However, it requires

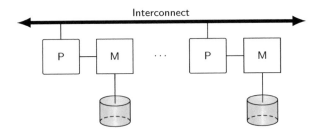

Fig. 8.7 Shared-nothing architecture

careful partitioning of the data on multiple disks. Furthermore, the addition of new nodes in the system presumably requires reorganizing and repartitioning the database to deal with the load balancing issues. Finally, node fault-tolerance is difficult (requires replication) as a failed node will make its data on disk unavailable.

Many parallel database system prototypes have adopted the shared-nothing architecture, e.g., Bubba, Gamma, Grace, and Prisma/DB. The first major parallel DBMS product was Teradata's database machine. Other major DBMS companies such as IBM, Microsoft, and Sybase and vendors of column-store DBMS such as MonetDB and Vertica provide shared-nothing implementations for high-end OLAP applications. Finally, NoSQL DBMSs and big data systems typically use shared-nothing.

Note that it is possible to have a hybrid architecture, where part of the cluster is shared-nothing, e.g., for OLAP workloads, and part is shared-disk, e.g., for OLTP workloads. For instance, Teradata supports the concept of *clique*, i.e., a set of nodes that share a common set of disks, to its shared-nothing architecture to improve availability.

8.3 Data Placement

In the rest of this chapter, we consider a shared-nothing architecture because it is the most general case and its implementation techniques also apply, sometimes in a simplified form, to the other architectures. Data placement in a parallel database system exhibits similarities with data fragmentation in distributed databases (see Chap. 2). An obvious similarity is that fragmentation can be used to increase parallelism. As noted in Chap. 2, parallel DBMSs mostly use horizontal partitioning, although vertical fragmentation can also be used to increase parallelism and load balancing much as in distributed databases and has been employed in column-store DBMSs, such as MonetDB or Vertica. Another similarity with distributed databases is that since data is much larger than programs, execution should occur, as much as possible, where the data resides. As noted in Chap. 2, there are two important differences with the distributed database approach. First, there is no need to maximize local processing (at each node) since users are not associated with particular nodes. Second, load balancing is much more difficult to achieve in the presence of a large number of nodes. The main problem is to avoid resource contention, which may result in the entire system thrashing (e.g., one node ends up doing all the work, while the others remain idle). Since programs are executed where the data resides, data placement is critical for performance.

The most common data partitioning strategies that are used in parallel DBMSs are the round-robin, hashing, and range-partitioning approaches discussed in Sect. 2.1.1. Data partitioning must scale with the increase in database size and load. Thus, the degree of partitioning, i.e., the number of nodes over which a relation is partitioned, should be a function of the size and access frequency of the relation. Therefore, increasing the degree of partitioning may result in placement reorganization. For example, a relation initially placed across eight nodes may have its cardinality doubled by subsequent insertions, in which case it should be placed across 16 nodes.

In a highly parallel system with data partitioning, periodic reorganizations for load balancing are essential and should be frequent unless the workload is fairly static and experiences only a few updates. Such reorganizations should remain transparent to compiled queries that run on the database server. In particular, queries should not be recompiled because of reorganization and should remain independent of data location, which may change rapidly. Such independence can be achieved if the runtime system supports associative access to distributed data. This is different from a distributed DBMS, where associative access is achieved at compile time by the query processor using the data directory.

One solution to associative access is to have a global index mechanism replicated on each node. The global index indicates the placement of a relation onto a set of nodes. Conceptually, the global index is a two-level index with a major clustering on the relation name and a minor clustering on some attribute of the relation. This global index supports variable partitioning, where each relation has a different degree of partitioning. The index structure can be based on hashing or on a B-tree like organization. In both cases, exact-match queries can be processed efficiently with a single node access. However, with hashing, range queries are processed by accessing all the nodes that contain data from the queried relation. Using a B-tree index (usually much larger than a hash index) enables more efficient processing of range queries, where only the nodes containing data in the specified range are accessed.

Example 8.1 Figure 8.8 provides an example of a global index and a local index for relation EMP(ENO, ENAME, TITLE) of the engineering database example we have been using in this book.

Suppose that we want to locate the elements in relation EMP with ENO value "E50." The first-level index maps the name EMP onto the index on attribute ENO

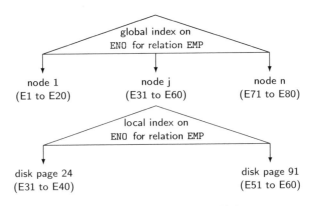

Fig. 8.8 Example of global and local indexes

for relation EMP. Then, the second-level index further maps the cluster value "E50" onto node number j. A local index within each node is also necessary to map a relation onto a set of disk pages within the node. The local index has two levels, with a major clustering on relation name and a minor clustering on some attribute. The minor clustering attribute for the local index is the *same* as that for the global index. Thus, *associative routing* is improved from one node to another based on (relation name, cluster value). This local index further maps the cluster value "E5" onto page number 91.   ♦

A serious problem in data placement is dealing with skewed data distributions that may lead to nonuniform partitioning and hurt load balancing. A solution is to treat nonuniform partitions appropriately, e.g., by further fragmenting large partitions. This is easy with range partitioning, since a partition can be split as a B-tree leaf, with some local index reorganization. With hashing, the solution is to use a different hash function on a different attribute. The separation between logical and physical nodes is useful here since a logical node may correspond to several physical nodes.

A final complicating factor for data placement is data replication for high availability, which we discussed at length in Chap. 6. In parallel DBMSs, simpler approaches might be adopted, such as the *mirrored disks* architecture where two copies of the same data are maintained: a primary and a backup copy. However, in case of a node failure, the load of the node with the copy may double, thereby hurting load balance. To avoid this problem, several high-availability data replication strategies have been proposed for parallel database systems. An interesting solution is Teradata's interleaved partitioning that further partitions the backup copy on a number of nodes. Figure 8.9 illustrates the interleaved partitioning of relation R over four nodes, where each primary copy of a partition, e.g., R_1, is further divided into three partitions, e.g., $R_{1,1}$, $R_{1,2}$, and $R_{1,3}$, each at a different backup node. In failure mode, the load of the primary copy gets balanced among the backup copy nodes. But if two nodes fail, then the relation cannot be accessed, thereby hurting availability. Reconstructing the primary copy from its separate backup copies may be costly. In normal mode, maintaining copy consistency may also be costly.

An alternative solution is Gamma's *chained partitioning*, which stores the primary and backup copy on two adjacent nodes (Fig. 8.10). The main idea is that

Node	1	2	3	4
Primary copy	R_1	R_2	R_3	R_4
Backup copies		$R_{1,1}$	$R_{1,2}$	$R_{1,3}$
	$R_{2,1}$		$R_{2,2}$	$R_{2,3}$
	$R_{3,1}$	$R_{3,2}$		$R_{3,3}$
	$R_{4,1}$	$R_{4,2}$	$R_{4,3}$	

Fig. 8.9 Example of interleaved partitioning

Node	1	2	3	4
Primary copy	R_1	R_2	R_3	R_4
Backup copy	R_4	R_1	R_2	R_3

Fig. 8.10 Example of chained partitioning

the probability that two adjacent nodes fail is much lower than the probability that any two nodes fail. In failure mode, the load of the failed node and the backup nodes is balanced among all remaining nodes by using both primary and backup copy nodes. In addition, maintaining copy consistency is cheaper. An open issue is how to perform data placement taking into account data replication. Similar to the fragment allocation in distributed databases, this should be considered an optimization problem.

8.4 Parallel Query Processing

The objective of parallel query processing is to transform queries into execution plans that can be efficiently executed in parallel. This is achieved by exploiting parallel data placement and the various forms of parallelism offered by high-level queries. In this section, we first introduce the basic parallel algorithms for data processing. Then, we discuss parallel query optimization.

8.4.1 Parallel Algorithms for Data Processing

Partitioned data placement is the basis for the parallel execution of database queries. Given a partitioned data placement, an important issue is the design of parallel algorithms for efficient processing of database operators (i.e., relational algebra operators) and database queries that combine multiple operators. This issue is difficult because a good trade-off between parallelism and communication cost must be reached since increasing parallelism involves more communication among processors.

Parallel algorithms for relational algebra operators are the building blocks necessary for parallel query processing. The objective of these algorithms is to maximize the degree of parallelism. However, according to Amdahl's law, only part of an algorithm can be parallelized. Let seq be the ratio of the sequential part of a program (a value between 0 and 1), i.e., which cannot be parallelized, and let p be the number of processors. The maximum speed-up that can be achieved is given by the following formula:

$$MaxSpeedup(seq, p) = \frac{1}{seq + \left(\frac{1-seq}{p}\right)}$$

For instance, with $seq = 0$ (the entire program is parallel) and $p = 4$, we obtain the ideal speed-up, i.e., 4. But with $seq = 0.3$, the speed-up goes down to 2.1. And even if we double the number of processors, i.e., $p = 8$, the speed-up increases only slightly to 2.5. Thus, when designing parallel algorithms for data processing, it is important to minimize the sequential part of an algorithm and to maximize the parallel part, by exploiting intraoperator parallelism.

The processing of the select operator in a partitioned data placement context is identical to that in a fragmented distributed database. Depending on the select predicate, the operator may be executed at a single node (in the case of an exact-match predicate) or, in the case of arbitrarily complex predicates, at all the nodes over which the relation is partitioned. If the global index is organized as a B-tree-like structure (see Fig. 8.8), a select operator with a range predicate may be executed only by the nodes that store relevant data. In the rest of this section, we focus on the parallel processing of the two major operators used in database queries, i.e., sort and join.

8.4.1.1 Parallel Sort Algorithms

Sorting relations is necessary for queries that require an ordered result or involve aggregation and grouping. And it is hard to do efficiently as any item needs to be compared with every other item. One of the fastest single processor sort algorithms is *quicksort* but it is highly sequential and thus, according to Amdahl's law, inappropriate for parallel adaptation. Several other centralized sort algorithms can be made parallel. One of the most popular algorithms is the parallel merge sort algorithm, because it is easy to implement and does not have strong requirements on the parallel system architecture. Thus, it has been used in both shared-disk and shared-nothing clusters. It can also be adapted to take advantage of multicore processors.

We briefly review the b-way merge sort algorithm. Let us consider a set of n elements to be sorted. A run is defined as an ordered sequence of elements; thus, the set to be sorted contains n runs of one element. The method consists of iteratively merging b runs of K elements into a sorted run of $K * b$ elements, starting with $K = 1$. For pass i, each set of b runs of b^{i-1} elements is merged into a sorted run of b^i elements. Starting from $i = 1$, the number of passes necessary to sort n elements is $log_b n$.

We now describe the application of this method in a shared-nothing cluster. We assume the popular master–worker model for executing parallel tasks, with one master node coordinating the activities of the worker nodes, by sending them tasks and data and receiving back notifications of tasks done.

Let us suppose we have to sort a relation of p disk pages partitioned over n nodes. Each node has a local memory of $b+1$ pages, where b pages are used as input pages and 1 is used as an output page. The algorithm proceeds in two stages. In the first stage, each node locally sorts its fragment, e.g., using quicksort if the node is single processor or a parallel b-way merge sort if the node is a multicore processor. This stage is called the optimal stage since all nodes are fully busy. It generates n runs of p/n pages, and if n equals b, one node can merge them in a single pass. However, n can be very much greater than b, in which case the solution is for the master node to arrange the worker nodes as a tree of order b during the last stage, called the postoptimal stage. The number of necessary nodes is divided by b at each pass. At the last pass, one node merges the entire relation. The number of passes for the postoptimal stage is $log_b p$. This stage degrades the degree of parallelism.

8.4.1.2 Parallel Join Algorithms

Assuming two arbitrary partitioned relations, there are three basic parallel algorithms to join them: the parallel merge sort join algorithm , the parallel nested loop (PNL) algorithm, and the parallel hash join (PHJ) algorithm. These algorithms are variations of their centralized counterpart. The parallel merge sort join algorithm simply sorts both relations on the join attribute using a parallel merge sort and joins them using a merge like operation done by a single node. Although the last operation is sequential, the result joined relation is sorted on the join attribute, which can be useful for the next operation.

The other two algorithms are fully parallel. We describe them in more details using a pseudoconcurrent programming language with three main constructs: parallel-do, send, and receive. Parallel-do specifies that the following block of actions is executed in parallel. For example,

```
for i from 1 to n in parallel-do action  A
```

indicates that action A is to be executed by n nodes in parallel. The send and receive constructs are basic data communication primitives: send sends data from one node to one or more nodes, while receive gets the content of the data sent at a particular node. In what follows we consider the join of two relations R and S that are partitioned over m and n nodes, respectively. For the sake of simplicity, we assume that the m nodes are distinct from the n nodes. A node at which a fragment of R (respectively, S) resides is called an R-node (respectively, S-node).

Parallel Nested Loop Join Algorithm

The parallel nested loop algorithm is simple and general. It implements the fragment-and-replicate method described in Sect. 4.5.1. It basically composes the

---

Algorithm 8.1: Parallel Nested Loop (PNL)

Input: $R_1, R_2, \ldots, R_m$: fragments of relation R
$S_1, S_2, \ldots, S_n$: fragments of relation S ;
JP: join predicate
Output: $T_1, T_2, \ldots, T_n$: result fragments
begin
    for i *from* 1 *to m in parallel* **do**   {send R entirely to each S-node}
    | send R_i to each node containing a fragment of S
    end for
    for j *from* 1 *to n in parallel* **do**   {perform the join at each S-node}
    | $R \leftarrow \bigcup_{i=1}^{m} R_i$;   {$R_i$ from R-nodes; R is fully replicated at S-nodes}
    | $T_j \leftarrow R \bowtie_{JP} S_j$
    end for
end

Cartesian product of relations R and S in parallel. Therefore, arbitrarily complex join predicates, not only equijoin, may be supported.

The algorithm performs two nested loops. One relation is chosen as the inner relation, to be accessed in the inner loop, and the other relation as the outer relation, to be accessed in the outer loop. This choice depends on a cost function with two main parameters: relation sizes, which impacts communication cost, and presence of indexes on join attributes, which impacts local join processing cost.

This algorithm is described in Algorithm 8.1, where the join result is produced at the S-nodes, i.e., S is chosen as inner relation. The algorithm proceeds in two phases.

In the first phase, each fragment of R is sent and replicated at each node that contains a fragment of S (there are n such nodes). This phase is done in parallel by m nodes; thus, $(m * n)$ messages are necessary.

In the second phase, each S-node j receives relation R entirely, and locally joins R with fragment S_j. This phase is done in parallel by n nodes. The local join can be done as in a centralized DBMS. Depending on the local join algorithm, join processing may or may not start as soon as data is received. If a nested loop join algorithm, possibly with an index on the join attribute of S , is used, join processing can be done in a pipelined fashion as soon as a tuple of R arrives. If, on the other hand, a sort-merge join algorithm is used, all the data must have been received before the join of the sorted relations begins.

To summarize, the parallel nested loop algorithm can be viewed as replacing the operator R $\bowtie$ S by $\bigcup_{i=1}^{n}(R \bowtie S_i)$.

Example 8.2 Figure 8.11 shows the application of the parallel nested loop algorithm with $m = n = 2$.   ◆

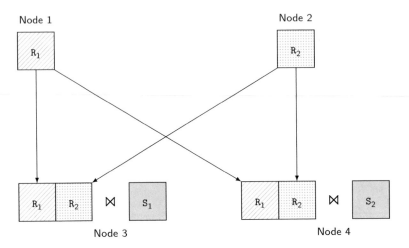

Fig. 8.11 Example of parallel nested loop

Parallel Hash Join Algorithm

The parallel hash join algorithm shown in Algorithm 8.2 applies only in the case of equijoin and does not require any particular partitioning of the operand relations. It has been first proposed for the Grace database machine, and is known as the Grace hash join.

The basic idea is to partition relations R and S into the same number p of mutually exclusive sets (fragments) $R_1, R_2, \ldots, R_p$, and $S_1, S_2, \ldots, S_p$, such that

$$R \bowtie S = \bigcup_{i=1}^{p} (R_i \bowtie S_i)$$

The partitioning of R and S is based on the same hash function applied to the join attribute. Each individual join $(R_i \bowtie S_i)$ is done in parallel, and the join result is produced at p nodes. These p nodes may actually be selected at runtime based on the load of the system.

The algorithm can be divided into two main phases, a *build* phase and a *probe* phase. The build phase hashes R used as inner relation, on the join attribute, sends it to the target p nodes that build a hash table for the incoming tuples. The probe phase sends S, the outer relation, associatively to the target p nodes that probe the hash table for each incoming tuple. Thus, as soon as the hash tables have been built for R the S tuples can be sent and processed in pipeline by probing the hash tables.

Example 8.3 Figure 8.12 shows the application of the parallel hash join algorithm with $m = n = 2$. We assume that the result is produced at nodes 1 and 2. Therefore, an arrow from node 1 to node 1 or node 2 to node 2 indicates a local transfer.   ◆

Algorithm 8.2: Parallel Hash Join (PHJ)

Input: $R_1, R_2, \ldots, R_m$: fragments of relation R ;
$S_1, S_2, \ldots, S_n$: fragments of relation S ;
JP: join predicate $R.A = S.B$;
h: hash function that returns an element of $[1, p]$
Output: $T_1, T_2, \ldots, T_p$: result fragments
begin
    {Build phase}
    for i *from* 1 *to* m *in parallel* **do**
        $R_i^j \leftarrow$ apply $h(A)$ to R_i $(j = 1, \ldots, p)$;   {hash R on A)}
        send R_i^j to node j
    end for
    for j *from* 1 *to* p *in parallel* **do**
        $R_j \leftarrow \bigcup_{i=1}^{m} R_j^i$ {receive R_j fragments from R-nodes}
        build local hash table for R_j
    end for
    {Probe phase}
    for i *from* 1 *to* n *in parallel* **do**
        $S_i^j \leftarrow$ apply $h(B)$ to S_i $(j = 1, \ldots, p)$;   {hash S on B)}
        send S_i^j to node j
    end for
    for j *from* 1 *to* p *in parallel* **do**
        $S_j \leftarrow \bigcup_{i=1}^{n} S_j^i$;   {receive S_j fragments from S-nodes}
        $T_j \leftarrow R_j \bowtie_{JP} S_j$ {probe S_j for each tuple of R_j}
    end for
end

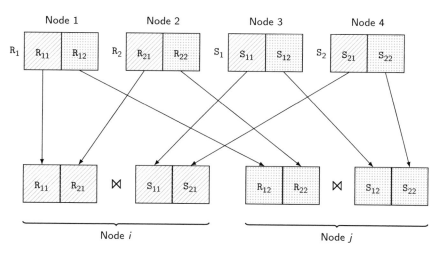

Fig. 8.12 Example of parallel hash join

The parallel hash join algorithm is usually much more efficient than the parallel nested loop join algorithm, since it requires less data transfer and less local join processing in the probe phase. Furthermore, one relation, say R may already be partitioned by hashing on the join attribute. In this case, no build phase is needed and the S fragments are simply sent associatively to corresponding R nodes. It is also generally more efficient than the parallel sort-merge join algorithm. However, this later algorithm is still useful as it produces a result relation sorted on the join attribute.

The problem with the parallel hash join algorithm and its many variants is that the data distribution on the join attribute may be skewed, thus leading to load unbalancing. We discuss solutions to this problem in Sect. 8.5.2.

Variants

The basic parallel join algorithms have been used in many variants, in particular to deal with adaptive query processing or exploit main memories and multicore processors. We discuss these extensions below.

When considering adaptive query processing (see Sect. 4.6), the challenge is to dynamically order pipelined join operators at runtime, while tuples from different relations are flowing in. Ideally, when a tuple of a relation participating in a join arrives, it should be sent to a join operator to be processed on the fly. However, most join algorithms cannot process some incoming tuples on the fly because they are asymmetric with respect to the way inner and outer tuples are processed. Consider PHJ, for instance: the inner relation is fully read during the build phase to construct a hash table, whereas tuples in the outer relation can be pipelined during the probe phase. Thus, an incoming inner tuple cannot be processed on the fly as it must be stored in the hash table and the processing will be possible only when the entire hash table is built. Similarly, the nested loop join algorithm is asymmetric as only the inner relation must be read entirely for each tuple of the outer relation. Join algorithms with some kind of asymmetry offer little opportunity for alternating input relations between inner and outer roles. Thus, to relax the order in which join inputs are consumed, symmetric join algorithms are needed, whereby the role played by the relations in a join may change without producing incorrect results.

The earlier example of symmetric join algorithm is the symmetric hash join, which uses two hash tables, one for each input relation. The traditional build and probe phases of the basic hash join algorithm are simply interleaved. When a tuple arrives, it is used to probe the hash table corresponding to the other relation and find matching tuples. Then, it is inserted in its corresponding hash table so that tuples of the other relation arriving later can be joined. Thus, each arriving tuple can be processed on the fly. Another popular symmetric join algorithm is the ripple join, which is a generalization of the nested loop join algorithm where the roles of inner and outer relation continually alternate during query execution. The main idea is to keep the probing state of each input relation, with a pointer that indicates the last tuple used to probe the other relation. At each toggling point, a change of roles between inner and outer relations occurs. At this point, the new outer relation starts to probe the inner input from its pointer position onwards, to a specified number of tuples. The inner relation, in turn, is scanned from its first tuple to its pointer position minus 1. The number of tuples processed at each stage in the outer relation gives the toggling rate and can be adaptively monitored.

Exploiting processors' main memories is also important for the performance of parallel join algorithms. The hybrid hash join algorithm improves on the Grace hash join by exploiting the available memory to hold an entire partition (called partition 0) during partitioning, thus avoiding disk accesses. Another variation is to modify the built phase so that the resulting hash tables fit into the processor's main memory. This improves performance significantly as the number of cache misses while probing the hash table is reduced. The same idea is used in the radix hash join algorithm for multicore processors, where access to a core's memory is much faster than access to the remote shared-memory. A multipass partitioning scheme is used to divide both input relations into disjoint partitions based on the join attribute, so they fit into the cores' memories. Then, hash tables are built over each partition of the inner relation and probed using the data from the corresponding partition of the outer relation. The parallel merge sort join, which is generally considered inferior to the parallel hash join can also be optimized for multicore processors.

8.4.2 Parallel Query Optimization

Parallel query optimization exhibits similarities with distributed query processing. However, it focuses much more on taking advantage of both intraoperator parallelism (using the algorithms described above) and interoperator parallelism. As any query optimizer, a parallel query optimizer has three components: a search space, a cost model, and a search strategy. In this section, we describe the parallel techniques for these components.

8.4.2.1 Search Space

Execution plans are abstracted by means of operator trees, which define the order in which the operators are executed. Operator trees are enriched with *annotations*, which indicate additional execution aspects, such as the algorithm of each operator. In a parallel DBMS, an important execution aspect to be reflected by annotations is the fact that two subsequent operators can be executed in *pipeline*. In this case, the second operator can start before the first one is completed. In other words, the second operator starts *consuming* tuples as soon as the first one *produces* them. Pipelined executions do not require temporary relations to be materialized, i.e., a tree node corresponding to an operator executed in pipeline is not *stored*.

Some operators and some algorithms require that one operand be stored. For example, in PHJ (Algorithm 8.2), in the build phase, a hash table is constructed in

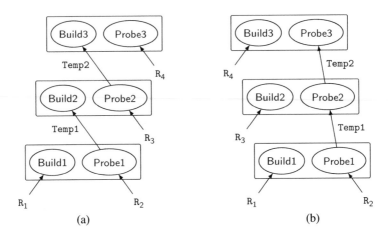

Fig. 8.13 Two hash join trees with a different scheduling. (**a**) No pipeline. (**b**) Pipeline of R_2, `Temp1`, and `Temp2`

parallel on the join attribute of the smallest relation. In the probe phase, the largest relation is sequentially scanned and the hash table is consulted for each of its tuples. Therefore, pipeline and stored annotations constrain the *scheduling* of execution plans by splitting an operator tree into nonoverlapping subtrees, corresponding to execution phases. Pipelined operators are executed in the same phase, usually called *pipeline chain*, whereas a storing indication establishes the boundary between one phase and a subsequent phase.

Example 8.4 Figure 8.13 shows two execution trees, one with no pipeline (Fig. 8.13a) and one with pipeline (Fig. 8.13b). In Fig. 8.13a, the temporary relation `Temp1` must be completely produced and the hash table in Build2 must be built before Probe2 can start consuming R_3. The same is true for `Temp2`, Build3, and Probe3. Thus, the tree is executed in four consecutive phases: (1) build R_1's hash table, (2) probe it with R_2 and build `Temp1`'s hash table, (3) probe it with R_3 and build `Temp2`'s hash table, (4) probe it with R_3 and produce the result. Figure 8.13b shows a pipeline execution. The tree can be executed in two phases if enough memory is available to build the hash tables: (1) build the tables for R_1 R_3 and R_4, (2) execute Probe1, Probe2, and Probe3 in pipeline.   ◆

The set of nodes where a relation is stored is called its *home*. The *home of an operator* is the set of nodes where it is executed and it must be the home of its operands in order for the operator to access its operand. For binary operators such as join, this might imply repartitioning one of the operands. The optimizer might even sometimes find that repartitioning both the operands is of interest. Operator trees bear execution annotations to indicate repartitioning.

Figure 8.14 shows four operator trees that represent execution plans for a three-way join. Operator trees may be *linear*, i.e., at least one operand of each join node is a base relation or *bushy*. It is convenient to represent pipelined relations as the

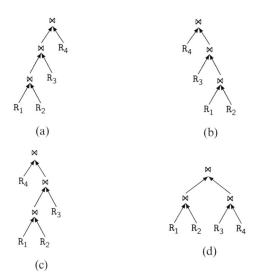

Fig. 8.14 Execution plans as operator trees. (**a**) Left deep. (**b**) Right deep. (**c**) Zigzag. (**d**) Bushy

right-hand side input of an operator. Thus, right-deep trees express full pipelining, while left-deep trees express full materialization of all intermediate results. Thus, assuming enough memory to hold the left-hand side relations, long right-deep trees are more efficient then corresponding left-deep trees. In a left-deep tree such as that of Fig. 8.14a, only the last operator can consume its right input relation in pipeline provided that the left input relation can be entirely stored in main memory.

Parallel tree formats other than left or right deep are also interesting. For example, bushy trees (Fig. 8.14d) are the only ones to allow independent parallelism and some pipeline parallelism. Independent parallelism is useful when the relations are partitioned on disjoint homes. Suppose that the relations in Fig. 8.14d are partitioned such that R_1 and R_2 have the same home h_1 and R_3 and R_4 have the same home h_2 that is different than h_1. Then, the two joins of the base relations could be independently executed in parallel by the set of nodes that constitutes h_1 and h_2.

When pipeline parallelism is beneficial, *zigzag trees*, which are intermediate formats between left-deep and right-deep trees, can sometimes outperform right-deep trees due to a better use of main memory. A reasonable heuristic is to favor right-deep or zigzag trees when relations are partially fragmented on disjoint homes and intermediate relations are rather large. In this case, bushy trees will usually need more phases and take longer to execute. On the contrary, when intermediate relations are small, pipelining is not very efficient because it is difficult to balance the load between the pipeline stages.

With the operator trees above, operators must capture parallelism, which requires repartitioning input relations. This is exemplified in the PHJ algorithm (see Sect. 8.4.1.2), where input relations are partitioned based on the same hash function applied to the join attribute, followed by a parallel join on local partitions.

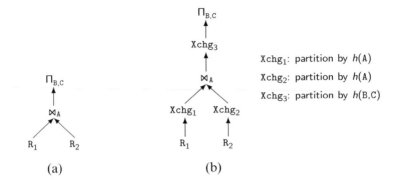

Fig. 8.15 Operator tree with exchange operators. (**a**) Sequential operator tree. (**b**) Parallel operator tree

To ease navigation in the search space by the optimizer, data repartitioning can be encapsulated in an *exchange operator*. Depending on how partitioning is done, we can have different exchange operators such as hashed partitioning, range partitioning, or replicating data to a number of nodes. Examples of uses of exchange operators are:

- Parallel hash join: hashed partitioning of the input relations on join attribute followed by local join;
- Parallel nested loop join: replicating the inner relation on the nodes where the outer relation is partitioned, followed by local join;
- Parallel range sort: range partitioning followed by local sort.

Figure 8.15 shows an example of operator tree with exchange operators. The join operation is done by hashed partitioning of the input relations on A (operators Xchg₁ and Xchg₂) followed by local join. The project operations are done by duplicate elimination by hashing (operator Xchg₃), followed by local project.

8.4.2.2   Cost Model

Recall that the optimizer cost model is responsible for estimating the cost of a given execution plan. It consists of two parts: architecture-dependent and architecture-independent. The architecture-independent part is constituted by the cost functions for operator algorithms, e.g., nested loop for join and sequential access for select. If we ignore concurrency issues, only the cost functions for data repartitioning and memory consumption differ and constitute the architecture-dependent part. Indeed, repartitioning a relation's tuples in a shared-nothing system implies transfers of data across the interconnect, whereas it reduces to hashing in shared-memory systems. Memory consumption in the shared-nothing case is complicated by interoperator parallelism. In shared-memory systems, all operators read and write data through a global memory, and it is easy to test whether there is enough space to execute them in parallel, i.e., the sum of the memory consumption of individual operators is less than the available memory. In shared-nothing, each processor has its own memory, and it becomes important to know which operators are executed in parallel on the same processor. Thus, for simplicity, we can assume that the set of processors (home) assigned to operators do not overlap, i.e., either the intersection of the set of processors is empty or the sets are identical.

The total time of a plan can be computed by a formula that simply adds all CPU, I/O, and communication cost components as in distributed query optimization. The response time is more involved as it must take pipelining into account.

The response time of plan p, scheduled in phases (each denoted by ph), is computed as follows:

$$RT(p) = \sum_{ph \in p} (max_{Op \in ph}(respTime(Op) + pipe\_delay(Op))$$

$$+ store\_delay(ph))$$

where Op denotes an operator, $respTime(Op)$ is the response time of Op, $pipe\_delay(Op)$ is the waiting period of Op necessary for the producer to deliver the first result tuples (it is equal to 0 if the input relations of Op are stored), $store\_delay(ph)$ is the time necessary to store the output result of phase ph (it is equal to 0 if ph is the last phase, assuming that the results are delivered as soon as they are produced).

To estimate the cost of an execution plan, the cost model uses database statistics and organization information, such as relation cardinalities and partitioning, as with distributed query optimization.

8.4.2.3 Search Strategy

The search strategy does not need to be different from either centralized or distributed query optimization. However, the search space tends to be much larger because there are more parameters that impact parallel execution plans, in particular, pipeline and store annotations. Thus, randomized search strategies such as Iterative Improvement and Simulated Annealing generally outperform traditional deterministic search strategies in parallel query optimization. Another interesting, yet simple approach to reduce the search space is the two phase optimization strategy proposed for XPRS, a shared-memory parallel DBMS. First, at compile time, the optimal query plan based on a centralized cost model is produced. Then, at execution time, runtime parameters such as available buffer size and number of free processors are considered to parallelize the query plan. This approach is shown to almost always produce optimal plans.

8.5   Load Balancing

Good load balancing is crucial for the performance of a parallel system. The response time of a set of parallel operators is that of the longest one. Thus, minimizing the time of the longest one is important for minimizing response time. Balancing the load of different nodes is also essential to maximize throughput. Although the parallel query optimizer incorporates decisions on how to execute a parallel execution plan, load balancing can be hurt by several problems incurring at execution time. Solutions to these problems can be obtained at the intra and interoperator levels. In this section, we discuss these parallel execution problems and their solutions.

8.5.1   Parallel Execution Problems

The principal problems introduced by parallel query execution are initialization, interference, and skew.

Initialization

Before the execution takes place, an initialization step is necessary. This step is generally sequential and includes task (or thread) creation and initialization, communication initialization, etc. The duration of this step is proportional to the degree of parallelism and can actually dominate the execution time of simple queries, e.g., a select query on a single relation. Thus, the degree of parallelism should be fixed according to query complexity.

A formula can be developed to estimate the maximal speed-up reachable during the execution of an operator and to deduce the optimal number of processors. Let us consider the execution of an operator that processes N tuples with n processors. Let c be the average processing time of each tuple and a the initialization time per processor. In the ideal case, the response time of the operator execution is

$$ResponseTime = (a * n) + \frac{c * N}{n}$$

By derivation, we can obtain the optimal number of processors n_{opt} to allocate and the maximal achievable speed-up ($Speed_{max}$).

$$n_{opt} = \sqrt{\frac{c * N}{a}} \qquad Speed_{max} = \frac{n_{opt}}{2}$$

The optimal number of processors (n_{opt}) is independent of n and only depends on the total processing time and initialization time. Thus, maximizing the degree of parallelism for an operator, e.g., using all available processors, can hurt speed-up because of the overhead of initialization.

Interference

A highly parallel execution can be slowed down by *interference*. Interference occurs when several processors simultaneously access the same resource, hardware, or software. A typical example of hardware interference is the contention created on the interconnect of a shared-memory system. When the number of processors is increased, the number of conflicts on the interconnect increases, thus limiting the extensibility of shared-memory systems. A solution to these interferences is to duplicate shared resources. For instance, disk access interference can be eliminated by adding several disks and partitioning the relations.

Software interference occurs when several processors want to access shared data. To prevent incoherence, mutual exclusion variables are used to protect shared data, thus blocking all but one processor that accesses the shared data. This is similar to the locking-based concurrency control algorithms (see Chap. 5). However, shared variables may well become the bottleneck of query execution, creating hot spots. A typical example of software interference is the access of database internal structures such as indexes and buffers. For simplicity, the earlier versions of database systems were protected by a unique mutual exclusion variable, which incurred much overhead.

A general solution to software interference is to partition the shared resource into several independent resources, each protected by a different mutual exclusion variable. Thus, two independent resources can be accessed in parallel, which reduces the probability of interference. To further reduce interference on an independent resource (e.g., an index structure), replication can be used. Thus, access to replicated resources can also be parallelized.

Skew

Load balancing problems can arise with intraoperator parallelism (variation in partition size), namely *data skew*, and interoperator parallelism (variation in the complexity of operators).

The effects of skewed data distribution on a parallel execution can be classified as follows: *Attribute value skew (AVS)* is skew inherent in the data (e.g., there are more citizens in Paris than in Waterloo), while *tuple placement skew (TPS)* is the skew introduced when the data is initially partitioned (e.g., with range partitioning). *Selectivity skew (SS)* is introduced when there is variation in the selectivity of select predicates on each node. *Redistribution skew (RS)* occurs in the redistribution step between two operators. It is similar to TPS. Finally *join product skew (JPS)* occurs because the join selectivity may vary between nodes. Figure 8.16 illustrates this classification on a query over two relations R and S that are poorly partitioned.

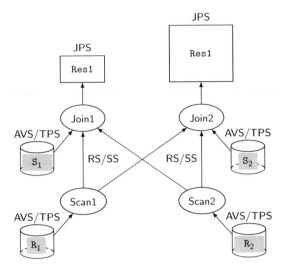

Fig. 8.16 Data skew example

The boxes are proportional to the size of the corresponding partitions. Such poor partitioning stems from either the data (AVS) or the partitioning function (TPS). Thus, the processing times of the two instances Scan1 and Scan2 are not equal. The case of the join operator is worse. First, the number of tuples received is different from one instance to another because of poor redistribution of the partitions of R (RS) or variable selectivity according to the partition of R processed (SS). Finally, the uneven size of S partitions (AVS/TPS) yields different processing times for tuples sent by the scan operator and the result size is different from one partition to the other due to join selectivity (JPS).

8.5.2 Intraoperator Load Balancing

Good intraoperator load balancing depends on the degree of parallelism and the allocation of processors for the operator. For some algorithms, e.g., PHJ, these parameters are not constrained by the placement of the data. Thus, the home of the operator (the set of processors where it is executed) must be carefully decided. The skew problem makes it hard for the parallel query optimizer to make this decision statically (at compile time) as it would require a very accurate and detailed cost model. Therefore, the main solutions rely on adaptive or specialized techniques that can be incorporated in a hybrid query optimizer. We describe below these techniques in the context of parallel join processing, which has received much attention. For simplicity, we assume that each operator is given a home as decided by the query processor (either statically or just before execution).

Adaptive Techniques

The main idea is to statically decide on an initial allocation of the processors to the operator (using a cost model) and, at execution time, adapt to skew using load reallocation. A simple approach to load reallocation is to detect the oversized partitions and partition them again onto several processors (among the processors already allocated to the operation) to increase parallelism. This approach is generalized to allow for more dynamic adjustment of the degree of parallelism. It uses specific *control operators* in the execution plan to detect whether the static estimates for intermediate result sizes will differ from the runtime values. During execution, if the difference between the estimate and the real value is sufficiently high, the control operator performs relation redistribution in order to prevent join product skew and redistribution skew. Adaptive techniques are useful to improve intraoperator load balancing in all kinds of parallel architectures. However, most of the work has been done in the context of shared-nothing where the effects of load unbalance are more severe on performance. DBS3 has pioneered the use of an adaptive technique based on relation partitioning (as in shared-nothing) for shared-memory. By reducing processor interference, this technique yields excellent load balancing for intraoperator parallelism.

Specialized Techniques

Parallel join algorithms can be specialized to deal with skew. One approach is to use multiple join algorithms, each specialized for a different degree of skew, and to determine, at execution time, which algorithm is best. It relies on two main techniques: range partitioning and sampling. Range partitioning is used instead of hash partitioning (in the parallel hash join algorithm) to avoid redistribution skew of the building relation. Thus, processors can get partitions of equal numbers of tuples, corresponding to different ranges of join attribute values. To determine the values that delineate the range values, sampling of the building relation is used to produce a histogram of the join attribute values, i.e., the numbers of tuples for each attribute value. Sampling is also useful to determine which algorithm to use and which relation to use for building or probing. Using these techniques, the parallel hash join algorithm can be adapted to deal with skew as follows:

1. Sample the building relation to determine the partitioning ranges.
2. Redistribute the building relation to the processors using the ranges. Each processor builds a hash table containing the incoming tuples.
3. Redistribute the probing relation using the same ranges to the processors. For each tuple received, each processor probes the hash table to perform the join.

This algorithm can be further improved to deal with high skew using additional techniques and different processor allocation strategies. A similar approach is to modify the join algorithms by inserting a scheduling step that is in charge of redistributing the load at runtime.

8.5.3   Interoperator Load Balancing

In order to obtain good load balancing at the interoperator level, it is necessary to choose, for each operator, how many and which processors to assign for its execution. This should be done taking into account pipeline parallelism, which requires interoperator communication. This is harder to achieve in shared-nothing for the following reasons: First, the degree of parallelism and the allocation of processors to operators, when decided in the parallel optimization phase, are based on a possibly inaccurate cost model. Second, the choice of the degree of parallelism is subject to errors because both processors and operators are discrete entities. Finally, the processors associated with the latest operators in a pipeline chain may remain idle a significant time. This is called the pipeline delay problem.

The main approach in shared-nothing is to determine dynamically (just before the execution) the degree of parallelism and the localization of the processors for each operator. For instance, the rate match algorithm uses a cost model in order to match the rate at which tuples are produced and consumed. It is the basis for choosing the set of processors that will be used for query execution (based on available memory, CPU, and disk utilization). Many other algorithms are possible for the choice of the number and localization of processors, for instance, by maximizing the use of several resources, using statistics on their usage.

In shared-disk and shared-memory, there is more flexibility since all processors have equal access to the disks. Since there is no need for physical relation partitioning, any processor can be allocated to any operator. In particular, a processor can be allocated all the operators in the same pipeline chain, thus, with no interoperator parallelism. However, interoperator parallelism is useful for executing independent pipeline chains. The approach proposed in XPRS for shared-memory allows the parallel execution of independent pipeline chains, called tasks. The main idea is to combine I/O-bound and CPU-bound tasks to increase system resource utilization. Before execution, a task is classified as I/O-bound or CPU-bound using cost model information as follows. Let us suppose that, if executed sequentially, task t generates disk accesses at rate $IO_{rate}(t)$, e.g., in numbers of disk accesses per second. Let us consider a shared-memory system with n processors and a total disk bandwidth of B (numbers of disk accesses per second). Task t is defined as I/O-bound if $IO_{rate}(t) > B/n$ and CPU-bound otherwise. CPU-bound and I/O-bound talks can then be run in parallel at their optimal I/O-CPU balance point. This is accomplished by dynamically adjusting the degree of intraoperator parallelism of the tasks in order to reach maximum resource utilization.

8.5.4   Intraquery Load Balancing

Intraquery load balancing must combine intra and interoperator parallelism. To some extent, given a parallel architecture, the techniques for either intra or interoperator load balancing we just presented can be combined. However, in shared-nothing clusters with shared-memory nodes (or multicore processors), the

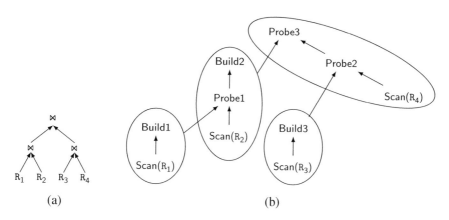

Fig. 8.17 A join tree and associated operator tree. (**a**) Join tree. (**b**) Operator tree (ellipses are pipeline chains)

problems of load balancing are exacerbated because they must be addressed at two levels, locally among the processors or cores of each shared-memory node (SM-node) and globally among all nodes. None of the approaches for intra and interoperator load balancing just discussed can be easily extended to deal with this problem. Load balancing strategies for shared-nothing would experience even more severe problems worsening (e.g., complexity and inaccuracy of the cost model). On the other hand, adapting dynamic solutions developed for shared-memory systems would incur high communication overhead.

A general solution to load balancing is the execution model called *Dynamic Processing (DP)*. The fundamental idea is that the query is decomposed into self-contained units of sequential processing, each of which can be carried out by any processor. Intuitively, a processor can migrate horizontally (intraoperator parallelism) and vertically (interoperator parallelism) along the query operators. This minimizes the communication overhead of internode load balancing by maximizing intra and interoperator load balancing within shared-memory nodes. The input to the execution model is a parallel execution plan as produced by the optimizer, i.e., an operator tree with operator scheduling and allocation of computing resources to operators. The operator scheduling constraints express a partial order among the operators of the query: $Op_1 \prec Op_2$ indicates that operator Op_1 cannot start before operator Op_2.

Example 8.5 Figure 8.17 shows a join tree with four relations R_1, R_2, R_3, and R_4, and the corresponding operator tree with the pipeline chains clearly identified. Assuming that parallel hash join is used, the operator scheduling constraints are between the associated build and probe operators:

  Build1 $\prec$ Probe1
  Build2 $\prec$ Probe3
  Build3 $\prec$ Probe2

There are also scheduling heuristics between operators of different pipeline chains that follow from the scheduling constraints :

Heuristic1: Build1 $\prec$ Scan(R_2) Build3 $\prec$ Scan(R_4), Build2 $\prec$ Scan(R_3)
Heuristic2: Build2 $\prec$ Scan(R_3)

Assuming three SM-nodes i, j, and k with R_1 stored at node i, R_2 and R_3 at node j, and R_4 at node k, we can have the following operator homes:

home (Scan(R_1)) = i
home (Build1, Probe1, Scan(R_2), Scan(R_3)) = j
home (Scan(R_4)) = k
home (Build2, Build3, Probe2, Probe3) = j and k

$\blacklozenge$

Given such an operator tree, the problem is to produce an execution that minimizes response time. This can be done by using a dynamic load balancing mechanism at two levels: (i) within an SM-node, load balancing is achieved via fast interprocess communication; (ii) between SM-nodes, more expensive message-passing communication is needed. Thus, the problem is to come up with an execution model so that the use of local load balancing is maximized, while the use of global load balancing (through message passing) is minimized.

We call *activation* the smallest unit of sequential processing that cannot be further partitioned. The main property of the DP model is to allow any processor to process any activation of its SM-node. Thus, there is no static association between threads and operators. This yields good load balancing for both intraoperator and interoperator parallelism within an SM-node, and thus reduces to the minimum the need for global load balancing, i.e., when there is no more work to do in an SM-node.

The DP execution model is based on a few concepts: activations, activation queues, and threads.

Activations

An activation represents a sequential unit of work. Since any activation can be executed by any thread (by any processor), activations must be self-contained and reference all information necessary for their execution: the code to execute and the data to process. Two kinds of activations can be distinguished: trigger activations and data activations. A *trigger activation* is used to start the execution of a leaf operator, i.e., scan. It is represented by an ($Operator, Partition$) pair that references the scan operator and the base relation partition to scan. A *data activation* describes a tuple produced in pipeline mode. It is represented by an ($Operator, Tuple, Partition$) triple that references the operator to process. For a build operator, the data activation specifies that the tuple must be inserted in the hash table of the bucket and for a probe operator, that the tuple must be probed with the partition's hash table. Although activations are self-contained, they can only be executed on the SM-node where the associated data (hash tables or base relations) are.

Activation Queues

Moving data activations along pipeline chains is done using *activation queues* associated with operators. If the producer and consumer of an activation are on the same SM-node, then the move is done via shared-memory. Otherwise, it requires message passing. To unify the execution model, queues are used for trigger activations (inputs for scan operators) as well as tuple activations (inputs for build or probe operators). All threads have unrestricted access to all queues located on their SM-node. Managing a small number of queues (e.g., one for each operator) may yield interference. To reduce interference, one queue is associated with each thread working on an operator. Note that a higher number of queues would likely trade interference for queue management overhead. To further reduce interference without increasing the number of queues, each thread is given priority access to a distinct set of queues, called its primary queues. Thus, a thread always tries to first consume activations in its *primary queues*. During execution, operator scheduling constraints may imply that an operator is to be blocked until the end of some other operators (the blocking operators). Therefore, a queue for a blocked operator is also blocked, i.e., its activations cannot be consumed but they can still be produced if the producing operator is not blocked. When all its blocking operators terminate, the blocked queue becomes consumable, i.e., threads can consume its activations. This is illustrated in Fig. 8.18 with an execution snapshot for the operator tree of Fig. 8.17.

Threads

A simple strategy for obtaining good load balancing inside an SM-node is to allocate a number of threads that is much higher than the number of processors and let the operating system do thread scheduling. However, this strategy incurs high numbers of system calls due to thread scheduling and interference. Instead of relying on the operating system for load balancing, it is possible to allocate only one thread per processor per query. This is made possible by the fact that any thread can execute any operator assigned to its SM-node. The advantage of this one thread per processor allocation strategy is to significantly reduce the overhead of interference and synchronization, provided that a thread is never blocked.

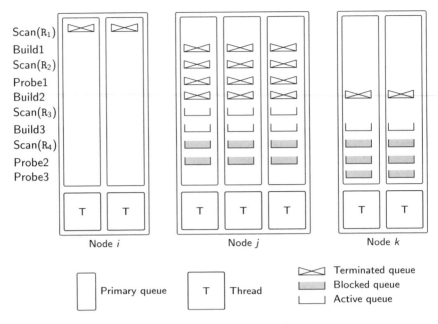

Fig. 8.18 Snapshot of an execution

Load balancing within an SM-node is obtained by allocating all activation queues in a segment of shared-memory and by allowing all threads to consume activations in any queue. To limit thread interference, a thread will consume as much as possible from its set of primary queues before considering the other queues of the SM-node. Therefore, a thread becomes idle only when there is no more activation of any operator, which means that there is no more work to do on its SM-node that is starving.

When an SM-node starves, we share the load of another SM-node by acquiring some of its workload. However, acquiring activations (through message passing) incurs communication overhead. Furthermore, activation acquisition is not sufficient since associated data, i.e., hash tables, must also be acquired. Thus, the benefit of acquiring activations and data should be dynamically estimated.

The amount of load balancing depends on the number of operators that are concurrently executed, which provides opportunities for finding some work to share in case of idle times. Increasing the number of concurrent operators can be done by allowing concurrent execution of several pipeline chains or by using nonblocking hash join algorithms, which allows the concurrent execution of all the operators of the bushy tree. On the other hand, executing more operators concurrently can increase memory consumption. Static operator scheduling as provided by the optimizer should avoid memory overflow and solve this trade-off.

8.6   Fault-Tolerance

In this section, we discuss what happens in the advent of failures. There are several issues raised by failures. The first is how to maintain consistency despite failures. Second, for outstanding transactions, there is the issue of how to perform failover. Third, when a failed replica is reintroduced (following recovery), or a fresh replica is introduced in the system, the current state of the database needs to be recovered. The main concern is how to cope with failures. To start with, failures need to be detected. In group communication based approaches (see Chap. 6), failure detection is provided by the underlying group communication (typically based on some kind of heartbeat mechanism). Membership changes are notified as events.[1] By comparing the new membership with the previous one, it becomes possible to learn which replicas have failed. Group communication also guarantees that all the connected replicas share the same membership notion. For approaches that are not based on group communication failure detection can be either delegated to the underlying communication layer (e.g., TCP/IP) or implemented as an additional component of the replication logic. However, some agreement protocol is needed to ensure that all connected replicas share the same membership notion of which replicas are operational and which ones are not. Otherwise, inconsistencies can arise.

Failures should also be detected at the client side by the client API. Clients typically connect through TCP/IP and can suspect of failed nodes via broken connections. Upon a replica failure, the client API must discover a new replica, reestablish a new connection to it, and, in the simplest case, retransmit the last outstanding transaction to the just connected replica. Since retransmissions are needed, duplicate transactions might be delivered. This requires a duplicate transaction detection and removal mechanism. In most cases, it is sufficient to have a unique client identifier, and a unique transaction identifier per client. The latter is incremented for each new submitted transaction. Thus, the cluster can track whether a client transaction has already been processed and if so, discard it.

Once a replica failure has been detected, several actions should be taken. These actions are part of the failover process, which must redirect the transactions from a failed node to another replica node, in a way that is as transparent as possible for the clients. Failover highly depends on whether or not the failed replica was a master. If a nonmaster replica fails, no action needs to be taken on the cluster side. Clients with outstanding transactions connect to a new replica node and resubmit the last transactions. However, the interesting question is which consistency definition is provided. Recall from Sect. 6.1 that, in a replicated database, one-copy serializabil-itycan be violated as a result of serializing transactions at different nodes in reverse order. Due to failover, the transactions may also be processed in such a way that one-copy serializability is compromised.

---

[1]Group communication literature uses the term *view change* to denote the event of a membership change. Here, we will not use the term to avoid confusion with the database *view* concept.

In most replication approaches, failover is handled by aborting all ongoing transactions to prevent these situations. However, this way of handling failures has an impact on clients that must resubmit the aborted transactions. Since clients typically do not have transactional capabilities to undo the results of a conversational interaction, this can be very complex. The concept of *highly available transactions* makes failures totally transparent to clients so they do not observe transaction aborts due to failures.

The actions to be taken in the case of a master replica failure are more involved as a new master should be appointed to take over the failed master. The appointment of a new master should be agreed upon by all the replicas in the cluster. In group-based replication, thanks to the membership change notification, it is enough to apply a deterministic function over the new membership to assign masters (all nodes receive exactly the same list of up and connected nodes).

Another essential aspect of fault-tolerance is recovery after failure. High availability requires to tolerate failures and continue to provide consistent access to data despite failures. However, failures diminish the degree of redundancy in the system, thereby degrading availability and performance. Hence, it is necessary to reintroduce failed or fresh replicas in the system to maintain or improve availability and performance. The main difficulty is that replicas do have state and a failed replica may have missed updates while it was down. Thus, a recovering failed replica needs to receive the lost updates before being able to start processing new transactions. A solution is to stop transaction processing. Thus, a quiescent state is directly attained that can be transferred by any of the working replicas to the recovering one. Once the recovering replica has received all the missed updates, transaction processing can resume and all replicas can process new transactions.

8.7   Database Clusters

A parallel database system typically implements the parallel data management functions in a tightly coupled fashion, with all homogeneous nodes under the full control of the parallel DBMS. A simpler (yet not as efficient) solution is to use a *database cluster*, which is a cluster of autonomous databases, each managed by an off-the-shelf DBMS. A major difference with a parallel DBMS implemented on a cluster is the use of a "black-box" DBMS at each node. Since the DBMS source code is not necessarily available and cannot be changed to be "cluster-aware," parallel data management capabilities must be implemented via middleware. This approach has been successfully adopted in the MySQL or PostgreSQL clusters.

Much research has been devoted to take full advantage of the cluster environment (with fast, reliable communication) in order to improve performance and availability by exploiting data replication. The main results of this research are new techniques for replication, load balancing, and query processing. In this section, we present these techniques after introducing a database cluster architecture.

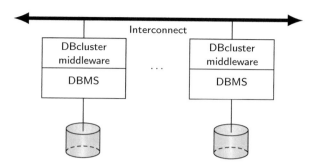

Fig. 8.19 A shared-nothing database cluster

8.7.1 Database Cluster Architecture

Figure 8.19 illustrates a database cluster with a shared-nothing architecture. Parallel
data management is done by independent DBMSs orchestrated by a middleware
replicated at each node. To improve performance and availability, data can be
replicated at different nodes using the local DBMS. Client applications interact
with the middleware in a classical way to submit database transactions, i.e.,
ad hoc queries, transactions, or calls to stored procedures. Some nodes can be
specialized as access nodes to receive transactions, in which case they share a global
directory service that captures information about users and databases. The general
processing of a transaction to a single database is as follows. First, the transaction
is authenticated and authorized using the directory. If successful, the transaction is
routed to a DBMS at some, possibly different, node to be executed. We will see
in Sect. 8.7.4 how this simple model can be extended to deal with parallel query
processing, using several nodes to process a single query.

As in a parallel DBMS, the database cluster middleware has several software
layers: transaction load balancer, replication manager, query processor, and fault-
tolerance manager. The transaction load balancer triggers transaction execution at
the best node, using load information obtained from node probes. The "best" node
is defined as the one with lightest transaction load. The transaction load balancer
also ensures that each transaction execution obeys the ACID properties, and then
signals to the DBMS to commit or abort the transaction. The replication manager
manages access to replicated data and assures strong consistency in such a way
that transactions that update replicated data are executed in the same serial order
at each node. The query processor exploits both inter and intraquery parallelism.
With interquery parallelism, the query processor routes each submitted query to one
node and, after query completion, sends results to the client application. Intraquery
parallelism is more involved. As the black-box DBMSs are not cluster-aware, they
cannot interact with one another in order to process the same query. Then, it is
up to the query processor to control query execution, final result composition, and

load balancing. Finally, the fault-tolerance manager provides online recovery and failover.

8.7.2   Replication

As in distributed DBMSs, replication can be used to improve performance and availability. In a database cluster, the fast interconnect and communication system can be exploited to support one-copy serializability while providing scalability (to achieve performance with large numbers of nodes) and autonomy (to exploit black-box DBMS). A cluster provides a stable environment with little evolution of the topology (e.g., as a result of added nodes or communication link failures). Thus, it is easier to support a group communication system that manages reliable communication between groups of nodes. Group communication primitives (see Sect. 6.4) can be used with either eager or lazy replication techniques as a means to attain atomic information dissemination (i.e., instead of the expensive 2PC).

We present now another protocol, called *preventive replication*, which is lazy and provides support for one-copy serializability and scalability. Preventive replication also preserves DBMS autonomy. Instead of using total ordered multicast, it uses FIFO reliable multicast that is simpler and more efficient. The principle is the following. Each incoming transaction T to the system has a chronological timestamp $ts(T) = C$, and is multicast to all other nodes where there is a copy. At each node, a time delay is introduced before starting the execution of T. This delay corresponds to the upper bound of the time needed to multicast a message (a synchronous system with bounded computation and transmission time is assumed). The critical issue is the accurate computation of the upper bounds for messages (i.e., delay). In a cluster system, the upper bound can be computed quite accurately. When the delay expires, all transactions that may have committed before C are guaranteed to be received and executed before T, following the timestamp order (i.e., total order). Hence, this approach prevents conflicts and enforces strong consistency in database clusters. Introducing delay times has also been exploited in several lazy centralized replication protocols for distributed systems. The validation of the preventive replication protocol using experiments with the TPC-C benchmark over a cluster of 64 nodes running the PostgreSQL DBMS have shown excellent scale-up and speed-up.

8.7.3   Load Balancing

In a database cluster, replication offers good load balancing opportunities. With eager or preventive replication (see Sect. 8.7.2), query load balancing is easy to achieve. Since all copies are mutually consistent, any node that stores a copy of the transaction data, e.g., the least loaded node, can be chosen at runtime by a conventional load balancing strategy. Transaction load balancing is also easy in the case of lazy distributed replication since all master nodes need to eventually perform the transaction. However, the total cost of transaction execution at all nodes may be high. By relaxing consistency, lazy replication can better reduce transaction execution cost and thus increase performance of both queries and transactions. Thus, depending on the consistency/performance requirements, eager and lazy replication are both useful in database clusters.

8.7.4   Query Processing

In a database cluster, parallel query processing can be used successfully to yield high performance. Interquery parallelism is naturally obtained as a result of load balancing and replication as discussed in the previous section. Such parallelism is primarily useful to increase the throughput of transaction-oriented applications and, to some extent, to reduce the response time of transactions and queries. For OLAP applications that typically use ad hoc queries, which access large quantities of data, intraquery parallelism is essential to further reduce response time. Intraquery parallelism consists of processing the same query on different partitions of the relations involved in the query.

There are two alternative solutions for partitioning relations in a database cluster: physical and virtual. Physical partitioning defines relation partitions, essentially as horizontal fragments, and allocates them to cluster nodes, possibly with replication. This resembles fragmentation and allocation design in distributed databases (see Chap. 2) except that the objective is to increase intraquery parallelism, not locality of reference. Thus, depending on the query and relation sizes, the degree of partitioning should be much finer. Physical partitioning in database clusters for decision-support can use small grain partitions. Under uniform data distribution, this solution is shown to yield good intraquery parallelism and outperform interquery parallelism. However, physical partitioning is static and thus very sensitive to data skew conditions and the variation of query patterns that may require periodic repartitioning.

Virtual partitioning avoids the problems of static physical partitioning using a dynamic approach and full replication (each relation is replicated at each node). In its simplest form, which we call *simple virtual partitioning (SVP)* , virtual partitions are dynamically produced for each query and intraquery parallelism is obtained by sending subqueries to different virtual partitions. To produce the different subqueries, the database cluster query processor adds predicates to the incoming query in order to restrict access to a subset of a relation, i.e., a virtual partition. It may also do some rewriting to decompose the query into equivalent subqueries followed by a composition query. Then, each DBMS that receives a subquery is forced to process a different subset of data items. Finally, the partitioned result needs to be combined by an aggregate query.

Example 8.6 Let us illustrate SVP with the following query Q:

```
SELECT PNO, AVG(DUR)
FROM    WORKS
WHERE   SUM(DUR) > 200
GROUP BY PNO
```

A generic subquery on a virtual partition is obtained by adding to Q's where clause the predicate "**and** PNO >= 'P1' and PNO < 'P2'." By binding ['P1', 'P2'] to n subsequent ranges of PNO values, we obtain n subqueries, each for a different node on a different virtual partition of WORKS. Thus, the degree of intraquery parallelism is n. Furthermore, the **AVG**(DUR) operation must be rewritten as **SUM**(DUR), **COUNT**(DUR) in the subquery. Finally, to obtain the correct result for **AVG**(DUR), the composition query must perform **SUM**(DUR)/**SUM**(**COUNT**(DUR)) over the n partial results.

The performance of each subquery's execution depends heavily on the access methods available on the partitioning attribute (PNO). In this example, a clustered index on PNO would be best. Thus, it is important for the query processor to know the access methods available to decide, according to the query, which partitioning attribute to use.   ◆

SVP allows great flexibility for node allocation during query processing since any node can be chosen for executing a subquery. However, not all kinds of queries can benefit from SVP and be parallelized. We can classify OLAP queries such that queries of the same class have similar parallelization properties. This classification relies on how the largest relations, called fact tables in a typical OLAP application, are accessed. The rationale is that the virtual partitioning of such relations yields higher intraoperator parallelism. Three main classes are identified:

1. Queries without subqueries that access a fact table.
2. Queries with a subquery that are equivalent to a query of Class 1.
3. Any other queries.

Queries of Class 2 need to be rewritten into queries of Class 1 in order for SVP to apply, while queries of Class 3 cannot benefit from SVP.

SVP has some limitations. First, determining the best virtual partitioning attributes and value ranges can be difficult since assuming uniform value distribution is not realistic. Second, some DBMSs perform full table scans instead of indexed access when retrieving tuples from large intervals of values. This reduces the benefits of parallel disk access since one node could read an entire relation to access a virtual partition. This makes SVP dependent on the underlying DBMS query capabilities. Third, as a query cannot be externally modified while being executed, load balancing is difficult to achieve and depends on the initial partitioning.

Fine-grained virtual partitioning addresses these limitations by using a large number of subqueries instead of one per DBMS. Working with smaller subqueries avoids full table scans and makes query processing less vulnerable to DBMS idiosyncrasies. However, this approach must estimate the partition sizes, using database statistics and query processing time estimates. In practice, these estimates are hard to obtain with black-box DBMSs.

Adaptive virtual partitioning (AVP) solves this problem by dynamically tuning partition sizes, thus without requiring these estimates. AVP runs independently at each participating cluster node, avoiding internode communication (for partition size determination). Initially, each node receives an interval of values to work with. These intervals are determined exactly as for SVP. Then, each node performs the following steps:

1. Start with a very small partition size beginning with the first value of the received interval.
2. Execute a subquery with this interval.
3. Increase the partition size and execute the corresponding subquery while the increase in execution time is proportionally smaller than the increase in partition size.
4. Stop increasing. A stable size has been found.
5. If there is performance degradation, i.e., there were consecutive worse executions, decrease size and go to Step 2.

Starting with a very small partition size avoids full table scans at the very beginning of the process. This also avoids having to know the threshold after which the DBMS does not use clustered indices and starts performing full table scans. When partition size increases, query execution time is monitored allowing determination of the point after which the query processing steps that are data size independent do not influence too much total query execution time. For example, if doubling the partition size yields an execution time that is twice the previous one, this means that such a point has been found. Thus the algorithm stops increasing the size. System performance can deteriorate due to DBMS data cache misses or overall system load increase. It may happen that the size being used is too large and has benefited from previous data cache hits. In this case, it may be better to shrink partition size. That is precisely what step 5 does. It gives a chance to go back and inspect smaller partition sizes. On the other hand, if performance deterioration was due to a casual and temporary increase of system load or data cache misses, keeping a small partition size can lead to poor performance. To avoid such a situation, the algorithm goes back to Step 2 and restarts increasing sizes.

AVP and other variants of virtual partitioning have several advantages: flexibility for node allocation, high availability because of full replication, and opportunities for dynamic load balancing. But full replication can lead to high cost in disk usage. To support partial replication, hybrid solutions have been proposed to combine physical and virtual partitioning. The hybrid design uses physical partitioning for the largest and most important relations and fully replicates the small tables. Thus, intraquery parallelism can be achieved with lesser disk space requirements. The hybrid solution combines AVP with physical partitioning. It solves the problem of disk usage while keeping the advantages of AVP, i.e., full table scan avoidance and dynamic load balancing.

8.8   Conclusion

Parallel database systems have been exploiting multiprocessor architectures to provide high-performance, high-availability, extensibility, and scalability with a good cost/performance ratio. Furthermore, parallelism is the only viable solution for supporting very large databases and applications within a single system.

Parallel database system architectures can be classified as shared-memory, shared-disk, and shared-nothing. Each architecture has its advantages and limitations. Shared-memory is used in tightly coupled NUMA multiprocessors or multicore processors, and can provide the highest performance because of fast memory access and great load balancing. However, it has limited extensibility and scalability. Shared-disk and shared-nothing are used in computer clusters, typically using multicore processors. With low latency networks (e.g., Infiniband and Myrinet), they can provide high performance and scale up to very large configurations (with thousands of nodes). Furthermore, the RDMA capability of those networks can be exploited to make cost-effective NUMA clusters. Shared-disk is typically used for OLTP workloads as it is simpler and has good load balancing. However, shared-nothing remains the only choice for highly scalable systems, as need in OLAP or big data, with the best cost/performance ratio.

Parallel data management techniques extend distributed database techniques. However, the critical issues for such architectures are data partitioning, replication, parallel query processing, load balancing, and fault-tolerance. The solutions to these issues are more involved than in distributed DBMS because they must scale to high numbers of nodes. Furthermore, recent advances in hardware/software such as low latency interconnect, multicore processor nodes, large main memory, and RDMA provide new opportunities for optimization. In particular, parallel algorithms for the most demanding operators such as join and sort need be made NUMA-aware.

A database cluster is an important kind of parallel database system that uses a black-box DBMS at each node. Much research has been devoted to take full advantage of the cluster stable environment in order to improve performance and availability by exploiting data replication. The main results of this research are new techniques for replication, load balancing, and query processing.

8.9   Bibliographic Notes

The earlier proposal of a database machine dates back to [Canaday et al. 1974], mainly to address the "I/O bottleneck" [Boral and DeWitt 1983], induced by high disk access time with respect to main memory access time. The main idea was to push database functions closer to disk. CAFS-ISP is an early example of hardware-based filtering device [Babb 1979] that was bundled within disk controllers for fast associative search. The introduction of general-purpose microprocessors in disk controllers also led to intelligent disks [Keeton et al. 1998].

The first parallel database system products were Teradata and Tandem Non-StopSQL in the early 1980s. Since then, all major DBMS players have delivered a parallel version of their product. Today, the field is still the subject of intensive research to deal with big data and exploit new hardware capabilities, e.g., low latency interconnects, multicore processor nodes, and large main memories.

Comprehensive surveys of parallel database systems are provided in [DeWitt and Gray 1992, Valduriez 1993, Graefe 1993]. Parallel database system architectures are discussed in [Bergsten et al. 1993, Stonebraker 1986, Pirahesh et al. 1990], and compared using a simple simulation model in [Breitbart and Silberschatz 1988]. The first NUMA architectures are described in [Lenoski et al. 1992, Goodman and Woest 1988]. A more recent approach based on Remote Direct Memory Access (RDMA) is discussed in [Novakovic et al. 2014, Leis et al. 2014, Barthels et al. 2015].

Examples of parallel database system prototypes are Bubba [Boral et al. 1990], DBS3 [Bergsten et al. 1991], Gamma [DeWitt et al. 1986], Grace [Fushimi et al. 1986], Prisma/DB [Apers et al. 1992], Volcano [Graefe 1990], and XPRS [Hong 1992].

Data placement, including replication, in a parallel database system is treated in [Livny et al. 1987, Copeland et al. 1988, Hsiao and DeWitt 1991]. A scalable solution is Gamma's *chained partitioning* [Hsiao and DeWitt 1991], which stores the primary and backup copy on two adjacent nodes. Associative access to a partitioned relation using a global index is proposed in [Khoshafian and Valduriez 1987].

Parallel query optimization is treated in [Shekita et al. 1993], [Ziane et al. 1993], and [Lanzelotte et al. 1994]. Our discussion of cost model in Sect. 8.4.2.2 is based on [Lanzelotte et al. 1994]. Randomized search strategies are proposed in [Swami 1989, Ioannidis and Wong 1987]. XPRS uses a two phase optimization strategy [Hong and Stonebraker 1993]. The exchange operator, which is the basis for parallel repartitioning in parallel query processing, was proposed in the context of the Volcano query evaluation system [Graefe 1990].

There is an extensive literature on parallel algorithms for database operators, in particular sort and join. The objective of these algorithms is to maximize the degree of parallelism, following Amdahl's law [Amdahl 1967] that states that only part of an algorithm can be parallelized. The seminal paper by [Bitton et al. 1983] proposes and compares parallel versions of merge sort, nested loop join, and sort-merge join algorithms. Valduriez and Gardarin [1984] propose the use of hashing for parallel join and semijoin algorithms. A survey of parallel sort algorithms can be found in [Bitton et al. 1984]. The specification of two main phases, *build* and *probe*, [DeWitt and Gerber 1985] has been useful to understand parallel hash join algorithms. The Grace hash join [Kitsuregawa et al. 1983], the hybrid hash join algorithm [DeWitt et al. 1984, Shatdal et al. 1994], and the radix hash join [Manegold et al. 2002] have been the basis for many variations in particular to exploit multicore processors and NUMA [Barthels et al. 2015]. Other important join algorithms are the symmetric hash join [Wilschut and Apers 1991] and the Ripple join [Haas and Hellerstein 1999b]. In [Barthels et al. 2015], the authors show that a radix hash join can perform very well in large-scale shared-nothing clusters using RDMA.

The parallel sort-merge join algorithm is gaining renewed interest in the context of multicore and NUMA systems [Albutiu et al. 2012, Pasetto and Akhriev 2011].

Load balancing in parallel database systems has been extensively studied both in the context of shared-memory and shared-disk [Lu et al. 1991, Shekita et al. 1993] and shared-nothing [Kitsuregawa and Ogawa 1990, Walton et al. 1991, DeWitt et al. 1992, Shatdal and Naughton 1993, Rahm and Marek 1995, Mehta and DeWitt 1995, Garofalakis and Ioannidis 1996]. The presentation of the Dynamic Processing execution model in Sect. 8.5 is based on [Bouganim et al. 1996, 1999]. The rate match algorithm is described in [Mehta and DeWitt 1995].

The effects of skewed data distribution on a parallel execution are introduced in [Walton et al. 1991]. A general adaptive approach to dynamically adjust the degree of parallelism using control operators is proposed in [Biscondi et al. 1996]. A good approach to deal with data skew is to use multiple join algorithms, each specialized for a different degree of skew, and to determine, at execution time, which algorithm is best [DeWitt et al. 1992].

The content of Sect. 8.6 on fault-tolerance is based on [Kemme et al. 2001, Jiménez-Peris et al. 2002, Perez-Sorrosal et al. 2006].

The concept of database cluster is defined in [Röhm et al. 2000, 2001]. Several protocols for scalable eager replication in database clusters using group communication are proposed in [Kemme and Alonso 2000b,a, Patiño-Martínez et al. 2000, Jiménez-Peris et al. 2002]. Their scalability has been studied analytically in [Jiménez-Peris et al. 2003]. Partial replication is studied in [Sousa et al. 2001]. The presentation of preventive replication in Sect. 8.7.2 is based on [Pacitti et al. 2005]. Load balancing in database clusters is addressed in [Milán-Franco et al. 2004, Gançarski et al. 2007].

Most of the content of Sect. 8.7.4 is based on the work on adaptive virtual partitioning [Lima et al. 2004] and hybrid partitioning [Furtado et al. 2008]. Physical partitioning in database clusters for decision-support is addressed by [Stöhr et al. 2000], using small grain partitions. Akal et al. [2002] propose a classification of OLAP queries such that queries of the same class have similar parallelization properties.

Exercises

Problem 8.1 (*) Consider a shared-disk cluster and very big relations that need to be partitioned across several disk units. How you would adapt the various partitioning and replication techniques in Sect. 8.3 to take advantage of shared-disk? Discuss the impact on query performance and fault-tolerance.

Problem 8.2 (**) Order-preserving hashing [Knuth 1973] could be used to partition a relation on an attribute A, so that the tuples in any partition $i+1$ have A values higher than those of the tuples in partition i. Propose a parallel sort algorithm that exploits order-preserving hashing. Discuss it advantages and limitations, compared with the b-way merge sort algorithm in Sect. 8.4.1.1.

Problem 8.3 Consider the parallel hash join algorithm in Sect. 8.4.1.2. Explain what the build phase and probe phase are. Is the algorithm symmetric with respect to its input relations?

Problem 8.4 (*) Consider the join of two relations R and S in a shared-nothing cluster. Assume that S is partitioned by hashing on the join attribute. Modify the parallel hash join algorithm in Sect. 8.4.1.2 to take advantage of this case. Discuss the execution cost of this algorithm.

Problem 8.5 (**) Consider a simple cost model to compare the performance of the three basic parallel join algorithms (nested loop join, sort-merge join, and hash join). It is defined in terms of total communication cost (C_{COM}) and processing cost (C_{PRO}). The total cost of each algorithm is therefore

$$Cost(Alg.) = C_{COM}(Alg.) + C_{PRO}(Alg.)$$

For simplicity, C_{COM} does not include control messages, which are necessary to initiate and terminate local tasks. We denote by $msg(\#tup)$ the cost of transferring a message of $\#tup$ tuples from one node to another. Processing costs (that include total I/O and CPU cost) are based on the function $C_{LOC}(m, n)$ that computes the local processing cost for joining two relations with cardinalities m and n. Assume that the local join algorithm is the same for all three parallel join algorithms. Finally, assume that the amount of work done in parallel is uniformly distributed over all nodes allocated to the operator. Give the formulas for the total cost of each algorithm, assuming that the input relations are arbitrary partitioned. Identify the conditions under which an algorithm should be used.

Problem 8.6 Consider the following SQL query:

```
SELECT ENAME, DUR
FROM    EMP, ASG, PROJ
WHERE   EMP.ENO=ASG.ENO
AND     ASG.PNO=PROJ.PNO
AND     RESP="Manager"
AND     PNAME="Instrumentation"
```

Give four possible operator trees: right-deep, left-deep, zigzag, and bushy. For each one, discuss the opportunities for parallelism.

Problem 8.7 Consider a nine way join (ten relations are to be joined), calculate the number of possible right-deep, left-deep, and bushy trees, assuming that each relation can be joined with anyone else. What do you conclude about parallel optimization?

Problem 8.8 (**) Propose a data placement strategy for a NUMA cluster (using RDMA) that maximizes a combination of *intranode* parallelism (intraoperator parallelism within shared-memory nodes) and *internode* parallelism (interoperator parallelism across shared-memory nodes).

Problem 8.9 (**) How should the DP execution model presented in Sect. 8.5.4 be changed to deal with interquery parallelism?

Problem 8.10 (**) Consider a multiuser centralized database system. Describe the main change to allow interquery parallelism from the database system developer and administrator's points of view. What are the implications for the end-user in terms of interface and performance?

Problem 8.11 (*) Consider the database cluster architecture in Fig. 8.19. Assuming that each cluster node can accept incoming transactions, make precise the database cluster middleware box by describing the different software layers, and their components and relationships in terms of data and control flow. What kind of information need be shared between the cluster nodes? how?

Problem 8.12 (**) Discuss the issues of fault-tolerance for the preventive replication protocol (see Sect. 8.7.2).

Problem 8.13 (**) Compare the preventive replication protocol with the eager replication protocol (see Chap. 6) in the context of a database cluster in terms of: replication configurations supported, network requirements, consistency, performance, fault-tolerance.

Problem 8.14 (**) Consider two relations R(A,B,C,D,E) and S(A,F,G,H). Assume there is a clustered index on attribute A for each relation. Assuming a database cluster with full replication, for each of the following queries, determine whether Virtual Partitioning can be used to obtain intraquery parallelism and, if so, write the corresponding subquery and the final result composition query.

(a) SELECT B, COUNT(C)
     FROM   R
     GROUP BYB

(b) SELECT C, SUM(D), AVG(E)
     FROM   R
     WHERE   B=:v1
     GROUP BY C

(c) SELECT B, SUM(E)
     FROM.   R, S
     WHERE. R.A=S.A
     GROUP BY B
     HAVING COUNT(*) > 50

(d) SELECT B, MAX(D)
     FROM+. R, S
     WHERE C = (SELECT SUM(G) FROM S WHERE S.A=R.A)
     GROUP BY B

(e) SELECT B, MIN(E)
     FROM.   R
     WHERE   D > (SELECT MAX(H) FROM S WHERE G >= :v1)
     GROUP BY B

Chapter 9
Peer-to-Peer Data Management

In this chapter, we discuss the data management issues in the "modern" peer-to-peer (P2P) data management systems. We intentionally use the phrase "modern" to differentiate these from the early P2P systems that were common prior to client/server computing. As indicated in Chap. 1, early work on distributed DBMSs had primarily focused on P2P architectures where there was no differentiation between the functionality of each site in the system. So, in one sense, P2P data management is quite old—if one simply interprets P2P to mean that there are no identifiable "servers" and "clients" in the system. However, the "modern" P2P systems go beyond this simple characterization and differ from the old systems that are referred to by the same name in a number of important ways, as mentioned in Chap. 1.

The first difference is the massive distribution in current systems. While the early systems focused on a few (perhaps at most tens of) sites, current systems consider thousands of sites. Furthermore, these sites are geographically very distributed, with possible clusters forming at certain locations.

The second is the inherent heterogeneity of every aspect of the sites and their autonomy. While this has always been a concern of distributed databases, coupled with massive distribution, site heterogeneity and autonomy take on added significance, disallowing some of the approaches from consideration.

The third major difference is the considerable volatility of these systems. Distributed DBMSs are well-controlled environments, where additions of new sites or the removal of existing sites are done very carefully and rarely. In modern P2P systems, the sites are (quite often) people's individual machines and they join and leave the P2P system at will, creating considerable hardship in the management of data.

In this chapter, we focus on this modern incarnation of P2P systems. In these systems, the following requirements are:

The original version of this chapter was revised. The correction to this chapter is available at https://doi.org/10.1007/978-3-030-26253-2_13

© Springer Nature Switzerland AG 2020
M. T. Özsu, P. Valduriez, *Principles of Distributed Database Systems*, https://doi.org/10.1007/978-3-030-26253-2_9

- **Autonomy.** An autonomous peer should be able to join or leave the system at any time without restriction. It should also be able to control the data it stores and which other peers can store its data (e.g., some other trusted peers).
- **Query expressiveness.** The query language should allow the user to describe the desired data at the appropriate level of detail. The simplest form of query is key lookup, which is only appropriate for finding files. Keyword search with ranking of results is appropriate for searching documents, but for more structured data, an SQL-like query language is necessary.
- **Efficiency.** The efficient use of the P2P system resources (bandwidth, computing power, storage) should result in lower cost, and, thus, higher throughput of queries, i.e., a higher number of queries can be processed by the P2P system in a given time interval.
- **Quality of service.** This refers to the user-perceived efficiency of the system, such as completeness of query results, data consistency, data availability, and query response time.
- **Fault-tolerance.** Efficiency and quality of service should be maintained despite the failures of peers. Given the dynamic nature of peers that may leave or fail at any time, it is important to properly exploit data replication.
- **Security.** The open nature of a P2P system gives rise to serious security challenges since one cannot rely on trusted servers. With respect to data management, the main security issue is access control which includes enforcing intellectual property rights on data contents.

A number of different uses of P2P systems have been developed for sharing computation (e.g., SETI@home), communication (e.g., ICQ), or data (e.g., BitTorrent, Gnutella, and Kazaa). Our interest, naturally, is on data sharing systems. Popular systems such as BitTorrent, Gnutella, and Kazaa are quite limited when viewed from the perspective of database functionality. First, they provide only file level sharing with no sophisticated content-based search/query facilities. Second, they are single-application systems that focus on performing one task, and it is not straightforward to extend them for other applications/functions. In this chapter, we discuss the research activities towards providing proper database functionality over P2P infrastructures. Within this context, data management issues that must be addressed include the following:

- Data location: peers must be able to refer to and locate data stored in other peers.
- Query processing: given a query, the system must be able to discover the peers that contribute relevant data and efficiently execute the query.
- Data integration: when shared data sources in the system follow different schemas or representations, peers should still be able to access that data, ideally using the data representation used to model their own data.
- Data consistency: if data is replicated or cached in the system, a key issue is to maintain the consistency between these duplicates.

Figure 9.1 shows a reference architecture for a peer participating in a data sharing P2P system. Depending on the functionality of the P2P system, one or more of the

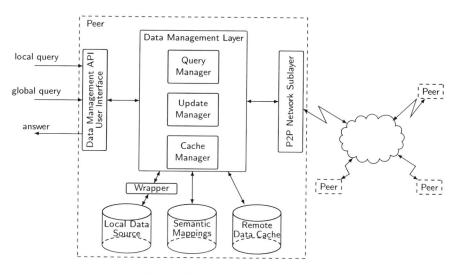

Fig. 9.1 Peer reference architecture

components in the reference architecture may not exist, may be combined together, or may be implemented by specialized peers. The key aspect of the proposed architecture is the separation of the functionality into three main components: (1) an interface used for submitting the queries; (2) a data management layer that handles query processing and metadata information (e.g., catalogue services); and (3) a P2P infrastructure, which is composed of the P2P network sublayer and P2P network. In this chapter, we focus on the P2P data management layer and P2P infrastructure.

Queries are submitted using a user interface or data management API and handled by the data management layer. They may refer to data stored locally or globally in the system. The query request is processed by a query manager module that retrieves semantic mapping information from a repository when the system integrates heterogeneous data sources. This semantic mapping repository contains metainformation that allows the query manager to identify peers in the system with data relevant to the query and to reformulate the original query in terms that other peers can understand. Some P2P systems may store the semantic mapping in specialized peers. In this case, the query manager will need to contact these specialized peers or transmit the query to them for execution. If all data sources in the system follow the same schema, neither the semantic mapping repository nor its associated query reformulation functionality is required.

Assuming a semantic mapping repository, the query manager invokes services implemented by the P2P network sublayer to communicate with the peers that will be involved in the execution of the query. The actual execution of the query is influenced by the implementation of the P2P infrastructure. In some systems, data is sent to the peer where the query was initiated and then combined at this peer. Other systems provide specialized peers for query execution and coordination. In either case, result data returned by the peers involved in the execution of the query may be cached locally to speed up future executions of similar queries. The cache manager maintains the local cache of each peer. Alternatively, caching may occur only at specialized peers.

The query manager is also responsible for executing the local portion of a global query when data is requested by a remote peer. A wrapper may hide data, query language, or any other incompatibilities between the local data source and the data management layer. When data is updated, the update manager coordinates the execution of the update between the peers storing replicas of the data being updated.

The P2P network infrastructure, which can be implemented as either structured or unstructured network topology, provides communication services to the data management layer.

In the remainder of this chapter, we will address each component of this reference architecture, starting with infrastructure issues in Sect. 9.1. The problems of data mapping and the approaches to address them are the topics of Sect. 9.2. Query processing is discussed in Sect. 9.3. Data consistency and replication issues are discussed in Sect. 9.4. In Sect. 9.5, we introduce Blockchain, a P2P infrastructure for recording transactions efficiently, safely, and permanently.

9.1   Infrastructure

The infrastructure of all P2P systems is a P2P network, which is built on top of a physical network (usually the Internet); thus, it is commonly referred to as the *overlay network*. The overlay network may (and usually does) have a different topology than the physical network and all the algorithms focus on optimizing communication over the overlay network (usually in terms of minimizing the number of "hops" that a message needs to go through from a source node to a destination node—both in the overlay network). The distinction between the overlay network and the physical network may be a problem in that two nodes that are neighbors in the overlay network may, in some cases, be considerably far apart in the physical network. Therefore, the cost of communication within the overlay network may not reflect the actual cost of communication in the physical network. We address this issue at the appropriate points during the infrastructure discussion.

Overlay networks can be of two general types: pure and hybrid. *Pure overlay networks* (more commonly referred to as *pure P2P networks*) are those where there is no differentiation between any of the network nodes—they are all equal. In *hybrid P2P networks*, on the other hand, some nodes are given special tasks to perform. Hybrid networks are commonly known as *superpeer systems*, since some of the peers are responsible for "controlling" a set of other peers in their domain. The pure networks can be further divided into structured and unstructured networks. *Structured networks* tightly control the topology and message routing, whereas in *unstructured networks* each node can directly communicate with its neighbors and can join the network by attaching themselves to any node.

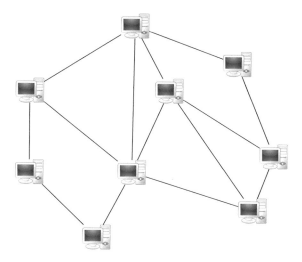

Fig. 9.2 Unstructured P2P network

9.1.1 Unstructured P2P Networks

Unstructured P2P networks refer to those with no restriction on data placement in the overlay topology. The overlay network is created in a nondeterministic (ad hoc) manner and the data placement is completely unrelated to the overlay topology. Each peer knows its neighbors, but does not know the resources that they have. Figure 9.2 shows an example unstructured P2P network.

Unstructured networks are the earliest examples of P2P systems whose core functionality remains file sharing. In these systems, replicated copies of popular files are shared among peers, without the need to download them from a centralized server. Examples of these systems are Gnutella, Freenet, Kazaa, and BitTorrent.

A fundamental issue in all P2P networks is the type of index to the resources that each peer holds, since this determines how resources are searched. Note that what is called "index management" in the context of P2P systems is very similar to catalog management that we studied in Chap. 2. Indexes are stored metadata that the system maintains. The exact content of the metadata differs in different P2P systems. In general, it includes, at a minimum, information on the resources and sizes.

There are two alternatives to maintaining indices: centralized, where one peer stores the metadata for the entire P2P system, and distributed, where each peer maintains metadata for resources that it holds. Again, the alternatives are identical to those for directory management.

The type of index supported by a P2P system (centralized or distributed) impacts how resources are searched. Note that we are not, at this point, referring to running queries; we are merely discussing how, given a resource identifier, the underlying P2P infrastructure can locate the relevant resource. In systems that maintain a centralized index, the process involves consulting the central peer to find the location

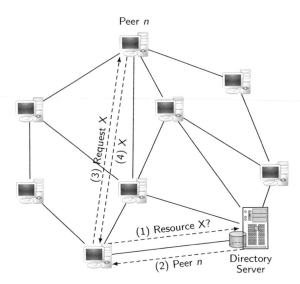

Fig. 9.3 Search over a centralized index. (1) A peer asks the central index manager for resource, (2) The response identifies the peer with the resource, (3) The peer is asked for the resource, (4) It is transferred

of the resource, followed by directly contacting the peer where the resource is located (Fig. 9.3). Thus, the system operates similar to a client/server one up to the point of obtaining the necessary index information (i.e., the metadata), but from that point on, the communication is only between the two peers. Note that the central peer may return a set of peers who hold the resource and the requesting peer may choose one among them, or the central peer may make the choice (taking into account loads and network conditions, perhaps) and return only a single recommended peer.

In systems that maintain a distributed index, there are a number of search alternatives. The most popular one is flooding, where the peer looking for a resource sends the search request to all of its neighbors on the overlay network. If any of these neighbors have the resource, they respond; otherwise, each of them forwards the request to its neighbors until the resource is found or the overlay network is fully spanned (Fig. 9.4).

Naturally, flooding puts very heavy demands on network resources and is not scalable—as the overlay network gets larger, more communication is initiated. This has been addressed by establishing a Time-to-Live (TTL) limit that restricts the number of hops that a request message makes before it is dropped from the network. However, TTL also restricts the number of nodes that are reachable.

There have been other approaches to address this problem. A straightforward method is for each peer to choose a subset of its neighbors and forward the request only to those. There are different ways to determine this subset. For example, the concept of random walks can be used where each peer chooses a neighbor at random

Peer *n*

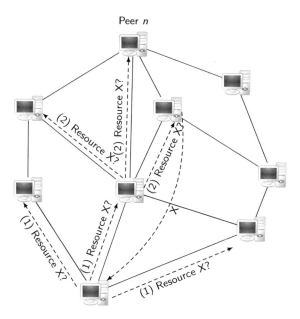

Fig. 9.4 Search over a Decentralized Index. (1) A peer sends the request for resource to all its neighbors, (2) Each neighbor propagates to its neighbors if it does not have the resource, (3) The peer who has the resource responds by sending the resource

and propagates the request only to it. Alternatively, each neighbor can maintain not only indices for local resources, but also for resources that are on peers within a radius of itself and use the historical information about their performance in routing queries. Still another alternative is to use similar indices based on resources at each node to provide a list of neighbors that are most likely to be in the direction of the peer holding the requested resources. These are referred to as routing indices and are used more commonly in structured networks, where we discuss them in more detail.

Another approach is to exploit *gossip protocols*, also known as *epidemic protocols*. Gossiping has been initially proposed to maintain the mutual consistency of replicated data by spreading replica updates to all nodes over the network. It has since been successfully used in P2P networks for data dissemination. Basic gossiping is simple. Each node in the network has a complete view of the network (i.e., a list of all nodes' addresses) and chooses a node at random to spread the request. The main advantage of gossiping is robustness over node failures since, with very high probability, the request is eventually propagated to all the nodes in the network. In large P2P networks, however, the basic gossiping model does not scale as maintaining the complete view of the network at each node would generate very heavy communication traffic. A solution to scalable gossiping is to maintain at each node only a partial view of the network, e.g., a list of tens of neighbor nodes. To gossip a request, a node chooses, at random, a node in its partial view and sends it the request. In addition, the nodes involved in a gossip exchange their partial views to reflect network changes in their own views. Thus, by continuously refreshing their partial views, nodes can self-organize into randomized overlays that scale up very well.

The final issue that we would like to discuss with respect to unstructured networks is how peers join and leave the network. The process is different for centralized versus distributed index approaches. In a centralized index system, a peer that wishes to join simply notifies the central index peer and informs it of the resources that it wishes to contribute to the P2P system. In the case of a distributed index, the joining peer needs to know one other peer in the system to which it "attaches" itself by notifying it and receiving information about its neighbors. At that point, the peer is part of the system and starts building its own neighbors. Peers that leave the system do not need to take any special action, they simply disappear. Their disappearance will be detected in time, and the overlay network will adjust itself.

9.1.2   Structured P2P Networks

Structured P2P networks have emerged to address the scalability issues faced by unstructured P2P networks. They achieve this goal by tightly controlling the overlay topology and the placement of resources. Thus, they achieve higher scalability at the expense of lower autonomy as each peer that joins the network allows its resources to be placed on the network based on the particular control method that is used.

As with unstructured P2P networks, there are two fundamental issues to be addressed: how are the resources indexed, and how are they searched. The most popular indexing and data location mechanism that is used in structured P2P networks is a *distributed hash table* (DHT). DHT-based systems provide two APIs: put(key, data) and get(key), where key is an object identifier. Each key (k_i) is hashed to generate a peer id (p_i), which stores the data corresponding to object contents (Fig. 9.5).

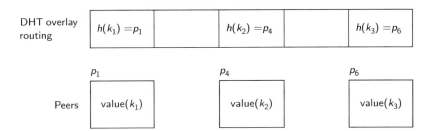

Fig. 9.5 DHT network

A straightforward approach could be to use the URI of the resource as the IP address of the peer that would hold the resource. However, one of the important design requirements is to provide a uniform distribution of resources over the overlay network and URIs/IP addresses do not provide sufficient flexibility. Consequently, *consistent hashing* techniques that provide uniform hashing of values are used to evenly place the data on the overlay. Although many hash functions may be employed for generating *virtual address mappings* for the resource, SHA-1 has become the most widely accepted *base*[1] hash function that supports both uniformity and security (by supporting data integrity for the keys). The actual design of the hash function may be implementation dependent and we will not discuss that issue any further.

Search (commonly called "lookup") over a DHT-based structured P2P network also involves the hash function: the key of the resource is hashed to get the id of the peer in the overlay network that is responsible for that key. The lookup is then initiated on the overlay network to locate the target node in question. This is referred to as the *routing protocol*, and it differs between different implementations and is closely associated with the overlay structure used. We will discuss one example approach shortly.

While all routing protocols aim to provide efficient lookups, they also try to minimize the *routing information* (also called *routing state*) that needs to be maintained in a routing table at each peer in the overlay. This information differs between various routing protocols and overlay structures, but it needs to provide sufficient directory-type information to route the put and get requests to the appropriate peer on the overlay. All routing table implementations require the use of maintenance algorithms in order to keep the routing state up-to-date and consistent. In contrast to routers on the Internet that also maintain routing databases, P2P systems pose a greater challenge since they are characterized by high node volatility and undependable network links. Since DHTs also need to support perfect recall (i.e., all the resources that are accessible through a given key have to be found), routing state consistency becomes a key challenge. Therefore, the maintenance of consistent routing state in the face of concurrent lookups and during periods of high network volatility is essential.

Many DHT-based overlays have been proposed. These can be categorized according to their *routing geometry* and *routing algorithm*. Routing geometry essentially defines the manner in which neighbors and routes are arranged. The routing algorithm corresponds to the routing protocol discussed above and is defined as the manner in which next-hops/routes are chosen on a given routing geometry. The more important existing DHT-based overlays can be categorized as follows:

- **Tree.** In the tree approach, the leaf nodes correspond to the node identifiers that store the keys to be searched. The height of the tree is $\log n$, where n is the number of nodes in the tree. The search proceeds from the root to the leaves by

---

[1] A base hash function is defined as a function that is used as a basis for the design of another hash function.

doing a longest prefix match at each of the intermediate nodes until the target node is found. Therefore, in this case, matching can be thought of as correcting bit values from left-to-right at each successive hop in the tree. A popular DHT implementation that falls into this category is Tapestry, which uses *surrogate routing* in order to forward requests at each node to the closest digit in the routing table. Surrogate routing is defined as routing to the *closest* digit when an exact match in the longest prefix cannot be found. In Tapestry, each unique identifier is associated with a node that is the root of a unique spanning tree used to route messages for the given identifier. Therefore, lookups proceed from the base of the spanning tree all the way to the root node of the identifier. Although this is somewhat different from traditional tree structures, Tapestry routing geometry is very closely associated with a tree structure and we classify it as such.

In tree structures, a node in the system has 2^{i-1} nodes to choose from as its neighbor from the subtree with whom it has $\log(n - i)$ prefix bits in common. The number of potential neighbors increases exponentially as we proceed further up in the tree. Thus, in total there are $n^{\log n/2}$ possible routing tables per node (note, however that, only one such routing table can be selected for a node). Therefore, the tree geometry has good neighbor selection characteristics that would provide it with fault-tolerance. However, routing can only be done through one neighboring node when sending to a particular destination. Consequently, the tree-structured DHTs do not provide any flexibility in the selection of routes.

- **Hypercube.** The hypercube routing geometry is based on d-dimensional Cartesian coordinate space that is partitioned into an individual set of zones such that each node maintains a separate zone of the coordinate space. An example of hypercube-based DHT is the Content Addressable Network (CAN). The number of neighbors that a node may have in a d-dimensional coordinate space is $2d$ (for the sake of discussion, we consider $d = \log n$). If we consider each coordinate to represent a set of bits, then each node identifier can be represented as a bit string of length $\log n$. In this way, the hypercube geometry is very similar to the tree since it also simply *fixes* the bits at each hop to reach the destination. However, in the hypercube, since the bits of neighboring nodes only differ in *exactly* one bit, each forwarding node needs to modify only a single bit in the bit string, which can be done in any order. Thus, if we consider the correction of the bit string, the first correction can be applied to any $\log n$ nodes, the next correction can be applied to any $(\log n) - 1$ nodes, etc. Therefore, we have $(\log n)!$ possible routes between nodes, which provides high route flexibility in the hypercube routing geometry. However, a node in the coordinate space does not have any choice over its neighbors' coordinates since adjacent coordinate zones in the coordinate space cannot change. Therefore, hypercubes have poor neighbor selection flexibility.
- **Ring.** The ring geometry is represented as a one-dimensional circular identifier space where the nodes are placed at different locations on the circle. The distance between any two nodes on the circle is the numeric identifier difference (clockwise) around the circle. Since the circle is one-dimensional, the data identifiers can be represented as single decimal digits (represented as binary bit strings) that map to a node that is closest in the identifier space to the given

decimal digit. Chord is a popular example of the ring geometry. Specifically, in Chord, a node whose identifier is a maintains information about $\log n$ other neighbors on the ring where the ith neighbor is the node closest to $a + 2^{i-1}$ on the circle. Using these links (called *fingers*), Chord is able to route to any other node in $\log n$ hops.

A careful analysis of Chord's structure reveals that a node does not necessarily need to maintain the node closest to $a + 2^{i-1}$ as its neighbor. In fact, it can still maintain the $\log n$ lookup upper bound if any node from the range $[(a + 2^{i-1}), (a + 2^i)]$ is chosen. Therefore, in terms of route flexibility, it is able to select between $n^{\log n/2}$ routing tables for each node. This provides a great deal of neighbor selection flexibility. Moreover, for routing to any node, the first hop has $\log n$ neighbors that can route the search to the destination and the next node has $(\log n) - 1$ nodes, and so on. Therefore, there are typically $(\log n)!$ possible routes to the destination. Consequently, ring geometry also provides good route selection flexibility.

In addition to these most popular geometries, there have been many other DHT-based structured overlays that use different topologies.

DHT-based overlays are efficient in that they guarantee finding the node on which to place or find the data in $\log n$ hops, where n is the number of nodes in the system. However, they have several problems, in particular when viewed from the data management perspective. One of the issues with DHTs that employ consistent hashing functions for better distribution of resources is that two peers that are "neighbors" in the overlay network because of the proximity of their hash values may be geographically quite apart in the actual network. Thus, communicating with a neighbor in the overlay network may incur high transmission delays in the actual network. There have been studies to overcome this difficulty by designing *proximity-aware* or *locality-aware* hash functions. Another difficulty is that they do not provide any flexibility in the placement of data—a data item has to be placed on the node that is determined by the hash function. Thus, if there are P2P nodes that contribute their own data, they need to be willing to have data moved to other nodes. This is problematic from the perspective of node autonomy. The third difficulty is in that it is hard to run range queries over DHT-based architectures since, as is well-known, it is hard to run range queries over hash indices. There have been studies to overcome this difficulty that we discuss later.

These concerns have caused the development of structured overlays that do not use DHT for routing. In these systems, peers are mapped into the data space rather than the hash key space. There are multiple ways to partition the data space among multiple peers.

- **Hierarchical structure.** Many systems employ hierarchical overlay structures, including tree, balanced trees, randomized balance trees (e.g., skip list), and others. Specifically PHT and P-Grid employ a binary tree structure, where peers whose data share common prefixes cluster under common branches. Balanced trees are also widely used due to their guaranteed routing efficiency (the expected "hop length" between arbitrary peers is proportional to the tree height). For instance, BATON, VBI-tree, and BATON* employ k-way balanced tree structure to manage peers, and data is evenly partitioned among peers at the leaf-level. In comparison, P-Tree uses a B-tree structure with better flexibility on tree structural changes. SkipNet and Skip Graph are based on the skip list, and they link peers according to a randomized balanced tree structure where the node order is determined by each node's data values.

- **Space-filling curve.** This architecture is usually used to linearize sort data in multidimensional data space. Peers are arranged along the space-filling curve (e.g., Hilbert curve) so that sorted traversal of peers according to data order is possible.
- **Hyperrectangle structure.** In these systems, each dimension of the hyperrectangle corresponds to one attribute of the data according to which an organization is desired. Peers are distributed in the data space either uniformly or based on data locality (e.g., through data intersection relationship). The hyperrectangle space is then partitioned by peers based on their geometric positions in the space, and neighboring peers are interconnected to form the overlay network.

9.1.3 Superpeer P2P Networks

Superpeer P2P systems are hybrid between pure P2P systems and the traditional client–server architectures. They are similar to client–server architectures in that not all peers are equal; some peers (called *superpeers*) act as dedicated serves for some other peers and can perform complex functions such as indexing, query processing, access control, and metadata management. If there is only one superpeer in the system, then this reduces to the client–server architecture. They are considered P2P systems, however, since the organization of the superpeers follows a P2P organization, and superpeers can communicate with each other in sophisticated ways. Thus, unlike client–server systems, global information is not necessarily centralized and can be partitioned or replicated across superpeers.

In a superpeer network, a requesting peer sends the request, which can be expressed in a high-level language, to its responsible superpeer. The superpeer can then find the relevant peers either directly through its index or indirectly using its neighbor superpeers. More precisely, the search for a resource proceeds as follows (see Fig. 9.6):

1. A peer, say Peer 1, asks for a resource by sending a request to its superpeer.
2. If the resource exists at one of the peers controlled by this superpeer, it notifies Peer 1, and the two peers then communicate to retrieve the resource. Otherwise, the superpeer sends the request to the other superpeers.
3. If the resource does not exist at one of the peers controlled by this superpeer, the superpeer asks the other superpeers. The superpeer of the node that contains the resource (say Peer n) responds to the requesting superpeer.

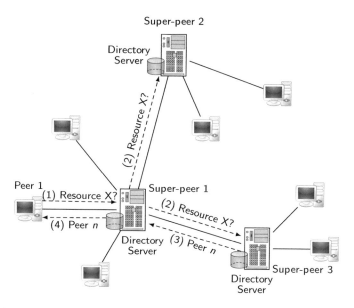

Fig. 9.6 Search over a superpeer system. (1) A peer sends the request for resource to all its superpeer, (2) The superpeer sends the request to other superpeers if necessary, (3) The superpeer one of whose peers has the resource responds by indicating that peer, (4) The superpeer notifies the original peer

4. Peer n's identity is sent to Peer 1, after which the two peers can communicate directly to retrieve the resource.

The main advantages of superpeer networks are efficiency and quality of service (e.g., completeness of query results, query response time). The time needed to find data by directly accessing indices in a superpeer is very small compared with flooding. In addition, superpeer networks exploit and take advantage of peers' different capabilities in terms of CPU power, bandwidth, or storage capacity as superpeers take on a large portion of the entire network load. Access control can also be better enforced since directory and security information can be maintained at the superpeers. However, autonomy is restricted since peers cannot log in freely to any superpeer. Fault-tolerance is typically lower since superpeers are single points of failure for their subpeers (dynamic replacement of superpeers can alleviate this problem).

Examples of superpeer networks include Edutella and JXTA.

Requirements	Unstructured	Structured	Superpeer
Autonomy	Low	Low	Moderate
Query expressiveness	High	Low	High
Efficiency	Low	High	High
QoS	Low	High	High
Fault-tolerance	High	High	Low
Security	Low	Low	High

Fig. 9.7 Comparison of approaches

9.1.4 Comparison of P2P Networks

Figure 9.7 summarizes how the requirements for data management (autonomy, query expressiveness, efficiency, quality of service, fault-tolerance, and security) are possibly attained by the three main classes of P2P networks. This is a rough comparison to understand the respective merits of each class. Obviously, there is room for improvement in each class of P2P networks. For instance, fault-tolerance can be improved in superpeer systems by relying on replication and fail-over techniques. Query expressiveness can be improved by supporting more complex queries on top of structured networks.

9.2 Schema Mapping in P2P Systems

We discussed the importance of, and the techniques for, designing database integration systems in Chap. 7. Similar issues arise in data sharing P2P systems.

Due to specific characteristics of P2P systems, e.g., the dynamic and autonomous nature of peers, the approaches that rely on centralized global schemas no longer apply. The main problem is to support decentralized schema mapping so that a query expressed on one peer's schema can be reformulated to a query on another peer's schema. The approaches which are used by P2P systems for defining and creating the mappings between peers' schemas can be classified as follows: pairwise schema mapping, mapping based on machine learning techniques, common agreement mapping, and schema mapping using information retrieval (IR) techniques.

9.2.1 Pairwise Schema Mapping

In this approach, each user defines the mapping between the local schema and the schema of any other peer that contains data that are of interest. Relying on the transitivity of the defined mappings, the system tries to extract mappings between schemas that have no defined mapping.

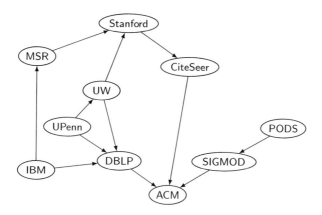

Fig. 9.8 An example of pairwise schema mapping in piazza

Piazza follows this approach (see Fig. 9.8). The data is shared as XML documents, and each peer has a schema that defines the terminology and the structural constraints of the peer. When a new peer (with a new schema) joins the system for the first time, it maps its schema to the schema of some other peers in the system. Each mapping definition begins with an XML template that matches some path or subtree of an instance of the target schema. Elements in the template may be annotated with query expressions that bind variables to XML nodes in the source.

The Local Relational Model (LRM) is another example that follows this approach. LRM assumes that the peers hold relational databases, and each peer knows a set of peers with which it can exchange data and services. This set of peers is called peer's *acquaintances*. Each peer must define semantic dependencies and translation rules between its data and the data shared by each of its acquaintances. The defined mappings form a semantic network, which is used for query reformulation in the P2P system.

Hyperion generalizes this approach to deal with autonomous peers that form acquaintances at runtime, using mapping tables to define value correspondences among heterogeneous databases. Peers perform local querying and update processing, and also propagate queries and updates to their acquainted peers.

PGrid also assumes the existence of pairwise mappings between peers, initially constructed by skilled experts. Relying on the transitivity of these mappings and using a gossip algorithm, PGrid extracts new mappings that relate the schemas of the peers between which there is no predefined schema mapping.

9.2.2 Mapping Based on Machine Learning Techniques

This approach is generally used when the shared data is defined based on ontologies and taxonomies as proposed for the semantic web. It uses machine learning techniques to automatically extract the mappings between the shared schemas. The extracted mappings are stored over the network, in order to be used for processing future queries. GLUE uses this approach. Given two ontologies, for each concept in one, GLUE finds the most similar concept in the other. It gives well-founded probabilistic definitions to several practical similarity measures, and uses multiple learning strategies, each of which exploits a different type of information either in the data instances or in the taxonomic structure of the ontologies. To further improve mapping accuracy, GLUE incorporates commonsense knowledge and domain constraints into the schema mapping process. The basic idea is to provide classifiers for the concepts. To decide the similarity between two concepts X and Y, the data of concept Y is classified using X's classifier and vice versa. The number of values that can be successfully classified into X and Y represent the similarity between X and Y.

9.2.3 Common Agreement Mapping

In this approach, the peers that have a common interest agree on a common schema description for data sharing. The common schema is usually prepared and maintained by expert users. The APPA P2P system makes the assumption that peers wishing to cooperate, e.g., for the duration of an experiment, agree on a Common Schema Description (CSD). Given a CSD, a peer schema can be specified using views. This is similar to the LAV approach in data integration systems, except that queries at a peer are expressed in terms of the local views, not the CSD. Another difference between this approach and LAV is that the CSD is not a global schema, i.e., it is common to a limited set of peers with a common interest (see Fig. 9.9). Thus, the CSD does not pose scalability challenges. When a peer decides to share data, it needs to map its local schema to the CSD.

Example 9.1 Given two CSD relation definitions R_1 and R_2, an example of peer mapping at peer p is

$$p : R(A, B, D) \subseteq csd : R_1(A, B, C), csd : R_2(C, D, E)$$

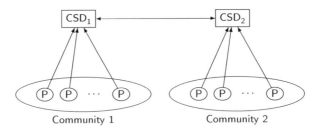

Fig. 9.9 Common agreement schema mapping in APPA

In this example, the relation R(A, B, D) that is shared by peer p is mapped to relations R_1(A, B, C), R_2(C, D, E) both of which are involved in the CSD. In APPA, the mappings between the CSD and each peer's local schema are stored locally at the peer. Given a query Q on the local schema, the peer reformulates Q to a query on the CSD using locally stored mappings. ◆

9.2.4 Schema Mapping Using IR Techniques

This approach extracts the schema mappings at query execution time using IR techniques by exploring the schema descriptions provided by users. PeerDB follows this approach for query processing in unstructured P2P networks. For each relation that is shared by a peer, the description of the relation and its attributes is maintained at that peer. The descriptions are provided by users upon creation of relations, and serve as a kind of synonymous names of relation names and attributes. When a query is issued, a request to find out potential matches is produced and flooded to the peers that return the corresponding metadata. By matching keywords from the metadata of the relations, PeerDB is able to find relations that are potentially similar to the query relations. The relations that are found are presented to the issuer of the query who decides whether or not to proceed with the execution of the query at the remote peer that owns the relations.

Edutella also follows this approach for schema mapping in superpeer networks. Resources in Edutella are described using the RDF metadata model, and the descriptions are stored at superpeers. When a user issues a query at a peer p, the query is sent to p's superpeer where the stored schema descriptions are explored and the addresses of the relevant peers are returned to the user. If the superpeer does not find relevant peers, it sends the query to other superpeers such that they search relevant peers by exploring their stored schema descriptions. In order to explore stored schemas, superpeers use the RDF-QEL query language, which is based on Datalog semantics and thus compatible with all existing query languages, supporting query functionalities that extend the usual relational query languages.

9.3 Querying Over P2P Systems

P2P networks provide basic techniques for routing queries to relevant peers and this is sufficient for supporting simple, exact-match queries. For instance, as noted earlier, a DHT provides a basic mechanism to efficiently look up data based on a key-value. However, supporting more complex queries in P2P systems, particularly in DHTs, is difficult and has been the subject of much recent research. The main types of complex queries which are useful in P2P systems are top-k queries, join queries, and range queries. In this section, we discuss the techniques for processing them.

9.3.1   Top-k Queries

Top-k queries have been used in many domains such as network and system monitoring, information retrieval, and multimedia databases. With a top-k query, the user requests k most relevant answers to be returned by the system. The degree of relevance (score) of the answers to the query is determined by a scoring function. Top-k queries are very useful for data management in P2P systems, in particular when the complete answer set is very large.

Example 9.2 Consider a P2P system with medical doctors who want to share some (restricted) patient data for an epidemiological study. Assume that all doctors agreed on a common Patient description in relational format. Then, one doctor may want to submit the following query to obtain the top 10 answers ranked by a scoring function over height and weight:

```
SELECT *
FROM     Patient P
WHERE    P.disease = "diabetes"
AND      P.height < 170
AND      P.weight > 160
ORDER BY scoring-function(height,weight)
STOP AFTER 10
```

The scoring function specifies how closely each data item matches the conditions. For instance, in the query above, the scoring function could compute the ten most overweight people.   ◆

Efficient execution of top-k queries in P2P systems is difficult because of the scale of the network. In this section, we first discuss the most efficient techniques proposed for top-k query processing in distributed systems. Then, we present the techniques proposed for P2P systems.

9.3.1.1   Basic Techniques

An efficient algorithm for top-k query processing in centralized and distributed systems is the Threshold Algorithm (TA) . TA is applicable for queries where the scoring function is monotonic, i.e., any increase in the value of the input does not decrease the value of the output. Many of the popular aggregation functions such as Min, Max, and Average are monotonic. TA has been the basis for several algorithms, and we discuss these in this section.

Threshold Algorithm (TA)

TA assumes a model based on lists of data items sorted by their local scores. The model is as follows. Suppose we have m lists of n data items such that each data item has a local score in each list and the lists are sorted according to the local scores of their data items. Furthermore, each data item has an overall score that is computed based on its local scores in all lists using a given scoring function. For example, consider the database (i.e., three sorted lists) in Fig. 9.10. Assuming the scoring function computes the sum of the local scores of the same data item in all lists, the overall score of item d_1 is $30 + 21 + 14 = 65$.

Then the problem of top-k query processing is to find the k data items whose overall scores are the highest. This problem model is simple and general. Suppose we want to find the top-k tuples in a relational table according to some scoring function over its attributes. To answer this query, it is sufficient to have a sorted (indexed) list of the values of each attribute involved in the scoring function, and return the k tuples whose overall scores in the lists are the highest. As another example, suppose we want to find the top-k documents whose aggregate rank is the highest with respect to some given set of keywords. To answer this query, the solution is to have, for each keyword, a ranked list of documents, and return the k documents whose aggregate rank over all lists are the highest.

TA considers two modes of access to a sorted list. The first mode is sorted (or sequential) access that accesses each data item in their order of appearance in the list. The second mode is random access by which a given data item in the list is directly looked up, for example, by using an index on item id.

Given m sorted lists of n data items, TA (see Algorithm 9.1) goes down the sorted lists in parallel, and, for each data item, retrieves its local scores in all lists through random access and computes the overall score. It also maintains in a set Y, the k data

Position	List 1 Data Item	List 1 Local score s_1	List 2 Data Item	List 2 Local score s_2	List 3 Data Item	List 3 Local score s_3
1	d_1	30	d_2	28	d_3	30
2	d_4	28	d_6	27	d_5	29
3	d_9	27	d_7	25	d_8	28
4	d_3	26	d_5	24	d_4	25
5	d_7	25	d_9	23	d_2	24
6	d_8	23	d_1	21	d_6	19
7	d_5	17	d_8	20	d_{13}	15
8	d_6	14	d_3	14	d_1	14
9	d_2	11	d_4	13	d_9	12
10	d_{11}	10	d_{14}	12	d_7	11
. . .	. . .	. . .	. . .	. . .	. . .	. . .

Fig. 9.10 Example database with 3 sorted lists

Algorithm 9.1: Threshold Algorithm (TA)

Input: $L_1, L_2, \ldots, L_m$: m sorted lists of n data items
f: scoring function
Output: Y: list of top-k data items
begin
   | $j \leftarrow 1$
   | $threshold \leftarrow 1$
   | $min\_overall\_score \leftarrow 0$
   | **while** $j \neq n + 1$ *and* $min\_overall\_score < threshold$ **do**
   | | {Do sorted access in parallel to each of the m sorted lists}
   | | **for** i *from* 1 *to* m *in parallel* **do**
   | | | {Process each data item at position j}
   | | | **for** *each data item d at position j in L_i* **do**
   | | | | {access the local scores of d in the other lists through random access}
   | | | | $overall\_score(d) \leftarrow f(\text{scores of } d \text{ in each } L_i)$
   | | | **end for**
   | | **end for**
   | | $Y \leftarrow k$ data items with highest score so far
   | | $min\_overall\_score \leftarrow$ smallest overall score of data items in Y
   | | $threshold \leftarrow f(\text{local scores at position } j \text{ in each } L_i)$
   | | $j \leftarrow j + 1$
   | **end while**
end

---

items whose overall scores are the highest so far. The stopping mechanism of TA uses a threshold that is computed using the last local scores seen under sorted access in the lists. For example, consider the database in Fig. 9.10. At position 1 for all lists (i.e., when only the first data items have been seen under sorted access) assuming that the scoring function is the sum of the scores, the threshold is $30 + 28 + 30$. At position 2, it is 84. Since data items are sorted in the lists in decreasing order of local score, the threshold decreases as one moves down the list. This process continues until k data items are found whose overall scores are greater than a threshold.

Example 9.3 Consider again the database (i.e., three sorted lists) shown in Fig. 9.10. Assume a top-3 query Q (i.e., $k = 3$), and suppose the scoring function computes the sum of the local scores of the data item in all lists. TA first looks at the data items which are at position 1 in all lists, i.e., d_1, d_2, and d_3. It looks up the local scores of these data items in other lists using random access and computes their overall scores (which are 65, 63, and 70, respectively). However, none of them has an overall score that is as high as the threshold of position 1 (which is 88). Thus, at position 1, TA does not stop. At this position, we have $Y = \{d_1, d_2, d_3\}$, i.e., the k highest scored data items seen so far. At positions 2 and 3, Y is set to $\{d_3, d_4, d_5\}$ and $\{d_3, d_5, d_8\}$, respectively. Before position 6, none of the data items involved in Y has an overall score higher than or equal to the threshold value. At position 6, the threshold value is 63, which is less than the overall score of the three data items involved in Y, i.e., $Y = \{d_3, d_5, d_8\}$. Thus, TA stops. Note that the contents of Y at position 6 are exactly the same as at position 3. In other words, at position 3, Y already contains all top-k answers. In this example, TA does three additional sorted accesses in each list that do not contribute to the final result. This is a characteristic of TA algorithm in that it has a conservative stopping condition that causes it to stop later than necessary—in this example, it performs 9 sorted accesses and $18 = (9 * 2)$ random accesses that do not contribute to the final result.

$\blacklozenge$

TA-Style Algorithms

Several TA-style algorithms, i.e., extensions of TAThreshold Algorithm, have been proposed for distributed top-k query processing. We illustrate these by means of the Three Phase Uniform Threshold (TPUT) algorithm that executes top-k queries in three round trips, assuming that each list is held by one node (which we call the *list holder*) and that the scoring function is sum. The TPUT algorithm executed by the query originator is detailed in Algorithm 9.2.

TPUT works as follows:

1. The query originator first gets from each list holder its k top data items. Let f be the scoring function, d be a received data item, and $s_i(d)$ be the local score of d in list L_i. Then the partial sum of d is defined as $psum(d) = \sum_{i=1}^{m} s_i'(d)$, where $s_i'(d) = s_i(d)$ if d has been sent to the coordinator by the holder of L_i, else $s_i'(d) = 0$. The query originator computes the partial sums for all received data items and identifies the items with the k highest partial sums. The partial sum of the k−th data item (called *phase-1 bottom*) is denoted by λ_1.

2. The query originator sends a threshold value $\tau = \lambda_1/m$ to every list holder. In response, each list holder sends back all its data items whose local scores are not less than τ. The intuition is that if a data item is not reported by any node in this phase, its score must be less than λ_1, so it cannot be one of the top-k data items. Let Y be the set of data items received from list holders. The query originator computes the new partial sums for the data items in Y, and identifies the items with the k highest partial sums. The partial sum of the k-th data item (called phase-2 bottom) is denoted by λ_2. Let the upper bound score of a data item d be defined as $u(d) = \sum_{i=1}^{m} u_i(d)$, where $u_i(d) = s_i(d)$ if d has been received, else $u_i(d) = \tau$. For each data item $d \in D$, if $u(d)$ is less than λ_2, it is removed from Y. The data items that remain in Y are called top-k candidates because there may be some data items in Y that have not been obtained from all list holders. A third phase is necessary to retrieve those.

3. The query originator sends the set of top-k candidate data items to each list holder that returns their scores. Then, it computes the overall score, extracts the k data items with highest scores, and returns the answer to the user.

Example 9.4 Consider the first two sorted lists (List 1 and List 2) in Fig. 9.10. Assume a top-2 query Q, i.e., $k = 2$, where the scoring function is sum. Phase 1

Algorithm 9.2: Three Phase Uniform Threshold (TPUT)

Input: $L_1, L_2, \ldots, L_m$: m sorted lists of n data items, each at a different list holder
f: scoring function
Output: Y: list of top-k data items
begin
    {Phase 1}
    for i *from* 1 *to* m *in parallel* **do**
      | $Y \leftarrow$ receive top-k data items from L_i holder
    end for
    $Z \leftarrow$ data items with the k highest partial sum in Y
    $\lambda_1 \leftarrow$ partial sum of k-th data item in Z
    {Phase 2}
    for i *from* 1 *to* m *in parallel* **do**
      send λ_1/m to L_i's holder
      $Y \leftarrow$ all data items from L_i's holder whose local scores are not less than λ_1/m
    end for
    $Z \leftarrow$ data items with the k highest partial sum in Y
    $\lambda_2 \leftarrow$ partial sum of k-th data item in Z
    $Y \leftarrow Y -$ {data items in Y whose upper bound score is less than λ_2}
    {Phase 3}
    for i *from* 1 *to* m *in parallel* **do**
      send Y to L_i holder
      $Z \leftarrow$ data items from L_i's holder that are in both Y and L_i
    end for
    $Y \leftarrow k$ data items with highest overall score in Z
end

---

produces the sets $Y = \{d_1, d_2, d_4, d_6\}$ and $Z = \{d_1, d_2\}$. The k−th (i.e., second) data item is d_2, whose partial sum is 28. Thus we get $\lambda_1/2 = 28/2 = 14$. Let us now denote each data item d in Y as $(d$, score in List 1, score in List 2$)$. Phase 2 produces

$Y = \{(d_1, 30, 21), (d_2, 0, 28), (d_3, 26, 14), (d_4, 28, 0), (d_5, 17, 24), (d_6, 14, 27), (d_7, 25, 25), (d_8, 23, 20), (d_9, 27, 23)\}$ and $Z = \{(d_1, 30, 21), (d_7, 25, 25)\}$. Note that d_9 could also have been picked instead of d_7 because it has same partial sum. Thus we get $\lambda_2/2=50$. The upper bound scores of the data items in Y are obtained as:

$$u(d_1) = 30 + 21 = 51$$
$$u(d_2) = 14 + 28 = 42$$
$$u(d_3) = 26 + 14 = 40$$
$$u(d_4) = 28 + 14 = 42$$
$$u(d_5) = 17 + 24 = 41$$
$$u(d_6) = 14 + 27 = 41$$
$$u(d_7) = 25 + 25 = 50$$
$$u(d_8) = 23 + 20 = 43$$
$$u(d_9) = 27 + 23 = 50$$

After removal of the data items in Y whose upper bound score is less than λ_2, we have $Y = \{d_1, d_7, d_9\}$. The third phase is not necessary in this case as all data items have all their local scores. Thus the final result is $Y = \{d_1, d_7\}$ or $Y = \{d_1, d_9\}$. ◆

When the number of lists (i.e., m) is high, the response time of TPUT is much better than that of the basic TA algorithm.

Best Position Algorithm (BPA)

There are many database instances over which TA keeps scanning the lists although it has seen all top-k answers (as in Example 9.3). Thus, it is possible to stop much sooner. Based on this observation, best position algorithms (BPA) that execute top-k queries much more efficiently than TA have been proposed. The key idea of BPA is that the stopping mechanism takes into account special positions in the lists, called the *best positions*. Intuitively, the best position in a list is the highest position such that any position before it has also been seen. The stopping condition is based on the overall score computed using the best positions in all lists.

The basic version of BPA (see Algorithm 9.3) works like TA, except that it keeps track of all positions that are seen under sorted or random access, computes best positions, and has a different stopping condition. For each list L_i, let P_i be the set of positions that are seen under sorted or random access in L_i. Let bp_i, the best position in L_i, be the highest position in P_i such that any position of L_i between 1 and bp_i is also in P_i. In other words, bp_i is best because we are sure that all positions of L_i between 1 and bpi have been seen under sorted or random access. Let $s_i(bp_i)$ be the local score of the data item that is at position bp_i in list L_i. Then, BPA's threshold is $f(s_1(bp_1), s_2(bp_2), \ldots, s_m(bp_m))$ for some function f.

Example 9.5 To illustrate basic BPA, consider again the three sorted lists shown in Fig. 9.10 and the query Q in Example 9.3.

1. At position 1, BPA sees the data items d_1, d_2, and d_3. For each seen data item, it does random access and obtains its local score and position in all the lists. Therefore, at this step, the positions that are seen in list L_1 are positions 1, 4, and 9, which are, respectively, the positions of d_1, d_3, and d_2. Thus, we have $P_1 = \{1, 4, 9\}$ and the best position in L_1 is $bp_1 = 1$ (since the next position is 4 meaning that positions 2 and 3 have not been seen). For L_2 and L_3 we have $P_2 = \{1, 6, 8\}$ and $P_3 = \{1, 5, 8\}$, so $bp_2 = 1$ and $bp_3 = 1$. Therefore, the best positions overall score is $\lambda = f(s_1(1), s_2(1), s_3(1)) = 30 + 28 + 30 = 88$. At position 1, the set of the three highest scored data items is $Y = \{d_1, d_2, d_3\}$, and since the overall score of these data items is less than λ, BPA cannot stop.
2. At position 2, BPA sees d_4, d_5, and d_6. Thus, we have $P_1 = \{1, 2, 4, 7, 8, 9\}$, $P_2 = \{1, 2, 4, 6, 8, 9\}$, and $P_3 = \{1, 2, 4, 5, 6, 8\}$. Therefore, we have $bp_1 = 2$, $bp_2 = 2$, and $bp_3 = 2$, so $\lambda = f(s_1(2), s_2(2), s_3(2)) = 28 + 27 + 29 = 84$. The overall score of the data items involved in $Y = \{d_3, d_4, d_5\}$ is less than 84, so BPA does not stop.

Algorithm 9.3: Best Position Algorithm (BPA)

Input: $L_1, L_2, \ldots, L_m$: m sorted lists of n data items
f: scoring function
Output: Y: list of top-k data items
begin

    $j \leftarrow 1$
    $threshold \leftarrow 1$
    $min\_overall\_score \leftarrow 0$
    for i *from* 1 *to* m *in parallel* **do**
      | $P_i \leftarrow \emptyset$
    end for
    while $j \neq n+1$ *and* $min\_overall\_score < threshold$ **do**
      {Do sorted access in parallel to each of the m sorted lists}
      for i *from* 1 *to* m *in parallel* **do**
        {Process each data item at position j}
        for *each data item d at position j in* L_i **do**
          {access the local scores of d in the other lists through random access}
          $overall\_score(d) \leftarrow f(\text{scores of } d \text{ in each } L_i)$
        end for
        $P_i \leftarrow P_i \cup$ {positions seen under sorted or random access}
        $bp_i \leftarrow$ best position in L_i
      end for
      $Y \leftarrow k$ data items with highest score so far
      $min\_overall\_score \leftarrow$ smallest overall score of data items in Y
      $threshold \leftarrow f(\text{local scores at position } bp_i \text{ in each } L_i)$
      $j \leftarrow j+1$
    end while
end

---

3. At position 3, BPA sees d_7, d_8, and d_9. Thus, we have $P_1 = P_2 = \{1, 2, 3, 4, 5, 6, 7, 8, 9\}$ and $P_3 = \{1, 2, 3, 4, 5, 6, 7, 8, 10\}$. Thus, we have $bp_1 = 9$, $bp_2 = 9$, and $bp_3 = 8$. The best positions overall score is $\lambda = f(s_1(9), s_2(9), s_3(8)) = 11 + 13 + 14 = 38$. At this position, we have $Y = \{d_3, d_5, d_8\}$. Since the score of all data items involved in Y is higher than λ, BPA stops, i.e., exactly at the first position where BPA has all top-k answers.

Recall that over this database, TA stops at position 6.   ◆

It has been proven that, for any set of sorted lists, BPA stops as early as TA, and its execution cost is never higher than TA. It has also been shown that the execution cost of BPA can be $(m - 1)$ times (where m is the number of sorted lists) lower than that of TA. Although BPA is quite efficient, it still does redundant work. One of the redundancies with BPA (and also TA) is that it may access some data items several times under sorted access in different lists. For example, a data item that is accessed at a position in a list through sorted access and thus accessed in other lists via random access may be accessed again in the other lists by sorted access at the next positions. An improved algorithm, BPA2, avoids this and is therefore much more efficient than BPA. It does not transfer the seen positions from list owners to the query originator. Thus, the query originator does not need to maintain the seen positions and their local scores. It also accesses each position in a list at most once. The number of accesses to the lists done by BPA2 can be about $(m - 1)$ times lower than that of BPA.

9.3.1.2 Top-k Queries in Unstructured Systems

One possible approach for processing top-k queries in unstructured systems is to route the query to all the peers, retrieve all available answers, score them using the scoring function, and return to the user the k highest scored answers. However, this approach is not efficient in terms of response time and communication cost.

The first efficient solution that has been proposed is that of PlanetP, which is an unstructured P2P system. In PlanetP, a content-addressable publish/subscribe service replicates data across P2P communities of up to ten thousand peers. The top-k query processing algorithm works as follows. Given a query Q, the query originator computes a relevance ranking of peers with respect to Q, contacts them one by one in decreasing rank order, and asks them to return a set of their top-scored data items together with their scores. To compute the relevance of peers, a global fully replicated index is used that contains term-to-peer mappings. This algorithm has very good performance in moderate-scale systems. However, in a large P2P system, keeping the replicated index up-to-date may hurt scalability.

We describe another solution that was developed within the context of APPA, which is a P2P network-independent data management system. A fully distributed framework to execute top-k queries has been proposed that also addresses the volatility of peers during query execution, and deals with situations where some peers leave the system before finishing query processing. Given a top-k query Q with a specified TTL, the basic algorithm called Fully Decentralized Top-k (FD) proceeds as follows (see Algorithm 9.4):

1. **Query forward.** The query originator forwards Q to the accessible peers whose hop-distance from the query originator is less than TTL.
2. **Local query execution and wait.** Each peer p that receives Q executes it locally: it accesses the local data items that match the query predicate, scores them using a scoring function, selects the k top data items, and saves them as well as their scores locally. Then p waits to receive its neighbors' results. However, since some of the neighbors may leave the P2P system and never send a score-list to p, the wait time has a limit that is computed for each peer based on the received TTL, network parameters, and peer's local processing parameters.
3. **Merge-and-backward.** In this phase, the top scores are bubbled up to the query originator using a tree-based algorithm as follows. After its wait time has expired, p merges its k local top scores with those received from its neighbors and sends the result to its parent (the peer from which it received Q) in the form of a score-list. In order to minimize network traffic, FD does not bubble up the top data

---

Algorithm 9.4: Fully Decentralized Top-k (FD)

Input: Q: top-k query
f: scoring function
TTL: time to live
w: wait time
Output: Y: list of top-k data items
begin

    At query originator peer
    begin
        send Q to neighbors
        $Final\_score\_list$ ← merge local score lists received from neighbors
        for *each peer p in $Final\_score\_list$* **do**
          | Y ← retrieve top-k data items in p
        end for
    end
    for *each peer that receives Q from a peer p* **do**
        TTL ← $TTL - 1$
        if $TTL > 0$ **then**
          | send Q to neighbors
        end if
        $Local\_score\_list$ ← extract top-k local scores
        Wait a time w
        $Local\_score\_list$ ← $Local\_score\_list$ ∪ top-k received scores
        Send $Local\_score\_list$ to p
    end for
end

---

items (which could be large), only their scores and addresses. A score-list is simply a list of k pairs (a, s), where a is the address of the peer owning the data item and s its score.

4. **Data retrieval.** After receiving the score-lists from its neighbors, the query originator forms the final score-list by merging its k local top scores with the merged score-lists received from its neighbors. Then it directly retrieves the k top data items from the peers that hold them.

The algorithm is completely distributed and does not depend on the existence of certain peers, and this makes it possible to address the volatility of peers during query execution. In particular, the following problems are addressed: peers becoming inaccessible in the merge-and-backward phase; peers that hold top data items becoming inaccessible in the data retrieval phase; late reception of score-lists by a peer after its wait time has expired. The performance evaluation of FD shows that it can achieve major performance gains in terms of communication cost and response time.

9.3.1.3 Top-k Queries in DHTs

As we discussed earlier, the main functionality of a DHT is to map a set of keys to the peers of the P2P system and lookup efficiently the peer that is responsible for a given key. This offers efficient and scalable support for exact-match queries. However, supporting top-k queries on top of DHTs is not easy. A simple solution is to retrieve all tuples of the relations involved in the query, compute the score of each retrieved tuple, and finally return the k tuples whose scores are the highest. However, this solution cannot scale up to a large number of stored tuples. Another solution is to store all tuples of each relation using the same key (e.g., relation's name), so that all tuples are stored at the same peer. Then, top-k query processing can be performed at that central peer using well-known centralized algorithms. However, the peer becomes a bottleneck and a single point of failure.

A solution has been proposed as part of APPA project that is based on TA (see Sect. 9.3.1.1) and a mechanism that stores the shared data in the DHT in a fully distributed fashion. In APPA, peers can store their tuples in the DHT using two complementary methods: tuple storage and attribute value storage. With tuple storage, each tuple is stored in the DHT using its identifier (e.g., its primary key) as the storage key. This enables looking up a tuple by its identifier similar to a primary index. Attribute value storage individually stores in the DHT the attributes that may appear in a query's equality predicate or in a query's scoring function. Thus, as in secondary indices, it allows looking up the tuples using their attribute values. Attribute value storage has two important properties: (1) after retrieving an attribute value from the DHT, peers can retrieve easily the corresponding tuple of the attribute value; (2) attribute values that are relatively "close" are stored at the same peer. To provide the first property, the key, which is used for storing the entire tuple, is stored along with the attribute value. The second property is provided using the concept of domain partitioning as follows. Consider an attribute a and let D_a be its domain of values. Assume that there is a total order $\prec$ on D_a (e.g., D_a is numeric). D_a is partitioned into n nonempty subdomains $d_1, d_2, \ldots, d_n$ such that their union is equal to D_a, the intersection of any two different subdomains is empty, and for each $v_1 \in d_i$ and $v_2 \in d_j$, if $i < j$, then we have $v_1 \prec v_2$. The hash function is applied on the subdomain of the attribute value. Thus, for the attribute values that fall in the same subdomain, the storage key is the same and they are stored at the same peer. To avoid attribute storage skew (i.e., skewed distribution of attribute values within subdomains), domain partitioning is done in such a way that attribute values are uniformly distributed in subdomains. This technique uses histogram-based information that describes the distribution of values of the attribute.

Using this storage model, the top-k query processing algorithm, called DHTop (see Algorithm 9.5), works as follows. Let Q be a given top-k query, f be its scoring function, and p_0 be the peer at which Q is issued. For simplicity, let us assume that f is a monotonic scoring function. Let scoring attributes be the set of attributes that are passed to the scoring function as arguments. DHTop starts at p_0 and proceeds in two phases: first it prepares ordered lists of candidate subdomains, and then it

---

Algorithm 9.5: DHT Top-k (DHTop)

Input: Q: top-k query;
f: scoring function;
A: set of m attributes used in f
Output: Y: list of top-k tuples
begin
      {Phase 1: prepare lists of attributes' subdomains}
      for *each scoring attribute* A_i *in* A **do**
          $L_{A_i} \leftarrow$ all subdomains of A_i
          $L_{A_i} \leftarrow L_{A_i} -$ subdomains which do not satisfy Q's condition
          Sort L_{A_i} in descending order of its subdomains
      end for
      {Phase 2: continuously retrieve attribute values and their tuples until finding k top
       tuples}
      Done $\leftarrow$ false
      for *each scoring attribute* A_i *in* A *in parallel* **do**
          $i \leftarrow 1$
          while ($i <$ *number of subdomains of* A) *and not Done* **do**
              send Q to peer p that maintains the attribute values of subdomain i in L_{A_i}
              $Z \leftarrow A_i$ values (in descending order) from p that satisfy Q's condition,
               along with their corresponding data storage keys
              for *each received value* v **do**
                 get the tuple of v
                 $Y \leftarrow k$ tuples with highest score so far
                 threshold $\leftarrow f(v_1, v_2, \ldots, v_m)$ such that v_i is the last value received
                  for attribute A_i in A
                 min_overall_score $\leftarrow$ smallest overall score of tuples in Y
                 if *min_overall_score* $\leq$ *threshold* **then**
                   Done $\leftarrow$ true
                 end if
                 $i \leftarrow i + 1$
              end for
          end while
      end for
end

---

continuously retrieves candidate attribute values and their tuples until it finds k top
tuples. The details of the two steps are as follows:

1. For each scoring attribute A_i, p_0 prepares the list of subdomains and sorts them in
   descending order of their positive impact on the scoring function. For each list,
   p_0 removes from the list the subdomains in which no member can satisfy Q's
   conditions. For instance, if there is a condition that enforces the scoring attribute
   to be equal to a constant, (e.g., $A_i = 10$), then p_0 removes from the list all the
   subdomains except the subdomain to which the constant value belongs. Let us
   denote by L_{A_i} the list prepared in this phase for a scoring attribute A_i.
2. For each scoring attribute A_i, in parallel, p_0 proceeds as follows. It sends Q
   and A_i to the peer, say p, that is responsible for storing the values of the first
   subdomain of L_{A_i}, and requests it to return the values of A_i at p. The values are

returned to p_0 in order of their positive impact on the scoring function. After receiving each attribute value, p_0 retrieves its corresponding tuple, computes its score, and keeps it if the score is one of the k highest scores yet computed. This process continues until k tuples are obtained whose scores are higher than a threshold that is computed based on the attribute values retrieved so far. If the attribute values that p returns to p_0 are not sufficient for determining the k top tuples, p_0 sends Q and A_i to the site that is responsible for the second subdomain of L_{A_i} and so on until k top tuples are found.

Let $A_1, A_2, \ldots, A_m$ be the scoring attributes and $v_1, v_2, \ldots, v_m$ be the last values retrieved, respectively, for each of them. The threshold is defined to be $\tau = f(v_1, v_2, \ldots, v_m)$. A main feature of DHTop is that after retrieving each new attribute value, the value of the threshold decreases. Thus, after retrieving a certain number of attribute values and their tuples, the threshold becomes less than k of the retrieved data items and the algorithm stops. It has been analytically proven that DHTop works correctly for monotonic scoring functions and also for a large group of nonmonotonic functions.

9.3.1.4   Top-k Queries in Superpeer Systems

A typical algorithm for top-k query processing in superpeer systems is that of Edutella. In Edutella, a small percentage of nodes are superpeers and are assumed to be highly available with very good computing capacity. The superpeers are responsible for top-k query processing and the other peers only execute the queries locally and score their resources. The algorithm is quite simple and works as follows. Given a query Q, the query originator sends Q to its superpeer, which then sends it to the other superpeers. The superpeers forward Q to the relevant peers connected to them. Each peer that has some data items relevant to Q scores them and sends its maximum scored data item to its superpeer. Each superpeer chooses the overall maximum scored item from all received data items. For determining the second best item, it only asks one peer, the one that has returned the first top item, to return its second top-scored item. The superpeer selects the overall second top item from the previously received items and the newly received item. Then, it asks the peer which has returned the second top item and so on until all k top items are retrieved. Finally the superpeers send their top items to the superpeer of the query originator, to extract the overall k top items, and send them to the query originator. This algorithm minimizes communication between peers and superpeers since, after having received the maximum scored data items from each peer connected to it, each superpeer asks only one peer for the next top item.

9.3.2 Join Queries

The most efficient join algorithms in distributed and parallel databases are hash-based. Thus, the fact that a DHT relies on hashing to store and locate data can be naturally exploited to support join queries efficiently. A basic solution has been proposed in the context of the PIER P2P system that provides support for complex queries on top of DHTs. The solution is a variation of the parallel hash join algorithm (PHJ) (see Sect. 8.4.1) which we call PIERjoin. As in the PHJ algorithm, PIERjoin assumes that the joined relations and the result relations have a home (called *namespace* in PIER), which are the nodes that store horizontal fragments of the relation. Then it makes use of the put method for distributing tuples onto a set of peers based on their join attribute so that tuples with the same join attribute values are stored at the same peers. To perform joins locally, PIER implements a version of the symmetric hash join algorithm (see Sect. 8.4.1.2) that provides efficient support for pipelined parallelism. In symmetric hash join, with two joining relations, each node that receives tuples to be joined maintains two hash tables, one per relation. Thus, upon receiving a new tuple from either relation, the node adds the tuple into the corresponding hash table and probes it against the opposite hash table based on the tuples received so far. PIER also relies on the DHT to deal with the dynamic behavior of peers (joining or leaving the network during query execution) and thus does not give guarantees on result completeness.

For a binary join query Q (which may include select predicates), PIERjoin works in three phases (see Algorithm 9.6): multicast, hash, and probe/join.

1. **Multicast phase.** The query originator peer multicasts Q to all peers that store tuples of the join relations R and S, i.e., their homes.
2. **Hash phase.** Each peer that receives Q scans its local relation, searching for the tuples that satisfy the select predicate (if any). Then, it sends the selected tuples to the home of the result relation, using put operations. The DHT key used in the put operation is calculated using the home of the result relation and the join attribute.
3. **Probe/join phase.** Each peer in the home of the result relation, upon receiving a new tuple, inserts it in the corresponding hash table, probes the opposite hash table to find tuples that match the join predicate (and a select predicate if any), and constructs the result joined tuples. Recall that the "home" of a (horizontally partitioned) relation was defined in Chap. 4 as a set of peers where each peer has a different partition. In this case, the partitioning is by hashing on the join attribute. The home of the result relation is also a partitioned relation (using put operations) so it is also at multiple peers.

This basic algorithm can be improved in several ways. For instance, if one of the relations is already hashed on the join attributes, we may use its home as result home, using a variation of the parallel associative join algorithm (PAJ) (see Sect. 8.4.1), where only one relation needs to be hashed and sent over the DHT.

Algorithm 9.6: PIERjoin

Input: Q: join query over relations R and S on attribute A;
h: hash function;
H_R, H_S: homes of R and S
Output: T: join result relation;
H_T: home of T
begin
> {Multicast phase}
> At query originator peer send Q to all peers in H_R and H_S
> {Hash phase}
> **for** *each peer p in H_R that received Q in parallel* **do**
> > **for** *each tuple r in R_p that satisfies the select predicate* **do**
> > > place r using $h(H_T, A)$
> > **end for**
> **end for**
> **for** *each peer p in H_S that received Q in parallel* **do**
> > **for** *each tuple s in S_p that satisfies the select predicate* **do**
> > > place s using $h(H_T, A)$
> > **end for**
> **end for**
> {Probe/join phase}
> **for** *each peer p in H_T in parallel* **do**
> > **if** *a new tuple i has arrived* **then**
> > > **if** *i is an r tuple* **then**
> > > > probe s tuples in S_p using $h(A)$
> > > **else**
> > > > probe r tuples in R_p using $h(A)$
> > > **end if**
> > > $T_p \leftarrow r \bowtie s$
> > **end if**
> **end for**
end

9.3.3   Range Queries

Recall that range queries have a **WHERE** clause of the form "attribute A in range $[a, b]$," with a and b being numerical values. Structured P2P systems, in particular, DHTs are very efficient at supporting exact-match queries (of the form "$A = a$") but have difficulties with range queries. The main reason is that hashing tends to destroy the ordering of data that is useful in finding ranges quickly.

There are two main approaches for supporting range queries in structured P2P systems: extend a DHT with proximity or order-preserving properties, or maintain the key ordering with a tree-based structure. The first approach has been used in several systems. Locality sensitive hashing is an extension to DHTs that hashes similar ranges to the same DHT node with high probability. However, this method can only obtain approximate answers and may cause unbalanced loads in large networks.

The Prefix Hash Tree (PHT) is a tree-based distributed data structure that supports range queries over a DHT, by simply using the DHT lookup operation. The data being indexed are binary strings of length D. Each node has either 0 or 2 children, and a key k is stored at a leaf node whose label is a prefix of k. Furthermore, leaf nodes are linked to their neighbors. PHT's lookup operation on key k must return the unique leaf node $leaf(k)$ whose label is a prefix of k. Given a key k of length D, there are $D+1$ distinct prefixes of k. Obtaining $leaf(k)$ can be performed by a linear scan of these potential $D+1$ nodes. However, since a PHT is a binary tree, the linear scan can be improved using a binary search on prefix length. This reduces the number of DHT lookups from $(D+1)$ to $(\log D)$. Given two keys a and b such as $a \leq b$, two algorithms for range queries are supported, using PHT's lookup. The first one is sequential: it searches $leaf(a)$ and then scans sequentially the linked list of leaf nodes until the node $leaf(b)$ is reached. The second algorithm is parallel: it first identifies the node which corresponds to the smallest prefix range that completely covers the range $[a, b]$. To reach this node, a simple DHT lookup is used and the query is forwarded recursively to those children that overlap with the range $[a, b]$.

As in all hashing schemes, the first approach suffers from data skew that can result in peers with unbalanced ranges, which hurts load balancing. To overcome this problem, the second approach exploits tree-based structures to maintain balanced ranges of keys. The first attempt to build a P2P network based on a balanced tree structure is BATON (BAlanced Tree Overlay Network). We now present BATON and its support for range queries in more detail.

BATON organizes peers as a balanced binary tree (each node of the tree is maintained by a peer). The position of a node in BATON is determined by a (level, number) tuple, with level starting from 0 at the root, number starting from 1 at the root and sequentially assigned using in-order traversal. Each tree node stores links to its parent, children, adjacent nodes, and selected neighbor nodes that are nodes at the same level. Two routing tables: a *left routing table* and a *right routing table* store links to the selected neighbor nodes. For a node numbered i, these routing tables contain links to nodes located at the same level with numbers that are less (left routing table) and greater (right routing table) than i by a power of 2. The jth element in the left (right) routing table at node i contains a link to the node numbered $i - 2^{j-1}$ (respectively, $i + 2^{j-1}$) at the same level in the tree. Figure 9.11 shows the routing table of node 6.

In BATON, each leaf and internal node (or peer) is assigned a range of values. For each link this range is stored at the routing table and when its range changes, the link is modified to record the change. The range of values managed by a peer is required to be to the right of the range managed by its left subtree and less than the range managed by its right subtree (see Fig. 9.12). Thus, BATON builds an effective distributed index structure. The joining and departure of peers are processed such that the tree remains balanced by forwarding the request upward in the tree for joins

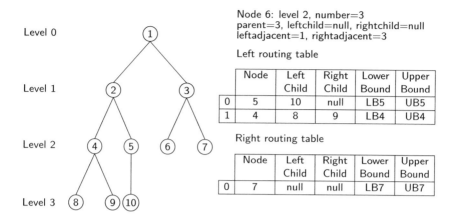

Node 6: level 2, number=3
parent=3, leftchild=null, rightchild=null
leftadjacent=1, rightadjacent=3

Left routing table

	Node	Left Child	Right Child	Lower Bound	Upper Bound
0	5	10	null	LB5	UB5
1	4	8	9	LB4	UB4

Right routing table

	Node	Left Child	Right Child	Lower Bound	Upper Bound
0	7	null	null	LB7	UB7

Fig. 9.11 BATON structure-tree index and routing table of node 6

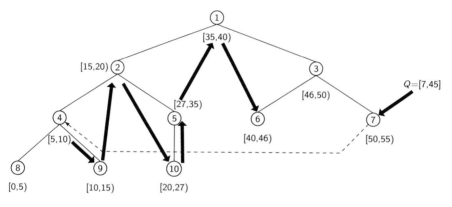

Fig. 9.12 Range query processing in BATON

and downward in the tree for leaves, thus with no more than $O(\log n)$ steps for a tree of n nodes.

A range query is processed as follows (Algorithm 9.7). For a range query Q with range $[a, b]$ submitted by node i, it looks for a node that intersects with the lower bound of the searched range. The peer that stores the lower bound of the range checks locally for tuples belonging to the range and forwards the query to its right adjacent node. In general, each node receiving the query checks for local tuples and contacts its right adjacent node until the node containing the upper bound of the range is reached. Partial answers obtained when an intersection is found are sent to the node that submits the query. The first intersection is found in $O(\log n)$ steps using an algorithm for exact-match queries. Therefore, a range query with X nodes covering the range is answered in $O(\log n + X)$ steps.

Algorithm 9.7: BatonRange

Input: Q: a range query in the form $[a, b]$
Output: T: result relation
begin
  {Search for the peer storing the lower bound of the range}
  At query originator peer
  begin
    find peer p that holds value a
    send Q to p
  end
  for *each peer p that receives Q* **do**
    $T_p \leftarrow Range(p) \cap [a, b]$
    send T_p to query originator
    if $Range(Right Adjacent(p)) \cap [a, b] \neq \emptyset$ **then**
      let p be right adjacent peer of p
      send Q to p
    end if
  end for
end

Example 9.6 Consider the query Q with range $[7, 45]$ issued at node 7 in Fig. 9.12. First, BATON executes an exact-match query looking for a node containing the lower bound of the range (see dashed line in the figure). Since the lower bound is in the range assigned to node 4, it checks locally for tuples belonging to the range and forwards the query to its adjacent right node (node 9). Node 9 checks for local tuples belonging to the range and forwards the query to node 2. Nodes 10, 5, 1, and 6 receive the query, they check for local tuples and contact their respective right adjacent node until the node containing the upper bound of the range is reached.   ◆

9.4 Replica Consistency

To increase data availability and access performance, P2P systems replicate data. However, different P2P systems provide very different levels of replica consistency. The earlier, simple P2P systems such as Gnutella and Kazaa deal only with static data (e.g., music files) and replication is "passive" as it occurs naturally as peers request and copy files from one another (basically, caching data). In more advanced P2P systems where replicas can be updated, there is a need for proper replica management techniques. Unfortunately, most of the work on replica consistency has been done only in the context of DHTs. We can distinguish three approaches to deal with replica consistency: basic support in DHTs, data currency in DHTs, and replica reconciliation. In this section, we introduce the main techniques used in these approaches.

9.4.1 Basic Support in DHTs

To improve data availability, most DHTs rely on data replication by storing $(key, data)$ pairs at several peers by, for example, using several hash functions. If one peer is unavailable, its data can still be retrieved from the other peers that hold a replica. Some DHTs provide basic support for the application to deal with replica consistency. In this section, we describe the techniques used in two popular DHTs: CAN and Tapestry.

CAN provides two approaches for supporting replication. The first one is to use m hash functions to map a single key onto m points in the coordinate space, and, accordingly, replicate a single $(key, data)$ pair at m distinct nodes in the network. The second approach is an optimization over the basic design of CAN that consists of a node proactively pushing out popular keys towards its neighbors when it finds it is being overloaded by requests for these keys. In this approach, replicated keys should have an associated TTL field to automatically undo the effect of replication at the end of the overloaded period. In addition, the technique assumes immutable (read-only) data.

Tapestry is an extensible P2P system that provides decentralized object location and routing on top of a structured overlay network. It routes messages to logical endpoints (i.e., endpoints whose identifiers are not associated with physical location), such as nodes or object replicas. This enables message delivery to mobile or replicated endpoints in the presence of instability of the underlying infrastructure. In addition, Tapestry takes latency into account to establish each node's neighborhood. The location and routing mechanisms of Tapestry work as follows. Let o be an object identified by $id(o)$; the insertion of o in the P2P network involves two nodes: the server node (noted n_s) that holds o and the root node (noted n_r) that holds a mapping in the form $(id(o), n_s)$ indicating that the object identified by $id(o)$ is stored at node n_s. The root node is dynamically determined by a globally consistent deterministic algorithm. Figure 9.13a shows that when o is inserted into n_s, n_s publishes $id(o)$ at its root node by routing a message from n_s to n_r containing the mapping $(id(o), n_s)$. This mapping is stored at all nodes along the message path. During a location query, e.g., "$id(o)$?" in Fig. 9.13a, the message that looks for $id(o)$ is initially routed towards n_r, but it may be stopped before reaching it once a node containing the mapping $(id(o), n_s)$ is found. For routing a message to $id(o)$'s root, each node forwards this message to its neighbor whose logical identifier is the most similar to $id(o)$.

Tapestry offers the entire infrastructure needed to take advantage of replicas, as shown in Fig. 9.13b. Each node in the graph represents a peer in the P2P network and contains the peer's logical identifier in hexadecimal format. In this example, two replicas O_1 and O_2 of object O (e.g., a book file) are inserted into distinct peers ($O_1 \rightarrow$ peer 4228 and $O_2 \rightarrow$ peer $AA93$). The identifier of O_1 is equal to that of O_2 (i.e., 4378 in hexadecimal) as O_1 and O_2 are replicas of the same object O. When O_1 is inserted into its server node (peer 4228), the mapping $(4378, 4228)$ is routed from peer 4228 to peer 4377 (the root node for

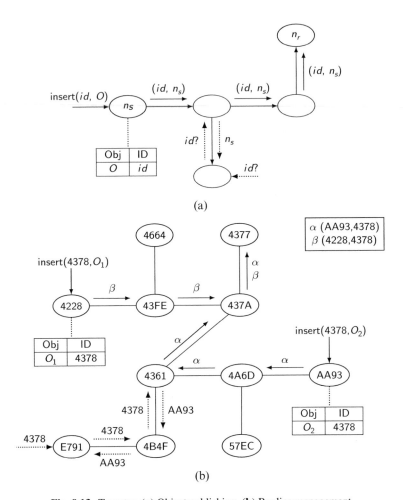

Fig. 9.13 Tapestry. (a) Object publishing. (b) Replica management

O_1's identifier). As the message approaches the root node, the object and the node identifiers become increasingly similar. In addition, the mapping $(4378, 4228)$ is stored at all peers along the message path. The insertion of O_2 follows the same procedure. In Fig. 9.13b, if peer E791 looks for a replica of O, the associated message routing stops at peer 4361. Therefore, applications can replicate data across multiple server nodes and rely on Tapestry to direct requests to nearby replicas.

9.4.2   Data Currency in DHTs

Although DHTs provide basic support for replication, the mutual consistency of the replicas after updates can be compromised as a result of peers leaving the network or concurrent updates. Let us illustrate the problem with a simple update scenario in a typical DHT.

Example 9.7 Let us assume that the operation put(k, d_0) (issued by some peer) maps onto peers p_1 and p_2 both of which get to store data d_0. Now consider an update (from the same or another peer) with the operation put(k, d_1) that also maps onto peers p_1 and p_2. Assuming that p_2 cannot be reached (e.g., because it has left the network), only p_1 gets updated to store d_1. When p_2 rejoins the network later on, the replicas are not consistent: p_1 holds the current state of the data associated with k, while p_2 holds a stale state.

Concurrent updates also cause problems. Consider now two updates put(k, d_2) and put(k, d_3) (issued by two different peers) that are sent to p_1 and p_2 in reverse order, so that p_1's last state is d_2, while p_2's last state is d_3. Thus, a subsequent get(k) operation will return either stale or current data depending on which peer is looked up, and there is no way to tell whether it is current or not.   ◆

For some applications (e.g., agenda management, bulletin boards, cooperative auction management, reservation management, etc.) that could take advantage of a DHT, the ability to get the current data is very important. Supporting data currency in replicated DHTs requires the ability to return a current replica despite peers leaving the network or concurrent updates. Of course, replica consistency is a more general problem, as discussed in Chap. 6, but the issue is particularly difficult and important in P2P systems, since there is considerable dynamism in the peers joining and leaving the system.

A solution has been proposed that considers both data availability and data currency. To provide high data availability, data is replicated in the DHT using a set of independent hash functions H_r, called *replication hash functions*. The peer that is responsible for key k with respect to hash function h at the current time is denoted by $rsp(k, h)$. To be able to retrieve a current replica, each pair ($k, data$) is stamped with a logical timestamp, and for each $h \in H_r$, the pair ($k, newData$) is replicated at $rsp(k, h)$, where $newData = \{data, timestamp\}$, i.e., newdata is composed of the initial data and the timestamp. Upon a request for the data associated with a key, we can return one of the replicas that are stamped with the latest timestamp. The number of replication hash functions, i.e., H_r, can be different for different DHTs. For instance, if in a DHT the availability of peers is low, a high value of H_r (e.g., 30) can be used to increase data availability.

This solution is the basis for a service called *Update Management Service* (UMS) that deals with efficient insertion and retrieval of current replicas based on timestamping. Experimental validation has shown that UMS incurs very little overhead in terms of communication cost. After retrieving a replica, UMS detects whether it is current or not, i.e., without having to compare with the other replicas, and returns it as output. Thus, UMS does not need to retrieve all replicas to find a current one; it only requires the DHT's lookup service with put and get operations.

To generate timestamps, UMS uses a distributed service called *Key-based Timestamping Service* (KTS). The main operation of KTS is gen_ts(k), which, given a key k, generates a real number as a timestamp for k. The timestamps generated by KTS are *monotonic* such that if ts_i and ts_j are two timestamps generated for the same key at times t_i and t_j, respectively, $ts_j > ts_i$ if t_j is later than t_i. This property allows ordering the timestamps generated for the same key according to the time at which they have been generated. KTS has another operation denoted by *last_ts(k)*, which, given a key k, returns the last timestamp generated for k by KTS. At any time, gen_ts(k) generates at most one timestamp for k, and different timestamps for k are monotonic. Thus, in the case of concurrent calls to insert a pair $(k, data)$, i.e., from different peers, only the one that obtains the latest timestamp will succeed to store its data in the DHT.

9.4.3   Replica Reconciliation

Replica reconciliation goes one step further than data currency by enforcing mutual consistency of replicas. Since a P2P network is typically very dynamic, with peers joining or leaving the network at will, eager replication solutions (see Chap. 6) are not appropriate; lazy replication is preferred. In this section, we describe the reconciliation techniques used in OceanStore, P-Grid, and APPA to provide a spectrum of proposed solutions.

9.4.3.1   OceanStore

OceanStore is a data management system designed to provide continuous access to persistent information. It relies on Tapestry and assumes an infrastructure composed of untrusted powerful servers that are connected by high-speed links. For security reasons, data is protected through redundancy and cryptographic techniques. To improve performance, data is allowed to be cached anywhere in the network.

OceanStore allows concurrent updates on replicated objects and relies on reconciliation to assure data consistency. A replicated object can have multiple primary replicas and secondary replicas at different nodes. The primary replicas are all linked and cooperate among themselves to achieve replica mutual consistency by ordering updates. Secondary replicas provide a lesser degree of consistency in order to gain performance and availability. Thus, secondary replicas may be less up-to-date and can be in higher numbers than primary replicas. Secondary replicas communicate among themselves and primary replicase via an epidemic algorithm.

Figure 9.14 illustrates update management in OceanStore. In this example, R is the (only) replicated object, whereas R and R$_{sec}$ denote, respectively, a primary and

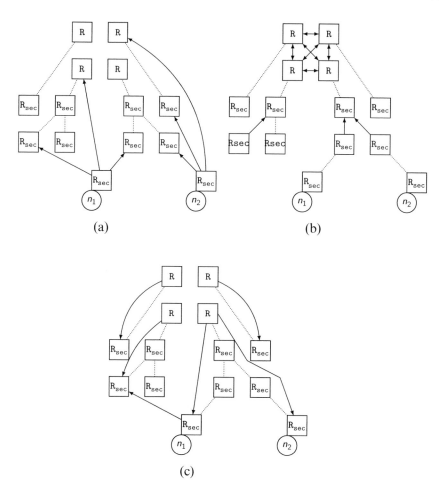

Fig. 9.14 OceanStore reconciliation. (**a**) Nodes n_1 and n_2 send updates to the master group of R and to several random secondary replicas. (**b**) The master group of R orders updates while secondary replicas propagate them epidemically. (**c**) After the master group agreement, the result of updates is multicast to secondary replicas

a secondary copy of R. The four nodes holding a primary copy are linked to each other (not shown in the figure). Dotted lines represent links between nodes holding primary or secondary replicas. Nodes n_1 and n_2 are concurrently updating R. Such updates are managed as follows. Nodes that hold primary copies of R, called the *master group of* R, are responsible for ordering updates. So, n_1 and n_2 perform tentative updates on their local secondary replicas and send these updates to the master group of R as well as to other random secondary replicas (see Fig. 9.14a). The tentative updates are ordered by the master group based on timestamps assigned by n_1 and n_2; at the same time, these updates are epidemically propagated among secondary replicas (Fig. 9.14b). Once the master group obtains an agreement, the result of updates is multicast to secondary replicas (Fig. 9.14c), which contain both tentative[2] and committed data.

Replica management adjusts the number and location of replicas in order to serve requests more efficiently. By monitoring the system load, OceanStore detects when a replica is overwhelmed and creates additional replicas on nearby nodes to alleviate load. Conversely, these additional replicas are eliminated when they are no longer needed.

9.4.3.2   P-Grid

P-Grid is a structured P2P network based on a binary tree structure. A decentralized and self-organizing process builds P-Grid's routing infrastructure which is adapted to a given distribution of data keys stored by peers. This process addresses uniform load distribution of data storage and uniform replication of data to support availability.

To address updates of replicated objects, P-Grid employs gossiping, without strong consistency guarantees. P-Grid assumes that quasiconsistency of replicas (instead of full consistency which is too hard to provide in a dynamic environment) is enough.

The update propagation scheme has a push phase and a pull phase. When a peer p receives a new update to a replicated object R, it pushes the update to a subset of peers that hold replicas of R, which, in turn, propagate it to other peers holding replicas of R, and so on. Peers that have been disconnected and get connected again, peers that do not receive updates for a long time, or peers that receive a pull request but are not sure whether they have the latest update, enter the pull phase to reconcile. In this phase, multiple peers are contacted and the most up-to-date among them is chosen to provide the object content.

9.4.3.3   APPA

APPA provides a general lazy distributed replication solution that assures eventual consistency of replicas. It uses the IceCube action-constraint framework to capture the application semantics and resolve update conflicts.

The application semantics is described by means of constraints between update actions. An *action* is defined by the application programmer and represents an application-specific operation (e.g., a write operation on a file or document, or a database transaction). A *constraint* is the formal representation of an application invariant. For instance, the *predSucc*(a_1, a_2) constraint establishes causal ordering between actions (i.e., action a_2 executes only after a_1 has succeeded); the *mutuallyExclusive*(a_1, a_2) constraint states that either a_1 or a_2 can be executed. The aim of

---

[2]Tentative data is data that the primary replicas have not yet committed.

reconciliation is to take a set of actions with the associated constraints and produce a *schedule*, i.e., a list of ordered actions that do not violate constraints. In order to reduce the schedule production complexity, the set of actions to be ordered is divided into subsets called *clusters*. A cluster is a subset of actions related by constraints that can be ordered independently of other clusters. Therefore, the *global schedule* is composed by the concatenation of clusters' ordered actions.

Data managed by the APPA reconciliation algorithm are stored in data structures called *reconciliation objects*. Each reconciliation object has a unique identifier in order to enable its storage and retrieval in the DHT. Data replication proceeds as follows. First, nodes execute local actions to update a replica of an object while respecting user-defined constraints. Then, these actions (with the associated constraints) are stored in the DHT based on the object's identifier. Finally, reconciler nodes retrieve actions and constraints from the DHT and produce the global schedule, by reconciling conflicting actions based on the application semantics. This schedule is locally executed at every node, thereby assuring eventual consistency.

Any connected node can try to start reconciliation by inviting other available nodes to engage with it. Only one reconciliation can run at-a-time. The reconciliation of update actions is performed in 6 distributed steps as follows. Nodes at step 2 start reconciliation. The outputs produced at each step become the input to the next one.

- **Step 1—node allocation:** a subset of connected replica nodes is selected to proceed as reconcilers based on communication costs.
- **Step 2—action grouping:** reconcilers take actions from the action logs and put actions that try to update common objects into the same group since these actions are potentially in conflict. Groups of actions that try to update object R are stored in the *action log R* reconciliation object (L_R).
- **Step 3—cluster creation:** reconcilers take action groups from the action logs and split them into clusters of semantically dependent conflicting actions: two actions a_1 and a_2 are semantically independent if the application judges it safe to execute them together, in any order, even if they update a common object; otherwise, a_1 and a_2 are semantically dependent. Clusters produced in this step are stored in the cluster set reconciliation object.
- **Step 4—clusters extension:** user-defined constraints are not taken into account in cluster creation. Thus, in this step, reconcilers extend clusters by adding to them new conflicting actions, according to user-defined constraints.
- **Step 5—cluster integration:** cluster extensions lead to cluster overlapping (an overlap occurs when the intersection of two clusters results in a nonnull set of actions). In this step, reconcilers bring together overlapping clusters. At this point, clusters become mutually independent, i.e., there are no constraints involving actions of distinct clusters.
- **Step 6—cluster ordering:** in this step, reconcilers take each cluster from the cluster set and order the cluster's actions. The ordered actions associated with each cluster are stored in the *schedule* reconciliation object. The concatenation

of all clusters' ordered actions makes up the global schedule that is executed by all replica nodes.

At every step, the reconciliation algorithm takes advantage of data parallelism, i.e., several nodes perform simultaneously independent activities on a distinct subset of actions (e.g., ordering of different clusters).

9.5   Blockchain

Popularized by bitcoin and other cryptocurrencies, blockchain is a recent P2P infrastructure that can record transactions between two parties efficiently and safely. It has become a hot topic, subject to much hype and controversy. On the one hand, we find enthusiastic proponents such as Ito, Narula, and Ali claiming in 2017 that blockchain is a disruptive technology that "will do to the financial system what the Internet did to media." On the other hand, we find strong opponents, e.g., famous economist N. Roubini who calls blockchain in 2018 the most "overhyped and least useful technology in human history." As always, the truth is probably somewhere in between.

Blockchain was invented for bitcoin to solve the double spending problem of previous digital currencies without the need of a trusted, central authority. On January 3, 2009, Satoshi Nakamoto[3] created the first source block with a unique transaction of 50 bitcoins to himself. Since then, there have been many other blockchains such as Ethereum in 2013 and Ripple in 2014. The success has been significant and cryptocurrencies have been used a lot for money transfer or high-risk investment, e.g., initial coin offerings (ICOs) as an alternative to initial public offerings (IPOs). The potential advantages of using a blockchain-based cryptocurrency are the following:

- Low transaction fee (set by the sender to speed up processing), which is independent of the amount of money transferred;
- Fewer risks for merchants (no fraudulent chargebacks);
- Security and control (e.g., protection from identity theft);
- Trust through the blockchain, without any central authority.

However, cryptocurrencies have also been used a lot for scams and illegal activities (purchases on the dark web, money laundering, theft, etc.), which has triggered warnings from market authorities and beginning of regulation in some countries. Other problems are that it is:

- unstable: as there is no backing by a state or federal bank (unlike strong currencies like Dollar or Euro);

---

[3]Pseudo for the person or people who developed bitcoin, which generated much speculation about their true identity.

- unrelated to real economy, which fosters speculation;
- highly volatile, e.g., the exchange rate with a real currency (as set by cryptocurrency marketplaces) can greatly vary in a few hours;
- subject to severe crypto-bubble bursts, as in 2017.

Thus, there are pros and cons to blockchain-based cryptocurrencies. However, we should avoid restricting the blockchain to cryptocurrency, as there are many other useful applications. The original blockchain is a public, distributed ledger that can record and share transactions among a number of computers in a secure and permanent way. It is a complex distributed database infrastructure, combining several technologies such as P2P, data replication, consensus, and public key encryption. The term Blockchain 2.0 refers to new applications that can be programmed into the blockchain to go beyond transactions and enable exchange of assets without powerful intermediaries. Examples of such applications are smart contracts, persistent digital ids, intellectual property rights, blogging, voting, reputation, etc.

9.5.1 Blockchain Definition

Recording financial transactions between two parties has been traditionally done using an intermediary centralized ledger, i.e., a database of all transactions, controlled by a trusted authority, e.g., a clearing house. In a digital world, this centralized approach has several problems. First, it creates single points of failure and makes it an attractive target for attackers. Second, it favors concentration of actors such as big financial institutions. Third, complex transactions that require multiple intermediaries, typically with heterogeneous systems and rules, may be difficult and take time to execute.

A blockchain is essentially a distributed ledger shared among a number of participant nodes in a P2P network. It is organized as an append-only, replicated database of blocks. Blocks are digital containers for transactions and are secured through public key encryption. The code of each new block is built on that of the preceding block, which guarantees that it cannot be tampered with. The blockchain is viewed by all participants that maintain database copies in multimaster mode (see Chap. 6) and collaborate through consensus in validating the transactions in the blocks. Once validated and recorded in a block, a transaction cannot be modified or deleted, making the blockchain tamper-proof. The participant nodes may not fully trust each other and some may even behave in malicious (Byzantine) manner, i.e., give different values to different observer nodes. Thus, in the general case, i.e., public blockchain as in bitcoin, the blockchain must tolerate Byzantine failures.

Note that the objective of a typical P2P data structure such as a DHT is to provide fast and scalable lookup. The purpose of a blockchain is quite different, i.e., to manage a continuously growing list of blocks in a secure and tamper-proof manner. But scalability is not an objective as the blockchain is not partitioned across P2P nodes.

Compared with the centralized ledger approach, the blockchain can bring the following advantages:

- Increased trust in transactions and value exchange, by trusting the data, not the participants.
- Increased reliability (no single point of failure) through replication.
- Built-in security through chaining of blocks and public key encryption.
- Efficient and cheaper transactions between participants, in particular, compared with relying on a long chain of intermediaries.

Blockchains can be used in two different kinds of markets: public, e.g., cryptocurrency, public auction, where anybody can join in, and private, e.g., supply chain management, healthcare, where participants are known. Thus, an important distinction to make is between public and private (also called permissioned) blockchains.

A public blockchain (like bitcoin) is an open P2P nonpermissioned network and can be very large scale. Participants are unknown and untrusted, and can join and leave the network without notification. They are typically pseudonymized which makes it possible to track a participant's entire transaction history and sometimes even to identify the participant.

A private blockchain is a closed permissioned network, so its scale is typically much smaller than a public blockchain. Control is regulated to ensure that only identified, approved participants can validate transactions. Access to blockchain transactions can be restricted to authorized participants, which increases data protection. Although the underlying infrastructure can be the same, the main difference between public and private blockchain is who (person, group, or company) is allowed to participate in the network and who controls it.

9.5.2 Blockchain Infrastructure

In this section, we introduce the blockchain infrastructure as originally proposed for bitcoin, focusing on the process of transaction processing. Participant nodes are called *full nodes* to distinguish from other nodes, e.g., lightweight client nodes that handle digital wallets. When a new full node joins the network, it synchronizes with known nodes using Domain Name System (DNS) to obtain a copy of the blockchain. Then, it can create transactions and become a "miner," i.e., participate in the validation of blocks called "mining" process.

Transaction processing is done in three main steps:

1. Creating a transaction after two users have agreed on transaction information exchange: wallet addresses, public keys, etc.
2. Grouping of transactions in a block and linking with a previous block.
3. Validation of the block (and of the transactions) using "mining," addition of the validated block in the blockchain and replication in the network.

In the rest of this section, we present each step in more detail.

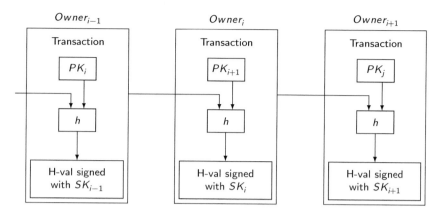

Fig. 9.15 Chaining of transactions

9.5.2.1 Creating a Transaction

Let us consider a bitcoin transaction between a coin owner and a coin recipient that receives the money. The transaction is secured with public key encryption and digital signature. Each owner has a public and private key. The coin owner signs the transaction by

- creating a hash digest of a combination of the previous transaction (with which it receives the coins) and of the public key of the next owner;
- signing the hash digest with its private key.

This signature is then appended to the end of the transaction, thus making a chain of transactions between all owners (see Fig. 9.15). Then, the coin owner publishes the transaction in the network by multicasting it to all other nodes. Given the public key of the coin owner who created the transaction, any node in the network can verify the transaction's signature.

9.5.2.2 Grouping Transactions into Blocks

Double spending is a potential flaw in a digital cash scheme in which the same single digital token can be spent more than once. Unlike physical cash, a digital token consists of a digital file that can be duplicated or falsified.

Each miner node (which maintains a copy of the blockchain) receives the transactions that get published, validates them, and groups them into blocks. To accept a transaction and include it in a block, the miners follow some rules such as checking that the inputs are valid and that a coin is not double-spent (spent more than once) as a result of an attack (see 51% attack next). It may be possible that a malicious miner tries to accept a transaction that violates some rules and include it in a block. In this case, the block will not obtain the consensus of other miners

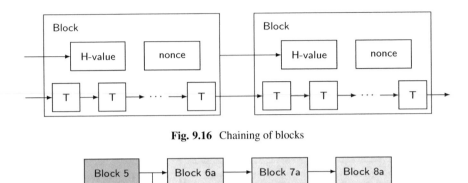

Fig. 9.16 Chaining of blocks

Fig. 9.17 Longest chain rule

that follow the rules and will not be accepted and included in the blockchain. Thus, if a majority of miners follow the rule, the system works. As shown in Fig. 9.16, each new block is built on a previous block of the chain by producing a hash digest (h−value) of the previous block's address, thus protecting the block from tampering or change. The current size of a bitcoin block is 1 Megabyte, reflecting a compromise between efficiency and security.

A problem that can arise is an accidental or intentional fork. As different blocks are validated in parallel by different nodes, one node can see several candidate chains at any time. For instance, in Fig. 9.17, a node may see blocks 7a and 6b, both originated from block 5. The solution is to apply the longest chain rule, i.e., choose the block which is in the longest chain. In the example of Fig. 9.17, the block 7a will be chosen to build the next block 7b. The rationale for this rule is to minimize the number of transactions that need to be resubmitted. For instance, transactions in Block 6b have to be resubmitted by the client (who will see that the block has not been validated). Thus, transactions in a validated block are only provisionally validated and confirmation must be awaited. Each new block accepted in the chain after the validation of the transaction is considered as a confirmation. Bitcoin considers a transaction mature after 6 confirmations (1 hour on average). In Fig. 9.17, transaction maturity is illustrated by the darkness of the boxes (Block 6b is lighter because its transactions will not be confirmed).

In addition to accidental forks, there are also intentional forks, which are useful to add new features to the blockchain code base (protocol changes) or to reverse the effects of hacking or catastrophic bugs. Two kinds of fork are possible: *soft fork* versus *hard fork*. A soft fork is backward compatible: the old software recognizes blocks created with new rules as valid. However, it makes it easy for attackers. A famous occurrence of a hard fork is that of the Ethereum blockchain in 2016, after an attack against a complex smart contract for venture capital. Ethereum forked but without momentum from the community managing the software, thus leading to two blockchains: (new) Ethereum and (old) Ethereum Classic. Note that the battle has been more philosophical and ethical than technical.

9.5.2.3 Block Validation by Consensus

Since blocks are being produced in parallel by competing nodes, a consensus is needed to validate and add them to the blockchain. Note that in the general case of the public blockchain where participants are unknown, traditional consensus protocols such as Paxos (see Sect. 5.4.5) are not applicable. The consensus protocol of the bitcoin blockchain is based on *mining*.[4] We can summarize the consensus protocol as follows:

1. Miner nodes compete (as in a lottery) to produce new blocks. Using much computing power, each miner tries to produce a nonce (number used once) for the block (see Fig. 9.16).
2. Once a miner has found the nonce, it adds the block to the blockchain and multicasts it to all network nodes.
3. Other nodes verify the new block, by checking the nonce (which is easy).
4. Since many nodes try to be the first to add a block to the blockchain, a lottery-based reward system selects one of the competing blocks, based on some probability, and the winner gets paid, e.g., 12.5 bitcoins today (originally 50). This increases the money supply.

Mining is designed to be difficult. The more mining power the network has, the harder it is to compute the nonce. This allows controlling the injection of new blocks ("inflation") in the system, on average 1 block every 10 minutes. The mining difficulty consists in producing a Proof of Work (PoW), i.e., a piece of data that is difficult to calculate but easy to verify, to calculate the nonce. PoW was first proposed to prevent DoS attacks. The bitcoin blockchain uses the Hashcash PoW, which is based on the SHA-256 hash function. The goal is to produce a value v such that $h(f(block, v)) < T$, where

1. h is the SHA-256 hash function;
2. f is a function that combines v with information in the block, so the nonce cannot be precomputed;
3. T is a target value shared by all nodes and reflects the size of the network;
4. v is a 256-bit number starting with n zero bits.

The average effort to produce the PoW is exponential in the number of zero bits required, i.e., the probability of success is low and can be approximated as $1/2^n$.

---

[4]The term is used by analogy to gold mining as the process of bringing out coins that exist in the protocol's design.

This advantages powerful nodes, which now use big clusters of GPUs. However, verification is very simple and can be done by executing a single hash function.

A potential problem with PoW based mining is the *51% attack*, which enables the attacker to invalidate valid transactions and double spend funds. To do so, the attacker (a miner or miner coalition) must hold more than 50% of the total computing power for mining. It then becomes possible to modify a received chain (e.g., by removing a transaction) and produce a longer chain that will be selected by the majority according to the longest chain rule.

9.5.3 Blockchain 2.0

The first generation blockchain, pioneered by bitcoin, enables recording of transactions and exchange of cryptocurrencies without powerful intermediaries. Blockchain 2.0 is a major evolution of the paradigm to go beyond transactions and enable exchange of all kinds of assets. Pioneered by Etherum, it makes blockchain programmable, allowing application developers to build APIs and services directly on the blockchain.

Critical characteristics of the applications are that asset and value are exchanged (through transactions), there are multiple participants, possibly unknown to each other, and trust (in the data) is critical. There are many applications of Blockchain 2.0 in many industries, e.g., financial services and micropayments, digital rights, supply chain management, healthcare record keeping, Internet of Things (IoT), food provenance. Most of these applications can be supported by a private blockchain. In this case, the major advantages are increased privacy and control, and more efficient transaction validation since participants are trusted and there is no need to produce a PoW.

An important capability that can be supported in Blockchain 2.0 is smart contracts. A smart contract is a self-executing contract, with code that embeds the terms and conditions of a contract. An example of simple smart contract is a service contract between two parties, one that requests the service with an associated payment, and the other that fulfills the service and once executed gets the payment. In a blockchain, contracts can be partially or fully executed without human interaction and involve many participants, e.g., IoT devices. A major advantage of having smart contracts in the blockchain is that the code, which implements the contract, becomes visible to all for verification. However, once on a blockchain the contract cannot be changed. From a technical point of view, the main challenge is to produce bug-free code, which would best be done using code verification.

An important collaborative initiative to produce open source blockchains and related tools is the Hyperledger project of the Linux Foundation that was started in 2015 by IBM, Intel, Cisco, and others. The major frameworks are:

- Hyperledger Fabric (IBM, digital Asset): a permissioned blockchain infrastructure with smart contracts, configurable consensus, and membership services.

- Sawtooth (Intel): a novel consensus mechanism, "Proof of Elapsed Time," that builds on trusted execution environments.
- Hyperledger Iroha (Soramitsu): based on Hyperledger Fabric, with a focus on mobile applications.

9.5.4 Issues

Blockchain is often advertised as a disruptive technology for recording transactions and verifying records, with much impact on the finance industry. In particular, the ability to program applications and business logic in the blockchain opens up many possibilities for developers, e.g., smart contracts. Some proponents, e.g., cypherpunk activists, even consider it as a potential disruptive power that will establish a sense of democracy and equality, where individuals and small businesses will be able to compete with corporate powers.

However, there are important limitations, in particular in the case of the public blockchain, as is the most general infrastructure. The limitations are:

- Complexity and scalability, in particular, difficult evolution of operating rules that require forking the blockchain.
- Ever increasing chain size and high energy consumption (with PoW).
- Potential for a 51% attack.
- Low privacy as users are only pseudonymized. For instance, making a transaction with a user may reveal all its other transactions.
- Unpredictable duration of transactions, from a few minutes to days.
- Lack of control and regulation, which makes it hard for states to watch and tax transactions.
- Security concerns: if a private key is lost or stolen, an individual has no recourse.

To address these limitations, several research issues in distributed systems, software engineering, and data management can be identified:

- Scalability and security of the public blockchain. This issue has triggered renewed interest on consensus protocols, with more efficient alternatives to PoW: proof-of-stake, proof-of-hold, proof-of-use, proof-of-stake/time. Furthermore, there are other performance bottlenecks beside consensus. However, a major issue remains the trade-off between performance and security. Bitcoin-NG is a new generation blockchain with two types of blocks: key blocks that include PoW, a reference to previous block, and mining reward, which makes PoW computing more efficient; and microblocks that include transactions, but no PoW.
- Smart contract management, including code certification and verification, contract evolution (change propagation), optimization, and execution control.
- Blockchain and data management. As a blockchain is merely a distributed database structure, it can be improved by drawing from design principles of database systems. For instance, a declarative language could make it easier

to define, verify, and optimize complex smart contracts. BigchainDB is a
new DBMS that applies distributed database concepts, in particular, a rich
transaction model, role-based access control, and queries, to support a scalable
blockchain. Understanding the performance bottlenecks also requires benchmarking. BLOCKBENCH is a benchmarking framework for understanding the
performance of private blockchains against data processing workloads.
• Blockchain interoperability. There are many blockchains, each with different
protocols and APIs. The Blockchain Interoperability Alliance (BIA) has been
established to define standards in order to promote cross-blockchain transactions.

9.6 Conclusion

By distributing data storage and processing across autonomous peers in the network,
P2P systems can scale without the need for powerful servers. Today, major data
sharing applications such as BitTorrent, eDonkey, or Gnutella are used daily by
millions of users. P2P has also been successfully used to scale data management
in the cloud, e.g., DynamoDB key-value store (see Sect. 11.2.1). However, these
applications remain limited in terms of database functionality.

Advanced P2P applications such as collaborative consumption (e.g., car sharing)
must deal with semantically rich data (e.g., XML or RDF documents, relational
tables, etc.). Supporting such applications requires significant revisiting of distributed database techniques (schema management, access control, query processing, transaction management, consistency management, reliability, and replication).
When considering data management, the main requirements of a P2P data management system are autonomy, query expressiveness, efficiency, quality of service, and
fault-tolerance. Depending on the P2P network architecture (unstructured, structured DHT, or superpeer), these requirements can be achieved to varying degrees.
Unstructured networks have better fault-tolerance but can be quite inefficient
because they rely on flooding for query routing. Hybrid systems have better potential
to satisfy high-level data management requirements. However, DHT systems are
best for key-based search and could be combined with superpeer networks for more
complex searching.

Most of the work on data sharing in P2P systems has initially focused on schema
management and query processing, in particular to deal with semantically rich data.
However, more recently with blockchain, there has been much more work on update
management, replication, transactions, and access control, yet over relatively simple
data. P2P techniques have also received some attention to help scaling up data
management in the context of Grid Computing or to help protecting data privacy
in the context of information retrieval or data analytics.

Research on P2P data management is having renewed interest in two major
contexts: blockchain and edge computing. In the context of blockchain, the major
research issues, which we discussed at length at the end of Sect. 9.5, have to do with
scalability and security of the public blockchain (e.g., consensus protocols), smart

contract management, in particular, using declarative query languages, benchmarking, and blockchain interoperability. In the context of edge computing, typically with IoT devices, mobile edge servers could be organized as a P2P network to offload data management tasks. Then, the issues are at the crossroads of mobile and P2P computing.

9.7   Bibliographic Notes

Data management in "modern" P2P systems is characterized by massive distribution, inherent heterogeneity, and high volatility. The topic is fully covered in several books including [Vu et al. 2009, Pacitti et al. 2012]. A shorter survey can be found in [Ulusoy 2007]. Discussions on the requirements, architectures, and issues faced by P2P data management systems are provided in [Bernstein et al. 2002, Daswani et al. 2003, Valduriez and Pacitti 2004]. A number of P2P data management systems are presented in [Aberer 2003].

In unstructured P2P networks, the problem of flooding is handled using one of two methods as noted. Selecting a subset of neighbors to forward requests is due to Kalogeraki et al. [2002]. The use of random walks to choose the neighbor set is proposed by Lv et al. [2002], using a neighborhood index within a radius is due to Yang and Garcia-Molina [2002], and maintaining a resource index to determine the list of neighbors most likely to be in the direction of the searched peer is proposed by Crespo and Garcia-Molina [2002]. The alternative proposal to use epidemic protocol is discussed in [Kermarrec and van Steen 2007] based on gossiping that is discussed in [Demers et al. 1987]. Approaches to scaling gossiping are given in [Voulgaris et al. 2003].

Structured P2P networks are discussed in [Ritter 2001, Ratnasamy et al. 2001, Stoica et al. 2001]. Similar to DHTs, dynamic hashing has also been successfully used to address the scalability issues of very large distributed file structures [Devine 1993, Litwin et al. 1993]. DHT-based overlays can be categorized according to their routing geometry and routing algorithm [Gummadi et al. 2003]. We introduced in more details the following DHTs: Tapestry[Zhao et al. 2004], CAN [Ratnasamy et al. 2001], and Chord [Stoica et al. 2003]. Hierarchical structured P2P networks that we discussed and their source publications are the following: PHT [Ramabhadran et al. 2004], P-Grid [Aberer 2001, Aberer et al. 2003a], BATON [Jagadish et al. 2005], BATON* [Jagadish et al. 2006], VBI-tree [Jagadish et al. 2005], P-Tree [Crainiceanu et al. 2004], SkipNet [Harvey et al. 2003], and Skip Graph [Aspnes and Shah 2003]. Schmidt and Parashar [2004] describe a system that uses space-filling curves for defining structure, and Ganesan et al. [2004] propose one based on hyperrectangle structure.

Examples of superpeer networks include Edutella [Nejdl et al. 2003] and JXTA.

A good discussion of the issues of schema mapping in P2P systems can be found in [Tatarinov et al. 2003]. Pairwise schema mapping is used in Piazza [Tatarinov et al. 2003], LRM [Bernstein et al. 2002], Hyperion [Kementsietsidis et al. 2003], and PGrid [Aberer et al. 2003b]. Mapping based on machine learning techniques is used in GLUE [Doan et al. 2003b]. Common agreement mapping is used in APPA [Akbarinia et al. 2006, Akbarinia and Martins 2007] and AutoMed [McBrien and Poulovassilis 2003]. Schema mapping using IR techniques is used in PeerDB [Ooi et al. 2003] and Edutella [Nejdl et al. 2003]. Semantic query reformulation using pairwise schema mappings in social P2P systems is addressed in [Bonifati et al. 2014].

An extensive survey of query processing in P2P systems is provided in [Akbarinia et al. 2007b] and has been the basis for writing Sections 9.2 and 9.3. An important kind of query in P2P systems is top-k queries. A survey of top-k query processing techniques in relational database systems is provided in [Ilyas et al. 2008]. An efficient algorithm for top-k query processing is the Threshold Algorithm (TA) which was proposed independently by several researchers [Nepal and Ramakrishna 1999, Güntzer et al. 2000, Fagin et al. 2003]. TA has been the basis for several algorithms in P2P systems, in particular in DHTs [Akbarinia et al. 2007a]. A more efficient algorithm than TA is the Best Position Algorithm [Akbarinia et al. 2007c]. Several TA-style algorithms have been proposed for distributed top-k query processing, e.g., TPUT[Cao and Wang 2004].

Top-k query processing in P2P systems has received much attention: in unstructured systems, e.g., PlanetP [Cuenca-Acuna et al. 2003] and APPA [Akbarinia et al. 2006]; in DHTs, e.g., APPA [Akbarinia et al. 2007a]; and in superpeer systems, e.g., Edutella [Balke et al. 2005]. Solutions to P2P join query processing are proposed in PIER [Huebsch et al. 2003]. Solutions to P2P range query processing are proposed in locality sensitive hashing [Gupta et al. 2003], PHT [Ramabhadran et al. 2004], and BATON [Jagadish et al. 2005].

The survey of replication in P2P systems by Martins et al. [2006b] has been the basis for Sect. 9.4. A complete solution to data currency in replicated DHTs, i.e., providing the ability to find the most current replica, is given in [Akbarinia et al. 2007d]. Reconciliation of replicated data is addressed in OceanStore [Kubiatowicz et al. 2000], P-Grid [Aberer et al. 2003a], and APPA [Martins et al. 2006a, Martins and Pacitti 2006, Martins et al. 2008]. The action-constraint framework has been proposed for IceCube [Kermarrec et al. 2001].

P2P techniques have also received attention to help scaling up data management in the context of Grid Computing [Pacitti et al. 2007] or edge/mobile computing [Tang et al. 2019], or to help protecting data privacy in data analytics [Allard et al. 2015].

Blockchain is a relatively recent, polemical topic, featuring enthusiastic proponents [Ito et al. 2017] and strong opponents, e.g., famous economist N. Roubini [Roubini 2018]. The concepts are defined in the pioneering paper on the bitcoin blockchain [Nakamoto 2008]. Since then, many other blockchains for other cryptocurrencies have been proposed, e.g., Etherum and Ripple. Most of the initial contributions have been made by developers, outside the academic world. Thus, the main source of information is on web sites, white papers, and blogs. Academic research on blockchain has recently started. In 2016, Ledger, the first academic journal dedicated to various aspects (computer science, engineering, law, economics, and philosophy) related to blockchain technology was launched. In the distributed system community, the focus has been on improving the security or performance of the protocols, e.g., Bitcoin-NG [Eyal et al. 2016]. In the data management community, we can find useful tutorials in major conferences, e.g., [Maiyya et al. 2018], survey papers, e.g., [Dinh et al. 2018], and system designs such as BigchainDB. Understanding the performance bottlenecks also requires benchmarking, as shown in BLOCKBENCH [Dinh et al. 2018].

Exercises

Problem 9.1 What is the fundamental difference between P2P and client–server architectures? Is a P2P system with a centralized index equivalent to a client–server system? List the main advantages and drawbacks of P2P file sharing systems from different points of view:

- end-users;
- file owners;
- network administrators.

Problem 9.2 (**) A P2P overlay network is built as a layer on top of a physical network, typically the Internet. Thus, they have different topologies and two nodes that are neighbors in the P2P network may be far apart in the physical network. What are the advantages and drawbacks of this layering? What is the impact of this layering on the design of the three main types of P2P networks (unstructured, structured, and superpeer)?

Problem 9.3 (*) Consider the unstructured P2P network in Fig. 9.4 and the bottom-left peer that sends a request for resource. Illustrate and discuss the two following search strategies in terms of result completeness:

- flooding with TTL=3;
- gossiping with each peer has a partial view of at most 3 neighbors.

Problem 9.4 (*) Consider Fig. 9.7, focusing on structured networks. Refine the comparison using the scale 1–5 (instead of low, moderate, high) by considering the three main types of DHTs: tree, hypercube, and ring.

Problem 9.5 (**) The objective is to design a P2P social network application, on top of a DHT. The application should provide basic functions of social networks: register a new user with her profile; invite or retrieve friends; create lists of friends; post a message to friends; read friends' messages; post a comment on a message. Assume a generic DHT with put and get operations, where each user is a peer in the DHT.

Problem 9.6 (**) Propose a P2P architecture of the social network application, with the (key, data) pairs for the different entities which need be distributed.

Describe how the following operations: create or remove a user; create or remove a friendship; read messages from a list of friends. Discuss the advantages and drawbacks of the design.

Problem 9.7 (**) Same question, but with the additional requirement that private data (e.g., user profile) must be stored at the user peer.

Problem 9.8 Discuss the commonalities and differences of schema mapping in multidatabase systems and P2P systems. In particular, compare the local-as-view approach presented in Chap. 7 with the pairwise schema mapping approach in Sect. 9.2.1.

Problem 9.9 (*) The FD algorithm for top-k query processing in unstructured P2P networks (see Algorithm 9.4) relies on flooding. Propose a variation of FD where, instead of flooding, random walk or gossiping is used. What are the advantages and drawbacks?

Problem 9.10 (*) Apply the TPUT algorithm (Algorithm 9.2) to the three lists of the database in Fig. 9.10 with k=3. For each step of the algorithm, show the intermediate results.

Problem 9.11 (*) Same question applied to Algorithm DHTop (see Algorithm 9.5).

Problem 9.12 (*) Algorithm 9.6 assumes that the input relations to be joined are placed arbitrarily in the DHT. Assuming that one of the relations is already hashed on the join attributes, propose an improvement of Algorithm 9.6.

Problem 9.13 (*) To improve data availability in DHTs, a common solution is to replicate $(k, data)$ pairs at several peers using several hash functions. This produces the problem illustrated in Example 9.7. An alternative solution is to use a nonreplicated DHT (with a single hash function) and have the nodes replicating (k, data) pairs at some of their neighbors. What is the effect on the scenario in Example 9.7? What are the advantages and drawbacks of this approach, in terms of availability and load balancing?

Problem 9.14 (*) Discuss the commonalities and differences of public versus private (permissioned) blockchain. In particular, analyze the properties that need be provided by the transaction validation protocol.

Chapter 10
Big Data Processing

The past decade has seen an explosion of "data-intensive" or "data-centric" applications where the analysis of large volumes of heterogeneous data is the basis of solving problems. These are commonly known as *big data applications* and special systems have been investigated to support the management and processing of this data—commonly referred to as *big data processing systems*. These applications arise in many domains, from health sciences to social media to environmental studies and many others. Big data is a major aspect of data science, which combines various disciplines such as data management, data analysis and statistics, machine learning, and others to produce new knowledge from data. The more the data, the better the results of data science can be with the attendant challenges in managing and processing these data.

There is no precise definition of big data applications or systems, but they are typically characterized by the "four Vs" (although others have also been specified, such as value, validity, etc.):

1. **Volume.** The datasets that are used in these applications are very large, typically in the petabyte (PB; $10^{15} bytes$) range and with the growth of Internet-of-Things applications soon to reach zettabytes (ZB; $10^{21} bytes$). To put this in perspective, Google has reported that in 2016, user uploads to YouTube required 1PB of *new* storage capacity *per day*. They expect this to grow exponentially, with $10\times$ increase every five years (so by the time you read this book, their daily storage addition may be 10PB). Facebook stores about 250 billion images (as of 2018) requiring exabytes of storage. Alibaba has reported that during a heavy period in 2017, 320 PB of log data was generated in a six hour period as a result of customer purchase activity.

2. **Variety.** Traditional (usually meaning relational) DBMSs are designed to work on well-structured data—that is what the schema describes. In big data appli-

---

The original version of this chapter was revised. The correction to this chapter is available at https://doi.org/10.1007/978-3-030-26253-2_13

© Springer Nature Switzerland AG 2020
M. T. Özsu, P. Valduriez, *Principles of Distributed Database Systems*,
https://doi.org/10.1007/978-3-030-26253-2_10

cations, this is no longer the case, and multimodal data has to be managed and processed. In addition to structured, the data may include images, text, audio, and video. It has been claimed that 90% of generated data today is unstructured. The big data systems need to be able to manage and process all of these data types seamlessly.

3. **Velocity.** An important aspect of big data applications is that they sometimes deal with data that is arriving at the system at high-speed requiring systems to be able to process the data as they arrive. Following the examples we gave above for volume, Facebook has to process 900 million photos that users upload per day; Alibaba has reported that during a peak period, they had to process 470 million event logs per second. These numbers do not normally allow systems to store the data before processing, requiring real-time capabilities.

4. **Veracity.** The data used by big data applications comes from many sources, each of which may not be entirely reliable or trustworthy—there could be noise, bias, inconsistencies among the different copies and deliberate misinformation. This is commonly referred to as "dirty data" and it is unavoidable as the data sources grow along with the volume. It is claimed that dirty data costs upwards of $3 billion per year in US economy alone. Big data systems need to "clean" the data and maintain their provenance in order to reason about their trustworthiness. Another important dimension of veracity is "truthfulness" of the data to ensure that the data is not altered by noise, biases, or intentional manipulation. The fundamental point is that the data needs to be trustable.

These characteristics are quite different than the data that traditional DBMSs (which we have focused on up to this point) have to deal with—they require new systems, methodologies, and approaches. Perhaps it can be argued that parallel DBMSs (Chap. 8) handle volume reasonably well as there are very large datasets managed by these systems; however, the systems that can address **all** of the dimensions highlighted above require attention. These are topics of active research and development and our objective in this chapter and the next is to highlight the system infrastructure approaches that are currently being considered to address the first three points; veracity can be considered orthogonal to our discussion and is a complete topic in itself, and we will not consider it further. In the Bibliographic Notes, we will point to some of the literature in that area. Readers will recall that we briefly discussed it in Chap. 7 (specifically in Sect. 7.1.5); we will also address the issue in the context of web data management in Chap. 12 (specifically, Sect. 12.6.3).

Compared to traditional DBMSs, big data management uses a different software stack with the following layers (see Fig. 10.1). Big data management relies on a distributed storage layer, whereby data is typically stored in files or objects distributed over the nodes of a shared-nothing cluster. Data stored in distributed files is accessed directly by a data processing framework that enables programmers to express parallel processing code without an intervening DBMS. There could be scripting and declarative (SQL-like) querying tools on top of the data processing frameworks. For the management of multimodal data, typically NoSQL systems are deployed as part of the data access layer, or a streaming engine may be used, or even search engines can be employed. Finally, at the top various tools are provided that can be used to build more complex big data analytics, including machine learning

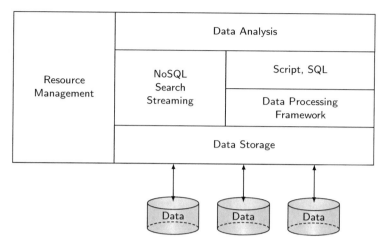

Fig. 10.1 Big data management software stack

(ML) tools. This software stack, as exemplified by Hadoop that we discuss shortly, fosters the integration of loosely-coupled (typically open source) components. For instance, a NoSQL DBMS typically supports different storage systems (e.g., HDFS, etc.). These systems are commonly deployed in a public or private cloud computing environment. This software stack architecture will guide our discussion in this and the following chapter.

The rest of this chapter is focused on components of this architecture going bottom-up, and, in the process, we address two of the V's that characterize big data systems. Section (10.1) focuses on distributed storage systems. Section 10.2, covers two important big data processing frameworks, focusing on MapReduce and Spark. Together with Sect. 10.1, this section addresses scalability concerns, i.e., the "volume" dimension. In Sect. 10.3 we discuss data processing for stream data—this addresses the "velocity" dimension. In Sect. 10.4 we cover graph systems focusing on graph analytics, addressing some of the "variety" issues. Variety issues are also addressed in Sect. 10.5 where we discuss the emerging field of data lakes. Data lakes integrate data from many sources that may or may not be structured. We leave the NoSQL side of this architecture to the next chapter (Chap. 11).

10.1   Distributed Storage Systems

Big data management relies on a distributed storage layer, whereby data is typically stored in files or objects distributed over the nodes of a shared-nothing cluster. This is one major difference with the software stack of current DBMSs that relies on block storage. The history of DBMSs is interesting to understand the evolution of this software stack. The very first DBMSs, based on the hierarchical or network models, were built as extensions of a file system, such as COBOL, with inter-file links, and the first relational DBMSs too were built on top of a file system. For instance, the famous INGRES DBMS was implemented atop the Unix file system. But using a general-purpose file system was making data access quite inefficient, as the DBMS could have no control over data clustering on disk or cache management in main memory. The main criticism for this file-based approach was the lack of operating system support for database management (at that time). As a result, the architecture of relational DBMSs evolved from file-based to block-based, using a raw disk interface provided by the operating system. A block-based interface provides direct, efficient access to disk blocks (the unit of storage allocation on disks). Today all relational DBMSs are block-based, and thus have full control over disk management. The evolution towards parallel DBMSs kept the same approach, primarily to ease the transition from centralized systems. A primary reason for the return to the use of a file system is that the distributed storage can be made fault-tolerant and scalable, which makes it easier to build the upper data management layers.

Within this context, the distributed storage layer typically provides two solutions to store data, objects, or files, distributed over cluster nodes. These two solutions are complementary, as they have different purposes and can be combined.

Object storage manages data as objects. An object includes its data along with a variable amount of metadata, and a unique identifier (oid) in a flat object space. Thus, an object can be represented as a triple ⟨oid, data, metadata⟩, and once created, it can be directly accessed by its oid. The fact that data and metadata are bundled within each object makes it easy to move objects between distributed locations. Unlike in file systems where the type of metadata is the same for all files, objects can have variable amounts of metadata. This allows much user flexibility to express how objects are protected, how they can be replicated, when they can be deleted, etc. Using a flat object space allows managing massive amounts (e.g., billions or trillions) of unstructured data objects. Finally, objects can be easily accessed with a simple REST-based API with put and get commands easy to use on Internet protocols. Object stores are particularly useful to store a very high number of relatively small data objects, such as photos, mail attachments, etc. Therefore, this approach has been popular with most cloud providers who serve these applications.

File storage manages data within unstructured files (i.e., sequences of bytes) on top of which data can be organized as fixed-length or variable-length records. A file system organizes files in a directory hierarchy and maintains for each file its metadata (file name, folder position, owner, length of the content, creation time, last update time, access permissions, etc.), separate from the content of the file. Thus, the file metadata must first be read to locate the file's content. Because of such metadata management, file storage is appropriate for sharing files locally within a data center and when the number of files are limited (e.g., in the hundreds of thousands). To deal with big files that may contain high numbers of records, files need to be split and distributed on multiple cluster nodes, using a distributed file system. One of the most influential distributed file systems is Google File System (GFS). In the rest of this section, we describe GFS. We also discuss the combination of object storage and file storage, which is typically useful in the cloud.

10.1.1 Google File System

GFS has been developed by Google for its internal use and is used by many Google applications and systems, such as Bigtable.

Similar to other distributed file systems, GFS aims at providing performance, scalability, fault-tolerance, and availability. However, the targeted systems, shared-nothing clusters, are challenging as they are made of many (e.g., thousands of) servers built from inexpensive hardware. Thus, the probability that any server fails at a given time is high, which makes fault-tolerance difficult. GFS addresses this problem through replication and failover as we discuss later. It is also optimized for Google data-intensive applications such as search engine or data analysis. These applications have the following characteristics. First, their files are very large, typically several gigabytes, containing many objects such as web documents. Second, workloads consist mainly of read and append operations, while random updates are rare. Read operations consist of large reads of bulk data (e.g., 1 MB) and small random reads (e.g., a few KBs). The append operations are also large and there may be many concurrent clients that append the same file. Third, because workloads consist mainly of large read and append operations, high throughput is more important than low latency.

GFS organizes files as a tree of directories and identifies them by pathnames. It provides a file system interface with traditional file operations (create, open, read, write, close, and delete file) and two additional operations: snapshot, which allows creating a copy of a file or of a directory tree, and record append, which allows appending data (the "record") to a file by concurrent clients in an efficient way.

A record is appended atomically, i.e., as a continuous byte string, at a byte location determined by GFS. This avoids the need for distributed lock management that would be necessary with the traditional write operation (which could be used to append data).

The architecture of GFS is illustrated in Fig. 10.2. Files are divided into fixed-size partitions, called *chunks*, of large size, i.e., 64 MB. The cluster nodes consist of GFS clients that provide the GFS interface to applications, chunk servers that store chunks, and a single GFS master that maintains file metadata such as namespace,

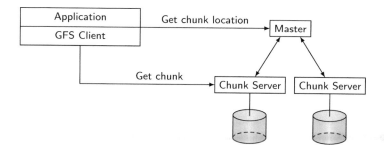

Fig. 10.2 GFS Architecture

access control information, and chunk placement information. Each chunk has a unique id assigned by the master at creation time and, for reliability reasons, is replicated on at least three chunk servers. To access chunk data, a client must first ask the master for the chunk locations, needed to answer the application file access. Then, using the information returned by the master, the client can request the chunk data to one of the replicas.

This architecture using single master is simple, and since the master is mostly used for locating chunks and does not hold chunk data, it is not a bottleneck. Furthermore, there is no data caching at either clients or chunk servers, since it would not benefit large reads. Another simplification is a relaxed consistency model for concurrent writes and record appends. Thus, the applications must deal with relaxed consistency using techniques such as checkpointing and writing self-validating records. Finally, to keep the system highly available in the face of frequent node failures, GFS relies on replication and automatic failover. Each chunk is replicated at several servers (by default, GFS stores three replicas). The master periodically sends each chunk server heartbeat messages. Then, upon a chunk server's failure, the master performs automatic failover, by redirecting all file accesses to an alive server that holds a replica. GFS also replicates all the master's data to a shadow master, so that in case of a master's failure, the shadow master automatically takes over.

There are open source implementations of GFS, such as Hadoop Distributed File System (HDFS), which we discuss in Sect. 10.2.1. There are other important open source distributed file systems for cluster systems, such as GlusterFS for shared-nothing and Global File System 2 (GFS2) for shared-disk, both being now developed by Red Hat for Linux.

10.1.2   Combining Object Storage and File Storage

An important trend is to combine object and file storage in a single system, in order to support both high numbers of objects and large files. The first system that combined object and file storage is Ceph. Ceph is an open source software storage platform, now developed by Red Hat in a shared-nothing cluster at exabyte scale. Ceph decouples data and metadata operations by eliminating file allocation tables and replacing them with data distribution functions designed for heterogeneous and dynamic clusters of unreliable object storage devices (OSDs). This allows Ceph to leverage the intelligence present in OSDs to distribute the complexity surrounding data access, update serialization, replication and reliability, failure detection, and recovery. Ceph and GlusterFS are now the two major storage platforms offered by Red Hat for shared-nothing clusters.

HDFS, on the other hand, has become the de facto standard for scalable and reliable file system management for big data. Thus, there is much incentive to add object storage capabilities to HDFS, in order to make data storage easier for cloud providers and users. In Azure HDInsight, Microsoft's Hadoop-based solution for big data management in the cloud, HDFS is integrated with Azure Blob Storage, the object storage manager, to operate directly on structured or unstructured data. Blob storage containers store data as key-value pairs, and there is no directory hierarchy.

10.2   Big Data Processing Frameworks

An important class of big data applications requires data management without the overhead of full database management, and cloud services require scalability for applications that are easy to partition into a number of parallel but smaller tasks—the so-called embarrassingly parallelizable applications. For these cases where scalability is more important than declarative querying, transaction support, and database consistency, a parallel processing platform called MapReduce has been proposed. The fundamental idea is to simplify parallel processing using a distributed computing platform that offers only two interfaces: map and reduce. Programmers implement their own map and reduce functions, while the system is responsible for scheduling and synchronizing the map and reduce tasks. This architecture is further optimized in Spark, so much of the following discussion applies to both frameworks. We start discussing basic MapReduce (Sect. 10.2.1), and then introduce Spark optimizations (Sect. 10.2.2).

The commonly cited advantages of this type of processing framework are as follows:

1. **Flexibility**. Since the code for map and reduce functions is written by the user, there is considerable flexibility in specifying the exact processing that is required over the data rather than specifying it using SQL. Programmers can write simple map and reduce functions to process large volumes of data on many machines (or nodes, as is commonly used in parallel DBMSs)[1] without the knowledge of how to parallelize the processing of a MapReduce job.
2. **Scalability**. A major challenge in many existing applications is to be able to scale with increasing data volumes. In particular, in cloud applications *elastic scalability* is desired, which requires the system to be able to scale its performance up and down dynamically as the computation requirements change. Such a "pay-as-you-go" service model is now widely adopted by the cloud computing service providers, and MapReduce can support it seamlessly through data parallel execution.
3. **Efficiency**. MapReduce does not need to load data into a database, avoiding the high cost of data ingest. It is, therefore, very efficient for applications that require processing the data only once (or only a few times).

---

[1] In MapReduce literature, these are commonly referred as *workers*, while we use the term *node* in our discussions in the parallel DBMS chapter and the following chapter on NoSQL. The reader should note that we use the terms interchangeably.

4. **Fault-tolerance**. In MapReduce, each job is divided into many small tasks that are assigned to different machines. Failure of a task or a machine is compensated by assigning the task to a machine that is able to handle the load. The input of a job is stored in a distributed file system where multiple replicas are kept to ensure high availability. Thus, the failed map task can be repeated correctly by reloading the replica. The failed reduce task can also be repeated by repulling the data from the completed map tasks.

The criticisms of MapReduce center on its reduced functionality, requiring considerable amount of programming effort, and its unsuitability for certain types of applications (e.g., those that require iterative computations). MapReduce does not require the existence of a schema and does not provide a high-level language such as SQL. The flexibility advantage mentioned above comes at the expense of considerable (and usually sophisticated) programming on the part of the user. Consequently, a job that can be performed using relatively simple SQL commands may require considerable amount of programming in MapReduce, and this code is generally not reusable. Moreover, MapReduce does not have built-in indexing and query optimization support, always resorting to scans (this is highlighted both as an advantage and as a disadvantage depending on the viewpoint).

10.2.1   MapReduce Data Processing

As noted above, MapReduce is a simplified parallel data processing approach for execution on a computer cluster. It enables programmers to express in a simple, functional style their computations on large datasets and hides the details of parallel data processing, load balancing, and fault-tolerance. Its programming model consists of two user-defined functions, map() and reduce() with the following semantics:

map	$(k1, v1) \rightarrow list(k2, v2)$
reduce	$(k2, list(v2)) \rightarrow list(v3)$

The map function is applied to each record in the input dataset to compute zero or more intermediate (key,value) pairs. The reduce function is applied to all the values that share the same unique key in order to compute a combined result. Since they work on independent inputs, map and reduce can be automatically processed in parallel, on different data partitions using many cluster nodes.

Figure 10.3 gives an overview of MapReduce execution in a cluster. The inputs of the map function are a set of key/value pairs. When a MapReduce job is submitted to the system, the map tasks (which are processes that are referred to as *mappers*) are started on the compute nodes and each map task applies the map function to every key/value pair $(k1, v1)$ that is allocated to it. Zero or more intermediate

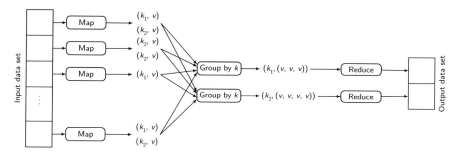

Fig. 10.3 Overview of MapReduce Execution

key/value pairs $(list(k2, v2))$ can be generated for the same input key/value pair. These intermediate results are stored in the local file system and sorted by the keys. After all the map tasks complete, the MapReduce engine notifies the reduce tasks (which are also processes that are referred to as *reducers*) to start their processing. The reducers will pull the output files from the map tasks in parallel, and merge-sort the files obtained from the map tasks to combine the key/value pairs into a set of new key/value pair $(k2, list(v2))$, where all values with the same key $k2$ are grouped into a list and used as the input for the reduce function—this is commonly known as the *shuffle* process, which is, in effect, a parallel sort. The reduce function applies the user-defined processing logic to process the data. The results, normally a list of values, are written back to the storage system.

In addition to writing the map and reduce functions, programmers can exert further control (e.g., input/output formats and partitioning function) by means of user-defined functions (UDFs) that these systems provide.

Example 10.1 Let us consider relation EMP(ENO, ENAME, TITLE, CITY) and the following SQL query that returns for each city, the number of employees whose name contains "Smith."

```
SELECT CITY, COUNT(*)
FROM   EMP
WHERE  ENAME LIKE "%Smith"
GROUP BY CITY
```

Processing this query with MapReduce can be done with the following Map and Reduce functions (which we give in pseudo code).

```
Map (Input: (TID,EMP), Output: (CITY,1))
    if EMP.ENAME like ''\%Smith'' return (CITY,1)
Reduce (Input: (CITY,list(1)), Output: (CITY, SUM(list(1))))
    return (CITY,SUM(1))
```

map is applied in parallel to every tuple in EMP. It takes one pair (TID,EMP), where the key is the EMP tuple identifier (TID) and the value being the EMP tuple, and, if applicable, returns one pair (CITY,1). Note that the parsing of the tuple format to extract attributes needs to be done by the map function. Then all (CITY,1) pairs with the same CITY are grouped together and a pair (CITY,list(1)) is created for each CITY. reduce is then applied in parallel to compute the count for each CITY and produce the result of the query.   ♦

10.2.1.1 MapReduce Architecture

In discussing specifics of MapReduce, we will focus on one particular implementation: Hadoop. The Hadoop stack is shown in Fig. 10.4, which is a particular realization of the big data architecture depicted in Fig. 10.1. Hadoop uses Hadoop Distributed File System (HDFS) as its storage, although it can be deployed on different storage systems. HDFS and the Hadoop processing engine are loosely connected; they can either share the same set of compute nodes, or be deployed on different nodes. In HDFS, two types of nodes are created: *name node* and *data node*. The name node records how data is partitioned, and monitors the status of data nodes in HDFS. Data imported into HDFS is split into equal-size chunks and the name node distributes the data chunks to different data nodes that store and manage the chunks assigned to them. The name node also acts as the dictionary server, providing partitioning information to applications that search for a specific chunk of data.

The decoupling of the Hadoop processing engine from the underlying storage system allows the processing and the storage layers to scale up and down independently as needed. In Sect. 10.1, we discussed different approaches to distributed storage system design and gave examples. Each data chunk that is stored at each machine in the cluster is an input to one mapper. Therefore, if the dataset is partitioned into k chunks, Hadoop will create k mappers to process the data (or vice versa).

Hadoop processing engine has two types of nodes, the *master* node and the *worker* nodes, as shown in Fig. 10.5. The master node controls the execution flow

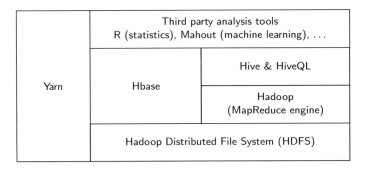

Fig. 10.4 Hadoop stack

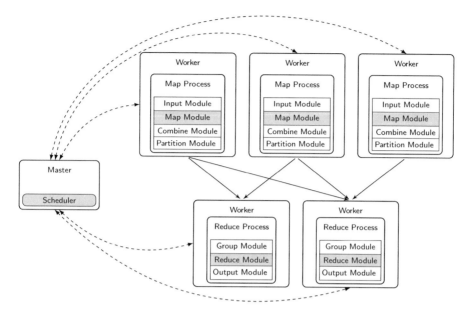

Fig. 10.5 Master-Worker Architecture of MapReduce

of the tasks at the worker nodes via the *scheduler* module (in Hadoop, this is known as the *job tracker*). Each worker node is responsible for a map or reduce task. The basic implementation of MapReduce engine needs to include the following modules the first three of which are essential modules; the remaining ones are extensions:

1. *Scheduler.* The *scheduler* is responsible for assigning the map and reduce tasks to the worker nodes based on data locality, network state, and other statistics of the worker nodes. It also controls fault-tolerance by rescheduling a failed process to other worker nodes (if possible). The design of the *scheduler* significantly affects the performance of the MapReduce system.
2. *Map module.* The *map module* scans a data chunk and invokes the user-defined map() function to process the input data. After generating the intermediate results (a set of key/value pairs), it groups the results based on the partition keys, sorts the tuples in each partition, and notifies the master node about the positions of the results.
3. *Reduce module.* The *reduce module* pulls data from the mappers after receiving the notification from the master. Once all intermediate results are obtained from the mappers, the reducer merges the data by keys and all values with the same key are grouped together. Finally, the user-defined function is applied to each key/value pair, and the results are output to distributed storage.
4. *Input and Output modules.* The *input module* is responsible for recognizing the input data with different input formats, and splitting the input data into key/value pairs. This module allows the processing engine to work with different storage systems by allowing different input formats to be used to parse different data

sources, such as text files, binary files, and even database files. The *output module* similarly specifies the output format of mappers and reducers.

5. *Combine module*. The purpose of this module is to reduce the shuffling cost by performing a local reduce process for the key/value pairs generated by the mapper.

6. *Partition module*. This is used to specify how to shuffle the key/value pairs from mappers to reducers. The default partition function is defined as $f(key) = h(key)\%numOfReducer$, where % indicates the mod operator and $h(key)$ is the hash value of the key. A key/value pair (k, v) is sent to the $f(k)$-th reducer. Users can define different partition functions to support more sophisticated behavior.

7. *Group module*. *Group module* specifies how to merge the data received from different map processes into one sorted run in the reduce phase. By specifying the group function, which is a function of the map output key, the data can be merged more flexibly. For example, if the map output key is a composition of several attributes (sourceIP,destURL), the group function can only compare a subset of the attributes (sourceIP). As a result, in the reducer module, the reduce function is applied to the key/value pairs with the same sourceIP.

Given its stated purpose of scaling over a large number of processing nodes, a MapReduce system needs to support fault-tolerance efficiently. When a map or reduce task fails, another task on a different machine is created to reexecute the failed task. Since the mapper stores the results locally, even a completed map task needs to be reexecuted in case of a node failure. In contrast, since the reducer stores the results in the distributed storage, a completed reduce task does not need to be reexecuted when a node failure occurs.

10.2.1.2   High-Level Languages for MapReduce

The design philosophy of MapReduce is to provide a flexible framework that can be exploited to solve different problems. Therefore, MapReduce does not provide a query language, expecting the users to implement their customized map() and reduce() functions. While this provides considerate flexibility, it adds to the complexity of application development. To make MapReduce easier to use, a number of high-level languages have been developed, some of which are declarative (HiveQL, Tenzing, JAQL), others are data flow languages (Pig Latin), procedural languages (Sawzall), Java library (FlumeJava), and still others are declarative machine learning languages (SystemML). From a database system perspective, perhaps the declarative languages are of more interest. Although these languages are different, they generally follow a similar architecture, as shown in Fig. 10.6. The upper level consists of multiple query interfaces such as command line interface, web interface, or JDBC/ODBC server. Currently, only Hive supports all these query interfaces. After a query is issued from one of the interfaces, the query compiler parses this query to generate a logical plan using the metadata. Then, the rule

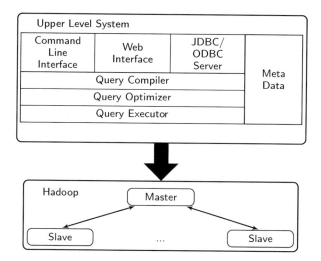

Fig. 10.6 Architecture of Declarative Query Implementations

based optimization, such as pushing projection down, is applied to optimize the logical plan. Finally, the plan is transformed into a directed acyclic graph (DAG) of MapReduce jobs, which are subsequently submitted to the execution engine one-by-one.

10.2.1.3 MapReduce Implementation of Database Operators

If MapReduce implementations such as Hadoop are to be used for data management going beyond the "embarrassingly parallelizable" applications, it is important to implement typical database operators in these systems, and this has been the subject of some research. Simple operators such as select and project can be easily supported in the map function, while complex ones, such as theta-join, equijoin, multiway join require significant effort. In this section, we discuss these implementations.

The projection and selection can be easily implemented by adding a few conditions to the map function to filter the unnecessary columns and tuples. The implementation of aggregation can be easily achieved using the map() and reduce() functions; Fig. 10.7 illustrates the data flow of the MapReduce job for the aggregation operator. The mapper extracts an aggregation key (Aid) for each incoming tuple (transformed into key/value pair). The tuples with the same aggregation key are shuffled to the same reducers, and the aggregation function (e.g., sum, min) is applied to these tuples.

Join operator implementations have attracted by far the most attention, as it is one of the more expensive operators, and a better implementation may potentially lead to

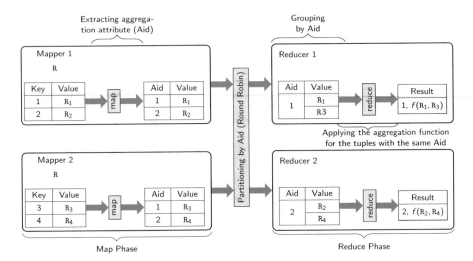

Fig. 10.7 Data flow of aggregation

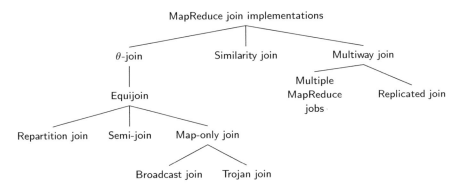

Fig. 10.8 Join implementations on MapReduce

significant performance improvement. The existing join algorithms are summarized in Fig. 10.8. We will describe theta-join and equijoin implementations as examples.

Recall that theta-join (θ-join) is a join operator where the join condition θ is one of $\{<, \leq, =, \geq, >, \neq\}$. A binary (natural) join of relations R(A, B) and S(B, C) can be performed using MapReduce in the following manner. Relation R is partitioned and each partition is assigned to a set of mappers. Each mapper takes tuples $\langle a, b \rangle$ and converts them to a list of key/value pairs of the form $(b, \langle a, R \rangle)$, where the key is the join attribute and the value includes the relation name R. These key/value pairs are shuffled and sent to the reducers so that all pairs with the same join key value are collected at the same reducer. The same process is applied to S. Each reducer then joins tuples of R with tuples of S (the inclusion of relation name in the value ensures that tuples of R or S are not joined with each other).

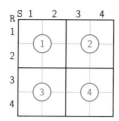

Fig. 10.9 Matrix-to-Reducer Mapping for Cross Product

To efficiently implement theta-join on MapReduce, the $|R| \times |S|$ tuples should be evenly distributed on the R reducers, so that each reducer generates about the same number of results: $\frac{|R| \times |S|}{r}$. 1-Bucket-Theta algorithm achieves this by evenly partitioning the join matrix into buckets (Fig. 10.9) and assigning each bucket to only one reducer to eliminate duplicate computation. This algorithm, at the same time, ensures that all the reducers are assigned the same number of buckets to balance the load. In Fig. 10.9, both tables R and S are evenly partitioned into 4 parts, resulting in a matrix with 16 buckets that are grouped into 4 regions. Each region is assigned to a reducer.

Figure 10.10 illustrates the data flow of the theta-join when θ equals "$\neq$" for the case depicted in Fig. 10.9. The map and reduce phases are implemented as follows:

1. *Map.* On the map side, for each tuple from R or S, a row id or column id (call it *Bid*) between 1 and the number of regions (4 in the above example) is randomly selected as the map output key, and the tuple is concatenated with a tag indicating the origin of the tuple as the map output value. The *Bid* specifies which row or column in the matrix (of Fig. 10.9) the tuple belongs to, and the output tuples of the map() function are shuffled to all the reducers (each reducer corresponds to one region) that intersect with the row or column.

2. *Reduce.* On the reduce side, the tuples from the same table are grouped together based on the tags. The local theta-join computation is then applied to the two partitions. The qualified results ($R.key \neq S.key$) are output to storage. Since each bucket is assigned to only one reducer, no redundant results are generated.

   In Fig. 10.9 there are 16 buckets organized into 4 regions; there are 4 reducers in Fig. 10.10, each responsible for one region. Since Reducer 1 is in charge of region 1, all R tuples where Bid $= 1$ or 2 and S tuples with Bid $= 1$ or 2 are sent to it. Similarly, Reducer 2 gets R tuples with Bid $= 1$ or 2 and S tuples with Bid $= 3$ or 4. Each reducer partitions the tuples it receives into two parts based on the origins, and joins these parts.

Let us now consider equijoin, which is a special case of θ-join where θ is "$=$". There are three variations of equijoin implementations: repartition join, semijoin-based join, and map-only join. We discuss repartition join in some detail below. Semijoin-based implementation consists of three MapReduce jobs: The first is a full

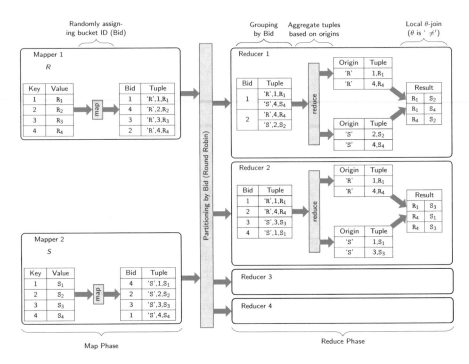

Fig. 10.10 Data flow of theta-join (theta equals "$\neq$")

MapReduce job that extracts the unique join keys from one of the relations, say R, where the map task extracts the join key of each tuple and shuffles the identical keys to the same reducer, and the reduce task eliminates the duplicate keys and stores the results in DFS as a set of files $(u_0, u_1, \ldots, u_k)$. The second job is a map-only job that produces the semijoin results $S' = S \ltimes R$. In this job, since the files that store the unique keys of R are small, they are broadcast to each mapper and locally joined with the part of S (called *data chunk*) assigned to that mapper. The third job is also a map-only job where S' is broadcast to all the mappers and locally joined with R. Map-only join requires only map side processing. If the inner relation is much smaller than the outer relation, then shuffling can be avoided (as proposed in broadcast join) by using a map task similar to the third job of semijoin-based algorithm. Assuming S is the inner and R is the outer relation, each mapper loads the full S table to build an in-memory hash and scans its assigned data chunk of R (i.e., R_i). The local hash join is performed between S and R_i.

Repartition join is the default join algorithm for MapReduce in Hadoop. The two tables are partitioned in the map phase, followed by shuffling the tuples with the same key to the same reducer that joins the tuples. As shown in Fig. 10.11, repartition join can be implemented as one MapReduce job.

1. *Map.* Two types of mappers are created in the map phase, each of which is responsible for processing one of the tables. For each tuple of the table, the

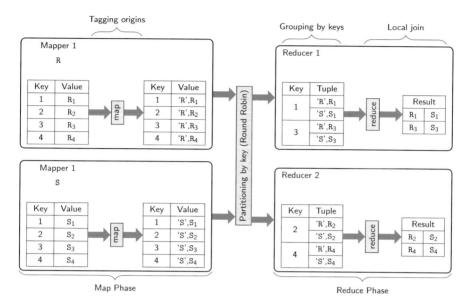

Fig. 10.11 Data flow of repartition join

mapper outputs a key/value pair $(k, \langle t, v \rangle)$, where k is the join attribute value, v is the entire tuple, and t is the tag indicating the source relation of the key/value pair. More specifically, the map phase consists of the following steps:

(a) Scanning the data from HDFS and generating the key/value pair.
(b) Sorting the map output (i.e., set of key/value pairs). On the map side, the output of each mapper needs to be sorted before being shuffled to the reducers.

2. *Shuffle.* After the map tasks are finished, the generated data is shuffled to the reduce tasks.
3. *Reduce.* The reduce phase includes the following steps:

(a) Merge. Each reducer merges the data that it receives using the sort-merge algorithm. Assume that the memory is sufficient for processing all sorted runs together. Then the reducer only needs to read and write data into local file systems once.
(b) Join. After the sorted runs are merged, the reducer needs two phases to complete the join. First, the tuples with the same key are split into two parts based on the tag indicating its source relation. Second, the two parts are joined locally. Assuming that the number of tuples for the same key are small and can fit in memory, this step only needs to scan the sorted run once.
(c) Write to HDFS. Finally, the results generated by the reducer should be written back to the HDFS.

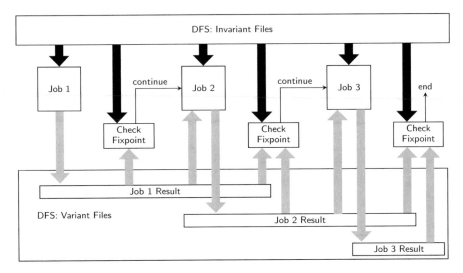

Fig. 10.12 MapReduce Processing for Iterative Computation

10.2.2 Data Processing Using Spark

Basic MapReduce, as discussed in the previous section, is not well suited for a class of data-intensive applications that are characterized by iterative computation requiring a chain of (i.e., multiple) MapReduce jobs (e.g., data mining) or online aggregation. In this section, we discuss an important extension of MapReduce to deal with this class of applications—this extension is the Spark system. We first start by discussing how iterative computing can be performed in a basic MapReduce system and why this is problematic.

Figure 10.12 shows an iterative job with three iterations that have two features: (1) the data source of each iteration consists of a variant part and an invariant part—the variant part consists of the files generated from the previous MapReduce jobs (the gray arrows in Fig. 10.12), and the invariant part is the original input file (the black arrows in Fig. 10.12); (2) a progress check might be needed at the end of each iteration to detect whether a fixpoint has been reached. The fixpoint has different meanings in different applications; in the k-means clustering algorithm that we discuss in Example 10.2, it may reflect whether the within-cluster sum-of-squares is minimized, or in the PageRank computation discussed in Example 10.4 it might reflect that the rank computation of each vertex has converged. This figure identifies three important issues in using MapReduce for these types of tasks. The first is that after each job (i.e., iteration), the intermediate results have to be written to the distributed file system (e.g., HDFS) and read again at the start of the next job (iteration). The second point is that there are no guarantees for subsequent jobs to be assigned to the same machines. Consequently, invariant data that do not change between iterations cannot be kept at the worker nodes and may have to be reread.

The third point is that an additional job is needed at the end of each iteration to compare the results generated between the current job and the previous one (i.e., check for convergence). All of these have high overhead, making it inefficient to use MapReduce for these applications. There have been a number of approaches to address these problems, some of which are task-specific, such as graph analytics that we discuss in the next section, while others, such as Spark, are more general.

An example of a workload that is problematic in MapReduce is the k-means clustering algorithm that is used quite frequently in big data analysis. We present this workload in Example 10.2 and discuss the difficulties in accomplishing it using MapReduce.

Example 10.2 The k-means algorithm takes a set X of values and partitions them in k clusters by placing each value $x_i \in X$ in cluster C_j whose centroid has the lowest distance to x_i. The centroid of a cluster is the mean of the values in that cluster. The distance computation is the within-cluster-sum-of-squares, i.e., $\sum_{j=1}^{k} \sum_{x_i \in C_j} (x_i - \mu_j)^2$ where μ_j is the centroid of cluster C_j. So, we are trying to find the allocation that minimizes this function for each x_i.

The standard k-means algorithm takes as input the value set $X = \{x_1, x_2, \ldots, x_r\}$, and an initial set of centroids $M = \{\mu_1, \mu_2, \ldots, \mu_m\}$ (usually $r \gg m$) and iteratively performs the following three steps:

1. Compute the distance of each $x_i \in X$ to every centroid $\mu_j \in M$ and assign x_i to cluster C_z if μ_z minimizes the above function.
2. Calculate a new set of centroids M according to the new value assignment to clusters.
3. For each of the clusters in C, check if the new and old centroid values are the same; if they are, convergence has been reached and the algorithms stops. Otherwise another iteration is needed with the new centroid values.

The implementation of this algorithm in MapReduce is straightforward: the first step is performed during map phase with each worker (mapper) performing the computation on a subset of X, while the second step is performed during reduce phase. The third step, checking for convergence, is another job as discussed above. One thing to note is that all of the mappers need the full set of centroids M; therefore, the convergence-checking job (step 3) needs to broadcast the new centroids if convergence has not been reached.

The problems with implementing iterative jobs using MapReduce are exhibited in this example: the results of computation at the end of each iteration (i.e., the newly computed centroids M and the current configuration of the clusters C) have to be written to HDFS so that they can be read by the mappers and reducers in the next iteration; since the assignment of the subsequent iteration job can go to any machine, the invariant data (i.e., X) has to be repartitioned and read again; and there is an extra convergence-check job at the end of each iteration.   ◆

Spark addresses this shortcoming of MapReduce by providing an abstraction for sharing data across multiple stages of an iterative computation. The abstraction is called *resilient distributed dataset* (RDD). It accomplishes efficient sharing in two ways: the first is that it ensures that the partitions that are assigned to each worker node are maintained between iterations to avoid shuffling data; the second is that it avoids writing and reading from HDFS in between iteration jobs by keeping the RDDs in memory—since the assignment to workers is maintained from one iteration to the next, this is feasible.

An RDD is a data structure that users can create, decide how it is partitioned among the worker nodes of a cluster, and explicitly decide whether it is stored on disk or kept in memory. If it is kept in memory, it serves as the working set cache of the application. An RDD is immutable (i.e., read-only) collection of data records; performing an update over an RDD is accomplished by a *transformation* (e.g., map(), filter(), groupByKey()) that results in the generation of a new RDD. Thus, an RDD can be created either from the data read from the file system or from another RDD through a transformation.

Example 10.3 Let us consider the implementation of k-means clustering (Example 10.2) in Spark. We will not give the full algorithm here[2] but will highlight how it addresses the issues:

1. Create an RDD for the invariant data (set X), and cache it in memory to bypass the I/O that has to be performed in between each iteration.
2. Create an RDD for variant data (chosen centroids M).
3. Compute the distance between $x_i \in X$ and each $\mu_j \in M$; save these distances as an RDD D.
4. Create a new RDD that includes each x_i and the μ_j with minimum distance from D.
5. Create an RDD M_{new} that includes the mean value of x_i assigned to each μ_j.
6. Compare M and M_{new}, and decide if convergence has been achieved (check fixpoint).
7. If not converged yet, then $M \leftarrow M_{new}$. There is no need to reload invariant data again, Spark can proceed to step 10.3.

◆

An important aspect of an RDD is whether it persists across iterations (or MapReduce jobs). If this is desired, then one of the two transforms have to be applied to the RDD: cache or persist. If it is desired for the RDD to remain in main memory across jobs, then cache is used; if flexibility is needed in specifying the "storage level" (e.g., disk only, disk and memory, etc.), then persist is used with the appropriate options with the default being persistence in memory.

Computation of RDDs is done lazily, when the program requires an *action*. Actions (e.g., collect(), count()) are different than transforms in that they materialize

---

[2]The full implementation of a variant of the algorithm we discussed above can be found at https://github.com/apache/spark/blob/master/mllib/src/main/scala/org/apache/spark/mllib/clustering/KMeans.scala (accessed January 2018).

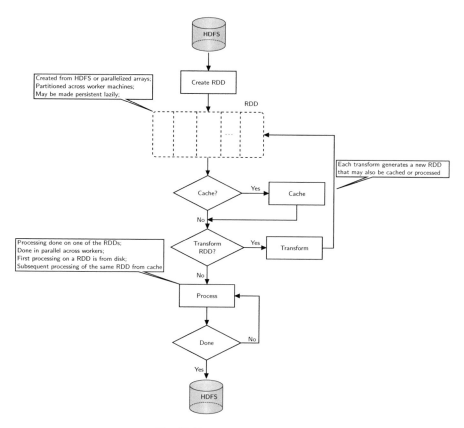

Fig. 10.13 Spark Program Flow

the RDD when the first action is performed, and the specified action is executed
on the RDD at all the nodes where it is partitioned. We will discuss the execution
aspect later.

Let us now look at the workflow of a Spark program execution—this is depicted
in Fig. 10.13. The first thing that the program does is to create an RDD from the
raw data on HDFS. Then, based on the user decision as to whether to cache/persist
the RDD, the system takes appropriate preparations. Then, there may be additional
transforms to generate other RDDs and, for each, cache/persist decision is specified.
Finally, the processing starts with the actions indicated in the program. As noted
above, the first action on an RDD materializes it, and then applies the action. The
processing iterates over multiple actions and jobs.

Let us now discuss Spark support for executing programs written using the
RDD concept. Spark expects to have a controller machine that executes the driver
software. The driver generates the RDDs indicated in the program, and upon the
first action on an RDD, materializes it, partitions it across the worker nodes, and
then executes the action on the workers. The controller corresponds to the master

node in MapReduce while the driver performs the schedule function. Based on the cache/persist decision for each RDD, the driver instructs the workers to take appropriate action. When the workers indicate that the execution of the action is completed, the driver initiates the subsequent action. There are usual optimizations with respect to how RDDs are managed, how to deal with straggler workers, etc., but these are outside our scope.

Spark adds to standard MapReduce fault-tolerance by maintaining the lineage of the RDDs. In other words, it maintains a graph of how each RDD is generated from other RDDs. The lineage is constructed as an object and stored persistently for recovery. When a failure occurs and an RDD is lost, it can be recomputed based on the lineage. Furthermore, as discussed below, each RDD is partitioned across worker machines, so it is likely that the loss is restricted to some partitions of an RDD, and the recomputation can be restricted to those.

An important objective of Spark is to implement the reference architecture we discussed in a uniform way but providing a common ecosystem. This has resulted in the development of a relational DBMS on top of Spark (Spark SQL), a data stream system (Spark Streaming), and a graph processing system (GraphX). We discuss Spark Stream and GraphX in subsequent sections.

10.3   Stream Data Management

The traditional data management systems that we have been considering until now consist of a set of unordered objects that are relatively static, with insertions, updates, and deletions occurring less frequently than queries. They are sometimes called *snapshot databases* since they show a snapshot of the values of data objects at a given point in time.[3] Queries over these systems are executed when posed and the answer reflects the current state of the database. The typical paradigm is executing *transient* queries over *persistent* data.

A class of applications has emerged that does not fit this data model and querying paradigm. These include, among others, sensor networks, network traffic analysis, Internet-of-Things (IoT), financial tickers, on-line shopping and auctions, and applications that analyze transaction logs (such as web usage logs and telephone call records). In these applications, data is generated in real time, taking the form of an unbounded sequence (stream) of values. These are referred to as the *data stream* applications. In this section, we discuss systems that support these applications. Data stream applications are reflective of the velocity characteristic of big data.

Systems that process data streams usually come in two flavors: *data stream management systems* (DSMSs) that provide the functionalities of a typical DBMS

---

[3]Recall from our earlier discussion that data warehouses typically store historical data to allow analysis over time. Most systems we have been considering are OLTP ones, which deal with snapshots.

including a query language (declarative or data flow-based), and *data stream processing systems* (DSPSs) that do not claim to embody full DBMS functionality. Early systems were typically DSMSs, some of which had declarative languages (e.g., STREAM, Gigascope, TelegraphCQ) whereas others (e.g., Aurora and its distributed version Borealis) had a data flow language. More recent ones are typically in the DSPS class (e.g., Apache Storm, Heron, Spark Streaming, Flink, MillWheel, TimeStream). Many of the early DSMSs were single machine systems (except Borealis), while the more recent DSPSs are all distributed/parallel systems.

A fundamental assumption of the data stream model is that new data is generated continually and in a fixed order, although the arrival rates may vary across applications from millions of items per second (e.g., Internet traffic monitoring) down to several items per hour (e.g., temperature and humidity readings from a weather monitoring station). The ordering of streaming data may be implicit (by arrival time at the processing site) or explicit (by generation time, as indicated by a *timestamp* appended to each data item by the source). As a result of these assumptions, data stream systems (DSSs)[4] face the following requirements.

1. Much of the computation performed by a DSS is push-based, or data-driven. Newly arrived stream items are continually (or periodically) pushed into the system for processing. On the other hand, a traditional DBMS employs a mostly pull-based, or query-driven computation model, where processing is initiated when a query is posed.
2. As a consequence of the above, DSS queries and workloads are usually *persistent* (also referred to as *continuous*, *long-running*, or *standing* queries) in that they are issued once, but remain active in the system for possibly a long period of time. This means that a stream of updated results must be produced over time. These systems may, of course, accept and run transient ad-hoc queries as a traditional DBMS, but the persistent queries are their identifying characteristic.
3. A data stream is assumed to have unbounded, or at least unknown, length. Therefore, it is not possible to follow the usual approach and store the data completely before executing the queries; queries need to be executed as the data arrives at the system. Some systems employ *continuous processing model* where each new data item is processed as soon as it arrives in the system (e.g., Apache Storm, Heron). Others employ *windowed processing model* where incoming data items are batched and processed as a batch (e.g., , STREAM, Spark Streaming). From the user's point of view, recently arrived data may be more interesting and useful, leading to window definitions at the application level. Systems that follow a continuous processing model may (and usually do) provide windowing in their API. Therefore, from a user's perspective, they do both. Systems may also implement windows internally to overcome blocking operations as we discuss shortly.

---

[4]We will use this more general term when the separation between DSMS and DSPS is not important for the discussion.

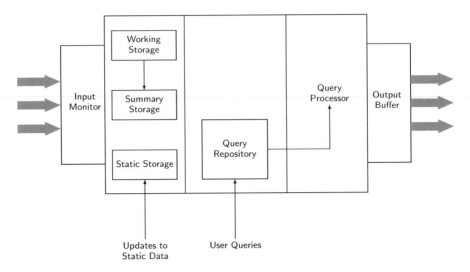

Fig. 10.14   Abstract reference architecture for a data stream management system

4. The system conditions may not be stable during the *lifetime* of a persistent query. For example, the stream arrival rates may fluctuate and the query workload may change.

An abstract single-node reference architecture for DSSs is shown in Fig. 10.14. Data arrives from one or more external sources. An input monitor regulates the input rates, perhaps by dropping items if the system is unable to keep up data is typically stored in three partitions: temporary working storage (e.g., for window queries that will be discussed shortly), summary storage for stream synopses (which is optional since some systems do not expose stream state to applications and therefore do not need this), and static storage for metadata (e.g., physical location of each source). Long-running queries are registered in the query repository and placed into groups for shared processing, though one-time queries over the current state of the stream may also be posed. The query processor communicates with the input monitor and may reoptimize the query plans in response to changing input rates. Results are streamed to the users or temporarily buffered. Users may then refine their queries based on the latest results. In a distributed/parallel DSS, this architecture would be replicated at each node and additional components are added for communication and distributed data management.

10.3.1   Stream Models, Languages, and Operators

We now focus on the fundamental model issues of stream systems. There is rich literature on this subject that we will point to in the Bibliographic Notes; our objective at this point is to highlight and explain the fundamental concepts to understand the subsequent discussion.

10.3.1.1 Data Models

A data stream is an append-only sequence of timestamped items that arrive in some order. While this is the commonly accepted definition, there are more relaxed versions; for example, *revision tuples*, which are understood to replace previously reported (presumably erroneous) data, may be considered so that the sequence is not append-only. In publish/subscribe systems, where data is produced by some sources and consumed by those who subscribe to those data feeds, a data stream may be thought of as a sequence of events that are being reported continually. Since items may arrive in bursts, a stream may instead be modeled as a sequence of sets (or bags) of elements, with each set storing elements that have arrived during the same unit of time (no order is specified among data items that have arrived at the same time). In relation-based stream models (e.g., STREAM), individual items take the form of relational tuples such that all tuples arriving on the same stream have the same schema. In object-based models (e.g., COUGAR and Tribeca), sources and item types may be instantiations of (hierarchical) data types with associated methods. In more recent systems such as Apache Storm, Spark Streaming and others, data items can be any application-specific data—so, sometimes the generic term *payload* is used. Stream items may contain explicit source-assigned timestamps or implicit timestamps assigned by the DSMS upon arrival, so each data item is a tuple ⟨timestamp, payload⟩. In either case, the timestamp attribute may or may not be part of the stream schema, and therefore may or may not be visible to users. Stream items may arrive out-of-order (if explicit timestamps are used) and/or in preprocessed form. For instance, rather than propagating the header of each IP packet, one value (or several partially preaggregated values) may be produced to summarize the length of a connection between two IP addresses and the number of bytes transmitted.

A number of different classifications of window models have been defined, but two criteria are the most important and prevalent:

1. *Direction of movement of the endpoints:* Two fixed endpoints define a *fixed window*, two sliding endpoints (either forward or backward, replacing old items as new items arrive) define a *sliding window*, and one fixed endpoint and one moving endpoint (forward or backward) define a *landmark window*,.
2. *Definition of window size:* Logical or *time-based* windows are defined in terms of a time interval, whereas physical (also known as *count-based*) windows are defined in terms of the number of data items. Moreover, *partitioned windows* may be defined by splitting a window into groups and defining a separate count-based window on each group. The most general type is a *predicate window*, in which an arbitrary predicate specifies the contents of the window; e.g., all the packets from TCP connections that are currently open. A predicate window is

analogous to a materialized view and are also called *session windows* or *user-defined windows*.

Using this classification, the more important window models are time-based and count-based sliding windows. These have attracted the most attention and most of our discussions will focus on them.

10.3.1.2   Stream Query Models and Languages

An important issue is what the semantics of persistent (continuous) queries are, i.e., how do they generate answers. Persistent queries may be monotonic or non-monotonic. A *monotonic query* is one whose results can be updated incrementally. That is, it is sufficient to reevaluate the query over newly arrived items and append qualifying tuples to the result. Consequently, the answer of a monotonic persistent query is a continuous, append-only stream of results. Optionally, the output may be periodically updated by appending a batch of new results. *Non-monotonic queries* may produce results that cease to be valid as new data is added and existing data changed (or deleted). Consequently, they may need to be recomputed from scratch during every reevaluation.

As noted earlier, DSMSs provide a query language for access. Two fundamental querying paradigms can be identified: declarative and procedural. *Declarative languages* have SQL-like syntax, but stream-specific semantics. The languages in this class include CQL, GSQL, and StreaQuel. *Procedural languages* construct queries by defining an acyclic graph of operators (e.g., Aurora).

Languages that support windowed execution provide two language primitives: `size` and `slide`. The first specifies the length of the window and the second specifies how frequently the window moves. For example, for a time-based sliding window query, `size=10min, slide=5sec` would mean that we are interested in operating on data in a window that is 10 minutes long, and the window "moves" every 5 seconds. These have an impact on the way the content of the window is managed and we discuss the issue in Sect. 10.3.2.1.

10.3.1.3   Streaming Operators and Their Implementation

The applications that generate data streams also have similarities in the type of operations they perform. We list below a set of fundamental operations over streaming data.

- **Selection:** All streaming applications require support for complex filtering.
- **Complex aggregation:** Complex aggregates, including nested aggregates (e.g., comparing a minimum with a running average), frequent item queries, etc. are needed to compute trends in the data.

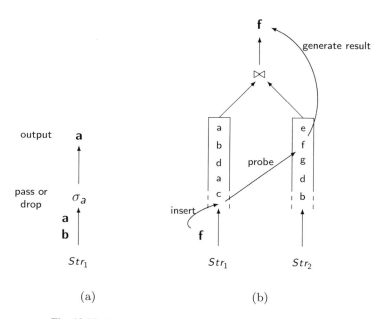

Fig. 10.15 Continuous query operators: (a) Selection, (b) Join

- **Multiplexing and demultiplexing:** Physical streams may need to be decomposed into a series of logical streams and conversely logical streams may need to be fused into one physical stream (similar to group-by and union, respectively).
- **Stream mining:** Operations such as pattern matching, similarity searching, and forecasting are needed for on-line mining of streaming data.
- **Joins:** Support should be included for multistream joins and joins of streams with static metadata.
- **Windowed queries:** All of the above query types may be constrained to return results inside a window (e.g., the last 24 hours or the last one hundred packets).

While these look, by and large, as ordinary relational query operators, their implementation and optimization present novel challenges that we discuss below.

Some of these operators are stateless (e.g., projection and selection) and their relational implementations may be used in streaming queries without significant modifications. Figure 10.15(a) depicts the implementation of selection operator as an example. Incoming tuples are simply filtered based on the select condition.

However, stateful operators (e.g., joins) have blocking behavior in their relational implementations that is not suitable in DSSs. For instance, prior to returning the next tuple, the Nested Loops Join (NLJ) may potentially scan the entire inner relation and compare each tuple therein with the current outer tuple. Given the unbounded nature of streaming data, such blocking is problematic. It has been proven that a query is monotonic if and only if it is *non-blocking*, which means that it does not need to wait until the end-of-input marker before producing results. Some operators have non-blocking counterparts, such as joins and simple aggregates. For example, a non-blocking pipelined symmetric hash join (of two character streams, Str_1 and Str_2) builds hash tables on the fly for each of Str_1 and Str_2 (see Fig. 10.15(b)). Hash tables are stored in main memory and when a tuple from one of the relations arrives, it is inserted into its table and the other tables are probed for matches to generate results involving the new tuple, if any. Joins of more than two streams and joins of streams with a static relation are straightforward extensions. In the former, for each arrival on one input, the states of all the other inputs are probed in some order. In the latter, new arrivals on the stream trigger the probing of the relation. Since maintaining hash tables on unbounded streams is not practical, most DSMSs only support window joins, where the windows over each input stream are defined and joins are computed over the data in these windows based on the specific window semantics.

Unblocking a query operator may be accomplished by reimplementing it in an incremental form, restricting it to operate over a window, and exploiting stream constraints such as *punctuations*, which are constraints (encoded as data items) that specify conditions for all future items. We return to punctuations soon. Sliding window operators process two types of events: arrivals of new data and expirations of old data. We discuss this at length in the next section when we discuss query processing issues.

10.3.2   Query Processing over Data Streams

With some modifications, the query processing methodology over streaming data is similar to its relational counterpart: declarative queries are translated into execution plans that map logical operators specified in the query into physical implementations. However, a number of differences arise in the details.

An important difference is the introduction of persistent queries and the fact that operations consume data pushed into the plan by the sources, rather than pulling data from sources as in a traditional DBMS. Furthermore, as discussed above, the operations may be (and often are) more complicated than relational operators and involve UDFs. Queues allow sources to push data into the query plan and operations to retrieve data as needed. A simple scheduling strategy allocates a time slice to each operation, during which it extracts tuples from its input queue(s), processes them in timestamp order, and deposits output tuples into the next operation's input queue (Fig. 10.16).

As noted earlier, DSSs can follow either the continuous processing model or the windowed execution model. A fundamental concern in the latter case is how the windows are managed—specifically, the addition and deletion of data items to/from the current window. This represents another distinction from relational DBMSs and we discuss it in Sect. 10.3.2.1. Two other issues arise in stream systems that we discuss: load management when data arrival rate exceeds the system's processing capacity (Sect. 10.3.2.2), and dealing with out-of-order data

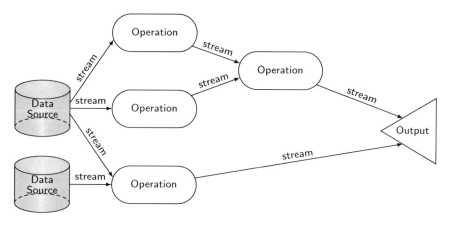

Fig. 10.16 Stream query plan example

items (Sect. 10.3.2.3). Finally, persistent queries provide additional opportunities for multiquery processing, and we discuss this topic in Sect. 10.3.2.4.

Distributed and parallel DSSs follow different paths, similar to their relational counterparts. In the distributed case, the fundamental technique is partitioning the query plan across multiple processing nodes on data that reside on those nodes. Partitioning the query plan involves assigning query operators to nodes and may require rebalancing over time. The issues here are analogous to distributed DBMSs that we have discussed at length earlier in the book. In parallel systems, data-parallel processing is typically followed where the stream data is partitioned and each processing node executes the same query on a subset of the data. Most modern systems follow the latter approach so we discuss those further in Sect. 10.3.2.5.

10.3.2.1 Windowed Query Execution

We noted earlier that in windowed execution, the system has to deal with the arrival of new data and expiration of old data. The actions taken upon arrival and expiration vary across operators. A new data item may generate new results (e.g., join) or remove previously generated results (e.g., negation). Furthermore, an expired data item may cause removal of data items from the result (e.g., aggregation) or addition of new data to the result (e.g., duplicate elimination and negation). Note that we are not discussing here the case where an application deletes a data item. This discussion is about removal of data items from query results as a consequence of window operations.

Consider, for example, the sliding window join: a newly arrived data on one of the inputs probes the state of the other input, as in a join of unbounded streams. Additionally, expired data is removed from the state.

Expiration from an individual time-based window is simple: a data item expires if its timestamp falls out of the range of the window.

In a count-based window, the number of data items remains constant over time. Therefore, expiration can be implemented by overwriting the oldest data item with a newly arrived one. However, if an operator stores state corresponding to the output of a count-based window join, then the number of data items in the state may change, depending upon the join attribute values of new tuples.

In general, there are two techniques for sliding window query processing and state maintenance: the negative tuple approach and the direct approach. In the negative tuple approach, each window referenced in the query is assigned an operator that explicitly generates a negative tuple for every expiration, in addition to pushing newly arrived tuples into the query plan. Thus, each window must be materialized so that the appropriate negative tuples are produced. Negative tuples propagate through the query plan and are processed by operators in a similar way as regular tuples, but they also cause operators to remove corresponding "real" tuples from their state. The negative tuple approach can be implemented efficiently using hash tables as operator state so that expired tuples can be looked up quickly in response to negative tuples. The downside is that twice as many tuples must be processed by the query because every tuple eventually expires from its window and generates a corresponding negative tuple. Furthermore, additional operators must be present in the plan to generate negative tuples as the window slides forward.

Direct approach handles negation-free queries over time-based windows. These queries have the property that the expiration times of base tuples and intermediate results can be determined via their expiry timestamps, which is the arrival time plus the window length. Hence, operators can access their state directly and find expired tuples without the need for negative tuples. The direct approach does not incur the overhead of negative tuples and does not have to store the base windows referenced in the query. However, it may be slower than the negative tuple approach for queries over multiple windows since state buffers may require a sequential scan during insertions or deletions.

10.3.2.2   Load Management

The stream arrival rates may be so high that not all tuples can be processed, regardless of the (static or run-time) optimization techniques used. In this case, two types of load shedding may be applied: random or semantic, with the latter making use of stream properties or quality-of-service parameters to drop tuples believed to be less significant than others. For an example of semantic load shedding, consider performing an approximate sliding window join with the objective of attaining the maximum result size. The idea is that tuples that are about to expire or tuples that are not expected to produce many join results should be dropped (in case of memory limitations), or inserted into the join state but ignored during the probing step (in case of CPU limitations). Note that other objectives are possible, such as obtaining a random sample of the join result.

In general, it is desirable to shed load in such a way as to minimize the drop in accuracy. This problem becomes more difficult when multiple queries with many operators are involved, as it must be decided where in the query plan the tuples should be dropped. Clearly, dropping tuples early in the plan is effective because all of the subsequent operators enjoy reduced load. However, this strategy may adversely affect the accuracy of many queries if parts of the plan are shared. On the other hand, load shedding later in the plan, after the shared subplans have been evaluated and the only remaining operators are specific to individual queries, may have little or no effect in reducing the overall system load.

One issue that arises in the context of load shedding and query plan generation is whether an optimal plan chosen without load shedding is still optimal if load shedding is used. It has been shown that this is indeed the case for sliding window aggregates, but not for queries involving sliding window joins.

Note that instead of dropping tuples during periods of high load, it is also possible to put them aside (e.g., spill to disk) and process them when the load has subsided. Finally, note that in the case of periodic reexecution of persistent queries, increasing the reexecution interval may be thought of as a form of load shedding.

10.3.2.3   Out-of-Order Processing

Our discussion so far has assumed that the DSS processes incoming data items in-order, usually in timestamp order. However, this is not always realistic. Since the data arrives from external sources, some items may arrive late, or out-of-order with respect to their generation time. Furthermore, no data may be received from a source (e.g., a remote sensor or a router) for some time, which could mean that there are no new data to report, or that the source is down. Particularly in distributed systems, this should be considered the normal operating condition due to network disconnections, length of recovery, etc. Consequently, out-of-order processing needs to be considered.

One early approach to deal with this issue is to build in a "slack" that establishes an upper bound on how much unordered the data can be. This is followed in Aurora that has, for example, a buffered sort operator where the incoming stream is buffered for this slack time before being processed. The operator outputs the stream in sorted order on some attribute. Data that arrives later than the slack time units are dropped. Truviso introduces the concept of "drift" to accommodate the case where streams from the same data source are ordered within themselves, but delays may occur in data feed from some sources. When the input monitor detects this, it starts a drift period during which it buffers data from other sources. The difference between the two is that Aurora can define slack on a per-operator basis whereas Truviso has drift management at the input monitor.

Another solution is to use punctuations introduced previously. In this case, a punctuation is a special tuple that contains a predicate that is guaranteed to be satisfied by the remainder of the data stream. For instance, a punctuation with the predicate `timestamp > 1262304000` guarantees that no more tuples will

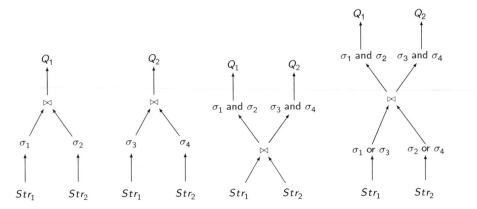

Fig. 10.17 Separate and shared query plans for Q_1 and Q_2

arrive with timestamps below the given Unix time; of course, if this punctuation is generated by the source, then it is useful only if tuples arrive in timestamp order. Punctuations that govern the timestamps of future tuples are typically referred to as *heartbeats*.

10.3.2.4 Multiquery Optimization

Database queries may share parts that are identical and techniques for optimizing a batch of queries have long been of interest and this is referred to as *multiquery optimization*. In streaming systems that support persistent queries, there is more opportunity to detect and exploit shared components and state in processing them. For example, aggregate queries over different window lengths and possibly different SLIDE intervals may share state and data structures. Similarly, state and computation may be shared across similar predicates and joins. Therefore, a DSS may group similar queries and run a single query plan per group.

Figure 10.17 shows some of the issues involved in shared query plans. The first two plans correspond to executing queries Q_1 and Q_2 separately, in which selections are evaluated before joins. The third plan executes both queries and evaluates the join first, then the selections (note that the join operator effectively creates two copies of its output stream). Despite sharing work across two queries, the third plan may be less efficient than separate execution if only a small fraction of the join result satisfies the selection predicates σ_1 through σ_4. If so, then the join operator will perform a great deal of unnecessary work over time. The fourth plan addresses this problem by "prefiltering" the streams before they are joined.

10.3.2.5   Parallel Data Stream Processing

Most of the modern DSSs run on large-scale parallel clusters; so, these are parallel data stream processing systems (PDSPS). These systems have significant similarities to parallel databases we discussed in Chap. 8 and, perhaps more importantly to the big data processing frameworks in Sect. 10.2 of this chapter. Therefore in the following discussion we rely on those discussions and appeal to the specific characteristics of data stream systems discussed earlier.

The typical execution environment in these systems can be characterized as parallel execution of continuous operators. Referring to Fig. 10.16, each vertex is a different continuous operation that is assigned to a number of worker nodes. To simplify the discussion, let us assume that each worker only executes one operation. In this context, each worker machine executes the operation assigned to it on a partition of the data stream and produces results that are streamed to the workers that execute the subsequent operation in the query plan. The important point to note here is that partitioning of the stream happens in between each pair of operations. So, the execution of each operation follows three steps:

1. Partitioning of the incoming stream;
2. Execution of the operation on the partition; and
3. (Optionally) aggregation of the results from the workers.

Stream Partitioning

As with all parallel systems, a particular objective of partitioning is to obtain a balanced load across the workers to avoid stragglers. The differentiating characteristic here is that the dataset that is assigned to each worker arrives in a streaming fashion; therefore the partitioning of the data (according to a key attribute) to multiple workers needs to be done on the fly rather than as an offline process as in the systems discussed in Sect. 10.2.

The simplest load balancing approach in distributed systems is to randomly distribute the load among workers. *Shuffle partitioning* routes incoming data items among the workers in a round-robin fashion (hence, it is also referred to as *round-robin partitioning*). Such partitioning results in a perfectly balanced workload. For stateless applications, this works well, but stateful ones require more care. Since data items with the same key may be assigned to different workers, an aggregation step is required for stateful operations to combine the partial results of each worker for each key at each step of the execution (more on this in Sect. 10.3.2.5). The aggregation is expensive and needs to be taken into account. Additionally, shuffle partitioning also has high space demands for stateful operations as each worker has to maintain the state of each key.

The other extreme is hash partitioning—a technique we have seen a number of times. Hashing ensures that data items with the same key are assigned to one worker, eliminating the expensive aggregation step, and minimizing space requirements since only one worker maintains the state for each key value. However, it may result in heavily imbalanced load distribution, particularly for skewed (in terms of key values) data streams.

For stateful applications, shuffle and hash partitioning constitute upper-bounds for key splitting cost and load imbalance, respectively. Most recent work has focused on finding partitioning algorithms within these extremes. An approach that is promising is key-splitting, whereby hash partitioning is followed by splitting each key among a small number of workers to reduce the load imbalance. The objective is to reduce the overhead of aggregation while also reducing imbalance, particularly in skewed data streams. Partial Key Grouping (PKG) algorithm aims to reduce the load imbalance of hash partitioning by adapting key splitting. PKG utilizes the "power of two choices" by allowing each key to be split between two workers. That enables PKG to achieve significantly better load balance compared to hash partitioning and bounds the replication factor and the aggregation cost. For heavily skewed data, PKG has been extended to use more than two choices for the head of the distribution. Although it is shown to further improve load balance, its replication factor is upper bounded by the number of worker nodes in the worst case. Another approach to deal with heavily skewed data is to use a hybrid partitioning technique where the tuples in the head (frequent) and tail (less frequent) of the key distribution are treated differently, perhaps with a preference for well-balanced assignment of the heavy hitters from the head.

Parallel Stream Workload Execution

Let us first focus on the execution of individual operations. For stateless operations there are no specific issues raised as a consequence of streaming and the aggregation step is unnecessary. Stateful operations require more care and that is what we discuss below.

If shuffle partitioning is used for a stateful operation, as discussed above, data items with the same key may be located on different workers each of which will store only partial results. Therefore, shuffle partitioning requires an aggregation step to produce the final results. As an example, Fig. 10.18 depicts a counting operation over three workers where different colors indicate different keys. As can be observed, data items with the same keys may go to different workers, each of which maintain the count for each key (state) that are aggregated at the end.

If hash partitioning is used for a stateful operation, all data items with identical keys are assigned to the same worker, so there is no aggregation step. Figure 10.19 demonstrates hash partitioning for the same counting example we used earlier.

When these points are incorporated into the query plan, each operation is typically treated individually, with partitioning decisions performed for each as in Apache Storm and Heron. Consequently, the example query plan given in Fig. 10.16 takes the shape of Fig. 10.20.

An issue that arises is in terms of highly skewed data streams. As we discussed in Sect. 10.3.2.5, the commonly accepted current approach is to use key-splitting possibly with certain optimizations for highly skewed data. Another approach is stream repartitioning in between operations in the query plan. The fundamental issue here is to reroute the dataflow between operations in the query plan, which also requires state migration (since another worker will be taking over parts of the stream). A number of alternative strategies have been developed, but the seminal work on this is Flux, and we use that as an exemplar to discuss how this repartitioning works. Flux is a dataflow operator that is placed between two operations in the query plan; it monitors the worker loads and dynamically reroutes data and migrates state from one worker to another. This process has two phases: rerouting the data and migrating the state. Rerouting requires update to internal routing tables. State migration requires more care since the state that is maintained at the "old" worker with respect to that partition has to be marshaled and moved to the "new" worker. This involves the following steps: stopping new tuples from being accepted into the partition; marshaling the state at the "old" worker, which involves extracting this information from internal data structures; moving the state to the "new" worker; unmarshaling the state and installing it by populating the data structures of the "new" machine; and restarting the receipt of data to the stream. This state migration needs to be fast, obviously, but it is a heavyweight task that involves complex synchronization protocols. That is one reason modern systems do not typically provide built-in support for state migration.

10.3.3 DSS Fault-Tolerance

Distributed/parallel DSS reliability has similarity to the relational DBMSs, but the issues are exacerbated by the fact that it is necessary to deal with streams flowing

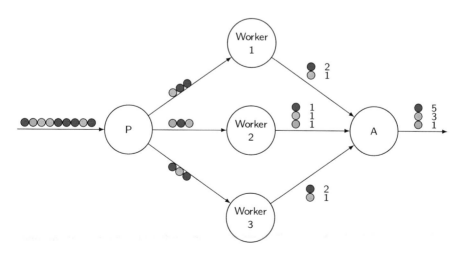

Fig. 10.18 Round-robin stream partitioning

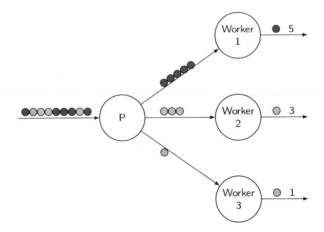

Fig. 10.19 Hash-based stream partitioning

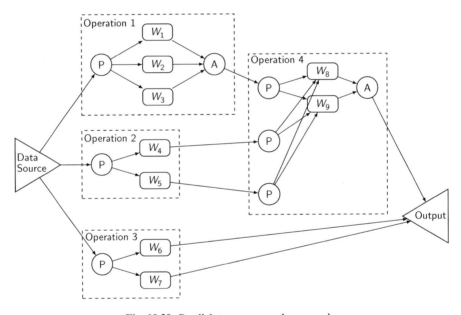

Fig. 10.20 Parallel stream query plan example

through the query plans. Let us first revisit the distinction that we made earlier between systems that partition the query plan and execute each part on a different server node and those that partition the data and replicate the query plan at each node (i.e., the data parallel execution). In the latter, failures can be handled by worker replication techniques that we discussed in Sect. 10.2.1. However, in the former case, the servers are "connected" as they execute parts of the query plan and data flows from upstream servers to downstream ones. A failure of a node can, therefore, disrupt query execution due to the loss of significant (transient) state information and halting the downstream servers that no longer receive data. Consequently, these systems need to implement strong availability techniques.

An important issue is the query execution semantics a system provides as data flows through the network of servers (or through the query plan). There are three alternatives: at-least-once, at-most-once, and exactly-once. *At-least-once* semantics (also called *rollback recovery*) indicates that the system guarantees to process each data item at least once, but makes no guarantees about duplicates. So, if, a data item is forwarded again by a failed node after recovery, that data item may be processed again and produce a duplicate output. In contrast, if *at-most-once* semantics (also called *gap recovery*) is adopted, the system guarantees that duplicate data items would be detected and not processed, but certain data items may not be executed at all. This can be due to load management as discussed earlier, or as a result of the failure of a node that ignores, upon recovery, all the data items that it might have received while it was down. Finally, *exactly-once* semantics (also called *precise recovery*) means that the system executes each data item exactly once— so nothing gets dropped and nothing gets executed more than once. Each of these require different system functionality obviously. Each of these are supported in the existing systems: Apache Storm and Heron provide applications with a choice of at-least-once and at-most-once semantics, whereas Spark Streaming, Apache Flink, and MillWheel enforce exactly-once semantics.

The types of recovery techniques for DSSs can be classified into two main approaches: replication and upstream backup. In the case of *replication*, for each node that executes a portion of the query plan there is a replica node that is also responsible for that portion of the query plan. This is a primary-secondary arrangement where the primary node services the query plan as long as it is operational, and the secondary node picks up the work if the primary fails. The arrangement between the two could be active standby where both the primary and the secondary get data items from upstream nodes and process them at the same time with only the primary sending outputs downstream, or passive standby where the primary periodically sends the delta difference in its state to the secondary and the secondary updates its state accordingly. Both can be supported by checkpointing to speed up recovery. This approach has been proposed as part of the Flux operator discussed above and used in Borealis. The other alternative is *upstream backup* where upstream nodes buffer the data items that they flow to the downstream nodes until they are processed. If a downstream node fails and recovers, it obtains the buffered data items from its upstream node and reprocesses them. A design difficulty is determining how big these buffers should be to accommodate data that is gathered during failure and recovery. This is complicated because it is affected by data arrival rate as well as other considerations. Systems such as Apache Storm and TimeStream adopt this approach.

10.4   Graph Analytics Platforms

Graph data is of growing importance in many applications. In this section, we discuss *property graph*, which are graphs that have attributes associated with vertices and edges. Another type of graph is Resource Description Framework graph (RDF graph) that we discuss in Chap. 12. Property graphs are used to model entities and relationships in many domains such as bioinformatics, software engineering, e-commerce, finance, trading, and social networks. A graph $G = (V, E, D_V, D_E)$ is defined by a set of vertices V and a set of edges E,[5] D_V and D_E are defined below. The distinguishing characteristics of property graphs are the following:

- Each vertex in the graph represents an entity, and each edge between a pair of vertices represents a relationship between those two entities. For example, in a social network graph representing Facebook, each vertex might represent a user and each edge might represent the "friendship" relationship.
- It is possible to have multiple edges between a pair of vertices, each representing a different relationship; these graphs are commonly called *multigraphs*.
- Edges may have weights attached to them (*weighted graphs*), where the weight of an edge might have different semantics in different graphs.
- The graphs can be *directed* or *undirected*. For example Facebook graph is normally undirected, representing the symmetric friendship relationship between two users: if user A is friend of user B, then user B is a friend of user A. However, a Twitter graph, where the edges represent "follows" relationship, is directed representing that user A is following user B, but the inverse may not necessarily be true. As you will recall, RDF graphs are directed by definition.
- As noted, each vertex and each edge may have a set of attributes (properties) to encode the properties of the entity (in case of vertex) or the relationship (in case of edge). If edges have properties, these graphs are usually called *edge-labeled graphs*. D_V and D_E in the graph definition given above represent the set of vertex and edge properties, respectively. Each vertex/edge may have different properties, and when we refer to the properties of the graph in general, we will write D or D_G.

Real-life graphs that are the subject of graph analytics (such as social network graphs, road network graphs, as well as web graphs we discussed earlier) have a number of properties that are important and affect many aspects of system design:

1. These graphs are very large, some with billions of vertices and edges. Processing graphs with this number of vertices and, especially, edges, requires care.
2. Many of these graphs are known as the power-law or scale-free graphs in which there is significant variation in vertex degrees (known as *degree distribution*

---

[5]In this section, when necessary, we will write V_G and E_G to specifically refer to the vertices and edges, respectively, of graph G, but, we will omit the subscripts when it is obvious.

skew). For example, while the average vertex degree in Twitter graph is 35, the "supernodes" in that graph have maximum degree of 2.9 million.[6]

3. Following the point above, the average vertex degree in many real-world graphs is quite high with high-density cores. For example, the average vertex degree in Friendster graph is about 55 and in Facebook graph is 190.

4. Some of the real-world graphs have very large diameters (i.e., the number of hops between two farthest vertices). These include the spatial graphs (e.g., the road network graphs) and web graphs: the web graph diameters can be in the hundreds, while some road networks are much larger. The graph diameter affects graph analytics algorithms that depend on visiting and doing computation on each vertex iteratively (we discuss this further below).

Efficiently running workloads on these graphs is an essential part of big data platforms. As with many big data frameworks, these are mostly parallel/distributed (scale-out) platforms that rely on the data graph being partitioned across nodes of a cluster or sites of a distributed system.

Graph workloads are typically separated into two classes. The first is *analytical queries* (or *analytical workloads*) whose evaluation typically requires processing each vertex in the graph over multiple iterations until a fixpoint is reached. Examples of analytical workloads include PageRank computation (see Example 10.4), clustering, finding connected components (see Example 10.5), and many machine learning algorithms that utilize graph data (e.g., belief propagation). We focus on the different computational approaches that have been developed for these tasks, and the systems that have been built to support them. These are the specialized iterative computation platforms that we referred to when we discussed Spark in the previous section. They are our focus in this section. The second class of workloads is *online queries* (or *online workloads*), which are not iterative and usually require access to a portion of the graph and whose execution can be assisted by properly designed auxiliary data structures such as indexes. Examples of online workloads are reachability queries (e.g., whether a target vertex is reachable from a given source vertex), single-source shortest path (finding the shortest path between two vertices), and subgraph matching (graph isomorphism). We postpone the treatment of these workloads to Chap. 11 where we discuss graph DBMSs.

Example 10.4 PageRank is a well-known algorithm for computing the importance of web pages. It is based on the principle that the importance of a page is determined by the number and quality of other pages pointing to it. Quality, in this case, is measured as the PageRank of a page (hence the recursive definition). Each web page is represented as a vertex in the web graph (see Fig. 10.21), with each directed edge representing a "pointing to" relationship. Thus, the PageRank of a web page P_i, denoted $PR(P_i)$ is the summation of the PageRank of all the pages P_j pointing to it, normalized by the number of pages that each P_j points to. The idea is that if

---

[6]We caution that these values change as the graphs evolve over time. They should be taken as indicative of the point we are making rather than as definitive values.

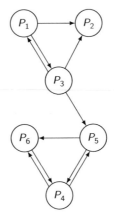

Fig. 10.21 Web Graph Representation for PageRank Computation

a page P_i points to n pages (one of which is P_i), its PageRank contributes to the PageRank computation of n pages equally. The PageRank formula also includes a damping factor based on the theory of random walks: if a user starts from a web page and continues clicking on the links to reach other web pages, this "walk" will eventually stop. So, when the user is at page P_i, there is a probability d that the user will continue clicking and $(1-d)$ that the walk will stop; the typical value for d is 0.85 determined as a result of empirical studies. Therefore, if the set of in-neighbors of P_i is B_{P_i} (these are P_i's backward links), and the set of out-neighbors is F_{P_i} (forward links), the PageRank formula is

$$PR(P_i) = (1-d) + d \sum_{P_j \in B_{P_i}} \frac{PR(P_j)}{|F_{P_j}|}.$$

We discuss PageRank in more detail in Chap. 12 when we consider web data management. For the time being, we will simply focus on the computation of the values using Fig. 10.21 as an example. Let us consider page P_2; the PageRank of this page is $PR(P_2) = 0.15 + 0.85(\frac{PR(P_1)}{2} + \frac{PR(P_3)}{3})$. Clearly, this is a recursive formula since it depends on the computation of the PageRank values for P_1 and P_3. The computation typically starts with assigning each vertex equal PageRank values (in this case $1/6$ since there are 6 vertices), and iterates to compute the values of each node until a fixpoint is reached (i.e., the values no longer change). Therefore, PageRank computation exhibits both of the properties we identified for analytical workloads: iterative computation, and involvement of each vertex at each iteration.[7]

♦

---

[7]There are various optimizations that have been developed for PageRank computation, but we ignore them in this discussion.

Example 10.5 As a second example, let us consider the computation of connected components of a graph. First some basics. A graph is said to be *connected* if there is a path between every pair of vertices. A maximal connected subgraph of the graph is called a *connected component*—every vertex in this component is reachable from every other vertex. Finding the set of connected components in a graph is an important graph analytics problem that can be used for a number of applications such as clustering. If the graph is directed, then a subgraph where there is a directed path from every pair of vertices in both directions (i.e., a path from vertex v to u and a path from u to v) is called a *strongly connected component*. For example, in Fig. 10.21, $\{P_1, P_3\}$ and $\{P_4, P_5, P_6\}$ are two strongly connected components. If all directed edges in this graph are replaced by undirected edges, and then the maximal connected components are determined, this produces the set of *weakly connected components*. The entire graph in Fig. 10.21 is one weakly connected component (in this case, the graph is said to be *weakly connected*).

Finding weakly connected component is an iterative algorithm that uses depth-first search (DFS). Given a graph $G = (V, E)$ for each $v \in V$, one conducts DFS to determine the component in which v is in.   ♦

10.4.1 Graph Partitioning

As noted earlier, most graph analytics systems are parallel, requiring the data graph to be partitioned and assigned to worker nodes. We have dealt with data partitioning earlier, considering it within the context of distributed relational systems in Chap. 2, and in the context of parallel database systems in Chap. 8. Partitioning graphs is different, because of the connections among the vertices; this is, in some sense, similar to worrying about cross-fragment integrity constraints in distribution design, but graphs require more care due to the heavy communication between vertices, as we will discuss in the upcoming sections. Thus, special algorithms have been designed for graph partitioning, and the literature on this topic is very rich.

Graph partitioning can follow either the *edge-cut* approach (also known as *vertex-disjoint*) or the *vertex-cut* approach (also called *edge-disjoint*). In the former, each vertex is assigned to a partition, but edges may be replicated among partitions if they connect boundary vertices. In the latter, each edge is assigned to a partition, but vertices may be replicated among partitions if they are incident to edges that are allocated to different partitions. In both of these approaches, three objectives are pursued: (1) allocate each vertex or edge to partitions such that the partitions are mutually exclusive, (2) ensure that the partitions are balanced, and (3) minimize the cuts (either edge-cuts or vertex-cuts) so as to minimize the communication between machines to which each partition is assigned. Balancing these requirements is the difficult part; if, for example, we only had to worry about balancing the workload while getting mutually exclusive partitions, a round-robin allocation of vertices (or edges) to machines might be sufficient. However, there is no guarantee that this would not cause large number of cuts.

Partitioning can be formulated as an optimization problem as follows. Given a graph $G(V, E)$ (ignoring properties for the time being), we wish to obtain a partitioning $P = \{P_1, \ldots, P_k\}$ of G into k partitions where the sizes of P_i are balanced, which can be formulated as the following optimization problem:

$$\text{minimize } C(P)$$

subject to:

$$w(P_i) \leq \beta * \frac{\sum_{j=1}^{k} w(P_j)}{k}, \forall i \in \{1 \ldots k\}.$$

where $C(P)$ represents the total communication cost of partitioning, and $w(P_i)$ is the abstract overhead of processing partition P_i. The two approaches (vertex-cut and edge-cut) differ in the definition of $C(P)$ and $w(P_i)$, as we discuss below. In the above formulation β is introduced as a slackness parameter to allow partitioning that is not exactly balanced; if $\beta = 1$, then the solution is an exactly balanced partitioning, and the problem is known as k-balanced graph partitioning optimization problem; if $\beta > 1$, then some deviation from exact balance is allowed, and this is known as the (k, β)-balanced graph partitioning optimization problem. This problem has been proven to be NP-hard, and researchers have proposed heuristics methods to achieve an approximate solution.

The heuristics for edge-cut (vertex-disjoint) approach attempt to achieve a balanced allocation of vertices to partitions while minimizing edge-cuts; thus each P_i contains a set of vertices. In these approaches, $w(P_i)$ is defined in terms of the number of vertices per partition (i.e., $w(P_i) = |P_i|$) while the communication cost is computed as a fraction of edge-cuts:

$$C(P) = \frac{\sum_{i=1}^{k} |e(P_i, V \setminus P_i)|}{|E|}.$$

where $|e(P_i, P_j)|$ is the number of edges between partitions P_i and P_j.

The best-known vertex-disjoint heuristic algorithm is METIS, which provides near-optimal partitioning. It consists of three steps:

1. Given a graph $G_0 = (V, E)$ a hierarchy of successively coarsened graphs $G_1, \ldots, G_n$ are produced such that $|V(G_i)| > |V(G_j)|$ for $i < j$. There are a number of possible ways of coarsening, but the most popular is what is called *contraction* where a set of vertices in G_i are replaced by a single vertex in G_j $(i < j)$. The coarsening usually stops when G_n is sufficiently small that a high-cost partitioning algorithm can still be applied. A graph G_i is coarsened to G_{i+1} by finding the *maximal match*, which is the set of edges where no two edges share a vertex. Then the endpoints of each of these edges are represented by a vertex in G_{i+1}.

2. G_n is partitioned using some partitioning algorithm—as noted above, G_n should by now be sufficiently small to use any desired partitioning algorithm regardless of its computational cost.

3. G_n is iteratively uncoarsened to G_0, and at each step:

(a) the partitioning solution on graph G_j is projected to graph G_{j-1} (note that the smaller subscript indicates finer granularity of the graph) and

(b) the partitioning of G_{j-1} is improved by various techniques.

Although METIS and related algorithms improve graph analytics workload processing times considerably, they are not practical for even medium-sized graphs because of their high computation cost. The partitioning overhead is an important consideration in graph analytic systems, as the loading and partitioning time of a graph can account for a large portion of the processing time.

A simple vertex-disjoint partitioning heuristic based on hashing is incorporated in the repertoire of most graph analytics systems we discuss below. In this case, a vertex is assigned to the partition to which its identifier hashes. This is simple, and very fast, and would work reasonably well, in terms of balancing the load, in graphs with uniform degree distribution. However, in real-life graphs that have degree skew as discussed above, the result may be unbalanced workload. Edge-cut partitioning models distribute the load in terms of vertices, but for some algorithms the load is proportional to the number of edges, which would not be balanced for skewed graphs. For these cases more sophisticated heuristics that pay attention to the structure of the graph would be appropriate.

One such approach is *label propagation*, where one starts with each vertex having its own label that it iteratively exchanges with its neighbors. At each iteration, each vertex assumes the most frequent label of its "neighborhood"; when the frequencies are identical, a method is used to select the label. This iterative process stops when vertex labels no longer change. This technique is sensitive to the graph structure, but is not guaranteed to produce a balanced partitioning. One way to achieve balance is to start with a non-balanced partitioning, and then use a greedy label propagation algorithm to relocate vertices to achieve balance (or near balance). The greedy algorithm moves vertices to maximize a relocation utility function subject to constraints for balance. The utility function might be, for example, the number of neighbors of the graph that are going to be in the same partition. It is possible to combine METIS with label propagation by incorporating the latter in the coarsening phase. Again, the problem is modeled as a constrained partitioning problem that maximizes a utility function that pays attention to the vertex neighborhood to minimize edge-cuts.

Example 10.6 Consider the graph in Fig. 10.22a. A vertex-disjoint partitioning of this graph is shown in Fig. 10.22(b), where the edge-cuts are shown by dashed lines. This partitioning was achieved by hashing as described above. Notice that this causes 10 out of 12 total edges to be cut. This example demonstrates the difficulty of partitioning graphs with high-degree vertices (in this graph vertices v_3, and in particular v_4 are high degree), leading to high edge-cuts. METIS does better on this graph, but it cannot generate three partitions, and instead produces

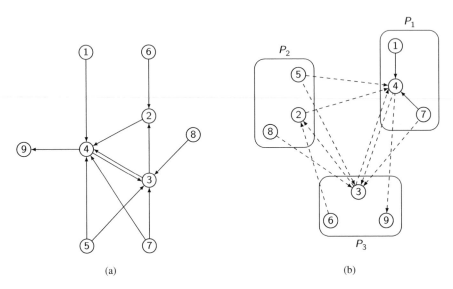

Fig. 10.22 Partitioning example. (**a**) Example graph. (**b**) Vertex-disjoint (edge-cut) partitioning

two: $\{v_1, v_3, v_4, v_7, v_9\}$ and $\{v_2, v_5, v_6, v_8\}$ resulting in five edge-cuts (a two-way partitioning based on hashing results in 8 edge-cuts).   ♦

It has been demonstrated that edge-cut heuristics perform well for graphs with low-degree vertices, but perform poorly on power-law graphs causing high number of edge-cuts. METIS has been modified to deal with this particular problem, but its performance in dealing with very large graphs remains an issue. It is generally accepted that vertex-cut approaches that allocate edges to individual partitions while partitioning (replicating) the vertices incident to these edges handle power-law graphs more easily (i.e., each P_i contains a set of edges). The definition of $w(P_i)$, in this case, is the number of edges in partition P_i, i.e., $w(P_i) = |e(P_i)|$. For these heuristics, the communication $C(P)$ is going to be affected by the replication factor of each vertex (defined as the number of partitions to which that vertex is assigned); this can be formulated as follows:

$$C(P) = \frac{\sum_{v \in V} |A(v)|}{|V|}.$$

where $A(v) \subseteq \{P_1, \ldots, P_k\}$ represent the set of partitions in which vertex v is assigned.

Hashing is also an option as a vertex-cut heuristic: in this case the hashing is done on the ids of the two vertices incident on an edge. It is simple, fast (since it can be easily parallelized), and would provide a good balanced partitioning. However, it may lead to high vertex replication. It is possible to use hashing, but control the replication factor. One approach that has been proposed is to define, for edge $e_{u,v}$, *constraint sets* C_u and C_v, respectively, for its incident vertices u and v. These are the sets of partitions over which u and v can be replicated. Obviously, edge $e_{u,v}$ has to be assigned to a partition that is common to the constraint sets of both u and v, i.e., $C_u \cap C_u$. The constraint sets a limit on the number of partitions to which a vertex can be assigned, thereby controlling the upper bound of the replication factor. One way to generate these constraint sets is to define a square matrix of partitions, and assign as S_u (similarly S_v) by hashing u (similarly v) to one of the partitions (say P_i), and taking the partitions that lie on the same row and column as P_i.

Vertex-cut heuristics that are cognizant of the graph characteristics have also been designed. A greedy algorithm decides how to allocate $(I+1)$-st edge to a partition such that the replication factor is minimized. Of course, the allocation of $(I+1)$-st edge is dependent on the allocation of the first R edges, so past history is important. The location of edge $e_{u,v}$ is decided using the following heuristic rules:

1. If the intersection of $A(u)$ and $A(v)$ is not empty (i.e., there are some partitions that contain both u and v), then assign $e_{u,v}$ to one of the partitions in the intersection.
2. If the intersection of $A(u)$ and $A(v)$ is empty, but if $A(u)$ and $A(v)$ are not individually empty, then assign $e_{u,v}$ to one of the partitions in $A(u) \cup A(v)$ with the most unassigned edges.
3. If only one of $A(u)$ and $A(v)$ is not empty (i.e., only one of u or v has been assigned to partitions), then assign $e_{u,v}$ to one of the partitions of the assigned vertex.
4. If both $A(u)$ and $A(v)$ are empty, then assign $e_{u,v}$ to the smallest partition.

This algorithm takes the graph structure into account, but is hard to parallelize for high performance, since it relies on past history. Parallelizing requires either the maintenance of a global state that is periodically updated, or an approximation where each machine only considers its local state history without maintaining a global one.

It is also possible to use both vertex-cut and edge-cut approaches within one partitioning algorithm. PowerLyra, for example, uses an edge-cut algorithm for lower-degree vertices, and a vertex-cut algorithm for high-degree ones. Specifically, given a directed edge $e_{u,v}$, if the degree of v is low, then it hashes on v, and if it is high, then it hashes on u.

Example 10.7 Again consider the graph in Fig. 10.22a. An edge-disjoint partitioning of this graph is shown in Fig. 10.23, where the replicated vertices are shown by dotted circles. This partitioning was achieved by hashing as described above. Notice that this causes 6 out of 9 vertices to be replicated.   ◆

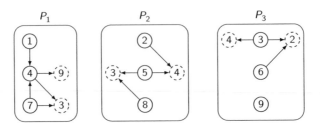

Fig. 10.23 Edge-disjoint (vertex-cut) partitioning

10.4.2   *MapReduce and Graph Analytics*

It is possible to use a MapReduce system such as Hadoop for graph processing
and analytics. However, as noted in Sect. 10.2.1, MapReduce systems do not deal
with iterative computation particularly well and we discussed the main issues
in that section. In graph systems, there is the additional problem of balanced
assignment of vertices across the workers due to the skewed degree distribution
in many real-life graphs, as discussed in Sect. 10.4.1, that leads to variations in
the communication overhead among worker nodes. All of these cause significant
overhead that negatively impacts the performance of MapReduce systems for graph
analytics. However, most of the special-purpose graph analytics systems that we
discuss in the next section require the entire graph to be maintained in memory;
when this is not possible, MapReduce might be a reasonable alternative, and there
are studies that look at its use for various workloads, as well as modifications that
would allow better scalability. There are also systems that modify MapReduce
to better fit iterative graph analytics workloads. As noted earlier, Spark is an
improvement of MapReduce to deal with iteration, and GraphX has been developed
as a graph processing system on top of Spark. Another MapReduce variant for
graph processing is exemplified by the HaLoop system. Both of these separate the
state that changes over iterations from the invariant data that does not and cache
the invariant data to avoid unnecessary I/O. They also modify the scheduler to
ensure that the same data gets mapped to the same workers in multiple iterations.
The approaches to implementing these obviously differ with HaLoop modifying
the Hadoop task scheduler at the master and task tracker in workers and by
implementing a loop control in the master to check for fixpoint. GraphX, on the
other hand, uses modifications incorporated into Spark to better deal with iterative
workloads. It performs an edge-disjoint partitioning of the graph and creates vertex
tables and edge tables at each worker. Each entry in the vertex table includes the
vertex identifier along with the vertex properties, while each entry in the edge table
includes the endpoints of each edge as well as the edge properties. These tables
are realized as Spark RDDs. Any graph computation involves a two-step process
(with iteration): join vertex and edge tables, and performs an aggregation. The join
involves moving vertex tables to the workers that hold the appropriate edge tables,
since the number of vertices are smaller than the number of edges. In order to avoid

broadcasting each vertex table to all of the edge table worker nodes, GraphX creates a routing table that specifies, for each vertex, the edge tables worker nodes where it exists; this is implemented as an RDD as well.

10.4.3 Special-Purpose Graph Analytics Systems

We now turn our attention to systems that have been specifically developed for graph analytics. These systems can be characterized along their *programming models* and their *computation models*. Programming models specify how an application developer would write the algorithms to execute on a system, while computation models indicate how the underlying system would execute these algorithms.

There are three fundamental programming models: vertex-centric, partition-centric, and edge-centric:

- **Vertex-centric model**
  Vertex-centric approach requires the programmer to focus on the computation to be performed on each vertex. Therefore, this is commonly referred to as "think-like-a-vertex" approach. A vertex v bases its computation only on its own state and the states of its neighbor vertices. For example, in the computation of PageRank, each vertex is programmed to receive the rank computation from its neighbors, and to calculate its own rank based on these. The results of the state computation is then available to neighbor vertices so that they can perform their computation.
- **Partition-centric model**
  In systems that follow this programming model, the programmer is expected to specify the computation that is to be performed on an entire partition rather than on each vertex. This is also referred to as *block-centric*, since computation is over blocks of vertices. The approach is also known as "think-like-a-block" or "think-like-a-graph."

  Partition-centric approach typically uses a serial algorithm within each block and only relies on the states of entire neighbor blocks rather than states of individual vertices. This characteristic of using separate computation algorithms within a partition and across partitions (for the vertices at the boundaries) may result in more complicated algorithms, but reduces dependence on neighbor states and communication overhead.
- **Edge-centric model**
  A third approach is the dual of vertex-centric model in that the operations are specified for each edge rather than each vertex. In this case, the principle object of attention is an edge rather than a vertex. Following the same naming scheme, this can be called "think-like-an-edge."

The computation models are bulk synchronous parallel (BSP), asynchronous parallel (AP), and gather-apply-scatter (GAS):

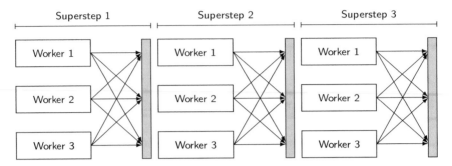

Fig. 10.24 BSP Computation Model

- **Bulk Synchronous Parallel**

  Bulk synchronous parallel (BSP) is a parallel computation model in which a computation is divided into a series of supersteps separated by global barriers. At each superstep, all of the processing nodes (i.e., the worker machines) perform the computation in parallel, and at the end of the superstep, they synchronize before starting the next superstep. Synchronization involves sharing state computed in that superstep with others so that this state can be used by all the worker nodes in the following superstep. The computation proceeds in multiple supersteps until a fixpoint is reached. Figure 10.24 shows an example BSP computation that reaches fixpoint in three supersteps involving three processor nodes.

  Since most of these systems run on parallel clusters, the communication is usually in terms of message passing (this is true for all computational models that we discuss). The BSP model implements a push-based communication approach: messages are pushed by the sender and buffered at the receiver. The receipt of a message at the end of one superstep causes the receiver to be automatically scheduled for execution in the next superstep. The BSP model simplifies parallel computation, but it requires care in task partitioning so that the worker machines are reasonably balanced to avoid stragglers. It also incurs synchronization overhead at the end of each superstep.

- **Asynchronous Parallel**

  The asynchronous parallel (AP) model removes the restriction of the BSP model that requires synchronization between worker machines at the global barrier—states computed at superstep k are available to be used in computation in superstep $k + 1$ even if they arrive at the destination within superstep k. The AP model retains global barriers to separate supersteps, but allows the received states to be seen and used immediately. Therefore, computation in state k may be based on the states of neighbors that were computed in superstep $k - 1$ but were delayed and not received until the end of superstep $k - 1$, or in superstep k.

  The fact that computation of state in one superstep may overlap with the receipt of states from neighbors gives rise to consistency concerns: state changes and state reads require careful control. This is usually handled by the application of locks on states while they are being read or written; given that the states are distributed over multiple worker nodes, there is a need to have distributed locking solutions.

An important objective of the AP model is to improve performance by allowing faster' processing units to continue their processing without having to wait until the synchronization barrier.[8] This may result in fewer number of supersteps. However, since it still retains the synchronization barriers, the synchronization and communication overheads are not completely eliminated.

- **Gather-Apply-Scatter**
  As its name suggests, the gather-apply-scatter (GAS) model consists of three phases: In the gather phase, a graph element (vertex, block, or edge) receives (or pulls) information about its neighborhood; in the apply phase, it uses the gathered data to compute its own state; and in the scatter phase, it updates the states of its neighborhood. An important differentiating characteristic of GAS is the separation of state update from activation. In both BSP and AP, when a state update is communicated to neighbors, they are automatically activated (i.e., scheduled for execution), whereas in GAS, the two actions are separate. This separation is important as it allows the scheduler to make its own decisions as to which graph elements to execute next (perhaps based on priorities).

  GAS can be synchronous or asynchronous. Synchronous GAS is similar to the BSP model in that the global barriers are maintained, but there is one important difference: in BSP, each graph element pushes its state to its neighbors at the end of a superstep, while in GAS, a graph element that is activated pulls the state of its neighbors at the beginning of a superstep.

  The asynchronous GAS removes the global barriers, and therefore has the same consistency issue as the AP model that is addressed by distributed locking. However, it is different than the AP model, since it does not have any notion of supersteps in the same sense as the BSP model. It executes by iteratively scheduling a graph element for execution, gathering its neighbor states (called *scope*), computing its state, and updating the scope and the list of graph elements that require scheduling. The computation ends when there are no more graph elements that await scheduling.

Combination of programming and computation models define the design space with nine alternatives. However, systems have not been built, as of now, for each of the design alternatives. Most of the research and development efforts have focused on vertex-centric BSP systems (Sect. 10.4.4); consequently our discussion of this class will be more in-depth than the others. For those cases where there are no known actual systems, we briefly indicate how one might look like.

---

[8]We use the terms global barrier, global synchronization barrier, and synchronization barrier interchangeably.

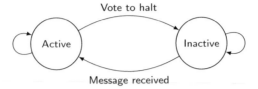

Fig. 10.25   Vertex States in Vertex-Centric Systems

10.4.4   *Vertex-Centric Block Synchronous*

As noted above, vertex-centric systems require the programmer to focus on the computation that is to be done on each vertex; edges are not first-class objects in these systems since there is no computation performed on them. When coupled with BSP computation model, these systems perform the computation iteratively (i.e., in supersteps) such that at each iteration, each vertex v accesses the state contained in the messages sent to it in the previous iteration, computes its new state based on these messages, and communicates its state to its neighbors (who will read the state in the subsequent superstep). The system then waits until all of the worker machines complete computation in that iteration (the global barrier) before starting the next iteration.

Each vertex is in either an "active" or "inactive" state. The computation starts with all vertices in active state and continues until all vertices reach fixpoint and enter inactive state and there are no pending messages in the system (Fig. 10.25). As each vertex reaches fixpoint it sends a "vote halt" message before it enters inactive state; once inactive, the vertex stays in that state unless it receives an external message to become active again.

This category has been the most popular one for system builders, as we noted earlier. The classical systems are Pregel and its open source counterpart Apache Giraph. Some of the others are GPS, Mizan, LFGraph, Pregelix, and Trinity. We focus on Pregel as an exemplar of this class of systems in discussing a number of details (these systems are commonly referred to as "Pregel-like").

To facilitate vertex-centric computation, a Compute() function is provided for each vertex, and the programmer needs to specify the computation that needs to be performed based on the application semantics. The system provides built-in functions such as GetValue() and WriteValue() to read the state associated with a vertex and modify the state of a vertex, as well as a SendMsg() function to push the vertex state updates to neighbor vertices. These are provided as the basic functionality and the programmer can focus on the computation that needs to be performed at each vertex. In this sense, the approach is similar to MapReduce where the programmer is expected to supply the specific codes for the map() and reduce() functions while the underlying system provides the execution and communication mechanism.

The Compute() function is quite general; in addition to computing a new state for the vertex, it can cause changes to the graph topology (called *mutations*) if the system supports this. For example, a clustering algorithm may replace a set of vertices with a single vertex. The mutations that are performed in one superstep are effective at the beginning of the following superstep. Naturally, conflicts can arise when multiple vertices require the same mutation, such as the addition of the same node with different values. These conflicts are resolved by partial ordering of the operations and by implementing user-defined handlers. The partial ordering of operations imposes the following order: edge removals are performed first, followed by vertex removals, followed by vertex additions, and, finally, edge additions. All of these mutations precede the call to the Compute() function.

Example 10.8 To demonstrate the vertex-centric BSP computation approach, we will compute the connected components of the graph given in Fig. 10.26a. For this example, we choose a simpler graph than the one we used for partitioning (Fig. 10.22a) to demonstrate the computation steps easily.

Note that, since this graph is directed, computing the connected component reduces to computing weakly connected component (WCC), where the directions are ignored (see Example 10.5). Furthermore, since this graph is fully connected, all of the vertices should be in one group, so we use that fact to check the correctness of the computation.

The vertex-centric BSP version of the WCC algorithm is as follows. Each vertex keeps information about the group it is in, and, in each superstep, it shares this information with its neighbors. At the beginning of the subsequent superstep each vertex gets these group ids from its neighbors and selects the smallest group id as its new group id—the Compute() = min{neighbor group ids, selfgroup id}. If its group id has not changed from the previous superstep, then the vertex enters inactive state (recall that inactive state represents that the vertex value has reached fixpoint). Otherwise, it pushes its new group id to its neighbors. When a vertex enters inactive state, it does not send any further messages to its neighbors, but it will receive messages from its active neighbors to determine if it should become active again. The computation continues in this fashion over multiple supersteps.

This execution is depicted in Fig. 10.26b. In the initialization step, the algorithm initializes by assigning each vertex to its own group identified by the vertex id (e.g., vertex v_1 is in group 1). Each vertex's value is the state at the end of the labeled superset. Then this group id is pushed to its neighbors. Each arrow shows when a message gets consumed by the recipient worker—so pointing to the next superset means the message is not accessed until then regardless of when it is delivered or received. In superstep 1, notice that vertices v_4, v_7, v_5, v_8, v_6, and v_9 change their group ids, while vertices v_1, v_2, and v_3 do not change their values and enter inactive state. The entire computation takes 9 supersteps in this example.

Notice that in some cases, vertices that are in inactive state become active as a result of messages they receive from neighbors. For example, vertex v_2 that becomes inactive in superstep 2 becomes active in superstep 4 when it receives a group id 1 from v_7 that causes it to update its own group id. This is a characteristic of this class of computation as discussed above.   ◆

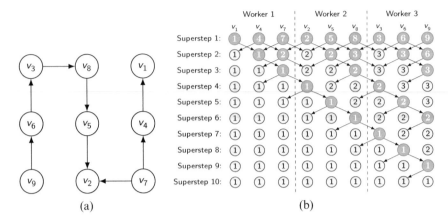

(a)   (b)

Fig. 10.26 Vertex-centric BSP example. (**a**) Example graph. (**b**) Vertex-centric BSP computation of WCC (gray vertices are inactive, blue vertices are active)

Recall that these systems perform parallel computations over a cluster where there is a master node and a number of worker nodes, with each worker hosting a set of graph vertices and implementing the Compute() function. In some systems (e.g., GPS and Giraph), there is an additional Master.Compute() function that allows for some parts of the algorithm to be executed serially at the master. The existence of these functions provides further flexibility for algorithm implementation and some optimizations (as we discuss below).

For some algorithms, it is important to capture the global state of the graph. To facilitate this, an *aggregator* can be implemented. Each vertex contributes a value to the aggregator, and the result of the aggregation is made available to all the vertices at the following superstep. Systems typically provide a number of basic aggregators such as min, max, and sum.

The performance of systems in this category is affected by two factors: communication cost and the number of supersteps. The properties of real-life graphs that we have discussed earlier impact the two cost factors mentioned above:

1. Power-law graphs with degree distribution skew: The problem with degree distribution skew is that the workers that hold these high-degree vertices receive and have to process far more messages than others, leading to load imbalances across workers that cause the straggler problem discussed earlier.
2. High average vertex degree: This results in each vertex having to deal with a high number of incoming messages, and having to communicate with a high number of neighbor vertices, leading to heavy communication overhead.
3. Large diameters: If, in the BSP computation, each superstep corresponds to one hop (i.e., one message) between vertices, these computations are going to take a large number of supersteps— proportional to the graph diameter. Although a few hundred hops as a graph diameter may not seem excessive, keep in mind that many of the analytics workloads require multiple passes over all the vertices in

these graphs, leading to high algorithmic cost. It has been reported, for example, that running strongly connected component algorithm over a graph of diameter 20 requires over 4,500 supersteps (without optimization).

A system optimization that can be implemented to reduce communication overhead between worker nodes is a *combiner* that combines the messages that are destined to vertex v based on application-defined semantics (e.g., if v only needs the sum of values from neighbors). This cannot be done automatically, since it is not possible for the system to determine when and how this aggregation is appropriate; instead, the system provides a Combine() function whose code the programmer needs to specify.

System-level optimizations to deal with skew include the implementation of graph partitioning algorithms that are sensitive to this skew. The partition-based systems we discuss in Sections 10.4.7–10.4.9 also address these issues by taking a dramatically different system design.

There have been proposals for algorithmic optimizations to deal with these problems as well, but these require modifications to the implementation of the workload algorithms. Although we will not get into these in any detail, we highlight one as an example. Some analytics workload algorithms may result in a small portion of the graph vertices to remain active after the others have become inactive, leading to many more supersteps before convergence. In this optimization, if the "active" part of the graph is sufficiently small, the computation is moved to the master node and executed serially using the Master.Compute() function. It has been shown experimentally that this can reduce the number of supersteps between 20% and 60%.

10.4.5   Vertex-Centric Asynchronous

These systems follow the same programming model as the previous case, but relax the synchronous execution model while maintaining synchronization barriers at the end of each superstep. Consequently, the Compute() function for each vertex is executed at each superstep as above, and the results are pushed to the neighbor vertices, but the messages available as input to the function are not restricted to those that were sent in the previous superstep; a vertex may see the messages it receives within the same superstep that it was sent. Messages that are not available at the time Compute() is executed are picked up at the beginning of the subsequent superstep as in BSP. This approach addresses an important problem with the BSP model, while maintaining the ease of vertex-centric programming: a vertex may see fresher messages that are not delayed until the subsequent superstep. This usually results in faster convergence than in BSP-based systems. GRACE and GiraphUC follow this approach.

Example 10.9 To demonstrate vertex-centric AP systems, we use the weakly connected component example from the previous section (Example 10.8). To

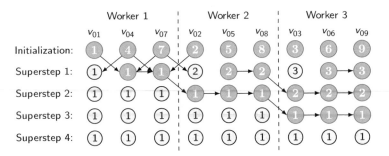

Fig. 10.27   Vertex-centric AP example

simplify matters, we assume that all the messages between vertices arrive to their destinations within the same superstep, and that the computation at each worker is also completed in the same superstep. Furthermore, we assume a single-threaded execution where each worker runs the Compute() on the vertices one-at-a-time. Under these assumptions, the calculation of the WCC over the graph in Fig. 10.26a is shown in Fig. 10.27. Note, for example, that during initialization step, v_1 pushes its group id (1) to v_4, and v_4 pushes its group id (4) to v_1 and v_7. Since we assume a single threaded execution, v_4.Compute is executed to change v_4's group id to 1, which is also pushed to v_7 in the same superstep (superset 1). So, when v_7.Compute() is executed, v_7's group id is set to 1. The access to the vertex states within the same superstep is the distinguishing feature of AP model.   ♦

As noted earlier, asynchronous execution requires consistency control by distributed locking. This exhibits itself in this class of systems in the following way. The state of a vertex may be accessed by other vertices while they execute their Compute() functions—vertex v_i may be executing its Compute() function while its neighbor vertex v_j is pushing its updates to v_i. To avoid this, locks are placed on each vertex. Since vertices are distributed across worker nodes, this requires a distributed locking mechanism to ensure state consistency.

Another issue with the AP approach is that it breaks a different type of consistent execution guarantee provided by BSP. Each vertex executes Compute() with all the message it has received since the last execution, and this will be a mix of old messages (from the previous superstep) and new messages (from the current superstep). Therefore, it is not possible to argue that, at each superstep, each vertex consistently computes a new state based on the states of the neighbor vertices at the end of the previous superstep. However, this relaxation allows a vertex to execute its Compute() function as soon as it receives a high priority message, for example.

Although the AP model addresses the message staleness problem of BSP, it still has performance bottlenecks due to the existence of global synchronization barriers, namely it has high communication overhead and it has to deal with stragglers. These can be overcome by eliminating some of the barriers as proposed in the *barrierless asynchronous parallel* (BAP) model of GiraphUC. BAP maintains *global barriers* between *global supersteps* when the worker nodes globally synchronize, but it

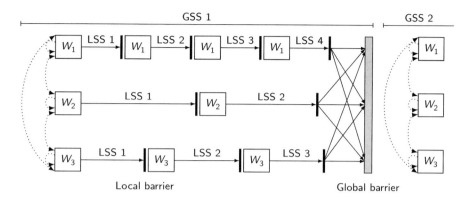

Fig. 10.28 BAP Model Over Three Worker Nodes

divides each global superstep into *logical supersteps* separated by very lightweight *local barriers*. This allows fast workers to execute Compute() function multiple times (once in each logical superstep) before it needs to globally synchronize with slower worker nodes. As in AP, vertices can immediately read the local and remote messages they have received, and this reduces the message staleness. Figure 10.28 demonstrates BAP over three worker nodes; the first worker (W_1) has four logical supersteps (LSS) within the first global superstep (GSS), the second worker has two, and the third worker has three. The dotted arrows represent messages received and processed in the same logical superstep, while solid arrows are messages that are picked up in the subsequent global superstep.

The BAP model requires care in determining termination. Recall that in both the BSP and AP models, the termination is checked at each synchronization barrier by checking that all the vertices are in inactive state and there are no messages in transmission. Since there is now a separation of local and global barriers, this check needs to occur at both the local and the global barriers. A simple approach is to check, at a local barrier, whether there are any more local or remote messages to process; if there are not, then there is no more work to do, and the vertices at this worker node arrive at the global barrier. When all the vertices in the graph arrive at the global barrier, a second check is performed, which is the same as in BSP and AP: the computation globally terminates if all vertices are inactive and there are no more messages.

10.4.6   Vertex-Centric Gather-Apply-Scatter

This category is characterized by GraphLab that combines vertex-centric programming model with the pull-based GAS computation model. As noted earlier, there can be a synchronous version of this approach (as implemented in GraphLab Sync) that is practically the same as vertex-centric BSP (except the pull aspect), so we will not discuss that further. The asynchronous version is different: in the gather phase, a vertex pulls data from its neighbors rather than the neighbors pushing their data.[9] For each vertex v a *scope* is defined [$Scope(v)$] that consists of the data stored in all adjacent edges and vertices as well as the data in v. The Compute() function (in GraphLab this is called the Update function) takes as input v and $Scope(v)$ and returns the updated $Scope'(v)$ as well as a set of vertices V' whose states have changed, and are candidates for scheduling. The execution follows three steps, taking as input a graph G and an initial set of vertices V':

1. Remove a vertex from V' according to the scheduling decision,
2. Execute the Compute() function and compute $Scope'(v)$ and V',
3. $V' \leftarrow V \cup V'$.

These three steps are executed iteratively until there are no more vertices in V. The separation of state updates in $Scope'(v)$ (i.e., states of neighbors) from the scheduling of vertex computations is a major distinction of GAS from the AP approach where the messages that update vertex states also schedule those vertices for computation. This separation allows flexibility in choosing the order of vertex computations, e.g., based on priorities or on load balancing. Furthermore, note that there is no explicit SendMsg() function in GAS execution; sharing state changes is done in the gather phase.

Since a vertex v can directly read data from its $Scope(v)$, inconsistency can arise as multiple vertex computations may cause conflicting updates of state, as noted earlier, requiring the deployment of distributed locking mechanisms. When vertex v is executing Compute, obtains locks over its $Scope(v)$, performs its computation, updates $Scope(v)$ and then releases its locks. In GraphLab, this is referred to as *full consistency*. In that particular system, two more relaxed consistency levels are provided to better accommodate applications whose semantics may not require full mutual exclusion: *edge consistency* and *vertex consistency*. Edge consistency ensures that v has read/write access to its own data and the data of its adjacent edges, but only read access to its neighboring vertices. For example, PageRank computation would only require edge consistency, since it only reads the ranks of the neighboring vertices. Vertex consistency simply ensures that while v is executing its Compute() function, no other vertex will be accessing it. Edge and vertex consistency allow application semantics to be taken into account for consistency.

10.4.7   Partition-Centric Block Synchronous Processing

As we noted in Sect. 10.4.4, many real-life graphs exhibit properties that are challenging for vertex-centric systems, and a number of optimizations have been

---

[9]GraphLab also differentiates itself by its distributed shared memory implementation, but that is not important in this discussion.

developed to deal with the issues that are raised. Partition-centric BSP systems constitute a different approach to deal with these problems. These systems exploit the partitioning of the graph over worker nodes so that, instead of each vertex communicating with others using message passing as in the vertex-centric approach, communication is limited to messages across blocks (partitions) with a simpler, serial algorithm implemented within each partition. The computation follows BSP, so multiple iterations are performed as supersteps until the system converges. This approach is exemplified by Blogel and Giraph++.

The critical point of these systems is they execute a serial algorithm within blocks, and only communicate between blocks. One way to reason about this is that given a graph $G = (V, E)$, after partitioning, we have a graph $G' = (B, E')$ where B is the set of blocks, and E' is the set of edges between blocks. In partition-centric algorithms, the communication overhead is bounded by $|E'|$, which is significantly smaller than $|E|$; therefore, graphs with high density have low communication overhead. For example, an experiment conducted on the Friendster graph to compute connected components show that a vertex-centric system takes 372 times more messages and 48 times longer computation time than a partition-centric system. Partition-based systems also reduce the diameter of the graphs since each block is represented by one vertex in G', and this results in a significantly reduced number of supersteps in BSP computation. A similar experiment for computing connected components over the USA road network graph (which has a diameter of about 9,000) demonstrates that the number of supersteps are reduced from over 6,000 to 22. Finally, dealing with skew in degree distribution is handled by the graph partitioning algorithm that ensures a balanced number of vertices in each block. Since a serial algorithm is executed within each block, higher degree vertices do not necessarily cause high number of messages—again the argument is that vertex-centric systems work on G while partition-centric systems work on the significantly smaller G'.

Example 10.10 Let us consider how the WCC computation we have been discussing would be performed in a partition-centric BSP system. The computation steps are shown in Fig. 10.29 where the graph segment at each worker is a partition denoted by shading. Since a serial algorithm is used within each partition, the algorithm we have been discussing, namely where each vertex starts out in its own group is not necessarily the one that might be used, but for comparison to previous approaches, we will assume the same algorithm. In superstep 1, each worker node performs a serial computation to determine the group ids for the vertices in its partition—for worker 1 the smallest group id is 1, so that becomes the group id of vertices v_1, v_4, and v_7. Similar computation takes places at other workers. At the end of the superstep, each worker pushes its group id to the other workers, and the computation repeats.

Notice that the number of supersteps in this case is the same as the vertex-centric AP (Example 10.9); in general, it could be lower, but this is not the main point. The savings is in the number of messages that are exchanged: partition-centric approach exchanges only 6 messages whereas vertex-centric AP exchanges 20 messages. The

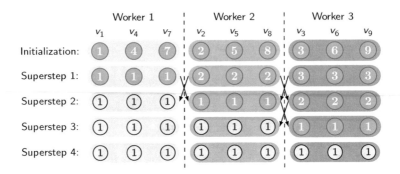

Fig. 10.29 Partition-centric BSP example

example graph we are using in these examples are not densely connected; if it were, the savings would have been more substantial. ◆

10.4.8 Partition-Centric Asynchronous

Systems in this category would partition the graph among worker nodes as in Sect. 10.4.7 and execute a serial algorithm within each partition, but communicate among workers asynchronously when inter-partition messages are sent. As noted earlier, the asynchronous communication is usually implemented using distributed locking. In that sense, these systems would be very similar to distributed DBMSs that we have been discussing in this book, if one treats each worker partition as a data fragment. At this point in time, there are no systems that have been developed in this category.

10.4.9 Partition-Centric Gather-Apply-Scatter

The only difference in this case to the partition-centric BSP described in Sect. 10.4.7 is the use of pull-based GAS rather than push-based BSP. Again, this class of systems are very similar to distributed DBMSs with appropriate changes to the data transfer operations in the query plans. So far, there are no systems that have been developed in this category.

10.4.10   Edge-Centric Block Synchronous Processing

Edge-centric systems focus on each edge as the primary object of interest; in this sense they are duals of vertex-centric approaches. The computation is done on each edge and iterates using supersteps until the fixpoint is reached. Note, however, that an edge in a graph is identified with its two incident vertices. Therefore, executing Compute() on an edge requires executing on that edge's incident vertices. The real difference, therefore, is that the system handles one edge at-a-time, rather than one vertex at-a-time as in the vertex-centric approach.

A natural question is why this would be preferable given that most graphs have far more edges than vertices. At first glance, it may seem that edge-centric approach would cause more computation. However, recall that the larger number of edges result in high messaging cost in vertex-centric systems. Furthermore, in vertex-centric systems, the edges are typically sorted by their originating vertex and an index is built upon them for easier access. When state updates are propagated to neighbor vertices, this index is then randomly accessed to locate edges incident to that vertex; this random access is expensive. Edge-centric systems aim to counter these problems by operating on unsorted sequence of edges where each edge identifies its source and target vertices—there is no random access to an index and when messages are pushed following computation on an edge, there is only one target vertex. Since we are considering BSP computation model, the updates that are computed at one superstep are available at the start of the subsequent superstep. X-Stream follows this approach over a shared memory parallel system and implements optimizations for both in-memory and disk-based graph processing.

10.4.11   Edge-Centric Asynchronous

The systems in this category would be modifications of vertex-centric asynchronous ones (Sect. 10.4.5) where the concern is on the consistent execution over each edge rather than over each vertex. Therefore, locks would be implemented on edges rather than on vertices. Currently, there are no known systems in this category.

10.4.12   Edge-Centric Gather-Apply-Scatter

Combining edge-centric programming with GAS computation model would entail changes to edge-centric BSP systems (Sect. 10.4.10) in the same way that vertex-centric GAS systems modify vertex-centric BSP systems. This would mean that the gather, apply, and scatter functions are implemented on edges with pull-based state read performed during the gather phase. At this point, there are no known systems that follow this approach.

10.5   Data Lakes

Big data technologies enable the storage and analysis of many different kinds of data, which can be structured, semistructured, or unstructured, in its natural format. This provides the opportunity to address in a new way the old problem of physical data integration (see Chap. 7, which has been typically solved using data warehouses. A data warehouse integrates data from different enterprises' data sources using a common format, usually the relational model, which requires data transformation. By contrast, a data lake stores data in its native format, using a big data store, such as Hadoop HDFS. Each data element can be directly stored, with a unique identifier and associated metadata (e.g., data source, format, etc.). Thus, there is no need for data transformation. The promise is that, for each business question, one can quickly find the relevant dataset to analyze it.

The term data lake was introduced to contrast with data warehouses and data marts. It is often associated with the Hadoop software ecosystem. It has become a hot, yet controversial, topic, in particular, in comparison with data warehouse.

In the rest of this section, we discuss in more details data lake versus data warehouse. Then, we introduce the principles and architecture of a data lake. Finally, we end with open issues.

10.5.1   Data Lake Versus Data Warehouse

As discussed in Chap. 7, a data warehouse follows physical database integration. It is central to OLAP and business analytics applications. Thus, it is generally at the heart of an enterprise's data-oriented strategy. When data warehousing started (in the 1980s), such enterprise data was located in OLTP operational databases. Today, more and more useful data is coming from many other big data sources, such as web logs, social networks, and emails. As the result, the traditional data warehouse suffers from several problems:

- **Long development process.** Developing a data warehouse is typically a long, multiyear process. The main reason is that it requires upfront a precise definition and modeling of the data that is needed. Once the needed data is found, often in enterprise information silos, a global schema and associated metadata need be carefully defined and data cleaning and transformation procedures must be designed.
- **Schema-on-write.** A data warehouse typically relies on a relational DBMS to manage the data, which is structured according to a relational schema. Relational DBMSs adopt what has been recently called a *schema-on-write* approach, to contrast with *schema-on-read* (discussed shortly). With schema-on-write, the data is written to the database with a fixed format, as defined by the schema. This helps enforce database consistency. Then, users can express queries based on the

schema to retrieve the data, which is already in the right format. Query processing is efficient in this case, as there is no need to parse the data at runtime. However, this is at the expense of difficult and costly evolution to adapt to changes in the business environment. For instance, introducing new data may imply schema modifications (e.g., adding new columns), which in turn may imply changes in applications and predefined queries.

- **OLAP workload data processing.** A data warehouse is typically optimized for OLAP workloads only, where data analysts can interactively query the data across different dimensions, e.g., through data cubes. Most OLAP applications, such as trend analysis and forecasting, need to analyze historical data and do not need the most current versions of the data. However, more recent OLAP applications may need real-time access to the operational data, which is hard to support in a data warehouse.

- **Complex development with ETL.** The integration of heterogeneous data sources through a global schema requires developing complex ETL programs, to deal with data cleaning, data transformation and manage data refreshment. With more and more diverse data sources to integrate, ETL development becomes even more difficult.

A data lake is a central repository of all the enterprise data in its natural format. Like a data warehouse, it can be used for OLAP and business analytics applications, as well as for batch or realtime data analysis using big data technologies. Compared with data warehouse, a data lake can provide the following advantages.

- **Schema-on-read.** Schema-on-read refers to the "load-first" approach to big data analysis, as exemplified by Hadoop. With schema-on-read, the data is loaded as is, in its native format, e.g., in Hadoop HDFS. Then, when the data is read, a schema is applied to identify the data fields of interest. Thus, the data can be queried in its native format. This provides much flexibility as new data can be added at any time in the data lake. However, more work is necessary to write the code that applies the schema to the data, for instance, as part of the Map function in MapReduce. Furthermore, data parsing is performed during query execution.

- **Multiworkload data processing.** The big data management software stack (see Fig. 10.1) provides support for multiple access methods to the same data, e.g., batch analysis with a framework like MapReduce, interactive OLAP, or business analytics with a framework like Spark, realtime analysis with a data streaming framework. Thus, by assembling these different frameworks, a data lake can support multiworkload data processing.

- **Cost-effective architecture.** By relying on open source technologies to implement the big data management software stack and shared-nothing clusters, a data lake provides excellent cost/performance ratio and return on investment.

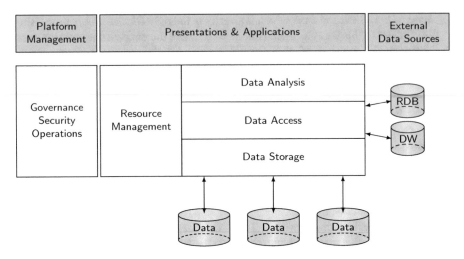

Fig. 10.30 Data Lake Architecture

10.5.2 Architecture

A data lake should provide the following main capabilities:

- Collect all useful data: raw data, transformed data, data coming from external data sources, etc.;
- Allow users from different business units to explore the data and enrich it with metadata;
- Access shared data through different methods: batch, interactive, realtime, etc.
- Govern, secure, and manage data and tasks.

Figure 10.30 shows the data lake architecture, with its main components.

At the center of the architecture is the big data management components (data storage, data access, data analysis, and resource management), on top of which different presentations and applications can be built. These components are those of the big data management software stack and can be found as Apache open source software. Note that many BI tools are now available to work with Hadoop, where we can distinguish new tools or extensions of traditional BI tools for RDBMSs. We can also distinguish between two approaches (which can be combined in one tool):

1. SQL-on-Hadoop, i.e., using an Hadoop SQL driver such as HiveQL or Spark SQL. Examples of tools are Tableau, Platfora, Pentaho, Power BI, and DB2 BigSQL.
2. Function library that provides HDFS access through high-level operators. Examples of tools are Datameer, Power BI, and DB2 BigSQL.

At the left-hand side of the architecture is platform management, which includes data governance, data security, and task operations. These components supplement big data management with functions that are critical to share data at the enterprise's scale (across multiple business units). Data governance has growing importance in a data lake as it is necessary to manage the data according to the enterprise's policy, with special attention to data privacy laws, e.g., the famous General Data Protection Regulation (GDPR) adopted by the European Union in May 2018). This policy is typically supervised by a data governance committee and implemented by data stewards, who are in charge of organizing data for business needs. Data security includes user authentication, access control, and data protection. Task operations include provisioning, monitoring, and scheduling of tasks (typically in a SN cluster). Like for the BI tools for big data, one can now find Apache tools for data governance, e.g., Falcon, data security, e.g., Ranger and Sentry, and task operations, e.g., Ambari and Zookeeper.

Finally, the right-hand side of the architecture shows that different kinds of external data sources, e.g., SQL, NoSQL, etc., can be integrated, typically using the wrappers of the tools for data access, e.g., Spark connectors.

10.5.3 Challenges

Building and operating a data lake remain challenging, both for methodological and technical reasons. The methodology for a data warehouse is now well-understood. It consists of a combination of prescriptive data modeling (schema-on-write), metadata management, and data governance, which altogether yield strong data consistency. Then, with powerful OLAP or business analytics tools, different users, even with limited data analysis skills can get value out of the data. In particular, a data mart will make it easier to analyze data that is specific to a business need.

In contrast, a data lake lacks data consistency, which makes data analysis at the enterprise's scale much more difficult. This is the main reason skilled data scientists and data stewards are needed. Another reason is that the big data technology landscape is complex and keeps changing. Therefore, the following methodology and best practices to build a data lake should be considered:

- Set a list of priorities and business added values, in comparison with the enterprise's data warehouse. This should include the definition of precise business objectives, and the corresponding data requirements for the data lake.
- Have a global vision of the data lake architecture which should be extensible (to accommodate technical evolutions) and include data governance and metadata management.
- Define a security and privacy policy, which is critical if data is shared between business lines.
- Define a compute/storage model that supports the global vision. In particular, the extensibility and scalability aspects will drive the technical choices.
- Define an operational plan with service level agreements (SLAs) in terms of uptime, volume, variety, velocity, and veracity.

The technical reasons that make a data lake challenging are due to the issues of data integration and data quality. Traditional data integration (see Chap. 7) focuses on the problem of schema integration, including schema matching and mapping, in order to produce a global schema. In the context of big data integration, the problem of schema integration, with many heterogeneous data sources, gets more difficult. The data lake approach simply avoids the problem of schema integration, by managing schemaless data. However, as data lakes mature the issue of schema integration may arise, in order to improve data consistency. Then, an interesting solution is the automatic extraction of metadata and schema information from many related data items, e.g., within the same dataset. One way to do this is by combining techniques from machine learning, matching, and clustering.

10.6 Conclusion

Big data and its role in data science have become important topics in data management, although they are hard to define precisely. Consequently, there is no unifying framework within which developments in this area can be presented—perhaps the reference architecture we provided in Fig. 10.1 is the best that can be done. Therefore, in this chapter, we focused on the properties that characterize these systems and focused on the fundamental platforms that have been proposed to address them. To summarize, we discussed distributed storage systems and MapReduce and Spark processing platforms that address the issues with managing and processing large volumes of data; we discussed data streams that deal with the velocity property associated with big data applications; and we discussed graph analytics that, together with data streams, highlight the issues of variety. Data lakes discussion addresses the variety and scale issues in terms of data integration, and it highlights the data quality problems (veracity) and the need for data cleaning when the source data is not well-curated to begin with.

It is unavoidable that the topics covered in this chapter will continue to evolve and change—this is an area where technology moves fast. We have covered the fundamentals and have pointed to the foundational publications. We give more references in the following section, but the reader would be well-advised to monitor publications for developments.

10.7 Bibliographic Notes

Statistics about big data are scattered and there is no single publication that reports comprehensive statistics. YouTube statistics are from [Brewer et al. 2016] while Alibaba statistics are from personal correspondence. Many more numbers are reported in various blogs and web publications.

A good early discussion of problems with operating system support for DBMSs is Stonebraker [1981] which also explains why early DBMSs moved from file system based storage to block storage. Among the more recent storage systems that we discussed, Google File System is described in [Ghemawat et al. 2003] and Ceph in [Weil et al. 2006].

Our discussion on big data processing platforms (in particular MapReduce) is based primarily on Li et al. [2014]. Sakr et al. [2013] and Lee et al. [2012] also provide overviews of the topic. The original MapReduce proposal is in [Dean and Ghemawat 2004, 2010]. Criticism of MapReduce are discussed in [DeWitt et al. 2008, Dewitt and Stonebraker 2009, Pavlo et al. 2009, Stonebraker et al. 2010]. Sources for MapReduce languages are as follows: HiveQL [Thusoo et al. 2009], Tenzing [Chattopadhyay et al. 2011], JAQL [Beyer et al. 2009], Pig Latin [Olston et al. 2008], Sawzall [Pike et al. 2005]), FlumeJava [Chambers et al. 2010], and SystemML [Ghoting et al. 2011]. The MapReduce join implementation 1-Bucket-Theta algorithm is due to Okcan and Riedewald [2011], broadcast join is due to Blanas et al. [2010], and repartition join is proposed by Blanas et al. [2010].

Spark is proposed in [Zaharia et al. 2010, Zaharia 2016]. As part of the Spark ecosystem, Spark SQL is discussed in [Armbrust et al. 2015], Spark Streaming in [Zaharia et al. 2013], and GraphX in [Gonzalez et al. 2014].

On data stream systems, the rich literature is covered in a number of books. Golab and Özsu [2010] mostly focus on the earlier systems and data and query modeling issues. The book also discusses stream warehouses. Aggarwal [2007] contains a wide range of topics (including stream mining that we omitted) focusing on earlier work. More discussion on stream mining can be found in [Bifet et al. 2018]. Muthukrishnan [2005] focuses on the theoretical foundations of these systems. Generalization of data stream systems to event processing is another direction that has been followed; although we have not discussed this issue in this chapter, Etzion and Niblett [2010] is a good starting point to investigate this direction. In addition to the systems that we discuss, there are DSS deployments in the cloud, as exemplified by StreamCloud[Gulisano et al. 2010, 2012].

The definition of a data stream as an append-only sequence of timestamped items that arrive in some order [Guha and McGregor 2006]. Other definitions of a data stream are given in [Wu et al. 2006, Tucker et al. 2003]. The concept of revision tuples are introduced in data streams by Ryvkina et al. [2006]. Streaming query semantics are discussed by Arasu et al. [2006] within the context of CQL language and more generally by Law et al. [2004]. These languages are classified as either declarative (QL [Arasu et al. 2006, Arasu and Widom 2004], GSQL [Cranor et al. 2003], and StreaQuel [Chandrasekaran et al. 2003]) or procedural (Aurora [Abadi et al. 2003]). Operator executions in stream systems are important due to their non-blocking requirements. Non-blocking joins are topics of [Haas and Hellerstein 1999a, Urhan and Franklin 2000, Viglas et al. 2003, Wilschut and Apers 1991] and aggregation of [Hellerstein et al. 1997, Wang et al. 2003]. Joins of more than two streams (multistream joins) are discussed in [Golab and Özsu 2003, Viglas et al. 2003] and joins of streams with static data is the topic of [Balazinska et al. 2007]. The topic of punctuations as a means of unblocking is presented by

Tucker et al. [2003]. Punctuations can also be used to reduce the amount of state that operators need to support [Ding and Rundensteiner 2004, Ding et al. 2004, Fernández-Moctezuma et al. 2009, Li et al. 2006, 2005]. Heartbeats which are punctuations that govern the timestamps of future tuples are discussed in [Johnson et al. 2005, Srivastava and Widom 2004a].

Query processing over data streams is the topic of [Abadi et al. 2003, Adamic and Huberman 2000, Arasu et al. 2006, Madden and Franklin 2002, Madden et al. 2002a]. Windowed query processing is discussed in [Golab and Özsu 2003, Hammad et al. 2003a, 2005, Kang et al. 2003, Wang et al. 2004, Arasu et al. 2006, Hammad et al. 2003b, 2004]. Load management approaches when stream rate exceeds processing capacity are presented in [Tatbul et al. 2003, Srivastava and Widom 2004b, Ayad and Naughton 2004, Liu et al. 2006, Reiss and Hellerstein 2005, Babcock et al. 2002, Cammert et al. 2006, Wu et al. 2005].

There have been a number of stream processing systems proposed and developed as prototypes and production systems. We classified some of these as Data Stream Management Systems (DSMS): STREAM [Arasu et al. 2006], Gigascope [Cranor et al. 2003], TelegraphCQ [Chandrasekaran et al. 2003], COUGAR [Bonnet et al. 2001], Tribeca [Sullivan and Heybey 1998], Aurora [Abadi et al. 2003], Borealis [Abadi et al. 2005]. We classified others as Data Stream Processing Systems (DSPS): Apache Storm [Toshniwal et al. 2014], Heron [Kulkarni et al. 2015], Spark Streaming [Zaharia et al. 2013], Flink [Carbone et al. 2015], MillWheel [Akidau et al. 2013], and TimeStream [Qian et al. 2013]. As noted, all DSMSs except Borealis were single machine systems, while all of the DSPSs are distributed/parallel.

Partitioning streaming data in parallel/distributed systems is discussed in [Xing et al. 2006] and [Johnson et al. 2008]. Key-splitting is proposed by Azar et al. [1999], Partial Key Grouping (PKG) by Nasir et al. [2015] (the "power of two choices" that PKG is based on is discussed in [Mitzenmacher 2001]). PKG has been extended to use more than two choices for the head of the distribution [Nasir et al. 2016]. Hybrid partitioning to deal with skewed data is given in [Gedik 2014, Pacaci and Özsu 2018]. Repartitioning in between operations in the query plan is discussed in [Zhu et al. 2004, Elseidy et al. 2014, Heinze et al. 2015, Fernandez et al. 2013, Heinze et al. 2014]. In this context, the seminal work flux is proposed by Shah et al. [2003].

Recovery semantics of parallel/distributed stream systems is the topic of [Hwang et al. 2005].

There are many books that focus on the specific aspects of graph analytics platforms, and these typically address how to perform analytics using one of the platforms that we discuss. For a more general book on graph processing, [Deshpande and Gupta 2018] is a good source. Graph analytics is discussed in an extensive survey [Yan et al. 2017]. The survey by Larriba-Pey et al. [2014] is also a very good reference. The real challenges in graph processing is discussed by Lumsdaine et al. [2007]. McCune et al. [2015] provide a good survey of vertex-centric systems.

Graph characteristics, in particular skew in degree distribution, plays a significant role in graph processing. This is discussed in [Newman et al. 2002]. An important first step in parallel/distributed graph processing is graph partitioning, which takes up a large portion of processing time [Verma et al. 2017] and is computationally expensive [Andreev and Racke 2006]. Graph partitioning techniques can be of two classes: vertex-disjoint (edge-cut) and edge-disjoint (vertex-cut). The main algorithm in the first class is METIS [Karypis and Kumar 1995] whose computation cost is analyzed by McCune et al. [2015].Hashing is another possibility when vertices are hashed to different partitions. These techniques distribute vertices in a balanced way, but they do not deal well with power-law graphs. Extensions to METIS have developed for this case [Abou-Rjeili and Karypis 2006]. Alternatively, label propagation Ugander and Backstrom [2013] is an alternative approach to deal with this problem. Combining METIS with label propagation by incorporating the latter in the coarsening phase of METIS has also been proposed [Wang et al. 2014]. Another alternative is to start from an unbalanced partitioning and incrementally achieving balance [Ugander and Backstrom 2013]. For edge-disjoint partitioning, hashing can be possible. It is also possible to combine both vertex-disjoint and edge-disjoint approaches as in PowerLyra [Chen et al. 2015].

MapReduce has been proposed as a possible approach to process graphs [Cohen 2009, Kiveris et al. 2014, Rastogi et al. 2013, Zhu et al. 2017] as well as modifications that would allow better scalability [Qin et al. 2014]. HaLoop system [Bu et al. 2010, 2012] is a specially tailored MapReduce approach to graph analytics. GraphX [Gonzalez et al. 2014] is a Spark-based system that follows the MapReduce approach.

In native graph analytics systems, the classification we discussed in Sect. 10.4.3 is based on [Han 2015, Corbett et al. 2013]. Bulk synchronous parallel (BSP) computation model is due to Valiant [1990]. Vertex-centric BSP systems include Pregel [Malewicz et al. 2010] and its open source counterpart Apache Giraph [Apache], GPS [Salihoglu and Widom 2013], Mizan [Khayyat et al. 2013], LFGraph [Hoque and Gupta 2013], Pregelix [Bu et al. 2014], and Trinity [Shao et al. 2013]. System-level optimizations to deal with skew are discussed in [Lugowski et al. 2012, Salihoglu and Widom 2013, Gonzalez et al. 2012]. Some algorithmic optimizations are presented in [Salihoglu and Widom 2014]. Vertex-centric asynchronous systems include GRACE [Wang et al. 2013] and GiraphUC [Han and Daudjee 2015]. The primary example of vertex-centric gather-apply-scatter systems is GraphLab [Low et al. 2012, 2010]. Blogel [Yan et al. 2014] and Giraph++ [Tian et al. 2013] follow the partition-centric BSP approach. X-Stream [Roy et al. 2013] is the only edge-centric BSP system that has been developed so far.

Data lake is a new topic and, thus, it is too early to see many technical books on the topic. Pasupuleti and Purra [2015] provide a good introduction to data lake architectures, with a focus on data governance, security, and data quality. One can also find useful information in white papers, e.g., [Hortonworks 2014] from companies that provide data lake components and services. Some of the challenges facing data lakes are in big data integration. Dong and Srivastava Dong and Srivastava [2015] provide an excellent survey of the recent techniques for big data integration. The broader issue of big data integration, which includes the web, is the topic of [Dong and Srivastava 2015]. Within this context, [Coletta et al. 2012] suggest combining techniques from machine learning, matching, and clustering to address integration issues in data lakes.

Exercises

Problem 10.1 Compare and contrast the different approaches to storage system design in terms of scalability, ease of use (ingesting data, etc.), architecture (shared, shared-nothing, etc.), consistency scheme, fault-tolerance, meta-data management. Try to generate a comparison table in addition to a short discussion.

Problem 10.2 (*) Consider the big data management software stack (Fig. 10.1) and compare it with the traditional relational DBMS software stack, for instance, based on that in Fig. 1.9. In particular, discuss the main differences in terms of storage management.

Problem 10.3 (*) In the distributed storage layer of the big data management software stack, data is typically stored in files or objects. Discuss when to use object storage versus object storage based on the characteristics of the data, e.g., large size or small objects, high number of objects, similar records, and application requirements, e.g., easy to move across machines, scalability, fault-tolerance.

Problem 10.4 (*) In a distributed file system like GFS or HDFS, the files are divided into fixed-size partitions, called chunks. Explain the differences between the concept of chunk and horizontal partition as defined in Chap. 2.

Problem 10.5 Consider the various MapReduce implementations for equijoin given in Sect. 10.2.1.3. Compare broadcast join and repartition join in terms of generality and shuffling cost.

Problem 10.6 (*) Section 10.2.1.1 describes how the combine module is used to reduce the shuffling cost.

(a) Provide pseudo-code of such combiner function for the SQL query example given in Example 10.1.
(b) Describe how it would reduce the shuffling cost.

Problem 10.7 Consider the MapReduce implementation of the theta-join operator and its dataflow given in Fig. 10.10. Discuss the performance implication of such dataflow for equijoin (where θ is $=$).

Problem 10.8 Consider the Spark implementation of the k-means clustering algorithm presented in Example 10.3. Describe which steps of the algorithms result in shuffling of data across multiple workers.

Problem 10.9 We discussed PageRank computation in Example 10.4. A version, called personalized PageRank, computes the value of a page around a user-selected set of pages by assigning more importance to edges in the neighborhood of certain pages that the user has identified. In this question, assume that the set of pages that the user has identified is a single page, called the *source*. It is with respect to this source page that the computation is conducted. The differences from usual PageRank are as follows:

- Recall that in PageRank when the random walk lands on a page, with probably d the walk jumps to a random page in the graph. In personalized PageRank, the jump is not to a random page, but always to the source page, i.e., with probability d, the walk jumps back to the *source*.
- When computation is initialized, instead of assigning equal PageRank values to all of the vertices of the graph, *source* is assigned a rank of 1, the rest of the pages are assigned a rank of 0.

Compute (by hand) the personalized PageRank of the web graph shown in Fig. 10.21.

Problem 10.10 (**) Implement personalized PageRank as defined in Problem 10.9 in MapReduce (use Hadoop).

Problem 10.11 (**) Implement personalized PageRank as defined in Problem 10.9 in Spark.

Problem 10.12 (**) Consider a DSPS as described in Sect. 10.3. Describe an algorithm to implement at-least-once delivery semantics.

Problem 10.13 (**) Consider the DSS as described in Sect. 10.3.

(a) Design an intra-operator parallel version of the filter streaming operator.
(b) Design an intra-operator parallel version of the aggregate operator. Hint: Unlike the filter operator above, the aggregate operator is stateful. What do you need to take into account that was not necessary for the (stateless) filter operator? How is data split across instances of the operator? What shall be done at the output of the previous operator to guarantee each streaming tuple goes to the right instance?

Problem 10.14 (**) Design a sliding window join operator for two streams. Is it deterministic? Why not? Can you propose an alternative design of the operator that guarantees determinism independently of the relative speed/interleaving of the input streams?

Problem 10.15 Consider the vertex-centric programming model for graph processing as described in Sect. 10.4.3. Compare BSP and GAS computation models in terms of

(a) generality and expressiveness of graph algorithms and
(b) performance optimizations

Problem 10.16 (**) Give an algorithm for personalized PageRank as defined in Problem 10.9 using vertex-centric BSP model.

Problem 10.17 (*) Example 10.8 describes an iterative label-propagation based algorithm for finding connected components of the input graph in the vertex-centric programming model. Consider a streaming application where each incoming tuple in the stream represents an undirected edge of the input graph. Design an incremental algorithm that finds connected components of the graph that is formed by the edges in the stream.

Problem 10.18 (*) Consider the greedy vertex-cut edge placement heuristics defined in Sect. 10.4.10. Such greedy partitioning heuristics are known to suffer from load-imbalance if the edge steam is presented in some adversarial order.

(a) Create an ordering of the vertices in Fig. 10.23 such that the described heuristics results in highly imbalanced partitioning, i.e., entire set of edges is assigned to a single partition.
(b) Propose a strategy to mitigate the load imbalance in case of such adversarial stream ordering.

Problem 10.19 (*) A data lake resembles a data warehouse (see Chap. 7), but for unstructured schemaless data, e.g., stored in HDFS. Consider the Spark big data system, which provides SQL access to HDFS data (through SparkSQL) and many other data sources. Is Spark sufficient to build a data lake? What functionality would be missing?

Problem 10.20 (**) Recent parallel DBMSs used in modern data warehousing have added support for external tables (see, for instance, Polybase in Chap. 11), which make the correspondence with the HDFS files and can be manipulated together with native relational tables using SQL queries. On the other hand, data lakes provide access to external data sources, e.g., SQL, NoSQL, etc., using wrappers, e.g., Spark connectors. Compare the two approaches (data lake and modern data warehouse) from the point of view of data integration. What is similar? What is different?

Chapter 11
NoSQL, NewSQL, and Polystores

For managing data in the cloud, one can always rely on a relational DBMS. All relational DBMSs have a distributed version, and most of them operate in the cloud. However, these systems have been criticized for their "one size fits all" approach. Although they have been able to integrate support for all kinds of data (e.g., multimedia objects, documents) and new functions, this has resulted in a loss of performance, simplicity, and flexibility for applications with specific, tight performance requirements. Therefore, it has been argued that more specialized DBMS engines are needed. For instance, column-oriented DBMSs which store column data together rather than rows in traditional row-oriented relational DBMSs have been shown to perform more than an order of magnitude better on OLAP workloads. Similarly, data stream management systems (see Sect. 10.3) are specifically architected to deal efficiently with data streams.

Thus, many different data management solutions have been proposed, specialized for different kinds of data and tasks, and able to perform orders of magnitude better than traditional relational DBMSs. Examples of new data management technologies include distributed file systems and parallel data processing frameworks for big data (see Chap. 10).

An important kind of new data management technology is NoSQL, meaning "Not Only SQL" to contrast with the "one size fits all" approach of relational DBMS. NoSQL systems are specialized data stores that address the requirements of web and cloud data management. The term data store is often used as it is quite general, including not only DBMSs but also simpler file systems or directories. As an alternative to relational DBMSs, NoSQL systems support different data models and different languages other than standard SQL. They also emphasize scalability, fault-tolerance, and availability, sometimes at the expense of consistency. There are different types of NoSQL systems, including key-value, document, wide column, and graph, as well as hybrid (multimodel or NewSQL).

The original version of this chapter was revised. The correction to this chapter is available at https://doi.org/10.1007/978-3-030-26253-2_13

© Springer Nature Switzerland AG 2020
M. T. Özsu, P. Valduriez, *Principles of Distributed Database Systems*,
https://doi.org/10.1007/978-3-030-26253-2_11

These new data management technologies have led to a rich offering of services that can be used to build cloud data-intensive applications that can scale and exhibit high performance. However, this has also led to a wide diversification of data store interfaces and the loss of a common programming paradigm. Thus, this makes it very hard for a user to build applications that use multiple data stores, e.g., distributed file system, relational DBMS, and NoSQL DBMS. This has motivated the design of *polystores*, also called multistore systems, that provide integrated access to a number of cloud data stores through one or more query languages.

This chapter is organized as follows: Section 11.1 discusses the motivations for NoSQL systems, in particular, the CAP theorem that helps to understand the trade-off between different properties. We then introduce the different types of NoSQL systems: key-value in Sect. 11.2, document in Sect. 11.3, wide column in Sect. 11.4, graph in Sect. 11.5. Section 11.6 presents the hybrid systems, i.e., multimodel NoSQL systems and NewSQL DBMSs. Section 11.7 discusses the polystores.

11.1 Motivations for NoSQL

There are several (complementary) reasons that have motivated the need for NoSQL systems. The first obvious one is the "one size fits all" limitation of relational DBMSs, which we discussed above.

A second reason is the limited scalability and availability of the early database architecture that has been used in the cloud. This architecture is a traditional 3-tier architecture with web clients accessing a data center that features a load balancer, web/application servers, and database servers. The data center typically uses a shared-nothing cluster, which is the most cost-effective solution for the cloud. For a given application, there is one database server, typically a relational DBMS, which provides fault-tolerance and data availability through replication. As the number of web clients increases, it is relatively easy to add web/application servers, typically using virtual machines, to absorb the incoming load and scale up. However, the database server becomes the bottleneck, and adding new database servers would require to replicate the entire database, which would take much time. In a shared-nothing cluster, a solution could be to use a parallel relational DBMS to provide scalability. However, this solution would be appropriate only for OLAP (read-intensive) workloads (see Sect. 8.2) and not cost-effective as parallel relational DBMSs are high-end products.

A third reason that has been used to motivate the need for NoSQL systems is that supporting strong database consistency as relational DBMSs do, i.e., through ACID transactions, hurts scalability. Therefore, some NoSQL systems have relaxed strong database consistency in favor of scalability. An argument to support this approach has been the famous CAP theorem from distributed systems theory. However, the argument is simply wrong as the CAP theorem has nothing to do with database scalability: it is related to replication consistency in the presence of network partitioning. Furthermore, it is quite possible to provide both strong database consistency and scalability, as some NewSQL systems do (see Sect. 11.6.2).

The CAP theorem states that a distributed data store with replication can only provide two out of the following three properties: (C) consistency, (A) availability, and (P) partition tolerance. Note there is no (S) scalability. These properties are defined as follows:

- Consistency: all nodes see the same data values at the same time, i.e., each read request returns the last written value. This property corresponds to linearizability (consistency over individual operations) and not serializability (consistency over groups of operations).
- Availability: any replica has to reply to any received request.
- Partition tolerance: the system continues to operate despite a partitioning of the network due to a failure.

A common misunderstanding of the CAP theorem is that one of these properties needs to be abandoned. However, only in the case of a network partitioning does one have to choose between consistency and availability.

NoSQL (Not Only SQL) is an overloaded term, which leaves much room for interpretation and definition. For instance, it can be applied to the early hierarchical and network DBMS, or the object or XML DBMSs. However, the term first appeared in the late 1990s for the new data stores built to address the requirements of web and cloud data management. As an alternative to relational databases, they support different data models and languages other than standard SQL. These systems typically emphasize scalability, fault-tolerance, and availability, sometimes at the expense of consistency.

In this chapter, we introduce the four main categories of NoSQL systems based on the underlying data model, i.e., key-value, wide column, document, and graph. We also consider the hybrid data stores: multimodel, to combine multiple data models in one system, and NewSQL, to combine the scalability of NoSQL with the strong consistency of relational DBMS. For each category, we illustrate with a representative system.

11.2 Key-Value Stores

In the key-value data model, all data is represented as key-value pairs, where the key uniquely identifies the value. Key-values stores are schemaless, which yields great flexibility and scalability. They typically provide a simple interface such as put (key, value), value=get (key), delete (key).

An extended form of key-value store is able to store records, as lists of attribute-value pairs. The first attribute is called major key or primary key, e.g., a social security number, and uniquely identifies the record among a collection of records, e.g., people. The keys are usually sorted, which enables range queries as well as ordered processing of keys.

A popular key-value store is Amazon DynamoDB, which we introduce below.

11.2.1   DynamoDB

DynamoDB is used by some of Amazon's core services that need high availability and key-based data access. Examples of services are those that provide shopping carts, seller lists, customer preferences, and product catalogs. To achieve scalability and availability, Dynamo sacrifices consistency under some failure scenarios and uses a synthesis of well-known P2P techniques (see Chap. 9) in a shared-nothing cluster.

DynamoDB stores data as database tables, which are collections of individual items. Each item is a list of attribute-value pairs. An attribute value can be of type scalar, set, or JSON. The items are analogous to rows in a relational table, and the attributes are analogous to columns. However, since attributes are self-describing, there is no need for a relational schema. Furthermore, items may be heterogeneous, i.e., with different attributes.

The original design of DynamoDB provides the P2P distributed hash table (DHT) abstraction (see Sect. 9.1.2). The primary key (the first attribute) is hashed over the different partitions, which allows efficient key-based read and write operations to an item as well as load balancing. More recently, DynamoDB has been extended to support composite primary keys, which are made of two attributes. The first attribute is the hash key and is not necessarily unique. The second attribute is the range key and allows range operations within the hash partition corresponding to the hash key. To access database tables, DynamoDB provides a Java API with the following operations:

- PutItem, UpdateItem, DeleteItem: adds, updates, or deletes an item in a table based on its primary key (either a hash primary key or a composite primary key).
- GetItem: returns an item based on its primary key in a table.
- BatchGetItem: returns all items that have the same primary key, but in several tables.
- Scan: returns all items in a table.
- Range query: returns all items based on a hash key and a range on the range key.
- Indexed query: returns all items based on an indexed attribute.

Example 11.1 Consider table Forum_Thread in Fig. 11.1. This table is made of homogeneous items that have four attributes: Forum, Subject, Date of last post, and Tags. It has a composite key, made of a hash key (Forum) and a range key (Subject). An example of primary key access is

> GetItem(Forum="EC2," Subject="xyz")

which returns the last item. An example of range query is

> Query(Forum="S3," Subject >"ac")

which returns the second and third items.   ◆

DynamoDB builds an unordered hash index on the hash key, i.e., a DHT, and a sorted range index on the range (ordered) key. Furthermore, DynamoDB provides

Table: Forum_Thread

Forum	Subject	Date of last post	Tags
"S3"	"abc"	"2017 . . ."	"a" "b"
"S3"	"acd"	"2017 . . ."	"c"
"S3"	"cbd"	"2017 . . ."	"d" "e"

"RDS"	"xyz"	"2017 . . ."	"f"

"EC2"	"abc"	"2017 . . ."	"a" "e"
"EC2"	"xyz"	"2017 . . ."	"f"

| Hash | Range | | |
| key | key | | |

Fig. 11.1 DynamoDB table example

two kinds of secondary indexes to allow fast access to items based on nonkey attributes: local secondary indexes, to retrieve items within a hash partition, i.e., items that have the same value in their hash key, and global secondary indexes, to retrieve items in the whole DynamoDB table.

Data is partitioned and replicated across multiple cluster nodes in several data centers, which provides both load balancing and high availability. Data partitioning relies on consistent hashing , a popular hashing scheme that has been used in DHTs with ring geometry, e.g., Chord (see Sect. 9.1.2). The DHT is represented as a one-dimensional circular identifier space, i.e., a "ring," where each node in the system is assigned a random value within this space which represents its position on the ring. Each item is assigned to a node by hashing the item's key to yield its position on the ring, and then finding the first node clockwise with a position higher than the item position. Thus, each node becomes responsible for the interval in the ring between its predecessor node and itself. The main advantage of consistent hashing is that the addition (joins) and removal (leaves/failures) of nodes only affect the nodes' immediate neighbor, with no impact on other nodes.

DynamoDB also exploits consistent hashing to provide high availability, by replicating each item at n nodes, n being a system-configured parameter. Each item is assigned a coordinator node, as described above, and is replicated on the $n - 1$ clockwise successor nodes. Thus, each node is responsible for the interval of the ring between its nth predecessor and itself.

Example 11.2 Figure 11.2 shows a ring with 6 nodes, each named by its position (hash value). For instance, node B is responsible for the hash value interval (A,B] and node A for the interval (F,A]. The put(c,v) operation yields a hash value for key c between A and B, so node B becomes responsible for the item. In addition, assuming replication parameter $n = 3$, the item would be replicated at nodes C and

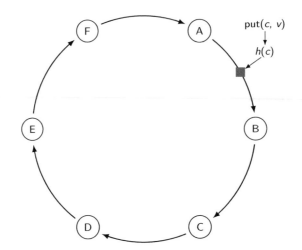

Fig. 11.2 DynamoDB consistent hashing. Node B is responsible for the hash value interval (A,B].
Thus, item (c,v) is assigned to node B

D. Thus, node D will store the items whose keys fall in the intervals (A, B], (B, C],
and (C, D].   ◆

DynamoDB trades strong data consistency for scalability and availability, but
with different ways of controlling consistency. It provides eventual consistency of
replicas (see Sect. 6.1.1), which is achieved by an asynchronous update propagation
protocol and a gossip-based distributed failure detection protocol.

Write consistency in a concurrent multiuser environment can be controlled
through conditional writes. By default, the write operations (PutItem, UpdateItem,
DeleteItem) will overwrite an existing item that has the given primary key. A
conditional write specifies a condition over the item's attributes to succeed. For
instance, a condition for a PutItem to succeed is that there is not already an item
with the same primary key. Thus, conditional writes are useful in case of concurrent
updates.

DynamoDB supports eventually consistent and strongly consistent reads. By
default, reads are eventually consistent, i.e., may not return the latest data which
is being asynchronously replicated. Strongly consistent reads return the most up-to-
date data, which may not be possible in the case of network failures, because not all
replica updates have been propagated.

11.2.2   Other Key-Value Stores

Other popular key-value stores are Cassandra, Memcached, Riak, Redis, Amazon
SimpleDB, and Oracle NoSQL Database. Many systems provide further extensions

so that we can see a smooth transition to wide column store and document stores, which we discuss next.

11.3   Document Stores

Document stores are advanced key-value stores, where keys are mapped to values of document type, such as JSON, YAML, or XML. Documents are typically grouped into collections, which play a role similar to relational tables. However, documents are different from relational tuples. Documents are self-describing, storing data and metadata (e.g., markups in XML, field names in JSON objects) altogether and can be different from one another within a collection. Furthermore, the document structures are hierarchical, using nested constructs, e.g., nested objects and arrays in JSON. Thus, modeling a database using documents requires fewer collections than with (flat) relational tables, and also avoids expensive join operations.

In addition to the simple key-value interface to retrieve documents, document stores offer an API or query language that retrieve documents based on their contents. Document stores make it easier to deal with change and optional values, and to map into program objects. This makes them attractive for modern web applications, which are subject to continual change, and where speed of deployment is important.

A popular NoSQL document store is MongoDB, which we introduce below.

11.3.1   MongoDB

MongoDB is an open source system written in C++. It provides a JSON-based data model for documents, schema flexibility, high availability, fault-tolerance, and scalability in shared-nothing clusters.

MongoDB stores data as documents in BSON (Binary JSON), a binary encoded serialization of JSON to include additional types such as binary, int, long, and floating point. BSON documents contain one or more fields, and each field has a name and contains a value of a specific data type, including arrays, binary data, and subdocuments. Each document is a BSON object, i.e., with multiple fields, and uniquely identified by its first field of type ObjectId, whose value is automatically generated by MongoDB.

Documents that have a similar structure are organized as collections, like relational tables, document fields being similar to columns. However, documents in the same collection can have different structures, since there is no imposed schema.

MongoDB provides a rich query language to update and retrieve BSON data using functions expressed in JSON. Representing queries as JSON allows unifying both the way data is stored and manipulated. The query language can be used with APIs in various programming languages, such as Java, PHP, JavaScript, and Scala.

Since queries are implemented as methods or functions within the API of a specific programming language, the integration within application programs is natural and simple for developers.

MongoDB supports many kinds of queries to insert, update, delete, and retrieve documents. A query may return documents, subsets of specific fields within documents, or complex aggregations of values from many documents. Queries can also include user-defined JavaScript functions. The general form of a query is

> db.collection.function (JSON expression)

where *db* is a global variable corresponding to the database connection, and *function* is the database operation applied to the collection. The JSON expression can be arbitrary and used as a criterion to select data. The different kinds of queries are

- Insert, delete, and update operations on documents. For delete and update operations, the JSON expression specifies the criteria to select the documents.
- Exact-match queries return results based on the equality of a value for a field in the documents, typically the primary key.
- Range queries return results based on values of a field in a given range.
- Geospatial queries return results based on proximity, intersection, and inclusion of geographical objects, such as point, line, circle, or polygon in GeoJSON format.
- Text search queries return results in relevance order based on text arguments using Boolean operators.
- Aggregation queries return aggregated values from a collection with operators such as count, min, max, and average. Furthermore, documents from two collections can be combined using a left outer join operation.

Example 11.3 Consider collection Posts in Fig. 11.3. Each post item in the collection is uniquely identified by its key of type ObjectId (generated by MongoDB) and its value is a JSON object, with nested arrays such as tags and comments. Examples of update operations are

> db.posts.insert(author:"alex," title:"No Free Lunch")
> db.posts.update(author:"alex," $set:age:30)
> db.posts.update(author:"alex," $push:tags:"music")

_id: ObjectId("abc")	author: "alex", title: "No Free Lunch", text: "This is …", tags: ["business", "ramblings"], comments: [{who:"jane", what:"I agree."},{who:"joe", what:"No…"}]
_id: ObjectId("abd")	A post by X
_id: ObjectId("acd")	A post by Y
Unique key generated by MongoDB	Value = JSON object with nested arrays

Fig. 11.3 MongoDB posts collection example

where $set (sets a specified value for a field) and $push (appends a specified value to an array) are MongoDB instructions within JSON.

The following queries:

> db.posts.find(author:"alex")
> db.posts.find(comments.who:"jane")

are exact-match queries. The first one returns all the posts from Alex, while the second one returns all the posts for which Jane made a comment   ♦

To provide efficient access to data, MongoDB includes support for many kinds of secondary indexes that can be declared on any field in the document, including fields within arrays. The different kinds of indexes are:

- Unique indexes, where the value of the indexed field is enforced to be unique.
- Multikey (compound) indexes on multiple fields.
- Array indexes for array fields, with a separate index entry for each array value.
- TTL indexes that should expire automatically after a certain Time-to-Live (TTL).
- Geospatial indexes to optimize queries based on proximity, intersection, and inclusion of geographical objects, such as point, line, circle, or polygon.
- Partial indexes that are created for a subset of documents that satisfy a condition specified by the user.
- Sparse indexes that index only documents that contain the specified field.
- Text search indexes use language-specific linguistic rules to optimize text search queries.

To scale out in shared-nothing clusters, MongoDB supports different kinds of data partitioning (or sharding) schemes: hash-based, range-based, and location-aware (whereby the user specifies key-ranges and associated nodes). High availability is provided through a variation of primary-copy replication, called replica sets, with asynchronous update propagation. If a master goes down, one of the replicas becomes the new master and continues to accept update operations. A MongoDB cluster consists of: shards (data partitions) where each shard can be a unit of replication (a replica set); mongos that act as query processors between client applications and the cluster; and configuration servers that store metadata and configuration settings for the cluster. Applications can optionally read from secondary replicas, where data is eventually consistent.

MongoDB has recently introduced support for ACID transactions on multiple documents, in addition to single document transactions. This is achieved through snapshot isolation. One or more fields in a document may be written in a single transaction, including updates to multiple subdocuments and elements of an array. Multidocument transactions can be used across multiple collections, databases, documents, and shards.

MongoDB also provides an option called *write concern* that allows users to specify a guarantee level for reporting the success of a write operation, i.e., with a desired trade-off between level of persistence and performance, on database replicas. There are four guarantee levels for clients to adjust the control of a

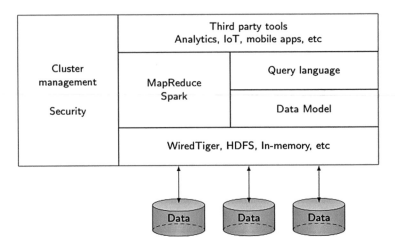

Fig. 11.4 MongoDB architecture

write operation, in order from weakest to strongest. These are unacknowledged (no guarantee), acknowledged (the write to disk has been done), journaled (the write has been recorded in the log), and replica acknowledged (the write has been propagated to replicas).

MongoDB's architecture fits in the big data management software stack (see Fig. 10.1). It supports pluggable storage engines, e.g., HDFS, or in-memory, for dealing with unique application demands, interfaces with big data frameworks like MapReduce and Spark, and supports third-party tools for analytics, IoT, mobile applications, etc. (see Fig. 11.4). It makes extensive use of main memory to speed up database operations and native compression, using its storage engine (WiredTiger).

11.3.2 Other Document Stores

Other popular document stores are AsterixDB, Couchbase, CouchDB, and RavenDB , which all support the JSON data model in a scalable shared-nothing cluster architecture. However, AsterixDB and Couchbase support a dialect of SQL++, an elegant extension of SQL with a few simple features to query JSON data. Couchbase's SQL++ dialect is called N1QL (Non-first normal form Query Language, pronounced "nickel"). Couchbase supports restricted transactions (atomic document writes) and allows to trade some properties for performance, e.g., relaxing durability by acknowledging write operations done in memory and then asynchronously writing to disk. In addition to the Couchbase server, which is used for queries and transactions, the Couchbase platform has an analytics service that allows online data analytics, without hurting transaction performance, and also without requiring a different data model or (as a result) ETL. This is kind of Hybrid

Transaction and Analytics Processing (HTAP) for NoSQL (see the introduction
of HTAP in Sect. 11.6.2). The implementation of this analytics service is based
on AsterixDB's storage engine and parallel query processor. AsterixDB is a high-
performance JSON document store with a combination of techniques from parallel
databases and document databases.

11.4   Wide Column Stores

Wide column stores combine some of the nice properties of relational databases
(e.g., representing data as tables) with the flexibility of key-value stores (e.g.,
schemaless data within columns). Each row in a wide column table is uniquely
identified by a key and has a number of named columns. But unlike in a relational
table, where columns can only contain atomic values, a column can be wide and
contain multiple key-value pairs.

Wide column stores extend the key-value store interface with more declarative
constructs that allow scans, exact-match and range queries over column families.
They typically provide an API for these constructs to be used in a programming
language. Some systems also provide an SQL-like query language, e.g., Cassandra
Query Language (CQL).

At the origin of the wide column stores is Google Bigtable, which we introduce
below.

11.4.1   Bigtable

Bigtable is a wide column store for shared-nothing clusters. Bigtable uses Google
File System (GFS) for storing structured data in distributed files, which provides
fault-tolerance and availability (see Sect. 10.1 on block-based distributed file
systems). It also uses a form of dynamic data partitioning for scalability. Like GFS,
it is used by popular Google applications, such as Google Earth, Google Analytics,
and Google+.

Bigtable supports a simple data model that resembles the relational model, with
multivalued, timestamped attributes. We briefly describe this model as it is the basis
for Bigtable implementation that combines aspects of row-store and column-store
DBMS. For consistency with the concepts we have used so far, we present the
Bigtable data model as a slightly extended relational model.[1]

A Bigtable instance is a collection of (key, value) pairs where the key identifies
a row and the value is the set of columns, organized as column families. Bigtable

---

[1]In the original proposal, a Bigtable is defined as a multidimensional map, indexed by a row key, a
column key, and a timestamp, each cell of the map being a single value (a string).

Row key	Name	Email	Web page
100	"Prefix": "Dr." "Last": "Dobb"	"email: gmail.com": "dobb@gmail.com"	<!DOCTYPE html PUBLIC... >
101	"First": "Alice" "Last": "Martin"	"email: gmail.com": "amartin@gmail.com" "email: free.fr": "amartin@free.fr"	<!DOCTYPE html PUBLIC... >

Fig. 11.5 A Bigtable with 3 column families and 2 rows

sorts its data by keys, which helps clustering rows of the same range in the same cluster node.

Each row in a Bigtable is uniquely identified by a *row key*, which is an arbitrary string (of up to 64KB in the original system). Thus, a row key is like a single attribute key in a relation. A Bigtable is always sorted by row keys, A row can have multiple *column families*, which form the unit of access control and storage. A column family is a set of columns of the same type. To create a Bigtable, only the table name and the column family names need to be specified. However, within a column family, arbitrary columns (of same type) can be dynamically added.

To access data in a Bigtable, it is necessary to identify columns within column families using *column keys*. A column key is a fully qualified name of the form **column-family-name:column-name**. The column family name is like a relation attribute name. The column name is like a relation attribute value, but used as a name as part of the column key to represent a single item. This allows the equivalent of multivalued attributes within a relation. In addition, the data identified by a column key within a row can have multiple versions, each identified by a timestamp (a 64 bit integer).

Example 11.4 Figure 11.5 shows an example of a Bigtable with 3 column families and 2 rows, as a relational style representation. The Name and EMail column families have heterogeneous columns. To access a column value, the row key and column key must be specified, e.g., row key = "111" and column key = "Email:gmail.com" which yields "am@gmail.com." ◆

Bigtable provides a basic API for defining and manipulating tables, within a programming language such as C++. It also provides functions for changing table, and column family metadata, such as access control rights. The API offers various operators to write and update values, and to iterate over subsets of data, produced by a scan operator. There are various ways to restrict the rows, columns, and timestamps produced by a scan, as in a relational select operator. However, there are no complex operators such as join or union, which need to be programmed using the scan operator.

Transactional atomicity is supported for single row updates only. Thus, for more complex multiple row updates, it is up to the programmer to write the appropriate code to control atomicity using an interface for batching writes across row keys at the clients.

To store a table in GFS, Bigtable uses range partitioning on the row key. Each table is divided into partitions called *tablets*, each corresponding to a row range. Partitioning is dynamic, starting with one tablet (the entire table range) that is subsequently split into multiple tablets as the table grows. To locate the (user) tablets in GFS, Bigtable uses a metadata table, which is itself partitioned in metadata tablets, with a single root tablet stored at a master server, similar to GFS's master. In addition to exploiting GFS for scalability and availability, Bigtable uses various techniques to optimize data access and minimize the number of disk accesses, such as compression of column families, grouping of column families with high locality of access, and aggressive caching of metadata information by clients.

Bigtable relies on a highly available and persistent distributed lock service called Chubby . A Chubby service consists of five active replicas, one of which is elected to be the master and actively serves requests. Bigtable uses Chubby for several tasks: to ensure that there is at most one active master at any time; to store the bootstrap location of Bigtable data; to discover tablet servers and finalize tablet server removals; and to store Bigtable schemas. If Chubby becomes unavailable for an extended period of time, Bigtable becomes unavailable.

11.4.2   Other Wide Column Stores

There are popular open source implementations of Bigtable, such as Hadoop Hbase, a popular Java implementation that runs on top of HDFS, and Cassandra that combines techniques from Bigtable and DynamoDB.

11.5   Graph DBMSs

We introduced graph analytics in Chap. 10, where the entire graph can be processed multiple time until a fixpoint is reached. In contrast, graph DBMSs support queries that are not iterative and might access only a portion of the graph, allowing indexes to be effective. Graph databases represent and store data directly as graphs which allows easy expression and fast processing of graph-like queries, e.g., computing the shortest path between two elements in the graph. This is much more efficient than with a relational database where graph data need be stored as separated tables and graph-like queries require repeated, expensive join operations. Graph DBMSs typically provide a powerful graph query language. They have become popular with data-intensive web-based applications such as social networks and recommender systems.

Graph DBMSs can provide a flexible schema by specifying vertex and edge types with their properties. This facilitates the definition of indexes to provide fast access to vertices, based on some property value, e.g., a city name, in addition to structural indexes. Graph queries can be expressed using graph operators through a specific API or a declarative query language.

As we have seen above, in order to scale up to very large databases, key-value, document, and wide column stores partition data across a number of cluster nodes. The reason that such data partitioning works well is that it deals with individual items. However, graph data partitioning is much more difficult since the problem of optimally partitioning a graph is NP-complete (see Sect. 10.1). In particular, recall that we may get items in different partitions that are connected by edges. Traversing such interpartition edges incurs communication overhead which hurts the performance of graph traversal operations. Thus, the number of interpartition edges should be minimized. But, at the same time, this may produce unbalanced partitions.

In the following, we illustrate graph DBMSs with Neo4j, which is a popular one with many deployments.

11.5.1   Neo4j

Neo4j is a commercial open source system introduced as a scalable and high-performance graph DBMS with native graph storage and processing in shared-nothing clusters. It provides a rich graph data model with integrity constraints, a powerful query language, called Cypher, with indexes, ACID transactions, and support for high availability and load balancing.

The data model is based on directed graphs, with separated storage for edges (called relationships), vertices (called nodes), or attributes (called properties). Each node can have any number of properties, in the form of (attribute, value) pairs. A relationship must have a type, which gives semantics, and a direction from one node to another (or to itself). An important capability of Neo4j is that relationships can be traversed in both directions with the same performance. This simplifies the modeling of graph DBMSs since there is no need to create two different relationships between nodes, if one implies the other, e.g., a mutual relationship such as friend (whose reverse is also friend) or a 1-1 relationship such as owns (whose reverse is owned-by).

Updating a graph involves updating nodes, relationships, and properties, which needs to be done in a consistent manner. This is done using ACID transactions.

Example 11.5   Figure 11.6 shows an example of a simple graph for a social network. The friend relationship from Bob to Mary (meaning "Bob is a friend of Mary") is sufficient to represent the mutual relationship (hopefully, Mary is also a friend of Bob). It could have also been represented the other way (from Mary to Bob). This makes the graph model simple.

The following transaction, using the Java API, creates nodes Bob and Mary, their properties, and the friend relationship from Bob to Mary.

```
Transaction tx = neo.beginTx();
Node n1 = neo.CreateNode();
n1.setProperty(''name'', ''Bob'');
```

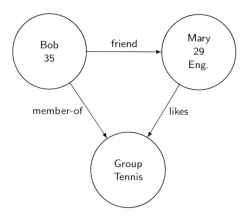

Fig. 11.6 Example of Neo4j graph

```
n1.setProperty(''age'', 35);
Node n2 = neo.createNode();
n2.setProperty(''name'', ''Mary'');
n1.setProperty(''age'', 29);
n1.setProperty(''job'', ''engineer'');
n1.createRelationshipTo(n2, RelTypes.friend);
tx.Commit();
```

◆

Neo4j imposes no schema on the graph, which provides much flexibility in allowing data to be created without having to fully understand upfront the way data will be used. However, schemas in other data models (relational, object, XML, etc.) have proved to be useful for database consistency and efficient query processing. Therefore, Neo4j introduces an optional schema based on the concept of labels and a data definition language to manipulate it. A label is like a tag, useful to group similar nodes. A node may be assigned any number of labels, e.g., person, student, and user. This allows Neo4j to query only some subset of the graph, e.g., the students in a given city. Labels are used when defining integrity constraints and indexes. Integrity constraints can be defined on nodes and relationships, e.g., unique node property, node property existence, or relationship property existence.

Indexes can be created based on labels and combinations of properties. They provide efficient node lookup, which is an important operation used to start graph traversals at specific nodes based on predicates that involve labels and properties. The Neo4j-spatial library also provides n-dimensional polygon indexes to optimize geospatial queries.

To query and manipulate graph data, Neo4j provides a Java API and a query language, called Cypher. The Java API gives the Java programmer access to the graph operations of nodes, relationships, properties, and labels, with ACID transactions. This API provides tight integration with the programming language.

Cypher is a powerful graph DBMS query language with SQL flavor. It can be used to manipulate graph data. For instance, the transaction in Example 11.5 could be simply written by the following **CREATE** statement:

```
CREATE (:Person {name:''Bob'', age:35}) <- [:FRIEND]
  -(:Person {name:''Mary'', age:29, job:''engineer''})
```

Cypher is easy to use through graph pattern matching: the user specifies a graph pattern as when drawing a diagram and queries the database to find the data that matches the pattern. Cypher provides clauses such as **MATCH, MERGE, WHERE, RETURN**, which can manipulate node variables (like tuple variables in SQL) and a few others. **MATCH** does graph pattern matching. Nodes are expressed with parentheses, and relationships using pairs of dashes with greater-than or less-than signs to indicate relationship direction. Node and relationship property key-value pairs are then specified within curly braces. **MERGE** is useful to create or match graphs. WHERE specifies a predicate on nodes and **RETURN** the result nodes, relationships, and properties to be returned.

Example 11.6 The following Cypher query returns all direct and indirect friends of Bob whose name starts with "M." The **MATCH** expression defines a recursive pattern for the friend-of-friend relationship with the node variables bob and follower. The **WHERE** expression looks up the node whose name is "Bob," which may be done through an index, and selects its follower nodes of whose name starts with "M." The **RETURN** expressions return all pairs of nodes bound to the bob and follower variables.

```
MATCH bob-[:FRIEND]-> ()-[:FRIEND] -> follower
WHERE bob.name = ''Bob'' AND follower.name =~ ''M.*''
RETURN bob, follower.name
```

◆

Neo4j provides a cost-based query compiler that produces optimized query plans for Cypher queries, both read-only and update queries. The compiler first performs logical rewriting of the query plan using unnesting, merging, and simplification of various parts of the query. Then, based on statistical information on index and label selectivity, it chooses the best access methods for operators and produces the query execution plan, using nested iterators to be executed in a pipelined, top-down fashion.

Neo4j provides extensive support for high availability through full replication both at the cluster level and across data centers. Within a cluster, a variation of multimaster replication (see Chap. 6), called causal clustering, is used to scale out to large configurations. Causal clustering supports *causal consistency*, a consistency model that guarantees that causally related operations are seen in the same order by all client applications. Thus, a client application is guaranteed to read its own writes. Causal clustering architecture is shown in Fig. 11.7, with three kinds of cluster nodes: application server, core server, and read server. Application servers execute

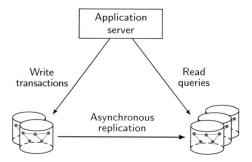

Fig. 11.7 Neo4j causal clustering architecture

application code, and issue write transactions to core servers and read queries to read servers. The core servers replicate all transactions asynchronously using the Raft protocol. Raft ensures transaction durability using a majority of the core servers to acknowledge a write before it is safely committed. Core servers replicate transactions to read servers by shipping transaction logs. The Raft protocol is also used to implement various replication architectures across data centers to support disaster recovery.

In addition to high availability, causal clustering allows scaling out graph queries using many read servers. To optimize RAM memory utilization, Neo4j employs cache-based sharding, which mandates that all queries from the same user always be sent to the same read server. This naturally improves locality of reference at each read server, and allows scaling to very large graphs.

From the discussion above, it follows that the maximum size of a database graph is constrained to that of a core server disk. This constraint makes it possible to provide linear performance for path traversals while at the same time requiring to push compact graph storage to the limits. Neo4j uses dynamic pointer compression to expand the available address space as needed while allowing locating a node's adjacent nodes and relationships via a pointer hop. Finally, Neo4j's separation of storage for nodes, relationships, and properties allows further optimization. This allows the first two stores to keep only basic information and have fixed size node and relationship records, which yields efficient $O(1)$ path traversals. The property store allows for dynamic length records.

11.5.2   Other Graph Databases

Other popular graph DBMSs are Infinite Graph, Titan, GraphBase, Trinity, and Sparksee.

11.6   Hybrid Data Stores

Hybrid data stores combine capabilities typically found in different data stores and DBMS. We distinguish between multimodel NoSQL systems and NewSQL DBMSs.

11.6.1   Multimodel NoSQL Stores

Multimodel NoSQL systems are designed to reduce the need to deal with multiple systems when building complex applications. We illustrate multimodel NoSQL stores with OrientDB, a popular NoSQL data store that combines concepts from object-oriented and NoSQL document and graph data models. Other popular multimodel systems are ArangoDB and Microsoft Azure Cosmos DB.

OrientDB originated as a Java implementation of the storage layer of the Orient Object-Oriented DBMS (initially written in C++) for shared-nothing clusters. It provides a rich data model with schemas, a powerful SQL-based query language, optimistic ACID transactions, and support for high availability and load balancing.

The data model is a graph data model, with direct connections between records. There are four types of records: Document, RecordBytes (binary data), Vertex, and Edge. When OrientDB generates a record, which is the smallest unit of storage, it assigns it a unique identifier, called Record ID.

The query language is an extension of SQL with graph path traversals. It supports different kinds of indexes: SB-Tree, which is the default index; hashed index for efficient exact-match queries; Lucene full-text index for text-based search; and Lucene spatial index for spatial queries.

Schema management follows from the object-orientation with class inheritance. A class defines a set of similar records and can be schemaless, schema-full (as in object-oriented databases), or schema-hybrid. The schema-hybrid mode enables classes to define some attributes, but some records can have specific attributes. Class inheritance is based on structure, i.e., a subclass extends a parent class, inheriting all of its attributes.

Classes are the basis for clustering and partitioning records on multiple nodes. Each class can have one or more partitions, called clusters. When inserting a new record in a class, OrientDB selects the cluster to store it in using one of the following preconfigured strategies:

- default: selects the cluster using a default cluster identifier specified in the class;
- round-robin: arranges the clusters for the class into sequence and assigns each new record to the next cluster in order;
- balanced: checks the number of records in the clusters for the class and assigns the new record to the smallest cluster;
- local: when the database is replicated, it selects the master cluster on the current node (that is processing the insertion).

OrientDB supports multimaster replication, i.e., all nodes of the shared-nothing cluster can write to the database in parallel. Transactions are processed using optimistic multiversion concurrency control, based on the assumption that there are few update conflicts. So transactions proceed without any looking until commit time. When a transaction commits, each record version is checked to see if there are conflicting updates from another transaction, which may yield to aborting some transactions.

11.6.2 NewSQL DBMSs

NewSQL is a recent class of DBMS that seeks to combine the scalability of NoSQL systems with the strong consistency and usability of relational DBMSs. The main objective is to address the requirements of enterprise information systems, which have been supported by traditional relational DBMS, but also need to be able to scale. NoSQL systems provide scalability, as well as availability, flexible schemas, and practical APIs for programming complex data-intensive applications. As we have seen in the previous sections, this is typically achieved by exploiting data partitioning in shared-nothing clusters of commodity servers and relaxing database consistency. On the other hand, relational DBMSs provide strong database consistency with ACID transactions and make it easy for tools and applications to use with standard SQL. They can also scale, using their parallel version, but typically at a high price, even using a shared-nothing cluster.

An important class of NewSQL is Hybrid Transaction and Analytics Processing (HTAP) whose objective is to perform OLAP and OLTP on the same data. HTAP allows performing real-time analysis on operational data, thus avoiding the traditional separation between operational database and data warehouse and the complexity of dealing with ETL.

NewSQL systems are recent and have different architectures. However, we can identify the following common features: relational data model and standard SQL; ACID transactions; scalability using data partitioning in shared-nothing clusters; and availability using data replication.

In the rest of this section, we illustrate NewSQL with Google F1 and LeanX-cale. Other kinds of NewSQL systems are Apache Ignite, CockroachDB, Esgyn, GridGain, MemSQL, NuoDB, Splice Machine, VoltDB, and SAP HANA.

11.6.2.1 F1

F1 is a NewSQL system from Google that combines the scalability of Bigtable and the consistency and usability of relational DBMSs. It has been built to support the AdWords application, which is a very large-scale update-intensive application. F1 provides a relational data model with some extensions, full SQL query support, with indexes and ad hoc querying, and optimistic transactions. It is built on top of Spanner, a scalable data storage system for shared-nothing clusters (see Sect. 5.5.1).

The F1 data model is the relational model, with a hierarchical implementation inspired from Bigtable. Several relational tables, with foreign key dependencies, can be organized as a nested relation, where the rows of each child table are clustered with the rows from their parent table based on the join key. This makes updates of multiple rows of same foreign key efficient and speeds up join processing. F1 also supports table columns with structured data types using protocol buffers, which is Google's language-neutral extensible mechanism for serializing structured data. Using protocol buffers makes it easy to write transformations between database rows and in-memory data structures.

The primary interface is SQL, which is used for both OLTP transactions and large OLAP queries. It extends standard SQL with constructs for accessing data stored in Protocol Buffer columns. F1 also provides support for joining Spanner data with other data sources including Bigtable and CSV files. F1 supports a NoSQL key/value interface with fast access to rows, through exact-match and range queries, and updates based on primary key. Secondary indexes are stored in Spanner tables, keyed by a concatenation of the index key and the indexed table's primary key. F1 indexes can be local or global. Local indexes are local to a table hierarchy and include in their index keys the root row primary key as a prefix. Their index entries are colocated with the rows they index, which makes index updates efficient. In contrast, global indexes are global to multiple tables and do not include the root row primary key as a prefix. Thus, they cannot be colocated with the rows they index.

F1 supports both centralized and distributed query execution. Centralized execution is used for short OLTP queries, where an entire query runs on one F1 server node. Distributed execution is used for OLAP queries, with a high degree of parallelism, using hash-based repartitioning and streaming techniques.

In Sect. 5.5.1, we introduced Spanner's approach to scale out transaction management. Spanner also provides fault-tolerance, data partitioning within data centers, geographical synchronous replication across data centers, and ACID transactions. In Spanner, every transaction is assigned a commit timestamp that is used for the global total ordering of commits. F1 supports three types of transactions, on top of Spanner's strong transaction support:

- Snapshot transactions, for read-only transactions with snapshot isolation semantics, using Spanner snapshot timestamps.
- Pessimistic transactions, using ACID locking-based transactions provided by Spanner.
- Optimistic transactions, with a read phase that does not take locks, and then a validation phase that detects row-level conflicts, using rows' last modification timestamps, to decide whether to commit or abort.

11.6.2.2   LeanXcale

LeanXcale is a NewSQL/HTAP system with full SQL and polystore support in a shared-nothing cluster. It has three main subsystems: storage engine, query engine, and transactional engine, all three distributed and highly scalable (i.e., to 100s of nodes).

LeanXcale provides full SQL functionality over relational tables with JSON columns. Clients can access LeanXcale with any analytics tool using a JDBC driver. An important capability of LeanXcale is polystore access using the scripting mechanism of the CloudMdsQL query language (see Sect. 11.7.3.2). The data stores that can be accessed range from distributed raw data files (e.g., HDFS) through parallel SQL databases, to NoSQL databases (e.g., MongoDB, where queries can be expressed as JavaScript programs).

The storage engine is a proprietary relational key-value store, KiVi, which allows for efficient horizontal partitioning of tables and indexes, based on the primary key or index key. Each table is stored as a KiVi table, where the key corresponds to the primary key of the LeanXcale table and all the columns are stored as they are in KiVi columns. Indexes are also stored as KiVi tables, where the index keys are mapped to the corresponding primary keys. This model enables high scalability of the storage layer by partitioning tables and indexes across KiVi data nodes. KiVi provides the typical put and get operations of key-value stores as well as all single table operations such as predicate-based selection, aggregation, grouping, and sorting, i.e., any algebraic operator but join. Multitable operations, i.e., joins, are performed by the query engine and any algebraic operator above the join in the query plan. Thus, all algebraic operators below a join are pushed down to the KiVi storage engine.

The query engine processes OLAP workloads over operational data, so that analytical queries are answered over real-time data. The parallel implementation of the query engine follows the single-program multiple data (SPMD) approach, which combines interquery and intraoperator parallelism. With SPMD, multiple symmetric workers (threads) on different query instances execute the same query/operator, but each of them deals with different portions of the data.

The query engine optimizes queries using two-step optimization. As queries are received, query plans are broadcast and processed by all workers. For parallel execution, an optimization step is added, which transforms a generated sequential query plan into a parallel one. This transformation involves replacing table scans with parallel table scans, and adding shuffle operators to make sure that, in stateful operators (such as group by or join), related rows are handled by the same worker. Parallel table scans divide the rows from the base tables among all workers, i.e., each worker will retrieve a disjoint subset of the rows during table scan. This is done by dividing the rows and scheduling the obtained subsets to the different query engine instances. Each worker then processes the rows obtained from subsets scheduled to its query engine instance, exchanging rows with other workers as determined by the shuffle operators added to the query plan. To process joins, the query engine supports two strategies for data exchange (shuffle and broadcast) and various join methods (hash, nested loop, etc.), performed locally at each worker after the data exchange takes place.

The query engine is designed to integrate with arbitrary data stores, where data resides in its natural format and can be retrieved (in parallel) by running specific scripts or declarative queries. This makes it a powerful polystore that can process data from its original format, taking full advantage of both expressive scripting and massive parallelism. Moreover, joins across any native datasets, such as HDFS or MongoDB, including LeanXcale tables, can be applied, exploiting efficient parallel join algorithms. To enable ad hoc querying of an arbitrary dataset, the query engine processes queries in the CloudMdsQL query language, where scripts are wrapped as native subqueries (Sect. 11.7.3.2).

In Sect. 5.5.2, we introduced LeanXcale's approach to scale out transaction management. LeanXcale scales out transactional management by decomposing the ACID properties and scaling each of them independently but in a composable manner. The transactional engine provides strong consistency with snapshot isolation. Thus, reads are not blocked by writes, using multiversion concurrency control. It supports timestamp-based ordering and conflict detection just before commit. The distributed algorithm for providing transactional consistency is able to commit transactions fully in parallel without any coordination by making a smart separation of concerns. Thus, the visibility of the committed data is separated from the commit processing. In this way, commit processing can adopt a fully parallel approach without compromising consistency that is regulated by the visibility of the committed updates. Thus, commits happen in parallel, and whenever there is a longer prefix of committed transactions without gaps the current snapshot is advanced to that point.

11.7 Polystores

Polystores provide integrated access to multiple cloud data stores such as NoSQL, relational DBMS, or HDFS. They typically support only read-only queries, as supporting distributed transactions across heterogeneous data stores is a hard problem. We can divide polystores based on the level of coupling with the underlying data stores: loosely coupled, tightly coupled, and hybrid. In this section, we introduce for each class a set of representative systems, with their architecture and query processing. We end the section with some remarks.

11.7.1 Loosely Coupled Polystores

Loosely coupled polystores are reminiscent of multidatabase systems in that they can deal with autonomous data stores, which can be accessed through the polystore common interface as well as separately through their local API. They follow the

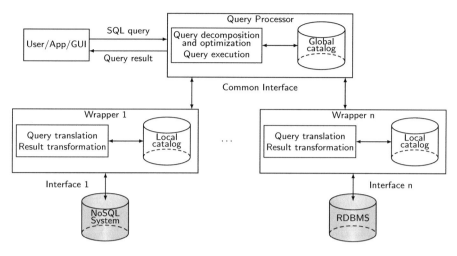

Fig. 11.8 Loosely coupled polystore architecture

mediator-wrapper architecture with several data stores (e.g., NoSQL and relational DBMS) as depicted in Fig. 11.8. Each data store is autonomous, i.e., locally controlled, and can be accessed by other applications. The mediator-wrapper architecture, which has been used in data integration systems, can scale to a high number of data stores.

There are two main modules: one query processor and one wrapper per data store. The query processor has a catalog of data stores, and each wrapper has a local catalog of its data store. After the catalogs and wrappers have been built, the query processor can start processing input queries from the users, by interacting with wrappers. The typical query processing is as follows:

1. Analyze the input query and translate it into subqueries (one per data store), each expressed in a common language, and an integration subquery.
2. Send the subqueries to the relevant wrappers, which trigger execution at the corresponding data stores and translate the results into the common language format.
3. Integrate the results from the wrappers (which may involve executing operators such as union and join), and return the results to the user. We describe below three loosely coupled polystores: BigIntegrator, Forward, and QoX.

11.7.1.1 BigIntegrator

BigIntegrator supports SQL-like queries and combines data in Bigtable data stores in the cloud with data in relational DBMS (not necessarily in the cloud). Bigtable is accessed through the Google Query Language (GQL), which has very limited query expressions, e.g., no join and only basic select predicates. To capture GQL's

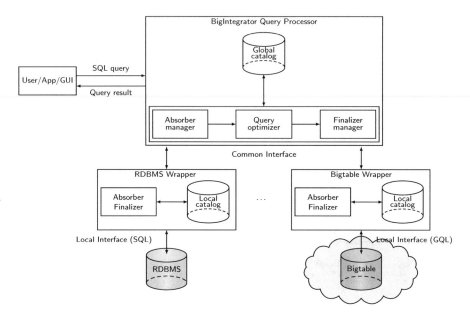

Fig. 11.9 BigIntegrator architecture

limited capabilities, BigIntegrator provides a query processing mechanism based on plugins, called absorber and finalizer, which enable to pre and postprocess those operations that cannot be done by Bigtable. For instance, a "LIKE" select predicate on a Bigtable or a join of two Bigtables will be processed through operations in BigIntegrator's query processor.

BigIntegrator uses the Local-As-View (LAV) approach (see Sect. 7.1.1) for defining the global schema of the Bigtable and relational data sources as flat relational tables. Each Bigtable or relational data source can contain several collections, each represented as a source table of the form "table-name_source-name," where table-name is the name of the table in the global schema and source-name is the name of the data source. For instance, "Employees_A" represents an Employees table at source A, i.e., a local view of Employees. The source tables are referenced as tables in the SQL queries.

Figure 11.9 illustrates the architecture of BigIntegrator with two data sources, one relational database and one Bigtable data store. Each wrapper has an importer module and absorber and finalizer plugins. The importer creates the source tables and stores them in the local catalog. The absorber extracts a subquery, called access filter, from a user query that selects data from a particular source table, based on the capabilities of the source. It translates each access filter (produced by the absorber) into an operator called interface function, specific for each kind of source. The interface function is used to send a query to the data source (i.e., a GQL or SQL query).

Query processing is performed in three steps, using an absorber manager, a query optimizer, and a finalizer manager. The absorber manager takes the (parsed) user query and, for each source table referenced in the query, calls the corresponding absorber of its wrapper. In order to replace the source table with an access filter, the absorber collects from the query the source tables and the possible other predicates, based on the capabilities of the data source. The query optimizer reorders the access filters and other predicates to produce an algebra expression that contains calls to both access filters and other relational operators. It also performs traditional transformations such as select push down and bind join. The finalizer manager takes the algebra expression and, for each access filter operator in the algebra expression, calls the corresponding finalizer of its wrapper. The finalizer transforms the access filters into interface function calls.

Finally, query execution is performed by the query processor that interprets the algebra expression, by calling the interface functions to access the different data sources and executing the subsequent relational operations, using in-memory techniques.

11.7.1.2 Forward

Forward supports SQL++, an SQL-like language designed to unify the data model and query language capabilities of NoSQL and relational databases. SQL++ has a powerful, semistructured data model that extends both the JSON and relational data models. Forward also provides a rich web development framework, which exploits its JSON compatibility to integrate visualization components (e.g., Google Maps).

The design of SQL++ is based on the observation that the concepts are similar across both data models, e.g., a JSON array is similar to an SQL table with order, and an SQL tuple to a JSON object literal. Thus, an SQL++ collection is an array or a bag, which may contain duplicate elements. An array is ordered (similar to a JSON array) and each element is accessible by its ordinal position while a bag is unordered (similar to an SQL table). Furthermore, SQL++ extends the relational model with arbitrary composition of complex values and element heterogeneity. As in nested data models, a complex value can be either a tuple or collection. Nested collections can be accessed by nesting **SELECT** expressions in the SQL **FROM** clause or composed using the **GROUP BY** operator. They can also be unnested using the FLATTEN operator. And unlike an SQL table that requires all tuples to have the same attributes, an SQL++ collection may also contain heterogeneous elements comprising a mix of tuples, scalars, and nested collections.

Forward uses the Global-As-View (GAV) approach (see Sect. 7.1.1), where each data source (SQL or NoSQL) appears to the user as an SQL++ virtual view, defined over SQL++ collections. Thus, the user can issue SQL++ queries involving multiple virtual views. The Forward architecture is that of Fig. 11.8, with a query processor and one wrapper per data source. The query processor performs SQL++ query decomposition, by exploiting the underlying data store capabilities as much as possible. However, given an SQL++ query that is not directly supported by the underlying data source, Forward will decompose it into one or more native queries that are supported and combine the native query results in order to compensate for the semantics or capabilities gap between SQL++ and the underlying data source. Cost-based optimization of SQL++ queries is possible, by reusing techniques from multidatabase systems when dealing with flat collections. However, it would be much harder considering the nesting and element heterogeneity capabilities of SQL++.

11.7.1.3 QoX

QoX is a special kind of loosely coupled polystore, where queries are analytical data-driven workflows (or data flows) that integrate data from relational databases, and various execution engines such as MapReduce or ETL tools. A typical data flow may combine unstructured data (e.g., tweets) with structured data and use both generic data flow operations like filtering, join, aggregation, and user-defined functions like sentiment analysis and product identification. A novel approach to ETL design incorporates a suite of quality metrics, termed QoX, at all stages of the design process. The QoX Optimizer deals with the QoX performance metrics, with the objective of optimizing the execution of dataflows that integrate both the back-end ETL integration pipeline and the front-end query operations into a single analytics pipeline.

The QoX Optimizer uses xLM, a proprietary XML-based language to represent data flows, typically created with some ETL tool. xLM allows capturing the flow structure, with nodes showing operations and data stores and edges interconnecting these nodes, and important operation properties such as operation type, schema, statistics, and parameters. Using appropriate wrappers to translate xLM to a tool-specific XML format and vice versa, the QoX Optimizer may connect to external ETL engines and import or export dataflows to and from these engines.

Given a data flow for multiple data stores and execution engines, the QoX Optimizer evaluates alternative execution plans, estimates their costs, and generates a physical plan (executable code). The search space of equivalent execution plans is defined by data flow transformations that model data shipping (moving the data to where the operation will be executed), function shipping (moving the operation to where the data is), and operation decomposition (into smaller operations). The cost of each operation is estimated based on statistics (e.g., cardinalities, selectivities). Finally, the QoX Optimizer produces SQL code for relational database engines, Pig and Hive code for MapReduce engines, and creates Unix shell scripts as the necessary glue code for orchestrating different subflows running on different engines. This approach could be extended to access NoSQL engines as well, provided the availability of SQL-like interfaces and wrappers.

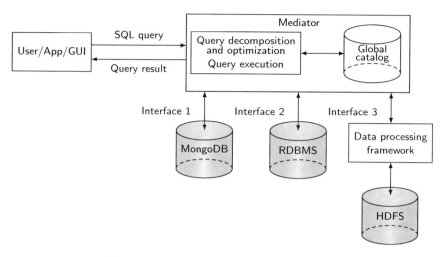

Fig. 11.10 Tightly coupled polystore architecture

11.7.2 Tightly Coupled Polystores

Tightly coupled polystores aim at efficient querying of structured and unstructured data for (big) data analytics. They may also have a specific objective, such as self-tuning or integration of HDFS and relational DBMS data. However, they all trade autonomy for performance, typically in a shared-nothing cluster, so that data stores can only be accessed through the polystore.

Like loosely coupled systems, they provide a single language for querying of structured and unstructured data. However, the query processor directly uses the data store local interfaces (see Fig. 11.10), or in the case of HDFS, can interface a data processing framework such as MapReduce or Spark. Thus, during query execution, the query processor directly accesses the data stores. This allows efficient data movement across data stores. However, the number of data stores that can be interfaced is typically very limited.

In the rest of this section, we describe three representative tightly coupled polystores: Polybase, HadoopDB, and Estocada. Three other interesting systems are Redshift Spectrum, Odyssey, and JEN. Amazon Redshift Spectrum is a feature of Amazon's Redshift data warehouse product in the cloud platform Amazon Web Services (AWS). This feature enables running SQL queries against big unstructured data residing in Amazon Simple Storage Service (S3). Odyssey is a polystore that can work with different analytic engines, such as parallel OLAP system or Hadoop. It enables storing and querying data within HDFS and relational DBMS, using opportunistic materialized views, based on MISO, a method for tuning the physical design of a polystore (Hive/HDFS and relational DBMS), i.e., deciding in which data store the data should reside, in order to improve the performance of big data query processing. The intermediate results of query execution are treated as opportunistic materialized views, which can then be placed in the underlying stores to optimize the evaluation of subsequent queries. JEN is a component on top of HDFS to provide tight-coupling with a parallel relational DBMS. It allows joining data from two data stores, HDFS and relational DBMS, with parallel join algorithms, in particular, an efficient zigzag join algorithm, and techniques to minimize data movement. As the data size grows, executing the join on the HDFS side appears to be more efficient.

11.7.2.1 Polybase

Polybase is a feature of Microsoft SQL Server Parallel Data Warehouse (PDW), which allows users to query unstructured (HDFS) data stored in a Hadoop cluster using SQL and integrate them with relational data in PDW. The HDFS data can be referenced in Polybase as external tables, which make the correspondence with the HDFS file on the Hadoop cluster, and thus be manipulated together with PDW native tables using SQL queries. Polybase leverages the capabilities of PDW, a shared-nothing parallel DBMS. Using the PDW query optimizer, SQL operators on HDFS data are translated into MapReduce jobs to be executed directly on the Hadoop cluster. Furthermore, the HDFS data can be imported/exported to/from PDW in parallel, using the same PDW service that allows shuffling PDW data among compute nodes.

The architecture of Polybase, which is integrated within PDW, is shown in Fig. 11.11. Polybase takes advantage of PDW's Data Movement Service (DMS), which is responsible for shuffling intermediate data across PDW nodes, e.g., to repartition tuples, so that any matching tuples of an equijoin be collocated at the same computing node that performs the join. DMS is extended with an HDFS Bridge component, which is responsible for all communications with HDFS. The HDFS Bridge enables DMS instances to also exchange data with HDFS in parallel (by directly accessing HDFS splits).

Polybase relies on the PDW cost-based query optimizer to determine when it is advantageous to push SQL operations on HDFS data to the Hadoop cluster for execution. Thus, it requires detailed statistics on external tables, which are obtained by exploring statistically significant samples of HDFS tables. The query optimizer enumerates the equivalent QEPs and selects the one with the least cost. The search space is obtained by considering the different decompositions of the query into two parts: one to be executed as MapReduce jobs at the Hadoop cluster and the other as regular relational operators at the PDW side. MapReduce jobs can be used to perform select and project operations on external tables, as well as joins of two external tables. The data produced by the MapReduce jobs can then be exported to PDW to be joined with relational data, using parallel hash-based join algorithms.

One strong limitation of pushing operations on HDFS data as MapReduce jobs is that even simple lookup queries have long latencies. A solution proposed for Polybase is to exploit an index built on the external HDFS data using a B+-tree that is stored inside PDW. This method leverages the robust and efficient indexing code in PDW without forcing a dramatic increase in the space that is required to store or cache the entire (large) HDFS data inside PDW. Thus, the index can be used as a prefilter by the query optimizer to reduce the amount of work that is carried out as MapReduce jobs. To keep the index synchronized with the data that is stored in HDFS, an incremental approach is used which records that the index is out-of-date, and lazily rebuilds it. Queries posed against the index before the rebuilding process is completed can be answered using a method that carefully executes parts of the query using the index in PDW, and the remaining part of the query is executed as a MapReduce job on just the changed data in HDFS. Apache AsterixDB uses a similar approach to accessing and indexing external data that lives in HDFS and allowing users' queries to span data that AsterixDB manages as well as external data in HDFS.

11.7.2.2 HadoopDB

The objective of HadoopDB is to provide the best of both parallel DBMS (high-performance data analysis over structured data) and MapReduce-based systems (scalability, fault-tolerance, and flexibility to handle unstructured data) with an SQL-like language (HiveQL) and a relational data model. To do so, HadoopDB

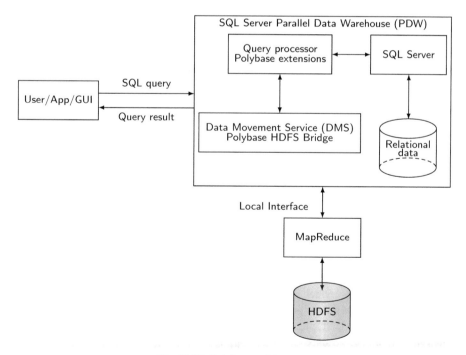

Fig. 11.11 Polybase architecture

tightly couples the Hadoop framework, including MapReduce and HDFS, with multiple single-node relational DBMS deployed across a cluster, as in a shared-nothing parallel DBMS.

HadoopDB extends the Hadoop architecture with four components: database connector, catalog, data loader, and SQL-MapReduce-SQL (SMS) planner. The database connector provides the wrappers to the underlying relational DBMS, using JDBC drivers. The catalog maintains information about the databases as an XML file in HDFS, and is used for query processing. The data loader is responsible for (re)partitioning (key, value) data collections using hashing on a key and loading the single-node databases with the partitions (or chunks). The SMS planner extends Hive, a Hadoop component that transforms HiveQL into MapReduce jobs that connect to tables stored as files in HDFS. This architecture yields a cost-effective parallel relational DBMS, where data is partitioned both in relational DBMS tables and in HDFS files, and the partitions can be collocated at cluster nodes for efficient parallel processing.

Query processing is simple, relying on the SMS planner for translation and optimization, and MapReduce for execution. The optimization consists in pushing as much work as possible into the single-node databases, and repartitioning data collections whenever needed. The SMS planner decomposes a HiveQL query to a QEP of relational operators. Then the operators are translated to MapReduce jobs, while the leaf nodes are again transformed into SQL to query the underlying relational DBMS instances. In MapReduce, repartitioning should take place before the reduce phase. However, if the optimizer detects that an input table is partitioned on a column used as aggregation key for Reduce, it will simplify the QEP by turning it to a single Map-only job, leaving all the aggregation to be done by the relational DBMS nodes. Similarly, repartitioning is avoided for equijoins as well, if both sides of the join are partitioned on the join key.

11.7.2.3 Estocada

Estocada is a self-tuning polystore with the goal of optimizing the performance of applications that must deal with data in multiple data models, including relational, key-value, document, and graph. To obtain the best possible performance from the available data stores, Estocada automatically distributes and partitions the data across the different data stores, which are entirely under its control and hence not autonomous. Hence, it is a tightly coupled polystore.

Data distribution is dynamic and decided based on a combination of heuristics and cost-based decisions, taking into account data access patterns as they become available. Each data collection is stored as a set of partitions, whose content may overlap, and each partition may be stored in any of the underlying data stores. Thus, it may happen that a partition is stored in a data store that has a different data model than its native one. To make Estocada applications independent of the data stores, each data partition is internally described as a materialized view over one or several data collections. Thus, query processing involves view-based query rewriting.

Estocada supports two kinds of requests, for storing data and querying, with four main modules: storage advisor, catalog, query processor and execution engine. These components can directly access the data stores through their local interface. The query processor deals with single model queries only, each expressed in the query language of the corresponding data source. However, to integrate various data sources, one would need a common data model and language on top of Estocada. The storage advisor is responsible for partitioning data collections and delegating the storage of partitions to the data stores. For self-tuning the applications, it may also recommend repartitioning or moving data from one data store to the other, based on access patterns. Each partition is defined as a materialized view expressed as a query over the collection in its native language. The catalog keeps track of information about partitions, including some cost information about data access operations by means of binding patterns which are specific to the data stores.

Using the catalog, the query processor transforms a query on a data collection into a logical QEP on possibly multiple data stores (if there are partitions of the collection in different stores). This is done by rewriting the initial query using the materialized views associated with the data collection, and selecting the best rewriting, based on the estimated execution costs. The execution engine translates the logical QEP into a physical QEP which can be directly executed by dividing the work between the data stores and Estocada's runtime engine, which provides its own operators (select, join, aggregate, etc.).

11.7.3 Hybrid Systems

Hybrid systems try to combine the advantages of loosely coupled systems (e.g., accessing many different data stores) and tightly coupled systems, e.g., accessing efficiently some data stores directly through their local interfaces. Therefore, the architecture (see Fig. 11.12) follows the mediator-wrapper architecture, while the query processor can also directly access some data stores, e.g., HDFS through MapReduce or Spark.

We describe below three hybrid polystores: Spark SQL, CloudMdsQL, and BigDAWG.

11.7.3.1 Spark SQL

Spark SQL is a module in Apache Spark that integrates relational data processing with Spark's functional programming API. It supports SQL-like queries that can integrate HDFS data accessed through Spark and external data sources (e.g., relational databases) accessed through a wrapper. Thus, it is a hybrid polystore with tight-coupling of Spark/HDFS and loose-coupling of external data sources.

Spark SQL has a nested relational data model. It supports all major SQL data types, as well as user-defined types and complex data types (structs, arrays, maps, and unions), which can be nested together. It also supports DataFrames, which are distributed collections of rows with the same schema, like a relational table. A DataFrame can be constructed from a table in an external data source or from an existing Spark Resilient Distributed Dataset (RDD) of native Java or Python objects. Once constructed, DataFrames can be manipulated with various relational operators, such as WHERE and GROUPBY, which take expressions in procedural Spark code.

Figure 11.13 shows the architecture of Spark SQL, which runs as a library on top of Spark. The query processor directly accesses the Spark engine through the Spark Java interface, while it accesses external data sources (e.g., a relational DBMS or a key-value store) through the Spark SQL common interface supported by wrappers

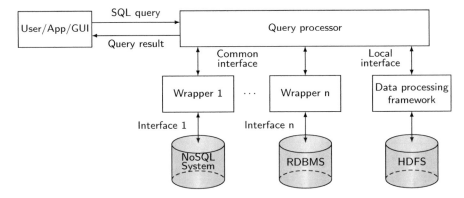

Fig. 11.12 Hybrid polystore architecture

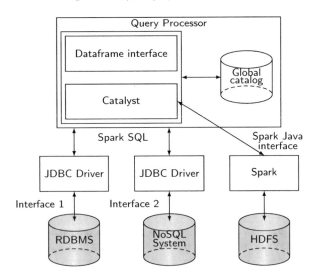

Fig. 11.13 Spark SQL architecture

(JDBC drivers). The query processor includes two main components: the DataFrame API and the Catalyst query optimizer. The DataFrame API offers tight integration between relational and procedural processing, allowing relational operations to be performed on both external data sources and RDDs. It is integrated into Spark's supported programming languages (Java, Scala, Python) and supports easy inline definition of user-defined functions, without the complicated registration process typically found in other database systems. Thus, the DataFrame API lets developers seamlessly mix relational and procedural programming, e.g., to perform advanced analytics (which is cumbersome to express in SQL) on large data collections (accessed through relational operations).

Catalyst is an extensible query optimizer that supports both rule-based and cost-based optimization. The motivation for an extensible design is to make it easy to add new optimization techniques, e.g., to support new features of Spark SQL, as well as to enable developers to extend the optimizer to deal with external data sources, e.g., by adding data source specific rules to push down select predicates. Although extensible query optimizers have been proposed in the past, they have typically required a complex language to specify rules and a specific compiler to translate the rules into executable code. In contrast, Catalyst uses standard features of the Scala functional programming language, such as pattern matching, to make it easy for developers to specify rules, which can be compiled to Java code.

Catalyst provides a general transformation framework for representing query trees and applying rules to manipulate them. This framework is used in four phases: (1) query analysis, (2) logical optimization, (3) physical optimization, and (4) code generation. Query analysis resolves name references using a catalog (with schema information) and produces a logical plan. Logical optimization applies standard rule-based optimizations to the logical plan, such as predicate pushdown, null propagation, and Boolean expression simplification. Physical optimization takes a logical plan and enumerates a search space of equivalent physical plans, using physical operators implemented in the Spark execution engine or in the external data sources. It then selects a plan using a simple cost model, in particular, to select the join algorithms. Code generation relies on the Scala language, in particular, to ease the construction of abstract syntax trees (ASTs) in the Scala language. ASTs can then be fed to the Scala compiler at runtime to generate Java bytecode to be directly executed by compute nodes.

To speed up query execution, Spark SQL exploits in-memory caching of hot data using a column-based storage (i.e., storing data collections as sections of columns of data rather than as rows of data). Compared with Spark's native cache, which simply stores data as Java native objects, this column-based cache can reduce memory footprint by an order of magnitude by applying column compression schemes (e.g., dictionary encoding and run-length encoding). Caching is particularly useful for interactive queries and for the iterative algorithms common in machine learning.

11.7.3.2   CloudMdsQL

CloudMdsQL supports a powerful functional SQL-like language, designed for
querying multiple heterogeneous data sources (e.g., relational and NoSQL). A
CloudMdsQL query may contain nested subqueries, and each subquery addresses
directly a particular data store and may contain embedded invocations to the data
store native query interface. Thus, the major innovation is that a CloudMdsQL query
can exploit the full power of local data stores, by simply allowing some local data
store native queries (e.g., a breadth-first search query against a graph database)
to be called as functions. CloudMdsQL has been extended to address distributed
processing frameworks such as Apache Spark by enabling the ad hoc usage of user-
defined map/filter/reduce operators as subqueries.

The CloudMdsQL language is SQL-based with extended capabilities for embed-
ding subqueries expressed in terms of each data store's native query interface. The
common data model is table-based, with support of rich data types that can capture a
wide range of the underlying data store data types, such as arrays and JSON objects,
in order to handle nonflat and nested data, with basic operators over such composite
data types. CloudMdsQL allows named table expressions to be defined as Python
functions, which is useful for querying data stores that have only API-based query
interface. A CloudMdsQL query is executed in the context of an ad hoc schema,
formed by all named table expressions within the query. This approach fills the gap
produced by the lack of a global schema and allows the query compiler to perform
semantic analysis of the query.

The design of the CloudMdsQL query engine takes advantage of the fact that it
operates in a cloud platform, with full control over where the system components
can be installed. The architecture of the query engine is fully distributed, so that
query engine nodes can directly communicate with each other, by exchanging code
(query plans) and data. This distributed architecture yields important optimization
opportunities, e.g., minimizing data transfers by moving the smallest intermediate
data for subsequent processing by one particular node. Each query engine node
consists of two parts (master and worker) and is collocated at each data store node
in a computer cluster. Each master or worker has a communication processor that
supports send and receive operators to exchange data and commands between nodes.
A master takes as input a query and produces, using a query planner and catalog
(with metadata and cost information on data sources) a query plan, which it sends to
one chosen query engine node for execution. Each worker acts as a lightweight
runtime database processor atop a data store and is composed of three generic
modules (i.e., same code library)—query execution controller, operator engine, and
table storage—and one wrapper module that is specific to a data store.

The query planner performs cost-based optimization. To compare alternative
rewritings of a query, the optimizer uses a simple catalog, which provides basic
information about data store collections such as cardinalities, attribute selectivities
and indexes, and a simple cost model. Such information can be exposed by
the wrappers in the form of cost functions or database statistics. The query
language also provides a possibility for the user to define cost and selectivity

functions whenever they cannot be derived from the catalog, mostly in the case of using native subqueries. The search space of alternative plans is obtained using traditional transformations, e.g., by pushing down select predicates, using bind join, performing join ordering, or planning intermediate data shipping.

11.7.3.3 BigDAWG

Like multidatabase systems, all the polystores we have seen so far provide transparent access across multiple data stores with the same data model and language. BigDAWG (Big Data Analytics Working Group) takes a different path, with the goal of unifying querying over a variety of data models and languages, Thus, there is no common data model and language. A key user abstraction in BigDAWG is an island of information, which is a collection of data stores accessed with a single query language. And there can be a variety of islands, including relational DBMSs, array DBMS, NoSQL, and data stream systems (DSSs). Within an island, there is loose-coupling of the data stores, which need to provide a wrapper (called a shim) to map the island language to their native one. When a query accesses more than one data store, objects may have to be copied between local databases, using a **CAST** operation, which provides a form of tight-coupling. This is why BigDAWG can be viewed as a hybrid polystore.

The architecture of BigDAWG is highly distributed, with a thin layer that interfaces the tools (e.g., visualization) and applications, with the islands of information. Since there is no common data model and language, there is no common query processor either. Instead, each island has its specific query processor. Query processing within an island is similar to that in multidatabase systems: most of the processing is pushed to the data stores and the query processor only integrates the results. The query optimizer does not use a cost model, but heuristics and some knowledge of the high performance of some data stores. For simple queries, e.g., select-project-join, the optimizer will use function shipping, in order to minimize data movement and network traffic among data stores. For complex queries, e.g., analytics, the optimizer may consider data shipping, to move the data to a data store that provides a high-performance implementation.

A query submitted to an island may involve multiple islands. In this case, the query must be expressed as multiple subqueries, each in a specific island language. To specify the island for which a subquery is intended, the user encloses the subquery in a SCOPE specification. Thus, a multiisland query will have multiple scopes to indicate the expected behavior of its subqueries. Furthermore, the user may insert **CAST** operations to move intermediate datasets between islands in an efficient way. Thus, the multiisland query processing is dictated by the way the subqueries, SCOPE, and **CAST** operations are specified by the user.

11.7.4 Concluding Remarks

Although all polystores share the same overall goal of querying multiple data stores, there are many different paths towards this goal, depending on the functional objective to be achieved. And this objective has important impact on the design choices. The major trend that dominates is the ability to integrate relational data (stored in relational DBMS) with other kinds of data in different data stores, such as HDFS (Polybase, HadoopDB, Spark SQL, JEN) or NoSQL (Bigtable only for BigIntegrator, document stores for Forward). Thus, an important difference lies in the kind of data stores that are supported. For instance, Estocada, BigDAWG, and CloudMdsQL can support a wide variety of data stores, while Polybase and JEN target the integration of relational DBMS with HDFS only. We can also note the growing importance of accessing HDFS within Hadoop, in particular, with MapReduce or Spark, which corresponds to major use cases in structured/unstructured data integration.

Another trend is the emergence of self-tuning polystores, such as Estocada and Odyssey, with the objective of leveraging the available data stores for performance. In terms of data model and query language, most systems provide a relational SQL-like abstraction. However, QoX has a more general graph abstraction to capture analytic data flows. And both Estocada and BigDAWG allow the data stores to be directly accessed with their native (or island) languages. CloudMdsQL also allows native queries, but as subqueries within an SQL-like language.

Most polystores provide some support for managing a global schema, using either the GAV or LAV approaches, with some variations, e.g., BigDAWG uses GAV within (single model) islands of information. However, QoX, Estocada, Spark SQL, and CloudMdsQL do not support global schemas, although they provide some way to deal with the data stores' local schemas.

The query processing techniques are extensions of known techniques from distributed database systems, e.g., data/function shipping, query decomposition (based on the data stores' capabilities, bind join, select pushdown). Query optimization is also generally supported, with either a (simple) cost model or heuristics.

11.8 Conclusion

Compared with traditional relational DBMSs, these new technologies promise better scalability, performance, and ease of use. They are also complementary to the new data management technologies for big data (see Chap. 10).

The main motivation for NoSQL is to address three major limitations of relational DBMSs: "one size fits all" approach for all kinds of data and applications; limited scalability and availability of the database architecture in the cloud; and, as shown by the CAP theorem, the trade-off between strong database consistency and service availability. The four main categories of NoSQL systems are based on their underlying data model, i.e., key-value, wide column, document, and graph. For each category, we illustrated with a representative system: DynamoDB (key-value), Bigtable (wide column), MongoDB (document), and Neo4j (graph). We also illustrated multimodel NoSQL systems with OrientDB, which combines concepts from object-oriented and NoSQL document and graph data models.

NoSQL systems provide scalability, as well as availability, flexible schemas, and practical APIs, but this is generally achieved by relaxing strong database consistency. NewSQL is a recent class of DBMS that seeks to combine the scalability of NoSQL systems with the strong consistency and usability of relational DBMS. The goal is to address the requirements of enterprise information systems, which have been supported by traditional relational DBMS, but also need to be able to scale. We illustrated NewSQL with the Google F1 and LeanXcale DBMSs.

Building cloud data-intensive applications often requires using multiple data stores (NoSQL, HDFS, relational DBMS, NewSQL), each optimized for one kind of data and tasks. In particular, many use cases exhibit the need to combine loosely structured data (e.g., log files, tweets, web pages) which are best supported by HDFS or NoSQL with more structured data in relational DBMS. Polystores provide integrated or transparent access to a number of cloud data stores through one or more query languages. We divided polystores based on the level of coupling with the underlying data stores, i.e., loosely coupled, tightly coupled, and hybrid. Then, we presented three representative polystores for each class: BigIntegrator, Forward, and QoX (loosely coupled); Polybase, HadoopDB, and Estocada (tightly coupled); Spark SQL, CloudMdsQL, and BigDAWG (hybrid).

The major trend that dominates is the ability to integrate relational data (stored in relational DBMS) with other kinds of data in different data stores, such as HDFS or NoSQL. However, an important difference between polystores lies in the kind of data stores that are supported. We also note the growing importance of accessing HDFS within Hadoop, in particular, with big data processing frameworks like MapReduce or Spark. Another trend is the emergence of self-tuning polystores, with the objective of leveraging the available data stores for performance. In terms of data model and query language, most systems provide a relational/ SQL-like abstraction. However, QoX has a more general graph abstraction to capture analytic data flows. And both Estocada and BigDAWG allow the data stores to be directly accessed with their native languages. The query processing techniques are extensions of known techniques from distributed database systems (see Chap. 4).

11.9 Bibliographic Notes

The landscape in NoSQL, NewSQL, and polystores keeps changing and lacks standards, which makes it difficult to come up with a good, up-to-date bibliography. There are many books and research papers on the topic but they become quickly outdated. Additional, up-to-date information can be found in systems' web sites and blogs. In this chapter, we focused on the systems' principles and architectures, rather than implementation details that may change over time.

An often cited motivation for NoSQL is the CAP theorem which helps understanding the trade-off between (C) consistency, (A) availability, and (P) partition tolerance. It started as a conjecture by [Brewer 2000], and was made a theorem by [Gilbert and Lynch 2002]. Although the CAP theorem says nothing about scalability, some NoSQL have used it to justify the lack of support for ACID transactions.

There are several books that introduce the NoSQL movement, in particular [Strauch 2011, Redmond and Wilson 2012], which illustrate well the topic with several representative systems presented in this chapter. There are also good books on particular systems. The presentation of the MongoDB document store is based on the book [Plugge et al. 2010] and other information on the MongoDB web site. AsterixDB [Alsubaiee et al. 2014] and Couchbase [Borkar et al. 2016] are JSON document stores that support a dialect of SQL++, initially proposed in [Ong et al. 2014]. There is also an excellent, practical book on SQL++ [Chamberlin 2018] written by Don Chamberlin, the coinventor of the original SQL language. AsterixDB's external data access and indexing mechanism is in [Alamoudi et al. 2015]. There are also good descriptions of DynamoDB [DeCandia et al. 2007] and Bigtable [Chang et al. 2008]. For an introduction to graph databases and Neo4j, there is the excellent book from the Neo4j team [Robinson et al. 2015]. Neo4j uses the causal consistency model [Elbushra and Lindström 2015] for multimaster replication and the Raft protocol for transaction durability [Ongaro and Ousterhout 2014].

The section on NewSQL systems is based on the description of the F1 DBMS [Shute et al. 2013] and the LeanXcale HTAP DBMS [Jimenez-Peris and Patiño Martinez 2011, Kolev et al. 2018].

A good motivation for polystores, or multistore systems, can be found in [Duggan et al. 2015, Kolev et al. 2016b]. The section on polystores is based on our survey paper on query processing in multistore systems [Bondiombouy and Valduriez 2016]. This paper identifies three classes of systems (1) loosely coupled, (2) tightly coupled, and (3) hybrid and illustrates each class with three representative systems: (1) BigIntegrator [Zhu and Risch 2011], Forward [Fu et al. 2014], and QoX [Simitsis et al. 2009, 2012]; (2) Polybase [DeWitt et al. 2013, Gankidi et al. 2014], HadoopDB [Abouzeid et al. 2009], and Estocada [Bugiotti et al. 2015]; (3) Spark SQL [Armbrust et al. 2015], BigDAWG [Gadepally et al. 2016], and CloudMdsQL [Bondiombouy et al. 2016, Kolev et al. 2016b,a]. Other important polystores are Amazon Redshift Spectrum, AsterixDB, AWESOME [Dasgupta et al. 2016], Odyssey [Hacigümüs et al. 2013], and JEN [Tian et al. 2016]. Odyssey uses opportunistic materialized views, based on MISO [LeFevre et al. 2014], a method for tuning the physical design of a polystore.

Exercises

Problem 11.1 Recall and discuss the motivations for NoSQL, in particular compared with relational DBMS.

Problem 11.2 (*) Explain why the CAP theorem is important. Consider a distributed architecture with multimaster replication (see Chap. 6). Assume a network partitioning in with asynchronous replication.

(a) Which of the CAP properties are preserved?
(b) What kind of consistency is achieved?

Same questions assuming synchronous replication.

Problem 11.3 (**) In this chapter, we divided NoSQL systems into four categories, i.e., key-value, wide column, document, and graph.

(a) Discuss the main similarities and differences in terms of data model, query language and interfaces, architectures, and implementation techniques.
(b) Identify the best use cases for each category of system.

Problem 11.4 (**) Consider the following simplified order-entry database schema (in nested relational format), with primary key attributes underlined:

```
CUSTOMERS(CID, NAME, ADDRESS (STREET, CITY, STATE,
   COUNTRY), PHONES)
ORDERS(OID, CID, O-DATE, O-TOTAL)
ORDER-ITEMS(OID, LINE-ID, PID, QTY)
PRODUCTS(PID, P-NAME, PRICE)
```

(a) Give the corresponding schemas in the four kinds of NoSQL systems (key-value, wide column, document, and graph). Discuss the respective advantages and disadvantages of each design in terms of ease of use, database administration, query complexity, and update performance.
(b) Consider now that a product can be made of several products, e.g., a six pack beer. Reflect this on the database schemas, and discuss the implications using the four kinds of NoSQL systems.

Problem 11.5 (**) As discussed in Chap. 10, there is no optimal solution for graph database partitioning. Elaborate on the impact on the scalability of graph databases? Propose ways around.

Problem 11.6 (**) Compare the F1 NewSQL system with a standard parallel relational DBMS, e.g., MySQL Cluster, in terms of data model, query language and interfaces, consistency, scalability, and availability.

Problem 11.7 Polystores provide integrated access through queries to multiple data stores such as NoSQL, relational DBMS, or HDFS. Compare polystores with the data integration systems we presented in Chap. 7.

Problem 11.8 (***) Polystores typically support only read-only queries, which satisfies the requirements of analytics. However, as more and more complex cloud data-intensive are built, the need for updating data across data stores will become important. Thus, the need for distributed transactions will arise. However, the transaction models of the data stores may be very different. In particular, most NoSQL systems do not provide ACID transaction support. Discuss the issue and propose directions for solutions.

Chapter 12
Web Data Management

The World Wide Web ("WWW" or "web" for short) has become a major repository of data and documents. Although measurements differ and change, the web has grown at a phenomenal rate.[1] Besides its size, the web is very dynamic and changes rapidly. For all practical purposes, the web represents a very large, dynamic, and distributed data store and there are the obvious distributed data management issues in accessing web data.

The web, in its present form, can be viewed as two distinct yet related components. The first of these components is what is known as the *publicly indexable web* (PIW) that is composed of all static (and cross-linked) web pages that exist on web servers. These can be easily searched and indexed. The other component, which is known as the *deep web* (or the *hidden web*), is composed of a huge number of databases that encapsulate the data, hiding it from the outside world. The data in the hidden web are usually retrieved by means of search interfaces where the user enters a query that is passed to the database server, and the results are returned to the user as a dynamically generated web page. A portion of the deep web has come to be known as the "dark web," which consists of encrypted data and requires a particular browser such as Tor to access.

The difference between the PIW and the hidden web is basically in the way they are handled for searching and/or querying. Searching the PIW depends mainly on crawling its pages using the link structure between them, indexing the crawled pages, and then searching the indexed data (as we discuss at length in Sect. 12.2). This may be either through the well-known keyword search or via question answering (QA) systems (Sect. 12.4). It is not possible to apply this approach to the hidden web directly since it is not possible to crawl and index those data (the techniques for searching the hidden web are discussed in Sect. 12.5).

The original version of this chapter was revised. The correction to this chapter is available at https://doi.org/10.1007/978-3-030-26253-2_13

[1] See http://www.worldwidewebsize.com/.

© Springer Nature Switzerland AG 2020
M. T. Özsu, P. Valduriez, *Principles of Distributed Database Systems*,
https://doi.org/10.1007/978-3-030-26253-2_12

Research on web data management has followed different threads in two separate but overlapping communities. Most of the earlier work in the web search and information retrieval community focused on keyword search and search engines. Subsequent work in this community focused on QA systems. The work in the database community focused on declarative querying of web data. There is an emerging trend that combines search/browse mode of access with declarative querying, but this work has not yet reached its full potential. In the 2000s, XML emerged as an important data format for representing and integrating data on the web. Thus, XML data management was a topic of significant interest. Although XML is still important in a number of application areas, its use in web data management has waned, mostly due to its perceived complexity. More recently, RDF has emerged as a common representation for Web data representation and integration.

The result of these different threads of development is that there is little in the way of a unifying architecture or framework for discussing web data management, and the different lines of research have to be considered somewhat separately. Furthermore, the full coverage of all the web-related topics requires far deeper and far more extensive treatment than is possible within a chapter. Therefore, we focus on issues that are directly related to data management.

We start by discussing how web data can be modeled as a graph. Both the structure of this graph and its management are important. This is discussed in Sect. 12.1. Web search is discussed in Sect. 12.2 and web querying is covered in Sect. 12.3. Section 12.4 summarizes question answering systems, and searching and querying the deep/hidden web is covered in Sect. 12.5. We then discuss web data integration in Sect. 12.6, focusing both on the fundamental problems and some of the representation approaches (e.g., web tables, XML, and RDF) that can assist with the task.

12.1 Web Graph Management

The web consists of "pages" that are connected by hyperlinks, and this structure can be modeled as a directed graph that reflects the hyperlink structure. In this graph, commonly referred to as the *web graph*, static HTML web pages are the vertices and the links between the pages are represented as directed edges. The characteristics of the web graph is important for studying data management issues since the graph structure is exploited in web search, categorization and classification of web content, and other web-related tasks. In addition, RDF representation that we discuss in Sect. 12.6.2.2 formalizes the web graph using a particular notation. The important characteristics of the web graph are the following:

(a) It is quite volatile. We already discussed the speed with which the graph is growing. In addition, a significant proportion of the web pages experience frequent updates.

(b) It is sparse. A graph is considered sparse if its average degree (i.e., the average of the degrees of all of its vertices) is less than the number of vertices. This

means that the each vertex of the graph has a limited number of neighbors, even
if the vertices are in general connected. The sparseness of the web graph implies
an interesting graph structure that we discuss shortly.

(c) It is "self-organizing." The web contains a number of communities, each
of which consists of a set of pages that focus on a particular topic. These
communities get organized on their own without any "centralized control," and
give rise to the particular subgraphs in the web graph.

(d) It is a "small-world graph." This property is related to sparseness—each node
in the graph may not have many neighbors (i.e., its degree may be small), but
many nodes are connected through intermediaries. Small-world networks were
first identified in social sciences where it was noted that many people who are
strangers to each other are connected by intermediaries. This holds true in web
graphs as well in terms of the connectedness of the graph.

(e) It is a power law graph. The in- and out-degree distributions of the web graph
follow power law distributions. This means that the probability that a vertex has
in- (out-) degree i is proportional to $1/i^{\alpha}$ for some $\alpha > 1$. The value of α is
about 2.1 for in-degree and about 7.2 for out-degree.

This brings us to a discussion of the structure of the web graph, which has a
"bowtie" shape (Fig. 12.1). It has a strongly connected component (the knot in
the middle) in which there is a path between each pair of pages. The numbers we
give below are from a study in 2000; while these numbers have possibly changed,
the structure depicted in the figure has persisted. Readers should treat numbers
as indicative of relative size and not as absolute values. The strongly connected
component (SCC) accounts for about 28% of the web pages. A further 21% of the
pages constitute the "IN" component from which there are paths to pages in SCC,
but to which no paths exist from pages in SCC. Symmetrically, "OUT" component
has pages to which paths exist from pages in SCC but not vice versa, and these
also constitute 21% of the pages. What is referred to as "tendrils" consist of pages
that cannot be reached from SCC and from which SCC pages cannot be reached

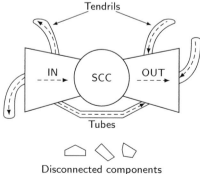

Fig. 12.1 The structure of the web as a bowtie (based on [Kumar et al. 2000])

either. These constitute about 22% of the web pages. These are pages that have not yet been "discovered" and have not yet been connected to the better known parts of the web. Finally, there are disconnected components that have no links to/from anything except their own small communities. This makes up about 8% of the web. This structure is interesting in that it determines the results that one gets from web searches and from querying the web. Furthermore, this graph structure is different than many other graphs that are normally studied, requiring special algorithms and techniques for its management.

12.2   Web Search

Web search involves finding "all" the web pages that are relevant (i.e., have content related) to keyword(s) that a user specifies. Naturally, it is not possible to find all the pages, or even to know if one has retrieved all the pages; thus the search is performed on a database of web pages that have been collected and indexed. Since there are usually multiple pages that are relevant to a query, these pages are presented to the user in ranked order of relevance as determined by the search engine.

The abstract architecture of a generic search engine is shown in Fig. 12.2. We discuss the components of this architecture in some detail.

In every search engine the *crawler* plays one of the most crucial roles. A crawler is a program used by a search engine to scan the web on its behalf and collect data about web pages. A crawler is given a starting set of pages—more accurately, it is given a set of Uniform Resource Locators (URLs) that identify these pages. The crawler retrieves and parses the page corresponding to that URL, extracts any

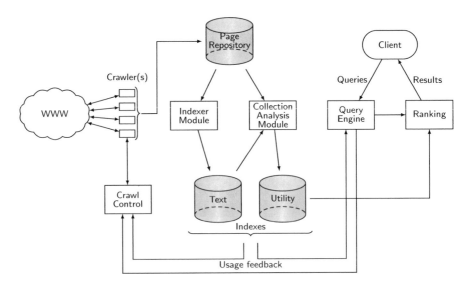

Fig. 12.2 Search engine architecture (based on [Arasu et al. 2001])

URLs in it, and adds these URLs to a queue. In the next cycle, the crawler extracts a URL from the queue (based on some order) and retrieves the corresponding page. This process is repeated until the crawler stops. A control module is responsible for deciding which URLs should be visited next. The retrieved pages are stored in a page repository. Section 12.2.1 examines crawling operations in more detail.

The *indexer module* is responsible for constructing indexes on the pages that have been downloaded by the crawler. While many different indexes can be built, the two most common ones are *text indexes* and *link indexes*. In order to construct a text index, the indexer module constructs a large "lookup table" that can provide all the URLs that point to the pages where a given word occurs. A link index describes the link structure of the web and provides information on the in-link and out-link state of pages. Section 12.2.2 explains current indexing technology and concentrates on ways indexes can be efficiently stored.

The *ranking module* is responsible for sorting a large number of results so that those that are considered to be most relevant to the user's search are presented first. The problem of ranking has drawn increased interest in order to go beyond traditional information retrieval (IR) techniques to address the special characteristics of the web—web queries are usually small and they are executed over a vast amount of data. Section 12.2.3 introduces algorithms for ranking and describes approaches that exploit the link structure of the web to obtain improved ranking results.

12.2.1   Web Crawling

As indicated above, a crawler scans the web on behalf of a search engine to extract information about the visited web pages. Given the size of the web, the changing nature of web pages, and the limited computing and storage capabilities of crawlers, it is impossible to crawl the entire web. Thus, a crawler must be designed to visit "most important" pages before others. The issue, then, is to visit the pages in some ranked order of importance.

There are a number of issues that need to be addressed in designing a crawler. Since the primary goal is to access more important pages before others, there needs to be some way of determining the importance of a page. This can be done by means of a measure that reflects the importance of a given page. These measures can be static, such that the importance of a page is determined independent of retrieval queries that will run against it, or dynamic in that they take the queries into consideration. Examples of static measures are those that determine the importance of a page P_i with respect to the number of pages that point to P_i (referred to as *backlink*), or those that additionally take into account the importance of the backlink pages as is done in the popular PageRank metric that is used by Google and others. A possible dynamic measure may be one that calculates the importance of a page P_i with respect its textual similarity to the query that is being evaluated using some of the well-known information retrieval similarity measures.

We had introduced PageRank in the Chap. 10 (Example 10.4). Recall that the PageRank of a page P_i, denoted $PR(P_i)$, is simply the normalized sum of the PageRank of all P_i's backlink pages (denoted as B_{P_i}) where the normalization for each $P_j \in B_{P_i}$ is over all of P_j's forward links F_{P_j}:

$$PR(P_i) = \sum_{P_j \in B_{P_i}} \frac{PR(P_j)}{|F_{P_j}|}$$

Recall also that this formula calculates the rank of a page based on the backlinks, but normalizes the contribution of each backlinking page P_j using the number of forward links that P_j has. The idea here is that it is more important to be pointed at by pages conservatively link to other pages than by those who link to others indiscriminately, but the "contribution" of a link from such a page needs to be normalized over all the pages that it points to.

A second issue is how the crawler chooses the next page to visit once it has crawled a particular page. As noted earlier, the crawler maintains a queue in which it stores the URLs for the pages that it discovers as it analyzes each page. Thus, the issue is one of ordering the URLs in this queue. A number of strategies are possible. One possibility is to visit the URLs in the order in which they were discovered; this is referred to as the *breadth-first approach*. Another alternative is to use random ordering whereby the crawler chooses a URL randomly from among those that are in its queue of unvisited pages. Other alternatives are to use metrics that combine ordering with importance ranking discussed above, such as backlink counts or PageRank.

Let us discuss how PageRank can be used for this purpose. A slight revision is required to the PageRank formula given above. We are now modeling a random surfer: when landed on a page P, a random surfer is likely to choose one of the URLs on this page as the next one to visit with some (equal) probability d or will jump to a random page with probability $1-d$. Then the above formula for PageRank is revised as follows:

$$PR(P_i) = (1 - d) + d \sum_{P_j \in B_{P_i}} \frac{PR(P_j)}{|F_{P_j}|}$$

The ordering of the URLs according to this formula allows the importance of a page to be incorporated into the order in which the corresponding page is visited. In some formulations, the first term is normalized with respect to the total number of pages in the web.

Example 12.1 Consider the web graph in Fig. 12.3 where each web page P_i is a vertex and there is a directed edge from P_i to P_j if P_i has a link to P_j. Assuming the commonly accepted value of $d = 0.85$, the PageRank of P_2 is $PR(P_2) = 0.15 + 0.85(\frac{PR(P_1)}{2} + \frac{PR(P_3)}{3})$. This is a recursive formula that is evaluated by initially assigning to each page equal PageRank values (in this case $\frac{1}{6}$ since there are 6

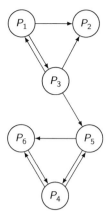

Fig. 12.3 Web graph representation for PageRank computation

pages) and iterating to compute each $PR(P_i)$ until a fixpoint is reached (i.e., the values no longer change).   ♦

Since many web pages change over time, crawling is a continuous activity and pages need to be revisited. Instead of restarting from scratch each time, it is preferable to selectively revisit web pages and update the gathered information. Crawlers that follow this approach are called *incremental crawlers*. They ensure that the information in their repositories are as fresh as possible. Incremental crawlers can determine the pages that they revisit based on the change frequency of the pages or by sampling a number of pages. *Change frequency-based* approaches use an estimate of the change frequency of a page to determine how frequently it should be revisited. One might intuitively assume that pages with high change frequency should be visited more often, but this is not always true—any information extracted from a page that changes frequently is likely to become obsolete quickly, and it may be better to increase revisit interval to that page. It is also possible to develop an adaptive incremental crawler such that the crawling in one cycle is affected by the information collected in the previous cycle. *Sampling-based approaches* focus on web sites rather than individual web pages. A small number of pages from a web site are sampled to estimate how much change has happened at the site. Based on this sampling estimate, the crawler determines how frequently it should visit that site.

Some search engines specialize in searching pages belonging to a particular topic. These engines use crawlers optimized for the target topic, and are referred to as *focused crawlers*. A focused crawler ranks pages based on their relevance to the target topic, and uses them to determine which pages it should visit next. Classification techniques that are widely used in information retrieval are used in evaluating relevance; learning techniques are used to identify the topic of a given page. These techniques are beyond our scope, but a number of them have been developed for this purpose, such as naïve Bayes classifier, and its extensions, reinforcement learning, and others.

To achieve reasonable scale-up, crawling can be parallelized by running *parallel crawlers*. Any design for parallel crawlers must use schemes to minimize the overhead of parallelization. For instance, two crawlers running in parallel may download the same set of pages. Clearly, such overlap needs to be prevented through coordination of the crawlers' actions. One method of coordination uses a *central coordinator* to dynamically assign each crawler a set of pages to download. Another coordination scheme is to logically partition the web. Each crawler knows its partition, and there is no need for central coordination. This scheme is referred to as the *static assignment*.

12.2.2   Indexing

In order to efficiently search the crawled pages and the gathered information, a number of indexes are built as shown in Fig. 12.2. The two more important indexes are the *structure* (or *link*) *index* and a *text* (or *content*) *index*.

12.2.2.1   Structure Index

The structure index is based on the graph model that we discussed in Sect. 12.1, with the graph representing the structure of the crawled portion of the web. The efficient storage and retrieval of these pages is important and two techniques to address these issues were discussed in Sect. 12.1. The structure index can be used to obtain important information about the linkage of web pages such as information regarding the *neighborhood* of a page and the siblings of a page.

12.2.2.2   Text Index

The most important and mostly used index is the *text index*. Indexes to support text-based retrieval can be implemented using any of the access methods traditionally used to search over text document collections. Examples include *suffix arrays*, *inverted files* or *inverted indexes*, and *signature files*. Although a full treatment of all of these indexes is beyond our scope, we will discuss how inverted indexes are used in this context since these are the most popular text indexes.

An inverted index is a collection of inverted lists, where each list is associated with a particular word. In general, an inverted list for a given word is a list of document identifiers in which that particular word occurs. The location of the word on a particular page can also be saved as part of the inverted list. This information is usually needed in proximity queries and query result ranking. Search algorithms also often make use of additional information about the occurrence of terms in a web page. For example, terms occurring in bold face (within ⟨strong⟩ tags), in section headings (within ⟨H1⟩ or ⟨H2⟩ tags in HTML), or as anchor text might be weighted differently in the ranking algorithms.

In addition to the inverted list, many text indexes also keep a *lexicon*, which is a list of all terms that occur in the index. The lexicon can also contain some term-level statistics that can be used by ranking algorithms.

Constructing and maintaining an inverted index has three major difficulties:

1. In general, building an inverted index involves processing each page, reading all the words and storing the location of each word. In the end, the inverted files are written to disk. This process, while trivial for small and static collections, becomes hard to manage when dealing with a vast and nonstatic collection like the web.
2. The rapid change of the web poses a challenge for maintaining the "freshness" of the index. Although we argued in the previous section that incremental crawlers should be deployed to ensure freshness, periodic index rebuilding is still necessary because most incremental update techniques do not perform well when dealing with the large changes often observed between successive crawls.
3. Storage formats of inverted indexes must be carefully designed. There is a tradeoff between a performance gain through a compressed index that allows portions of the index to be cached in memory and the overhead of decompression at query time. Achieving the right balance becomes a major concern when dealing with web-scale collections.

Addressing these challenges and developing a highly scalable text index can be achieved by distributing the index by either building a *local inverted index* at each machine where the search engine runs or building a *global inverted index* that is then shared. We do not discuss these further, as the issues are similar to the distributed data and directory management issues we have already covered in previous chapters.

12.2.3 Ranking and Link Analysis

A typical search engine returns a large number of web pages that are expected to be relevant to a user query. However, these pages are likely to be different in terms of their quality and relevance. The user is not expected to browse through this large collection to find a high-quality page. Clearly, there is a need for algorithms to rank these pages such that higher quality web pages appear as part of the top results.

Link-based algorithms can be used to rank a collection of pages. To repeat what we discussed earlier, the intuition is that if a page P_j contains a link to page P_i, then it is likely that the authors of page P_j think that page P_i is of good quality. Thus, a page that has a large number of incoming links is likely of high quality, and hence the number of incoming links to a page can be used as a ranking criterion. This intuition is the basis of ranking algorithms, but, of course, each specific algorithm implements this intuition in a different way. We already discussed the PageRank algorithm, and it is used for ranking of results in addition to crawling. We will discuss an alternative algorithm called HITS to highlight different ways of approaching the issue.

HITS is also a link-based algorithm. It is based on identifying "authorities" and "hubs." A good authority page receives a high rank. Hubs and authorities have a mutually reinforcing relationship: a good authority is a page that is linked to by many good hubs, and a good hub is a document that links to many authorities. Thus, a page pointed to by many hubs (a good authority page) is likely to be of high quality.

Let us start with a web graph, $G = (V, E)$, where V is the set of pages and E is the set of links among them. Each page P_i in V has a pair of nonnegative weights (a_{P_i}, h_{P_i}) that represent the authoritative and hub values of P_i respectively.

The authoritative and hub values are updated as follows. If a page P_i is pointed to by many good hubs, then a_{P_i} is increased to reflect all pages P_j that link to it (the notation $P_j \rightarrow P_i$ means that page P_j has a link to page P_i):

$$a_{P_i} = \sum_{\{P_j | P_j \rightarrow P_i\}} h_{P_j}$$

$$h_{P_i} = \sum_{\{P_j | P_j \rightarrow P_i\}} a_{P_j}$$

Thus, the authoritative value (hub value) of page P_i, is the sum of the hub values (authority values) of all the backlink pages to P_i.

12.2.4 Evaluation of Keyword Search

Keyword-based search engines are the most popular tools to search information on the web. They are simple, and one can specify fuzzy queries that may not have an exact answer, but may only be answered approximately by finding facts that are "similar" to the keywords. However, there are obvious limitations as to how much one can do by simple keyword search. The obvious limitation is that keyword search is not sufficiently powerful to express complex queries. This can be (partially) addressed by employing iterative queries where previous queries by the same user can be used as the context for the subsequent queries. A second limitation is that keyword search does not offer support for a global view of information on the web the way that database querying exploits database schema information. It can, of course, be argued that a schema is meaningless for web data, but the lack of an overall view of the data is an issue nevertheless. A third problem is that it is difficult to capture user's intent by simple keyword search—errors in the choice of keywords may result in retrieving many irrelevant answers.

Category search addresses one of the problems of using keyword search, namely the lack of a global view of the web. Category search is also known as web directory, catalogs, yellow pages, and subject directories. There are a number of public web directories available such as World Wide Web Virtual Library (http://vlib.org).[2] The web directory is a hierarchical taxonomy that classifies human knowledge. Although, the taxonomy is typically displayed as a tree, it is actually a directed acyclic graph since some categories are cross referenced.

If a category is identified as the target, then the web directory is a useful tool. However, not all web pages can be classified, so the user can use the directory for searching. Moreover, natural language processing cannot be 100% effective for categorizing web pages. We need to depend on human resource for judging the submitted pages, which may not be efficient or scalable. Finally, some pages change over time, so keeping the directory up-to-date involves significant overhead.

There have also been some attempts to involve multiple search engines in answering a query to improve recall and precision. A metasearcher is a web service that takes a given query from the user and sends it to multiple heterogeneous search engines. The metasearcher then collects the answers and returns a unified result to the user. It has the ability to sort the result by different attributes such as host, keyword, date, and popularity. Examples include Dogpile (http://www.dogpile.com/), MetaCrawler (http://www.metacrawler.com/), and IxQuick (http://www.ixquick.com/). Different metasearchers have different ways to unify results and translate the user query to the specific query languages of each search engines. The user can access a metasearcher through client software or a web page. Each search engine covers a smaller percentage of the web. The goal of a metasearcher is to cover more web pages than a single search engine by combining different search engines together.

12.3   Web Querying

Declarative querying and efficient execution of queries have been a major focus of database technology. It would be beneficial if the database techniques can be applied to the web. In this way, accessing the web can be treated, to a certain extent, similar to accessing a large database. We will discuss a number of the proposed approaches in this section.

There are difficulties in carrying over traditional database querying concepts to web data. Perhaps the most important difficulty is that database querying assumes the existence of a strict schema. As noted above, it is hard to argue that there is a schema for web data similar to databases.[3] At best, the web data are *semistructured*—data may have some structure, but this may not be as rigid, regular, or complete as that of databases, so that different instances of the data may be similar

---

[2] A list of these libraries is given in https://en.wikipedia.org/wiki/List_of_web_directories.

[3] We are focusing on the "open" web here; deep web data may have a schema, but it is usually not accessible to users.

but not identical (there may be missing or additional attributes or differences in structure). There are, obviously, inherent difficulties in querying schema-less data.

A second issue is that the web is more than the semistructured data (and documents). The links that exist between web data entities (e.g., pages) are important and need to be considered. Similar to search that we discussed in the previous section, links may need to be followed and exploited in executing web queries. This requires links to be treated as first-class objects.

A third major difficulty is that there is no commonly accepted language, similar to SQL, for querying web data. As we noted in the previous section, keyword search has a very simple language, but this is not sufficient for richer querying of web data. Some consensus on the basic constructs of such a language has emerged (e.g., path expressions), but there is no standard language. However, standardized languages for data models such as XML and RDF have emerged (XQuery for XML and SPARQL for RDF). We postpone discussion of these to Sect. 12.6 where we focus on web data integration

12.3.1 Semistructured Data Approach

One way to approach querying the web data is to treat it as a collection of semistructured data. Then, models and languages that have been developed for this purpose can be used to query the data. Semistructured data models and languages were not originally developed to deal with web data; rather they addressed the requirements of growing data collections that did not have as strict a schema as their relational counterparts. However, since these characteristics are also common to web data, later studies explored their applicability in this domain. We demonstrate this approach using a particular model (OEM) and a language (Lorel), but other approaches such as UnQL are similar.

OEM (Object Exchange Model) is a self-describing semistructured data model. Self-describing means that each object specifies the schema that it follows.

An OEM object is defined as a four-tuple ⟨label, type, value, oid⟩, where label is a character string describing what the object represents, type specifies the type of the object's value, value is obvious, and oid is the object identifier that distinguishes it from other objects. The type of an object can be atomic, in which case the object is called an *atomic object*, or complex, in which case the object is called a *complex object*. An atomic object contains a primitive value such as an integer, a real, or a string, while a complex object contains a set of other objects, which can themselves be atomic or complex. The value of a complex object is a set of oids.

Example 12.2 Let us consider a bibliographic database that consists of a number of documents. A snapshot of an OEM representation of such a database is given in Fig. 12.4. Each line shows one OEM object and the indentation is provided to simplify the display of the object structure. For example, the second line

```
<bib, complex, {&o2, &o22, &034}, &o1>
   <doc, complex, {&o3, &o6, &o7, &o20, &o22}, &o2>
      <authors, complex, {&o4, &o5}, &o3>
         <author, string, "M. Tamer Ozsu", &o4>
         <author, string, "Patrick Valduriez", &o5>
      <title, string, "Principles of Distributed ...", &o6>
      <chapters, complex, {&o8, &o11, &o14, &o9}, &o7>
         <chapter, complex, {&o9, &o10}, &o8>
            <heading, string, "...", &o9>
            <body, string, "...", &o10>
            ...
         <chapter, complex, {&o18, &o19}, &9>
            <heading, string, "...", &o18>
            <body, string, "...", &o19>
      <what, string, "Book", &o20>
      <price, float, 98.50, &o21>
   <doc, complex, {&o23, &o25, &o26, &o27, &o28}, &o22>
      <authors, complex, {&o24, &o4}, &o23>
         <author, string, "Yingying Tao", &o24>
      <title, string, "Mining data streams ...", &o25>
      <venue, string, "CIKM", &o26>
      <year, integer, 2009, &o27>
      <sections, complex, {&o29, &o30, &o31, &o32, &o33}, &28>
         <section, string, "...", &o29>
            ...
         <section, string, "...", &o33>
   <doc, complex, {&o16,&o9,&o7,&o18,&o19,&o20,&o21},&o34>
      <author, string, "Anthony Bonato", &o35>
      <title, string, "A Course on the Web Graph", &o36>
      <what, string, "Book", &o20>
      <ISBN, string, "TK5105.888.B667", &o37>
      <chapters, complex, {&o39, &o42, &o45}, &o38>
         <chapter, complex, {&o40, &o41}, &o39>
            <heading, string, "...", &o40>
            <body, string, "...", &o41>
         <chapter, complex, {&o43, &o44}, &o42>
            <heading, string, "...", &o43>
            <body, string, "...", &o44>
         <chapter, complex, {&o46, &o47}, &45>
            <heading, string, "...", &o46>
            <body, string, "...", &o47>
      <publisher, string, "AMS", &o48>
```

Fig. 12.4 An example OEM specification

<doc, complex, &o3, &o6, &o7, &o20, &o21, &o2> defines an object whose label is doc, type is complex, oid is &o2, and whose value consists of objects whose oids are &o3, &o6, &o7, &o20, and &o21.

This database contains three documents (&o2, &o22, &o34); the first and third are books and the second is an article. There are commonalities among the two books (and even the article), but there are differences as well. For example, &o2 has the price information that &o34 does not have, while &o34 has ISBN and publisher information that t&o2 does not have. .   ◆

As noted earlier, OEM data are self-describing, where each object identifies itself through its type and its label. It is easy to see that the OEM data can be represented as a vertex-labeled graph where the vertices correspond to OEM objects and the edges correspond to the subobject relationship. The label of a vertex is the oid and the label of the corresponding object vertex. However, it is quite common in literature to model the data as an edge-labeled graph: if object o_j is a subobject of object o_i, then o_j's label is assigned to the edge connecting o_i to o_j, and the oids are omitted as vertex labels. In Example 12.3, we use a vertex and edge-labeled representation that shows oids as vertex labels and assigns edge labels as described above.

Example 12.3 Figure 12.5 depicts the vertex and edge-labeled graph representation of the example OEM database given in Example 12.2. Normally, each terminal vertex (i.e., no outgoing edges) also contains the value of that object. To simplify exposition of the idea, we do not show the values.   ◆

The semistructured approach fits reasonably well for modeling web data since it can be represented as a graph. Furthermore, it accepts that data may have some structure, but this may not be as rigid, regular, or complete as that of traditional databases. The users do not need to be aware of the complete structure when they query the data. Therefore, expressing a query should not require full knowledge of the structure. These graph representations of data at each data source are generated by wrappers that we discussed in Sect. 7.2.

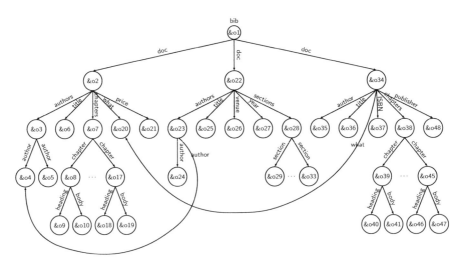

Fig. 12.5 The corresponding OEM graph for the OEM database of Example 12.2

A number of languages have been developed to query semistructured data. As noted above, we will focus our discussion by considering a particular language, Lorel, but other languages are similar in their basic approaches.

Lorel has the familiar SELECT-FROM-WHERE structure, but allows path expressions in the SELECT, FROM and WHERE clauses. The fundamental construct in forming Lorel queries is, therefore, a *path expression*. In its simplest form, a path expression in Lorel is a sequence of labels starting with an object name or a variable denoting an object. For example, bib.doc.title is a path expression whose interpretation is to start at bib and follow the edge-labeled doc and then follow the edge-labeled title. Note that there are three paths in Fig. 12.5 that would satisfy this expression: (i) &o1.doc:&o2.title:&o6, (ii) &o1.doc:&o22.title:&o25, and (iii) &o1.doc:&o34.title:&o36. Each of these is called a *data path*. In Lorel, path expressions can be more complex regular expressions such that what follows the object name or variable is not only a label, but more general expressions that can be constructed using conjunction, disjunction (|), iteration (? to mean 0 or 1 occurrences, + to mean 1 or more, and ∗ to mean 0 or more), and wildcards (#).

Example 12.4 The following are examples of acceptable path expressions in Lorel:

(a) bib.doc(.authors)?.author : start from bib, follow doc edge and the author edge with an optional authors edge in between.
(b) bib.doc.#.author : start from bib, follow doc edge, then an arbitrary number of edges with unspecified labels (using the wildcard #), and follow the author edge.
(c) bib.doc.%price : start from bib, follow doc edge, then an edge whose label has the string "price" preceded by some characters.

                                                             ♦

Example 12.5 The following are example Lorel queries that use some of the path expressions given in Example 12.4:

(a) Find the titles of documents written by Patrick Valduriez.

```
SELECT D.title
FROM   bib.doc D
WHERE  bib.doc(.authors)?.author =
       "Patrick Valduriez"
```

In this query, the **FROM** clause restricts the scope to documents (doc), and the **SELECT** clause specifies the nodes reachable from documents by following the title label. We could have specified the **WHERE** predicate as

```
D(.authors)?.author = "Patrick Valduriez".
```

(b) Find the authors of all books whose price is under $100.

```
SELECT  D(.authors)?.author
FROM    bib.doc D
WHERE   D.what = "Books" AND D.price < 100
```
                                                                                           ◆

Semistructured data approach to modeling and querying web data is simple and flexible. It also provides a natural way to deal with containment structure of web objects, thereby supporting, to some extent, the link structure of web pages. However, there are also deficiencies of this approach. The data model is too simple—it does not include a record structure (each vertex is a simple entity) nor does it support ordering as there is no imposed ordering among the vertices of an OEM graph. Furthermore, the support for links is also relatively rudimentary, since the model or the languages do not differentiate between different types of links. The links may show either subpart relationships among objects or connections between different entities that correspond to vertices. These cannot be separately modeled, nor can they be easily queried.

Finally, the graph structure can get quite complicated, making it difficult to query. Although Lorel provides a number of features (such as wildcards) to make querying easier, the examples above indicate that a user still needs to know the general structure of the semistructured data. The OEM graphs for large databases can become quite complicated, and it is hard for users to form the path expressions. The issue, then, is how to "summarize" the graph so that there might be a reasonably small schema-like description that might aid querying. For this purpose, a construct called a DataGuide has been proposed. A DataGuide is a graph where each path in the corresponding OEM graph occurs only once. It is dynamic in that as the OEM graph changes, the corresponding DataGuide is updated. Thus, it provides concise and accurate structural summaries of semistructured databases and can be used as a lightweight schema, which is useful for browsing the database structure, formulating queries, storing statistical information, and enabling query optimization.

Example 12.6 The DataGuide corresponding to the OEM graph in Example 12.3 is given in Fig. 12.6.   ◆

12.3.2   *Web Query Language Approach*

The approaches in this category are aimed to directly address the characteristics of web data, particularly focusing on handling *links* properly. Their starting point is to overcome the shortcomings of keyword search by providing proper abstractions for capturing the content structure of documents (as in semistructured data approaches)

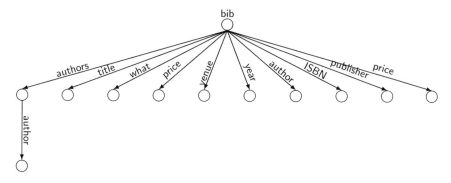

Fig. 12.6 The DataGuide corresponding to the OEM graph of Example 12.3

as well as the external links. They combine the content-based queries (e.g., keyword expressions) and structure-based queries (e.g., path expressions).

A number of languages have been proposed specifically to deal with web data, and these can be categorized as first generation and second generation. The first generation languages model the web as interconnected collection of *atomic* objects. Consequently, these languages can express queries that search the link structure among web objects and their textual content, but they cannot express queries that exploit the document structure of these web objects. The second generation languages model the web as a linked collection of *structured* objects, allowing them to express queries that exploit the document structure similar to semistructured languages. First generation approaches include WebSQL , W3QL, and WebLog, while second generation approaches include WebOQL and StruQL. We will demonstrate the general ideas by considering one first generation language (WebSQL) and one second generation language (WebOQL).

WebSQL is one of the early query languages that combines searching and browsing. It directly addresses web data as captured by web documents (usually in HTML format) that have some content and may include links to other pages or other objects (e.g., PDF files or images). It treats links as first-class objects, and identifies a number of different types of links that we will discuss shortly. As before, the structure can be represented as a graph, but WebSQL captures the information about web objects in two *virtual* relations:

```
DOCUMENT(URL, TITLE, TEXT, TYPE, LENGTH, MODIF)

LINK(BASE, HREF, LABEL)
```

DOCUMENT relation holds information about each web document where URL identifies the web object and is the primary key of the relation, TITLE is the title of the web page, TEXT is its text content of the web page, TYPE is the type of the web object (HTML document, image, etc.), LENGTH is self-explanatory, and MODIF is the last modification date of the object. Except URL, all other attributes can have null values. LINK relation captures the information about links where BASE is the URL of the HTML document that contains the link, HREF is the URL of the document that is referenced, and LABEL is the label of the link as defined earlier.

WebSQL defines a query language that consists of SQL plus path expressions. The path expressions are more powerful than their counterparts in Lorel; in particular, they identify different types of links:

(a) *interior link* that exists within the same document (#>)
(b) *local link* that is between documents on the same server (->)
(c) *global link* that refers to a document on another server (=>)
(d) *null path* (=)

These link types form the alphabet of the path expressions. Using them, and the usual constructors of regular expressions, different paths can be specified as in Example 12.7.

Example 12.7 The following are examples of possible path expressions that can be specified in WebSQL.

(a) -> | =>: a path of length one, either local or global
(b) ->*: local path of any length
(c) =>->*: as above, but in other servers
(d) (-> |=>)*: the reachable portion of the web

♦

In addition to path expressions that can appear in queries, WebSQL allows scoping within the **FROM** clause in the following way:

FROM Relation SUCH THAT domain-condition

where domain-condition can be either a path expression, or can specify a text search using **MENTIONS**, or can specify that an attribute (in the **SELECT** clause) is equal to a web object. Of course, following each relation specification, there could be a variable ranging over the relation—this is standard SQL. The following example queries (taken from with minor modifications) demonstrate the features of WebSQL.

Example 12.8 Following are some examples of WebSQL:

(a) The first example we consider simply searches for all documents about "hypertext" and demonstrates the use of MENTIONS to scope the query.

```
SELECT D.URL, D.TITLE
FROM   DOCUMENT D
       SUCH THAT D MENTIONS "hypertext"
WHERE  D.TYPE = "text/html"
```

(b) The second example demonstrates two scoping methods as well as a search for links. The query is to find all links to applets from documents about "Java."

```
SELECT A.LABEL, A.HREF
FROM   DOCUMENT D SUCH THAT D MENTIONS "Java"
       ANCHOR A SUCH THAT BASE=X
WHERE  A.LABEL = "applet"
```

(c) The third example demonstrates the use of different link types. It searches for documents that have the string "database" in their title that are reachable from the ACM Digital Library home page through paths of length two or less containing only local links.

```
SELECT D.URL, D.TITLE
FROM   DOCUMENT D SUCH THAT
           "http://www.acm.org/dl"=|->|->-> D
WHERE  D.TITLE CONTAINS "database"
```

(d) The final example demonstrates the combination of content and structure specifications in a query. It finds all documents mentioning "Computer Science" and all documents that are linked to them through paths of length two or less containing only local links.

```
SELECT D1.URL, D1.TITLE, D2.URL, D2.TITLE
FROM   DOCUMENT D1 SUCH THAT
           D1 MENTIONS "Computer Science",
       DOCUMENT D2 SUCH THAT D1=|->|->-> D2
```

                                                                                    ◆

WebSQL can query web data based on the links and the textual content of web documents, but it cannot query the documents based on their structure. This limitation is the consequence of its data model that treats the web as a collection of atomic objects.

The second generation languages, such as WebOQL, address this shortcoming by modeling the web as a graph of structured objects. In a way, they combine some features of semistructured data approaches with those of first generation web query models.

WebOQL's main data structure is a *hypertree*, which is an ordered edge-labeled tree with two types of edges: internal and external. An *internal edge* represents the internal structure of a web document, while an *external edge* represents a reference (i.e., hyperlink) among objects. Each edge is labeled with a record that consists of a number of attributes (fields). An external edge has to have a URL attribute in its record and cannot have descendants (i.e., they are the leaves of the hypertree).

Example 12.9 Let us revisit Example 12.2 and assume that instead of modeling the documents in a bibliography, it models the collection of documents about data management over the web. A possible (partial) hypertree for this example is given

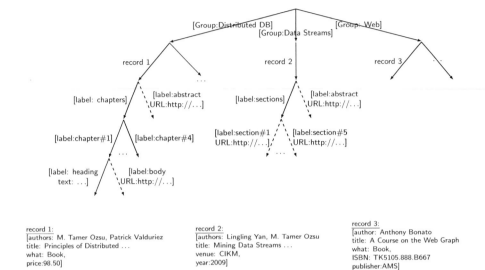

record 1:
[authors: M. Tamer Ozsu, Patrick Valduriez
title: Principles of Distributed ...
what: Book,
price:98.50]

record 2:
[authors: Lingling Yan, M. Tamer Ozsu
title: Mining Data Streams ...
venue: CIKM,
year:2009]

record 3:
[author: Anthony Bonato
title: A Course on the Web Graph
what: Book,
ISBN: TK5105.888.B667
publisher:AMS]

Fig. 12.7   The hypertree example

in Fig. 12.7. Note that we have made one revision to facilitate some of the queries
to be discussed later: we added an abstract to each document.

In Fig. 12.7, the documents are first grouped along a number of topics as
indicated in the records attached to the edges from the root. In this representation,
the internal links are shown as solid edges and external links as dashed edges.
Recall that in OEM (Fig. 12.5), the edges represent both attributes (e.g., author)
and document structure (e.g., chapter). In the WebOQL model, the attributes are
captured in the records that are associated with each edge, while the (internal) edges
represent the document structure.   ◆

Using this model, WebOQL defines a number of operators over trees:

Prime: returns the first subtree of its argument (denoted ′).
Peek: extracts a field from the record that labels the first outgoing edges of its
document. For example, if x points to the root of the subtree reached from the
"Groups = Distributed DB" edge, x.authors would retrieve "M. Tamer Ozsu,
Patrick Valduriez."
Hang: builds an edge-labeled tree with a record formed with the arguments
(denoted as []).

Example 12.10 Let us assume that the tree depicted in Fig. 12.8a is retrieved as a
result of a query (call it Q1). Then the expression ["Label: "Papers by Ozsu" / Q1]
results in the tree depicted in Fig. 12.8b.   ◆

Concatenate: combines two trees (denoted +).

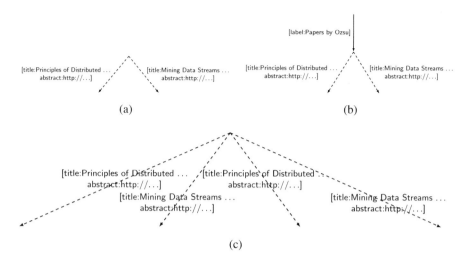

Fig. 12.8 Examples of Hang and Concatenate operators

Example 12.11 Again, assuming that the tree depicted in Fig. 12.8a is retrieved as a result of query Q1, Q1+Q2 produces tree in Fig. 12.8c.   ◆

Head: returns the first simple tree of a tree (denoted &). A simple tree of a tree
   t are the trees composed of one edge followed by a (possibly null) tree that
   originates from t's root.
Tail: returns all but the first simple tree of a tree (denoted !).

In addition to these, WebOQL introduces a string pattern matching operator (denoted $\sim$) whose left argument is a string and right argument is a string pattern. Since the only data type supported by the language is string, this is an important operator.

WebOQL is a functional language, so complex queries can be composed by combining these operators. In addition, it allows these operators to be embedded in the usual SQL (or OQL) style queries as demonstrated by the following example.

Example 12.12 Let dbDocuments denote the documents in the database shown in Fig. 12.7. Then the following query finds the titles and abstracts of all documents authored by "Ozsu" producing the result depicted in Fig. 12.8a.

```
SELECT  y.title, y'.URL
FROM    x IN dbDocuments, y IN x'
WHERE   y.authors ~ "Ozsu"
```

The semantics of this query is as follows: The variable x ranges over the simple trees of dbDocuments, and, for a given x value, y iterates over the simple trees of the single subtree of x. It peeks into the record of the edge and if the authors value matches "Ozsu" (using the string matching operator $\sim$), then it constructs a tree whose label is the `title` attribute of the record that `y` points to and the `URL` attribute value of the subtree.   ♦

The web query languages discussed in this section adopt a more powerful data model than the semistructured approaches. The model can capture both the document structure and the connectedness of web documents. The languages can then exploit these different edge semantics. Furthermore, as we have seen from the WebOQL examples, the queries can construct new structures as a result. However, formation of these queries still requires some knowledge about the graph structure.

12.4   Question Answering Systems

In this section, we discuss an interesting and unusual (from a database perspective) approach to accessing web data: question answering (QA) systems. These systems accept natural language questions that are then analyzed to determine the specific query that is being posed. They then conduct a search to find the appropriate answer.

Question answering systems have grown within the context of IR systems where the objective is to determine the answer to posed queries within a well-defined corpus of documents. These are usually referred to as *closed domain* systems. They extend the capabilities of keyword search queries in two fundamental ways. First, they allow users to specify complex queries in natural language that may be difficult to specify as simple keyword search requests. In the context of web querying, they also enable asking questions without a full knowledge of the data organization. Sophisticated natural language processing (NLP) techniques are then applied to these queries to understand the specific query. Second, they search the corpus of documents and return explicit answers rather than links to documents that may be relevant to the query. This does not mean that they return exact answers as traditional DBMSs do, but they may return a (ranked) list of explicit responses to the query, rather than a set of web pages. For example, a keyword search for "President of USA" using a search engine would return the (partial) result in Fig. 12.9. The user is expected to find the answer within the pages whose URLs and short descriptions (called snippets) are included on this page (and several more). On the other hand, a similar search using a natural language question "Who is the president of USA?" might return a ranked list of presidents' names (the exact type of answer differs among different systems).

Question answering systems have been extended to operate on the web. In these systems, the web is used as the corpus (hence they are called *open domain* systems). The web data sources are accessed using wrappers that are developed for them to obtain answers to questions. A number of question answering systems have been developed with different objectives and functionalities, such as Mulder, WebQA, Start, and Tritus. There are also commercial systems with varying capabilities (e.g., Wolfram Alpha http://www.wolframalpha.com/).

Fig. 12.9 Keyword search example

We describe the general functionality of these systems using the reference architecture given in Fig. 12.10. Preprocessing, which is not employed in all systems, is an offline process to extract and enhance the rules that are used by the systems. In many cases, these are analyses of documents extracted from the web or returned as answers to previously asked questions in order to determine the most effective query structures into which a user question can be transformed. These transformation rules are stored in order to use them at runtime while answering the user questions. For example, Tritus employs a learning-based approach that uses

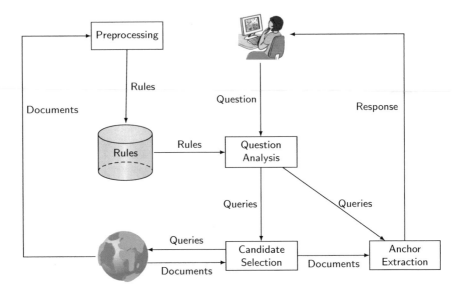

Fig. 12.10 General architecture of QA systems

a collection of frequently asked questions and their correct answers as a training dataset. In a three-stage process, it attempts to guess the structure of the answer by analyzing the question and searching for the answer in the collection. In the first stage, the question is analyzed to extract the *question phrase* (e.g., in the question "What is a hard disk?," "What is a" is a question phrase). This is used to classify the question. In the second phase, it analyzes the question-answer pairs in the training data and generates *candidate transforms* for each question phrase (e.g., for the question phrase "What is a," it generates "refers to," "stands for," etc.). In the third stage, each candidate transform is applied to the questions in the training dataset, and the resulting transformed queries are sent to different search engines. The similarities of the returned answers with the actual answers in the training data are calculated, and, based on these, a ranking is done for candidate transforms. The ranked transformation rules are stored for later use during runtime execution of questions.

The natural language question that is posed by a user first goes through the question analysis process. The objective is to understand the question issued by the user. Most of the systems try to guess the type of the answer in order to categorize the question, which is used in translating the question into queries and also in answer extraction. If preprocessing has been done, the transformation rules that have been generated are used to assist the process. Although the general goals are the same, the approaches used by different systems vary considerably depending on the sophistication of the NLP techniques employed by the systems (this phase is usually all about NLP). For example, question analysis in Mulder incorporates three phases: question parsing, question classification, and query generation. Query parsing generates a parse tree that is used in query generation and in answer extraction. Question classification, as its name implies, categorizes the question in one of a number of classes: e.g., *nominal* is for nouns, *numerical* is for numbers, and *temporal* is for dates. This type of categorization is done in most of the QA systems because it eases the answer extraction. Finally, query generation phase uses the previously generated parse tree to construct one or more queries that can be executed to obtain the answers to the question. Mulder uses four different methods in this phase.

- Verb conversion: Auxiliary and main verb is replaced by the conjugated verb (e.g., "When did Nixon visit China?" is converted to "Nixon visited China").
- Query expansion: Adjective in the question phrase is replaced by its attribute noun (e.g., "How tall is Mt. Everest?" is converted to "The height of Everest is").
- Noun phrase formation: Some noun phrases are quoted in order to give them together to the search engine in the next stage.
- Transformation: Structure of the question is transformed into the structure of the expected answer type ("Who was the first American in space?" is converted to "The first American in space was").

Mulder is an example of a system that uses a sophisticated NLP approach to question analysis. At the other end of the spectrum is WebQA, which follows a lightweight approach in question parsing.

Once the question is analyzed and one or more queries are generated, the next step is to generate candidate answers. The queries that were generated at question analysis stage are used at this step to perform keyword search for relevant documents. Many of the systems simply use the general-purpose search engines in this step, while others also consider additional data sources that are available on the web. For example, CIA's World Factbook (https://www.cia.gov/library/publications/the-world-factbook/) is a very popular source for reliable factual data about countries. Similarly, weather information may be obtained very reliably from a number of weather data sources such as the Weather Network (http://www.theweathernetwork.com/) or Weather Underground (http://www.wunderground.com/). These additional data sources may provide better answers in some cases and different systems take advantage of these to differing degrees. Since different queries can be better answered by different data sources (and, sometimes, even by different search engines), an important aspect of this processing stage is the choice of the appropriate search engine(s)/data source(s) to consult for a given query. The naive alternative of submitting the queries to all search engines and data sources is not a wise decision, since these operations are quite costly over the web. Usually, the category information is used to assist the choice of the appropriate sources, along with a ranked listing of sources and engines for different categories. For each search engine and data source, wrappers need to be written to convert the query into the format of that data source/search engine and convert the returned result documents into a common format for further analysis.

In response to queries, search engines return links to the documents together with short snippets, while other data sources return results in a variety of formats.

The returned results are normalized into "records." The direct answers need to be extracted from these records, which is the function of the answer extraction phase. Various text processing techniques can be used to match the keywords to (possibly parts of) the returned records. Subsequently, these results need to be ranked using various information retrieval techniques (e.g., word frequencies, inverse document frequency). In this process, the category information that is generated during question analysis is used. Different systems employ different notions of the appropriate answer. Some return a ranked list of direct answers (e.g., if the question is "Who invented the telephone," they would return "Alexander Graham Bell" or "Graham Bell" or "Bell," or all of them in ranked order[4]), while others return a ranked order of the portion of the records that contain the keywords in the query (i.e., a summary of the relevant portion of the document).

Question answering systems are very different than the other web querying approaches we have discussed in previous sections. They are more flexible in what they offer users in terms of querying without any knowledge of the organization of web data. On the other hand, they are constrained by idiosynchrocies of natural language, and the difficulties of natural language processing.

12.5 Searching and Querying the Hidden Web

Currently, most general-purpose search engines only operate on the PIW while a considerable amount of the valuable data are kept in hidden databases, either as relational data, as embedded documents, or in many other forms. The current trend in web search is to find ways to search the hidden web as well as the PIW, for two main reasons. First is the size—the size of the hidden web (in terms of generated HTML pages) is considerably larger than the PIW, therefore the probability of finding answers to users' queries is much higher if the hidden web can also be searched. The second is in data quality—the data stored in the hidden web are usually of much higher quality than those found on public web pages since they are properly curated. If they can be accessed, the quality of answers can be improved.

However, searching the hidden web faces many challenges, the most important of which are the following:

1. Ordinary crawlers cannot be used to search the hidden web, since there are neither HTML pages, nor hyperlinks to crawl.
2. Usually, the data in hidden databases can be only accessed through a search interface or a special interface, requiring access to this interface.
3. In most (if not all) cases, the underlying structure of the database is unknown, and the data providers are usually reluctant to provide any information about their data that might help in the search process (possibly due to the overhead

---

[4]The inventor of the telephone is a subject of controversy, with multiple claims to the invention. We'll go with Bell in this example since he was the first one to patent the device.

of collecting this information and maintaining it). One has to work through the interfaces provided by these data sources.

In the remainder of this section, we discuss these issues as well as some proposed solutions.

12.5.1   Crawling the Hidden Web

One approach to address the issue of searching the hidden web is to try crawling in a manner similar to that of the PIW. As already mentioned, the only way to deal with hidden web databases is through their search interfaces. A hidden web crawler should be able to perform two tasks: (a) submit queries to the search interface of the database, and (b) analyze the returned result pages and extract relevant information from them.

12.5.1.1   Querying the Search Interface

One approach is to analyze the search interface of the database, and build an internal representation for it. This internal representation specifies the fields used in the interface, their types (e.g., text boxes, lists, checkboxes, etc.), their domains (e.g., specific values as in lists, or just free text strings as in text boxes), and also the labels associated with these fields. Extracting these labels requires an exhaustive analysis of the HTML structure of the page.

Next, this representation is matched with the system's task-specific database. The matching is based on the labels of the fields. When a label is matched, the field is then populated with the available values for this field. The process is repeated for all possible values of all fields in the search form, and the form is submitted with every combination of values and the results are retrieved.

Another approach is to use agent technology. In this case, *hidden web agents* are developed that interact with the search forms and retrieve the result pages. This involves three steps: (a) finding the forms, (b) learning to fill the forms, and (c) identifying and fetching the target (result) pages.

The first step is accomplished by starting from a URL (an entry point), traversing links, and using some heuristics to identify HTML pages that contain forms, excluding those that contain password fields (e.g., login, registration, purchase pages). The form filling task depends on identifying labels and associating them with form fields. This is achieved using some heuristics about the location of the label relative to the field (on the left or above it). Given the identified labels, the agent determines the application domain that the form belongs to, and fills the fields with values from that domain in accordance with the labels (the values are stored in a repository accessible to the agent).

12.5.1.2   Analyzing the Result Pages

Once the form is submitted, the returned page has to be analyzed, for example, to see if it is a data page or a search-refining page. This can be achieved by matching values in this page with values in the agent's repository. Once a data page is found, it is traversed, as well as all pages that it links to (especially pages that have more results), until no more pages can be found that belong to the same domain.

However, the returned pages usually contain a lot of irrelevant data, in addition to the actual results, since most of the result pages follow some template that has a considerable amount of text used only for presentation purposes. A method to identify web page templates is to analyze the textual contents and the adjacent tag structures of a document in order to extract query-related data. A web page is represented as a sequence of text segments, where a text segment is a piece of tag encapsulated between two tags. The mechanism to detect templates is as follows:

1. Text segments of documents are analyzed based on textual contents and their adjacent tag segments.
2. An initial template is identified by examining the first two sample documents.
3. The template is then generated if matched text segments along with their adjacent tag segments are found from both documents.
4. Subsequent retrieved documents are compared with the generated template. Text segments that are not found in the template are extracted for each document to be further processed.
5. When no matches are found from the existing template, document contents are extracted for the generation of future templates.

12.5.2   Metasearching

Metasearching is another approach for querying the hidden web. Given a user query, a metasearcher performs the following tasks:

1. Database selection: selecting the databases(s) that are most relevant to the user's query. This requires collecting some information about each database. This information is known as a *content summary*, which is statistical information, usually including the *document frequencies* of the words that appear in the database.
2. Query translation: translating the query to a suitable form for each database (e.g., by filling certain fields in the database's search interface).
3. Result merging: collecting the results from the various databases, merging them (and most probably, ordering them), and returning them to the user.

We discuss the important phases of metasearching in more detail below.

12.5.2.1 Content Summary Extraction

The first step in metasearching is to compute content summaries. In most of the cases, the data providers are not willing to go through the trouble of providing this information. Therefore, the metasearcher itself extracts this information.

A possible approach is to extract a document sample set from a given database D and compute the frequency of each observed word w in the sample, $SampleDF(w)$. The technique works as follows:

1. Start with an empty content summary where $SampleDF(w) = 0$ for each word w, and a general (i.e., not specific to D), comprehensive word dictionary.
2. Pick a word and send it as a query to database D.
3. Retrieve the top-k documents from among the returned documents.
4. If the number of retrieved documents exceeds a prespecified threshold, stop. Otherwise continue the sampling process by returning to Step 2.

There are two main versions of this algorithm that differ in how Step 2 is executed. One of the algorithms picks a random word from the dictionary. The second algorithm selects the next query from among the words that have been already discovered during sampling. The first constructs better profiles, but is more expensive.

An alternative is to use a focused probing technique that can actually classify the databases into a hierarchical categorization. The idea is to preclassify a set of training documents into some categories, and then extract different terms from these documents and use them as query probes for the database. The single-word probes are used to determine the *actual* document frequencies of these words, while only *sample* document frequencies are computed for other words that appear in longer probes. These are used to estimate the actual document frequencies for these words.

Yet another approach is to start by randomly selecting a term from the search interface itself, assuming that, most probably, this term will be related to the contents of the database. The database is queried for this term, and the top-k documents are retrieved. A subsequent term is then randomly selected from terms extracted from the retrieved documents. The process is repeated until a predefined number of documents are retrieved, and then statistics are calculated based on the retrieved documents.

12.5.2.2 Database Categorization

A good approach that can help the database selection process is to categorize the databases into several categories (for example, as Yahoo directory). Categorization facilitates locating a database given a user's query, and makes most of the returned results relevant to the query.

If the focused probing technique is used for generating content summaries, then the same algorithm can probe each database with queries from some category and count the number of matches. If the number of matches exceeds a certain threshold, the database is said to belong to this category.

Database Selection

Database selection is a crucial task in the metasearching process, since it has a critical impact on the efficiency and effectiveness of query processing over multiple databases. A database selection algorithm attempts to find the best set of databases, based on information about the database contents, on which a given query should be executed. Usually, this information includes the number of different documents that contain each word (known as the document frequency), as well as some other simple related statistics, such as the number of documents stored in the database. Given these summaries, a database selection algorithm estimates how relevant each database is for a given query (e.g., in terms of the number of matches that each database is expected to produce for the query).

GlOSS is a simple database selection algorithm that assumes that query words are independently distributed over database documents to estimate the number of documents that match a given query. GlOSS is an example of a large family of database selection algorithms that rely on content summaries. Furthermore, database selection algorithms expect such content summaries to be accurate and up-to-date.

The focused probing algorithm discussed above exploits the database categorization and content summaries for database selection. This algorithm consists of two basic steps: (1) propagate the database content summaries to the categories of the hierarchical classification scheme, and (2) use the content summaries of categories and databases to perform database selection hierarchically by zooming in on the most relevant portions of the topic hierarchy. This results in more relevant answers to the user's query since they only come from databases that belong to the same category as the query itself.

Once the relevant databases are selected, each database is queried, and the returned results are merged and sent back to the user.

12.6   Web Data Integration

In Chap. 7 we discussed the integration of databases, each of which have well-defined schemas. The techniques discussed in that chapter are mostly appropriate when enterprise data is considered. When we wish to provide integrated access to web data sources, the problem becomes more complex—all the characteristics of "big data" play a role. In particular, the data may not have a proper schema, and if it does, the data sources are so varied that the schemas are widely different, making schema matching a real challenge. In addition, the amount of data and even the number of data sources are significantly higher than in an enterprise environment, making manual curation all but impossible. The quality of the data on the web is also far more suspect than the enterprise data collections that we considered previously, and this increases the importance of data cleaning solutions.

An appropriate approach to web data integration is what is called *pay-as-you-go integration* where the up-front investment to integrate data is significantly reduced, eliminating some of the stages discussed in Chap. 7. Instead, a framework and basic infrastructure is provided for data owners to easily integrate their datasets into a federation. One proposal for the pay-as-you-go approach to web data integration is *data spaces*, which advocates that there should be lightweight integration platform with perhaps rudimentary access opportunities (e.g., keyword search) to start with, and ways to improve the value of the integration over time by providing the opportunity to develop tools for more sophisticated use. Perhaps the *data lakes* that have started to receive attention and that we discussed in Chap. 10, are more advanced versions of the data space proposal.

In this section, we cover some of the approaches that have been developed to address these challenges. In particular, we will look at web tables and fusion tables (Sect. 12.6.1) as a low-overhead integration approach for tabular structured data. We then look at the semantic web and the Linked Open Data (LOD) approach to web data integration (Sect. 12.6.2.3). Finally, we discuss the issues of data cleaning and the use of machine learning techniques in data integration and cleaning at web-scale integration in Sect. 12.6.3.

12.6.1 Web Tables/Fusion Tables

Two popular approaches to lightweight web data integration are *web portals* and *mashups* that aggregate web and other data on specific topics such as travel, hotel bookings, etc. The two differ in the technologies that they use, but that is not important for our discussion. These are examples of "vertically integrated" systems where each mashup or portal targets one domain.

A first question that comes up in developing a mashup is how to find the relevant web data. Web tables project is an early attempt at finding data on the web that has relational table structure and provide access over these tables (the so-called "database-like" tables). The focus is on the open web, and tables in the deep web are not considered as their discovery is a much more difficult problem. Even finding the database-like tables in the open web is not easy since the usual relational table structures (i.e., attribute names) may not exist. Web tables employ a classifier that can group HTML tables as relational and nonrelational. It then provides tools to extract a schema and maintain statistics about the schemas that can be used in search over these tables. Join opportunities across tables are introduced to allow more sophisticated navigation across the discovered tables. Web tables can be viewed as a method to retrieve and query web data, but they also serve as a virtual integration framework for web data with global schema information.

Fusion tables project at Google takes web tables a step further by allowing users to upload their own tables (in various formats) in addition to the discovered

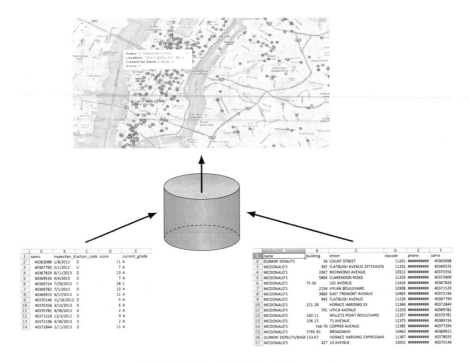

Fig. 12.11 Web tables/fusion tables example

web tables. The fusion table's infrastructure can automatically discover the join attribute across tables and produce integration opportunities. An example is given in Fig. 12.11 which depicts two datasets contributed by two different owners, one on eateries and the other about the scores and grades given to these eateries as a result of inspection. The system would determine that the two datasets can be joined over a common attribute and provide integrated access. Although in this case both tables were contributed by users, in other cases one or both of the tables can be discovered from the web by using the techniques developed by web tables project.

12.6.2   Semantic Web and Linked Open Data

A fundamental contribution of the web is to produce a repository of *machine processable* data. Semantic web aims to convert this data into *machine understandable* form by integrating both structured and unstructured data on the web and marking it up semantically. The original semantic web vision includes three components:

- Markup web data so that metadata is captured as annotations;
- Use ontologies for making different data collections understandable; and
- Use logic-based technologies to access both the metadata and the ontologies.

Linked Open Data (LOD) was introduced in 2006 as a clarification of this vision emphasizing the linkages among the data that is part of the semantic web. It set out guidelines for how data should be published on the web to achieve the vision of the semantic web. Thus, the semantic web is a web data integration vision realized through LOD. LOD requirements for publishing (and hence integrating) data on the web are based on four principles:

- All web resources (data) are locally identified by their URIs that serve as names;
- These names are accessible by HTTP;
- Information about web resources/entities are encoded as RDF (Resource Description Framework) triples. In other words, RDF is the semantic web data model (and we discuss it below);
- Connections among datasets are established by data links and publishers of datasets should establish these links so that more data is discoverable.

The LOD, therefore, generates a graph where the vertices are web resources and the edges are the relationships. A simplified form of "LOD graph" as of 2018 is shown in Fig. 12.12 where each vertex represents a dataset (not a web resource) categorized according to by color (e.g., publications, life sciences, social networking) and the size of each vertex represents its in-degree. At that time, LOD consisted of 1,234 datasets with 16,136 links.[5] We will come back to LOD and the LOD graph shortly.

Semantic web consists of a number of technologies that build upon each other (Fig. 12.13). At the bottom layer, XML provides the language for writing structured web documents and exchanging them easily. On top of this is the RDF that, as noted above, establishes the data model. Although it is not necessary, if a schema over this data is specified, the RDF Schema provides the necessary primitives. Ontologies extend RDF schema with more powerful constructs to specify the relationships among web data. Finally, logic-based declarative rule languages allow applications to define their own rules.

In the remainder we discuss the technologies in the lower layers as these are the minimal requirements.

12.6.2.1 XML

The predominant encoding for web documents has been HTML (which stands for HyperText Markup Language). A web document encoded in HTML consists of *HTML elements* encapsulated by tags as discussed in Sect. 12.6.1 where we also presented approaches to discover structured data in HTML-encoded web documents and integrating them. As noted above, within the context of semantic web, the preferred representation for encoding and exchanging web documents is XML

---

[5]Statistics obtained from https://lod-cloud.net, which should be consulted for up-to-date statistics.

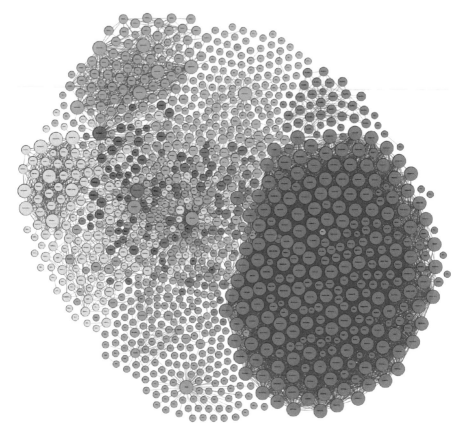

Fig. 12.12   LOD graph as of 2018

Declarative Rule Languages
Ontology Languages
RDF Schema
RDF
XML

Fig. 12.13   Semantic web technologies. Simplified from [Antoniou and Plexousakis 2018]

(which stands for Extensive Markup Language) proposed by the World Wide Web Consortium (W3C).

XML tags (also called markups) divide data into pieces called *elements*, with the objective to provide more semantics to the data. Elements can be nested but they cannot be overlapped. Nesting of elements represents hierarchical relationships between them. As an example, Fig. 12.14 is the XML representation, with slight revisions, of the bibliography data that we had given earlier.

An XML document can be represented as a tree that contains a *root element*, which has zero or more nested subelements (or *child elements*), which can recursively contain subelements. For each element, there are zero or more *attributes* with atomic values assigned to them. An element also contains an optional value. Due to the textual representation of the tree, a total order, called *document order*, is defined on all elements corresponding to the order in which the first character of the elements occurs in the document.

For instance, the root element in Fig. 12.4 is `bib`, which has three child elements: two `book` and one `article`. The first `book` element has an attribute `year` with atomic value "1999", and also contains subelements (e.g., the `title` element). An element can contain a value (e.g., "`Principles of Distributed Database Systems`" for the element `title`).

Standard XML document definition is a bit more complicated: it can contain ID-IDREFs, which define references between elements in the same document or in another document. In that case, the document representation becomes a graph. However, it is quite common to use the simpler tree representation, and we'll assume the same in this section and we define it more precisely below.[6]

An XML document is modeled as an ordered, node-labeled tree $T = (V, E)$, where each node $v \in V$ corresponds to an element or attribute and is characterized by:

- a unique identifier denoted by $ID(v)$;
- a unique *kind* property, denoted as $kind(v)$, assigned from the set {`element`, `attribute`, `text`};
- a label, denoted by $label(v)$, assigned from some alphabet Σ;
- a content, denoted by $content(v)$, which is empty for nonleaf nodes and is a strong for leaf nodes.

A directed edge $e = (u, v)$ is included in E if and only if:

- $kind(u) = kind(v) = $ `element`, and v is a subelement of u; or
- $kind(u) = $ `element` $\land kind(v) = $ `attribute`, and v is an attribute of u.

Now that an XML document tree is properly defined, we can define an instance of XML data model as an ordered collection (sequence) of XML document tree nodes or atomic values. A schema may or may not be defined for an XML document, since it is a self-describing format. If a schema is defined for a collection of

---

[6]In addition, we omit the comment nodes, namespace nodes, and PI nodes from the model.

```
<bib>
<book year = "1999">
<author> M. Tamer Ozsu </author>
<author> Patrick Valduriez </author>
<title> Principles of Distributed ... </title>
<chapters>
<chapter>
<heading> ... </heading>
<body> ... </body>
</chapter>
...
<chapter>
<heading> ... </heading>
<body> ... </body>
</chapter>
</chapters>
<price currency= "USD"> 98.50 </price>
</book>
<article year = "2009">
<author> M. Tamer Ozsu </author>
<author> Yingying Tao </author>
<title> Mining data streams ... </title>
<venue> "CIKM" </venue>
<sections>
<section> ... </section>
...
<section> ... </section>
</sections>
</article>
<book>
<author> Anthony Bonato </author>
<title> A Course on the Web Graph </title>
<ISBN> TK5105.888.B667 </ISBN>
<chapters>
<chapter>
<heading> ... </heading>
<body> ... </body>
</chapter>
<chapter>
<heading> ... </heading>
<body> ... </body>
</chapter>
<chapter>
<heading> ... </heading>
<body> ... </body>
</chapter>
</chapters>
<publisher> AMS </publisher>
</book>
</bib>
```

Fig. 12.14 An example XML document

XML documents, then each document in this collection conforms to that schema; however, the schema allows for variations in each document, since not all elements or attributes may exist in each document. XML schemas can be defined either using the Document Type Definition (DTD) or XMLSchema. In this section, we will use a simpler schema definition that exploits the graph structure of XML documents as defined above.

An XML *schema graph* is defined as a 5-tuple $\langle \Sigma, \Psi, s, m, \rho \rangle$ where Σ is an alphabet of XML document node types, ρ is the root node type, $\Psi \subseteq \Sigma \times \Sigma$ is a set of edges between node types, $s : \Psi \rightarrow$ {ONCE, OPT, MULT} and $m : \Sigma \rightarrow$ {string}. The semantics of this definition are as follows: An edge $\psi = (\sigma_1, \sigma_2) \in \Psi$ denotes that an item of type σ_1 may contain an item of type σ_2. $s(\psi)$ denotes the cardinality of the containment represented by this edge: If $s(\psi) = $ ONCE, then an item of type σ_1 must contain exactly one item of σ_2. If $s(\psi) = $ OPT, then an item of type σ_1 may or may not contain an item of type σ_2. If $s(\psi) = $ MULT, then an item of type σ_1 may contain multiple items of type σ_2. $m(\sigma)$ denotes the domain of the text content of an item of type σ, represented as the set of all strings that may occur inside such an item.

Using the definition of XML data model and instances of this data model, it is now possible to define the query languages. Expressions in XML query languages take an instance of XML data as input and produce an instance of XML data as output. XPath and XQuery are two query languages proposed by the W3C. Path expressions, that we introduced earlier, are present in both query languages and are arguably the most natural way to query the hierarchical XML data. XQuery defines for more powerful constructs. Although XQuery was the subject of intense research and development efforts in the 2000s, it is not widely used any longer. It is complicated, hard to formulate by users and difficult to optimize by systems. JSON has replaced both XML and XQuery for many applications, as we discussed in Chap. 11, although XML representation remains important for the semantic web (but not XQuery).

12.6.2.2   RDF

RDF is the data model on top of XML and forms a fundamental building block of the semantic web (Fig. 12.13). Although it was originally proposed by W3C as a component of the semantic web, its use is now wider. For example, Yago and DBPedia extract facts from Wikipedia automatically and store them in RDF format to support structural queries over Wikipedia; biologists encode their experiments and results using RDF to communicate among themselves leading to RDF data collections, such as Bio2RDF (bio2rdf.org) and Uniprot RDF (dev.isb-sib.ch/projects/uniprot-rdf). Related to semantic web, LOD project builds a RDF data cloud by linking a large number of datasets, as noted earlier.

RDF models each "fact" as a set of triples (subject, **p**roperty (or **p**redicate), **o**bject), denoted as $\langle s, p, o \rangle$, where *subject* is an entity, class or blank node, a *property*[7] denotes one attribute associated with one entity, and *object* is an entity, a class, a blank node, or a literal value. According to the RDF standard, an entity is denoted by a URI (Uniform Resource Identifier) that refers to a named *resource* in the environment that is being modeled. Blank nodes, by contrast, refer to anonymous resources that do not have a name.[8] Thus, each triple represents a named relationship; those involving blank nodes simply indicate that "something with the given relationship exists, without naming it."

It is appropriate at this point to briefly talk about the next layer in the semantic web technology stack (Fig. 12.13), namely the RDF Schema (RDFS). It is possible to annotate RDF data with semantic metadata using RDFS, which is also a W3C standard.[9] This annotation primarily enables reasoning over the RDF data (called *entailment*), and also impacts data organization in some cases, and the metadata can be used for semantic query optimization. We illustrate the fundamental concepts by simple examples using RDFS, which allows the definition of *classes* and *class hierarchies*. RDFS has built-in class definitions—the more important ones being rdfs:Class and rdfs:subClassOf that are used to define a class and a subclass, respectively (another one, rdfs:label is used in our query examples below). To specify that an individual resource is an element of the class, a special property, rdf:type is used.

Example 12.13 For example, if we wanted to define a class called Movies and two subclasses ActionMovies and Dramas, this would be accomplished in the following way:

```
Movies rdf:type rdfs:Class .
ActionMovies rdfs:subClassOf Movies .
Dramas rdfs:subClassOf Movies .
```

◆

Formally, a RDF dataset can be defined as follows. Let $\mathcal{U}$, $\mathcal{B}$, and $\mathcal{L}$, denote the sets of all URIs, blank nodes, and literals, respectively. A tuple $(s, p, o) \in (\mathcal{U} \cup \mathcal{B}) \times \mathcal{U} \times (\mathcal{U} \cup \mathcal{B} \cup \mathcal{L})$ is an *RDF triple*. A set of RDF triples form a *RDF dataset*.

Example 12.14 An example RDF dataset is shown in Fig. 12.15 where the data comes from a number of sources as defined by the URI prefixes.

◆

RDF data can be modeled as an RDF graph as follows. A *RDF graph* is a six-tuple $G = \langle V, L_V, f_V, E, L_E, f_E \rangle$, where

---

[7]In literature, the terms "property" and "predicate" are used interchangeably; in this paper, we will use "property" consistently.

[8]In much of the research, blank nodes are ignored. Unless explicitly stated otherwise, we will ignore them in this paper as well.

[9]The same annotation can also be done using the ontology languages such as OWL (also a W3C standard) but we will not discuss that topic further.

Prefixes:
mdb=http://data.linkedmdb.org/resource/geo=http://sws.geonames.org/
bm=http://wifo5-03.informatik.uni-mannheim.de/bookmashup/
exvo=http://lexvo.org/id/
wp=http://en.wikipedia.org/wiki/

Subject	Property	Object
mdb: film/2014	rdfs:label	"The Shining"
mdb:film/2014	movie:initial_release_date	"1980-05-23"'
mdb:film/2014	movie:director	mdb:director/8476
mdb:film/2014	movie:actor	mdb:actor/29704
mdb:film/2014	movie:actor	mdb: actor/30013
mdb:film/2014	movie:music_contributor	mdb: music_contributor/4110
mdb:film/2014	foaf:based_near	geo:2635167
mdb:film/2014	movie:relatedBook	bm:0743424425
mdb:film/2014	movie:language	lexvo:iso639-3/eng
mdb:director/8476	movie:director_name	"Stanley Kubrick"
mdb:film/2685	movie:director	mdb:director/8476
mdb:film/2685	rdfs:label	"A Clockwork Orange"
mdb:film/424	movie:director	mdb:director/8476
mdb:film/424	rdfs:label	"Spartacus"
mdb:actor/29704	movie:actor_name	"Jack Nicholson"
mdb:film/1267	movie:actor	mdb:actor/29704
mdb:film/1267	rdfs:label	"The Last Tycoon"
mdb:film/3418	movie:actor	mdb:actor/29704
mdb:film/3418	rdfs:label	"The Passenger"
geo:2635167	gn:name	"United Kingdom"
geo:2635167	gn:population	62348447
geo:2635167	gn:wikipediaArticle	wp:United_Kingdom
bm:books/0743424425	dc:creator	bm:persons/Stephen+King
bm:books/0743424425	rev:rating	4.7
bm:books/0743424425	scom:hasOffer	bm:offers/0743424425amazonOffer
lexvo:iso639-3/eng	rdfs:label	"English"
lexvo:iso639-3/eng	lvont:usedIn	lexvo:iso3166/CA
lexvo:iso639-3/eng	lvont:usesScript	lexvo:script/Latn

Fig. 12.15 Example RDF dataset. Prefixes are used to identify the data sources

1. $V = V_c \cup V_e \cup V_l$ is a collection of vertices that correspond to all subjects and objects in RDF data, where V_c, V_e, and V_l are collections of class vertices, entity vertices, and literal vertices, respectively.
2. L_V is a collection of vertex labels.
3. A *vertex labeling function* $f_V : V \to L_V$ is an bijective function that assigns to each vertex a label. The label of a vertex $u \in V_l$ is its literal value, and the label of a vertex $u \in V_c \cup V_e$ is its corresponding URI.
4. $E = \{\overrightarrow{u_1, u_2}\}$ is a collection of directed edges that connect the corresponding subjects and objects.
5. L_E is a collection of edge labels.
6. An *edge labeling function* $f_E : E \to L_E$ is an bijective function that assigns to each edge a label. The label of an edge $e \in E$ is its corresponding property.

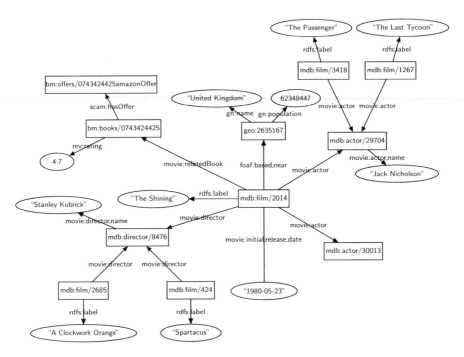

Fig. 12.16 RDF graph corresponding to the dataset in Fig. 12.15

An edge $\overrightarrow{u_1, u_2}$ is an *attribute property* edge if $u_2 \in V_l$; otherwise, it is a *link* edge.

Note that RDF graph structure is different than the property graphs we discussed in Chap. 10. As you will recall, property graphs have attributes attached to vertices and edges allowing sophisticated value-based predicates to be specified in queries. In RDF graphs, the only attribute of a vertex or an edge is the vertex/edge label. What would be vertex attributes in a property graph become edges whose labels are the attribute names. Therefore, RDF graphs are simpler and more regular, but generally larger in terms of the number of vertices and edges.

Figure 12.16 shows an example of an RDF graph. The vertices that are denoted by boxes are entity or class vertices, and the others are literal vertices.

The W3C standard language for RDF is SPARQL, which can be defined as follows [Hartig 2012]. Let $\mathcal{U}, \mathcal{B}, \mathcal{L}$, and $\mathcal{V}$ denote the sets of all URIs, blank nodes, literals, and variables, respectively. A SPARQL expression is expressed recursively

1. A *triple pattern* $(\mathcal{U} \cup \mathcal{B} \cup \mathcal{V}) \times (\mathcal{U} \cup \mathcal{V}) \times (\mathcal{U} \cup \mathcal{B} \cup \mathcal{L} \cup \mathcal{V})$ is a SPARQL expression,
2. (optionally) If P is a SPARQL expression, then $P \ FILTER \ R$ is also a SPARQL expression where R is a built-in SPARQL filter condition,
3. (optionally) If P_1 and P_2 are SPARQL expressions, then $P_1 \ AND|OPT|OR \ P_2$ are also SPARQL expressions.

A set of triple patterns is called *basic graph pattern* (BGP) and SPARQL expressions that only contain these are called *BGP queries*. These are the subject of most of the research in SPARQL query evaluation.

Example 12.15 An example SPARQL query that finds the names of the movies directed by "Stanley Kubrick" and have a related book that has a rating greater than 4.0 is specified as follows:

```
SELECT ?name
WHERE {
?m rdfs:label ?name. ?m movie:director ?d.
?d movie:director_name "Stanley Kubrick".
?m movie:relatedBook ?b. ?b rev:rating ?r.
FILTER(?r > 4.0)
}
```

In this query, the first three lines in the **WHERE** clause form a BGP consisting of five triple patterns. All triple patterns in this example have *variables*, such as "?m", "?name" and "?r", and "?r" has a filter: **FILTER(?r > 4.0)**.

◆

A SPARQL query can also be represented as a *query graph*. A *query graph* is a seven-tuple $Q = \langle V^Q, L_V^Q, E^Q, L_E^Q, f_V^Q, f_E^Q, FL \rangle$, where

1. $V^Q = V_c^Q \cup V_e^Q \cup V_l^Q \cup V_p^Q$ is a collection of vertices that correspond to all subjects and objects in a SPARQL query, where V_p^Q is a collection of variable vertices (corresponding to variables in the query expression), and V_c^Q and V_e^Q and V_l^Q are collections of class vertices, entity vertices, and literal vertices in the query graph Q, respectively.
2. E^Q is a collection of edges that correspond to properties in a SPARQL query.
3. L_V^Q is a collection of vertex labels in Q and L_E^Q is the edge labels in E^Q.
4. $f_V^Q : V^Q \rightarrow L_V^Q$ is a bijective vertex labeling function that assigns to each vertex in Q a label from L_V^Q. The label of a vertex $v \in V_p^Q$ is the variable; that of a vertex $v \in V_l^Q$ is its literal value; and that of a vertex $v \in V_c^Q \cup V_e^Q$ is its corresponding URI.
5. $f_E^Q : V^Q \rightarrow L_E^Q$ is a bijective vertex labeling function that assigns to each edge in Q a label from L_V^Q. An edge label can be a property or an edge variable.
6. FL are constraint filters.

The query graph for Q_1 is given in Fig. 12.17.

The semantics of SPARQL query evaluation can, therefore, be defined as subgraph matching using graph homomorphism whereby all subgraphs of an RDF graph G are found that are homomorphic to the SPARQL query graph Q.

It is usual to talk about SPARQL query types based on the shape of the query graph (we will refer to these types in the following discussion). Typically, three

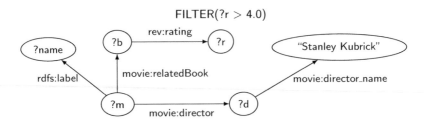

Fig. 12.17 SPARQL query graph corresponding to query Q_1

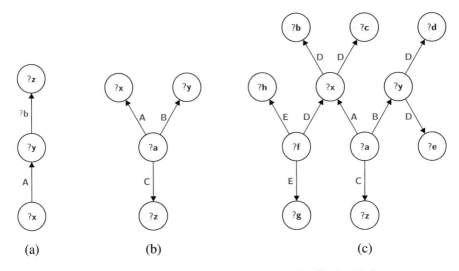

Fig. 12.18 Sample SPARQL query shapes. (a) Q_L. (b) Q_S. (c) Q_K

query types are observed: (i) linear (Fig. 12.18a), where the variable in the object field of one triple pattern appears in the subject of another triple pattern (e.g., ?y in Q_L) (ii) star-shaped (Fig. 12.18b), where the variable in the object field of one triple pattern appears in the subject of multiple other triple patterns (e.g., ?a in Q_S), and (iii) snowflake-shaped (Fig. 12.18c), which is a combination of multiple star queries.

A number of RDF data management systems have been developed. These can be broadly classified into five groups: those that map the RDF data directly into a relational system, those that use a relational schema with extensive indexing (and a native storage system), those that denormalize the triples table into clustered properties, those that use column-store organization, and those that exploit the native graph pattern matching semantics of SPARQL.

Direct Relational Mapping

Direct relational mapping systems take advantage of the fact that RDF triples have a
natural tabular structure. Therefore, they create a single table with three columns
(Subject, Property, Object) that holds the triples (there usually are additional
auxiliary tables, but we ignore them here). The SPARQL query can then be
translated into SQL and executed on this table. It has been shown that SPARQL
1.0 can be full translated to SQL; whether the same is true for SPARQL 1.1 with
its added features is still open. This approach aims to exploit the well-developed
relational storage, query processing and optimization techniques in executing
SPARQL queries. Systems such as Sesame SQL92SAIL[10] and Oracle follow this
approach.

Example 12.16 Assuming that the table given in Fig. 12.15 is a relational table, the
example SPARQL query in Example 12.15 can be translated to the following SQL
query (where s,p,o correspond to column names: Subject, Property, Object):

```
SELECT T1.object
FROM  T AS T1, T AS T2, T AS T3,
T AS T4, T AS T5
WHERE T1.p="rdfs:label"
AND T2.p="movie:relatedBook"
AND T3.p="movie:director"
AND T4.p="rev:rating"
AND T5.p="movie:director_name"
AND T1.s=T2.s
AND T1.s=T3.s
AND T2.o=T4.s
AND T3.o=T5.s
AND T4.o > 4.0
AND T5.o="Stanley Kubrick"
```

◆

   As can be seen from this example, this approach results in a high number of self-
joins that are not easy to optimize. Furthermore, in large datasets, this single triples
table becomes very large, further complicating query processing.

---

[10]Sesame is built to interact with any storage system since it implements a Storage and Inference
Layer (SAIL) to interface with the particular storage system on which it sits. SQL92SAIL is the
specific instantiation to work on relational systems.

Single Table Extensive Indexing

One alternative to the problems created by direct relational mapping is to develop native storage systems that allow extensive indexing of the triple table. Hexastore and RDF-3X are examples of this approach. The single table is maintained, but extensively indexed. For example, RDF-3X creates indexes for all six possible permutations of the subject, property, and object: (spo, sop,ops,ops,sop,pos). Each of these indexes is sorted lexicographically by the first column, followed by the second column, followed by the third column. These are then stored in the leaf pages of a clustered B^+-tree.

The advantage of this type of organization is that SPARQL queries can be efficiently processed regardless of where the variables occur (subject, property, object) since one of the indexes will be applicable. Furthermore, it allows for index-based query processing that eliminates some of the self-joins—they are turned into range queries over the particular index. Even when joins are required, fast merge-join can be used since each index is sorted on the first column. The obvious disadvantages are, of course, the space usage, and the overhead of updating the multiple indexes if data is dynamic.

Property Tables

Property tables approach exploits the regularity exhibited in RDF datasets where there are repeated occurrence of patterns of statements. Consequently, it stores "related" properties in the same table. The first system that proposed this approach is Jena; IBM's DB2RDF also follows the same strategy. In both of these cases, the resulting tables are mapped to a relational system and the queries are converted to SQL for execution.

Jena defines two types of property tables. The first type, which can be called *clustered property table*, group together the properties that tend to occur in the same (or similar) subjects. It defines different table structures for single-valued properties versus multivalued properties. For single-valued properties, the table contains the subject column and a number of property columns (Fig. 12.19a). The value for a given property may be null if there is no RDF triple that uses the subject and that property. Each row of the table represents a number of RDF triples—the same number as the nonnull property values. For these tables, the subject is the primary key. For multivalued properties, the table structure includes the subject and the multivalued property (Fig. 12.19b). Each row of this table represents a single RDF triple; the key of the table is the compound key (subject, property). The mapping of the single triple table to property tables is a database design problem that is done by a database administrator.

Jena also defines a *property class table* that cluster the subjects with the same *type* of property into one property table (Fig. 12.19c). In this case, all members of a class (recall our discussion of class structure within the context of RDFS) together

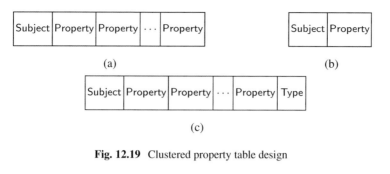

Fig. 12.19   Clustered property table design

Fig. 12.20   DB2RDF table design. (a) DPH. (b) DS

in one table. The "Type" column is the value of rdf:type for each property in that row.

Example 12.17 The example dataset in Example 12.14 may be organized to create one table that includes the properties of subjects that are films, one table for properties of directors, one table for properties of actors, one table for properties of books and so on.   ◆

IBM DB2RDF also follows the same strategy, but with a more dynamic table organization (Fig. 12.20). The table, called *direct primary hash* (DPH) is organized by each subject, but instead of manually identifying "similar" properties, the table accommodates k property columns, each of which can be assigned a different property in different rows. Each property column is, in fact, two columns: one that holds the property label, and the other that holds the value. If the number of properties for a given subject is greater than k, then the extra properties are spilled onto a second row and this is marked on the "spill" column. For multivalued properties, a *direct secondary hash* (DSH) table is maintained—the original property value stores a unique identifier l_id, which appears in the DS table along with the values.

The advantage of property table approach is that joins in star queries (i.e., subject-subject joins) become single table scans. Therefore, the translated query has fewer joins. The disadvantages are that in either of the two forms discussed above, there could be a significant number of null values in the tables, and dealing with multivalued properties requires special care. Furthermore, although star queries can be handled efficiently, this approach may not help much with other query types. Finally, when manual assignment is used, clustering "similar" properties is nontrivial and bad design decisions exacerbate the null value problem.

Binary Tables

Binary tables approach follows column-oriented database schema organization and defines a two-column table for each property containing the subject and object. This results in a set of tables each of which is ordered by the subject. This is a typical column-oriented database organization and benefits from the usual advantages of such systems such as reduced I/O due to reading only the needed properties and reduced tuple length, compression due to redundancy in the column values, etc. In addition, it avoids the null values that is experienced in property tables as well as the need for manual or automatic clustering algorithms for "similar" properties, and naturally supports multivalued properties—each becomes a separate row as in the case of Jena's DS table. Furthermore, since tables are ordered on subjects, subject-subject joins can be implemented using efficient merge-joins. The shortcomings are that the queries require more join operations some of which may be subject-object joins that are not helped by the merge-join operation. Furthermore, insertions into the tables have higher overhead since multiple tables need to be updated. It has been argued that the insertion problem can be mitigated by batch insertions, but in dynamic RDF repositories the difficulty of insertions is likely to remain a significant problem. The proliferation of the number of tables may have a negative impact on the scalability (with respect to the number of properties) of binary tables approach.

Example 12.18 For example, the binary table representation of the dataset given in Example 12.14 would create one table for each unique property—there are 18 of them. Two of these tables are shown in Fig. 12.21.   ◆

Graph-Based Processing

Graph-based RDF processing approaches fundamentally implement the semantics of RDF queries as defined at the beginning of this section. In other words, they maintain the graph structure of the RDF data (using some representation such as adjacency lists), convert the SPARQL query to a query graph, and do subgraph

Subject	Object
film/2014	"The Shining"
film/2685	"A Clockwork Orange"
film/424	"Spartacus"
film/1267	"The Last Tycoon"
film/3418	"The Passenger"
iso639-3/eng	"English"

(a)

Subject	Object
film/2014	actor/29704
film/2014	actor/30013
film/1267	actor/29704
film/3418	actor/29704

(b)

Fig. 12.21 Binary table organization of properties (**a**) "rdfs:label" and (**b**) "movie:actor" from the example dataset (prefixes are removed)

matching using homomorphism to evaluate the query against the RDF graph. Systems such as gStore, and chameleon-db follow this approach.

The advantage of this approach is that it maintains the original representation of the RDF data and enforces the intended semantics of SPARQL. The disadvantage is the cost of subgraph matching—graph homomorphism is NP-complete. This raises issues with respect to the scalability of this approach to large RDF graphs; typical database techniques including indexing can be used to address this issue. In the remainder, we present the approach within the context of the gStore system to highlight the issues.

gStore uses adjacency list representation of graphs. It encodes each entity and class vertex into a fixed length bit string that captures the "neighborhood" information for each vertex and exploits this during graph matching. This results is the generation of a *data signature graph* G^*, in which each vertex corresponds to a class or an entity vertex in the RDF graph G. Specifically, G^* is induced by all entity and class vertices in the original RDF graph G together with the edges whose endpoints are either entity or class vertices. Figure 12.22a shows the data signature graph G^* that corresponds to RDF graph G in Fig. 12.16. An incoming SPARQL query is also represented as a *query graph* Q that is similarly encoded into a *query*

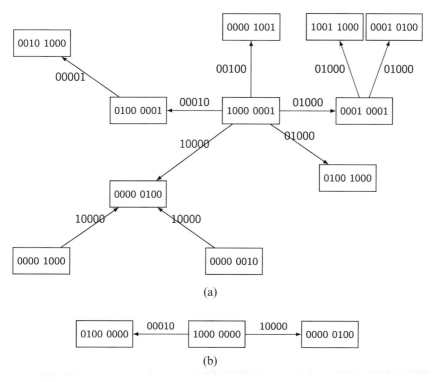

Fig. 12.22   Signature graphs. (a) Data signature graph G^*. (b) Query signature graph Q^*

signature graph Q^*. The encoding of query graph depicted in Fig. 12.17 into a query signature graph Q_2^* is shown in Fig. 12.22b.

The problem now turns into finding matches of Q^* over G^*. Although both the RDF graph and the query graph are smaller as a result of encoding, the NP-completeness of the problem remains. Therefore, gStore uses a filter-and-evaluate strategy to reduce the search space over which matching is applied. The objective is to first use a false-positive pruning strategy to find a set of candidate subgraphs (denoted as CL), and then validate these using the adjacency list to find answers (denoted as RS). Accordingly, two issues need to be addressed. First, the encoding technique should guarantee that $RS \subseteq CL$—the encoding described above provably achieves this. Second, an efficient subgraph matching algorithm is required to find matches of Q^* over G^*. For this, gStore uses an index structure called VS*-tree that is a summary graph of G^*. VS*-tree is used to efficiently process queries using a pruning strategy to reduce the search space for finding matches of Q^* over G^*.

Distributed and Federated SPARQL Execution

As RDF collections grow, scale-out solutions to scaling have been developed involving parallel and distributed processing. Many of these solutions divide an RDF graph G into several fragments and place each at a different site in a parallel/distributed system. Each site hosts a centralized RDF store of some kind. At runtime, a SPARQL query Q is decomposed into several subqueries such that each subquery can be answered locally at one site, and the results are then aggregated. Each of these papers proposes its own data partitioning strategy, and different partitioning strategies result in different query processing methods. Some of the approaches use MapReduce-based solutions where RDF triples are stored in HDFS and each triple pattern is evaluated by scanning the HDFS files followed by a MapReduce join implementation. Other approaches follow more or less the distributed/parallel query processing methodologies described in detail in various chapters of this book whereby the query is partitioned into subqueries and evaluated across the sites.

An alternative that has been proposed is to use partial query evaluation for executing distributed SPARQL queries. Partial function evaluation is a well-known programming language strategy whose basic idea is the following: given a function $f(s, d)$, where s is the known input and d is the yet unavailable input, the part of f's computation that depends only on s generates a partial answer. In this approach, data is partitioned, but queries are not—each site receives the full SPARQL query Q and executes it on the local RDF graph fragment providing data parallel computation. In this particular setting, the partial evaluation strategy is applied as follows: each site S_i treats fragment F_i as the known input in the partial evaluation stage; the unavailable input is the rest of the graph ($\overline{G} = G \setminus F_i$). There are two important issues to be addressed in this framework. The first is to compute the partial evaluation results at each site S_i given a query graph Q—in other words, addressing the graph homomorphism of Q over F_i; this is called the *local partial match* since it finds the matches internal to fragment F_i. Since ensuring edge disjointness is not possible in vertex-disjoint partitioning, there will be *crossing edges* between graph fragments. The second task is the assembly of these local partial matches to compute crossing matches. This assembly task can be executed either on a control site or similar to distributed join.

The above approaches take a centralized RDF dataset and partition it for distributed/parallel execution. In many RDF settings, concerns arise similar to what we discussed in database integration requiring a federated solution. In the RDF world, some of the sites that host RDF data also have the capability to process SPARQL queries; these are called *SPARQL endpoints*. A typical example is LOD, where different RDF repositories are interconnected, providing a *virtually integrated distributed database*. A common technique in federated RDF environments is to precompute metadata for each individual SPARQL endpoint. The metadata can specify the capabilities of the end point or a description of the triple patterns (i.e., property) that can be answered at that endpoint, or other information that the particular algorithm uses. Based on the metadata, the original SPARQL query is decomposed into several subqueries, where each subquery is sent to its relevant SPARQL endpoints. The results of subqueries are then joined together to answer the original SPARQL query.

An alternative to precomputing metadata is to make use of SPARQL ASK queries to gather information about each endpoint and to construct the metadata on the fly. Based on the results of these queries, a SPARQL query is decomposed into subqueries and assigned to endpoints.

12.6.2.3   Navigating and Querying the LOD

LOD consists of a set of *web documents*. The starting point, therefore, is a web document with embedded RDF triples that encode web resources. The RDF triples contain *data links* to other documents that allow web documents to be interconnected to get the graph structure.

The semantics of SPARQL queries over the LOD becomes tricky. One possibility is to adopt *full web semantics* that specifies the scope of evaluating a SPARQL query expression to be all linked data. There is no known (terminating) query execution algorithm that can guarantee result completeness under this semantics. The alternative is a family of *reachability-based semantics* that define the scope of evaluating a SPARQL query in terms of the documents that can be reached: given a set of seed URIs and a reachability condition, the scope is all data along the paths of the data links from the seeds and that satisfy the reachability condition. The family is defined by different reachability conditions. In this case, there are computationally feasible algorithms.

There are three approaches to SPARQL query execution over LOD: traversal-based, index-based, and hybrid. *Traversal approaches* basically implement a reachability-based semantics: starting from seed URIs, they recursively discover relevant URIs by traversing specific data links at query execution runtime. For these algorithms, the selection of the seed URIs is critical for performance. The advantage of traversal approaches is their simplicity (to implement) since they do not need to maintain any data structures (such as indexes). The disadvantages are the latency of query execution since these algorithms "browse" web documents, and repeated data retrieval from each document introduces significant latency. They also have limited possibility for parallelization—they can be parallelized to the same extent that crawling algorithms can.

The *index-based approaches* use an index to determine relevant URIs, thereby reducing the number of linked documents that need to be accessed. A reasonable index key is triple patterns in which case the "relevant" URIs for a given query are determined by accessing the index, and the query is evaluated over the data retrieved by accessing those URIs. In these approaches, data retrieval can be fully parallelized, which reduces the negative impact of data retrieval on query execution time. The disadvantages of the approach are the dependence on the index—both in terms of the latency that index construction introduces and in terms of the restriction the index imposes on what can be selected—and the freshness issues that result from the dynamicity of the web and the difficulty of keeping the index up-to-date.

Hybrid approaches perform a traversal-based execution using prioritized listing of URIs for look-up. The initial seeds come from a prepopulated index; new discovered URIs that are not in the index are ranked according to number of referring documents.

12.6.3   Data Quality Issues in Web Data Integration

In Chap. 7 (specifically in Sect. 7.1.5) we discussed data quality and data cleaning issues in the case of database integration (mainly data warehousing) systems. Data quality issues in web data are only more severe due to the sheer number of web data sources, the uncontrolled data entry process of web information sources, and the increased data diversity. Data quality encompasses both data consistency and veracity (authenticity and conformity of data with reality). In a data warehouse, data consistency is obtained through data cleaning, which deals with detecting and removing errors and inconsistencies from data. Data cleaning in the web context (and also in data lakes) is made difficult by the lack of schema information and the limited number of integrity constraints that can be defined without a schema.

Checking for data veracity remains a big challenge. However, if many different data sources overlap, as it is often the case with data coming from the web for instance, there will be a high-level of redundancy. It may be possible to use efficient data fusion techniques (to be discussed shortly) to detect the correct values for the same data items, and thus discover the truth.

In this section, we highlight some of the main data quality and data cleaning issues in web data and discuss current solutions for addressing them.

12.6.3.1   Cleaning Structured Web Data

Structured data represents an important category of data on the web, and they suffer from numerous data quality issues. In the following, we first summarize the techniques proposed in cleaning structured data in general. Then, we point out the unique challenges in cleaning structured data on the web.

Figure 12.23 shows a typical workflow for cleaning structured data, consisting of an optional discovery and profiling step, an error detection step, and an error repair step. To clean a dirty dataset, we often need to model various aspects of this data (metadata), e.g., schema, patterns, probability distributions, and other metadata. One way to obtain such metadata is by consulting domain experts, which is usually a costly and a time-consuming process, hence a discovery and profiling step is often used to discover these metadata automatically. Given a dirty dataset and the associated metadata, the error detection step finds part of the data that do not conform to the metadata, and declares this subset to contain errors. The errors surfaced by the error detection step can be in various forms, such as outliers, violations of integrity constraints, and duplicates. Finally, the error repair step produces data updates that are applied to the dirty dataset to remove detected errors. Since there are many uncertainties in the data cleaning process, external sources such as knowledge bases and human experts are consulted whenever possible to ensure the accuracy of the cleaning workflow.

The above process works well for structured tables that have a rich set of metadata, e.g., large schema with enough constraints to model columns and rows interactions. Also, the cleaning and error detection process works better when there are enough examples (tuples) for automatic algorithms to compare various instances to detect possible errors, and to leverage the redundancy in the data to correct these

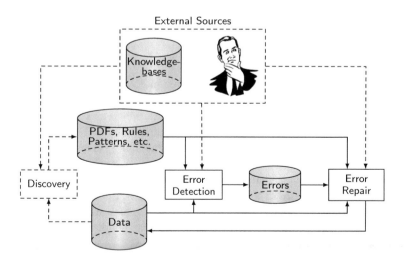

Fig. 12.23 A typical workflow for cleaning structured data

Sevilla - Jerez de la Frontera-Cádiz	1861
Córdoba - Málaga	1865.
Bobadilla - Granada	1874
Córdoba - Bélmez	1874
Osuna	La Roda

(a)

Polaco	15.04.1983	194	84
Vini	29.09.1982	N/A	N/A
Caiao	30/11/1982	N/A	N/A
Jairo	17.02.1990	N/A	N/A
Michael	20.04.1983	N/A	N/A
Ricardinho	19.11.1975	192	94

(b)

2002[12]	10.300 oz	899,500 oz
2005[13]	25.272	2.174.620 oz
2006[13]	49.354 oz	3.005.611 oz
2007[13]	48.807 oz	3.165408 oz
2008[9]	47.755 oz	3.157.837 oz
2009^2	0.9 million oz	818.050 oz

(c)

WARRIORS@Susses Thunder	13-28	—
WARRIORS@Hampshire Thrashers	42-13	—
Essex Spartans@WARRIORS	P-P	Postponed
WARRIORS@Cambridgeshire Cats	36-44	—
East Kent Mavericks@WARRIORS	12-18	—
WARRIORS@East Kent Mavericks	15-17	—

(d)

Fig. 12.24 Data quality issues on structured web data (erroneous data is marked in red cells). Adapted from [Huang and He 2018]. (**a**) Extra dot. (**b**) Mixed dates. (**c**) Inconsistent weights. (**d**) Score placeholder

errors. However, in web tables, both of these premises are not satisfied, as most of the tables are short (few tuples) and skinny (limited number of attributes). o make matters worse, the number of web tables is far greater than the number of tables in a data warehouse. This means that manual cleaning, though relatively for a single web table, is not feasible for all structured web tables. Figure 12.24 shows some sample errors found on Wikipedia tables, and there is an estimated 300K such errors.

12.6.3.2   Web Data Fusion

A common problem that arises often in web data integration is data fusion, namely deciding what is the correct value for an item that has different representations from multiple web sources. The problem is that different web sources can provide conflicting representations, and thus making data fusion hard. There are two types of data conflicts: *uncertainty* and *contradiction*. Uncertainty is a conflict between a nonnull value and one or more null values that are used to describe the same property of a real world entity. Uncertainty is caused by missing information, usually represented by null values in a source. Contradiction is a conflict between two or more different nonnull values that represent different values of the same property of a real world entity. Contradiction is caused by different sources providing different values for the same attribute.

Automatic cleaning of web tables is thus particularly challenging. While cleaning techniques developed in the context of data warehouse can be applied to clean some

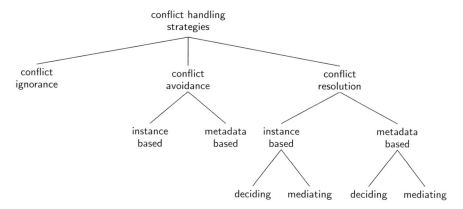

Fig. 12.25 Classification of strategies for data fusion. From [Bleiholder and Naumann 2009]

errors, cleaning web tables deserve more dedicated techniques. Auto-Detect is a recent proposal that aims at detecting such errors on web tables. Auto-Detect is a data-driven statistics-based techniques that leverage value co-occurrence statistics from large corpora for error detection. The main assumption is that if a certain value combination is extremely rare (quantified using point-wise mutual information), then it suggests a potential error. While Auto-Detect is able to detect many errors, it does not suggest data fixes. We have yet to see proposals that automatically repair errors (or even suggest fixes) in web table.

Figure 12.25 shows the classification of different data fusing strategies. *Conflict ignorance* strategies ignore the conflicts and simply pass the conflicts to the users or applications. *Conflict avoidance* strategies acknowledge the existence of conflicting representations, and apply a simple rule to take a unique decision based on either the data instance or the metadata. An example of instance based conflict avoidance strategy is to prefer nonnull values over null values. An example of metadata based conflict avoidance strategy is to prefer values from one source over values from another. *Conflict resolution* strategies resolve the conflicts, by picking a value from the already present values (deciding) or by choosing a value that does not necessarily exist among present values (mediating). An example of instance based, deciding conflict resolution strategy is to take the most frequent value. An example of instance based, mediating conflict resolution strategy is to take the average of all present values.

12.6.3.3 Web Source Quality

These basic conflict resolution strategies described above mostly rely on participating values to resolve conflicts, and they can fall short in the following three aspects. First, web sources have different qualities; data values provided by more accurate web sources are usually more accurate. However, more accurate web sources can also provide incorrect values, therefore, an advanced resolution strategy is often needed to take source quality into consideration when predicting the correct value. Second, web sources can copy from each other, and ignoring these kinds of dependencies between web sources can cause wrong resolution decisions. For example, the majority vote strategy to resolve conflicts would be affected if some data items in a source are copied. Third, the correct value for a data item may evolve over time as well (e.g., a person's affiliation), hence, it is therefore crucial to distinguish between incorrect value and *outdated* value when evaluating source accuracies and making resolution decisions.

The building block of advanced data fusion strategies is to evaluate the trustworthiness or quality of a source. In this section, we discuss how the accuracy of a data source is modeled, and we mention how that model is extended to handle source dependencies and source freshness.

Source Accuracy

The accuracy of a source can be measured as the fraction of true values provided by a source. The accuracy of a source S is denoted by $A(S)$, which can be considered as the probability that a value provided by S is the true value. Let $V(S)$ denote the values provided by S. For each $v \in V(S)$, let $Pr(v)$ denote the probability that v is the true value. Then $A(S)$ is computed as follows:

$$A(S) = Avg_{v \in V(S)} Pr(v)$$

Consider a data item D. Let $Dom(D)$ be the domain of D, including one true value and n false values. Let S_D be the set of sources that provide a value for D, and let $S_D(v) \subseteq S_D$ be the set of sources that provide the value v for D. Let $\Phi(D)$ denote the observation of which value each $S \in S_D$ provides for D. The probability $Pr(v)$ can be computed as follows:

$$Pr(v) = Pr(v \text{ is true value}|\Phi(D)) \propto Pr(\Phi(D)|v \text{ is true value})$$

Assume that sources are independent and that the n false values are equally likely to happen, $Pr(\Phi(D)|v \text{ is true value})$ can be computed as follows:

$$Pr(\Phi(D)|v \text{ is true value}) = \prod_{S \in S_D(v)} A(S) \prod_{S \in S_D \backslash S_D(v)} \frac{1 - A(S)}{n}$$

which can be rewritten as

$$Pr(\Phi(D)|v \text{ is true value}) = \prod_{S \in S_D(v)} \frac{nA(S)}{1 - A(S)} \prod_{S \in S_D} \frac{1 - A(S)}{n}$$

Since $\prod_{S\in S_D} \frac{1-A(S)}{n}$ is the same for all values, we have

$$Pr(\Phi(D)|v \text{ is true value}) \propto \prod_{S\in S_D(v)} \frac{nA(S)}{1-A(S)}$$

Accordingly, the *vote count* of a data source S is defined as:

$$C(S) = ln\frac{nA(S)}{1-A(S)}$$

The *vote count* of a value v is defined as:

$$C(v) = \sum_{S\ in S_D(v)} C(S)$$

Intuitively, a source with a higher vote count is more accurate and a value with a higher vote count is more likely to be true. Combining the above analysis, the probability of each value v can be computed as follows:

$$Pr(v) = \frac{exp(C(v))}{\sum_{v_0\ in Dom(v)} exp(C(v_0))}$$

Obviously, for a data item D, the value $v \in Dom(D)$ with the highest probability $Pr(v)$ would be selected as the true value. As we can see, the computation of the source accuracy $A(S)$ depends on the probability $Pr(v)$, and the computation of the probability $Pr(v)$ depends on the source accuracy $A(S)$. An algorithm is possible that starts with the same accuracy for every source and the same probability for every value, and iteratively computes probabilities for all sources and probabilities for all values until convergence. The convergence criteria is set to be when there is no change in source accuracies and no oscillation in decided true values.

Source Dependency

The above computation for source accuracy assumes that sources are independent. In reality, sources copy from each other, which creates dependencies. There are two intuitions for copy detection between sources. First, for a particular data item, there is only one true value, but there are usually multiple false values. Two sources sharing the same true value does not necessarily imply dependency; however, two sources sharing the same false value is typically a rare event, and thus would more likely imply source dependency. Second, a random subset of values provided by a data source would typically have similar accuracies as the full set of values provided by the data source. However, for a copier data source, the subset of values it copies may have different accuracies than the rest of the values it provides independently.

Thus, between two dependent sources where one copies another, the source whose own data values' accuracies differ significantly from the values shared with the other source is more likely to be the copier. Based on these intuitions, a Bayesian model can be developed to compute the probability of copying between two sources S_1 and S_2 given the observations Φ on all data items; this probability is then used to adjust the computation of the vote count for a value $C(v)$ to account for source dependencies.

Source Freshness

We have so far assumed that data fusion is done on a static snapshot of the data. However, in reality, data evolves over time and the true value for an item might change as well. For example, the scheduled departure time for a flight might change in different months; a person's affiliation might change over time; and the CEO of a company could also change. To capture such changes, data sources will need to update their data. In this dynamic setting, data errors occur for these several reasons: (1) the sources may provide wrong values, similar to the static setting; (2) the sources may fail to update their data at all; and (3) some sources may not update their data in time. Data fusion, in this context, aims at finding all correct values and their valid periods in the history, when the true values evolve over time. While the source quality can be capture by accuracy in the static case, the metrics for evaluating source quality are more complicated in the dynamic setting—a high-quality source should provide a new value for a data item *if and only if*, and *right after* the value becomes the true value. Three metrics can be used to capture this intuition: the *coverage* of a source measures the transitions of different data items that it captures; the *exactness* measures the percentage of transitions a source mis-captures (by providing a wrong value); and the *freshness* measures how quickly a value change is captured by a source. Again, it is possible to rely on Bayesian analysis to decide both the time and the value of each transition for a data item.

Machine learning and probabilistic models have also been used in data fusion and modeling data source quality. In particular, SLiMFast is a framework that expresses data fusion as a statistical learning problem over discriminative probabilistic models. In contrast to previous learning-based fusion approaches, SLiMFast provides quality guarantees for the fused results, and it can also incorporate available domain knowledge in the fusion process. Figure 12.26 provides the system overview of SLiMFast. The input to SLiMFast includes (1) a collection of source observations, namely the possibly conflicting values provided for different objects by different sources; (2) an optional set of labeled ground truth, namely the true values for a subset of objects; and (3) some domain knowledge about sources that users deem to be informative of the accuracies of data sources. SLiMFast takes all of these information, and compiles them into a probabilistic graphical model for holistic learning and inference. Depending on the how much ground truth data is available, SLiMFast will decide which algorithm (expectation-maximization or empirical loss minimization) to use for learning the parameters of the graphical models. The

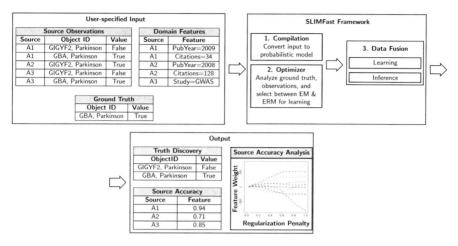

Fig. 12.26   Overview of SLiMFast. From [Rekatsinas et al. 2017]

learned model is then used for inferring both the value of objects and the source accuracies, as shown in the output.

12.7   Bibliographic Notes

There are a number of good sources on web topics, each with a slightly different focus. Abiteboul et al. [2011] focus on the use of XML and RDF for web data modeling and also contain discussions of search, and big data technologies such as MapReduce. A web data warehousing perspective is given in [Bhowmick et al. 2004]. Bonato [2008] primarily focuses on the modeling of the web as a graph and how this graph can be exploited. Early work on the web query languages and approaches are discussed in [Abiteboul et al. 1999].

A very good overview of web search issues is [Arasu et al. 2001], which we also follow in Sect. 12.2. Additionally, Lawrence and Giles [1998] provides an earlier discussion on the same topic focusing on the open web. Florescu et al. [1998] survey web search issues from a database perspective. Deep (hidden) web is the topic of [Raghavan and Garcia-Molina 2001]. Lage et al. [2002] and Hedley et al. [2004b] also discuss search over the deep web and the analysis of the results. Metasearch for accessing the deep web is discussed in [Ipeirotis and Gravano 2002, Callan and Connell 2001, Callan et al. 1999, Hedley et al. 2004a]. The metasearch-related problem of database selection is discussed by Ipeirotis and Gravano [2002] and Gravano et al. [1999] (GlOSS algorithm).

Statistics about the open web are taken from [Bharat and Broder 1998, Lawrence and Giles 1998, 1999, Gulli and Signorini 2005] and those related to the deep web are due to [Hirate et al. 2006] and [Bergman 2001].

The graph structure of the web and using graphs to model and query the web is the topic of many publications: [Kumar et al. 2000, Raghavan and Garcia-Molina 2003, Kleinberg et al. 1999] discuss web graph modeling, [Kleinberg et al. 1999, Brin and Page 1998, Kleinberg 1999] focus on graphs for search, and [Chakrabarti et al. 1998] for categorization and classification of web content. The discussion on the characteristics of the web graph and its bow-tie structure are due to Bonato [2008], Broder et al. [2000] and Kumar et al. [2000]. We did not discuss the important issues related to the management of the very large, dynamic, and volatile web graph. These are beyond the scope of this chapter, but two lines of research can be identified. The first one compresses the web graph for more efficient storage and manipulation [Adler and Mitzenmacher 2001], while the second one suggests a special representation for the web graph called S-nodes [Raghavan and Garcia-Molina 2003].

Issues on web crawling are the subject of [Cho et al. 1998, Najork and Wiener 2001] and [Page et al. 1998], the latter being the classical paper on PageRank whose revised form as discussed in this chapter is due to Langville and Meyer [2006]. Alternative crawling approaches are the subjects of [Cho and Garcia-Molina 2000] (change frequency-based), [Cho and Ntoulas 2002] (sampling-based) and [Edwards et al. 2001] (incremental). Classification techniques for evaluating relevance are discussed by [Mitchell 1997, Chakrabarti et al. 2002] (naïve Bayes), Passerini et al. [2001], Altingövde and Ulusoy [2004] (extensions of Beyesian), and by McCallum et al. [1999], Kaelbling et al. [1996] (reinforcement learning).

Web indexing is an important issue that we discussed in Sect. 12.2.2. Various text indexing methods are discussed in [Manber and Myers 1990] (suffix arrays), [Hersh 2001] [Lim et al. 2003] (inverted indexes), and [Faloutsos and Christodoulakis 1984] (signature files). Salton [1989] is probably the classical source for text processing and analysis. The challenges of building inverted indexes for the web and solutions are discussed by Arasu et al. [2001], Melnik et al. [2001], and Ribeiro-Neto and Barbosa [1998]. Related to this, ranking has been the topic of extensive research. In addition to the well-known PageRank, the HITS algorithm is due to Kleinberg [1999].

In our discussion of semistructured data approach to web querying we highlighted OEM data model and the Lorel language to expose the concepts. These are discussed in [Papakonstantinou et al. 1995] and [Abiteboul et al. 1997]. The data guides to simplify OEM are discussed in [Goldman and Widom 1997]. UnQL [Buneman et al. 1996] has similar concepts to Lorel. Our discussion of web query languages in Sect. 12.3.2 separated the languages into first and second generation; this is due to Florescu et al. [1998]. First generation languages include WebSQL [Mendelzon et al. 1997], W3QL [Konopnicki and Shmueli 1995], and WebLog [Lakshmanan et al. 1996]. The second generation languages include WebOQL [Arocena and Mendelzon 1998], and StruQL [Fernandez et al. 1997]. In the Query-Answering approach we referred to a number of systems: Mulder [Kwok et al. 2001], WebQA [Lam and Özsu 2002], Start [Katz and Lin 2002], and Tritus [Agichtein et al. 2004].

The components of the semantic web is presented by Antoniou and Plexousakis [2018]. The Linked Open Data (LOD) vision and its requirements are discussed by Bizer et al. [2018] and Berners-Lee [2006]. The topical domain separation of LOD is outlined in [Schmachtenberg et al. 2014].

Our discussion of RDF is primarily based on [Özsu 2016]. Five main approaches are described to managing RDF data: (1) direct relational mapping—Angles and Gutierrez [2008], Sequeda et al. [2014] discuss mapping SPARQL to SQL, Broekstra et al. [2002], and Chong et al. [2005] discuss Sesame SQL92SAIL and Oracle, respectively; (2) using a single table with extensive indexing (Hexastore [Weiss et al. 2008] and RDF-3X [Neumann and Weikum 2008, 2009]); (3) property tables (Jena [Wilkinson 2006]; IBM's DB2RDF [Bornea et al. 2013]); (4) binary tables (SW-Store [Abadi et al. 2009] based on the proposal by Abadi et al. [2007]) whose problems in terms of table proliferation is discussed in [Sidirourgos et al. 2008]; (5) graph-based ([Bönström et al. 2003], gStore [Zou et al. 2011, 2014], and chameleon-db [Aluç 2015]). Graph-based techniques are discussed in detail by Zou and Özsu [2017]. The distributed and cloud-based SPARQL execution is addressed in [Kaoudi and Manolescu 2015]. Three approaches are identified for SPARQL query execution over LOD [Hartig 2013a]: traversal-based [Hartig 2013b, Ladwig and Tran 2011], index-based [Umbrich et al. 2011], and hybrid [Ladwig and Tran 2010].

Cleaning structured data has been extensively studied in warehouse integration settings [Rahm and Do 2000] and [Ilyas and Chu 2015]. Expansion to a broader context, including the web, is covered in Ilyas and Chu [2019]. In our discussion of data fusion (Sect. 12.6.3.2), the separation of data conflicts into *uncertainty* and *contradiction* is due to Dong and Naumann [2009]. In the same section, the discussion of Auto-Detect is due to [Huang and He 2018] and the classification discussion (as well as Fig. 12.25) is from [Bleiholder and Naumann 2009]. The discussion of data source modeling accuracy in Sect. 12.6.3.3, its extension to handle source dependencies and source freshness are due to Dong et al. [2009b,a]. For a more comprehensive treatment on the subject of advanced data fusion, we refer readers to the tutorial [Dong and Naumann 2009] and the book [Dong and Srivastava 2015]. The SlimFAST system (see Fig. 12.26) is presented in [Rekatsinas et al. 2017] and [Koller and Friedman 2009].

One of the first systems to deal with data cleaning issues in data lakes is CLAMS [Farid et al. 2016], which allows discovering and enforcing integrity constraints over a data lake's data. CLAMS uses a graph data model, based on RDF, and a new integrity constraint formalism to capture both relational constraints and more expressive quality rules based on graph patterns as *denial constraints* [Chu et al. 2013]. CLAMS also uses Spark and parallel algorithms to enforce the constraints and detect data inconsistencies.

Exercises

Problem 12.1 How does web search differ from web querying?

Problem 12.2 (**) Consider the generic search engine architecture in Fig. 12.2. Propose an architecture for a web site with a shared-nothing cluster that implements all the components in this figure as well as web servers in an environment that will support very large sets of web documents and very large indexes, and very high numbers of web users. Define how web pages in the page directory and indexes should be partitioned and replicated. Discuss the main advantages of your architecture with respect to scalability, fault-tolerance, and performance.

Problem 12.3 (**) Consider your solution in Problem 12.2. Now consider a keyword search query from a web client to the web search engine. Propose a parallel execution strategy for the query that ranks the result web pages, with a summary of each web page.

Problem 12.4 (*) To increase locality of access and performance in different geographical regions, propose an extension of the web site architecture in Problem 12.3 with multiple sites, with web pages being replicated at all sites. Define how web pages are replicated. Define also how a user query is routed to a web site. Discuss the advantages of your architecture with respect to scalability, availability and performance.

Problem 12.5 (*) Consider your solution in Problem 12.4. Now consider a keyword search query from a web client to the web search engine. Propose a parallel execution strategy for the query that ranks the result web pages, with a summary of each web page.

Problem 12.6 (**) Consider two web data sources that we model as relations EMP1(Name, City, Phone) and EMP2(Firstname, Lastname, City). After schema integration, assume the view EMP(Firstname, Name, City, Phone) defined over EMP1 and EMP2, where each attribute in EMP comes from an attribute of EMP1 or EMP2, with EMP2. Lastname being renamed as Name. Discuss the limitations of such integration. Now consider that the two web data sources are XML. Give a corresponding definition of the XML schemas of EMP1 and EMP2. Propose an XML schema that integrates EMP1 and EMP2, and avoids the problems identified with EMP.

Correction to: Principles of Distributed Database Systems

Correction to:
M. T. Özsu, P. Valduriez,
***Principles of Distributed Database Systems*,**
https://doi.org/10.1007/978-3-030-26253-2

The figures included in the original version of this book has been replaced. The figures have been updated throughout the book in this version of the book. The updated figures can be accessed through the link below:

https://cs.uwaterloo.ca/~ddbook/errata.html

The updated version of the book can be found at
https://doi.org/10.1007/978-3-030-26253-2

© Springer Nature Switzerland AG 2020
M. T. Özsu, P. Valduriez, *Principles of Distributed Database Systems*,
https://doi.org/10.1007/978-3-030-26253-2_13

C1

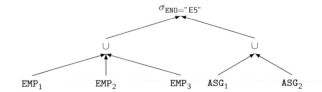

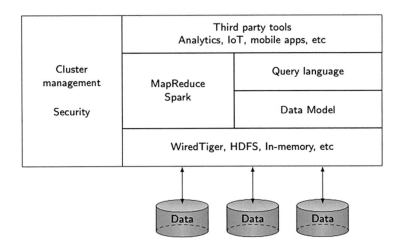

Appendix A
Overview of Relational DBMS

See https://cs.uwaterloo.ca/ddbs.

© Springer Nature Switzerland AG 2020

M. T. Özsu, P. Valduriez, *Principles of Distributed Database Systems*,
https://doi.org/10.1007/978-3-030-26253-2

Appendix B
Centralized Query Processing

See https://cs.uwaterloo.ca/ddbs.

© Springer Nature Switzerland AG 2020
M. T. Özsu, P. Valduriez, *Principles of Distributed Database Systems*,
https://doi.org/10.1007/978-3-030-26253-2

Appendix C
Transaction Processing Fundamentals

See https://cs.uwaterloo.ca/ddbs.

© Springer Nature Switzerland AG 2020   623
M. T. Özsu, P. Valduriez, *Principles of Distributed Database Systems*,
https://doi.org/10.1007/978-3-030-26253-2

Appendix D
Review of Computer Networks

See https://cs.uwaterloo.ca/ddbs.

© Springer Nature Switzerland AG 2020

M. T. Özsu, P. Valduriez, *Principles of Distributed Database Systems*,
https://doi.org/10.1007/978-3-030-26253-2

References

Abadi, D. J., Carney, D., Çetintemel, U., Cherniack, M., Convey, C., Lee, S., Stonebraker, M., Tatbul, N., and Zdonik, S. (2003). Aurora: a new model and architecture for data stream management. *VLDB J.*, 12(2):120–139.

Abadi, D. J., Ahmad, Y., Balazinska, M., Çetintemel, U., Cherniack, M., Hwang, J.-H., Lindner, W., Maskey, A., Rasin, A., Ryvkina, E., Tatbul, N., Xing, Y., and Zdonik, S. B. (2005). The design of the Borealis stream processing engine. In *Proc. 2nd Biennial Conf. on Innovative Data Systems Research*, pages 277–289.

Abadi, D. J., Marcus, A., Madden, S. R., and Hollenbach, K. (2007). Scalable semantic web data management using vertical partitioning. In *Proc. 33rd Int. Conf. on Very Large Data Bases*, pages 411–422.

Abadi, D. J., Marcus, A., Madden, S., and Hollenbach, K. (2009). SW-Store: a vertically partitioned DBMS for semantic web data management. *VLDB J.*, 18(2):385–406.

Aberer, K. (2001). P-grid: A self-organizing access structure for P2P information systems. In *Proc. Int. Conf. on Cooperative Inf. Syst.*, pages 179–194.

Aberer, K. (2003). Guest editor's introduction. *ACM SIGMOD Rec.*, 32(3):21–22.

Aberer, K., Cudré-Mauroux, P., Datta, A., Despotovic, Z., Hauswirth, M., Punceva, M., and Schmidt, R. (2003a). P-grid: a self-organizing structured P2P system. *ACM SIGMOD Rec.*, 32(3):29–33.

Aberer, K., Cudré-Mauroux, P., and Hauswirth, M. (2003b). Start making sense: The chatty web approach for global semantic agreements. *J. Web Semantics*, 1(1):89–114.

Abiteboul, S., Quass, D., McHugh, J., Widom, J., and Wiener, J. (1997). The Lorel query language for semistructured data. *Int. J. Digit. Libr.*, 1(1):68–88.

Abiteboul, S., Buneman, P., and Suciu, D. (1999). *Data on the Web: From Relations to Semistructured Data and XML*. Morgan Kaufmann.

Abiteboul, S., Manolescu, I., Rigaux, P., Rousset, M.-C., and Senellart, P. (2011). *Web Data Management*. Cambridge University Press.

Abou-Rjeili, A. and Karypis, G. (2006). Multilevel algorithms for partitioning power-law graphs. In *Proc. 20th IEEE Int. Parallel & Distributed Processing Symp.*, pages 124–124.

Abouzeid, A., Bajda-Pawlikowski, K., Abadi, D., Silberschatz, A., and Rasin, A. (2009). HadoopDB: an architectural hybrid of MapReduce and DBMS technologies for analytical workloads. *Proc. VLDB Endowment*, 2(1):922–933.

Adali, S., Candan, K. S., Papakonstantinou, Y., and Subrahmanian, V. S. (1996a). Query caching and optimization in distributed mediator systems. In *Proc. ACM SIGMOD Int. Conf. on Management of Data*, pages 137–148.

© Springer Nature Switzerland AG 2020
M. T. Özsu, P. Valduriez, *Principles of Distributed Database Systems*,
https://doi.org/10.1007/978-3-030-26253-2

Adali, S., Candan, K. S., Papakonstantinou, Y., and Subrahmanian, V. S. (1996b). Query caching and optimization in distributed mediator systems. In *Proc. ACM SIGMOD Int. Conf. on Management of Data*, pages 137–148.

Adamic, L. and Huberman, B. (2000). The nature of markets in the world wide web. *Quart. J. Electron. Comm.*, 1:5–12.

Adiba, M. (1981). Derived relations: A unified mechanism for views, snapshots and distributed data. In *Proc. 7th Int. Conf. on Very Data Bases*, pages 293–305.

Adiba, M. and Lindsay, B. (1980). Database snapshots. In *Proc. 6th Int. Conf. on Very Data Bases*, pages 86–91.

Adler, M. and Mitzenmacher, M. (2001). Towards compressing web graphs. In *Proc. Data Compression Conf.*, pages 203–212.

Aggarwal, C. C., editor. (2007). *Data Streams: Models and Algorithms*. Springer.

Agichtein, E., Lawrence, S., and Gravano, L. (2004). Learning to find answers to questions on the web. *ACM Trans. Internet Tech.*, 4(3):129—162.

Agrawal, D. and Sengupta, S. (1993). Modular synchronization in distributed, multiversion databases: Version control and concurrency control. *IEEE Trans. Knowl. and Data Eng.*, 5 (1):126 –137.

Agrawal, D., Das, S., and El Abbadi, A. (2012). *Data Management in the Cloud: Challenges and Opportunities*. Synthesis Lectures on Data Management. Morgan & Claypool Publishers.

Agrawal, S., Narasayya, V., and Yang, B. (2004). Integrating vertical and horizontal partitioning into automated physical database design. In *Proc. ACM SIGMOD Int. Conf. on Management of Data*.

Akal, F., Böhm, K., and Schek, H.-J. (2002). Olap query evaluation in a database cluster: A performance study on intra-query parallelism. In *Proc. 6th East European Conf. Advances in Databases and Information Systems*, pages 218–231.

Akal, F., Türker, C., Schek, H.-J., Breitbart, Y., Grabs, T., and Veen, L. (2005). Fine-grained replication and scheduling with freshness and correctness guarantees. In *Proc. 31st Int. Conf. on Very Large Data Bases*, pages 565–576.

Akbarinia, R. and Martins, V. (2007). Data management in the APPA system. *J. Grid Comp.*, 5 (3):303–317.

Akbarinia, R., Martins, V., Pacitti, E., and Valduriez, P. (2006). Design and implementation of Atlas P2P architecture. In Baldoni, R., Cortese, G., and Davide, F., editors, *Global Data Management*, pages 98–123. IOS Press.

Akbarinia, R., Pacitti, E., and Valduriez, P. (2007a). Processing top-k queries in distributed hash tables. In *Proc. 13th Int. Euro-Par Conf.*, pages 489–502.

Akbarinia, R., Pacitti, E., and Valduriez, P. (2007b). Query processing in P2P systems. Technical Report 6112, INRIA, Rennes, France.

Akbarinia, R., Pacitti, E., and Valduriez, P. (2007c). Best position algorithms for top-k queries. In *Proc. 33rd Int. Conf. on Very Large Data Bases*, pages 495–506.

Akbarinia, R., Pacitti, E., and Valduriez, P. (2007d). Data currency in replicated dhts. In *Proc. ACM SIGMOD Int. Conf. on Management of Data*, pages 211–222.

Akidau, T., Balikov, A., Bekiroglu, K., Chernyak, S., Haberman, J., Lax, R., McVeety, S., Mills, D., Nordstrom, P., and Whittle, S. (2013). MillWheel: Fault-tolerant stream processing at internet scale. *Proc. VLDB Endowment*, 6(11):1033–1044.

Alagiannis, I., Borovica, R., Branco, M., Idreos, S., and Ailamaki, A. (2012). NoDB: efficient query execution on raw data files. In *Proc. ACM SIGMOD Int. Conf. on Management of Data*, pages 241–252.

Alagiannis, I., Idreos, S., and Ailamaki, A. (2014). H2O: A hands-free adaptive store. In *Proc. ACM SIGMOD Int. Conf. on Management of Data*, pages 1103–1114.

Alamoudi, A. A., Grover, R., Carey, M. J., and Borkar, V. R. (2015). External data access and indexing in AsterixDB. In *Proc. 24th ACM Int. Conf. on Information and Knowledge Management*, pages 3–12.

Albutiu, M.-C., Kemper, A., and Neumann, T. (2012). Massively parallel sort-merge joins in main memory multi-core database systems. *Proc. VLDB Endowment*, 5(10):1064–1075.

Allard, T., Hébrail, G., Masseglia, F., and Pacitti, E. (2015). Chiaroscuro: Transparency and privacy for massive personal time-series clustering. In *Proc. ACM SIGMOD Int. Conf. on Management of Data*, pages 779–794.

Alomari, M., Cahill, M., Fekete, A., and Rohm, U. (2008). The cost of serializability on platforms that use snapshot isolation. In *Proc. 24th Int. Conf. on Data Engineering*, pages 576 –585.

Alomari, M., Fekete, A., and Rohm, U. (2009). A robust technique to ensure serializable executions with snapshot isolation DBMS. In *Proc. 25th Int. Conf. on Data Engineering*, pages 341–352.

Alsberg, P. A. and Day, J. D. (1976). A principle for resilient sharing of distributed resources. In *Proc. 2nd Int. Conf. on Software Engineering*, pages 562–570.

Alsubaiee, S., Altowim, Y., Altwaijry, H., Behm, A., Borkar, V. R., Bu, Y., Carey, M. J., Cetindil, I., Cheelangi, M., Faraaz, K., Gabrielova, E., Grover, R., Heilbron, Z., Kim, Y., Li, C., Li, G., Ok, J. M., Onose, N., Pirzadeh, P., Tsotras, V. J., Vernica, R., Wen, J., and Westmann, T. (2014). AsterixDB: A scalable, open source DBMS. *Proc. VLDB Endowment*, 7(14):1905–1916.

Altingövde, I. S. and Ulusoy, Ö. (2004). Exploiting interclass rules for focused crawling. *IEEE Intelligent Systems*, 19(6):66–73.

Aluç, G. (2015). *Workload Matters: A Robust Approach to Physical RDF Database Design*. PhD thesis, University of Waterloo.

Alvarez, V., Schuhknecht, F. M., Dittrich, J., and Richter, S. (2014). Main memory adaptive indexing for multi-core systems. In *Proc. 10th Workshop on Data Management on New Hardware*, pages 3:1—–3:10.

Amdahl, G. M. (1967). Validity of the single processor approach to achieving large scale computing capabilities. In *Proc. Spring Joint Computer Conf.*, pages 483–485.

Amsaleg, L., Franklin, M. J., Tomasic, A., and Urhan, T. (1996). Scrambling query plans to cope with unexpected delays. In *Proc. 4th Int. Conf. on Parallel and Distributed Information Systems*, pages 208–219.

Andreev, K. and Racke, H. (2006). Balanced graph partitioning. *Theor. Comp. Sci.*, 39(6):929–939.

Angles, R. and Gutierrez, C. (2008). The expressive power of SPARQL. In *Proc. 7th Int. Semantic Web Conf.*, pages 114–129.

Antoniou, G. and Plexousakis, D. (2018). Semantic web. In Liu, L. and Özsu, M. T., editors, *Encyclopedia of Database Systems*, pages 3425–3429. Springer New York, New York, NY.

Apache. (2016). Apache Giraph. http://giraph.apache.org. Last accessed June 2019.

Apers, P., van den Berg, C., Flokstra, J., Grefen, P., Kersten, M., and Wilschut, A. (1992). Prisma/DB: a parallel main-memory relational DBMS. *IEEE Trans. Knowl. and Data Eng.*, 4:541–554.

Apers, P. M. G. (1981). Redundant allocation of relations in a communication network. In *Proc. 5th Berkeley Workshop on Distributed Data Management and Computer Networks*, pages 245–258.

Arasu, A. and Widom, J. (2004). A denotational semantics for continuous queries over streams and relations. *ACM SIGMOD Rec.*, 33(3):6–11.

Arasu, A., Cho, J., Garcia-Molina, H., Paepcke, A., and Raghavan, S. (2001). Searching the web. *ACM Trans. Internet Tech.*, 1(1):2–43.

Arasu, A., Babu, S., and Widom, J. (2006). The CQL continuous query language: Semantic foundations and query execution. *VLDB J.*, 15(2):121–142.

Armbrust, M., Xin, R. S., Lian, C., Huai, Y., Liu, D., Bradley, J. K., Meng, X., Kaftan, T., Franklin, M. J., Ghodsi, A., and Zaharia, M. (2015). Spark SQL: Relational data processing in Spark. In *Proc. ACM SIGMOD Int. Conf. on Management of Data*, pages 1383–1394.

Arocena, G. and Mendelzon, A. (1998). WebOQL: Restructuring documents, databases and webs. In *Proc. 14th Int. Conf. on Data Engineering*, pages 24–33.

Asad, O. and Kemme, B. (2016). Adaptcache: Adaptive data partitioning and migration for distributed object caches. In *Proc. ACM/IFIP/USENIX 17th Int. Middleware Conf.*, pages 7:1–7:13.

Aspnes, J. and Shah, G. (2003). Skip graphs. In *Proc. 14th Annual ACM-SIAM Symp. on Discrete Algorithms*, pages 384–393.

Avnur, R. and Hellerstein, J. (2000). Eddies: Continuously adaptive query processing. In *Proc. ACM SIGMOD Int. Conf. on Management of Data*, pages 261–272.

Ayad, A. and Naughton, J. (2004). Static optimization of conjunctive queries with sliding windows over unbounded streaming information sources. In *Proc. ACM SIGMOD Int. Conf. on Management of Data*, pages 419–430.

Azar, Y., Broder, A. Z., Karlin, A. R., and Upfal, E. (1999). Balanced allocations. *SIAM J. on Comput.*, 29(1):180–200.

Babb, E. (1979). Implementing a relational database by means of specialized hardware. *ACM Trans. Database Syst.*, 4(1):1–29.

Babcock, B., Babu, S., Datar, M., Motwani, R., and Widom, J. (2002). Models and issues in data stream systems. In *Proc. ACM SIGACT-SIGMOD Symp. on Principles of Database Systems*, pages 1–16.

Balazinska, M., Kwon, Y., Kuchta, N., and Lee, D. (2007). Moirae: History-enhanced monitoring. In *Proc. 3rd Biennial Conf. on Innovative Data Systems Research*, pages 375–386.

Balke, W.-T., Nejdl, W., Siberski, W., and Thaden, U. (2005). Progressive distributed top-k retrieval in peer-to-peer networks. In *Proc. 21st Int. Conf. on Data Engineering*, pages 174–185.

Bancilhon, F. and Spyratos, N. (1981). Update semantics of relational views. *ACM Trans. Database Syst.*, 6(4):557–575.

Barbara, D., Garcia-Molina, H., and Spauster, A. (1986). Policies for dynamic vote reassignment. In *Proc. 6th IEEE Int. Conf. on Distributed Computing Systems*, pages 37–44.

Barbara, D., Molina, H. G., and Spauster, A. (1989). Increasing availability under mutual exclusion constraints with dynamic voting reassignment. *ACM Trans. Comp. Syst.*, 7(4):394–426.

Barthels, C., Loesing, S., Alonso, G., and Kossmann, D. (2015). Rack-scale in-memory join processing using RDMA. In *Proc. ACM SIGMOD Int. Conf. on Management of Data*, pages 1463–1475.

Batini, C. and Lenzirini, M. (1984). A methodology for data schema integration in entity-relationship model. *IEEE Trans. Softw. Eng.*, SE-10(6):650–654.

Batini, C., Lenzirini, M., and Navathe, S. B. (1986). A comparative analysis of methodologies for database schema integration. *ACM Comput. Surv.*, 18(4):323–364.

Beeri, C., Bernstein, P. A., and Goodman, N. (1989). A model for concurrency in nested transaction systems. *J. ACM*, 36(2):230–269.

Bell, D. and Grimson, J. (1992). *Distributed Database Systems*. Addison Wesley. Reading.

Bell, D. and Lapuda, L. (1976). Secure computer systems: Unified exposition and Multics interpretation. Technical Report MTR-2997 Rev.1, MITRE Corp, Bedford, MA.

Berenson, H., Bernstein, P., Gray, J., Melton, J., O'Neil, E., and O'Neil, P. (1995). A critique of ansi sql isolation levels. In *Proc. ACM SIGMOD Int. Conf. on Management of Data*, pages 1–10.

Bergamaschi, S. (2001). Semantic integration of heterogeneous information sources. *Data & Knowl. Eng.*, 36(3):215–249.

Bergman, M. K. (2001). The deep web: Surfacing hidden value. *J. Electronic Publishing*, 7(1).

Bergsten, B., Couprie, M., and Valduriez, P. (1991). Prototyping DBS3, a shared-memory parallel database system. In *Proc. Int. Conf. on Parallel and Distributed Information Systems*, pages 226–234.

Bergsten, B., Couprie, M., and Valduriez, P. (1993). Overview of parallel architectures for databases. *The Comp. J.*, 36(8):734–739.

Berkholz, C., Keppeler, J., and Schweikardt, N. (2017). Answering conjunctive queries under updates. In *Proc. ACM SIGACT-SIGMOD Symp. on Principles of Database Systems*, pages 303–318.

Berlin, J. and Motro, A. (2001). Autoplex: Automated discovery of content for virtual databases. In *Proc. Int. Conf. on Cooperative Inf. Syst.*, pages 108–122.

Berners-Lee, T. (2006). Linked data. Accessible at https://www.w3.org/DesignIssues/LinkedData.html. Last accessed June 2019.

Bernstein, P. and Blaustein, B. (1982). Fast methods for testing quantified relational calculus assertions. In *Proc. ACM SIGMOD Int. Conf. on Management of Data*, pages 39–50.

Bernstein, P. and Melnik, S. (2007). Model management: 2.0: Manipulating richer mappings. In *Proc. ACM SIGMOD Int. Conf. on Management of Data*, pages 1–12.

Bernstein, P., Blaustein, B., and Clarke, E. M. (1980a). Fast maintenance of semantic integrity assertions using redundant aggregate data. In *Proc. 6th Int. Conf. on Very Data Bases*, pages 126–136.

Bernstein, P., Shipman, P., and Rothnie, J. B. (1980b). Concurrency control in a system for distributed databases (SDD-1). *ACM Trans. Database Syst.*, 5(1):18–51.

Bernstein, P. A. and Chiu, D. M. (1981). Using semi-joins to solve relational queries. *J. ACM*, 28 (1):25–40.

Bernstein, P. A. and Goodman, N. (1981). Concurrency control in distributed database systems. *ACM Comput. Surv.*, 13(2):185–222.

Bernstein, P. A. and Goodman, N. (1983). Multiversion concurrency control — theory and algorithms. *ACM Trans. Database Syst.*, 8(4):465–483.

Bernstein, P. A. and Goodman, N. (1984). An algorithm for concurrency control and recovery in replicated distributed databases. *ACM Trans. Database Syst.*, 9(4):596–615.

Bernstein, P. A. and Newcomer, E. (1997). *Principles of Transaction Processing for the Systems Professional*. Morgan Kaufmann.

Bernstein, P. A., Goodman, N., Wong, E., Reeve, C. L., and Jr, J. B. R. (1981). Query processing in a system for distributed databases (SDD-1). *ACM Trans. Database Syst.*, 6(4):602–625.

Bernstein, P. A., Hadzilacos, V., and Goodman, N. (1987). *Concurrency Control and Recovery in Database Systems*. Addison Wesley.

Bernstein, P. A., Giunchiglia, F., Kementsietsidis, A., Mylopoulos, J., Serafini, L., and Zaihrayeu, I. (2002). Data management for peer-to-peer computing : A vision. In *Proc. 5th Int. Workshop on the World Wide Web and Databases*, pages 89–94.

Bernstein, P. A., Fekete, A., Guo, H., Ramakrishnan, R., and Tamma, P. (2006). Relexed concurrency serializability for middle-tier caching and replication. In *Proc. ACM SIGMOD Int. Conf. on Management of Data*, pages 599–610.

Beyer, K. S., Ercegovac, V., Krishnamurthy, R., Raghavan, S., Rao, J., Reiss, F., Shekita, E. J., Simmen, D. E., Tata, S., Vaithyanathan, S., and Zhu, H. (2009). Towards a scalable enterprise content analytics platform. *Q. Bull. IEEE TC on Data Eng.*, 32(1):28–35.

Bharat, K. and Broder, A. (1998). A technique for measuring the relative size and overlap of public web search engines. *Comp. Networks and ISDN Syst.*, 30:379 – 388. (Proc. 7th Int. World Wide Web Conf.).

Bhowmick, S. S., Madria, S. K., and Ng, W. K. (2004). *Web Data Management*. Springer.

Bifet, A., Gavaldà, R., Holmes, G., and Pfahringer, B. (2018). *Machine Learning for Data Streams: with Practical Examples in MOA*. MIT Press.

Binnig, C., Hildenbrand, S., Färber, F., Kossmann, D., Lee, J., and May, N. (2014). Distributed snapshot isolation: global transactions pay globally, local transactons pay locally. *VLDB J.*, 23:987–1011.

Biscondi, N., Brunie, L., Flory, A., and Kosch, H. (1996). Encapsulation of intra-operation parallelism in a parallel match operator. In *Proc. ACPC Conf.*, volume 1127 of *Lecture Notes in Computer Science*, pages 124–135.

Bitton, D., Boral, H., DeWitt, D. J., and Wilkinson, W. K. (1983). Parallel algorithms for the execution of relational database operations. *ACM Trans. Database Syst.*, 8(3):324–353.

Bitton, D., DeWitt, D. J., Hsiao, D. K., and Menon, J. (1984). A taxonomy of parallel sorting. *ACM Comput. Surv.*, 16(3):287–318.

Bizer, C., Vidal, M.-E., and Skaf-Molli, H. (2018). Linked open data. In Liu, L. and Özsu, M. T., editors, *Encyclopedia of Database Systems*, pages 2096–2101. Springer New York, New York, NY.

Blanas, S., Patel, J. M., Ercegovac, V., Rao, J., Shekita, E. J., and Tian, Y. (2010). A comparison of join algorithms for log processing in MapReduce. In *Proc. ACM SIGMOD Int. Conf. on Management of Data*, pages 975–986.

Blaustein, B. (1981). *Enforcing Database Assertions: Techniques and Applications*. PhD thesis, Harvard University, Cambridge, Mass.

Bleiholder, J. and Naumann, F. (2009). Data fusion. *ACM Comput. Surv.*, 41(1):1:1–1:41.

Bonato, A. (2008). *A Course on the Web Graph*. American Mathematical Society.

Bondiombouy, C. and Valduriez, P. (2016). Query processing in multistore systems: an overview. *Int. J. Cloud Computing*, 5(4):309–346.

Bondiombouy, C., Kolev, B., Levchenko, O., and Valduriez, P. (2016). Multistore big data integration with CloudMdsQL. *Trans. Large-Scale Data- and Knowledge-Centered Syst.*, 28: 48–74.

Bonifati, A., Summa, G., Pacitti, E., and Draidi, F. (2014). Query reformulation in PDMS based on social relevance. *Trans. Large-Scale Data- and Knowledge-Centered Syst.*, 13:59–90.

Bonnet, P., Gehrke, J., and Seshadri, P. (2001). Towards sensor database systems. In *Proc. 2nd Int. Conf. on Mobile Data Management*, pages 3–14.

Bönström, V., Hinze, A., and Schweppe, H. (2003). Storing RDF as a graph. In *Proc. 1st Latin American Web Congress*, pages 27 – 36.

Boral, H. and DeWitt, D. (1983). Database machines: An idea whose time has passed? A critique of the future of database machines. In *Proc. 3rd Int. Workshop on Database Machines*, pages 166–187.

Boral, H., Alexander, W., Clay, L., Copeland, G., Danforth, S., Franklin, M., Hart, B., Smith, M., and Valduriez, P. (1990). Prototyping bubba, a highly parallel database system. *IEEE Trans. Knowl. and Data Eng.*, 2(1):4–24.

Borkar, D., Mayuram, R., Sangudi, G., and Carey, M. J. (2016). Have your data and query it too: From key-value caching to big data management. In *Proc. ACM SIGMOD Int. Conf. on Management of Data*, pages 239–251.

Bornea, M. A., Dolby, J., Kementsietsidis, A., Srinivas, K., Dantressangle, P., Udrea, O., and Bhattacharjee, B. (2013). Building an efficient RDF store over a relational database. In *Proc. ACM SIGMOD Int. Conf. on Management of Data*, pages 121–132.

Borr, A. (1988). High performance SQL through low-level system integration. In *Proc. ACM SIGMOD Int. Conf. on Management of Data*, pages 342–349.

Bouganim, L., Florescu, D., and Valduriez, P. (1996). Dynamic load balancing in hierarchical parallel database systems. In *Proc. 22th Int. Conf. on Very Large Data Bases*, pages 436–447.

Bouganim, L., Florescu, D., and Valduriez, P. (1999). Multi-join query execution with skew in NUMA multiprocessors. *Distrib. Parall. Databases*, 7(1). in press.

Breitbart, Y. and Korth, H. F. (1997). Replication and consistency: Being lazy helps sometimes. In *Proc. ACM SIGACT-SIGMOD Symp. on Principles of Database Systems*, pages 173–184.

Breitbart, Y. and Silberschatz, A. (1988). Multidatabase update issues. In *Proc. ACM SIGMOD Int. Conf. on Management of Data*, pages 135–142.

Breitbart, Y., Olson, P. L., and Thompson, G. R. (1986). Database integration in a distributed heterogeneous database system. In *Proc. 2nd Int. Conf. on Data Engineering*, pages 301–310.

Brewer, E., Ying, L., Greenfield, L., Cypher, R., and T'so, T. (2016). Disks for data centers. Technical report, Google.

Brewer, E. A. (2000). Towards robust distributed systems (abstract). In *Proc. ACM SIGACT-SIGOPS 19th Symp. on the Principles of Distributed Computing*, page 7.

Bright, M. W., Hurson, A. R., and Pakzad, S. H. (1994). Automated resolution of semantic heterogeneity in multidatabases. *ACM Trans. Database Syst.*, 19(2):212–253.

Brill, D., Templeton, M., and Yu, C. (1984). Distributed query processing strategies in MERMAID: A front-end to data management systems. In *Proc. 1st Int. Conf. on Data Engineering*, pages 211–218.

Brin, S. and Page, L. (1998). The anatomy of a large-scale hypertextual web search engine. *Comp. Netw.*, 30(1-7):107 – 117.

Broder, A., Kumar, R., Maghoul, F., Raghavan, P., Rajagopalan, S., Stata, R., Tomkins, A., and Wiener, J. (2000). Graph structure in the web. *Comp. Netw.*, 33(1-6):309–320.

Broekstra, J., Kampman, A., and van Harmelen, F. (2002). Sesame: A generic architecture for storing and querying RDF and RDF schema. In *Proc. 1st Int. Semantic Web Conf.*, pages 54–68.

Bu, Y., Howe, B., Balazinska, M., and Ernst, M. D. (2010). HaLoop: efficient iterative data processing on large clusters. *Proc. VLDB Endowment*, 3(1):285–296.

Bu, Y., Howe, B., Balazinska, M., and Ernst, M. D. (2012). The HaLoop approach to large-scale iterative data analysis. *VLDB J.*, 21(2):169–190.

Bu, Y., Borkar, V. R., Jia, J., Carey, M. J., and Condie, T. (2014). Pregelix: Bigger graph analytics on a dataflow engine. *Proc. VLDB Endowment*, 8(2):161–172.

Bugiotti, F., Bursztyn, D., Deutsch, A., Ileana, I., and Manolescu, I. (2015). Invisible glue: Scalable self-tunning multi-stores. In *Proc. 7th Biennial Conf. on Innovative Data Systems Research*.

Buneman, P., Davidson, S., Hillebrand, G. G., and Suciu, D. (1996). A query language and optimization techniques for unstructured data. In *Proc. ACM SIGMOD Int. Conf. on Management of Data*, pages 505–516.

Cahill, M. J., Röhm, U., and Fekete, A. D. (2009). Serializable isolation for snapshot databases. *ACM Trans. Database Syst.*, 34(4):Article 20.

Calì, A. and Calvanese, D. (2002). Optimized querying of integrated data over the web. In *Engineering Information Systems in the Internet Context*, pages 285–301.

Callan, J. P. and Connell, M. E. (2001). Query-based sampling of text databases. *ACM Trans. Information Syst.*, 19(2):97–130.

Callan, J. P., Connell, M. E., and Du, A. (1999). Automatic discovery of language models for text databases. In *Proc. ACM SIGMOD Int. Conf. on Management of Data*, pages 479–490.

Cammert, M., Krämer, J., Seeger, B., and S.Vaupel. (2006). An approach to adaptive memory management in data stream systems. In *Proc. 22nd Int. Conf. on Data Engineering*, page 137.

Canaday, R. H., Harrisson, R. D., Ivie, E. L., Rydery, J. L., and Wehr, L. A. (1974). A back-end computer for data base management. *Commun. ACM*, 17(10):575–582.

Cao, P. and Wang, Z. (2004). Query processing issues in image (multimedia) databases. In *Proc. ACM SIGACT-SIGOPS 23rd Symp. on the Principles of Distributed Computing*, pages 206–215.

Carbone, P., Katsifodimos, A., Ewen, S., Markl, V., Haridi, S., and Tzoumas, K. (2015). Apache Flink^{TM}: Stream and batch processing in a single engine. *Q. Bull. IEEE TC on Data Eng.*, 38 (4):28–38.

Carey, M. and Lu, H. (1986). Load balancing in a locally distributed database system. In *Proc. ACM SIGMOD Int. Conf. on Management of Data*, pages 108–119.

Castano, S. and Antonellis, V. D. (1999). A schema analysis and reconciliation tool environment for heterogeneous databases. In *Proc. 3rd Int. Conf. on Database Eng. and Applications*, pages 53 – 62.

Castano, S., Fugini, M. G., Martella, G., and Samarati, P. (1995). *Database Security*. Addison Wesley.

Castro, M. and Liskov, B. (1999). Practical byzantine fault tolerance. In *Proc. 3rd USENIX Symp. on Operating System Design and Implementation*, pages 173–186.

Cellary, W., Gelenbe, E., and Morzy, T. (1988). *Concurrency Control in Distributed Database Systems*. North-Holland.

Ceri, S. and Owicki, S. (1982). On the use of optimistic methods for concurrency control in distributed databases. In *Proc. 6th Berkeley Workshop on Distributed Data Management and Computer Networks*, pages 117–130.

Ceri, S. and Pelagatti, G. (1983). Correctness of query execution strategies in distributed databases. *ACM Trans. Database Syst.*, 8(4):577–607.

Ceri, S. and Pernici, B. (1985). DATAID–D: Methodology for distributed database design. In Albano, V. d. A. and di Leva, A., editors, *Computer-Aided Database Design*, pages 157–183. North-Holland.

Ceri, S. and Widom, J. (1993). Managing semantic heterogeneity with production rules and persistent queues. In *Proc. 19th Int. Conf. on Very Large Data Bases*, pages 108–119.

Ceri, S., Martella, G., and Pelagatti, G. (1982a). Optimal file allocation in a computer network: A solution method based on the knapsack problem. *Comp. Netw.*, 6:345–357.

Ceri, S., Negri, M., and Pelagatti, G. (1982b). Horizontal data partitioning in database design. In *Proc. ACM SIGMOD Int. Conf. on Management of Data*, pages 128–136.

Ceri, S., Navathe, S. B., and Wiederhold, G. (1983). Distribution design of logical database schemes. *IEEE Trans. Softw. Eng.*, SE-9(4):487–503.

Ceri, S., Gottlob, G., and Pelagatti, G. (1986). Taxonomy and formal properties of distributed joins. *Inf. Syst.*, 11(1):25–40.

Ceri, S., Pernici, B., and Wiederhold, G. (1987). Distributed database design methodologies. *Proc. IEEE*, 75(5):533–546.

Chairunnanda, P., Daudjee, K., and Özsu, M. T. (2014). ConfluxDB: multi-master replication for partitioned snapshot isolation databases. *Proc. VLDB Endowment*, 7(11):947–958.

Chakrabarti, K., Keogh, E., Mehrotra, S., and Pazzani, M. (2002). Locally adaptive dimensionality reduction for indexing large time series databases. *ACM Trans. Database Syst.*, 27.

Chakrabarti, S., Dom, B., and Indyk, P. (1998). Enhanced hypertext classification using hyperlinks. In *Proc. ACM SIGMOD Int. Conf. on Management of Data*, pages 307 – 318.

Chamberlin, D. (2018). *SQL++ For SQL Users: A Tutorial*. CouchBase Inc.

Chamberlin, D., Gray, J., and Traiger, I. (1975). Views, authorization and locking in a relational database system. In *Proc. National Computer Conf*, pages 425–430.

Chambers, C., Raniwala, A., Perry, F., Adams, S., Henry, R. R., Bradshaw, R., and Weizenbaum, N. (2010). FlumeJava: easy, efficient data-parallel pipelines. In *Proc. ACM SIGPLAN 2010 Conf. on Programming Language Design and Implementation*, pages 363–375.

Chandra, T. D., Griesemer, R., and Redstone, J. (2007). Paxos made live: An engineering perspective. In *Proc. ACM SIGACT-SIGOPS 26th Symp. on the Principles of Distributed Computing*, pages 398–407.

Chandrasekaran, S., Cooper, O., Deshpande, A., Franklin, M. J., Hellerstein, J. M., Hong, W., Krishnamurthy, S., Madden, S., Raman, V., Reiss, F., and Shah, M. A. (2003). TelegraphCQ: Continuous dataflow processing for an uncertain world. In *Proc. 1st Biennial Conf. on Innovative Data Systems Research*.

Chang, F., Dean, J., Ghemawat, S., Hsieh, W., Wallach, D., Burrows, M., Chandra, T., Fikes, A., and Gruber, R. (2008). Bigtable: A distributed storage system for structured data. *ACM Trans. Comp. Syst.*, 26(2):Article 4.

Chang, S. K. and Liu, A. C. (1982). File allocation in a distributed database. *Int. J. Comput. Inf. Sci*, 11(5):325–340.

Chattopadhyay, B., Lin, L., Liu, W., Mittal, S., Aragonda, P., Lychagina, V., Kwon, Y., and Wong, M. (2011). Tenzing: A SQL implementation on the MapReduce framework. *Proc. VLDB Endowment*, 4(12):1318–1327.

Chaudhuri, S., Ganjam, K., Ganti, V., and Motwani, R. (2003). Robust and efficient fuzzy match for online data cleaning. In *Proc. ACM SIGMOD Int. Conf. on Management of Data*, pages 313–324.

Chen, R., Shi, J., Chen, Y., and Chen, H. (2015). PowerLyra: Differentiated graph computation and partitioning on skewed graphs. In *Proc. 10th ACM SIGOPS/EuroSys European Conf. on Comp. Syst.*, pages 1:1–1:15.

Chiu, D. M. and Ho, Y. C. (1980). A methodology for interpreting tree queries into optimal semi-join expressions. In *Proc. ACM SIGMOD Int. Conf. on Management of Data*, pages 169–178.

Cho, J. and Garcia-Molina, H. (2000). The evolution of the web and implications for an incremental crawler. In *Proc. 26th Int. Conf. on Very Large Data Bases*.

Cho, J. and Ntoulas, A. (2002). Effective change detection using sampling. In *Proc. 28th Int. Conf. on Very Large Data Bases*.

Cho, J., Garcia-Molina, H., and Page, L. (1998). Efficient crawling through URL ordering. *Comp. Networks and ISDN Syst.*, 30(1-7):161–172.

Chockler, G., Keidar, I., and Vitenberg, R. (2001). Group communication specifications: a comprehensive study. *ACM Comput. Surv.*, 33(4):427–469.

Chong, E., Das, S., Eadon, G., and Srinivasan, J. (2005). An efficient SQL-based RDF querying scheme. In *Proc. 31st Int. Conf. on Very Large Data Bases*, pages 1216–1227.

Chu, W. W. (1969). Optimal file allocation in a multiple computer system. *IEEE Trans. Comput.*, C-18(10):885–889.

Chu, W. W. (1973). Optimal file allocation in a computer network. In Abramson, N. and Kuo, F. F., editors, *Computer Communication Networks*, pages 82–94.

Chu, W. W. (1976). Performance of file directory systems for data bases in star and distributed networks. In *Proc. National Computer Conf.*, volume 45, pages 577–587.

Chu, W. W. and Nahouraii, E. E. (1975). File directory design considerations for distributed databases. In *Proc. 1st Int. Conf. on Very Data Bases*, pages 543–545.

Chu, X., Ilyas, I. F., and Papotti, P. (2013). Discovering Denial Constraints. *Proc. VLDB Endowment*, 6(13):1498–1509.

Chundi, P., Rosenkrantz, D. J., and Ravi, S. S. (1996). Deferred updates and data placement in distributed databases. In *Proc. ACM SIGACT-SIGMOD Symp. on Principles of Database Systems*, pages 469–476.

Civelek, F. N., Dogac, A., and Spaccapietra, S. (1988). An expert system approach to view definition and integration. In *Proc. 7th Int'l. Conf. on Entity-Relationship Approach*, pages 229–249.

Cohen, J. (2009). Graph twiddling in a MapReduce world. *Computing in Science & Engineering*, 11(4):29–41.

Cole, R. L. and Graefe, G. (1994). Optimization of dynamic query evaluation plans. In *Proc. ACM SIGMOD Int. Conf. on Management of Data*, pages 150–160.

Coletta, R., Castanier, E., Valduriez, P., Frisch, C., Ngo, D., and Bellahsene, Z. (2012). Public data integration with websmatch. In *Proc. Int. Workshop on Open Data*, pages 5–12.

Copeland, G., Alexander, W., Boughter, E., and Keller, T. (1988). Data placement in bubba. In *Proc. ACM SIGMOD Int. Conf. on Management of Data*, pages 99–108.

Corbett, J. C., Dean, J., Epstein, M., Fikes, A., Frost, C., Furman, J. J., Ghemawat, S., Gubarev, A., Heiser, C., Hochschild, P., Hsieh, W., Kanthak, S., Kogan, E., Li, H., Lloyd, A., Melnik, S., Mwaura, D., Nagle, D., Quinlan, S., Rao, R., Rolig, L., Saito, Y., Szymaniak, M., Taylor, C., Wang, R., and Woodford, D. (2013). Spanner: Google's globally distributed database. *ACM Trans. Database Syst.*, 31(3):8:1–8:22.

Crainiceanu, A., Linga, P., Gehrke, J., and Shanmugasundaram, J. (2004). Querying peer-to-peer networks using p-trees. In *Proc. 7th Int. Workshop on the World Wide Web and Databases*, pages 25–30.

Cranor, C., Johnson, T., Spatscheck, O., and Shkapenyuk, V. (2003). Gigascope: High performance network monitoring with an SQL interface. In *Proc. ACM SIGMOD Int. Conf. on Management of Data*, pages 647–651.

Crespo, A. and Garcia-Molina, H. (2002). Routing indices for peer-to-peer systems. In *Proc. 22nd IEEE Int. Conf. on Distributed Computing Systems*, pages 23–33.

Cuenca-Acuna, F., Peery, C., Martin, R., and Nguyen, T. (2003). PlanetP: using gossiping to build content addressable peer-to-peer information sharing communities. In *IEEE Int. Symp. on High Performance Distributed Computing*, pages 236–249.

Curino, C., Jones, E., Zhang, Y., and Madden, S. (2010). Schism: a workload-driven approach to database replication and partitioning. *Proc. VLDB Endowment*, 3(1):48–57.

Curino, C., Jones, E. P. C., Madden, S., and Balakrishnan, H. (2011). Workload-aware database monitoring and consolidation. In *Proc. ACM SIGMOD Int. Conf. on Management of Data*, pages 313–324.

Cusumano, M. A. (2010). Cloud computing and SaaS as new computing platforms. *Commun. ACM*, 53(4):27–29.

Dasgupta, S., Coakley, K., and Gupta, A. (2016). Analytics-driven data ingestion and derivation in the AWESOME polystore. In *Proc. 2016 IEEE Int. Conf. on Big Data*, pages 2555–2564.

Daswani, N., Garcia-Molina, H., and Yang, B. (2003). Open problems in data-sharing peer-to-peer systems. In *Proc. 9th Int. Conf. on Database Theory*, pages 1–15.

Daudjee, K. and Salem, K. (2004). Lazy database replication with ordering guarantees. In *Proc. 20th Int. Conf. on Data Engineering*, pages 424–435.

Daudjee, K. and Salem, K. (2006). Lazy database replication with snapshot isolation. In *Proc. 32nd Int. Conf. on Very Large Data Bases*, pages 715–726.

Davenport, R. A. (1981). Design of distributed data base systems. *Comp. J.*, 24(1):31–41.

Davidson, S. B. (1984). Optimism and consistency in partitioned distributed database systems. *ACM Trans. Database Syst.*, 9(3):456–481.

Davidson, S. B., Garcia-Molina, H., and Skeen, D. (1985). Consistency in partitioned networks. *ACM Comput. Surv.*, 17(3):341–370.

Dawson, J. L. (1980). A user demand model for distributed database design. In *Digest of Papers – COMPCON*, pages 211–216.

Dayal, U. and Bernstein, P. (1978). On the updatability of relational views. In *Proc. 4th Int. Conf. on Very Data Bases*, pages 368–377.

Dayal, U. and Hwang, H. (1984). View definition and generalization for database integration in MULTIBASE: A system for heterogeneous distributed database. *IEEE Trans. Softw. Eng.*, SE-10(6):628–644.

Dean, J. and Ghemawat, S. (2004). MapReduce: Simplified data processing on large clusters. In *Proc. 6th USENIX Symp. on Operating System Design and Implementation*, pages 137–149.

Dean, J. and Ghemawat, S. (2010). MapReduce: a flexible data processing tool. *Commun. ACM*, 53(1):72–77.

DeCandia, G., Hastorun, D., Jampani, M., Kakulapati, G., Lakshman, A., Pilchin, A., Sivasubramanian, S., Vosshall, P., and Vogels, W. (2007). Dynamo: Amazon's highly available key-value store. In *Proc. 21st ACM Symp. on Operating System Principles*, pages 205–220.

Demers, A. J., Greene, D. H., Hauser, C., Irish, W., Larson, J., Shenker, S., Sturgis, H. E., Swinehart, D. C., and Terry, D. B. (1987). Epidemic algorithms for replicated database maintenance. In *Proc. ACM SIGACT-SIGOPS 6th Symp. on the Principles of Distributed Computing*, pages 1–12.

Deshpande, A. and Gupta, A. (2018). *Principles of Graph Data Management and Analytics*. ACM Books. Forthcoming.

Devine, R. (1993). Design and implementation of DDH: A distributed dynamic hashing algorithm. In *Proc. 4th Int. Conf. on Foundations of Data Organization and Algorithms*, pages 101–114.

Dewitt, D. and Stonebraker, M. (2009). MapReduce: A major step backwards. https://homes.cs.washington.edu/~billhowe/mapreduce_a_major_step_backwards.html.

DeWitt, D., Naughton, J., Schneider, D., and Seshadri, S. (1992). Practical skew handling in parallel joins. In *Proc. 22th Int. Conf. on Very Large Data Bases*, pages 27–40.

DeWitt, D. J. and Gerber, R. (1985). Multi processor hash-based join algorithms. In *Proc. 11th Int. Conf. on Very Large Data Bases*, pages 151–164.

DeWitt, D. J. and Gray, J. (1992). Parallel database systems: The future of high performance database systems. *Commun. ACM*, 35(6):85–98.

DeWitt, D. J., Katz, R., Olken, F., Shapiro, L., Stonebraker, M., and Wood, D. (1984). Implementation techniques for main memory database systems. In *Proc. ACM SIGMOD Int. Conf. on Management of Data*, pages 1–8.

DeWitt, D. J., Gerber, R. H., Graek, G., Heytens, M. L., Kumar, K. B., and Muralikrishna, M. (1986). Gamma: A high performance dataflow database machine. In *Proc. 12th Int. Conf. on Very Large Data Bases*, pages 228–237.

DeWitt, D. J., Paulson, E., Robinson, E., Naughton, J., Royalty, J., Shankar, S., and Krioukov, A. (2008). Clustera: an integrated computation and data management system. *Proc. VLDB Endowment*, 1:28–41.

DeWitt, D. J., Halverson, A., Nehme, R. V., Shankar, S., Aguilar-Saborit, J., Avanes, A., Flasza, M., and Gramling, J. (2013). Split query processing in Polybase. In *Proc. ACM SIGMOD Int. Conf. on Management of Data*, pages 1255–1266.

Dhamankar, R., Lee, Y., Doan, A., Halevy, A. Y., and Domingos, P. (2004). iMAP: Discovering complex mappings between database schemas. In *Proc. ACM SIGMOD Int. Conf. on Management of Data*, pages 383–394.

Ding, L. and Rundensteiner, E. (2004). Evaluating window joins over punctuated streams. In *Proc. 13th ACM Int. Conf. on Information and Knowledge Management*, pages 98–107.

Ding, L., Mehta, N., Rundensteiner, E., and Heineman, G. (2004). Joining punctuated streams. In *Advances in Database Technology, Proc. 9th Int. Conf. on Extending Database Technology*, pages 587–604.

Dinh, T. T. A., Liu, R., Zhang, M., Chen, G., Ooi, B. C., and Wang, J. (2018). Untangling blockchain: A data processing view of blockchain systems. *IEEE Trans. Knowl. and Data Eng.*, 30(7):1366–1385.

Do, H. and Rahm, E. (2002). COMA: a system for flexible combination of schema matching approaches. In *Proc. 28th Int. Conf. on Very Large Data Bases*, pages 610–621.

Doan, A. and Halevy, A. Y. (2005). Semantic integration research in the database community: A brief survey. *AI Magazine*, 26(1):83–94.

Doan, A., Domingos, P., and Halevy, A. Y. (2001). Reconciling schemas of disparate data sources: A machine-learning approach. In *Proc. ACM SIGMOD Int. Conf. on Management of Data*, pages 509–520.

Doan, A., Domingos, P., and Halevy, A. (2003a). Learning to match the schemas of data sources: A multistrategy approach. *Machine Learning*, 50(3):279–301.

Doan, A., Madhavan, J., Dhamankar, R., Domingos, P., and Halevy, A. (2003b). Learning to match ontologies on the semantic web. *VLDB J.*, 12(4):303–319.

Doan, A., Halevy, A., and Ives, Z. (2012). *Principles of Data Integration*. Morgan Kaufmann.

Dogac, A., Kalinichenko, L., Özsu, M. T., and Sheth, A., editors. (1998). *Advances in Workflow Systems and Interoperability*. Springer.

Dong, X. L. and Naumann, F. (2009). Data fusion: resolving data conflicts for integration. *Proc. VLDB Endowment*, 2(2):1654–1655.

Dong, X. L. and Srivastava, D. (2015). *Big Data Integration*. Synthesis Lectures on Data Management. Morgan & Claypool Publishers.

Dong, X. L., Berti-Equille, L., and Srivastava, D. (2009a). Truth discovery and copying detection in a dynamic world. *Proc. VLDB Endowment*, 2(1):562–573.

Dong, X. L., Berti-Equille, L., and Srivastava, D. (2009b). Integrating conflicting data: the role of source dependence. *Proc. VLDB Endowment*, 2(1):550–561.

Dowdy, L. W. and Foster, D. V. (1982). Comparative models of the file assignment problem. *ACM Comput. Surv.*, 14(2):287–313.

Du, W., Krishnamurthy, R., and Shan, M. (1992). Query optimization in a heterogeneous DBMS. In *Proc. 18th Int. Conf. on Very Large Data Bases*, pages 277–291.

Du, W., Shan, M., and Dayal, U. (1995). Reducing multidatabase query response time by tree balancing. In *Proc. ACM SIGMOD Int. Conf. on Management of Data*, pages 293–303.

Duggan, J., Elmore, A. J., Stonebraker, M., Balazinska, M., Howe, B., Kepner, J., Madden, S., Maier, D., Mattson, T., and Zdonik, S. B. (2015). The BigDAWG polystore system. *ACM SIGMOD Rec.*, 44(2):11–16.

Duschka, O. M. and Genesereth, M. R. (1997). Answering recursive queries using views. In *Proc. ACM SIGACT-SIGMOD Symp. on Principles of Database Systems*, pages 109–116.

Eager, D. L. and Sevcik, K. C. (1983). Achieving robustness in distributed database systems. *ACM Trans. Database Syst.*, 8(3):354–381.

Edwards, J., McCurley, K., and Tomlin, J. (2001). An adaptive model for optimizing performance of an incremental web crawler. In *Proc. 10th Int. World Wide Web Conf.*

El Abbadi, A., Skeen, D., and Cristian, F. (1985). An efficient, fault–tolerant protocol for replicated data management. In *Proc. ACM SIGACT-SIGMOD Symp. on Principles of Database Systems*, pages 215–229.

Elbushra, M. M. and Lindström, J. (2015). Causal consistent databases. *Open Journal of Databases*, 2(1):17–35.

Elmagarmid, A., Rusinkiewicz, M., and Sheth, A., editors. (1999). *Management of Heterogeneous and Autonomous Database Systems*. Morgan Kaufmann.

Elmagarmid, A. K. (1986). A survey of distributed deadlock detection algorithms. *ACM SIGMOD Rec.*, 15(3):37–45.

Elmagarmid, A. K., editor. (1992). *Transaction Models for Advanced Database Applications*. Morgan Kaufmann.

Elmagarmid, A. K., Soundararajan, N., and Liu, M. T. (1988). A distributed deadlock detection and resolution algorithm and its correctness proof. *IEEE Trans. Softw. Eng.*, 14(10):1443–1452.

Elmasri, R., Larson, J., and Navathe, S. B. (1987). Integration algorithms for database and logical database design. Technical report, Honeywell Corporate Research Center, Golden Valley, Minn.

Elmore, A. J., Arora, V., Taft, R., Pavlo, A., Agrawal, D., and El Abbadi, A. (2015). Squall: Fine-grained live reconfiguration for partitioned main memory databases. In *Proc. ACM SIGMOD Int. Conf. on Management of Data*, pages 299–313.

Elseidy, M., Elguindy, A., Vitorovic, A., and Koch, C. (2014). Scalable and adaptive online joins. *Proc. VLDB Endowment*, 7(6):441–452.

Embley, D. W., Jackman, D., and Xu, L. (2001). Multifaceted exploitation of metadata for attribute match discovery in information integration. In *Proc. Workshop on Information Integration on the Web*, pages 110–117.

Embley, D. W., Jackman, D., and Xu, L. (2002). Attribute match discovery in information integration: exploiting multiple facets of metadata. *Journal of the Brazilian Computing Society*, 8(2):32–43.

Epstein, R., Stonebraker, M., and Wong, E. (1978). Query processing in a distributed relational database system. In *Proc. ACM SIGMOD Int. Conf. on Management of Data*, pages 169–180.

Eswaran, K. P. (1974). Placement of records in a file and file allocation in a computer network. In *Information Processing '74*, pages 304–307.

Etzion, O. and Niblett, P. (2010). *Event Processing in Action*. Manning.

Evrendilek, C., Dogac, A., Nural, S., and Ozcan, F. (1997). Multidatabase query optimization. *Distrib. Parall. Databases*, 5(1):77–114.

Eyal, I., Gencer, A. E., Sirer, E. G., and van Renesse, R. (2016). Bitcoin-ng: A scalable blockchain protocol. In *Proc. 13th USENIX Symp. on Networked Systems Design & Implementation*, pages 45–59.

Fagin, R. (2002). Combining fuzzy information: an overview. *ACM SIGMOD Rec.*, 31(2):109–118.

Fagin, R., Lotem, J., and Naor, M. (2003). Optimal aggregation algorithms for middleware. *Journal of Computer and System Sciences*, 66(4):614–656.

Fagin, R., Kolaitis, P. G., Miller, R. J., and Popa, L. (2005). Data exchange: semantics and query answering. *Theor. Comp. Sci.*, 336(1):89–124.

Faleiro, J. M. and Abadi, D. J. (2015). Rethinking serializable multiversion concurrency control. *Proc. VLDB Endowment*, 8(11):1190–1201.

Faloutsos, C. and Christodoulakis, S. (1984). Signature files: an access method for documents and its analytical performance evaluation. *ACM Trans. Information Syst.*, 2(4):267–288.

Farid, M. H., Roatis, A., Ilyas, I. F., Hoffmann, H., and Chu, X. (2016). CLAMS: bringing quality to data lakes. In *Proc. ACM SIGMOD Int. Conf. on Management of Data*, pages 2089–2092.

Farrag, A. A. and Özsu, M. T. (1989). Using semantic knowledge of transactions to increase concurrency. *ACM Trans. Database Syst.*, 14(4):503–525.

Fekete, A., Lynch, N., Merritt, M., and Weihl, W. (1987a). Nested transactions and read/write locking. Technical Memo MIT/LCS/TM–324, Massachusetts Institute of Technology, Cambridge, Mass.

Fekete, A., Lynch, N., Merritt, M., and Weihl, W. (1987b). Nested transactions, conflict-based locking, and dynamic atomicity. Technical Memo MIT/LCS/TM–340, Massachusetts Institute of Technology, Cambridge, Mass.

Fekete, A., Lynch, N., Merritt, M., and Weihl, W. (1989). Commutativity-based locking for nested transactions. Technical Memo MIT/LCS/TM-370b, Massachusetts Institute of Technology, Cambridge, Mass.

Fernandez, M., Florescu, D., and Levy, A. (1997). A query language for a web-site management system. *ACM SIGMOD Rec.*, 26(3):4–11.

Fernandez, R. C., Migliavacca, M., Kalyvianaki, E., and Pietzuch, P. (2013). Integrating scale out and fault tolerance in stream processing using operator state management. In *Proc. ACM SIGMOD Int. Conf. on Management of Data*, pages 725–736.

Fernández-Moctezuma, R., Tufte, K., and Li, J. (2009). Inter-operator feedback in data stream management systems via punctuation. In *Proc. 4th Biennial Conf. on Innovative Data Systems Research.*

Ferraiolo, D. and Kuhn, R. (1992). Role-based access control. In *Proc. National Computer Conf.*, pages 554–563.

Fisher, M. K. and Hochbaum, D. S. (1980). Database location in computer networks. *J. ACM*, 27 (4):718–735.

Fisher, P. S., Hollist, P., and Slonim, J. (1980). A design methodology for distributed data bases. In *Digest of Papers – COMPCON*, pages 199–202.

Florentin, J. J. (1974). Consistency auditing of databases. *Comp. J.*, 17(1):52–58.

Florescu, D., Levy, A., and Mendelzon, A. (1998). Database techniques for the World-Wide Web: a survey. *ACM SIGMOD Rec.*, 27(3):59–74.

Friedman, M., Levy, A. Y., and Millstein, T. D. (1999). Navigational plans for data integration. In *Proc. 16th National Conf. on Artificial Intelligence and 11th Innovative Applications of Artificial Intelligence Conf.*, pages 67–73.

Fu, Y., Ong, K. W., Papakonstantinou, Y., and Zamora, E. (2014). FORWARD: data-centric UIs using declarative templates that efficiently wrap third-party JavaScript components. *Proc. VLDB Endowment*, 7(13):1649–1652.

Furtado, C., Lima, A. A. B., Pacitti, E., Valduriez, P., and Mattoso, M. (2008). Adaptive hybrid partitioning for OLAP query processing in a database cluster. *Int. Journal of High Performance Computing and Networking*, 5(4):251–262.

Fushimi, S., Kitsuregawa, M., and Tanaka, H. (1986). An overview of the system software of a parallel relational database machine GRACE. In *Proc. 12th Int. Conf. on Very Large Data Bases*, pages 209–219.

Gadepally, V., Chen, P., Duggan, J., Elmore, A. J., Haynes, B., Kepner, J., Madden, S., Mattson, T., and Stonebraker, M. (2016). The BigDAWG polystore system and architecture. In *Proc. IEEE High Performance Extreme Computing Conf.*, pages 1–6.

Galhardas, H., Florescu, D., Shasha, D., Simon, E., and Saita, C.-A. (2001). Declarative data cleaning: Language, model, and algorithms. In *Proc. 27th Int. Conf. on Very Large Data Bases*, pages 371–380.

Gançarski, S., Naacke, H., Pacitti, E., and Valduriez, P. (2007). The leganet system: Freshness-aware transaction routing in a database cluster. *Inf. Syst.*, 32(7):320–343.

Ganesan, P., Yang, B., and Garcia-Molina, H. (2004). One torus to rule them all: Multidimensional queries in P2P systems. In *Proc. 7th Int. Workshop on the World Wide Web and Databases*, pages 19–24.

Gankidi, V. R., Teletia, N., Patel, J. M., Halverson, A., and DeWitt, D. J. (2014). Indexing HDFS data in PDW: splitting the data from the index. *Proc. VLDB Endowment*, 7(13):1520–1528.

Garcia-Molina, H. (1982). Elections in distributed computing systems. *IEEE Trans. Comput.*, C-31(1):48–59.

Garcia-Molina, H. (1983). Using semantic knowledge for transaction processing in a distributed database. *ACM Trans. Database Syst.*, 8(2):186–213.

Garcia-Molina, H. and Salem, K. (1987). Sagas. In *Proc. ACM SIGMOD Int. Conf. on Management of Data*, pages 249–259.

Garcia-Molina, H. and Wiederhold, G. (1982). Read–only transactions in a distributed database. *ACM Trans. Database Syst.*, 7(2):209–234.

Garcia-Molina, H., Gawlick, D., Klein, J., Kleissner, K., and Salem, K. (1990). Coordinating multi-transaction activities. Technical Report CS-TR-247-90, Department of Computer Science, Princeton University.

Garcia-Molina, H., Papakonstantinou, Y., Quass, D., Rajaraman, A., Sagiv, Y., Ullman, J. D., Vassalos, V., and Widom, J. (1997). The TSIMMIS approach to mediation: Data models and languages. *J. Intell. Information Syst.*, 8(2):117–132.

Garofalakis, M. N. and Ioannidis, Y. E. (1996). Multi-dimensional resource scheduling for parallel queries. In *Proc. ACM SIGMOD Int. Conf. on Management of Data*, pages 365–376.

Gavish, B. and Pirkul, H. (1986). Computer and database location in distributed computer systems. *IEEE Trans. Comput.*, C-35(7):583–590.

Gedik, B. (2014). Partitioning functions for stateful data parallelism in stream processing. *VLDB J.*, 23:517–539.

Georgakopoulos, D., Hornick, M., and Sheth, A. (1995). An overview of workflow management: From process modeling to workflow automation infrastructure. *Distrib. Parall. Databases*, 3: 119–153.

Ghemawat, S., Gobioff, H., and Leung, S. (2003). The Google file system. In *Proc. 19th ACM Symp. on Operating System Principles*, pages 29–43.

Ghoting, A., Krishnamurthy, R., Pednault, E. P. D., Reinwald, B., Sindhwani, V., Tatikonda, S., Tian, Y., and Vaithyanathan, S. (2011). SystemML: Declarative machine learning on MapReduce. In *Proc. 27th Int. Conf. on Data Engineering*, pages 231–242.

Gifford, D. K. (1979). Weighted voting for replicated data. In *Proc. 7th ACM Symp. on Operating System Principles*, pages 50–159.

Gilbert, S. and Lynch, N. A. (2002). Brewer's conjecture and the feasibility of consistent, available, partition-tolerant web services. *SIGACT News*, 33(2):51–59.

Glasbergen, B., Abebe, M., Daudjee, K., Foggo, S., and Pacaci. (2018). Apollo: Learning query correlations for predictive caching in geo-distributed systems. In *Proc. 21st Int. Conf. on Extending Database Technology*, pages 253–264.

Golab, L. and Özsu, M. T. (2003). Processing sliding window multi-joins in continuous queries over data streams. In *Proc. 29th Int. Conf. on Very Large Data Bases*, pages 500–511.

Golab, L. and Özsu, M. T. (2010). *Data Stream Systems*. Synthesis Lectures on Data Management. Morgan & Claypool.

Goldman, K. J. (1987). Data replication in nested transaction systems. Technical Report MIT/LCS/TR-390, Massachusetts Institute of Technology, Cambridge, Mass.

Goldman, R. and Widom, J. (1997). Dataguides: Enabling query formulation and optimization in semistructured databases. In *Proc. 23th Int. Conf. on Very Large Data Bases*, pages 436–445.

Gonzalez, J. E., Low, Y., Gu, H., Bickson, D., and Guestrin, C. (2012). PowerGraph: Distributed graph-parallel computation on natural graphs. In *Proc. 10th USENIX Symp. on Operating System Design and Implementation*, pages 17–30.

Gonzalez, J. E., Xin, R. S., Dave, A., Crankshaw, D., Franklin, M. J., and Stoica, I. (2014). GraphX: graph processing in a distributed dataflow framework graph processing in a distributed dataflow framework. In *Proc. 11th USENIX Symp. on Operating System Design and Implementation*, pages 599–613.

Goodman, J. R. and Woest, P. J. (1988). The Wisconsin multicube: A new large-scale cache-coherent multiprocessor. Technical Report TR766, University of Wisconsin-Madison.

Gounaris, A., Paton, N. W., Fernandes, A. A. A., and Sakellariou, R. (2002). Adaptive query processing: A survey. In *Proc. British National Conf. on Databases*, pages 11–25.

Graefe, G. (1990). Encapsulation of parallelism in the Volcano query processing systems. In *Proc. ACM SIGMOD Int. Conf. on Management of Data*, pages 102–111.

Graefe, G. (1993). Query evaluation techniques for large databases. *ACM Comput. Surv.*, 25(2): 73–170.

Graefe, G. (1994). Volcano - an extensible and parallel query evaluation system. *IEEE Trans. Knowl. and Data Eng.*, 6(1):120–135.

Graefe, G. and Kuno, H. (2010a). Self-selecting, self-tuning, incrementally optimized indexes. In *Proc. 13th Int. Conf. on Extending Database Technology*, pages 371–381.

Graefe, G. and Kuno, H. (2010b). Adaptive indexing for relational keys. In *Proc. Workshops of 26th Int. Conf. on Data Engineering*, pages 69–74.

Graefe, G., Idreos, S., Kuno, H., and Manegold, S. (2010). Benchmarking adaptive indexing. In *Proc. TPC Technology Conference on Performance Evaluation, Measurement and Characterization of Complex Systems*, pages 169–184.

Graefe, G., Halim, F., Idreos, S., Kuno, H., and Manegold, S. (2012). Concurrency control for adaptive indexing. *Proc. VLDB Endowment*, 5(7):656–667.

Graefe, G., Halim, F., Idreos, S., Kuno, H. A., Manegold, S., and Seeger, B. (2014). Transactional support for adaptive indexing. *VLDB J.*, 23(2):303–328.

Grapa, E. and Belford, G. G. (1977). Some theorems to aid in solving the file allocation problem. *Commun. ACM*, 20(11):878–882.

Gravano, L., Garcia-Molina, H., and Tomasic, A. (1999). Gloss: Text-source discovery over the internet. *ACM Trans. Database Syst.*, 24(2):229–264.

Gray, J. (1979). Notes on database operating systems. In Bayer, R., Graham, R., and Seegmüller, G., editors, *Operating Systems – An Advanced Course*, pages 393–481. Springer, New York.

Gray, J. and Lamport, L. (2006). Consensus on transaction commit. *ACM Trans. Database Syst.*, 31(1):133–160.

Gray, J. and Reuter, A. (1993). *Transaction Processing: Concepts and Techniques*. Morgan Kaufmann.

Gray, J., Helland, P., O'Neil, P. E., and Shasha, D. (1996). The dangers of replication and a solution. In *Proc. ACM SIGMOD Int. Conf. on Management of Data*, pages 173–182.

Gray, J. N., McJones, P., Blasgen, M., Lindsay, B., Lorie, R., Price, T., Putzolu, F., and Traiger, I. (1981). The recovery manager of the System R database manager. *ACM Comput. Surv.*, 13(2): 223–242.

Grefen, P. and Widom, J. (1997). Protocols for integrity constraint checking in federated databases. *Distrib. Parall. Databases*, 5(4):327–355.

Griffiths, P. P. and Wade, B. W. (1976). An authorization mechanism for a relational database system. *ACM Trans. Database Syst.*, 1(3):242–255.

Grossman, R. L. and Gu, Y. (2009). On the varieties of clouds for data intensive computing. *Q. Bull. IEEE TC on Data Eng.*, 32(1):44–50.

Guha, S. and McGregor, A. (2006). Approximate quantiles and the order of the stream. In *Proc. ACM SIGACT-SIGMOD Symp. on Principles of Database Systems*, pages 273–279.

Gulisano, V., Jiménez-Peris, R., Patino-Martinez, M., and Valduriez, P. (2010). StreamCloud: A large scale data streaming system. In *Proc. 30th IEEE Int. Conf. on Distributed Computing Systems*.

Gulisano, V., Jiménez-Peris, R., Patino-Martinez, M., and Valduriez, P. (2012). StreamCloud: An elastic and scalable data streaming system. *IEEE Trans. Parall. Dist. Sys.*, 23(12):2351–2365.

Gulli, A. and Signorini, A. (2005). The indexable web is more than 11.5 billion pages. In *Proc. 14th Int. World Wide Web Conf.*, pages 902–903.

Gummadi, P. K., Gummadi, R., Gribble, S. D., Ratnasamy, S., Shenker, S., and Stoica, I. (2003). The impact of DHT routing geometry on resilience and proximity. In *Proc. Conf. on Applications, Technologies, Architectures, and Protocols for Computer Communication*, pages 381–394.

Güntzer, U., Kießling, W., and Balke, W.-T. (2000). Optimizing multi-feature queries for image databases. In *Proc. 26th Int. Conf. on Very Large Data Bases*, pages 419–428.

Gupta, A. and Mumick, I. S., editors. (1999). *Materialized Views: Techniques, Implementations, and Applications*. M.I.T. Press.

Gupta, A., Mumick, I. S., and Subrahmanian, V. S. (1993). Maintaining views incrementally. In *Proc. ACM SIGMOD Int. Conf. on Management of Data*, pages 157–166.

Gupta, A., Jagadish, H., and Mumick, I. S. (1996). Data integration using self-maintainable views. In *Advances in Database Technology, Proc. 5th Int. Conf. on Extending Database Technology*, pages 140–144.

Gupta, A., Agrawal, D., and El Abbadi, A. (2003). Approximate range selection queries in peer-to-peer systems. In *Proc. 1st Biennial Conf. on Innovative Data Systems Research*, pages 141–151.

Haas, L. (2007). Beauty and the beast: The theory and practice of information integration. In *Proc. 11th Int. Conf. on Database Theory*, pages 28–43.

Haas, L., Kossmann, D., Wimmers, E., and Yang, J. (1997a). Optimizing queries across diverse data sources. In *Proc. 23th Int. Conf. on Very Large Data Bases*, pages 276–285.

Haas, L. M., Kossmann, D., Wimmers, E. L., and Yang, J. (1997b). Optimizing queries across diverse data sources. In *Proc. 23th Int. Conf. on Very Large Data Bases*, pages 276–285.

Haas, P. and Hellerstein, J. (1999a). Ripple joins for online aggregation. In *Proc. ACM SIGMOD Int. Conf. on Management of Data*, pages 287–298.

Haas, P. J. and Hellerstein, J. M. (1999b). Ripple joins for online aggregation. In *Proc. ACM SIGMOD Int. Conf. on Management of Data*, pages 287–298.

Hacigümüs, H., Sankaranarayanan, J., Tatemura, J., LeFevre, J., and Polyzotis, N. (2013). Odyssey: A multi-store system for evolutionary analytics. *Proc. VLDB Endowment*, 6(11): 1180–1181.

Haderle, C. M. D., Lindsay, B., Pirahesh, H., and Schwarz, P. (1992). Aries: A transaction recovery method supporting fine-granularity locking and partial rollbacks using write-ahead logging. *ACM Trans. Database Syst.*, 17(1):94–162.

Hadzilacos, V. (1988). A theory of reliability in database systems. *J. ACM*, 35(1):121–145.

Halevy, A., Rajaraman, A., and Ordille, J. (2006). Data integration: the teenage years. In *Proc. 32nd Int. Conf. on Very Large Data Bases*, pages 9–16.

Halevy, A. Y. (2001). Answering queries using views: A survey. *VLDB J.*, 10(4):270–294.

Halevy, A. Y., Etzioni, O., Doan, A., Ives, Z. G., Madhavan, J., McDowell, L., and Tatarinov, I. (2003). Crossing the structure chasm. In *Proc. 1st Biennial Conf. on Innovative Data Systems Research*.

Halici, U. and Dogac, A. (1989). Concurrency control in distributed databases through time intervals and short-term locks. *IEEE Trans. Softw. Eng.*, 15(8):994–995.

Halim, F., Idreos, S., Karras, P., and Yap, R. H. C. (2012). Stochastic database cracking: Towards robust adaptive indexing in main-memory column-stores. *Proc. VLDB Endowment*, 5(6):502–513.

Hammad, M., Aref, W., and Elmagarmid, A. (2003a). Stream window join: Tracking moving objects in sensor-network databases. In *Proc. 15th Int. Conf. on Scientific and Statistical Database Management*, pages 75–84.

Hammad, M., Aref, W., Franklin, M., Mokbel, M., and Elmagarmid, A. (2003b). Efficient execution of sliding window queries over data streams. Technical Report CSD TR 03-035, Purdue University.

Hammad, M., Mokbel, M., Ali, M., Aref, W., Catlin, A., Elmagarmid, A., Eltabakh, M., Elfeky, M., Ghanem, T., Gwadera, R., Ilyas, I., Marzouk, M., and Xiong, X. (2004). Nile: a query processing engine for data streams. In *Proc. 20th Int. Conf. on Data Engineering*, page 851.

Hammad, M., Aref, W., and Elmagarmid, A. (2005). Optimizing in-order execution of continuous queries over streamed sensor data. In *Proc. 17th Int. Conf. on Scientific and Statistical Database Management*, pages 143–146.

Hammer, M. and Niamir, B. (1979). A heuristic approach to attribute partitioning. In *Proc. ACM SIGMOD Int. Conf. on Management of Data*, pages 93–101.

Hammer, M. and Shipman, D. W. (1980). Reliability mechanisms for SDD-1: A system for distributed databases. *ACM Trans. Database Syst.*, 5(4):431–466.

Han, M. (2015). On improving distributed Pregel-like graph processing systems. Master's thesis, University of Waterloo, David R. Cheriton School of Computer Science.

Han, M. and Daudjee, K. (2015). Giraph unchained: Barrierless asynchronous parallel execution in Pregel-like graph processing systems. *Proc. VLDB Endowment*, 8(9):950–961.

Härder, T. and Reuter, A. (1983). Principles of transaction-oriented database recovery. *ACM Comput. Surv.*, 15(4):287–317.

Hartig, O. (2012). SPARQL for a web of linked data: Semantics and computability. In *Proc. 9th Extended Semantic Web Conf.*, pages 8–23.

Hartig, O. (2013a). An overview on execution strategies for linked data queries. *Datenbank-Spektrum*, 13(2):89–99.

Hartig, O. (2013b). SQUIN: a traversal based query execution system for the web of linked data. In *Proc. ACM SIGMOD Int. Conf. on Management of Data*, pages 1081–1084.

Harvey, N. J. A., Jones, M. B., Saroiu, S., Theimer, M., and Wolman, A. (2003). SkipNet: A scalable overlay network with practical locality properties. In *Proc. 4th USENIX Symp. on Internet Tech. and Systems*.

He, B., Chang, K. C.-C., and Han, J. (2004). Mining complex matchings across web query interfaces. In *Proc. ACM SIGMOD Workshop on Research Issues in Data Mining and Knowledge Discovery*, pages 3–10.

He, Q. and Ling, T. W. (2006). An ontology-based approach to the integration of entity-relationship schemas. *Data & Knowl. Eng.*, 58(3):299–326.

Hedley, Y. L., Younas, M., James, A., and Sanderson, M. (2004a). A two-phase sampling technique for information extraction from hidden web databases. In *WIDM04*, pages 1–8.

Hedley, Y.-L., Younas, M., James, A. E., and Sanderson, M. (2004b). Query-related data extraction of hidden web documents. In *Proc. 27th Annual Int. ACM SIGIR Conf. on Research and Development in Information Retrieval*, pages 558–559.

Heinze, T., Pappalardo, V., Jerzak, Z., and Fetzer, C. (2014). Auto-scaling techniques for elastic data stream processing. In *Proc. 8th Int. Conf. Distributed Event-Based Systems*, pages 318–321.

Heinze, T., Roediger, L., Meister, A., Ji, Y., Jerzak, Z., and Fetzer, C. (2015). Online parameter optimization for elastic data stream processing. In *Proc. 6th ACM Symp. on Cloud Computing*, pages 276–287.

Helal, A. A., Heddaya, A. A., and Bhargava, B. B. (1997). *Replication Techniques in Distributed Systems*. Kluwer Academic Publishers.

Hellerstein, J. M., Haas, P., and Wang, H. (1997). Online aggregation. In *Proc. ACM SIGMOD Int. Conf. on Management of Data*, pages 171–182.

Hellerstein, J. M., Franklin, M. J., Chandrasekaran, S., Deshpande, A., Hildrum, K., Madden, S., Raman, V., and Shah, M. A. (2000). Adaptive query processing: Technology in evolution. *Q. Bull. IEEE TC on Data Eng.*, 23(2):7–18.

Herlihy, M. (1987). Concurrency versus availability: Atomicity mechanisms for replicated data. *ACM Trans. Comp. Syst.*, 5(3):249–274.

Herman, D. and Verjus, J. P. (1979). An algorithm for maintaining the consistency of multiple copies. In *Proc. 1st IEEE Int. Conf. on Distributed Computing Systems*, pages 625–631.

Hersh, W. (2001). Managing gigabytes - compressing and indexing documents and images (second edition). *Inf. Retr.*, 4(1):79–80.

Hevner, A. R. and Schneider, G. M. (1980). An integrated design system for distributed database networks. In *Digest of Papers - COMPCON*, pages 459–465.

Hirate, Y., Kato, S., and Yamana, H. (2006). Web structure in 2005. In *Proc. 4th Int. Workshop on Algorithms and Models for the Web-Graph*, pages 36 – 46.

Hoffer, H. A. and Severance, D. G. (1975). The use of cluster analysis in physical data base design. In *Proc. 1st Int. Conf. on Very Data Bases*, pages 69–86.

Hoffer, J. A. (1975). *A Clustering Approach to the Generation of Subfiles for the Design of a Computer Data Base*. PhD thesis, Department of Operations Research, Cornell University, Ithaca, N.Y.

Hoffman, J. L. (1977). *Model Methods for Computer Security and Privacy*. Prentice-Hall.

Holze, M. and Ritter, N. (2008). Autonomic databases: Detection of workload shifts with n-gram-models. In *Proc. 12th East European Conf. Advances in Databases and Information Systems*, pages 127–142.

Hong, W. (1992). Exploiting inter-operation parallelism in XPRS. In *Proc. ACM SIGMOD Int. Conf. on Management of Data*, pages 19–28.

Hong, W. and Stonebraker, M. (1993). Optimization of parallel query execution plans in XPRS. *Distrib. Parall. Databases*, 1(1):9–32.

Hoque, I. and Gupta, I. (2013). LFGraph: simple and fast distributed graph analytics. In *Proc. 1st ACM SIGOPS Conf. on Timely Results in Operating Syst.*, pages 9:1–9:17.

Hortonworks. (2014). White paper: A modern data architecture with Apache Hadoop: the journey to the data lake. Technical report, Hortonworks. Last accessed August 2018.

Hsiao, H. I. and DeWitt, D. (1991). A performance study of three high-availability data replication strategies. In *Proc. Int. Conf. on Parallel and Distributed Information Systems*, pages 18–28.

Huang, Z. and He, Y. (2018). Auto-detect: Data-driven error detection in tables. In *Proc. ACM SIGMOD Int. Conf. on Management of Data*, pages 1377–1392.

Huebsch, R., Hellerstein, J., Lanham, N., Loo, B. T., Shenker, S., and Stoica, I. (2003). Querying the internet with pier. In *Proc. 29th Int. Conf. on Very Large Data Bases*, pages 321–332.

Hull, R. (1997). Managing semantic heterogeneity in databases: A theoretical perspective. In *Proc. ACM SIGACT-SIGMOD Symp. on Principles of Database Systems*, pages 51–61.

Hwang, J., Balazinska, M., Rasin, A., Cetintemel, U., Stonebraker, M., and Zdonik, S. (2005). High-availability algorithms for distributed stream processing. In *Proc. 21st Int. Conf. on Data Engineering*, pages 779–790.

Idreos, S. (2010). *Database Cracking: Towards Auto-tuning Database Kernels*. PhD thesis, University of Amsterdam.

Idreos, S., Kersten, M. L., and Manegold, S. (2007a). Updating a cracked database. In *Proc. ACM SIGMOD Int. Conf. on Management of Data*, pages 413–424.

Idreos, S., Kersten, M. L., and Manegold, S. (2007b). Database cracking. In *Proc. 3rd Biennial Conf. on Innovative Data Systems Research*, pages 68–78.

Idreos, S., Kersten, M. L., and Manegold, S. (2009). Self-organizing tuple reconstruction in column-stores. In *Proc. ACM SIGMOD Int. Conf. on Management of Data*, pages 297–308.

Idreos, S., Alagiannis, I., Johnson, R., and Ailamaki, A. (2011). Here are my data files. here are my queries. where are my results? In *Proc. 5th Biennial Conf. on Innovative Data Systems Research*, pages 57–68.

Ilyas, I. and Chu, X. (2019). *Principles of Data Cleaning*. ACM Books.

Ilyas, I. F. and Chu, X. (2015). Trends in cleaning relational data: Consistency and deduplication. *Foundations and Trends in Databases*, 5(4):281–393.

Ilyas, I. F., Beskales, G., and Soliman, M. A. (2008). A survey of top-k query processing techniques in relational database systems. *ACM Comput. Surv.*, 40(4):1–58.

Ioannidis, Y. and Wong, E. (1987). Query optimization by simulated annealing. In *Proc. ACM SIGMOD Int. Conf. on Management of Data*, pages 9–22.

Ipeirotis, P. G. and Gravano, L. (2002). Distributed search over the hidden web: Hierarchical database sampling and selection. In *Proc. 28th Int. Conf. on Very Large Data Bases*, pages 394–405.

Irani, K. B. and Khabbaz, N. G. (1982). A methodology for the design of communication networks and the distribution of data in distributed computer systems. *IEEE Trans. Comput.*, C-31(5): 419–434.

Isloor, S. and Marsland, T. (1980). The deadlock problem : An overview. *Computer*, 13(9):58–78.

Ito, J., Narula, N., and Ali, R. (2017). The blockchain will do to the financial system what the internet did to media. Accessible at https://hbr.org/2017/03/the-blockchain-will-do-to-banks-and-law-firms-what-the-internet-did-to-media/. Last accessed February 2019.

Jagadish, H. V., Ooi, B. C., and Vu, Q. H. (2005). BATON: A balanced tree structure for peer-to-peer networks. In *Proc. 31st Int. Conf. on Very Large Data Bases*, pages 661–672.

Jagadish, H. V., Ooi, B. C., Tan, K.-L., Vu, Q. H., and Zhang, R. (2006). Speeding up search in peer-to-peer networks with a multi-way tree structure. In *Proc. ACM SIGMOD Int. Conf. on Management of Data*, pages 1–12.

Jajodia, S. and Mutchler, D. (1987). Dynamic voting. In *Proc. ACM SIGMOD Int. Conf. on Management of Data*, pages 227–238.

Jajodia, S. and Sandhu, R. S. (1991). Towards a multilevel secure relational data model. In *Proc. ACM SIGMOD Int. Conf. on Management of Data*, pages 50–59.

Jajodia, S., Atluri, V., Keefe, T. F., McCollum, C. D., and Mukkamala, R. (2001). Multilevel security transaction processing. *J. Computer Security*, 9(3):165–195.

Jhingran, A. D., Mattos, N., and Pirahesh, H. (2002). Information integration: A research agenda. *IBM Systems J.*, 41(4):555–562.

Jimenez-Peris, R. and Patiño Martinez, M. (2011). System and method for highly scalable decentralized and low contention transactional processing. US Patent 9,760,597 B2, EU Patent 2780832.

Jiménez-Peris, R., Patiño-Martínez, M., and Alonso, G. (2002). Non-intrusive, parallel recovery of replicated data. In *Proc. 21st Symp. on Reliable Distributed Systems*, pages 150–159.

Jiménez-Peris, R., Patiño-Martínez, M., Kemme, B., and Alonso, G. (2002). Improving the scalability of fault-tolerant database clusters. In *Proc. 22nd IEEE Int. Conf. on Distributed Computing Systems*, pages 477–484.

Jiménez-Peris, R., Patiño-Martínez, M., Alonso, G., and Kemme, B. (2003). Are quorums an alternative for data replication? *ACM Trans. Database Syst.*, 28(3):257–294.

Johnson, T., Muthukrishnan, S., Shkapenyuk, V., and Spatscheck, O. (2005). A heartbeat mechanism and its application in Gigascope. In *Proc. 31st Int. Conf. on Very Large Data Bases*, pages 1079–1088.

Johnson, T., Muthukrishnan, S. M., Shkapenyuk, V., and Spatscheck, O. (2008). Query-aware partitioning for monitoring massive network data streams. In *Proc. ACM SIGMOD Int. Conf. on Management of Data*, pages 1135–1146.

Kaelbling, L. P., Littman, M. L., and Moore, A. P. (1996). Reinforcement learning: A survey. *J. Autom. Reasoning*, 4:237–285.

Kalogeraki, V., Gunopulos, D., and Zeinalipour-Yazti, D. (2002). A local search mechanism for peer-to-peer networks. In *Proc. 11th Int. Conf. on Information and Knowledge Management*, pages 300–307.

Kambayashi, Y., Yoshikawa, M., and Yajima, S. (1982). Query processing for distributed databases using generalized semi–joins. In *Proc. ACM SIGMOD Int. Conf. on Management of Data*, pages 151–160.

Kang, J., Naughton, J., and Viglas, S. (2003). Evaluating window joins over unbounded streams. In *Proc. 19th Int. Conf. on Data Engineering*, pages 341–352.

Kaoudi, Z. and Manolescu, I. (2015). RDF in the clouds: A survey. *VLDB J.*, 24:67–91.

Kara, A., Ngo, H. Q., Nikolic, M., Olteanu, D., and Zhang, H. (2019). Counting triangles under updates in worst-case optimal time. In *Proc. 22nd Int. Conf. on Database Theory*, pages 1:1–1:18.

Karlapalem, K. and Navathe, S. B. (1994). Materialization of redesigned distributed relational databases. Technical Report HKUST-CS94-14, Hong Kong University of Science and Technology, Department of Computer Science.

Karlapalem, K., Navathe, S. B., and Ammar, M. (1996). Optimal redesign policies to support dynamic processing of applications on a distributed relational database system. *Inf. Syst.*, 21 (4):353–367.

Karypis, G. and Kumar, V. (1995). Multilevel graph partitioning schemes. In *Proc. 1995 Int. Conf. on Parallel Processing*, pages 113–122.

Kashyap, V. and Sheth, A. P. (1996). Semantic and schematic similarities between database objects: A context-based approach. *VLDB J.*, 5(4):276–304.

Katz, B. and Lin, J. (2002). Annotating the world wide web using natural language. In *Proc. 2nd Workshop on NLP and XML*, pages 1–8.

Kazerouni, L. and Karlapalem, K. (1997). Stepwise redesign of distributed relational databases. Technical Report HKUST-CS97-12, Hong Kong University of Science and Technology, Department of Computer Science.

Keeton, K., Patterson, D., and Hellerstein, J. M. (1998). A case for intelligent disks (idisks). *ACM SIGMOD Rec.*, 27(3):42–52.

Keller, A. M. (1982). Update to relational databases through views involving joins. In *Proc. 2nd Int. Conf. on Databases: Improving Usability and Responsiveness*, pages 363–384.

Kementsietsidis, A., Arenas, M., and Miller, R. J. (2003). Managing data mappings in the hyperion project. In *Proc. 19th Int. Conf. on Data Engineering*, pages 732–734.

Kemme, B. and Alonso, G. (2000a). A new approach to developing and implementing eager database replication protocols. *ACM Trans. Database Syst.*, 25(3):333–379.

Kemme, B. and Alonso, G. (2000b). Don't be lazy, be consistent: Postgres-R, a new way to implement database replication. In *Proc. 26th Int. Conf. on Very Large Data Bases*, pages 134–143.

Kemme, B., Bartoli, A., and Babaoglu, O. (2001). Online reconfiguration in replicated databases based on group communication. In *Proc. Int. Conf. on Dependable Systems and Networks*, pages 117–130.

Kemme, B., Peris, R. J., and Patino-Martinez, M. (2010). *Database Replication*. Morgan & Claypool.

Kemper, A. and Neumann, T. (2011). HyPer: A hybrid OLTP&OLAP main memory database system based on virtual memory snapshots. In *Proc. 27th Int. Conf. on Data Engineering*, pages 195–206.

Kermarrec, A.-M. and van Steen, M. (2007). Gossiping in distributed systems. *Operating Systems Rev.*, 41(5):2–7.

Kermarrec, A.-M., Rowstron, A., Shapiro, M., and Druschel, P. (2001). The icecube approach to the reconciliation of diverging replicas. In *Proc. ACM SIGACT-SIGOPS 20th Symp. on the Principles of Distributed Computing*, pages 210–218.

Khayyat, Z., Awara, K., Alonazi, A., Jamjoom, H., Williams, D., and Kalnis, P. (2013). Mizan: A system for dynamic load balancing in large-scale graph processing. In *Proc. 8th ACM SIGOPS/EuroSys European Conf. on Comp. Syst.*, pages 169–182.

Khoshafian, S. and Valduriez, P. (1987). Sharing persistence and object-orientation: A database perspective. In *Int. Workshop on Database Programming Languages*, pages 181–205.

Kim, W. and Seo, J. (1991). Classifying schematic and data heterogeneity in multidatabase systems. *Computer*, 24(12):12–18.

Kirsch, J. and Amir, Y. (2008). Paxos for system builders: An overview. In *Proc. 2nd Workshop on Large-Scale Distributed Systems and Middleware*, pages 3:1–3:6.

Kitsuregawa, M. and Ogawa, Y. (1990). Bucket spreading parallel hash: A new, robust, parallel hash join method for data skew in the super database computer. In *Proc. 16th Int. Conf. on Very Large Data Bases*, pages 210–221.

Kitsuregawa, M., Tanaka, H., and Moto-Oka, T. (1983). Application of hash to data base machine and its architecture. *New Generation Computing*, 1(1):63–74.

Kiveris, R., Lattanzi, S., Mirrokni, V., Rastogi, V., and Vassilvitskii, S. (2014). Connected components in MapReduce and beyond. In *Proc. 5th ACM Symp. on Cloud Computing*, pages 18:1–18:13.

Kleinberg, J., Kumar, R., Raghavan, P., Rajagopalan, S., and Tomkins, A. (1999). The web as a graph: Measurements, models, and methods. In *Proc. 5th Annual Int. Conf. Computing and Combinatorics*, pages 1–17.

Kleinberg, J. M. (1999). Authoritative sources in a hyperlinked environment. *J. ACM*, 46(5): 604–632.

Knapp, E. (1987). Deadlock detection in distributed databases. *ACM Comput. Surv.*, 19(4):303–328.

Knuth, D. E. (1973). *The Art of Computer Programming, Volume III: Sorting and Searching*. Addison-Wesley.

Koch, C. (2001). *Data Integration against Multiple Evolving Autonomous Schemata*. Ph.D. thesis, Technical University of Vienna.

Koch, C. (2010). Incremental query evaluation in a ring of databases. In *Proc. 29th ACM SIGACT-SIGMOD-SIGART Symp. on Principles of Database Systems*, pages 87–98.

Koch, C., Ahmad, Y., Kennedy, O., Nikolic, M., Nötzli, A., Lupei, D., and Shaikhha, A. (2014). DBToaster: higher-order delta processing for dynamic, frequently fresh views. *VLDB J.*, 23(2): 253–278.

Kohler, W. H. (1981). A survey of techniques for synchronization and recovery in decentralized computer systems. *ACM Comput. Surv.*, 13(2):149–183.

Kolev, B., Bondiombouy, C., Valduriez, P., Jiménez-Peris, R., Pau, R., and Pereira, J. (2016a). The cloudmdsql multistore system. In *Proc. ACM SIGMOD Int. Conf. on Management of Data*, pages 2113–2116.

Kolev, B., Valduriez, P., Bondiombouy, C., Jiménez-Peris, R., Pau, R., and Pereira, J. (2016b). CloudMdsQL: querying heterogeneous cloud data stores with a common language. *Distrib. Parall. Databases*, 34(4):463–503.

Kolev, B., Levchenko, O., Pacitti, E., Valduriez, P., Vilaça, R., Gonçalves, R. C., Jiménez-Peris, R., and Kranas, P. (2018). Parallel polyglot query processing on heterogeneous cloud data stores with LeanXcale. In *Proc. 2018 IEEE Int. Conf. on Big Data*, pages 1757–1766.

Koller, D. and Friedman, N. (2009). *Probabilistic Graphical Models: Principles and Techniques.* The MIT Press.

Kollias, J. G. and Hatzopoulos, M. (1981). Criteria to aid in solving the problem of allocating copies of a file in a computer network. *Comp. J.*, 24(1):29–30.

Konopnicki, D. and Shmueli, O. (1995). W3QS: A query system for the World Wide Web. In *Proc. 21th Int. Conf. on Very Large Data Bases*, pages 54–65.

Kossmann, D. (2000). The state of the art in distributed query processing. *ACM Comput. Surv.*, 32 (4):422–469.

Krishnamurthy, R., Litwin, W., and Kent, W. (1991). Language features for interoperability of databases with schematic discrepancies. In *Proc. ACM SIGMOD Int. Conf. on Management of Data*, pages 40–49.

Kshemkalyani, A. and Singhal, M. (1994). On characterization and correctness of distributed deadlocks. *J. Parall. and Distrib. Comput.*, 22(1):44–59.

Kubiatowicz, J., Bindel, D., Chen, Y., Czerwinski, S., Eaton, P., Geels, D., Gummadi, R., Rhea, S., Weatherspoon, H., Weimer, W., Wells, C., and Zhao, B. (2000). Oceanstore: an architecture for global-scale persistent storage. In *ACM Int. Conf. on Architectural Support for Programming Languages and Operating Systems (ASPLOS)*, pages 190–201.

Kulkarni, S., Bhagat, N., Fu, M., Kedigehalli, V., Kellogg, C., Mittal, S., Patel, J. M., Ramasamy, K., and Taneja, S. (2015). Twitter heron: Stream processing at scale. In *Proc. ACM SIGMOD Int. Conf. on Management of Data*, pages 239–250.

Kumar, A. and Segev, A. (1993). Cost and availability tradeoffs in replicated data concurrency control. *ACM Trans. Database Syst.*, 18(1):102–131.

Kumar, R., Raghavan, P., Rajagopalan, S., Sivakumar, D., Tomkins, A., and Upfal, E. (2000). The Web as a graph. In *Proc. 19th ACM SIGACT-SIGMOD-SIGART Symp. on Principles of Database Systems*, pages 1–10.

Kumar, V., editor. (1996). *Performance of Concurrency Control Mechanisms in Centralized Database Systems*. Prentice-Hall.

Kung, H. and Robinson, J. (1981). On optimistic methods for concurrency control. *ACM Trans. Database Syst.*, 6(2):213–226.

Kwok, C. C. T., Etzioni, O., and Weld, D. S. (2001). Scaling question answering to the web. In *Proc. 10th Int. World Wide Web Conf.*, pages 150–161.

Ladwig, G. and Tran, T. (2010). Linked data query processing strategies. In *Proc. 9th Int. Semantic Web Conf.*, pages 453–469.

Ladwig, G. and Tran, T. (2011). SIHJoin: Querying remote and local linked data. In *Proc. 8th Extended Semantic Web Conf.*, pages 139–153.

Lage, J. P., da Silva, A. S., Golgher, P. B., and Laender, A. H. F. (2002). Collecting hidden web pages for data extraction. In *Proc. 4th Int. Workshop on Web Information and Data Management*, pages 69–75.

Lakshmanan, L. V. S., Sadri, F., and Subramanian, I. N. (1996). A declarative language for querying and restructuring the web. In *Proc. 6th Int. Workshop on Research Issues on Data Eng.*, pages 12–21.

Lam, S. S. and Özsu, M. T. (2002). Querying web data – the WebQA approach. In *Proc. 3rd Int. Conf. on Web Information Systems Eng.*, pages 139–148.

Lamport, L. (1998). The part-time parliament. *ACM Trans. Comp. Syst.*, 16(2):133–169.

Lamport, L. (2001). Paxos made simple. *ACM SIGACT News*, 32(4):51–58.

Lampson, B. and Sturgis, H. (1976). Crash recovery in distributed data storage system. Technical report, Xerox Palo Alto Research Center, Palo Alto, Calif.

Landers, T. and Rosenberg, R. L. (1982). An overview of multibase. In Schneider, H.-J., editor, *Distributed Data Bases*, pages 153–184. North-Holland, Amsterdam.

Langville, A. N. and Meyer, C. D. (2006). *Google's PageRank and Beyond*. Princeton University Press.

Lanzelotte, R., Valduriez, P., Zaït, M., and Ziane, M. (1994). Industrial-strength parallel query optimization: issues and lessons. *Inf. Syst.*, 19(4):311–330.

Larriba-Pey, J. L., Martínez-Bazán, N., and Domínguez-Sal, D. (2014). Introduction to graph databases. In Koubarakis, M., Stamou, G., Stoilos, G., Horrocks, I., Kolaitis, P., Lausen, G., and Weikum, G., editors, *Reasoning Web: Reasoning on the Web in the Big Data Era*, pages 171–194. Springer.

Larson, P.-Å., Blanas, S., Diaconu, C., Freedman, C., Patel, J. M., and Zwilling, M. (2011). High-performance concurrency control mechanisms for main-memory databases. *Proc. VLDB Endowment*, 5(4):298–309.

Law, Y.-N., Wang, H., and Zaniolo, C. (2004). Query languages and data models for database sequences and data streams. In *Proc. 30th Int. Conf. on Very Large Data Bases*, pages 492–503.

Lawrence, S. and Giles, C. L. (1998). Searching the world wide web. *Science*, 280(5360):98–100.

Lawrence, S. and Giles, C. L. (1999). Accessibility of information on the web. *Nature*, 400(6740): 107–9.

Lee, K.-H., Lee, Y.-J., Choi, H., Chung, Y. D., and Moon, B. (2012). Parallel data processing with mapreduce: A survey. *ACM SIGMOD Rec.*, 40(4):11–20.

LeFevre, J., Sankaranarayanan, J., Hacigumus, H., Tatemura, J., Polyzotis, N., and Carey, M. J. (2014). MISO: Souping up big data query processing with a multistore system. In *Proc. ACM SIGMOD Int. Conf. on Management of Data*, pages 1591–1602.

Leis, V., Boncz, P. A., Kemper, A., and Neumann, T. (2014). Morsel-driven parallelism: a NUMA-aware query evaluation framework for the many-core age. In *Proc. ACM SIGMOD Int. Conf. on Management of Data*, pages 743–754.

Lenoski, D., Laudon, J., Gharachorloo, K., Weber, W. D., Gupta, A., Henessy, J., Horowitz, M., and Lam, M. S. (1992). The Stanford Dash multiprocessor. *Computer*, 25(3):63–79.

Lenzerini, M. (2002). Data integration: a theoretical perspective. In *Proc. ACM SIGACT-SIGMOD Symp. on Principles of Database Systems*, pages 233–246.

Levandoski, J. J., Larson, P. Å., and Stoica, R. (2013). Identifying hot and cold data in main-memory databases. In *Proc. 29th Int. Conf. on Data Engineering*, pages 26–37.

Levin, K. D. and Morgan, H. L. (1975). Optimizing distributed data bases: A framework for research. In *Proc. National Computer Conf*, pages 473–478.

Levy, A. Y., Mendelzon, A. O., Sagiv, Y., and Srivastava, D. (1995). Answering queries using views. In *Proc. ACM SIGACT-SIGMOD Symp. on Principles of Database Systems*, pages 95–104.

Levy, A. Y., Rajaraman, A., and Ordille, J. J. (1996a). The world wide web as a collection of views: Query processing in the information manifold. In *Proc. Workshop on Materialized Views: Techniques and Applications*, pages 43–55.

Levy, A. Y., Rajaraman, A., and Ordille, J. J. (1996b). Querying heterogeneous information sources using source descriptions. In *Proc. 22th Int. Conf. on Very Large Data Bases*, pages 251–262.

Li, F., Ooi, B. C., Özsu, M. T., and Wu, S. (2014). Distributed data management using MapReduce. *ACM Comput. Surv.*, 46(3):Article No. 31.

Li, H.-G., Chen, S., Tatemura, J., Agrawal, D., Candan, K. S., and Hsiung, W.-P. (2006). Safety guarantee of continuous join queries over punctuated data streams. In *Proc. 32nd Int. Conf. on Very Large Data Bases*, pages 19–30.

Li, J., Maier, D., Tufte, K., Papadimos, V., and Tucker, P. a. (2005). Semantics and evaluation techniques for window aggregates in data streams. In *Proc. ACM SIGMOD Int. Conf. on Management of Data*, pages 311–322.

Li, W.-S. and Clifton, C. (2000). Semint: A tool for identifying attribute correspondences in heterogeneous databases using neural networks. *Data & Knowl. Eng.*, 33(1):49–84.

Li, W.-S., Clifton, C., and Liu, S.-Y. (2000). Database integration using neural networks: Implementation and experiences. *Knowl. and Information Syst.*, 2(1):73–96.

Lim, L., Wang, M., Padmanabhan, S., Vitter, J. S., and Agarwal, R. (2003). Dynamic maintenance of web indexes using landmarks. In *Proc. 12th Int. World Wide Web Conf.*, pages 102–111.

Lima, A., Mattoso, M., and Valduriez, P. (2004). OLAP query processing in a database cluster. In *Proc. 10th Int. Euro-Par Conf.*, pages 355–362.

Lin, Q., Chang, P., Chen, G., Ooi, B. C., Tan, K., and Wang, Z. (2016). Towards a Non-2PC transaction management in distributed database systems. In *Proc. ACM SIGMOD Int. Conf. on Management of Data*, pages 1659–1674.

Lin, Y., Kemme, B., Patiño Martínez, M., and Jiménez-Peris, R. (2005). Middleware based data replication providing snapshot isolation. In *Proc. ACM SIGMOD Int. Conf. on Management of Data*, pages 419–430.

Litwin, W., Neimat, M.-A., and Schneider, D. A. (1993). LH* – linear hashing for distributed files. In *Proc. ACM SIGMOD Int. Conf. on Management of Data*, pages 327–336.

Liu, B., Zhu, Y., and Rundensteiner, E. (2006). Run-time operator state spilling for memory intensive long running queries. In *Proc. ACM SIGMOD Int. Conf. on Management of Data*, pages 347–358.

Livny, M., Khoshafian, S., and Boral, H. (1987). Multi-disk management. In *Proc. ACM SIGMETRICS Conf. on Measurement and Modeling of Computer Systems*, pages 69–77.

Lohman, G., Mohan, C., Haas, L., Daniels, D., Lindsay, B., Selinger, P., and Wilms, P. (). Query processing in R*. pages 31–47.

Lomet, D., Feket, A., Wang, R., and Ward, P. (2012). Multi-version concurrency via timestamp range conflict management. In *Proc. 28th Int. Conf. on Data Engineering*, pages 714–725.

Low, Y., Gonzalez, J., Kyrola, A., Bickson, D., and Guestrin, C. (2010). GraphLab: new framework for parallel machine learning. In *Proc. 26th Conf. on Uncertainty in Artificial Intelligence*, pages 340–349.

Low, Y., Gonzalez, J., Kyrola, A., Bickson, D., Guestrin, C., and Hellerstein, J. M. (2012). Distributed graphlab: A framework for machine learning in the cloud. *Proc. VLDB Endowment*, 5(8):716–727.

Lu, H., Shan, M.-C., and Tan, K.-L. (1991). Optimization of multi-way join queries for parallel execution. In *Proc. 17th Int. Conf. on Very Large Data Bases*, pages 549–560.

Lu, H., Ooi, B., and Goh, C. (1992). On global multidatabase query optimization. *ACM SIGMOD Rec.*, 21(4):6–11.

Lu, H., Ooi, B., and Goh, C. (1993). Multidatabase query optimization: Issues and solutions. In *Proc. 3rd Int. Workshop on Res. Issues in Data Eng*, pages 137–143.

Lugowski, A., Alber, D., Buluç, A., Gilbert, J. R., Reinhardt, S., Teng, Y., and Waranis, A. (2012). A flexible open-source toolbox for scalable complex graph analysis. In *Proc. 2012 SIAM Int. Conf. on Data Mining*, pages 930–941.

Lumsdaine, A., Gregor, D., Hendrickson, B., and Berry, J. (2007). Challenges in parallel graph processing. *Parallel Processing Letters*, 17(01):5–20.

Lunt, T. F. and Fernández, E. B. (1990). Database security. *ACM SIGMOD Rec.*, 19(4):90–97.

Lv, Q., Cao, P., Cohen, E., Li, K., and Shenker, S. (2002). Search and replication in unstructured peer-to-peer networks. In *Proc. 16th Annual Int. Conf. on Supercomputing*, pages 84–95.

Lynch, N. (1983a). Multilevel atomicity: A new correctness criterion for database concurrency control. *ACM Trans. Database Syst.*, 8(4):484–502.

Lynch, N. (1983b). Concurrency control for resilient nested transactions. In *Proc. 2nd ACM SIGACT–SIGMOD Symp. on Principles of Database Systems*, pages 166–181.

Lynch, N. and Merritt, M. (1986). Introduction to the theory of nested transactions. Technical Report MIT/LCS/TR-367, Massachusetts Institute of Technology, Cambridge, Mass.

Lynch, N., Merritt, M., Weihl, W. E., and Fekete, A. (1993). *Atomic Transactions in Concurrent Distributed Systems*. Morgan Kaufmann.

Mackert, L. and Lohman, G. (1986a). R* optimizer validation and perfromance evaluation for distributed queries. In *Proc. 12th Int. Conf. on Very Large Data Bases*, pages 149–159.

Mackert, L. F. and Lohman, G. (1986b). R* optimizer validation and performance evaluation for local queries. In *Proc. ACM SIGMOD Int. Conf. on Management of Data*, pages 84–95.

Madden, S. and Franklin, M. J. (2002). Fjording the stream: An architecture for queries over streaming sensor data. In *Proc. 18th Int. Conf. on Data Engineering*, pages 555–566.

Madden, S., Shah, M., Hellerstein, J., and Raman, V. (2002a). Continuously adaptive continuous queries over streams. In *Proc. ACM SIGMOD Int. Conf. on Management of Data*, pages 49–60.

Madden, S., Shah, M. A., Hellerstein, J. M., and Raman, V. (2002b). Continuously adaptive continuous queries over streams. In *Proc. ACM SIGMOD Int. Conf. on Management of Data*, pages 49–60.

Madhavan, J., Bernstein, P., and Rahm, E. (2001). Generic schema matching with Cupid. In *Proc. 27th Int. Conf. on Very Large Data Bases*, pages 49–58.

Mahmoud, . A. and Riordon, J. S. (1976). Optimal allocation of resources in distributed information networks. *ACM Trans. Database Syst.*, 1(1):66–78.

Maiyya, S., Zakhary, V., Agrawal, D., and El Abbadi, A. (2018). Database and distributed computing fundamentals for scalable, fault-tolerant, and consistent maintenance of blockchains. *Proc. VLDB Endowment*, 11(12):2098–2101.

Malewicz, G., Austern, M. H., Bik, A. J. C., Dehnert, J. C., Horn, I., Leiser, N., and Czajkowski, G. (2010). Pregel: a system for large-scale graph processing. In *Proc. ACM SIGMOD Int. Conf. on Management of Data*, pages 135–146.

Manber, U. and Myers, G. (1990). Suffix arrays: a new method for on-line string searches. In *Proc. 1st Annual ACM-SIAM Symp. on Discrete Algorithms*, pages 319–327.

Manegold, S., Boncz, P. A., and Kersten, M. L. (2002). Optimizing main-memory join on modern hardware. *IEEE Trans. Knowl. and Data Eng.*, 14(4):709–730.

Manolescu, I., Florescu, D., and Kossmann, D. (2001). Answering XML queries on heterogeneous data sources. In *Proc. 27th Int. Conf. on Very Large Data Bases*, pages 241–250.

Martins, V. and Pacitti, E. (2006). Dynamic and distributed reconciliation in p2p-dht networks. In *uropean Conf. on Parallel Computing (Euro-Par)*, pages 337–349.

Martins, V., Akbarinia, R., Pacitti, E., and Valduriez, P. (2006a). Reconciliation in the APPA P2P system. In *Proc. IEEE Int. Conf. on Parallel and Distributed Systems*, pages 401–410.

Martins, V., Pacitti, E., and Valduriez, P. (2006b). Survey of data replication in P2P systems. Technical Report 6083, INRIA, Rennes, France.

Martins, V., Pacitti, E., Dick, M. E., and Jimenez-Peris, R. (2008). Scalable and topology-aware reconciliation on P2P networks. *Distrib. Parall. Databases*, 24(1–3):1–43.

McBrien, P. and Poulovassilis, A. (2003). Defining peer-to-peer data integration using both as view rules. In *Proc. 1st Int. Workshop on Databases, Information Systems and Peer-to-Peer Computing*, pages 91–107.

McCallum, A., Nigam, K., Rennie, J., and Seymore, K. (1999). A machine learning approach to building domain-specific search engines. In *Proc. 16th Int. Joint Conf. on AI*.

McCann, R., AlShebli, B., Le, Q., Nguyen, H., Vu, L., and Doan, A. (2005). Mapping maintenance for data integration systems. In *Proc. 31st Int. Conf. on Very Large Data Bases*, pages 1018–1029.

McCormick, W. T., Schweitzer, P. J., and White, T. W. (1972). Problem decomposition and data reorganization by a clustering technique. *Oper. Res.*, 20(5):993–1009.

McCune, R. R., Weninger, T., and Madey, G. (2015). Thinking like a vertex: A survey of vertex-centric frameworks for large-scale distributed graph processing. *ACM Comput. Surv.*, 48(2): 25:1–25:39.

Mehta, M. and DeWitt, D. (1995). Managing intra-operator parallelism in parallel database systems. In *Proc. 21th Int. Conf. on Very Large Data Bases*.

Melnik, S., Raghavan, S., Yang, B., and Garcia-Molina, H. (2001). Building a distributed full-text index for the web. In *Proc. 10th Int. World Wide Web Conf.*, pages 396–406.

Melnik, S., Garcia-Molina, H., and Rahm, E. (2002). Similarity flooding: A versatile graph matching algorithm and its application to schema matching. In *Proc. 18th Int. Conf. on Data Engineering*, pages 117–128.

Menasce, D. A. and Muntz, R. R. (1979). Locking and deadlock detection in distributed databases. *IEEE Trans. Softw. Eng.*, SE-5(3):195–202.

Mendelzon, A. O., Mihaila, G. A., and Milo, T. (1997). Querying the World Wide Web. *Int. J. Digit. Libr.*, 1(1):54–67.

Meng, W., Yu, C., Kim, W., Wang, G., Phan, T., and Dao, S. (1993). Construction of relational front-end for object-oriented database systems. In *Proc. 9th Int. Conf. on Data Engineering*, pages 476–483.

Milán-Franco, J. M., Jiménez-Peris, R., Patiño-Martínez, M., and Kemme, B. (2004). Adaptive middleware for data replication. In *Proc. ACM/IFIP/USENIX 5th Int. Middleware Conf.*, pages 175–194.

Miller, R. J., Haas, L. M., and Hernández, M. A. (2000). Schema mapping as query discovery. In *Proc. 26th Int. Conf. on Very Large Data Bases*, pages 77–88.

Miller, R. J., Hernández, M. A., Haas, L. M., Yan, L., Ho, C. T. H., Fagin, R., and Popa, L. (2001). The Clio project: Managing heterogeneity. *ACM SIGMOD Rec.*, 31(1):78–83.

Milo, T. and Zohar, S. (1998). Using schema matching to simplify heterogeneous data translation. In *Proc. 24th Int. Conf. on Very Large Data Bases*, pages 122–133.

Minoura, T. and Wiederhold, G. (1982). Resilient extended true-copy token scheme for a distributed database system. *IEEE Trans. Softw. Eng.*, SE-8(3):173–189.

Mitchell, T. (1997). *Machine Learning*. McGraw-Hill.

Mitzenmacher, M. (2001). The power of two choices in randomized load balancing. *IEEE Trans. Parall. Dist. Sys.*, 12(10):1094–1104.

Mohan, C. (1979). Data base design in the distributed environment. Working Paper WP-7902, Department of Computer Sciences, University of Texas at Austin.

Mohan, C. and Lindsay, B. (1983). Efficient commit protocols for the tree of processes model of distributed transactions. In *Proc. ACM SIGACT-SIGOPS 2nd Symp. on the Principles of Distributed Computing*, pages 76–88.

Mohan, C. and Yeh, R. T. (1978). *Distributed Data Base Systems: A Framework for Data Base Design. In Distributed Data Bases, Infotech State-of-the-Art Report*. Infotech.

Mohan, C., Lindsay, B., and Obermarck, R. (1986). Transaction management in the r* distributed database management system. *ACM Trans. Database Syst.*, 11(4):378–396.

Morgan, H. L. and Levin, K. D. (1977). Optimal program and data location in computer networks. *Commun. ACM*, 20(5):315–322.

Moss, E. (1985). *Nested Transactions*. M.I.T. Press.

Muthukrishnan, S. (2005). *Data Streams: Algorithms and Applications*. Foundations and Trends in Theoretical Computer Science. NOW Publishers.

Naacke, H., Tomasic, A., and Valduriez, P. (1999). Validating mediator cost models with DISCO. *Networking and Information Systems Journal*, 2(5):639–663.

Najork, M. and Wiener, J. L. (2001). Breadth-first crawling yields high-quality pages. In *Proc. 10th Int. World Wide Web Conf.*, pages 114–118.

Nakamoto, S. (2008). Bitcoin: A peer-to-peer electronic cash system. Accessible at https://bitcoin.org/bitcoin.pdf/. Last accessed February 2019.

Nasir, M. A. U., Morales, G. D. F., García-Soriano, D., Kourtellis, N., and Serafini, M. (2015). The power of both choices: Practical load balancing for distributed stream processing engines. In *Proc. 31st Int. Conf. on Data Engineering*, pages 137–148.

Nasir, M. A. U., Morales, G. D. F., Kourtellis, N., and Serafini, M. (2016). When two choices are not enough: Balancing at scale in distributed stream processing. In *Proc. 32nd Int. Conf. on Data Engineering*, pages 589–600.

Naumann, F., Ho, C.-T., Tian, X., Haas, L. M., and Megiddo, N. (2002). Attribute classification using feature analysis. In *Proc. 18th Int. Conf. on Data Engineering*, page 271.

Navathe, S. B., Ceri, S., Wiederhold, G., and Dou, J. (1984). Vertical partitioning of algorithms for database design. *ACM Trans. Database Syst.*, 9(4):680–710.

Nejdl, W., Siberski, W., and Sintek, M. (2003). Design issues and challenges for rdf- and schema-based peer-to-peer systems. *ACM SIGMOD Rec.*, 32(3):41–46.

Nepal, S. and Ramakrishna, M. (1999). Query processing issues in image (multimedia) databases. In *Proc. 15th Int. Conf. on Data Engineering*, pages 22–29.

Neumann, T. and Weikum, G. (2008). RDF-3X: a RISC-style engine for RDF. *Proc. VLDB Endowment*, 1(1):647–659.

Neumann, T. and Weikum, G. (2009). The RDF-3X engine for scalable management of RDF data. *VLDB J.*, 19(1):91–113.

Newman, M. E. J., Watts, D. J., and Strogatz, S. H. (2002). Random graph models of social networks. In *(Sackler NAS Colloquium) Self-Organized Complexity in the Physical, Biological, and Social Sciences*, pages 2566–2573. National Academy of Sciences.

Niamir, B. (1978). Attribute partitioning in a self–adaptive relational database system. Technical Report 192, Laboratory for Computer Science, Massachusetts Institute of Technology, Cambridge, Mass.

Nicolas, J. M. (1982). Logic for improving integrity checking in relational data bases. *Acta Informatica*, 18:227–253.

Nikolic, M. and Olteanu, D. (2018). Incremental view maintenance with triple lock factorization benefits. In *Proc. ACM SIGMOD Int. Conf. on Management of Data*, pages 365–380.

Novakovic, S., Daglis, A., Bugnion, E., Falsafi, B., and Grot, B. (2014). Scale-out NUMA. In *Architectural Support for Programming Languages and Operating Systems, ASPLOS*, pages 3–18.

Obermack, R. (1982). Distributed deadlock detection algorithm. *ACM Trans. Database Syst.*, 7 (2):187–208.

Okcan, A. and Riedewald, M. (2011). Processing theta-joins using MapReduce. In *Proc. ACM SIGMOD Int. Conf. on Management of Data*, pages 949–960.

Olston, C., Reed, B., Srivastava, U., Kumar, R., and Tomkins, A. (2008). Pig latin: a not-so-foreign language for data processing. In *Proc. ACM SIGMOD Int. Conf. on Management of Data*, pages 1099–1110.

Ong, K. W., Papakonstantinou, Y., and Vernoux, R. (2014). The SQL++ semi-structured data model and query language: A capabilities survey of SQL-on-Hadoop, NoSQL and NewSQL databases. CoRR/abs/1405.3631.

Ongaro, D. and Ousterhout, J. (2014). In search of an understandable consensus algorithm. In *Proc. USENIX 2014 Annual Technical Conf.*, pages 305–320.

Ooi, B., Shu, Y., and Tan, K.-L. (2003). Relational data sharing in peer-based data management systems. *ACM SIGMOD Rec.*, 32(3):59–64.

Ouksel, A. M. and Sheth, A. P. (1999). Semantic interoperability in global information systems: A brief introduction to the research area and the special section. *ACM SIGMOD Rec.*, 28(1):5–12.

Özsoyoglu, Z. M. and Zhou, N. (1987). Distributed query processing in broadcasting local area networks. In *Proc. 20th Hawaii Int. Conf. on System Sciences*, pages 419–429.

Özsu, M. T. (2016). A survey of RDF data management systems. *Front. Comput. Sci.*, 10(3):418–432.

Pacaci, A. and Özsu, M. T. (2018). Distribution-aware stream partitioning for distributed stream processing systems. In *Proc. 5th ACM SIGMOD Workshop on Algorithms and Systems for MapReduce and Beyond*, pages 6:1–6:10.

Pacitti, E. and Simon, E. (2000). Update propagation strategies to improve freshness in lazy master replicated databases. *VLDB J.*, 8(3-4):305–318.

Pacitti, E., Simon, E., and de Melo, R. (1998). Improving data freshness in lazy master schemes. In *Proc. 18th IEEE Int. Conf. on Distributed Computing Systems*, pages 164–171.

Pacitti, E., Minet, P., and Simon, E. (1999). Fast algorithms for maintaining replica consistency in lazy master replicated databases. In *Proc. 25th Int. Conf. on Very Large Data Bases*, pages 126–137.

Pacitti, E., Coulon, C., Valduriez, P., and Özsu, M. T. (2005). Preventive replication in a database cluster. *Distrib. Parall. Databases*, 18(3):223–251.

Pacitti, E., Valduriez, P., and Mattoso, M. (2007). Grid data management: open problems and new issues. *Journal of Grid Computing*, 5(3):273–281.

Pacitti, E., Akbarinia, R., and Dick, M. E. (2012). *P2P Techniques for Decentralized Applications*. Synthesis Lectures on Data Management. Morgan & Claypool Publishers.

Page, L., Brin, S., Motwani, R., and Winograd, T. (1998). The pagerank citation ranking: Bringing order to the web. Technical report, Stanford University.

Palopoli, L. (2003). Experiences using DIKE, a system for supporting cooperative information system and data warehouse design. *Inf. Syst.*, 28(7):835–865.

Palopoli, L., Saccà, D., and Ursino, D. (1998). Semi-automatic semantic discovery of properties from database schemas. In *Proc. 2nd Int. Conf. on Database Eng. and Applications*, pages 244–253.

Palopoli, L., Saccà, D., Terracina, G., and Ursino, D. (1999). A unified graph-based framework for deriving nominal interscheme properties, type conflicts and object cluster similarities. In *Proc. Int. Conf. on Cooperative Inf. Syst.*, pages 34–45.

Palopoli, L., Saccà, D., Terracina, G., and Ursino, D. (2003). Uniform techniques for deriving similarities of objects and subschemes in heterogeneous databases. *IEEE Trans. Knowl. and Data Eng.*, 15(2):271–294.

Papadimitriou, C. H. (1986). *The Theory of Concurrency Control*. Computer Science Press.

Papakonstantinou, Y., Garcia-Molina, H., and Widom, J. (1995). Object exchange across heterogeneous information sources. In *Proc. 11th Int. Conf. on Data Engineering*, pages 251–260.

Pape, C. L., Gançarski, S., and Valduriez, P. (2004). Refresco: Improving query performance through freshness control in a database cluster. In *Proc. Confederated Int. Conf. DOA, CoopIS and ODBASE*, Lecture Notes in Computer Science 3290, pages 174–193.

Paris, J. F. (1986). Voting with witnesses: A consistency scheme for replicated files. In *Proc. 6th IEEE Int. Conf. on Distributed Computing Systems*, pages 606–612.

Pasetto, D. and Akhriev, A. (2011). A comparative study of parallel sort algorithms. In *Proc. 26th ACM SIGPLAN Conf. on Object-Oriented Programming Systems, Languages & Applications*, pages 203–204.

Passerini, A., Frasconi, P., and Soda, G. (2001). Evaluation methods for focused crawling. In *Proc. 7th Congress of the Italian Association for Artificial Intelligence*, pages 33–39.

Pasupuleti, P. and Purra, B. S. (2015). *Data Lake Development with Big Data*. Packt Books.

Patiño-Martínez, M., Jiménez-Peris, R., Kemme, B., and Alonso, G. (2000). Scalable replication in database clusters. In *Proc. 14th Int. Symp. on Distributed Computing*, pages 315–329.

Pavlo, A., Paulson, E., Rasin, A., Abadi, D. J., DeWitt, D. J., Madden, S., and Stonebraker, M. (2009). A comparison of approaches to large-scale data analysis. In *Proc. ACM SIGMOD Int. Conf. on Management of Data*, pages 165–178.

Pavlo, A., Curino, C., and Zdonik, S. B. (2012). Skew-aware automatic database partitioning in shared-nothing, parallel OLTP systems. In *Proc. ACM SIGMOD Int. Conf. on Management of Data*, pages 61–72.

Perez-Sorrosal, F., Vuckovic, J., Patiño-Martínez, M., and Jiménez-Peris, R. (2006). Highly available long running transactions and activities for J2EE. In *Proc. 26th IEEE Int. Conf. on Distributed Computing Systems*, page 2.

Petraki, E., Idreos, S., and Manegold, S. (2015). Holistic indexing in main-memory column-stores. In *Proc. ACM SIGMOD Int. Conf. on Management of Data*, pages 1153–1166.

Pike, R., Dorward, S., Griesemer, R., and Quinlan, S. (2005). Interpreting the data: Parallel analysis with sawzall. *Sci. Program.*, 13(4):277–298.

Pirahesh, H., Mohan, C., Cheng, J. M., Liu, T. S., and Selinger, P. G. (1990). Parallelism in rdbms : Architectural issues and design. In *Proc. 2nd Int. Symp. on Databases in Distributed and Parallel Systems*, pages 4–29.

Pirk, H., Manegold, S., and Kersten, M. (2014). Waste not ... efficient co-processing of relational data. In *Proc. 30th Int. Conf. on Data Engineering*, pages 508–519.

Plattner, C. and Alonso, G. (2004). Ganymed: Scalable replication for transactional web applications. In *Proc. ACM/IFIP/USENIX 5th Int. Middleware Conf.*, pages 155–174.

Plugge, E., Membrey, P., and Hawkins, T. (2010). *The Definitive Guide to MongoDB: The NoSQL Database for Cloud and Desktop Computing*. Apress.

Popa, L., Velegrakis, Y., Miller, R. J., Hernandez, M. A., and Fagin, R. (2002). Translating web data. In *Proc. 28th Int. Conf. on Very Large Data Bases*.

Porto, F., Laber, E. S., and Valduriez, P. (2003). Cherry picking: A semantic query processing strategy for the evaluation of expensive predicates. In *Proc. Brazilian Symposium on Databases*, pages 356–370.

Ports, D. R. K. and Grittner, K. (2012). Serializable snapshot isolation in postgresql. *Proc. VLDB Endowment*, 5(12):1850–1861.

Pottinger, R. and Levy, A. Y. (2000). A scalable algorithm for answering queries using views. In *Proc. 26th Int. Conf. on Very Large Data Bases*, pages 484–495.

Pu, C. (1988). Superdatabases for composition of heterogeneous databases. In *Proc. 4th Int. Conf. on Data Engineering*, pages 548–555.

Pu, C. and Leff, A. (1991). Replica control in distributed systems: An asynchronous approach. In *Proc. ACM SIGMOD Int. Conf. on Management of Data*, pages 377–386.

Qian, Z., He, Y., Su, C., Wu, Z., Zhu, H., Zhang, T., Zhou, L., Yu, Y., and Zhang, Z. (2013). Timestream: Reliable stream computation in the cloud. In *Proc. 8th ACM SIGOPS/EuroSys European Conf. on Comp. Syst.*, pages 1–14.

Qin, L., Yu, J. X., Chang, L., Cheng, H., Zhang, C., and Lin, X. (2014). Scalable big graph processing in mapreduce. In *Proc. ACM SIGMOD Int. Conf. on Management of Data*, pages 827–838.

Quamar, A., Kumar, K. A., and Deshpande, A. (2013). Sword: Scalable workload-aware data placement for transactional workloads. In *Proc. 16th Int. Conf. on Extending Database Technology*, pages 430–441.

Raghavan, S. and Garcia-Molina, H. (2001). Crawling the hidden web. In *Proc. 27th Int. Conf. on Very Large Data Bases*.

Raghavan, S. and Garcia-Molina, H. (2003). Representing web graphs. In *Proc. 19th Int. Conf. on Data Engineering*, pages 405–416.

Rahal, A., Zhu, Q., and Larson, P.-Å. (2004). Evolutionary techniques for updating query cost models in a dynamic multidatabase environment. *VLDB J.*, 13(2):162–176.

Rahimi, S. (1987). Reference architecture for distributed database management systems. In *Proc. 3th Int. Conf. on Data Engineering*. Tutorial Notes.

Rahimi, S. K. and Haug, F. S. (2010). *Distributed Database Management Systems – A Practical Approach*. Wiley.

Rahm, E. and Bernstein, P. a. (2001). A survey of approaches to automatic schema matching. *VLDB J.*, 10(4):334–350.

Rahm, E. and Do, H. H. (2000). Data cleaning: Problems and current approaches. *Q. Bull. IEEE TC on Data Eng.*, 23(4):3–13.

Rahm, E. and Marek, R. (1995). Dynamic multi-resource load balancing in parallel database systems. In *Proc. 21th Int. Conf. on Very Large Data Bases*, pages 395–406.

Ramabhadran, S., Ratnasamy, S., Hellerstein, J. M., and Shenker, S. (2004). Brief announcement: prefix hash tree. In *Proc. ACM SIGACT-SIGOPS 23rd Symp. on the Principles of Distributed Computing*, page 368.

Ramamoorthy, C. V. and Wah, B. W. (1983). The isomorphism of simple file allocation. *IEEE Trans. Comput.*, 32:221–223.

Ramamritham, K. and Pu, C. (1995). A formal characterization of epsilon serializability. *IEEE Trans. Knowl. and Data Eng.*, 7(6):997–1007.

Raman, V. and Hellerstein, J. M. (2001). Potter's wheel: An interactive data cleaning system. In *Proc. 27th Int. Conf. on Very Large Data Bases*, pages 381–390.

Raman, V., Deshpande, A., and Hellerstein, J. M. (2003). Using state modules for adaptive query processing. In *Proc. 19th Int. Conf. on Data Engineering*, pages 353–365.

Rao, J., Zhang, C., Megiddo, N., and Lohman, G. (2002). Automating physical database design in a parallel database. In *Proc. ACM SIGMOD Int. Conf. on Management of Data*.

Rastogi, V., Machanavajjhala, A., Chitnis, L., and Sarma, A. D. (2013). Finding connected components in map-reduce in logarithmic rounds. In *Proc. 29th Int. Conf. on Data Engineering*, pages 50–61.

Ratnasamy, S., Francis, P., Handley, M., Karp, R., and Schenker, S. (2001). A scalable content-addressable network. *ACM SIGCOMM Computer Communication Review*, 31(4):161–172.

Ray, I., Mancini, L. V., Jajodia, S., and Bertino, E. (2000). Asep: A secure and flexible commit protocol for mls distributed database systems. *IEEE Trans. Knowl. and Data Eng.*, 12(6):880–899.

Redmond, E. and Wilson, J. R. (2012). *Seven Databases in Seven Weeks: A Guide to Modern Databases and the NoSQL Movement*. The Pragmatic Programmers.

Reed, D. P. (1978). *Naming and Synchronization in a Decentralized Computer System*. PhD thesis, MIT.

Reiss, F. and Hellerstein, J. (2005). Data triage: an adaptive architecture for load shedding in telegraphCQ. In *Proc. 21st Int. Conf. on Data Engineering*, pages 155–156.

Rekatsinas, T., Joglekar, M., Garcia-Molina, H., Parameswaran, A. G., and Ré, C. (2017). SLiMFast: Guaranteed results for data fusion and source reliability. In *Proc. ACM SIGMOD Int. Conf. on Management of Data*, pages 1399–1414.

Revilak, S., O'Neil, P. E., and O'Neil, E. J. (2011). Precisely serializable snapshot isolation (PSSI). In *Proc. 27th Int. Conf. on Data Engineering*, pages 482–493.

Ribeiro-Neto, B. A. and Barbosa, R. A. (1998). Query performance for tightly coupled distributed digital libraries. In *Proc. 3rd ACM Int. Conf. on Digital Libraries*, pages 182–190.

Richter, S., Quiané-Ruiz, J.-A., Schuh, S., and Dittrich, J. (2013). Towards zero-overhead static and adaptive indexing in Hadoop. *VLDB J.*, 23(3):469–494.

Ritter, J. (2001). Why Gnutella can't scale, no, really. http://www.darkridge.com/~jpr5/doc/gnutella.html. Last accessed June 2019.

Rivera-Vega, P., Varadarajan, R., and Navathe, S. B. (1990). Scheduling data redistribution in distributed databases. In *Proc. Int. Conf. on Data Eng*, pages 166–173.

Rjaibi, W. (2004). An introduction to multilevel secure relational database management systems. In *Proc. Conf. of the IBM Centre for Advanced Studies on Collaborative Research*, pages 232–241.

Robinson, I., Webber, J., and Eifrem, E. (2015). *Graph Databases*. O'Reilly, 2 edition.

Röhm, U., Böhm, K., and Schek, H.-J. (2000). OLAP query routing and physical design in a database cluster. In *Advances in Database Technology, Proc. 7th Int. Conf. on Extending Database Technology*, pages 254–268.

Röhm, U., Böhm, K., and Schek, H.-J. (2001). Cache-aware query routing in a cluster of databases. In *Proc. 17th Int. Conf. on Data Engineering*, pages 641–650.

Röhm, U., Böhm, K., Schek, H.-J., and Schuldt, H. (2002). FAS - A freshness-sensitive coordination middleware for a cluster of OLAP components. In *Proc. 28th Int. Conf. on Very Large Data Bases*, pages 754–765.

Roitman, H. and Gal, A. (2006). Ontobuilder: Fully automatic extraction and consolidation of ontologies from web sources using sequence semantics. In *Proc. EDBT Workshops*, volume 4254 of *LNCS*, pages 573–576.

Roth, M. and Schwartz, P. (1997). Don't scrap it, wrap it! a wrapper architecture for legacy data sources. In *Proc. 23th Int. Conf. on Very Large Data Bases*, pages 266–275.

Roth, M. T., Ozcan, F., and Haas, L. M. (1999). Cost models do matter: Providing cost information for diverse data sources in a federated system. In *Proc. 25th Int. Conf. on Very Large Data Bases*, pages 599–610.

Rothermel, K. and Mohan, C. (1989). Aries/nt: A recovery method based on write-ahead logging for nested transactions. In *Proc. 15th Int. Conf. on Very Large Data Bases*, pages 337–346.

Roubini, N. (2018). Testimony for the hearing of the US senate committee on banking, housing and community affairs on exploring the cryptocurrency and blockchain ecosystem. Accessible at https://www.banking.senate.gov/imo/media/doc/Roubini%20Testimony%2010-11-18.pdf/. Last accessed February 2019.

Roy, A., Mihailovic, I., and Zwaenepoel, W. (2013). X-stream: edge-centric graph processing using streaming partitions. In *Proc. 24th ACM Symp. on Operating System Principles*, pages 472–488.

Ryvkina, E., Maskey, A., Adams, I., Sandler, B., Fuchs, C., Cherniack, M., and Zdonik, S. (2006). Revision processing in a stream processing engine: A high-level design. In *Proc. 22nd Int. Conf. on Data Engineering*, page 141.

Sacca, D. and Wiederhold, G. (1985). Database partitioning in a cluster of processors. *ACM Trans. Database Syst.*, 10(1):29–56.

Sacco, M. S. and Yao, S. B. (1982). Query optimization in distributed data base systems. In Yovits, M., editor, *Advances in Computers*, volume 21, pages 225–273.

Saito, Y. and Shapiro, M. (2005). Optimistic replication. *ACM Comput. Surv.*, 37(1):42–81.

Sakr, S., Liu, A., and Fayoumi, A. G. (2013). The family of MapReduce and large-scale data processing systems. *ACM Comput. Surv.*, 46(1):11:1–11:44.

Salihoglu, S. and Widom, J. (2013). GPS: a graph processing system. In *Proc. 25th Int. Conf. on Scientific and Statistical Database Management*, pages 22:1–22:12.

Salihoglu, S. and Widom, J. (2014). Optimizing graph algorithms on Pregel-like systems. *Proc. VLDB Endowment*, 7(7):577–588.

Salton, G. (1989). *Automatic Text Processing – The Transformation, Analysis, and Retrieval of Information by Computer*. Addison–Wesley.

Sandhu, R. S., Coyne, E. J., Feinstein, H. L., and Youman, C. E. (1996). Role-based access control models. *IEEE Computer*, 29(2):38–47.

Schenkel, R., Weikum, G., Weißenberg, N., and Wu, X. (2000). Federated transaction management with snapshot isolation. In Saake, G., Schwarz, K., and Türker, C., editors, *Transactions and Database Dynamics*, pages 1–25. Springer.

Schmachtenberg, M., Bizer, C., and Paulheim, H. (2014). Adoption of best data practices in different topical domains. In *Proc. 13th Int. Semantic Web Conf.*, pages 245–260.

Schmidt, C. and Parashar, M. (2004). Enabling flexible queries with guarantees in P2P systems. *IEEE Internet Computing*, 8(3):19–26.

Schreiber, F. (1977). A framework for distributed database systems. In *Proc. Int. Computing Symposium*, pages 475–482.

Schuhknecht, F. M., Jindal, A., and Dittrich, J. (2013). The uncracked pieces in database cracking. *Proc. VLDB Endowment*, 7(2):97–108.

Selinger, P. G. and Adiba, M. (1980). Access path selection in distributed data base management systems. In *Proc. First Int. Conf. on Data Bases*, pages 204–215.

Selinger, P. G., Astrahan, M. M., Chamberlin, D. D., Lorie, R. A., and Price, T. G. (1979). Access path selection in a relational database management system. In *Proc. ACM SIGMOD Int. Conf. on Management of Data*, pages 23–34.

Sequeda, J. F., Arenas, M., and Miranker, D. P. (2014). OBDA: query rewriting or materialization? in practice, both! In *Proc. 13th Int. Semantic Web Conf.*, pages 535—551.

Shah, M. A., Hellerstein, J. M., Chandrasekaran, S., and Franklin, M. J. (2003). Flux: An adaptive partitioning operator for continuous query systems. In *Proc. 19th Int. Conf. on Data Engineering*, pages 25–36.

Shao, B., Wang, H., and Li, Y. (2013). Trinity: a distributed graph engine on a memory cloud. In *Proc. ACM SIGMOD Int. Conf. on Management of Data*, pages 505–516.

Shatdal, A. and Naughton, J. F. (1993). Using shared virtual memory for parallel join processing. In *Proc. ACM SIGMOD Int. Conf. on Management of Data*, pages 119–128.

Shatdal, A., Kant, C., and Naughton, J. F. (1994). Cache conscious algorithms for relational query processing. In *Proc. 20th Int. Conf. on Very Large Data Bases*, pages 510–521.

Shekita, E. J., Young, H. C., and Tan, K. L. (1993). Multi-join optimization for symmetric multiprocessor. In *Proc. 19th Int. Conf. on Very Large Data Bases*, pages 479–492.

Sheth, A., Larson, J., Cornellio, A., and Navathe, S. B. (1988a). A tool for integrating conceptual schemas and user views. In *Proc. 4th Int. Conf. on Data Engineering*, pages 176–183.

Sheth, A., Larson, J., and Watkins, E. (1988b). Tailor, a tool for updating views. In *Advances in Database Technology, Proc. 1st Int. Conf. on Extending Database Technology*, pages 190–213.

Sheth, A. P. and Kashyap, V. (1992). So far (schematically) yet so near (semantically). In *Proc. IFIP WG 2.6 Database Semantics Conf. on Interoperable Database Systems*, pages 283–312.

Sheth, A. P. and Larson, J. (1990). Federated database systems for managing distributed, heterogeneous, and autonomous databases. *ACM Comput. Surv.*, 22(3):183–236.

Shute, J., Vingralek, R., Samwel, B., Handy, B., Whipkey, C., Rollins, E., Oancea, M., Littlefield, K., Menestrina, D., Ellner, S., Cieslewicz, J., Rae, I., Stancescu, T., and Apte, H. (2013). F1: A distributed SQL database that scales. *Proc. VLDB Endowment*, 6(11):1068–1079.

Sidell, J., Aoki, P. M., Sah, A., Staelin, C., Stonebraker, M., and Yu, A. (1996). Data replication in Mariposa. In *Proc. 12th Int. Conf. on Data Eng*, pages 485–494.

Sidirourgos, L., Goncalves, R., Kersten, M., Nes, N., and Manegold, S. (2008). Column-store support for RDF data management: not all swans are white. *Proc. VLDB Endowment*, 1(2): 1553–1563.

Silberschatz, A., Korth, H., and Sudarshan, S. (2019). *Database System Concepts*. McGraw-Hill, 7 edition.

Simitsis, A., Wilkinson, K., Castellanos, M., and Dayal, U. (2009). QoX-driven ETL design: reducing the cost of ETL consulting engagements. In *Proc. ACM SIGMOD Int. Conf. on Management of Data*, pages 953–960.

Simitsis, A., Wilkinson, K., Castellanos, M., and Dayal, U. (2012). Optimizing analytic data flows for multiple execution engines. In *Proc. ACM SIGMOD Int. Conf. on Management of Data*, pages 829–840.

Simon, E. and Valduriez, P. (1984). Design and implementation of an extendible integrity subsystem. In *Proc. ACM SIGMOD Int. Conf. on Management of Data*, pages 9–17.

Simon, E. and Valduriez, P. (1986). Integrity control in distributed database systems. In *Proc. 19th Hawaii Int. Conf. on System Sciences*, pages 622–632.

Simon, E. and Valduriez, P. (1987). Design and analysis of a relational integrity subsystem. Technical Report DB-015-87, Microelectronics and Computer Corporation, Austin, Tex.

Singhal, M. (1989). Deadlock detection in distributed systems. *Computer*, 22(11):37–48.

Skarra, A. (1989). Concurrency control for cooperating transactions in an object-oriented database. In *Proc. ACM SIGPLAN Workshop on Object-Based Concurrent Programming*, pages 145–147.

Skarra, A., Zdonik, S., and Reiss, S. (1986). An object server for an object-oriented database system. In *Proc. of the 1st Int. Workshop on Object-Oriented Database Systems*, pages 196–204.

Skeen, D. (1981). Nonblocking commit protocols. In *ACM SIGMOD Int. Conf. on Management of Data*, pages 133–142.

Skeen, D. (1982a). A quorum-based commit protocol. In *Proc. 6th Berkeley Workshop on Distributed Data Management and Computer Networks*, pages 69–80.

Skeen, D. (1982b). *Crash Recovery in a Distributed Database Management System*. Ph.D. thesis, Department of Electrical Engineering and Computer Science, University of California at Berkeley, Berkeley, Calif.

Skeen, D. and Stonebraker, M. (1983). A formal model of crash recovery in a distributed system. *IEEE Trans. Softw. Eng.*, SE-9(3):219–228.

Skeen, D. and Wright, D. (1984). Increasing availability in partitioned networks. In *Proc. 3rd ACM SIGACT–SIGMOD Symp. on Principles of Database Systems*, pages 290–299.

Somani, A., Choy, D., and Kleewein, J. C. (2002). Bringing together content and data management systems: Challenges and opportunities. *IBM Systems J.*, 41(4):686–696.

Sousa, A., Oliveira, R., Moura, F., and Pedone, F. (2001). Partial replication in the database state machine. In *Proc. IEEE Int. Symp. Network Computing and Applications*, pages 298–309.

Srivastava, U. and Widom, J. (2004a). Flexible time management in data stream systems. In *Proc. ACM SIGACT-SIGMOD Symp. on Principles of Database Systems*, pages 263–274.

Srivastava, U. and Widom, J. (2004b). Memory-limited execution of windowed stream joins. In *Proc. 30th Int. Conf. on Very Large Data Bases*, pages 324–335.

Stanoi, I., Agrawal, D., and El Abbadi, A. (1998). Using broadcast primitives in replicated databases. In *Proc. 8th IEEE Int. Conf. on Distributed Computing Systems*, pages 148–155.

Stöhr, T., Märtens, H., and Rahm, E. (2000). Multi-dimensional database allocation for parallel data warehouses. In *Proc. 26th Int. Conf. on Very Large Data Bases*, pages 273–284.

Stoica, I., Morris, R., Karger, D., Kaashoek, M., and Balakrishnan, H. (2001). Chord: A scalable peer-to-peer lookup service for internet applications. In *Proc. 2001 Conf. on Applications, Technologies, Architectures, and Protocols for Computer Communication*, pages 149–160.

Stoica, I., Morris, R., Liben-Nowell, D., Karger, D., Kaashoek, M., Dabek, F., and Balakrishnan, H. (2003). Chord: a scalable peer-to-peer lookup protocol for internet applications. *IEEE/ACM Trans. Netw.*, 11(1):17–32.

Stonebraker, M. (1975). Implementation of integrity constraints and views by query modification. In *Proc. ACM SIGMOD Int. Conf. on Management of Data*, pages 65–78.

Stonebraker, M. (1981). Operating system support for database management. *Commun. ACM*, 24 (7):412–418.

Stonebraker, M. (1986). The case for shared nothing. *Q. Bull. IEEE TC on Data Eng.*, 9(1):4–9.

Stonebraker, M. and Neuhold, E. (1977). A distributed database version of INGRES. In *Proc. 2nd Berkeley Workshop on Distributed Data Management and Computer Networks*, pages 9–36.

Stonebraker, M., Abadi, D. J., DeWitt, D. J., Madden, S., Paulson, E., Pavlo, A., and Rasin, A. (2010). MapReduce and parallel DBMSs: friends or foes? *Commun. ACM*, 53(1):64–71.

Strauch, C. (2011). *NoSQL Databases*. Stuttgart Media University.

Sullivan, M. and Heybey, A. (1998). Tribeca: A system for managing large databases of network traffic. In *Proc. USENIX 1998 Annual Technical Conf.*

Swami, A. (1989). Optimization of large join queries: combining heuristics and combinatorial techniques. In *Proc. ACM SIGMOD Int. Conf. on Management of Data*, pages 367–376.

Taft, R., Mansour, E., Serafini, M., Duggan, J., Elmore, A. J., Aboulnaga, A., Pavlo, A., and Stonebraker, M. (2014). E-Store: Fine-Grained Elastic Partitioning for Distributed Transaction Processing. *Proc. VLDB Endowment*, 8(3):245–256.

Taft, R., El-Sayed, N., Serafini, M., Lu, Y., Aboulnaga, A., Stonebraker, M., Mayerhofer, R., and Andrade, F. (2018). P-store: An elastic database system with predictive provisioning. In *Proc. ACM SIGMOD Int. Conf. on Management of Data*, pages 205–219.

Tandem. (1987). NonStop SQL – a distributed high-performance, high-availability implementation of sql. In *Proc. Int. Workshop on High Performance Transaction Systems*, pages 60–104.

Tandem. (1988). A benchmark of NonStop SQL on the debit credit transaction. In *Proc. ACM SIGMOD Int. Conf. on Management of Data*, pages 337–341.

Tanenbaum, A. S. and van Renesse, R. (1988). Voting with ghosts. In *Proc. 8th IEEE Int. Conf. on Distributed Computing Systems*, pages 456–461.

Tang, W., Zhao, X., Rafique, W., Qi, L., Dou, W., and Ni, Q. (2019). An offloading method using decentralized P2P-enabled mobile edge servers in edge computing. *Journal of Systems Architecture – Embedded Systems Design*, 94:1–13.

Tatarinov, I., Ives, Z. G., Madhavan, J., Halevy, A. Y., Suciu, D., Dalvi, N. N., Dong, X., Kadiyska, Y., Miklau, G., and Mork, P. (2003). The piazza peer data management project. *ACM SIGMOD Rec.*, 32(3):47–52.

Tatbul, N., Cetintemel, U., Zdonik, S., Cherniack, M., and Stonebraker, M. (2003). Load shedding in a data stream manager. In *Proc. 29th Int. Conf. on Very Large Data Bases*, pages 309–320.

Thiran, P., Hainaut, J.-L., Houben, G.-J., and Benslimane, D. (2006). Wrapper-based evolution of legacy information systems. *ACM Trans. Softw. Eng. and Meth.*, 15(4):329–359.

Thomas, R. H. (1979). A majority consensus approach to concurrency control for multiple copy databases. *ACM Trans. Database Syst.*, 4(2):180–209.

Thomasian, A. (1996). *Database Concurrency Control: Methods, Performance, and Analysis.* Kluwer Academic Publishers.

Thomson, A. and Abadi, D. J. (2010). The case for determinism in database systems. *Proc. VLDB Endowment*, 3(1):70–80.

Thuraisingham, B. (2001). Secure distributed database systems. *Information Security Technical Report*, 6(2).

Thusoo, A., Sarma, J. S., Jain, N., Shao, Z., Chakka, P., Anthony, S., Liu, H., Wyckoff, P., and Murthy, R. (2009). Hive: a warehousing solution over a map-reduce framework. *Proc. VLDB Endowment*, 2(2):1626–1629.

Tian, F. and DeWitt, D. J. (2003). Tuple routing strategies for distributed eddies. In *Proc. 29th Int. Conf. on Very Large Data Bases*, pages 333–344.

Tian, Y., Balmin, A., Corsten, S. A., Tatikonda, S., and McPherson, J. (2013). From "think like a vertex" to "think like a graph". *Proc. VLDB Endowment*, 7(3):193–204.

Tian, Y., Özcan, F., Zou, T., Goncalves, R., and Pirahesh, H. (2016). Building a hybrid warehouse: Efficient joins between data stored in HDFS and enterprise warehouse. *ACM Trans. Database Syst.*, 41(4):21:1–21:38.

Tomasic, A., Raschid, L., and Valduriez, P. (1996). Scaling heterogeneous databases and the design of disco. In *Proc. 16th IEEE Int. Conf. on Distributed Computing Systems*, pages 449–457.

Tomasic, A., Amouroux, R., Bonnet, P., Kapitskaia, O., Naacke, H., and Raschid, L. (1997). The distributed information search component (DISCO) and the world-wide web – prototype demonstration. In *Proc. ACM SIGMOD Int. Conf. on Management of Data*, pages 546–548.

Tomasic, A., Raschid, L., and Valduriez, P. (1998). Scaling access to distributed heterogeneous data sources with Disco. In *IEEE Trans. Knowl. and Data Eng.* in press.

Toshniwal, A., Taneja, S., Shukla, A., Ramasamy, K., Patel, J. M., Kulkarni, S., Jackson, J., Gade, K., Fu, M., Donham, J., Bhagat, N., Mittal, S., and Ryaboy, D. (2014). Storm@twitter. In *Proc. ACM SIGMOD Int. Conf. on Management of Data*, pages 147–156.

Traiger, I. L., Gray, J., Galtieri, C. A., and Lindsay, B. G. (1982). Transactions and recovery in distributed database systems. *ACM Trans. Database Syst.*, 7(3):323–342.

Triantafillou, P. and Taylor, D. J. (1995). The location-based paradigm for replication: Achieving efficiency and availability in distributed systems. *IEEE Trans. Softw. Eng.*, 21(1):1–18.

Tu, S., Zheng, W., Kohler, E., Liskov, B., and Madden, S. (2013). Speedy transactions in multicore in-memory databases. In *Proc. 24th ACM Symp. on Operating System Principles*, pages 18–32.

Tucker, P., Maier, D., Sheard, T., and Faragas, L. (2003). Exploiting punctuation semantics in continuous data streams. *IEEE Trans. Knowl. and Data Eng.*, 15(3):555–568.

Ugander, J. and Backstrom, L. (2013). Balanced label propagation for partitioning massive graphs. In *Proc. 6th ACM Int. Conf. Web Search and Data Mining*, pages 507–516.

Ullman, J. (1997). Information integration using logical views. In *Proc. 6th Int. Conf. on Database Theory*, pages 19–40.

Ullman, J. D. (1982). *Principles of Database Systems*. Computer Science Press, 2nd edition.

Ulusoy, Ö. (2007). Research issues in peer-to-peer data management. In *Proc. 22nd Int. Symp. on Computer and Information Science*, pages 1–8.

Umbrich, J., Hose, K., Karnstedt, M., Harth, A., and Polleres, A. (2011). Comparing data summaries for processing live queries over linked data. *World Wide Web J.*, 14(5-6):495–544.

Urhan, T. and Franklin, M. (2000). XJoin: A reactively-scheduled pipelined join operator. *Q. Bull. IEEE TC on Data Eng.*, 23:27.

Urhan, T., Franklin, M. J., and Amsaleg, L. (1998). Cost based query scrambling for initial delays. In *Proc. ACM SIGMOD Int. Conf. on Management of Data*, pages 130–141.

Valduriez, P. (1982). Semi-join algorithms for distributed database machines. In Schneider, J.-J., editor, *Distributed Data Bases*. pages 23–37.

Valduriez, P. (1993). Parallel database systems: Open problems and new issues. *Distrib. Parall. Databases*, 1:137–16.

Valduriez, P. and Gardarin, G. (1984). Join and semi-join algorithms for a multi processor database machine. *ACM Trans. Database Syst.*, 9(1):133–161.

Valduriez, P. and Pacitti, E. (2004). Data management in large-scale P2P systems. In *Proc. 6th Int. Conf. High Performance Comp. for Computational Sci.*, pages 104–118.

Valiant, L. G. (1990). A bridging model for parallel computation. *Commun. ACM*, 33(8):103–111.

van Hee, K. (2002). *Workflow Management*. M.I.T. Press.

Van Renesse, R. and Altinbuken, D. (2015). Paxos made moderately complex. *ACM Comput. Surv.*, 47(3):42:1–42:36.

Varadarajan, R., Rivera-Vega, P., and Navathe, S. B. (1989). Data redistribution scheduling in fully connected networks. In *Proc. 27th Annual Allerton Conf. on Communication, Control, and Computing*.

Velegrakis, Y., Miller, R. J., and Popa, L. (2004). Preserving mapping consistency under schema changes. *VLDB J.*, 13(3):274–293.

Verhofstadt, J. S. (1978). Recovery techniques for database systems. *ACM Comput. Surv.*, 10(2): 168–195.

Verma, S., Leslie, L. M., Shin, Y., and Gupta, I. (2017). An experimental comparison of partitioning strategies in distributed graph processing. *Proc. VLDB Endowment*, 10(5):493–504.

Vermeer, M. (1997). *Semantic Interoperability for Legacy Databases*. Ph.D. thesis, Department of Computer Science, University of Twente, Enschede, Netherlands.

Viglas, S., Naughton, J., and Burger, J. (2003). Maximizing the output rate of multi-join queries over streaming information sources. In *Proc. 29th Int. Conf. on Very Large Data Bases*, pages 285–296.

Voulgaris, S., Jelasity, M., and van Steen, M. (2003). A robust and scalable peer-to-peer gossiping protocol. In *Agents and Peer-to-Peer Computing, Second Int. Workshop, (AP2PC)*, pages 47–58.

Vu, Q. H., Lupu, M., and Ooi, B. C. (2009). *Peer-to-Peer Computing: Principles and Applications*. Springer.

Wah, B. W. and Lien, Y. N. (1985). Design of distributed databases on local computer systems. *IEEE Trans. Softw. Eng.*, SE-11(7):609–619.

Walton, C., Dale, A., and Jenevin, R. (1991). A taxonomy and performance model of data skew effects in parallel joins. In *Proc. 17th Int. Conf. on Very Large Data Bases*, pages 537–548.

Wang, G., Xie, W., Demers, A. J., and Gehrke, J. (2013). Asynchronous large-scale graph processing made easy. In *Proc. 6th Biennial Conf. on Innovative Data Systems Research*.

Wang, H., Zaniolo, C., and Luo, R. (2003). Atlas: A small but complete SQL extension for data mining and data streams. In *Proc. 29th Int. Conf. on Very Large Data Bases*, pages 1113–1116.

Wang, L., Xiao, Y., Shao, B., and Wang, H. (2014). How to partition a billion-node graph. In *Proc. 30th Int. Conf. on Data Engineering*, pages 568–579.

Wang, W., Li, J., Zhang, D., and Guo, L. (2004). Processing sliding window join aggregate in continuous queries over data streams. In *Proc. 8th East European Conf. Advances in Databases and Information Systems*, pages 348–363.

Weikum, G. and Vossen, G. (2001). *Transactional Information Systems: Theory, Algorithms, and the Practice of Concurrency Control*. Morgan Kaufmann.

Weil, S. A., Brandt, S. A., Miller, E. L., Long, D. D. E., and Maltzahn, C. (2006). Ceph: A scalable, high-performance distributed file system. In *Proc. 7th USENIX Symp. on Operating System Design and Implementation*, pages 307–320.

Weiss, C., Karras, P., and Bernstein, A. (2008). Hexastore: sextuple indexing for semantic web data management. *Proc. VLDB Endowment*, 1(1):1008–1019.

Wiederhold, G. (1992). Mediators in the architecture of future information systems. *Computer*, 25 (3):38–49.

Wiesmann, M., Schiper, A., Pedone, F., Kemme, B., and Alonso, G. (2000). Database replication techniques: A three parameter classification. In *Proc. 28th Symp. on Reliable Distributed Systems*, pages 206–215.

Wilkinson, K. (2006). Jena property table implementation. Technical Report HPL-2006-140, HP Laboratories Palo Alto.

Wilms, P. F. and Lindsay, B. G. (1981). A database authorization mechanism supporting individual and group authorization. Research Report RJ 3137, IBM Almaden Research Laboratory, San Jose, Calif.

Wilschut, A. and Apers, P. (1991). Dataflow query execution in a parallel main-memory environment. In *Proc. 1st Int. Conf. on Parallel and Distributed Information Systems*, pages 68–77.

Wilson, B. and Navathe, S. B. (1986). An analytical framework for the redesign of distributed databases. In *Proc. 6th Advanced Database Symposium*, pages 77–83.

Wolfson, O. (1987). The overhead of locking (and commit) protocols in distributed databases. *ACM Trans. Database Syst.*, 12(3):453–471.

Wong, E. (1977). Retrieving dispersed data from SDD-1. In *Proc. 2nd Berkeley Workshop on Distributed Data Management and Computer Networks*, pages 217–235.

Wong, E. and Youssefi, K. (1976). Decomposition: A strategy for query processing. *ACM Trans. Database Syst.*, 1(3):223–241.

Wright, D. D. (1983). Managing distributed databases in partitioned networks. Technical Report TR83-572, Department of Computer Science, Cornell University, Ithaca, N.Y.

Wu, E., Diao, Y., and Rizvi, S. (2006). High-performance complex event processing over streams. In *Proc. ACM SIGMOD Int. Conf. on Management of Data*, pages 407–418.

Wu, K.-L., Yu, P. S., and Pu, C. (1997). Divergence control algorithms for epsilon serializability. *IEEE Trans. Knowl. and Data Eng.*, 9(2):262–274.

Wu, S., Yu, G., Yu, Y., Ou, Z., Yang, X., and Gu, Y. (2005). A deadline-sensitive approach for real-time processing of sliding windows. In *Proc. 6th Int. Conf. on Web-Age Information Management*, pages 566–577.

Xing, Y., Hwang, J.-H., Çetintemel, U., and Zdonik, S. (2006). Providing resiliency to load variations in distributed stream processing. In *Proc. 32nd Int. Conf. on Very Large Data Bases*, pages 775–786.

Yan, D., Cheng, J., Lu, Y., and Ng, W. (2014). Blogel: A block-centric framework for distributed computation on real-world graphs. *Proc. VLDB Endowment*, 7(14):1981–1992.

Yan, D., Bu, Y., Tian, Y., and Deshpande, A. (2017). Big graph analytics platforms. *Foundations and Trends in Databases*, 7(1-2):1–195.

Yan, L. L. (1997). Towards efficient and scalable mediation: The AURORA approach. In *Proc. IBM CASCON Conference*, pages 15–29.

Yan, L.-L., Özsu, M. T., and Liu, L. (1997). Accessing heterogeneous data through homogenization and integration mediators. In *Proc. Int. Conf. on Cooperative Inf. Syst.*, pages 130–139.

Yan, L. L., Miller, R. J., Haas, L. M., and Fagin, R. (2001). Data-driven understanding and refinement of schema mappings. In *Proc. ACM SIGMOD Int. Conf. on Management of Data*, pages 485–496.

Yang, B. and Garcia-Molina, H. (2002). Improving search in peer-to-peer networks. In *Proc. 22nd IEEE Int. Conf. on Distributed Computing Systems*, pages 5–14.

Yang, X., Lee, M.-L., and Ling, T. W. (2003). Resolving structural conflicts in the integration of XML schemas: A semantic approach. In *Proc. 22nd Int. Conf. on Conceptual Modeling*, pages 520–533.

Yao, S. B., Waddle, V., and Housel, B. (1982). View modeling and integration using the functional data model. *IEEE Trans. Softw. Eng.*, SE-8(6):544–554.

Yu, C. and Meng, W. (1998). *Principles of Query Processing for Advanced Database Applictions*. Morgan Kaufmann.

Zaharia, M. (2016). *An Architecture for Fast and General Data Processing on Large Clusters*. ACM Books.

Zaharia, M., Chowdhury, M., Franklin, M. J., Shenker, S., and Stoica, I. (2010). Spark: Cluster computing with working sets. In *Proc. 2nd USENIX Workshop on Hot Topics in Cloud Computing*, pages 10–10.

Zaharia, M., Das, T., an dTimothy Hunter, H. L., Shenker, S., and Stoica, I. (2013). Discretized streams: Fault-tolerant streaming computation at scale. In *Proc. 24th ACM Symp. on Operating System Principles*, pages 423–438.

Zhao, B., Huang, L., Stribling, J., Rhea, S., Joseph, A. D., and Kubiatowicz, J. (2004). Tapestry: A resilient global-scale overlay for service deployment. *IEEE J. Selected Areas in Comm.*, 22 (1):41–53.

Zhu, M. and Risch, T. (2011). Querying combined cloud-based and relational databases. In *Proc. 2011 Int. Conf. on Cloud and Service Comp.*, pages 330–335.

Zhu, Q. (1995). *Estimating Local Cost Parameters for Global Query Optimization in a Multidatabase System*. Ph.D. thesis, Department of Computer Science, University of Waterloo, Waterloo, Canada.

Zhu, Q. and Larson, P.-Å. (1994). A query sampling method of estimating local cost parameters in a multidatabase system. In *Proc. 10th Int. Conf. on Data Engineering*, pages 144–153.

Zhu, Q. and Larson, P. A. (1996a). Global query processing and optimization in the CORDS multidatabase system. In *Proc. Int. Conf. on Parallel and Distributed Computing Systems*, pages 640–647.

Zhu, Q. and Larson, P. A. (1996b). Developing regression cost models for multidatabase systems. In *Proc. 4th Int. Conf. on Parallel and Distributed Information Systems*, pages 220–231.

Zhu, Q. and Larson, P. A. (1998). Solving local cost estimation problem for global query optimization in multidatabase systems. *Distrib. Parall. Databases*, 6(4):373–420.

Zhu, Q., Sun, Y., and Motheramgari, S. (2000). Developing cost models with qualitative variables for dynamic multidatabase environments. In *Proc. 16th Int. Conf. on Data Engineering*, pages 413–424.

Zhu, Q., Motheramgari, S., and Sun, Y. (2003). Cost estimation for queries experiencing multiple contention states in dynamic multidatabase environments. *Knowledge and Information Systems*, 5(1):26–49.

Zhu, Y., Rundensteiner, E., and Heineman, G. (2004). Dynamic plan migration for continuous queries over data streams. In *Proc. ACM SIGMOD Int. Conf. on Management of Data*, pages 431–442.

Zhu, Y., Zhang, H., Qin, L., and Cheng, H. (2017). Efficient MapReduce algorithms for triangle listing in billion-scale graphs. *Distrib. Parall. Databases*, 35(2):149–176.

Ziane, M., Zaït, M., and Borla-Salamet, P. (1993). Parallel query processing with zigzag trees. *VLDB J.*, 2(3):277–301.

Zilio, D. C. (1998). *Physical Database Design Decision Algorithms and Concurrent Reorganization for Parallel Database Systems*. PhD thesis, University of Toronto.

Zou, L. and Özsu, M. T. (2017). Graph-based RDF data management. *Data Science and Engineering*, 2(1):56–70.

Zou, L., Mo, J., Chen, L., Özsu, M. T., and Zhao, D. (2011). gStore: answering SPARQL queries via subgraph matching. *Proc. VLDB Endowment*, 4(8):482–493.

Zou, L., Özsu, M. T., Chen, L., Shen, X., Huang, R., and Zhao, D. (2014). gStore: A graph-based SPARQL query engine. *VLDB J.*, 23(4):565–590.

Index

© Springer Nature Switzerland AG 2020
M. T. Özsu, P. Valduriez, *Principles of Distributed Database Systems*,
https://doi.org/10.1007/978-3-030-26253-2

O

Object exchange model, 570
Object storage, 454
Object store, 452
OceanStore, 432
Odyssey, 554, 556
OEM, *see* Object exchange model
OLAP, *see* On-line analytical processing
OLTP, *see* On-line transaction processing
One-copy equivalence, 247, 250
One-copy-serializability, 252
  strong, 254
On-line analytical processing, 96, 184, 244,
     282, 333, 349, 359, 387, 388, 390,
     392, 508, 509, 511, 519, 520,
     537–539, 545
Online graph query, 487
Online graph workload, 487
On-line transaction processing, 184, 244, 349,
     357, 359, 390, 470, 508, 537, 538
Ontology, 290
Operator tree, 149, 369
Optimistic concurrency control, 15
Oracle NoSQL, 524
OrientDB, 536, 537, 555
Overlay network, 398, 405
  pure, 398

P

PaaS, *see* Platform-as-a-Service
PageRank, 466, 487, 488, 495, 504, 563, 564,
     567
Parallel architecture, 352
Parallel associative join, 424
Parallel DBMS, 3, 16
Parallel hash join, 364, 366, 424
Parallel merge sort join, 364
Parallel nested loop join, 364
Parallel query optimization, 369
Partial function evaluation, 606
Partial key grouping, 482, 514
Partially duplicated database, *see* Partially
     replicated database
Partially replicated database, 13, 67, 95
Participant timeout, 221
Partition-centric approach, 495
Partition-centric graph processing
  asynchronous, 506
  block synchronous, 504
  gather-apply-scatter, 506
Partitioned database, 13, 67
Partitioning, 33, 62
Path expression, 573

Paxos, 231, 441
  basic, 232
Pay-as-you-go integration, 589
PeerDB, 411
Peer-to-peer, 17, 395
  computing, 16
  data management, 395
  DBMS, 22
  hierarchical structured, 445
  pure, 398
  replication, 428
  structured, 398, 402, 403, 425, 434, 447
  superpeer, 406, 444, 447
  systems, 4, 17, 19, 23, 24, 288, 395–399,
     401–403, 405, 406, 408–412, 419,
     421, 425, 426, 428, 429, 431, 432,
     436–438, 444–448, 522
  unstructured, 398, 399, 402, 411, 419,
     444–448
Pentaho, 510
Periodic data delivery, 6
Persistent query, 471
Pessimistic concurrency control, 15
PGrid, 405, 409, 432, 434, 445, 446
Phantom, 245
PHJ, *see* Parallel hash join
PHORIZONTAL, 44
PHT, 405
Piazza, 409
PIER, 424
PIERjoin, 424
Pig Latin, 460, 513
Pipelined symmetric hash join, 476
Pipeline parallelism, 12
PIW, *see* Publicly indexable web
PKG, *see* Partial key grouping
PlanetP, 419
Planning function, 326
Platfora, 510
Platform-as-a-Service, 5, 27, 29, 30
PNL, *see* Parallel nested loop join
Polybase, 545, 546, 554–556
Polystore, 519, 520, 539, 540, 544, 548,
     553–556
  hybrid, 549, 556
  loosely-coupled, 540, 556
  tightly-coupled, 545, 556
Posttest, 114
PoW, *see* Proof of Work
Power BI, 510
PowerLyra, 493
Precise recovery, *see* Exactly-once semantics
Precondition constraint, 112
Predefined constraint, 112